DISCARDED

Short Stories
for Students

Short Stories for Students

Presenting Analysis, Context and Criticism on Commonly Studied Short Stories

Volume 6

Tim Akers, Editor

The Gale Group

DETROIT • SAN FRANCISCO • LONDON • BOSTON • WOODBRIDGE, CT

National Advisory Board

Short Stories for Students

Staff

Editorial: Tim Akers,*Editor.* Donald Akers, Tim Akers, Thomas Bertonneau, Cynthia Bily, Paul Bodine, Carol Dell'Amico, Catherine V. Donaldson, Tom Faulkner, Benjamin Goluboff, Diane Andrews Henningfeld, Rena Korb, Oliver Lovesey, Sarah Madsen Hardy, Jacqueline Perret, Elisabeth Piedmont-Marton, Eric Rapp, *Sketchwriters.* Jeffrey W. Hunter, Maria Job, Daniel Jones, Deborah A. Schmitt, Polly Vedder, Timothy J. White, Kathleen Wilson, *Contributing Editors.* James P. Draper, *Managing Editor.*

Research: Victoria B. Cariappa, *Research Team Manager.* Andrew Malonis, *Research Specialist.*

Permissions: Maria Franklin, *Interim Permissions Manager.* Kimberly Smilay, *Permissions Specialist.* Kelly Quin, *Permissions Associate.* Sandra K. Gore, *Permissions Assistant.*

Production: Mary Beth Trimper, *Production Director.* Evi Seoud, *Assistant Production Manager.* Cindy Range, *Production Assistant.*

Graphic Services: Randy Bassett, *Image Database Supervisor.* Mikal Ansari, Robert Duncan, *Imaging Specialists.* Pamela A. Reed, *Photography Coordinator.*

Table of Contents

An Adventure in Reading

Sitting on top of my desk is a Pueblo storytelling doll. Her legs stick straight out before her and around her neck and flowing down into her lap are wide-eyed children. Her mouth is open as though she were telling the Zuni tale of the young husband who followed his wife to the Land of the Dead, a story strangely like the Greek myth of Orpheus and Euridice, as both teach the dangers of youthful impatience.

Although the Pueblo doll was created in New Mexico, she symbolizes a universal human activity. The pharaohs listened intently to tales of the goddess Isis, who traveled to foreign lands to rescue the dismembered body of her husband Osiris. Biblical narratives thrill the reader with stories like that of mortal combat between David and the giant Goliath. Greek and Roman myths immortalize the struggles of the wandering warriors Odysseus and Aeneas. In the Middle Ages, kings, queens and courtiers sat spellbound in drafty halls as troubadours sang of tragic lovers and pious pilgrims.

Around the world and down through the ages, myths, folktales, and legends have spoken to us about the human condition and our place in the world of nature and of spirit. Despite its ancient beginnings, however, there is no rigid criteria to which a story must adhere. It is one of the most protean literary forms. Though many scholars credit the nineteenth-century Romantic writers Edgar Allan Poe and Nathaniel Hawthorne with creating the modern short story, the form refuses to be frozen by a list of essential characteristics. Perhaps this is one of the reasons William Faulkner called it the ''most demanding form after poetry.'' Jack London felt it should be ''concrete, to the point, with snap and go and life, crisp and crackling and interesting.'' Eudora Welty wrote that each story should reveal something new yet also contain something ''as old as time.''

Below are some of the qualities you may observe as you explore the works discussed in *Short Stories for Students*. These characteristics also demonstrate some of the ways the short story differs from the novel:

1. Because time is compressed or accelerated, **unity** in plot, character development, tone, or mood is essential.

2. The author has chosen to **focus** on one character, event, or conflict within a limited time.

3. Poe wrote that **careful craftsmanship** serves unity by ensuring that every word must contribute to the story's design.

4. Poe also believed that reading should take place in **one sitting** so that the story's unity is not lost.

5. A character is **revealed** through a series of incidents or a conflict. The short story generally stops when it has achieved this purpose. A novel **develops** a character throughout its many chapters.

Now that we have briefly explored the history of the short story and heard from a few of its creators, let us consider the role of the reader. Readers are not empty vessels that wait, lids raised, to receive a teacher's or a critic's interpretation. They bring their unique life experiences to the story. With these associations, the best readers also bring their attention (a word that means ''leaning towards''), their reading skills, and, most importantly, their imagination to a reading of a story.

My students always challenged me to discuss, analyze, interpret, and evaluate the stories we read without destroying the thrill of being beamed up into another world. For years I grappled with one response after the other to this challenge. Then one day I read an article by a botanist who had explored the beauty of flowers by x-raying them. His illustrations showed the rose and the lily in their external beauty, and his x-rays presented the wonders of their construction. I brought the article to class, where we discussed the benefits of examining the internal design of flowers, relationships, current events, and short stories.

A short story, however, is not a fossil to admire. Readers must ask questions, guess at the answers, predict what will happen next, then read to discover. They and the author form a partnership that brings the story to life. Awareness of this partnership keeps the original excitement alive through discussion, analysis, interpretation, and evaluation. Literary explorations allow the reader to admire the authors' craftsmanship as well as their artistry. In fact, original appreciation may be enhanced by this x-ray vision. The final step is to appreciate once again the story in its entirety—to put the pieces back together.

Now it is your turn. Form a partnership with your author. During or following your adventure in reading, enter into a dialogue with the published scholars featured in *Short Stories for Students*. Through this dialogue with experts you will revise, enrich, and/or confirm your original observations and interpretations.

During this adventure, I hope you will feel the same awe that illuminates the faces of the listeners that surround the neck of my Pueblo storyteller.

Nancy Rosenberger
Conestoga High School
Berwyn, Pennsylvania

Introduction

Purpose of the Book

The purpose of *Short Stories for Students* (*SSfS*) is to provide readers with a guide to understanding, enjoying, and studying short stories by giving them easy access to information about the work. Part of Gale's "For Students" Literature line, *SSfS* is specifically designed to meet the curricular needs of high school and undergraduate college students and their teachers, as well as the interests of general readers and researchers considering specific short fiction. While each volume contains entries on classic stories frequently studied in classrooms, there are also entries containing hard-to-find information on contemporary stories, including works by multicultural, international, and women writers.

The information covered in each entry includes an introduction to the story and the story's author; a plot summary, to help readers unravel and understand the events in the work; descriptions of important characters, including explanation of a given character's role in the narrative as well as discussion about that character's relationship to other characters in the story; analysis of important themes in the story; and an explanation of important literary techniques and movements as they are demonstrated in the work.

In addition to this material, which helps the readers analyze the story itself, students are also provided with important information on the literary and historical background informing each work.

This includes a historical context essay, a box comparing the time or place the story was written to modern Western culture, a critical overview essay, and excerpts from critical essays on the story or author. A unique feature of *SSfS* is a specially commissioned overview essay on each story by an academic expert, targeted toward the student reader.

To further aid the student in studying and enjoying each story, information on media adaptations is provided, as well as reading suggestions for works of fiction and nonfiction on similar themes and topics. Classroom aids include ideas for research papers and lists of critical sources that provide additional material on the work.

Selection Criteria

The titles for each volume of *SSfS* were selected by surveying numerous sources on teaching literature and analyzing course curricula for various school districts. Some of the sources surveyed include: literature anthologies, *Reading Lists for College-Bound Students: The Books Most Recommended by America's Top Colleges; Teaching the Short Story: A Guide to Using Stories from Around the World,* by the National Council of Teachers of English (NTCE); and "A Study of High School Literature Anthologies," conducted by Arthur Applebee at the Center for the Learning and Teaching of Literature and sponsored by the National Endowment for the Arts and the Office of Educational Research and Improvement.

Input was also solicited from our expert advisory board, as well as educators from various areas. From these discussions, it was determined that each volume should have a mix of "classic" stories (those works commonly taught in literature classes) and contemporary stories for which information is often hard to find. Because of the interest in expanding the canon of literature, an emphasis was also placed on including works by international, multicultural, and women authors. Our advisory board members—current high-school teachers—helped pare down the list for each volume. Works not selected for the present volume were noted as possibilities for future volumes. As always, the editor welcomes suggestions for titles to be included in future volumes.

How Each Entry Is Organized

Each entry, or chapter, in *SSfS* focuses on one story. Each entry heading lists the title of the story, the author's name, and the date of the story's publication. The following elements are contained in each entry:

- **Introduction:** a brief overview of the story which provides information about its first appearance, its literary standing, any controversies surrounding the work, and major conflicts or themes within the work.

- **Author Biography:** this section includes basic facts about the author's life, and focuses on events and times in the author's life that may have inspired the story in question.

- **Plot Summary:** a description of the events in the story, with interpretation of how these events help articulate the story's themes.

- **Characters:** an alphabetical listing of the characters who appear in the story. Each character name is followed by a brief to an extensive description of the character's role in the story, as well as discussion of the character's actions, relationships, and possible motivation.

  Characters are listed alphabetically by last name. If a character is unnamed—for instance, the narrator in "The Eatonville Anthology"—the character is listed as "The Narrator" and alphabetized as "Narrator." If a character's first name is the only one given, the name will appear alphabetically by that name.

- **Themes:** a thorough overview of how the topics, themes, and issues are addressed within the story. Each theme discussed appears in a separate subhead, and is easily accessed through the boldface entries in the Subject/Theme Index.

- **Style:** this section addresses important style elements of the story, such as setting, point of view, and narration; important literary devices used, such as imagery, foreshadowing, symbolism; and, if applicable, genres to which the work might have belonged, such as Gothicism or Romanticism. Literary terms are explained within the entry, but can also be found in the Glossary of Literary Terms.

- **Historical and Cultural Context:** This section outlines the social, political, and cultural climate *in which the author lived and the work was created.* This section may include descriptions of related historical events, pertinent aspects of daily life in the culture, and the artistic and literary sensibilities of the time in which the work was written. If the story is historical in nature, information regarding the time in which the story is set is also included. Long sections are broken down with helpful subheads.

- **Critical Overview:** this section provides background on the critical reputation of the author and the story, including bannings or any other public controversies surrounding the work. For older works, this section may include a history of how story was first received and how perceptions of it may have changed over the years; for more recent works, direct quotes from early reviews may also be included.

- **Sources:** an alphabetical list of critical material quoted in the entry, with bibliographical information.

- **For Further Study:** an alphabetical list of other critical sources which may prove useful for the student. Includes full bibliographical information and a brief annotation.

- **Criticism:** an essay commissioned by *SSfS* which specifically deals with the story and is written specifically for the student audience, as well as excerpts from previously published criticism on the work.

In addition, each entry contains the following highlighted sections, if applicable, set separate from the main text:

- **Media Adaptations:** where applicable, a list of film and television adaptations of the story, including source information. The list also includes stage adaptations, audio recordings, musical adaptations, etc.

- **Compare and Contrast Box:** an ''at-a-glance'' comparison of the cultural and historical differences between the author's time and culture and late twentieth-century Western culture. This box includes pertinent parallels between the major scientific, political, and cultural movements of the time or place the story was written, the time or place the story was set (if a historical work), and modern Western culture. Works written after the mid-1970s may not have this box.

- **What Do I Read Next?:** a list of works that might complement the featured story or serve as a contrast to it. This includes works by the same author and others, works of fiction and nonfiction, and works from various genres, cultures, and eras.

- **Study Questions:** a list of potential study questions or research topics dealing with the story. This section includes questions related to other disciplines the student may be studying, such as American history, world history, science, math, government, business, geography, economics, psychology, etc.

Other Features

SSfS includes ''An Adventure in Reading,'' a foreword by Nancy Rosenberger, chair of the English department at Conestoga High School in Berwyn, Pennsylvania. This essay provides an enlightening look at how readers interact with literature and how *Short Stories for Students* can help students enrich their own reading experiences.

A Cumulative Author/Title Index lists the authors and titles covered in each volume of the *SSfS* series.

A Cumulative Nationality/Ethnicity Index breaks down the authors and titles covered in each volume of the *SSfS* series by nationality and ethnicity.

A Subject/Theme Index, specific to each volume, provides easy reference for users who may be studying a particular subject or theme rather than a single work. Significant subjects from events to broad themes are included, and the entries pointing to the specific theme discussions in each entry are indicated in **boldface.**

Entries may include illustrations, including an author portrait, stills from film adaptations (when available), maps, and/or photos of key historical events.

Citing Short Stories for Students

When writing papers, students who quote directly from any volume of *SSfS* may use the following general forms to document their source. These examples are based on MLA style; teachers may request that students adhere to a different style, thus, the following examples may be adapted as needed.

When citing text from *SSfS* that is not attributed to a particular author (for example, the Themes, Style, Historical Context sections, etc.) the following format may be used:

''The Celebrated Jumping Frog of Calaveras County.'' *Short Stories for Students.* Ed. Kathleen Wilson. Vol. 1. Detroit: Gale, 1997. 19-20.

When quoting the specially commissioned essay from *SSfS* (usually the first essay under the Criticism subhead), the following format may be used:

Korb, Rena. Essay on ''Children of the Sea.'' *Short Stories for Students.* Ed. Kathleen Wilson. Vol. 1. Detroit: Gale, 1997. 42.

When quoting a journal essay that is reprinted in a volume of *Short Stories for Students,* the following form may be used:

Schmidt, Paul. ''The Deadpan on Simon Wheeler.'' *The Southwest Review* XLI, No. 3 (Summer, 1956), 270-77; excerpted and reprinted in *Short Stories for Students,* Vol. 1, ed. Kathleen Wilson (Detroit: Gale, 1997), pp. 29-31.

When quoting material from a book that is reprinted in a volume of *SSfS,* the following form may be used:

Bell-Villada, Gene H. ''The Master of Short Forms,'' in *Garcia Marquez: The Man and His Work* (University of North Carolina Press, 1990); excerpted and reprinted in *Short Stories for Students,* Vol. 1, ed. Kathleen Wilson (Detroit: Gale, 1997), pp. 90-1.

We Welcome Your Suggestions

The editor of *Short Stories for Students* welcomes your comments and ideas. Readers who wish to suggest short stories to appear in future volumes, or who have other suggestions, are cordially invited to contact the editor. You may write to the editor at:

Editor, *Short Stories for Students*
The Gale Group
27500 Drake Rd.
Farmington Hills, MI 48331-3535

Literary Chronology

1821: Gustave Flaubert is born in France on December 12.

1843: Henry James is born in New York, New York, on April 15.

1861: The U.S. Civil War begins when Confederate forces capture Fort Sumter in South Carolina.

1862: Edith Wharton is born in New York, New York, on January 24.

1865: The U.S. Civil War ends; Abraham Lincoln is assassinated.

1877: "A Simple Heart" by Gustave Flaubert is published in his *Three Tales.*

1880: Gustave Flaubert dies on May 5.

1882: James Joyce is born in Dublin, Ireland, on February 2.

1885: Isak Dinesen is born in Rungsted, Denmark, on April 17.

1885: D. H. Lawrence is born in Eastwood, Nottinghamshire, England, on September 11.

1891: Zora Neale Hurston is born in Eatonville, Florida, on January 7.

1897: William Faulkner is born in New Albany, Mississippi on September 25.

1899: Vladimir Nabokov is born in St. Petersburg, Russia, on April 23.

1899: Ernest Hemingway is born in Oak Park, Illinois, on July 21.

1902: John Steinbeck is born in Salinas, California, on February 27.

1903: "The Beast in the Jungle" by Henry James is published in his short story collection, *The Better Sort.*

1911: "The Odour of Chrysanthemums" by D. H. Lawrence is published in the *English Review.*

1912: The *U.S.S. Titanic* sinks on her maiden voyage.

1914: With the assassination of Archduke Ferdinand of Austria, long-festering tensions in Europe erupt into what becomes known as the Great War.

1914: "The Dead" by James Joyce is published in his short story collection *Dubliners.*

1916: Henry James dies in London, England, on February 28.

1916: "The Easter Rising," in which Irish nationalists take control of the Dublin post office and declare a provisional government apart from British rule, takes place on April 24.

1917: Russian Revolution takes place. Czar Nicholas II abdicates the throne and a provisional government is established.

1918: World War I, the most deadly war in history, ends with the signing of the Treaty of Versailles.

1920: The 18th Amendment, outlawing the sale, manufacture, and transportation of alcohol--known as Prohibition--goes into effect. This law led to the creation of "speakeasies"--illegal bars--and an increase in organized crime. The law is repealed in 1933.

1920: The efforts of the Women's Suffrage movement, directed by women such as Susan B. Anthony and Elizabeth Cady Stanton, finally succeeds. The 19th Amendment, which granted the right to vote to women, is adopted.

1921: Edith Wharton wins the Pulitzer Prize for fiction for her novel *The Age of Innocence.*

1925: "Spunk" by Zora Neale Hurston is published in *Opportunity: A Journal of Negro Life.*

1925: "A Guide to Berlin" by Vladimir Nabokov is published.

1927: "Hills Like White Elephants" by Ernest Hemingway is published in the magazine *transition.*

1928: Gabriel Garcia Marquez is born in Aracataca, Columbia, on March 6.

1929: The stock market crash in October signals the beginning of a worldwide economic depression.

1929: *The Sound and the Fury* by William Faulkner is published.

1930: D. H. Lawrence dies of tuberculosis in Vence, France, on March 2.

1930: John Barth is born in Cambridge, Maryland, on May 27.

1930: "A Rose for Emily" by William Faulkner is published in *Forum.*

1931: "Pomegranate Seed" by Edith Wharton is published in *Ladies' Home Journal.*

1937: "The Chrysanthemums" by John Steinbeck is published in *Harper's* magazine.

1937: Edith Wharton dies in St. Brice-sous-Foret, France, on August 11.

1938: Raymond Carver is born in Clatskanie, Oregon, on May 25.

1939: World War II begins when Nazi Germany, led by Adolf Hitler, invades Poland; England and France declare war in response.

1940: John Steinbeck is awarded the Pulitzer Prize for Fiction for *The Grapes of Wrath.*

1941: James Joyce dies in Zurich, Switzerland, on January 13.

1941: John Edgar Wideman is born in Washington, D.C., on June 14.

1945: World War II ends in August with the atomic bombing of Hiroshima and Nagasaki, Japan.

1947: Octavia Butler is born in Pasadena, California, on June 22.

1949: William Faulkner wins Nobel Prize for literature.

1950: Senator Joseph McCarthy of Wisconsin sets off the "Red Scare" that leads to government hearings and blacklisting of suspected communists.

1952: Rohinton Mistry is born in Bombay, India.

1953: Ernest Hemingway is awarded the Nobel Prize for Literature.

1954: United States Supreme Court, in *Brown vs. Board of Education of Topeka,* rules unanimously that public school segregation is unconstitutional under the 14th amendment.

1958: "The Ring" by Isak Dinesen is published her short story collection *Anecdotes of Destiny.*

1960: Zora Neale Hurston dies in Fort Pierce, Florida, on January 28.

1961: Ernest Hemingway commits suicide in Ketchum, Idaho, on July 2.

1962: John Steinbeck is awarded the Nobel Prize for Literature.

1962: William Faulkner dies in Byhalia, Mississippi, on July 6.

1962: Isak Dinesen dies in Rungsted, Denmark, on September 7.

1963: President John F. Kennedy is assassinated in Dallas, Texas, on November 22.

1967: "Lost in the Funhouse" by John Barth is published in the *Atlantic Monthly.*

1968: "A Very Old Man with Enormous Wings" by Gabriel Garcia Marquez is published.

1968: John Steinbeck dies of heart disease in New York, New York, on December 20.

1972: President Richard Nixon resigns following the Watergate scandal.

1973: John Barth is awarded the National Book Award for his novel *Chimera.*

1975: Saigon, the South Vietnamese capital, falls to the North Vietnamese army, bringing an end to the Vietnam War.

1977: Vladimir Nabokov dies in Monteux, Switzerland, on July 2.

1981: "Cathedral" by Raymond Carver is published in *Atlantic Monthly.*

1982: Gabriel Garcia Marquez wins the Nobel Prize for Literature.

1984: John Edgar Wideman wins the PEN/Faulkner award for fiction for *Sent for You Yesterday.*

1984: "Bloodchild" by Octavia Butler is published in *Isaac Asimov's Science Fiction Magazine.*

1985: Octavia Butler is awarded both the Hugo and Nebula Awards for best novellette for "Bloodchild."

1987: "Swimming Lessons" by Rohinton Mistry is published in his short story collection *Tales from Firozsha Baag.*

1988: Raymond Carver dies of lung cancer in Port Angeles, Washington, on August 2.

1989: The Berlin Wall, a symbol of the 28 years of division between East and West Germany, is torn down.

1989: "Fever" by John Edgar Wideman is published in his short story collection *Fever.*

1990: Soviet leader Mikhail Gorbachev's policy of *glasnost* results in the fracturing of the Iron Curtain. By December the Soviet flag is lowered from the Kremlin.

Acknowledgments

The editors wish to thank the copyright holders of the excerpted criticism included in this volume and the permissions managers of many book and magazine publishing companies for assisting us in securing reproduction rights. We are also grateful to the staffs of the Detroit Public Library, the Library of Congress, the University of Detroit Mercy Library, Wayne State University Purdy/Kresge Library Complex, and the University of Michigan Libraries for making their resources available to us. Following is a list of the copyright holders who have granted us permission to reproduce material in this volume of SSFS. Every effort has been made to trace copyright, but if omissions have been made, please let us know.

COPYRIGHTED EXCERPTS IN *SSFS*, VOLUME 6, WERE REPRODUCED FROM THE FOLLOWING PERIODICALS:

African American Review, v. 28, 1994 for "'Would You Really Rather Die Than Bear My Young?': The Construction of Gender, Race, and Species in Octavia E. Butler's 'Bloodchild'" by Elyce Roe Helford. Copyright © 1994 Elyce Roe Helford. Reproduced by permission of the author.—*Arizona Quarterly,* v. 42, Winter, 1986 for "Imagery as Action in 'The Beast in the Jungle'" by James W. Gargano. Copyright © 1986 by Arizona Quarterly. Reproduced by permission of the publisher and the Literary Estate of James. W. Gargano.—*CLA Journal,* v. XXI, December, 1977; v. XXXI, June, 1988.

Copyright © 1977, 1988 by The College Language Association. Both used by permission of The College Language Association.—*College Literature,* v. XIV, 1987. Copyright © 1987 by West Chester University. Reproduced by permission.—*The Journal of Men's Studies,* v. 2, May, 1994. © 1994 by the Men's Studies Press. All rights reserved. Reproduced by permission.—*Modern Fiction Studies,* v. XIV, Winter, 1968/69. Copyright © 1968/69 by Purdue Research Foundation. All rights reserved. Reproduced by permission of The Johns Hopkins University.—*The Nation,* New York, v. 261, November 6, 1995. Copyright 1995 *The Nation magazine* / The Nation Company, Inc. Reproduced by permission.—*The North American Review,* v. 274, December, 1989. Copyright © 1989 by the University of Iowa. Reproduced by permission from *The North American Review.*—*Notes on Mississippi Writers,* v. VII, Fall, 1974. Reproduced by permission.—*Philosophy and Literature,* v. 16, April, 1992. © 1992. Reproduced by permission of The Johns Hopkins University Press.—*Slavic and East-European Journal,* v. 23, Fall, 1979. © 1979 by AATSEEL of the U.S., Inc. Reproduced by permission.—*Studies in American Fiction,* v. 10, Autumn, 1982. Copyright © 1982 Northeastern University. Reproduced by permission.—*Studies in Short Fiction,* v. 6, Fall, 1969; v. 7, Fall, 1970; v. 16, Summer, 1979; v. 17, Winter, 1980; v. 25, Winter, 1988; v. 27, Summer, 1990. Copyright 1969, 1970, 1979, 1980, 1988, 1990 by Newberry

College. All reproduced by permission.—*Texas Studies in Literature and Language,* v. 20, Winter, 1968. Copyright © 1968 by the University of Texas Press. Reproduced by permission of the publisher.—*The University Kansas City Review,* v. XXXVIII, Summer, 1971 for "Leitmotif and Irony in Hemingway's 'Hills Like White Elephants'" by Reid Maynard. © copyright 1971 The Curators of the University of Missouri. All rights reserved. Reproduced by permission of New Letters (formerly the UKC Review) and the Curators of the University of Missouri-Kansas City.—*The University of Mississippi Studies in English,* v. 8, 1990. Copyright © 1990 The University of Mississippi. Reproduced by permission.—*Wascana Review,* v. 21, Spring, 1986. Copyright, 1986 The University of Regina, Canada. Reproduced by permission.—*Women's Studies: An Interdisciplinary Journal, v. 20, 1991. © 1991 Gordon and Breach Science Publishers. Reproduced by permission.*

COPYRIGHTED EXCERPTS IN *SSFS,* VOLUME 6, WERE REPRODUCED FROM THE FOLLOWING BOOKS:

Bell, Millicent. From *Meaning in Henry James.* Cambridge, Mass.: Harvard University Press, 1991. Copyright © 1991 by the President and Fellows of Harvard College. All rights reserved. Reproduced by permission.—Black, Michael. From *D. H. Lawrence: The Early Fiction.* Cambridge University Press, 1986. © Michael Black, 1986. Reproduced with permission of the publisher and the author.—Butler, Octavia E. From an afterword to *Bloodchild and Other Stories.* Seven Stories Press, 1995. Copyright © 1995 Octavia E. Butler. Reproduced by permission of the publisher.—Connolly, Julian W. From *Nabokov's Early Fiction: Patterns of Self and Other.* Cambridge University Press, 1992. © Cambridge University Press 1992. Reprinted by permission of the publisher and the author.—Cushman, Keith. From "Blind, Intertextual Love: 'The Blind Man' and Raymond Carver's 'Cathedral'" in *D. H. Lawrence's Literary Inheritors.* Edited by Keith Cushman and Dennis Jackson. Macmillan, 1991. © Keith Cushman and Dennis Jackson. All rights reserved. Reproduced by permission of Macmillan, London and Basingstoke.—Gerlach, John. From "The Logic of Wings: Garcia Marquez, Todorov, and the Endless Resources of Fantasy" in *Bridges to Fantasy.* Edited by George E. Slusser, Eric S. Rabkin, and Robert Scholes. Southern Illinois University Press, 1982. Copyright © 1982 by the Board of Trustees, Southern Illinois University. All rights reserved. Reproduced by permission.—

Millington, Mard. From "Aspects of Narrative Structure in 'The Incredible and Sad Story of the Innocent Erendira and her Heartless Grandmother'" in *Gabriel Garcia Marquez: New Readings.* Edited by Bernard McGuirk and Richard Cardwell. Cambridge University Press, 1987. © The Nobel Foundation, 1987. Reproduced with permission of the publisher and the author.—Naumann, Marina Turkevich. From *Blue Evenings in Berlin: Nabokov's Short Stories of the 1920s.* New York University Press, 1978. Copyright © 1978 by New York University. Reproduced by permission of the author.—Saltzman, Arthur M. From *Understanding Raymond Carver.* University of South Carolina Press, 1988. Copyright © University of South Carolina 1988. Reproduced by permission.—Seidman, Barbara Kitt. From *Magill's Survey of American Literature. Salem Press, Inc., 1991. Copyright © 1991, by Salem Press, Inc. All rights reserved. Reproduced by permission.—Traub, Valerie. From "Rainbows of Darkness: Deconstructing Shakespeare in the Work of Gloria Naylor and Zora Neale Hurston" in Cross-Cultural Performances: Differences in Women's Re-Visions of Shakespeare.* Edited by Marianne Novy. University of Illinois Press, 1993. © 1993 by the Board of Trustees of the University of Illinois. Reproduced by permission.—Wagenknecht, Edward. From *The Tales of Henry James.* Frederick Ungar Publishing Co., 1984. Copyright © 1984 by Edward Wagenknecht. Reproduced by permission of the publisher.

PHOTOGRAPHS AND ILLUSTRATIONS APPEARING IN *SSFS,* VOLUME 6, WERE RECEIVED FROM THE FOLLOWING SOURCES:

19th-Century Print of Roses, a book illustration for *From Gold to Grey* (1886), photograph. CORBIS. Reproduced by permission.—A Heneritta Macaw, Florida's Sunken Gardens Aviary, photograph. Archive Photos, Inc./Sunken Gardens. Reproduced by permission.—A photograph of River Lilly from the roof of the Four Courts, Dublin City, Ushers Island is hidden by the statue, photograph. Bord Failte Eireann (The Irish Tourist Board). Reproduced by permission.—A view of Notre Dame Cathedral, Paris, France, 1998, photograph by Daniel L. Gore. © Daniel L. Gore. Reproduced by permission.—A view of the New Market from the corner of Shippen & Second Streets, 1787, Philadelphia, PA, photograph. Archive Photos, Inc. Reproduced by permission.—Amusement Park in Ocean City, Maryland, 1991, photograph by Douglas Peebles. CORBIS/

Douglas Peebles. Reproduced by permission.—'Autumn Days' Chrysanthemums, photograph by Patrick Johns. CORBIS/Patrick Johns. Reproduced by permission.—Barth, John, photograph. AP/Wide World Photos. Reproduced by permission.—Butler, Octavia E., photograph by O.M. Butler. Reproduced by permission.—Carver, Raymond, photograph by Jerry Bauer. © Jerry Bauer. Reproduced by permission.—Crops growing in Salinas Valley, California, photograph by Craig Lovell. CORBIS/Craig Lovell. Reproduced by permission.—Dinesen, Isak, 1957, photograph. Archive Photos, Inc. Reproduced by permission.—Face of a Black Panther, photograph by Tom Brakefield. CORBIS/Tom Brakefield. Reproduced by permission.—Faulkner, William, photograph by Neil Boenzi/New York Times. Archive Photos, Inc. Reproduced by permission.—Flaubert, Gustave, photograph. Library of Congress.—Hemingway, Ernest, photograph. Archive Photos, Inc. Reproduced by permission.—Hurston, Zora Neale, photograph. AP/Wide World Photos. Reproduced by permission.—James, Henry, photograph. The Library of Congress.—John Steinbeck's House, Salinas, California, photograph by Philip James Corwin. CORBIS/Philip James Corwin. Reproduced by permission.—Joyce, James (Ulysses), photograph. The Library of Congress.—Lawrence, D. H., photograph. AP/Wide World Photos. Reproduced by permission.—Marine Drive from Malibu Hill, Bombay, India, photograph. Archive Photos, Inc. Reproduced by permission.—Marquez, Gabriel Garcia, 1982, photograph. AP/Wide World Photos. Reproduced by permission.—Miner in Wales, photograph. Archive Photos, Inc. Reproduced by permission.—Nabokov, Vladimir, photograph. AP/Wide World Photos. Reproduced by permission.—New Gate in Berlin, photograph. UPI/Corbis-Bettmann. Reproduced by permission.—New York City Skyline, ca. 1925, photograph by E. O. Hoppe. CORBIS/E. O. Hoppe. Reproduced by permission.—Old Danish Farm, Faaborg, Fyn Island, Denmark, 1994, photograph by Philip Gould. CORBIS/Philip Gould. Reproduced by permission.—Oulpen Manor, built from the 1600s to 1800s, Gloustershire, England, photograph by Phillippa Lewis. CORBIS/Phillippa Lewis. Reproduced by permission.—Sculpture entitled "The Rape of Proserpina," by Italian Baroque sculptor Gian Lorenzo Bernini, Ca. 17th century, photograph. Corbis/Bettmann. Reproduced by permission.—Steinbeck, John, photograph. Archive Photos, Inc. Reproduced by permission.—The La Casa Verda visitor's center of the Ebro delta National Park, Spain, 5/31/95, photograph by Francesc Muntada. CORBIS/Francesc Muntada. Reproduced by permission.—Wharton, Edith, photograph. AP/Wide World Photos. Reproduced by permission.—Wideman, John Edgar, photograph by Jerry Bauer. © Jerry Bauer. Reproduced by permission.

Contributors

AKERS, Donald. Freelance writer and editor. Entry: "A Rose for Emily."

BARDEN, Thomas E. Professor of American Studies and Director of Graduate Studies at the University of Toledo. Entry: "Swimming Lessons."

BERTONNEAU, Thomas. Temporary Assistant Professor of English and the Humanities at Central Michigan University, and Senior Policy Analyst at the Mackinac Center for Public Policy. Entry: "The Ring."

BILY, Cynthia. Instructor at Adrian College in Michigan. Contributor to reference publications including *Feminist Writers, Gay and Lesbian Biography,* and *Chronology of Women Worldwide.* Entries: "The Chrysanthemums" and "Spunk."

BODINE, Paul Freelance writer, editor, and researcher and former instructor at the Milwaukee College of Business. Entry: "A Guide to Berlin."

DELL'AMICO, Carol. Ph.D. candidate in the Program of Literatures in English at Rutgers, The State University of New Jersey. Entry: "The Beast in the Jungle."

FAULKNER, Tom. Freelance writer and copyeditor. Entry: "A Very Old Man with Enormous Wings."

GOLUBOFF, Benjamin. Associate Professor of English at Lake Forest College. Entry: "Pomegranate Seed."

HENNINGFELD, Diane Andrews. Assistant professor of English at Adrian College in Michigan and contributor to reference works for Salem Press. Entries: "Hills Like White Elephants" and "Cathedral."

KORB, Rena. Freelance writer and editor with a master's degree in English literature and creative writing. Entry: "Fever."

LOVESEY, Oliver. Instructor at Okanagan University College in Kelowna, British Columbia. Entry: "Odour of Chrysanthemums."

MADSEN HARDY, Sarah. Ph.D. in English literature at the University of Michigan. Entry: "Bloodchild."

PERRET, Jacqueline. English instructor at Lake Forest College. Entry: "A Simple Heart."

PIEDMONT-MARTON, Elisabeth. Ph.D. in American literature. Entries: "Lost in the Funhouse," "Swimming Lessons," and "Fever."

The Beast in the Jungle

Henry James

1903

Literary critics generally agree that Henry James's career can be divided into three periods, the first from 1876 to the mid-1880s, the second from the mid-1880s to 1897, and the third from 1897 to his death. James's ''The Beast in the Jungle'' was written and published in the final phase of James's career (1903). Like other works composed during this period, this story's style is the product of James's desire to minutely render the permutations of an individual consciousness, in this case the mind of the story's protagonist, John Marcher. Thematically, this story can be linked to one of the greatest novels of his later period, *The Ambassadors,* which was also published in 1903.

Both ''The Beast in the Jungle'' and *The Ambassadors,* even if in different ways, present the reader with the idea of the failure to live life. ''The Beast in the Jungle'' is the story of John Marcher, who believes he is destined for a special fate. This conviction is so profound that instead of delving into life, Marcher chooses to live at life's fringe, waiting for this special event to occur. When, at the end of his life, Marcher decides that he was mistaken in his conviction, and that nothing of momentous import was in fact to be his destiny, he is left a broken man. He realizes that his exceptionality is of a purely negative aspect: ''The fate he had been marked for he met with a vengeance—he had emptied the cup to the lees; he had been the man of his time, *the* man, to whom nothing on earth was to have happened.''

Author Biography

Henry James, the second son of well-to-do parents, was born in New York City on April 15, 1843. Like his brother William James (the respected and influential pragmatist philosopher), Henry was destined for greatness. He was educated both in the United States and in Europe, and began his literary career writing fiction and literary criticism for prominent periodicals of his time such as the *Atlantic Monthly, Harper's Weekly,* and the *North American Review.* The great American writer William Dean Howells was an early and enthusiastic champion of James's prose, and James went on to win the admiration, friendship, or acquaintance, of many of the nineteenth and early twentieth centuries' leading literary talents. James wrote his first novel in 1878 (*Watch and Ward*) and went on to produce many novels, novellas, plays, and short stories during the rest of his life.

While James spent much of his early career in the United States, he traveled frequently to Europe and finally settled in London, which he made his permanent residence in 1875. (In protest of the initial reluctance of the United States to join the Allied cause in World War I, James became a naturalized British citizen in 1915, the year before his death.) James is most famous for his early novels, which have secured him the reputation of being a masterful portrayer of the American character. It was through some of these early works, such as *Daisy Miller* and *The Portrait of a Lady,* that James established himself as the originator of the international novel. These are narratives about Americans abroad who are depicted as naifs within a sophisticated and oftentimes corrupt European society. While James always found the clash of cultures an interesting subject, he moved on to other subjects as well, such as the moral education of children, the expanding consciousness of the individual, and the clash between subjective and external realities (such as is found in ''The Beast in the Jungle''). The prolific James was an impressive literary talent who was and is regarded today as a consummate literary craftsman.

Plot Summary

''The Beast in the Jungle'' is divided into six sections, each part designated by a roman numeral (I-VI). In the first section, James introduces the protagonist of the story, John Marcher. Marcher is at a manor house in the English countryside where he sees a woman whose face and manner stir his memory, although he is unable to recollect the circumstances of their acquaintance. Before he leaves, Marcher finds himself at close quarters with the woman. The moment she speaks to him he remembers where they met—in Italy where both were vacationing ten years previously. During this short renewal of their acquaintance, she reminds him that he had imparted to her a grave secret in Italy: he had told her that it was his conviction that he was destined to experience a monumental and devastating event, but as to the nature of this event, and when it might occur, he had no inkling. Marcher, who still fervently retains this conviction, is both pleased and shocked to meet the only human being to whom he has ever confided his deepest, and perhaps his only, secret. By the end of their conversation May Bartram has agreed to become his special friend, a friend who will wait and watch with him until the moment his fate is at last revealed.

In Section II Bartram receives an inheritance which allows her to set herself up in a London home. Bartram's and Marcher's proximity leads to a life in which they are constant companions. Most of this part of James's story details Marcher's pleased feelings over having a companion to keep him company during his ''vigil.'' There is a sense of much time passing quickly.

Section III opens with Marcher and Bartram discussing the oddity of their lives (spent waiting for Marcher's ''beast'' to spring), and the possibility that both of them might have long been a subject of especial interest to those who know them, since they have so long been such inseparable friends, and yet have never married. As in Section II, a sense of the passing of time is brought home to readers when it is learned that May Bartram has fallen ill from ''a deep disorder in her blood,'' a disease which will soon usher her to her death. This calamity leads Marcher to wonder, with some panic, if time is running out for him too, and whether he is correct in believing in a special fate. The section ends with Marcher's bleak hope that he has not been ''sold.''

Section IV opens with a description of one of Marcher's visits to Bartram. The sight of her wasted ''serene'' face, and a conversation they have about his ''beast,'' causes him once again to doubt his conviction. During this conversation, it occurs to Marcher that Bartram is attempting to ''save'' him from his beast, that she is trying to make him forget about it, because if he were to experience it he would not survive the revelation. This new perspective troubles him, and he becomes even more troubled when Bartram proceeds to suggest that he will never experience his beast, that his revelation was something that "*was* to" have happened.

In Section V Bartram is so ill that Marcher is rarely allowed to see her. Eventually, however, he is able to meet with her and, once again, they speak of his beast. This time Bartram tells him that what was to happen to him happened without his knowing it. She dies without telling him what the beast was, and he attends her funeral. Bartram's opinion about his beast convinces Marcher that he is a failure, a man who waited for an event but who missed its occurrence. He now views his life entirely differently. Since he can no longer wait for his beast, his life seems empty. He is now convinced that he will spend the remainder of his days wondering what it was that he missed. This, in effect, will be his new occupation; he will no longer wait—instead he will wonder what he missed. This desire to know gives rise to a deep feeling of restlessness in Marcher, and soon after Bartram's death, Marcher decides that he must travel.

In Part VI Marcher is once again in London after a year's travel in Asia, during which he did not, as he had hoped, find the answer to his question. He now takes to visiting Bartram's grave on a monthly basis. A year elapses in this manner until an event occurs at the graveyard which, for Marcher, turns out to be the culminating moment of his life. He notices a man nearby who appears to be mourning the recent death of a loved one. The two men leave the cemetery at the same time and their paths cross. As Marcher passes by this man he looks into his face and is shocked at the look of ravaged pain that marks the man's countenance. The man's profound look of one who suffers deeply for having loved deeply is the sight which induces Marcher's illumination. He suddenly realizes his terrible, ironic fate: he is a man to which nothing was to happen, a man who would wait, and who, in waiting, would miss all that life has to offer. In shock and horror Marcher perceives at last the true nature of his beast.

Henry James

nist, John Marcher. Very little is learned about her from the narrator, as the narrator is mostly concerned with conveying the thoughts of Marcher. (From Marcher's point of view she is an intelligent and charming woman.) And when the story departs from the narrator's rendering of Marcher's point of view, the various dialogues between Marcher and Bartram do little to reveal the depths of her character to the reader. Their exchanges are not only highly abstract and elliptical, with both Bartram and Marcher declining to make direct statements about any one thing, they also consistently revolve around the topic of Marcher's "beast," as he calls his anticipated fate, and never around things specific to Bartram's life. From these highly cautious and ambiguous exchanges, we gain the sense that she is a woman who never relinquishes control of her emotions, and who, very possibly, never expresses her deepest feelings to Marcher. At best, she hints at things, and when she hints she appears to know better than Marcher the truth of his fate. Thus, she can be said to be as reserved and aloof as Marcher, in her own way.

Characters

May Bartram

In "The Beast in the Jungle," May Bartram serves as a companion figure to the story's protago-

John Marcher

John Marcher is the protagonist of Henry James's "The Beast in the Jungle." He is a Londoner of modest private wealth who also holds a minor

Media Adaptations

- In 1978, renowned French film director Francois Truffaut adapted *The Altar of the Dead* and *The Beast in the Jungle* into a film entitled *La chambre vert (The Green Room)*. It is available with English subtitles from Metro Goldwyn Mayer/ United Artists Home Video.

governmental position. He is characterized by a conviction that he is destined to experience some type of event with consequences that will shake the very foundations of his being. This conviction shapes his character. He goes through life an outsider, quietly self-absorbed, and quietly but determinedly waiting for this moment to occur. Due to his abiding belief that he is different from all other humans, he remains fundamentally aloof from his friends and chooses never to marry. The only person with whom Marcher is truly close is the woman to whom he once confided his secret about his special fate, May Bartram. Since it is only at the story's end that Marcher discovers the truth of his destiny, the reader's sense of Marcher throughout the story is that of a man who dwells at life's fringe, watching what goes on about him.

Themes

Fate

"The Beast in the Jungle" is a story about a man who believes in fate, most particularly his own: "It isn't a matter as to which I can *choose,* I can decide for a change. It isn't one as to which there *can* be a change. It's in the lap of the gods. One's in the hands of one's law—there one is." Arguably, due to Marcher's fate turning out to be the opposite of what he expects, James could be said to be mocking the pretensions of his protagonist. Is his conviction about the "specialness" of his fate the flaw of an egotist? Or, is he a tragic figure who invents a grand fate due to his passion for a life which his circumstances cannot avail him?

Success and Failure

John Marcher believes he fails on two counts. On the one hand, he decides near the end of his life that he has failed to approach life with the correct attitude. He watched and waited and let life pass him by instead of participating directly within it. On the other hand, equally crushing to Marcher, is his having failed to apprehend the moment that his "beast" sprang. At the end of the story he realizes that it "sprang" in May's room on that day in April when she lay near death. This means that his realization of his overall failure would have been the same; that is, to realize that he should have spent his life loving May then, as she lay on her deathbed, would still amount to the realization that he failed to live life properly. Nevertheless, in missing what he believes should have been the "real" moment of this devastating illumination, he thus even fails to "properly" fulfill his negative destiny.

Doubt and Ambiguity

To read any of the dialogues between Marcher and Bartram is to be bereft of certainty as to what his characters have actually said. Readers attempt to decipher the prose but are confounded. What are these two characters referring to? What did May say with those words? The text is full of *lacunae,* passages of prose whose meaning remains opaque. The effect of these lacunae is to produce in the reader a feeling of doubt (what did they say?) and ambiguity (did they say this, or that?). Such a self-conscious authorial practice (James had to work hard at it) suggests that readers are to take note of their uncertainty, to consider themselves in the position of imperfectly knowing subjects. In this respect they are like Marcher, unable to read the signs, confounded in their search for clues.

Self and Other

As numerous critics point out, Marcher's guilty feelings and worries about his potential selfishness in regard to May Bartram, or about his egotistic self-involvement in the circumstances of his own fate, are telling. What he comes to believe, finally, is that it is precisely this self-involvement which robbed him of a full life. Marcher, then, fundamentally misunderstands his relationship to those around him. He learns that he cheated himself of contentment by isolating the significance of his own life and his own self from the lives and selves of all others.

Style

Point of View

Third-person narration, which consistently represents John Marcher's point of view, dominates James's story. The reader is privy to Marcher's thoughts, but the narrating voice declines to comment on these thoughts. In this respect, James is known as an innovator. In comparison with the third-person *omniscience* of the great nineteenth-century realists (for example, George Eliot), whose narration not only conveyed characters' thoughts and actions but also commentary and judgment regarding those thoughts and actions, James's third-person narration limits itself to presenting Marcher's thoughts and stops there. James's innovation, then, is to have introduced a narrative technique which is less regulative of the reader's experience: readers are not necessarily told what to think by James. However, this third-person narration in ''The Beast in the Jungle'' is occasionally disrupted. In the second section of the story, the narrating voice moves to encompass the reader by the introduction of the word ''[o]ur.'' After this first disruption, ''our'' and ''we'' begin to appear more frequently, and in section three, the narrating voice claims the first person singular pronoun, ''I.'' These occasional lapses in the third-person narration invite readers to distance themselves further from Marcher. Once the narrating voice explicitly draws the reader into the position of contemplating Marcher's development (''we''), or, when the narrating voice definitely detaches itself as an outsider looking in (''I''), Marcher becomes even more a subject of study, a man whose curious story is held up to the reader's scrutiny.

Setting

The settings which frame this story are highly evocative of the story's theme of a failure to live life. Marcher and Bartram renew their acquaintance and become friends in a manor house that is described as if it were a museum. It is full of treasures and precious old objects which visitors may respectfully contemplate, but since they are treasures, they may not be touched or used. In a way, life itself could be said to be a ''museum'' for Marcher. He watches life pass by, but does not partake of it, since he will not accept anything that is not the springing

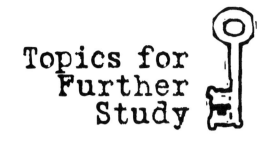

Topics for Further Study

- Analyze and discuss the seasonal and/or dark and light imagery in ''The Beast in the Jungle.'' Where does it appear, and how does it contribute to the story's effect?

- What can we discern about May Bartram's character, and what is her function in the story?

- Research the findings of archeologists at the sites of Pompeii, Carthage, or Troy. Aside from the suddenness of the destruction faced by these cities's inhabitants, what characteristics of their fates are in some ways similar to the fate of Marcher in ''The Beast in the Jungle'' ?

of his ''beast.'' That Marcher and Bartram have been together in Italy at the site of the buried city of Pompeii underscores this association of Marcher with a life never lived. This Italian city is most notable for its having been inundated in ancient times by a volcano. Much of its citizenry was buried alive, unable to escape the volcano's sudden and massive torrents of ash and lava. This buried city, then, also evokes Marcher's status of a man whose life is smothered by his passive waiting. It is perhaps no surprise then, that this story ends with Marcher in the cemetery near Bartram's grave. Marcher, who comes to the reader within a museum-like place and who is, still within this space, associated with a buried city, ends the story placed in a cemetery, a burial place for the dead.

Irony

''The Beast in the Jungle'' turns on its irony. John Marcher professes to expect an exceptional fate, but its exceptionality is that he is mistaken in his conviction. Literary critic Allen Tate deems James's irony in ''The Beast in the Jungle'' ''classic irony.'' By this, Tate means that Marcher's disappointment comes as no surprise to the reader, who is fully aware of the story's irony all along. If not after the first section, then probably after having read the second, the reader anticipates the story's (anti-)climax, and realizes that Marcher's perception is flawed. Thus the story's interest for the reader lies not so much in reading about Marcher's final revelation, but rather in watching him make his way to this final disappointment.

Symbolism

The titular "beast" of James's story is, in one respect, as ironic a symbol as the story itself is ironic. Since Marcher believes he is a man who is destined for something exceptional, but is rather a man "to whom nothing on earth was to have happened," it is ironic that the image that haunts his life is an image of a wild and vital creature. In this view, the pathos of Marcher's life is brought home vividly. As a minor governmental functionary, a reserved bachelor, a man who carefully lives within the bounds of middle-class respectability, Marcher lives the most staid of lives. However, insofar as we may imagine this beast as a creature hidden and enclosed within dense jungle growth, it is possible to consider it as a fitting symbol of that buried potential for an existence touched by real passion which lies within Marcher, but which due to his mistaken conviction, he never brings to light.

Historical Context

Character & Culture Change

If one agrees with Virginia Woolf's wry generalization that "in or about December 1910, human character changed," then one has to deem Henry James a man of America's bygone past, or, from the British point of view, "a Victorian" instead of "a Modern." His is the world which gave rise to our own. The years that bound the dates of his birth and death, 1843 and 1916, comprise an era of astounding movements and changes. James witnessed the abolitionist movement (Americans working for the end of slavery), industrialization (the era when John D. Rockefeller, John Pierpont Morgan, and Cornelius Vanderbilt built their fortunes), massive immigrant influxes into America, urbanization (the growth of cities), workers' rights movements, women's rights movements (the feminist movements and the suffragettes), and the pinnacle of European and American imperialism and colonialism. The American Civil War, which also occurred during this time period (when James was still living in New York, not in London), is related to this waning of European dominion, insofar as it resulted in the abolition of slavery, which was a legacy of European imperialism in Africa. The aristocrats who people James's novels were destined for the crash of World War I, which weakened their political power as did the Industrial Revolution's positive effect upon the growth of the middle class. But while the middle class grew in number so did the numbers of an urban working class, who began to demand universal suffrage (voting rights for all adults, regardless of sex). Denying the vote to women, thus, did not only concern feminists, but also working men who realized that their wives' political interests (wives who might have been working in the factories as well) coincided with their own. However, feminists interested in more than suffrage, such as Susan B. Anthony, inaugurated the women's movement, which began to work for equal opportunity and education for women. James's detailed depictions of the lives of his many female protagonists is therefore of great interest to feminist scholars eager to learn of the conditions within which middle- and upper-class women lived during this time.

This era also ushered in numerous new academic disciplines, such as anthropology, psychology, and sociology, all of which soon entered and flourished within university curriculums. James's elder brother, William James, is known mostly for being a philosopher of pragmatism, but he is also known for having been one of the earliest proponents of psychological study. This psychological "move into the interior" of human beings is present in James's own work, as he is known for his detailing of the thoughts, much more so than the actions or material environment, of his characters. This move into the interior of his characters can also be related to James's sensitivity to the anthropological leanings of his time. With imperialism and technology came travel and the comparative study of environments and peoples. Anthropologists cultivated an interest in the cultures and ways of life of diverse peoples. An added impetus to this interest in comparing cultures was the archeological excavations in Egypt, which astonished and enthralled the world. The way Henry James fixed his gaze so steadily upon his community amounts to something of an anthropological study. We learn to the last detail the social relations of his characters' class and world. Indeed, though certain commentators on James have said that his novels neglect that part of, and those doings of, the world beyond the immediate purview of his characters, one can nevertheless consider Henry James a man of his time.

Critical Overview

From the time of its first appearance in 1903 (in the short story collection *The Better Sort*) ''The Beast in the Jungle'' has been acclaimed as one of James's most accomplished short stories. Literary critics have found this story evocative and rich in imagery and insight. A reviewer writing in the *Nation* declared himself ''amazed at the display of an extensive and impartial observation of life, at the mastery of some dominant human motives with their thousand qualifications and modifications and at the variety of capacity for brilliant representation.'' Since 1903, ''The Beast in the Jungle'' has inspired numerous critical studies, many of which, including Allen Tate's in the 1950 *Sewanee Review* and Millicent Bell's in her *Meaning in Henry James,* respond to the story's fable-like quality. A fable is a short story with an easily understood moral thesis, the most common of which are ''beast fables,'' or those stories we read as children in which animals talk and act like human beings. Of course, the only beast in James's story is the beast of Marcher's imagination, and this story of two genteel upper-middle-class Britons creates an atmosphere far different from those of beast fables; yet, perhaps the story's enduring popularity arises, at least in part, from readers' and critics' clear apprehension of a moral thesis in this story. This thesis, in two words, might be deemed *Carpe Diem* (''seize the day'').

It has also been argued, however, that the story's allure derives from its element of pathos. In this view, the story of a man who desires the exceptional strikes a cord of recognition in many people who wish that their lives might be somehow extraordinary. In this reading, his final realization that the extraordinary is not to be his lot is less of a lesson and more of a comment on how lives are spent whiling away days in mundane pursuits. Critic Janice H. Harris presents an interesting twist on this question of passion versus passionlessness. She suggests that in *desiring* the extraordinary so intensely, Marcher can be said to have lived a life of intense passion.

Equally as interesting as critics' overarching view of the work is the analysis they do to get there. A critic such as James W. Gargano (writing in the *Arizona Quarterly,* Winter, 1986) for example, develops a reading of James's story from the launching point of John Marcher's and May Bartram's names (they evoke the seasons March and May), and pursues his reading through sustained attention

to seasonal imagery, in conjunction with an analysis of light and dark imagery (he argues that May is associated with light, and hence ''understanding,'' in contrast to Marcher's lifelong state of delusion, or state of ''darkness''). Other critics have also picked up on Bartram's status as the character who knows the truth before Marcher, and some of these writers have devoted entire essays to a discussion of the function and effect of her characterization within the story. Also of great interest are readings that discuss James's allusions to foreign monuments and locales (e.g. the Palace of the Caesars, Pompeii, and Asia).

Criticism

Carol Dell'Amico

Dell'Amico is a doctoral candidate in English literature at Rutgers University. Her areas of specialization include Modernism, the twentieth-century novel, feminist theory, and theories of Postmodernism. In the following essay, she surveys several of the prominent critical approaches by which ''The Beast in the Jungle'' has been read in the past, positing that it is a story destined for continued popularity.

Both literary critics and the general reading public find Henry James's short story ''The Beast in the Jungle'' to be evocative and rich. It has inspired numerous critical studies, many of which respond to the story's fable-like quality. Two well-known critics, for example, have even referred to the story as a ''fable.'' Allen Tate does so in his short, excellent commentary on the story that first appeared in the *Sewanee Review* in 1950 (also reprinted in *Critical Studies on Henry James*), and Millicent Bell does so in her *Meaning in Henry James* (1991). A fable is a short story with an easily understood moral thesis, the most common of which are ''beast fables,'' or those stories we read as children in which animals talk and act like human beings. Of course, the only beast in James's story is the Beast of John Marcher's imagination. Further, this story of two genteel upper-middle-class Britons creates an atmosphere far different from that created in most beast fables; yet, perhaps the story's enduring popularity arises, at least in part, from readers' and critics' clear apprehension of a moral thesis in this story. This thesis, in two words, might be deemed *carpe diem* (''seize the day''). In this view, Marcher's end-of-life insight is

Oulpen Manor, which is in Gloustershire, England, is typical of the type of home inhabited by those of John Marcher's social standing.

seen as this "fable's" final cautionary note and lesson: that he should have loved and cherished May Bartram, and lived a full life cultivating pleasure and passion from what life has to offer *any* human being, rather than waiting for something extraordinary to occur.

However, it is equally arguable that the story's allure derives from its element of pathos. In this view, the story of a man who desires the exceptional strikes a cord of recognition in all of us who wish that our lives might be somehow extraordinary. In this reading, his final realization that the extraordi-

nary is not to be his lot is less of a lesson and more of a comment on how our lives are, in fact, spent whiling away days in mundane pursuits. With the exception of an occasional skateboard adventure or trip to the Bahamas, how many people, after all, enjoy a life of consistently intense pleasure or passion? Critic Janice H. Harris presents an interesting twist on this question of passion versus passionlessness. She suggests that in *desiring* the extraordinary so intensely, Marcher can be said to have lived a life of intense passion. In Harris's essay, the story's irony does not lie in Marcher's

What Do I Read Next?

- *The Age of Innocence* (1920), by Edith Wharton, is a historical novel of aristocratic New York, in which the ranks of class propriety close around Newland Archer, preventing him from breaking his engagement to pursue a woman with whom he falls in love. This woman, though she is an American, has lived much of her life in Europe and returns to America following her estrangement from her aristocratic European husband. In this meeting of Archer and an Europeanized woman, Wharton, like James, stages a fascinating clash of cultures.

- *A Room with a View* (1908), by E. M. Forster, is another tale which treats the opposition between passion and repression. Like James, Forster was a traveler and writer who was often drawn to depicting the meeting of cultures. In this novel we read of Britons in Europe, and in his even more famous novel, *A Passage to India* (1924), Forster depicts the strained relations between the British imperial community and Indians.

- The short stories of Jorge Luis Borges and Julio Cortazar should attract any reader who enjoys Henry James. Borges and Cortazar are widely translated Latin American authors whose short stories are as artful as James's own.

- *Sister Carrie,* by Theodore Dreiser, was published in 1900, three years before James's "The Beast in the Jungle." Like James, Dreiser is a keen realist. As the reader follows the fortunes of Carrie Meeber from her small town to her success as an actress, glimpses at vivid scenes of late nineteenth-century Chicago and New York are offered.

---

realizing that his fate is the opposite of what he expected, but rather in his thinking that he "missed" life when in fact he lived a deeply passionate life. Harris's essay is also interesting for its focus on the significance of May Bartram in the story.

Equally as interesting as critics' overarching view of the work is the analysis they do to get there. A critic such as James W. Gargano, for example, develops a reading of James's story from the launching point of John Marcher's and May Bartram's names (they evoke the seasons March and May), and pursues his reading through sustained attention to seasonal imagery, in conjunction with an analysis of light and dark imagery (he argues that May is associated with light, and hence "understanding," in contrast to Marcher's lifelong state of delusion, or state of "darkness"). Other critics have also picked up on Bartram's status as the character who knows the truth before Marcher, and some of these writers have devoted entire essays to a discussion of the function and effect of her characterization within the story. Also of great interest are readings that discuss James's allusions to foreign monuments and locales.

One enduring problem for critics is the character of John Marcher. According to Millicent Bell, the reader "may interpret his aspiration for some tragic or heroic end as a recoil from the common goals of his society. At the same time, the story can be read as a representative Jamesian study of the selfishness and passionlessness that may accompany intellectual refinement and good breeding, a reading of fastidiousness as a mask for the evasion of social and personal responsibility." To read this commentary is to remember Marcher's egotism, his desire to shape life to his own ends, his annexing of May Bartram's life as his companion in waiting for nothing, and his self-congratulatory and complacent thoughts that in buying May birthday gifts that cost always a little more than he can afford, he is "paying off" any selfishness he could be accused of by drawing her into his web of "passionlessness." We are also reminded, in this respect, of Edith Wharton's *The House of Mirth* (Wharton and James

> ❝ Yet, perhaps the story's enduring popularity arises, at least in part, from readers' and critics' clear apprehension of a moral thesis in this story. This thesis, in two words, might be deemed carpe diem ('seize the day').❞

were long-time friends). *The House of Mirth* is the story of Lily Bart who dies young, and who is mourned by a young man who, it has been argued, could have saved her from her sad demise if he had only realized soon enough that he loved her.

Judgments of Marcher aside, James's method of presenting his reader with the tortuous thoughts of a human being attempting to read the signs around him for a message or messages pertaining to his hopes and desires, results in a story in which we are invited to contemplate the idea of the individual consciousness poised in relation to its environment. It is in this respect that James is considered to be an important precursor of certain early twentieth-century Modernist writers, because the Modernists, like James, are considered to be writers who believe that reality is something that comes "to mean" not because of any intrinsic qualities of its own, but only through the application of our subjective interpretation upon it.

Whether as a cautionary tale, for its pathos, or for its status as a literary work which presaged developments to come, James's "The Beast in the Jungle" will undoubtedly capture readers's attention for many years to come.

Source: Carol Dell'Amico, Overview of "The Beast in the Jungle," for *Short Stories for Students,* The Gale Group, 1999.

Millicent Bell

In the following excerpt, Bell looks at "The Beast in the Jungle" as a "dark fable" and examines its treatment of passivity and fate.

"The Beast in the Jungle" may be James's most extreme expression of the theme of human character as potentiality which cannot or will not move out into the world of action, of plot. Published in 1903, the same year as *The Ambassadors*, it bears, as will be seen, a certain relation to that novel, which arises, in a much more complicated way, from the idea of the failure to "live." But the short story is a dark fable, more abstract and pessimistic than the novel. Marcher (whose name differs from hers only by an initial letter) is the farthest James would ever go in illustrating the consequences of Isabel Archer's cult of Being; but where she is heroic in resisting the reductive expectations of others that she will enact herself in some way, he waits for his narrative in mere passive expectation, and—far from being a "marcher"—in the end is trapped in the story of his vain waiting. . . .

The world Marcher inhabits is a chamber of eternity. Like "The Turn of the Screw," the story is a mythical and moral tale, despite its modern tone. It is not for nothing that May . . . is called sphinxlike. Something must happen and, she even says, *has* happened, though Marcher can discover no evidence of it in his life. The conundrum is, like the sphinx's riddles, designed to be solved in a form least expected. The correct answer cannot be anticipated by the man to whom it has been told: "He had been the man of his time, *the* man, to whom nothing on earth was to have happened." His fate has arrived, it will turn out, precisely *because* nothing has happened. As allegory, the story is designed to illustrate the idea that no life escapes a destiny.

Mythically, the hero will encounter a "beast"—a figurative image which does not altogether, any more than the ghosts of "The Turn of the Screw," lose its relation to traditions of folklore—and recalls Hawthorne's "bosom serpent" (in "Egotism, or the Bosom Serpent") in its semi-literal, semi-symbolical presence in the story. A further resemblance to "The Turn of the Screw" resides in the fact that James seems to have conceived of Marcher as another absolutist who craves a fairy-tale plot of melodramatic simplicity, like the governess. Marcher, James explains in the New York Edition preface, found

> none of the mere usual and normal human adventures, whether delights or disconcertments, appearing to confirm to the great type of his fortune . . . No gathering appearance, no descried or interpreted promise or portent, affects his superstitious soul either as a damnation deep enough (if damnation be in question) for his appointed *quality* of consciousness, or as a translation into bliss sublime enough (on *that* hy-

pothesis) to fill, in vulgar parlance, the bill. Therefore, as each item of experience comes, with its possibilities, into view, he can but dismiss it under this sterilizing habit of the failure to find it good enough and thence to appropriate it.

"His career," James concludes, "thus resolves itself into a great negative adventure." Marcher himself seems to suspect and fear the utter negativity of his adventure when he asks May if she does not foresee that *nothing* will really happen to him.

James's problem, of course, was the difficult one, as Tate puts it, "of dramatizing the insulated ego, of making active what is incapable of action." James does not reduce this problem, however, by exhibiting as incident the succession of challenges summarized in the preface—the preface really promises more drama in the form of "descried or interpreted promises or portents" than the tale ever brings into view. What is suggested instead is simply the might-have-beens which Marcher and May both gaze into, a sweeping stream of negatives. "He knew each of the things of importance he was insidiously kept from doing, but she could add up the amount they made, understand how much, with a lighter weight on his spirit, he might have done." Between them, nearly eventless, flows the story, the *only* story, actually lived, though it is to prove the greatest might-have-been of all.

I say *nearly* eventless for, of course, there are *some* scenic moments which suggest to the reader that Marcher is making his way along a path not only of time but of development. He *has* been launched upon a plot, and James uses the same image of a boat put into the wind and current of its course that he used to describe the initiation of Isabel's destiny by Ralph's putting "wind in her sails": "The recovery, the first day at Weatherend, had served its purpose well, had given them quite enough; so that they were, to Marcher's sense, no longer hovering about the head-waters of their stream, but had felt their boat pushed sharply off and down the current." In the end the story disproves the idea that negativity can be maintained. It suggests that there is always a story, that in not writing one one writes another.

May's first assurance that something *will* happen is an occasion marked for him as "a date" or crisis which already gives some semblance of form to time; "again and again, even after long intervals, other things that passed between them wore in relation to this hour but the character of recalls and result." Marcher comes to believe that she knows what his catastrophe will be. He depends upon her

> **" James's problem, of course, was the difficult one, as Tate puts it, 'of dramatizing the insulated ego, of making active what is incapable of action.'"**

for the validation, somehow, of this ultimate revelation, and when she grows ill begins to fear that she may die without witnessing it at his side, and that perhaps it is already "Too Late" for his Event. He fears that he has been "sold." "It wouldn't have been failure to be bankrupt, dishonoured, pilloried, hanged; it was failure not to be anything." Time is threatening to stop—and all possibility of story cut short; "Since it was in Time that he was to have met his fate, so it was in Time that his fate was to have acted."

It is at this point that the story, which is enacting itself without Marcher's knowledge, exhibits its climax in the exquisite scene in which May seems already beyond time, mythically metamorphosed, *her* story completed and preserved like a lily under a bell jar. Their conversation convinces him that she knows his fate. She knows it as "the worst" thing conceivable, something they've never mentioned in reviewing possibilities. Her reassurance that he will not consciously suffer revives his fear that she has come back to his own early dread—that *nothing* will happen. But she can say no more. As at the start of their friendship, she cannot give him the "thread" of narrative continuity "without some putting forth of his hand for it." She stands before him with figure and face conveying her own offering before she collapses, with her despairing question, "Don't you know—now?" What has happened is "what *was* to." His story-less life has just achieved its catastrophe, though, as she had warned, he won't give it the right name.

He thinks that it is her death—and the solitude it means for him—that is the promised disaster. But in their last interview she tells him that disaster has already struck, though he asks, in bewilderment, "How can the thing I've never felt at all be the thing I was marked out to feel?" What he does experience, after her death, is extinction of the suspense which had filled his days for so many years. "What was to happen *had* so absolutely and finally happened that he was as little able to know a fear for his future as to know a hope; so absent in short was any question of anything still to come. He was to live entirely with the other question, that of his unidentified past, that of his having to see his fortune impenetrably muffled and masked." Again, as at the start of the story, we realize that the past and future only identify themselves to the kind of vision Marcher lacks. His catastrophe, now past, is as unknown to him as when it was a thing of the future.

A diminished man, with no sense of the shape which gives meaning to a life, he comes to worry less about "whatever had happened." Revelation does arrive at last at his dead friend's graveside, where the face of another mourner, unknown to him, is "the image of scarred passion." He realizes that "he had seen *outside* of his life, not learned it within, the way a woman was mourned when she had been loved for herself." Now he realizes that she had offered him an escape from the Beast; "the escape would have been to love her."

Yes, he had been "*the* man to whom nothing on earth was to have happened . . . That was the rare stroke—that was his visitation," the story states. But James's message is more subtle—or ambiguous. Marcher *is*, after all, the victim of the catastrophe he has been waiting for; the Beast springs at last. The Beast—like the sphinx's creature who walked on four, on two, and then on three feet—is only man, who must live the life of man. Marcher, like everyone, is the man to whom something *has* happened. His is only the disaster that is the outcome of a life that disdains a history but cannot escape one.

That plot overtakes the character who resists it seemed, in the case of Isabel Archer, an acknowledgment that the "free spirit" must be overtaken by a limiting, even diminishing story. James called Isabel "presumptuous," but indulged his heroine for the nobility of her presumptions. James contrasted that nobility with the destinies that would entrap and degrade her. But to presume that one can dispense with "adventure" of some sort, to imagine that there can be a tale without a plot, is delusive. In the story James so often seems to write, the story of the mere witness to life who refuses action, or of the person for whom opportunity comes "too late," refusal itself will turn out to constitute an adventure, for better or for worse. In "The Beast in the Jun-

gle," James redefines that word, "adventure"—a term used both for life's actual tale and for the literary narrative—and makes sense of the oxymoron, "negative adventure." More than Isabel's, Marcher's presumption amounts to arrogance in its indifference to life's best opportunities—and constitutes a critique of her attitude, from which the novel deliberately refrained.

The argument is perhaps conservative, a refutation of idealist intransigence, for it seems to say that we had better do the possible, after all. In the end, selfishly cherishing our essence, we will have acted somehow, and probably badly. To the literary artist the warning is obvious. There is no way to write stories but by resort to the old tales in the storeroom—tales of love and marriage or whatever, the stories men have been telling from the beginning of human time—stories so inescapable that they will express themselves in the most story-denying fiction we may invent.

Source: Millicent Bell, "The Inaccessible Future: 'The Beast in the Jungle'," in *Meaning in Henry James,* Harvard University Press, 1991, pp. 262–74.

James W. Gargano

In the following essay, Gargano provides a detailed analysis of the function of imagery in "The Beast in the Jungle," relating it to the story's themes and characterization.

In "The Beast in the Jungle," Henry James attempts to make a formidable dramatic action out of what he calls in one of his most interesting prefaces "a great negative adventure." The point of the story is the pointlessness of John Marcher's subordination of reality to his belief that a unique and possibly terrible destiny awaits him. Marcher's special fate (to be "*the* man, to whom nothing on earth was to have happened") is made vivid by his involvement or noninvolvement with May Bartram, a devoted companion who represents the possibility of a more fruitful life. In essence, "The Beast in the Jungle" traces Marcher's tortuous route to total negation through a series of episodes in which he fails to perceive, or, as James puts it, "is afraid to recognize what he incidentally misses." Appropriately, Marcher's deathlike withdrawal from life reaches its climax at May's grave where his adventure is completed not in a traditional physical ordeal, but in his shrinking from a monster created by his own psychic urgencies and imagination.

James faced the technical problem inherent in dramatizing nonlife by shifting his artistic focus from narrative incidents to clusters of images that mark the stages of his protagonist's psychological evasions. By filling the void resulting from Marcher's inaction, imagery itself becomes a kind of dominant action, an adumbration of the subconscious energies of Marcher's inner life. The inventiveness that most fiction writers expend on plot James thus invests in interrelated images and symbols that tell a tense story of omissions and possibilities rather than accomplished deeds. What emerges is an engrossing tapestry or mosaic made up of roads not taken, wrong turns fearfully followed, and chances missed. Ultimately, all the withdrawals, denials, and suppressions gather paradoxically into a symbol of startling emotional violence.

Both clear and suggestive, James's imagery possesses sharp immediacy and almost endless radiation. Even the most perfunctory reader will grasp the author's purport in naming his contrasting characters Marcher and May. More careful readers, however will see ramifications of meaning in other examples of seasonal imagery: the opening incident at Weatherend with its faint lure of October light; May and Marcher's comedy of terror in April; and the graveyard denouement in the fall that revives, with stunning variation, the April fiasco. The same mixture of obviousness and allusiveness controls most of the images in ''The Beast in the Jungle'' and keeps the novella from hardening into allegory or evaporating into supersubtle implications. Light, for instance, with all its elemental connotations and its association with seasonal change appears in the autumn sky, enters into the characters' language and shines in May's face. Light changes as seasons, moods, and human exigencies change, and its absence is as full of import as its many manifestations. Misleading, trustworthy, fierce, or positively revelatory, it is part of the labyrinth of images calculated to give readers a sense of mystery that cannot be fully rationalized away. The images, however, finally serve as the threads that conduct to understanding and awareness. Perhaps as convincingly as action in the traditional play or story, James's imagery quickens or retards narrative pace, provides ironic reversals, and creates climactic tensions.

An examination of James's imagery as the major vehicle of his thought in ''The Beast in the Jungle'' will reveal its pervasiveness, its closely woven texture, and its function in designating the phases of Marcher's fascinating psychological dis-

> "James faced the technical problem inherent in dramatizing nonlife by shifting his artistic focus from narrative incidents to clusters of images that mark the stages of his protagonist's psychological evasions."

integration. Clearly, James's art depends most heavily on images associated with seasons, links or connections, light, and burial. With metaphysical subtlety, he also employs a complex of sibyl-seeress-sphinx images to elaborate May Bartram's role as a counterintelligence whose glimpses into Marcher's mind date many of the crises of his inner history. Finally, to achieve his almost surrealistic climax, James relies on violent beast imagery to conclude Marcher's negative, actionless adventure.

Of course, other image-symbol patterns wind intricately through James's novella, sometimes fusing with the dominant ones and sometimes modifying them. ''The Beast in the Jungle'' is, indeed, so fine a web of connotation that it may be described as a vision of life ultimately inseparable from its metaphorical expression.

Although my study will be concerned with James's imagery, I recognize that its dramatic impact is heightened by a style at once elliptical, tortuous, and full of qualifications, intensifications, and suspensefully delayed referents. As David Smit has recently written [in ''The Leap of the Beast: The Dramatic Style of Henry James's 'The Beast in the Jungle','' *The Henry James Review* (Spring 1983)], the style of ''The Beast in the Jungle'' ''is not chaotic and it is not dull. It is as dramatic as the leap of the beast in our mind's eye.'' In fact, James's involute style is the perfect vehicle for his all-informing and, at times, untranslatable imagery.

Because seasonal imagery pervades almost every facet and nuance of the six sections of ''The Beast in the Jungle,'' it deserves special attention. James employs it in naming and defining his characters, setting his scenes, stressing motivation, and giving

> **As if to emphasize the consequences of his mock hero's insensitivity to May's appeals, James shows him as having less claim to be one of her mourners than 'the stupidest fourth cousin.'..."**

poetic coloration and resonance to his theme of the unlived life. It is so sensitively stitched into the texture of the work that it might be called the figure in the carpet.

The overall purpose of the seasonal imagery is to contrast the unnatural "law" of Marcher's life with the law governing natural processes. James, of course, associates Marcher with the end of winter and the possibility of spring, but unlike the month of March, the protagonist possesses no new or creative energies. Time passes and he remains immovably constant. James allows him occasional stirrings of life, but these stirrings occur in the depths of his being and are—until the end of the novella—overruled by an emotional rigidity stemming from his view of himself as someone mysteriously placed outside the context of ordinary humanity. Whereas the seasons flow into one another and are part of a changing order, James's main character is first seen at Weatherend, an English country house where natural fluidity seems to end and a kind of stasis prevails. Even May Bartram, who should symbolize growth, typifies pallid possibilities and has little energizing power for Marcher. She affects him as a faded memory to which he can attach no importance: having fully blotted out his past life because in a real sense it has not happened, he cannot even recall that he had met her in his youth and confided his obsession to her. Indeed, James shows him as pathetically desiring "to invent something, to get her to make-believe with him that some passage of a romantic or critical kind *had* originally occurred. He was really reaching out in imagination—as against time."

As the interval between March and May, April has a sinister importance in James's novella. It looms as the cruelest month not because, as in T. S.

Eliot's wasteland, it compels new growth, but because it acts as an unnatural, permanent barrier. For James, April does not serve as a bridge but as a lacuna, a gap never successfully spanned. It represents the germinal vigor almost entirely absent from Marcher's makeup. It represents the unruly and agitated time of the beast which in healthy lives must be lived through and thus accommodated to the procession of the months. To bypass it is to miss the initiating forces that stimulate and assure efflorescence and harvest. Predictably, then, what doesn't happen in "The Beast in the Jungle" actually does and does not take place in April: James shows that, though Marcher is physically present at his unique destiny, he witnesses no action as the beast springs. With his story beginning and ending in the fall, Marcher has more symbolic affinity with that season than with either April or May.

James places his climactic April scene with great care in the fourth section of "The Beast in the Jungle." It therefore begins the second half of the novella with the tragic assurance that the protagonist will never discover in May Bartram the quickening force of the month for which she is named. This conclusion is reached, however, only after three preparatory sections in which highly dramatic images establish the characters' identities, their relations to each other, and their reactions to seasonal change and time.

In the first and least pessimistic section of the novella, the seasonal imagery is closely interwoven with images of linkage, light, and burial. In staging the meeting between Marcher and May at Weatherend after a hiatus of ten years, James plays many imagistic changes on the themes of discontinuity and connection and opens up the slender possibility that his protagonist will end his self-inflicted isolation and enter life's mainstream. May's presence catches Marcher's attention and makes him feel in possession of the "sequel of something of which he had lost the beginning." He prods himself into imagining that the sound of May's voice furnishes him a "missing link," but for all his good will his memory draws a blank. With awkward earnestness, he fumbles toward knowledge as if it might forge a contact he apparently needs. Yet, James carefully shows that it is May and not Marcher who makes contact possible; her direct reminder that he had divulged his secret to her "cleared the air and supplied the link—the link it was so odd he should frivolously have managed to lose." A ray of hope appears when Marcher comforts himself that someone has shared his burden, "and so he wasn't alone a bit.'' Indeed, May's agreement to ''watch'' with him as he awaits his fate awakens speculation as to whether Marcher has made a saving connection with a vital woman and entered into what is referred to, at the beginning of the second section, as a ''goodly bond'' that will enable him to meet April's incitement to union with May when it comes.

Ironically, however, since Marcher has not changed with the years, his new meeting may become a mere reenactment of the earlier, forgotten one. He still practices detachment, entertains a ''theory'' that keeps him ''lost in the crowd,'' and affects colorless manners that secure him anonymity. His guarded language and circumspect behavior constitute an elaborate series of defenses against comradeship and other distractions that may weaken his commitment to his *idée fixe*. If the ''reunion'' at Weatherend begins with ''the feeling of an occasion missed'' and a sense that ''all the communities were wanting,'' it may already stamp Marcher as a hollow man to whom nothing can happen. Indeed, James does not encourage high hopes in his reader: when May stealthily leads up to her daring reminder of his confession, Marcher merely appraises her with ''wonder'' and stiffly gives ''no sign'' of support. The man who literally has no past to remember cannot be counted on to form a promising attachment. The question the whole novella will pose is, after all, what kind of link May can establish with someone so adept at dodges and expert in ego-preservation that he has, in a spiritual sense, converted life into an unalterable, arid autumn.

Light imagery, which James develops with a startling ''jump'' from images of links, affords a clue throughout the novella of the characters' clarity of perception and their fund of vitality. It is indicative of Marcher's original state of mind that he ''recalls'' the smallest detail of his earlier meeting with May and figuratively sees the dark past suddenly lit. In an artful use of light to give action and movement to his narrative, James compares Marcher's confidence in his memory to an ''impression operating like the torch of a lamplighter who touches into flame . . . a long row of gas-jets.'' Imagery shapes the scene into a neat drama of Marcher's psychic ineptitude and his need to believe he shared a past with May. His brilliant illumination, which should prove a transforming acuteness, only proves to be a trick of his imagination as she refutes his version of their original encounter, leaving him comically in the dark. Imagery continues to function actively when May informs him of his earlier confession and ''a light

broke for him.'' Already preparing for later developments, James characterizes the light coming from Marcher's unaided sight as weak and misleading and that coming from May as genuine and revelatory. Her perceptions are, and continue to be, trustworthy and illuminating; before the end of the first section, Marcher himself comes to place implicit faith in ''the light in her eyes.''

Like his imagery of links and light, James's burial imagery offers a slight hint that Marcher may emerge from his privacy and adopt a creative interest in life. For example, Marcher's conjectures about his first encounter with May turn on the possibility that what happened then may be ''too deeply buried—too deeply (didn't it seem?) to sprout after so many years.'' Yet, sprout it does as May attaches herself to a man whom she has a right to treat as a lunatic. It might not even be extravagant to propose, as some critics have, that James consciously staged one of the initial meetings between the ill-sorted pair ''at Pompeii, on an occasion when they had been present there at an important find''— when the past came unexpectedly to light in the present. Marcher, with May's necessary assistance, unearths something precious—a past confidence, a spontaneous approach to a shared life—that had been buried, if not for centuries, at least for ten round years. The vexing question inherent in the burial imagery is, however, whether he will use his knowledge to foster a new relationship or to serve his old monomania. Obviously, May's freedom to attach herself to him derives from her roots in reality—her roots, if it is not too much of a conceit, in April. Will Marcher, James appears to tease his readers into asking, improve upon the one generous act of his early life and be worthy of May's proffered aid?

In summary, the general effect of the imagery in the opening section of ''The Beast in the Jungle'' is to highlight the novella's immanent problem: will Marcher achieve the light or warmth and perception to form a link or bond subversive of his estranging narcissism? Except for the ominous implications of Weatherend and the October setting, the images are neither conclusive nor heavily oppressive. Marcher's severance from his own past and his inability to generate ''true'' light do not augur well for him, but he does constructively desire to be less alone and he does link himself to the potentially regenerative and light-giving May. Rather than pronounce doom on his protagonist at the outset of his fiction, James guides him to the crossroads where the future appears to be ''open'' and character will determine fate.

> "Unable to see that May comes to him like a new spring, Marcher is a striking example of what Henry Adams, in 'The Dynamo and the Virgin,' thought of as modern man's insensitivity to woman as a generative and dynamic force."

The second section, however, moves from the emergence of opportunity to near fatalism as James dramatizes May's certainty that Marcher will never outgrow the fatuity that makes him incapable of change. The section is framed by the opening declaration of May's knowledge ("The fact that she 'knew'") and her closing reliance on his inveterate blindness ("You'll never find out"). Unpromisingly, the goodly bond slackens into a loveless avoidance if not parody of marriage supported by the plausible argument, masking a fear of commitment, that a gentleman cannot ask a lady to accompany him on a "tiger-hunt." James's image patterns make it clear that as May desires the reality rather than the semblance of closeness, Marcher's sensibility narrows and his openness to the world's charm decreases; he retains his "dissimulation" toward the "people in London whose invitations he accepted and repaid," and, worst of all, he values his connection with May only because she supplies him with another pair of eyes with which to scrutinize his obsession. Link and bonding imagery paradoxically convicts Marcher of the cardinal Jamesian sin of exploiting a human being as if he or she were a means or tool to further egotistic ends.

In a little drama all its own, burial imagery also undergoes a radical change in the second section of "The Beast in the Jungle." James presents Marcher as at first buoyed up by the discovery that May is privy to his secret, which figures as "the buried treasure of her knowledge." Almost exuberantly, Marcher savors the good fortune of his new companionship: "He had with his own hands dug up this little hoard, brought to light . . . the object of value

the hiding place of which he had, after putting it into the ground himself, so strangely, so long forgotten." By the end of the section, however, James's imagery exposes Marcher's mismanagement of his excavated treasure. Moreover, in possibly the major twist of the second section, May now assumes importance as the possessor of a secret of her own, the closely guarded perception that by ceasing to respond to human vibrations Marcher is well on his way toward his destiny. This second secret, earned by shrewd observation and deeply hidden until the graveyard scene at the end of the novella, extends the burial imagery and serves as the dramatic center of Marcher's curiosity as he seeks to know what she knows. Still, he will pathologically fail to see that May and not any secret is the real treasure that might liberate him from his fate.

In perhaps the most audacious image in the second section, James begins to transform May into a Cassandra figure, one of the most penetrating of his uncommonly penetrating women. With a metaphysical elan worthy of John Donne, he ascribes to her an "indescribable" art which consists in the "feat of at once—or perhaps it was only alternately— meeting the [Marcher's] eyes from in front and mingling her own vision, as from over his shoulder, with their peep through the apertures." Obviously, May's vision has assumed an almost prophetesslike acuteness enabling her to formulate the law of Marcher's being: in possession of a light denied him, she penetrates his masks and hollow relationships and beholds him changeless and immovable in the flux of time. Indeed, as "they grew older together," her genuine attachment to him helps her to believe that he will never feel enough sympathy with another human being to "find out" what she has learned about him.

In the second section, James's skillful blurring of the time scheme of his novella emphasizes that for his protagonist the years accomplish nothing but their own passing. Though the beast crouches in "the twists and turns of the months and the years," Marcher exists physically *in* time while psychically *out* of it, sinking deeper and deeper into a temporal void, a constant autumn. No action takes place, but James's imagery invests his characters's inaction with developing drama. Unable to see that May comes to him like a new spring, Marcher is a striking example of what Henry Adams, in "The Dynamo and the Virgin," thought of as modern man's insensitivity to woman as a generative and dynamic force. By looking outside of time and beyond his own and May's innate energies, he perverts nature's laws instead of attuning himself to their rhythm. May, in contrast, achieves a kind of consummation through a life of effort and love even though she already assumes the burden of the sphinxlike intelligence who, in the fourth section, ponders the riddle of life and lost opportunities.

In the short third section, James's imagery pushes his vivid drama of consciousness toward its fatal turning point by intensifying the emptiness of the Marcher-May relationship and May's sibyl-like clairvoyance. All is artful preparation for the April scene in which the ''negative adventure'' reaches its climax of inaction, imperceptiveness, and unfulfillment. With acuteness couched in a wry tone of social satire, James presents May and Marcher almost jesting about the meaning of their long-standing tie. With a levity with undercurrents of mordant irony, she states that in the eyes of the world she seems a woman who has had her man (which she hasn't) while he passes for a man like another (which he isn't). Still, May's secret knowledge makes her sensitive to the double entendre in their banter: her language implies the truth and yet guards her secret, salves his doubts, and still gives him enough encouragement to make a closer and more binding approach. With subtle indirection, she addresses her words to his inner ear or to some recess in him uncontaminated by his obsession. Nevertheless, despite the tactful ministry of her love, he clings to his mock link with her and maintains his separateness under the guise of nearness. There is little likelihood that he will be capable of making use of his approaching April opportunity.

The seasonal imagery in this section, however, indicates that Marcher's sensibility is not impermeable. Although he fails to pick up May's subliminal messages, he begins to heed the increasingly overt lesson of time. He worries that the fleeting months and years will leave him ''no margin'' for his adventure. He discovers time's predatoriness in May's illness and aging: ''She looked older because, inevitably, after so many years, she *was old*, or almost; which was of course true in still greater measure of her companion.'' He is frightened by the bleak possibility that May will die unprivileged to see the enactment of his doom, and he is appalled that as a victim of time he may have been ''sold.'' Indeed, he almost achieves real feeling and knowledge when he experiences the ''dread of losing her by some catastrophe'': ultimately, though, his brooding and fear are only new forms of his vast emotional expenditure on the road to inaction.

Nevertheless, the time imagery of the third section marks an important milestone on Marcher's journey. After the first chapter launches him on a fresh start and the second, with a countermovement, exposes that start as false, the third chapter reveals an incompatibility between his rationalizations about himself and his deeper, subconscious stresses. James ingeniously suspends Marcher in an inconclusive state of semi-apprehension. May's subtle innuendos, the rapacity of the seasons, and the imminence of May's death have so upset his equilibrium that though his mind clings from habit to his own concerns, it is invaded by ambivalences and a new appreciation of May's humanity. He praises her for being ''kind'' and ''beautiful''; he feels ''sorry for her''; and he wonders before dismissing the thought, whether her death could be the fatality he has so long expected. He so identifies with her plight that as her health deteriorates, he imagines himself as suffering from ''some disfigurement of his outer person.'' The train of surprises set in motion by her helplessness before time causes him to dread existence without her as an empty prospect.

Clearly, James complicates Marcher's psychological state by showing him as a man of divided sensibility who knows that he does not know what his subconscious is trying to reveal to him; he cannot convert into thought what May has begun to make him grope toward. Marcher thus acts according to earlier, fixed assumptions no longer relevant to his altered situation. He cannot quite grasp the idea that May embodies the primal creativity operating with inevitability in nature but capable of being rejected by narcissistic man. With a greater than usual emphasis, James makes his heroine suggest both a season and a woman, a natural and a human impulse: she affirms an eternal principle of growth and fruition, but as a mere woman, she can only urge by gesture and circumlocution that Marcher break out of himself and live to the fullest reaches of his humanity. Her physical breakdown signals that Marcher is approaching his last chance to ''save'' himself through her. At the conclusion of the third chapter, however, with her secret intact and her light fading, he appears an unlikely candidate to restore her and himself to health.

With a heavy reliance on light and linkage imagery, James places his climactic April scene in the fourth section of ''The Beast in the Jungle.'' The strange couple meet on an April day whose ''light'' inauspiciously produces a ''sadness sharper than the greyest hours of autumn.'' The fireplace in May's house has no fire or light, and James declares

> **"** May's dual role as discerning intelligence and as the rejected spirit of spring culminates in two seemingly strained but entirely successful images."

that "it would never see a fire again." The cold fireplace corresponds to the "cold light" in May's eyes and both prefigure a fundamental loss of spirit as Marcher imagines that "her light might at any instant go out." With little light at her disposal (and with the "perfect old French clock" ticking time away), May still sees April as a possible saving link between herself and Marcher. Insisting that "It's never too late," she makes a last effort toward union (as she had made the first) and walks toward him "with a gliding step" that "diminishes the distance between them." The reverberations which James's imagery has by this time achieved lend a special emotional power to her desperate effort at connection: her movement brings her "nearer" and "close" to Marcher and all but speaks, with a language all its own, with "some finer emphasis." Nevertheless, he remains frozen in self-concern and, wondering what she has to give him, maintains his separateness.

The ingenuity of the April scene consists in James's creation of an episode of simultaneous action and nonaction, tragic recognition and comic blindness, springtime possibilities and autumnal bleakness. Marcher, who keeps waiting for the answer to his question, seals his doom on that crucial April day. For May, with her "face shining at him, her contact imponderably pressing," the negative adventure has been all too positive. His climax has the chill of anticlimax, but as he "gape[s] . . . for her revelation," she closes her eyes as if she has seen too much and then gives way to "a slow fine shudder." Although James does not belabor his point, any reader responsive to the pressure of the novella's imagery can interpret the quiet melodrama of May's "slow fine shudder" and Marcher's "fear that she might die without giving him light." She has seen the beast leap while Marcher innocently and expectantly questions the vacancy. In her resultant collapse, she surrenders her function and

all hope for him, and when he explicitly asks what has happened, she makes a sphinxlike pronouncement on his doom: "What *was* to." The light she brought to their affair has been extinguished and her bold experiment at linking him to life has been frustrated.

May's dual role as discerning intelligence and as the rejected spirit of spring culminates in two seemingly strained but entirely successful images. The first, May as sphinx, reveals her possession of the secret to the riddle that has puzzled Marcher since the end of the novella's opening pages; aged, and her face marked with innumerable "fine lines" that might have been "etched by a needle," she resembles "a serene and exquisite but impenetrable sphinx" who has attained ultimate wisdom. But the clue to her helpless sagacity is contained in the image almost implausibly intertwined with that of the sphinx. May's faded "green scarf, her wax-white face, and her soft white draperies" make her look like a lily: "She was a sphinx, yet with her white petals and green fronds she might have been a lily too—only an artificial lily, wonderfully imitated and constantly kept, without dust or stain, though not exempt from a slight droop and a complexity of faint creases, under some clear glass bell."

James's imagistic language resolves itself into a more compelling and intellectual drama than is usually conveyed by crude physical action. It leaves no doubt that Marcher has turned the natural woman into an artificial being preserved in an inviolate, inhuman state. Far from being the free germinal impulse she should naturally be, May is an object in a glass cage, a perfect victim of a monstrous egotist afraid to respond to her unspoken pleas.

The fifth section of "The Beast in the Jungle" begins with a variation on the sphinx motif and ends with Marcher's obsession with the buried secret (no longer likely to prove a treasure) that he must now exhume without May's help. James also weaves light imagery into his expanding psychological mosaic. However, the most moving motif in the special pathos of this section is that of the goodly bond established in the first section as Marcher's link to new possibilities is now permanently dissolved.

First, however, James refines upon the sphinx image and presents May, in her last conversation with Marcher, as a tender sibyl who speaks in riddles and mysteries. Although James describes her as communicating "with the perfect straightness of a sibyl," Marcher feels that her words are "all beyond him." The scene takes on structure, intellectual play, and emotional density from the energy of its controlling image. May tells Marcher strange and bewildering things that he believes without understanding: for instance, she convinces him that, despite his unawareness of it, he has met his fate; she assures him that he has crossed an unseen line and is now firmly established on "the other side" of his experience. She troubles him by warning him away from the knowledge of what has happened because "it's too much"; yet, she minimizes it by declaring it safely past. Her sibylline utterances leave him with the mournful sense of having had his ordeal and, at the same time, having been cheated of it. He suspects her of telling him that "his light has failed" but he ambivalently feels that as she speaks, "some light, hitherto hidden, had shimmered across his vision."

May's death functions as an ironic climax of the linking imagery by leaving Marcher stranded like some Hawthornian outcast of the universe. As if to emphasize the consequences of his mock hero's insensitivity to May's appeals, James shows him as having less claim to be one of her mourners than "the stupidest fourth cousin"; he is bereft, without the dignity of being able to claim any relationship with the woman who has been his mainstay. In terms of hard, practical reality, he and May had had no bond, no real intimacy. So Marcher deplores his outcast state, his banishment to the jungle that has grown more "spacious," stilled, and vacant. Even his visit to May's grave does not change his condition: it is as if the woman who offered him a link with life at Weatherend has broken all connection with him as "her two names [on the tombstone] became a pair of eyes that didn't know him."

The fifth section concludes with intermingled light and burial images that have the ring of a final verdict—Marcher beats "his forehead against the fact of the secret" kept in the grave and, in a bitter echo of May's Weatherend confession when a "light broke for him," now "no palest light broke." Nevertheless, James plants clues that these negative images will be replaced by unnaturally active ones: that his protagonist will see a lurid light, make an unexpected and catastrophic connection, and unearth a new and terrible "treasure." Before her death, May had been distressed that Marcher might be close to seeing his own folly and had put him off with kind ruses. But the accumulating data of his subconscious life will belatedly force him to see what she has seen. In fact, in his final colloquy with May, a "light . . . shimmered across his vision" only to be lost in darkness. Before it vanished,

however, "the gleam had already become for him an idea" that would take the shape of a beastly nemesis.

In the last section, James arrives at his psychological climax by recapitulating the major motifs of his novella: The fall day of the concluding graveyard scene recalls the dim October light at Weatherend, where Marcher's alliance with May began; light, however, returns with phantasmagoric effect; the riddle of the buried, sphinxlike woman is spelled out with brutal distinctness; and the April horror Marcher had once failed to see weirdly returns in the deadness of the autumn.

James sets the scene of his protagonist's epiphany in a "garden of death," where Marcher rests "on the low stone table that bore May Bartram's name." Having severed all connection with the world and even with himself, Marcher revisits the cemetery to renew his tie with "the creature beneath the sod" and to get "back into his own presence"; he is ready for the shock given him by a grief-stricken man at a nearby grave, a man whose "ravaged" face expresses the full meaning of the goodly bond. What the sphinxlike woman had tried to tell Marcher becomes manifest: "The sight that had just met his eyes named to him, as in letters of quick flame, something he had utterly, insanely missed." Obviously an alter ego who is blest in spite of his affliction, the mourner conveys a message that Marcher might have learned from Pompeii, from May's constant movement toward him, and from her once bright and then failing light. Significantly, Marcher's enlightenment comes as images of light succeed one another with ghastly coruscations: James refers to "a train of fire," a meaning which "flared," a "smoky torch," an "illumination" that "blazed to the zenith."

As already noted, the opening scene at Weatherend, like the final episode, takes place in the fall of the year "when the leaves were thick in the alleys." The major difference between the two scenes, however, is the difference between a promising prospect and a bitter harvest. May, the original light-bringer and spirit of the "goodly bond," is dead, and the fate she could not save Marcher from has been realized. The last incident also resembles and contrasts with the earlier April scene in section four: April, the symbol of possible connection and actual separation, returns as a surrogate for May and functions as the law of retribution. Moreover, Marcher's imaginary re-creation of the April day ironically completes James's book of hours and

> Marcher is the empty man with whom literature since James's time has become so tiresomely preoccupied, the embodiment of what Hemingway called 'Nada,' the man 'to whom nothing on earth was to have happened,' and this he becomes through his inability to love."

seasons with the conversion of a negative adventure into charged sensation. In direct contrast to the earlier April scene, the concluding fall-April episode contains an outburst of melodramatic imagery. The hush becomes a rush, Marcher's avoidances end in confrontation, and his deferred expectations shape themselves into an abnormal reality. In describing the "horror of awakening," James does not sentimentally grant his protagonist a reprieve or allow the violated May to make a redemptive speech from the grave: sickened with self-knowledge, Marcher experiences the full measure of his fate, and the beast, thwarted once, makes his destined leap.

There may, initially, seem to be some imagistic incongruity in the leap of the beast as the culmination of Marcher's anxious, self-probing inactivity and negation. It is almost as if an introspective drama has flared into histrionics. Superficially viewed, James's imagistic drama may have seemed to point to a conclusion in which his protagonist would wither into bewildered nihilism. The failed light, the lost connection, the buried secret, and the sphinxian double entendre have, however, given birth to half-formed alarms and insights in Marcher's subconscious. The beast, in a sense, is the emergence of those alarms to the level of awareness. James's resolution of his nonhero's negative quest with a sensational hallucinatory "action" does not reverse the drift of his imagistic narrative. He undoubtedly designed his ending to show that Marcher, the skillful evader, cannot in the logic of events escape the consequences of his inaction. Concealed as long as Marcher is not ready to see him, the beast

represents, as a metaphor of reality, the shocked recognition of self-devastation. It represents, too, the massed power of those primal energies Marcher had repressed in his offense against the spirit of May and time. In a sense, May, who in her human embodiment wished to protect him from knowledge, cannot shield him from his own nature, which had been slowly organizing a surge of energy in the covert lairs of his being. The beast, then, is only the active climactic image in a book of images remarkable for their intellectual content, emotional depth, and narrative accumulation of suspense and movement.

Source: James W. Gargano, ''Imagery as Action in 'The Beast in the Jungle','' in *Arizona Quarterly*, Vol. 42, No. 4, Winter, 1986, pp. 351–67.

Edward Wagenknecht

In the following excerpt, Wagenknecht analyzes the characters of John Marcher and May Bartram.

It must be clearly understood that Marcher is not a ''bad'' man. It is true that in effect May is sacrificed to him, but this is not his intention; he never deliberately exploits or victimizes anybody. He is ''tremendously mindful'' of all she does for him and worried over whether he is not receiving more than he gives. He escorts the lady to the opera and observes her birthday with more expensive gifts than he can really afford. He even thinks of asking her to marry him, and in a way it is only his consideration for her that prevents this: he is a man marked by destiny, but he is also a man of feeling, and he cannot believe that a man of feeling would ask a lady to accompany him on a tiger hunt. His egotism coexists with a naivete that almost makes it seem innocent; when she praises his attitude toward his ordeal, he asks, ''It's heroic?'' and again, ''I *am* then a man of courage?'' Nevertheless, his egotism is appalling. When May is stricken at last by mortal illness, he wonders momentarily whether her death might be the leap of the Beast for which he has been waiting, but he rejects this idea as he had previously rejected the love experience (it would be, for him, a ''drop of dignity'') and even goes the length of pitying the ''sphinx,'' the ''lily'' that May has become, because she may have to die without finding out what is going to happen to him!

While we must never forget in dealing with Marcher that his is a failure in understanding rather than good intentions, it is equally important to remember that this does not completely exonerate him. The consciousness of being set apart, even for misfortune, can easily become a force for distortion, especially when, as in Marcher's case, one does not see it as requiring any action or entailing any obligation. Gamaliel Bradford remarked of the poet Cowper, who thought he had committed the unpardonable sin, that he preferred being damned to being convinced that he had been mistaken, and theologians have always realized that the sinner who supposes his sins to have been so uniquely great as to carry him beyond the bounds of God's mercy is guilty of monstrous presumption as well as of the sin of despair.

May Bartram achieves the near miracle of knowing Marcher thoroughly, loving him, and yet viewing him almost objectively; at the same time she protects him by trying to help him ''to pass for a man like another.'' As for him, he realizes nothing except through her (he has not even grasped his own aging until he sees with the eyes of his flesh that she is visibly growing older), and it is a tragedy for both of them that she cannot communicate to him the most important piece of knowledge she has about him, for the simple reason that this is one of the things a man must learn for himself or die without knowing. For the Beast in Marcher's jungle is not imaginary; it is only different from any beast Marcher had conceived. Marcher is the empty man with whom literature since James's time has become so tiresomely preoccupied, the embodiment of what Hemingway called ''Nada,'' the man ''to whom nothing on earth was to have happened,'' and this he becomes through his inability to love. Life offers its best to him, and he passes it by, not because he does not value or desire it but simply because he does not recognize it. As children get ''warm'' from time to time when searching for a companion in a game of hide-and-seek and then veer off again, he experiences flashes of prescience that give us moments of hope for him: the fear of being too late; the thought that not to be anything would be worse than to be bankrupt, hanged, or dishonored. But he fails to follow up these clues because he cannot believe that such things could happen to so marked and exceptional a being as himself.

May, on the other hand, learns the truth as early as the end of the second of the six divisions of the tale, where Marcher accuses her of knowing what is to happen to him and of withholding her knowledge from him because it is too terrible to tell. She will only say that he will never know and never suffer. During her final illness she adds that it has already happened and that he has not recognized it. Why

should he seek to know that which he need not know? It is enough that *she* knows and that she can be grateful for having lived to learn what it is not. He continues to experience flashes of perception. He feels that she has more to give him than he has yet received. Once he even asks her if she is dying for him, and in a sense she is, as Milly Theale dies for her friends (or enemies) in *The Wings of the Dove*. But since he also accuses her of deserting him and leaving him alone to meet his fate, it is suitable that he should be left stranded on the periphery as he is at her funeral.

For if he is sometimes perceptive, he is more often blind. He can charge her with withholding information from him and, almost in the same breath, tell himself that, except for her feminine intuitions, she has no more knowledge than he has. Yet her own love and understanding never falter, and some hope remains to the end. ''The door's open,'' she tells him. ''It's never too late.'' She is right when she says, ''I've shown you, my dear, nothing,'' but this is merely because he has no eyes, and she is right again when she says, ''I haven't forsaken you'' and ''I'm with you—don't you see?''

But she is mistaken about one thing. Ultimately Marcher does ''know'' and suffer too, though this is not until after her death, when everything has become ''vulgar and vain'' without her, through a chance encounter near her grave, which has become to him something like Stransom's altar of the dead, with a desperately bereaved, ''deeply stricken'' young widower, visiting the grave of his young wife nearby. This man is one of those who, as Henry Adams, glancing obliquely at his own never-healing wound, once expressed it, ''suffer beyond the formulas of expression—who are crushed into silence and beyond pain,'' and Marcher envies him! ''What had the man had to make him by the loss of it so bleed and yet live?'' And, by the same token, what had Marcher himself missed? ''No passion had ever touched him, for this was what passion meant; he had survived and maundered and pined, but what had been *his* deep ravage? . . . He had seen *outside* of his life, not learned it within, the way a woman was mourned when she had been loved for herself.'' This man had lived, and May had lived, but Marcher had escaped living, and ''*she* was what he had missed.'' The Beast had sprung at last, and we leave Marcher, in his awakened anguish, flung face downward, upon May's grave. Knowledge has come at last.

Source: Edward Wagenknecht, in *The Tales of Henry James,* Frederick Ungar Publishing Co., 1984, pp. 145–60.

Sources

Harris, Janice H. ''Bushes, Bears, and 'The Beast in the Jungle'.'' *Studies in Short Fiction,* Vol. 18, No. 2 (Spring 1981): 147-54.

Tate, Allen. ''The Beast in the Jungle.'' In *Critics on Henry James,* J. Don Vann, editor, University of Miami Press, 1972, pp. 75-8.

Wharton, Edith. *The House of Mirth,* New York: Scribners, 1905.

Further Reading

Levenson, Michael H. ''Consciousness.'' In *A Genealogy of Modernism,* Cambridge University Press, 1984, pp. 1-22.
    Levenson's chapter explains how Joseph Conrad and Henry James introduced narrative innovations that the next generation of writers built on. A good comparative description of style and narrative point of view (nineteenth-century authorial omniscience versus limited-point-of-view technique).

James, Henry. *The Art of the Novel: Critical Prefaces,* New York: Scribners, 1934.
    An excellent companion text for the study of James. In this collected edition of critical prefaces, James presents the circumstances which gave rise to some of his narratives' composition, as well as wide-ranging commentary on diverse aspects of each work.

Woolf, Virginia. ''Modern Fiction.'' In *The Gender of Modernism,* edited by Bonnie Kime Scott, Indiana University Press, 1990, pp. 628-33.
    In this brief essay, Virginia Woolf, a Modernist writer, explains which techniques and concerns Modernist writers have in such a way as to make clear why James is considered an important Modernist precursor. While not mentioning James explicitly, Woolf's essay is nevertheless useful for those interested in the history of literary movements.

Bloodchild

Octavia Butler

1984

Octavia Butler, science fiction's most notable and influential African-American woman writer, first published "Bloodchild" in *Isaac Asimov's Science Fiction Magazine* in 1984. The story was well received and won two of science fiction's most prestigious awards, the Hugo and the Nebula. Butler, who is known primarily as a novelist, did not publish the story in book form until 1995, when she collected five of her short stories and two essays in *Bloodchild and Other Stories.* By this point, Butler had gained a much broader critical and popular reputation, and the collection was praised highly in distinguished mainstream forums such as the *New York Times* and *Booklist.* That same year, Butler was awarded the celebrated MacArthur Fellowship—commonly known as the "genius" award—for the body of her work.

Butler has described "Bloodchild" as a story about male pregnancy. Set on a foreign planet inhabited by giant, powerful, and intelligent insect-like beings, "Bloodchild" is the story of a young human male coming of age and coming to terms with his role as the carrier of an alien species' eggs. He witnesses the violent "delivery" of alien grubs from the abdomen of another man and is forced to question the relationship he has long taken for granted with the species whose planet he shares. Butler is acclaimed for her fully realized characters and her sensitivity toward the psychological dilemmas created by her imaginative science fiction scenarios. In the disconcerting world of "Bloodchild,"

Butler raises provocative questions about sex roles, self sacrifice, and the interdependence between different species.

Author Biography

Octavia Butler was born in Pasadena, California, on June 22, 1947, the only child of Laurice and Octavia Butler. Her father died when she was a baby, and she was raised by her mother and grandmother. Butler was a shy and solitary child who took refuge in reading. Her mother, a maid with a limited education, instilled in Butler a love of books and learning. From the age of ten, Butler knew that she wanted to be a writer. Despite the fact that she was unaware of the work of any black authors, she was determined to publish and began submitting stories to magazines in her teens. Her teachers gave her little encouragement, expressing no interest in Butler's science fiction themes.

Butler attended Pasadena City College and California State College in Los Angeles, after which she took several office, factory, and warehouse jobs. She continued to write and submit stories, which continued to be rejected by publishers. An important turn in Butler's career as a writer came when she attended the Clarion Science Fiction workshop in 1970. The workshop resulted in the publication of her first short story, ''Crossover,'' in a Clarion anthology. She did not publish any more of her work until she sold her first novel, *Patternmaster,* the first installment in her Patternist series, to Doubleday in 1976.

Over the next decade, Butler came out with four more Patternist novels, as well as a time travel novel about slavery, *Kindred,* which was published in 1979. Her next project was the Xenogenesis series, which includes the novels *Dawn, Adulthood Rites,* and *Imago.* Butler rose to prominence in the science fiction world during a time when women were just starting to assert a voice in the genre. She gained a particularly strong following of black women, among whom she was the only prominent sci-fi writer. But an increasingly wider audience soon came to enjoy and appreciate her work. After the publication of two more sci-fi novels and a collection of short stories, *Bloodchild and Other Stories,* she was awarded the prestigious MacArthur Fellowship (1995). Her most recent novels, *Parable of the Sower* (1993) and *Parable of the Talents* (1998), are part of her Earthseed series, which deals with a young woman's attempt to found a new religion in the twenty-first century.

Despite her growing fame, Butler has remained in her adult life the loner she was as a child. In a personal statement printed in *Women of Wonder,* Butler describes herself as ''comfortably asocial . . . a pessimist if I'm not careful, a feminist, an African-American, a former Baptist, and an oil-and-water combination of ambition, laziness, insecurity, certainty, and drive.''

Plot Summary

The protagonist of ''Bloodchild,'' Gan, is a Terran—a human—living on an alien planet among its powerful insect-like hosts, the Tlic, some time in the future. The story opens on Gan's ''last day of childhood.'' The events that unfold describe a rite of passage that takes place in a society where these two different species must depend on one another in order to survive. Gan's family has a special relationship with a particular Tlic named T'Gatoi. T'Gatoi has been a friend of Gan's mother, Lien, since childhood. When, generations earlier, Terrans arrived on the Tlic planet, the Tlic species was dying out. The Tlic needed Terrans in order to reproduce, using the Terrans' bodies to incubate their eggs. Despite the fact that the Tlic are more powerful physically and politically, they remain dependent on Terrans for the survival of their species. According to the arrangement between the Tlic and the Terrans, Lien would have to provide one of her children for Tlic reproduction. Gan's older sister Xuan Hoa had wanted to be chosen to play this special role, but T'Gatoi instead chose Gan and nurtured him from his first days.

The action begins with T'Gatoi bringing the family sterile Tlic eggs, which act on humans like both a drug and a medicine. The Tlic eggs make Terrans feel drunk and also prolong their lives. There is some tension between T'Gatoi and Gan's mother, Lien. Lien initially refuses to partake of the egg, but she eventually succumbs to T'Gatoi's wishes, sipping the egg and allowing T'Gatoi to embrace her. Gan does not understand why she does not want the egg. T'Gatoi comments that there was not enough egg left for Lien and so she stings her in order to sedate her. The sting loosens Lien's inhibitions and she refers to the fact that Gan is still hers, saying, ''Nothing can buy him from me.''

Suddenly T'Gatoi jumps up and goes outside, sensing something wrong. Gan follows and sees her bringing back a man named Bram Lomas who is N'Tlic, meaning that he is about to ''give birth'' to his Tlic's eggs as they hatch into flesh-consuming grubs. It is an emergency because his Tlic, T'Khotgif Teh, is sick and therefore unable to help with the ''delivery,'' putting the man in great pain and grave danger. T'Gatoi tries to send Gan to call for help, but he sends his older brother Qui instead, saying that he is willing to stay and help perform the procedure. T'Gatoi instructs him to go and slaughter a large animal. He does not know how to do this with a knife so he goes and retrieves a hidden rifle (Terrans are not allowed to own guns) and kills an achti, a local animal, then hides the rifle again.

Gan hesitates before returning to T'Gatoi with the carcass. He has seen diagrams of what a birth entails but now he is frightened. When T'Gatoi calls for him he enters the room and sees that Lomas is unconscious. Gan's mother steps into the room and offers to help, but Gan tells her not to worry and promises not to shame her. Lomas begins to regain consciousness and begs T'Gatoi to sting and sedate him again, but she cannot do this without risking the offspring. She ties him down and begins the ''delivery,'' cutting into his abdomen, retrieving the grubs, and placing them in the carcass of the animal Gan has slaughtered. At this stage the grubs eat any flesh except their mother's, so they must be extracted before they eat their way out of their host's flesh and kill him. Though Gan had known this, he is repulsed and alarmed when T'Gatoi licks Lomas's blood and appears indifferent to his agony. T'Gatoi suddenly seems alien to him.

T'Gatoi excuses Gan to go outside and vomit when Lomas loses consciousness. Gan sees the doctor arrive along with Qui and T'Khotgif Teh, whose eggs can save Lomas. He reports to her that her young are alive and she asks after Lomas, which Gan appreciates. After she rushes in, Qui stays behind and asks Gan about what he has just wit-

Octavia Butler

nessed. Qui has always been suspicious of the Tlic and hostile toward T'Gatoi. Qui tells his brother that he once saw a Tlic kill a man who was N'Tlic. He maintains that Terrans are merely ''host animals'' for the Tlic, but Gan insists that ''it's more than that.'' In part because he now understands Qui's point of view, Gan becomes furious. Qui asks if he has been implanted yet and Gan responds by hitting him. They fight and Qui wins.

Gan returns to the house, loads the rifle, and waits for T'Gatoi. She enters and reports that Lomas and the offspring will live, but that T'Khotgif will die of her disease. She asks if Gan means to shoot her and he does not answer, but asks, ''What are we to you?'' and moves the gun to his own throat. She responds that the answer to this question is up to him and asks if she should go to his sister, Xuan Hoa, for implantation. He at first agrees but then changes his mind. T'Gatoi tells him that she must implant an egg that night. They go into Gan's bedroom and she gives him her narcotic sting before painlessly implanting an egg. In her embrace, Gan admits that he had been afraid but that he had not wanted to give her up. He says he would not have killed her, though he'd almost killed himself. T'Gatoi reassures him that he will live and that she will stay with him and take care of him.

Characters

Gan

Gan, a young human male, is the protagonist of "Bloodchild." The story centers on Gan's growing knowledge and feelings of ambivalence regarding his special relationship with the insect-like extraterrestrial T'Gatoi, a member of the Tlic species. Gan and T'Gatoi live in a state of mutual dependence, according to which humans are guests on the Tlic planet and subject to the their greater power, and the Tlic are in turn dependent on humans to propagate their species through incubating Tlic eggs in their bodies. Gan has been chosen by T'Gatoi for this special responsibility and has been raised by her with this duty in mind.

"Bloodchild" is Gan's coming of age story. The action takes place on the night of his "impregnation" by T'Gatoi, signaling his passage to adulthood, his acceptance of responsibility, and his sacrifices for both his family and for T'Gatoi herself. On this night Gan witnesses an emergency "birth" procedure T'Gatoi performs on another Tlic's human host. He experiences a crisis when he confronts the procedure's violence and comprehends the implications of accepting an alien being into his body.

Lien

Lien is Gan's mother. She too is ambivalent about Gan's relationship to T'Gatoi. Lien has been close to T'Gatoi since her childhood and has accepted her into her family as part of a newer, less exploitative arrangement for the Tlic using human hosts for reproduction. Lien has taught her children to honor and respect T'Gatoi, but as the story opens she resists T'Gatoi's offers of restorative Tlic egg and challenges her with the comment that Gan is still hers, saying, "Nothing can buy him from me."

Bram Lomas

Bram Lomas is a human on whom T'Gatoi performs an emergency "delivery" of Tlic grubs. Lomas's Tlic, T'Khotgif, is too sick to participate in the birth, subjecting Lomas to extreme pain and danger. Gan witnesses the procedure and, as a result, sees T'Gatoi in a new light.

Qui

Qui is Gan's older brother. He is a rebel against the system that requires humans to carry Tlic eggs. He had attempted to run away from the Preserve where humans live before he realized that it was impossible to escape from the Tlic's dominance on their own planet. After Gan witnesses Lomas's suffering, Qui tells him that he too has seen an emergency birth—one that ended with the human's death. He maintains that humans are like animals to the Tlic and that T'Gatoi sees Gan as her property.

T'Gatoi

T'Gatoi is a Tlic who has had a close, ongoing relationship with Gan's family for two generations. Gan's father incubated T'Gatoi in his body and T'Gatoi later introduced him to Lien, who he married. She chose Gan at birth to live with her and to eventually carry her eggs. T'Gatoi believes in the system of familial relations between humans and Tlic. She appears unmoved when she must perform the violent procedure on Bram Lomas, which disgusts and frightens Gan, but she is emotionally invested in Gan and eventually regains his consent.

Ch'Khotgif Teh

See T'Khotgif Teh

T'Khotgif Teh

T'Khotgif Teh is a Tlic who has impregnated Bram Lomas with her eggs. She is old and ill so she is not there to protect Lomas with her sting during the painful removal of her grubs from his body. The fact that she asks after Lomas's well being after learning of the successful delivery of her grubs suggests that she has an emotional investment in him as well as a biological one. After she has produced offspring her name changes to Ch'Khotgif.

Xuan Hoa

Xuan Hoa is Gan's older sister. In contrast to Qui, she feels warmly toward T'Gatoi and she would be honored to carry her eggs. When Gan momentarily refuses to be impregnated, T'Gatoi suggests that she will turn to Xuan Hoa for the duty. Gan cannot tolerate the idea of Xuan Hoa as a host so he agrees to carry the eggs after all.

Themes

Coming of Age

"Bloodchild" opens with the line, "My last night of childhood began with a visit home." This

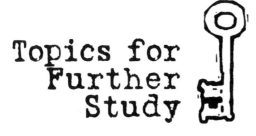

Topics for Further Study

- Do you think that the Tlic's use of humans to incubate their eggs is moral? Find evidence from the story to support or criticize the morality of the arrangement described in ''Bloodchild.''

- ''Bloodchild'' offers readers an imaginative scenario of male pregnancy set on another planet in the future. Here on earth, reproductive technology is advancing by leaps and bounds. Imagine that scientific advances made male pregnancy possible. How do you think that this would affect interactions between men and women? How would this change society? Do you think the changes would be positive or negative?

- Mary Shelley's classic novel *Frankenstein* can be interpreted, like ''Bloodchild,'' as being a story about reproduction gone awry. Compare themes of responsibility, sacrifice, fear and monstrosity in the two works.

- Until the 1970s, when women writers rose to prominence, science fiction was dominated by men. Do some research about one or more of the writers who might have influenced or inspired Butler. What concerns does their writing share? Does their gender make a difference?

- The United States continues to spend enormous amounts of money on its space program. Do some research about the experiments that are being performed by NASA and about its research objectives. How and when will this research render results that might affect the lives of common citizens? Specifically, are space colonies possible and are they desirable?

---

clearly signals that it is a coming of age story, concerning the protagonist's loss of innocence and his accession to an adult role of knowledge and responsibility. In the science-fiction fantasy world that Butler has created, Gan's rite of passage entails witnessing flesh-eating grubs hatch from a man's abdomen and then agreeing to be implanted with the eggs of a powerful, insect-like alien. Bizarre as these events may seem, the story's plot shares many elements that are common to coming of age stories.

At the beginning of the story Gan is innocent, not understanding his mother's or Qui's hostility toward T'Gatoi. At the end of the story, he is in a position of knowledge, agreeing to be implanted with T'Gatoi's eggs despite his new understanding of the fearsome risks involved. Gan undergoes a physical transformation that is also an emotional and social one. His implantation with T'Gatoi's eggs can be understood as a kind of loss of virginity. He agrees to the implantation for complicated reasons that suggest his new maturity. While T'Gatoi initially has a somewhat maternal relationship to Gan, this relationship changes when he challenges her with the gun, asserting his new status as her equal. When he chooses—despite his fear and disgust—to accept T'Gatoi's eggs, he not only protects his innocent sister from what he knows to be a terrifying experience, but he also assumes responsibility for maintaining the tenuous social order established between the human and Tlic species.

Morals and Morality

In her afterword to ''Bloodchild'' Butler asks, ''Who knows what we humans have that others might be willing to take in trade for a livable space on a world not our own?'' In the story she explores one such possibility, according to which a human society agrees to join into familial relations with an alien species and to offer some of their own members to carry alien eggs. Some complex moral questions are creatively posited by this situation—for instance, is it acceptable for one species to require another to help it survive and is such a relationship necessarily exploitative, or might it be possible for interdependence between two completely different kinds of beings to be mutually beneficial? Qui sees the relationship as exploitative, arguing that humans are nothing but host animals to the Tlic, and Gan struggles with this perspective. However, the story concludes with a strange kind of love scene in which T'Gatoi shows how much Gan means to her. Butler suggests that the power relations between humans and Tlic are complex, encompassing both fear and love.

Sex Roles

Butler is known as a feminist writer and many of her novels and stories have strong female protagonists who challenge traditional gender roles. In ''Bloodchild,'' T'Gatoi does serve as a strong and powerful female character, but the story's innovative exploration of sex roles goes even further. Rather than just presenting female characters in traditionally male roles, she creates drama by placing a male protagonist in what would normally be considered a quintessentially female dilemma. Gan is challenged with a sacrifice and a responsibility that is usually consigned to women: pregnancy. The story is not merely a reversal of masculine and feminine roles, however. T'Gatoi is powerful but is also both nurturing and dependent. And Gan's struggle requires traditionally masculine traits of courage and self-assertion as well as feminine ones of self-lessness and empathy. In a sense, in the world of ''Bloodchild,'' to allow oneself to be impregnated is to become a man.

Difference

The word *alien* signifies not only fantastic extra-terrestrials, but also anything that is extremely strange, foreign, or different from oneself. In ''Bloodchild,'' Butler has imaginatively created a society in which two species that are alien to each other live as intimates and depend upon one another for their very survival. At the beginning of the story Gan sees T'Gatoi as a member of his family. He finds it normal to lounge in the embrace of a giant insect and to get drunk on her species' eggs. The conflict of the story arises when Gan witnesses an emergency ''delivery'' of Tlic grubs from the abdomen of a human man. The process disgusts him in part because it highlights the differences between the two species. Gan can no longer see T'Gatoi as familiar and trusted after he witnesses her licking the man's blood and pulling the flesh eating grubs from his body. However, by the end of the story, Gan's relationship with T'Gatoi is reestablished on a more mature and equal level. He confronts his fear and accepts physical intimacy with her both out of

duty to his family and in the interest of harmony between the two societies.

Style

The Science Fiction Genre

The particular stylistic features that shape ''Bloodchild'' must be understood in terms of the story's genre. A genre is a category of art or literature distinguished by distinctive style, form, and content. As early as the second sentence of ''Bloodchild''—''T'Gatoi's sister had given us two sterile eggs''—most readers will recognize that it belongs to the genre of science fiction. Science fiction explores the implications of future scientific and technological advances for individuals and society as extrapolated from the current states of science and society. Science fiction represents fantastic material in a realistic manner, treating highly imaginative situations as hypothetically possible. Qualities that mark the story as science fiction include, most obviously, the fact that it is set in the future and involves an encounter with an alien race. However, Butler's emphasis on character and her development of the plot around psychological conflict are characteristics not typical of the genre, which often relies on conventions associated with the genre, such as space travel and high technology, as the driving force behind the narrative.

Setting

In keeping with the science fiction genre, the story's setting is detailed, dramatic, and fantastic. ''Bloodchild'' is set at an indeterminate point in the future, some generations after a colony of humans—known as Terrans—has fled oppression on earth and landed on a planet inhabited by powerful insect-like beings called Tlic. The Tlic control the planet, which is after all theirs, but they make special provisions for Terrans because the Tlic species is dependent on them for survival. Before the Terrans arrived, the Tlic were dying out. The animals they used to incubate their eggs had started to kill them. By taking on this role as incubators, Terrans saved the Tlic from extinction.

Terrans live in an area set aside for their use called the Preserve. It is theirs to live on and farm, but they are subject to Tlic government, including rules such as the prohibition of weapons. Before the Preserve was created, Terrans were exploited indiscriminately for their reproductive powers, so the Preserve offers a modicum of security to Terrans. Despite separate living arrangements, Tlic and Terran societies are closely intertwined. Tlic join with Terran families and choose one member to carry and incubate their eggs. This role is seen as both a sacrifice and an honor as it keeps the tenuous balance of power between the two species. These egg carriers live outside of the Preserve with their Tlic partners.

Point of View

"Bloodchild" is narrated in the first person by Gan, the Terran protagonist. Because it is described from his perspective, the situation, which seems bizarre to the reader, is treated as normal. Details of the setting and situation are revealed only as the action of the story unfolds, partly through Gan's narration of unfolding events and partly through the speech of other characters. Despite the fact that the story tells of a highly volatile personal situation, Gan's narration is rather matter-of-fact. As indicated by the first line of the story, "My last night of childhood began with a visit home," Gan narrates the story with the advantage of retrospective knowledge. He tells his story with the with the distance and coolness acquired by experience.

Symbolism

Some critics see science fiction in general and Butler's science fiction in particular as metaphoric explorations of contemporary social issues. In this way, all of the main features of the story can be understood as symbolic of present cultural tensions. For example, the relationship between the Tlic and Terrans may be interpreted as symbolic of the struggles between human groups who see each other as essentially different, yet who are forced to live together, such as racial groups in the United States and many other places in the world. This interpretation might be supported by the fact that many of Butler's other works take up racial themes more explicitly. On a more specific level, Tlic eggs are symbolic of the contradictory nature of Terran-Tlic relations. Sterile eggs are a source of pleasure and health for Terrans, signifying the Tlic's benevolent and nurturing qualities as well as the Tlic's

vulnerability to extinction. But when these eggs are fertile—necessary for the Tlic's own pleasure and health—they become an object of fear and disgust for Terrans, and soon hatch into violently self-preserving grubs.

Historical Context

Environmental Awareness

"The animals we once used began killing most of our eggs after implantation long before your ancestors arrived," T'Gatoi reminds Gan during the story's climactic scene. This suggests an environmental context for the psychological drama at the center of the story. Butler does not detail the reasons why the earlier host animals began killing Tlic eggs, but it is implicit that the tensions of plot have come about because the Tlic planet's ecosystem—that is, its ecological community and physical environment considered as a unit—is no longer in balance. "Bloodchild" explores the troubled interdependence between Tlic and human species during what might be understood as an environmental crisis on the Tlic planet. This reflects a sense of environmental crisis here on earth at the time that Butler wrote the story, when there was growing awareness of damage to the earth's ecosystem. Starting with the energy crisis of the mid-1970s, the direct consequences of human exploitation of the earth's resources increasingly occupied public consciousness. In 1979 the Three Mile Island nuclear power plant had a near meltdown, contaminating the immediate area with radioactive waste. In 1984 a large hole in the earth's protective ozone layer was discovered over Antarctica, caused by decades of pollution. In the 1980s many communities began recycling programs and there were visible protests of the development of rain forests and other wilderness areas, reflecting awareness of the relationship between the actions of individuals and the life of the planet.

Multiculturalism

Many of Butler's other works deal explicitly with racial oppression. In "Bloodchild" Butler refers to this issue only obliquely, when T'Gatoi reminds Gan that "your ancestors, fleeing from their homeworld, from their own kind who would have killed or enslaved them—they survived because of us." However, the story may be seen as a metaphor for the conflicted relations between racial

Compare & Contrast

- **1980s:** A chemical test to determine whether life exists on Mars renders inconclusive results.

  1990s: A meteorite from Mars is found in Antarctica that has structural features indicating the existence of microbes, providing evidence of life on Mars.

- **1980s:** Developments in space technology make it possible for astronauts to spend more time in space. In 1982 the Soviets set an endurance record of 211 days in space. In 1984 the first untethered space walks are performed using rocket packs.

  1990s: The Soviet Mir space station, where astronauts test long term effects of living in space, experiences technological problems and is phased out. A new space station is an international endeavor.

- **1980s:** After the first "test-tube" baby, Louise Brown, was born in England in 1978, clinics are established worldwide for in vitro fertilization as

a solution to infertility. Only about 200 test-tube babies have been born. The first successful embryo transfer and the first successful fetal surgery are performed.

  1990s: Infertility is on the rise worldwide. An estimated 4.9 million married couples in the Unites States want to be parents but are unable to conceive. There are over 300 in vitro fertilization clinics in the country. They perform more than forty thousand procedures each year.

- **1980s:** Steven Spielberg's *E.T.: The Extra-Terrestrial* becomes one of the most popular films in history. It portrays the special relationship between a sweet, gentle alien and a young boy.

  1990s: *The X-Files,* a tongue in cheek thriller about a government plot to cover up evidence of an alien invasion, attains cult status. The TV show gains widespread popularity and is made into a major motion picture.

---

and ethnic groups who live in the same society and share common interests, yet who see each other as irreconcilably different. This was the racial climate of 1980s Los Angeles where Butler lived and wrote. In this way, "Bloodchild" may be interpreted as a parable about the sacrifices and satisfactions of living in a multicultural society. Multiculturalism—the recognition and appreciation of cultural differences that exist within a larger society—became a catchword in the 1980s. Many workplaces and schools incorporated the value of multiculturalism into their training and curriculums.

Feminism

Butler has described "Bloodchild" as a story about male pregnancy. Gan's nurturing role as an egg carrier is also a fearsome one—something Gan realizes fully only when he witnesses the bloody delivery of grubs from Bram Lomas's body. Butler

challenges common ways of thinking about the meaning of pregnancy by placing a male character in this position. The inversion of sex roles that the story dramatizes may be understood as a feminist project. Butler redefines pregnancy as brave and heroic, qualities conventionally considered masculine. Such challenges to conventional thinking make sense in terms of the cultural climate in which Butler wrote. Despite the fact that the 1980s were not a moment of historical feminist solidarity, it was a time when women reaped some of the benefits of the legal and social progress of the feminist movement of the 1970s. It was also a time of backlash against feminism by men and women alike. In the 1980s the men's movement was born, which was intended to awaken "feminized" men to the masculine and powerful heroes inside of them. Butler, who describes herself as a feminist, may be responding to them with this story of heroic male pregnancy.

Surrogate Parenthood

At the center of "Bloodchild" is the drama of Gan's uncertainty over whether his role as an incubator to T'Gatoi's eggs is a matter of honor and sacrifice, or of power and exploitation. Surrogate parenthood—in which a woman agrees to be artificially inseminated and to carry a baby in exchange for monetary compensation—was one among a host of new options in the 1980s opening up to couples unable to conceive. One high profile court case in the 1980s revealed the complicated emotional and social issues surrounding surrogacy. A surrogate mother named Marybeth Whitehead broke her contract and decided to keep the child she had conceived and carried for another couple. Public opinion was sharply divided over whether the birth mother's connection to her offspring was more important than the father's. Feminists supported Whitehead, interpreting the contract as a form of exploitation of a working-class woman's body by a more powerful middle-class man. The father initially won custody of the child but this decision was overturned by a state Supreme Court. While in "Bloodchild" humans have no interest in parenting Tlic offspring, similar issues of power and exploitation are at the forefront.

Critical Overview

In 1982, early in Butler's career, black feminist scholar Francis Foster Smith summed up her critical reputation in *Extrapolation:* "Reviewers consider her a speculative fiction writer who is adequate, potentially outstanding, but at present neither particularly innovative nor interesting. However, Octavia Butler is not just another woman science fiction writer. Her major characters are black women, and through her characters and through the structure of her imagined social order, Butler consciously explores the impact of race and sex upon future society." Since then, Butler has apparently lived up to her potential. In 1995, the year that *Bloodchild and Other Stories* appeared, Butler won a prestigious MacArthur Fellowship. Popularly known as the "genius" award, MacArthur Fellowships are awarded to artists and thinkers in all mediums who push the boundaries of their fields.

Butler is known primarily as a novelist and her formidable critical reputation has been won on the strength of her Patternist and Xenogenesis series books. ("The truth is, I hate short story writing,"

she admits in the introduction to *Bloodchild and Other Stories.*) But "Bloodchild" is Butler's most prize-winning piece of writing. When the story first appeared in 1984, it won science fiction's two most prestigious awards, the Hugo and the Nebula, signaling Butler's ascension in the male-dominated world of science fiction. It was also recognized for awards by two science fiction magazines, *Locus* and *Science Fiction Chronicle Reader.* When *Bloodchild and Other Stories* was published more than a decade later, Butler had gained the attention of the mainstream literary establishment. The collection was widely and favorably reviewed, was selected as a *New York Times* Notable Book, and was placed on the Teenager List by the New York Public Library.

Butler has often been lauded for creating strong but believable female characters. Academic critics have embraced her, especially those interested in race and gender. Despite the fact that "Bloodchild" focuses on a male protagonist and a male rite of passage, the story is similar to her novels in its focus on gender relations and themes of interdependence and empathy. Writing in *Ms.,* novelist Sherley Anne Williams describes the themes of "Bloodchild" in feminist terms: "The story explores the paradoxes of power and inequality, and starkly portrays the experience of a class who, like women throughout history, are valued for their reproductive activities." In her afterword to the story, Butler expresses surprise that some scholars have interpreted "Bloodchild" as being about slavery. Butler herself characterizes it as "a love story between two very different beings," "a coming of age story in which a boy must absorb disturbing information and use it to make a decision that will affect the rest or his life," and "a pregnant man story."

Butler's following among sci-fi fans has broadened to include readers who would not normally be interested in fantasy novels. Reviews in mainstream publications have exposed an increasingly wider audience to her work and there is some critical consensus that Butler's fiction transcends the genre of science fiction. In fact, since Butler has gained such prestige, criticisms of Butler tend come from within the sci-fi community from critics who see Butler's science fiction as too "soft"—that is, too focused on delineating characters and exploring psychological and cultural issues to the exclusion of scientific plausibility and rigor. This is an accusation leveled against many of the female sci-fi writers who became visible in Butler's generation. However, the mainstream press has praised her writing for these same "soft" qualities. For exam-

ple, in the *Literary Review,* Burton Raffel describes
being compelled by the "rich dramatic textures, the
profound psychological insights and the strong,
challenging ideational matrices of virtually all of
her books." "Bloodchild," like her strongest novels, has been highly praised as a serious literary
study of character and of ideas. "Butler's imagination is strong—and so is her awareness of how to
work real issues subtly into the text of her fiction. . . . Although the book is small in size, its ideas
and aims are splendidly large," Janet St. John
writes in her *Booklist* review of *Bloodchild and
Other Stories.* Gerald Jonas of the *New York Times
Book Review* praises the collection for "never
ask[ing] easy questions or settl[ing] for easy answers" and for its power to "jar us into a new
appreciation of familiar truths."

Criticism

Sarah Madsen Hardy

*Madsen Hardy has a doctorate in English lit-
erature and is a freelance writer and editor. In the
following essay, she discusses some of the different models of dependence and exploitation in
"Bloodchild" discussed by Butler in her afterword
to the story.*

"I tried to write a story about paying the rent—
a story about an isolated colony of human beings in
an inhabited, extrasolar world," Butler explains in
her afterword to "Bloodchild." "Sooner or later,
the humans would have to make some kind of
accommodation with their um . . . their hosts. Chances
are this would be an unusual accommodation." In
"Bloodchild," Butler has created a compelling
imaginative world where adolescent boys give over
their bodies to carry the eggs of insect-like natives
of a distant planet—this is the "unusual accommodation" to which Butler refers. Readers of the story,
as well as characters within it, try to sort out the
meaning of this extreme measure. In this essay
I will look at several analogies for the arrangement between Terrans and Tlic, working toward an
understanding of the story's unsettling psychological drama.

Perhaps because several of Butler's novels,
Kindred and *Wild Seed,* deal explicitly with the
historical institution of slavery, some people have
interpreted "Bloodchild" as a parable about slavery, wherein the accommodation the Terrans make
is to be the Tlics' slaves. Upon reading the story,
one can see why slavery might come to mind, for
Terrans like Gan must allow the more powerful
Tlics to use their bodies, and Terran sacrifice leads
to Tlic gain. Gan's brother, Qui, can be seen as the
voice of this interpretation within the story. Despite
the fact that he has not been chosen to incubate Tlic
eggs himself, he deplores the social and biological
arrangement between the Terrans and the Tlic. Qui
tries to run away from the area of the Tlic planet set
aside for Terrans, the Preserve, until he realizes, in
Gan's words, that "there was no 'away'." The only
place away from the Preserve is the Tlic society
outside—which is, in Qui's eyes, the territory of his
exploiters. Personally he feels trapped and, as a
member of the human race, he feels exploited and
dehumanized by the use of his kind for Tlic reproduction. Terrans, he argues, are nothing but animals
to the Tlic.

However, the slavery interpretation is one to
which Butler herself has objected. And upon careful
thought, it does not really hold up. After all, Qui's
experience with the Tlic is limited. It is the protagonist Gan who has been chosen to live outside of the
Preserve with the Tlic T'Gatoi and to one day
incubate her young, and it is he who dramatizes
most fully the complexity of the humans' unusual
accommodation. Gan sees T'Gatoi as a family member rather than a master. While Gan's experiences
over the course of the story's actions cause him to
question his role as an incubator, his initial bond to
T'Gatoi survives the trauma and is transformed.
With full knowledge and new maturity he consents
to the implantation. If he were merely a slave, to be
used as an animal, his consent would be irrelevant.

So if "Bloodchild" is not a story about slavery,
how can we understand the strange power dynamic
between the two species? Butler offers a series of
clues. In her afterword, she describes "Bloodchild"
as "a love story between two very different beings," "a coming of age story" and a "pregnant
man story." She then goes on to spend most of the
short essay describing the habits of botflies. Botflies
are parasites—animals that live on the body of
another animal, called a host, from which they

What Do I Read Next?

- *Dawn* (1987), the first book of Octavia Butler's acclaimed Xenogenesis trilogy, takes place after a war on Earth has decimated the human race, making it necessary to engage in gene-swapping with an extraterrestrial race. The story centers on a heroic black woman and her biracial, half-alien offspring.

- *Women of Wonder: The Contemporary Years* (1995), edited by Pamela Sargent, offers a comprehensive collection of stories by the major women science fiction writers of the 1980s and 1990s.

- *Off Limits: Tales of Alien Sex* (1996), edited by Ellen Datlow, is a fascinating collection of science fiction short stories that take up the theme of sexual relations and relationships between humans and other species.

- *The Handmaid's Tale* (1986), by acclaimed novelist Margaret Atwood, tells a gripping story of surrogate reproduction in a dystopian future where class and gender divisions are exaggerated rather than minimized.

- *Woman on the Edge of Time* (1979), is a utopian sci-fi novel by Marge Piercy, who is known better as a poet and literary novelist. Piercy imagines a future where sex roles are fluid and where differences in gender and sexuality are divorced from power and exploitation, as well as from sexual reproduction.

- *Frankenstein* (1818), by Mary Shelley, a classic novel that may be seen as a precursor to modern science fiction, was a bestseller in its own time. Shelley tells of Dr. Frankenstein's overreaching scientific imagination and of the monster he creates and then abandons.

---

obtain the nutrients they needs to live. Botflies lay their eggs in the wounds left by other insect bites. When the eggs hatch and become maggots, these live on the flesh until they mature and are able to fly away. Once occupied by the botfly, a human host would be ill advised to squeeze the maggot out, for the maggot is so firmly attached to the flesh of its host that if it is removed, part of it stays behind and rots, leading to infection. Butler had spent time in Peru, where botflies are common, and the concept for "Bloodchild" grew out of her intolerable fear of them. The Tlic are botflies writ large.

Butler's afterword is fascinating, but also confusing. If "Bloodchild" is a love story, how can this be understood in relation to its inspiration—the disgusting habits of a reviled parasite? T'Gatoi and Gan do—as would characters in a conventional love story—love each other, face a crisis in their relationship, and transcend their difficulties, culminating in Gan's impregnation. However, the love Gan and T'Gatoi share is neither romantic nor sexual.

T'Gatoi begins this "love story" as a mother, telling Lien to eat her eggs and chiding Gan that he is too skinny. However, there is a strange doubleness to these nurturing nudges—she wants Lien to eat the egg so that she will give up Gan with less protest, and she wants Gan to fatten up so that he can nourish her eggs on his blood. In a way she seems caring and giving; in another she seems menacing and self-serving. Here, the unsettling figure of the parasite comes to mind. Mothers nourish their families and parasites steal nourishment from their hosts. T'Gatoi does both.

T'Gatoi's need for human hosts can be defined as repulsive and exploitative only if she is conceptualized as different, alien. After all, babies occupy and are nourished by the bodies of their mothers (who are by definition of the same species) in a way that is analogous to how parasites occupy and are nourished by the bodies of their hosts (which are by definition of a different species). T'Gatoi occupies a paradoxical position as completely familiar and, at

---

> Here, the unsettling figure of the parasite comes to mind. Mothers nourish their families and parasites steal nourishment from their hosts. T'Gatoi does both."

once, completely foreign. Butler's descriptions of T'Gatoi may evoke fear or disgust in the reader, who recognizes her as a giant insect, while they show that Gan sees her as simply part of the family. "One of my earliest memories is of my mother stretched alongside T'Gatoi, talking of things I could not understand, picking me up from the floor and laughing as she sat me on one of T'Gatoi's segments." T'Gatoi is characterized as something with *segments*—that is, totally inhuman—and, at once, to Gan, as a trusted aunt. While T'Gatoi's many-legged embraces are a testimony to her familiarity, her delivery of grubs renders her alien and thus fearsome. Gan's view of T'Gatoi changes when he witnesses Bram Lomas's alien "labor." The birth process is terrifying. Gan watches as T'Gatoi cuts into Lomas's flesh. He is horrified when he sees her bite the egg case in his abdomen and lick the dripping blood as she removes the grubs, fat and red with human blood. "The whole procedure was wrong, alien. I wouldn't have thought anything about her could seem alien to me." He fears her because he suddenly sees her as different from him.

Clearly the biological metaphor of parasitism, like the sociological metaphor of slavery, is too simple. Both slavery and parasitism are too one-way to describe the bonds and dependencies between T'Gatoi and Gan. Returning to Butler's afterword, it is important to note that she does not say that "Bloodchild" is a story *about* parasitism, but rather writing the story was a way to ease her fear of them. "When I have to deal with something that disturbs me as much as the botfly did, I write about it. I sort out my problems by writing about them." "Bloodchild" may then be understood best as a love story, a coming of age story, a male

pregnancy story, and a story about overcoming the fear of difference.

The story is resolved when Gan accepts the role of human host out of loyalty to his sister and also out of love for T'Gatoi. He recognizes her as an alien species, capable of cutting into a man's abdomen and licking his blood, but he also recognizes her as a part of a new improvised, adaptive kind of family that the two species have made together. Gan's father incubated T'Gatoi in his body and T'Gatoi in turn helped to raise Gan and to strengthen him with her eggs. Gan accepts her egg into his body as a continuation of this cycle. He makes this decision with a full knowledge of how she is different from him, and with a new mature love that accommodates this difference. Different beings need not have different interests. At the story's conclusion, two vastly different beings have seen their differences and have chosen each other anyway.

There is good reason make such a choice, Butler implies. In the climactic scene when Gan confronts T'Gatoi and threatens to kill himself rather than incubate her eggs, saying "I don't want to be a host animal," T'Gatoi reminds him that the relationship between their two species is mutually beneficial—*symbiotic* rather than parasitic. Terrans have saved the Tlic from extinction, she acknowledges, but the Tlic have also saved Terrans by sharing their planet with them. "[Y]our ancestors, fleeing from their homeworld, from their own kind who would have killed or enslaved them—they survived because of us," Butler writes, referring to the divisive kinds of fear of difference that exist within human society. By asking him to incubate her eggs T'Gatoi is asking him to be a host, but by acknowledging Terrans as people and sharing their planet with them, the Tlic have already acted as hosts themselves. The word *host* has a social definition as well as a biological one. A host is an organism that harbors and nourishes a parasite, but it is also a person who entertains and provides for his or her guests. In "Bloodchild" Butler creates a world where the biological and social go hand in hand.

Source: Sarah Madsen Hardy, "An Unusual Accommodation" for *Short Stories for Students,* The Gale Group, 1999.

Elyce Rae Helford

In the following excerpt, Helford examines "Bloodchild" in terms of Butler's treatment of issues of gender, race, and species.

Emphasis on the metaphoric impregnation of human males in "Bloodchild" makes the process of *gynesis* central to the story. In a 1986 article on Butler in *Ms.* magazine, Sherley Anne Williams reports that Butler "gleefully" describes "Bloodchild" as her "pregnant man story." Williams interprets the story as an exploration of "the paradoxes of power and inequality," as Butler portrays "the experience of a class who, like women throughout most of history, are valued chiefly for their reproductive capacities." I'd add that this "class" must be examined through issues of race and species as well as gender; however, Williams describes well the imaginative feminist space which makes the story so compelling a site for the study of *gynesis* in popular culture. Although human women tend to have more body fat—thus reducing their risk of damage or death at the bloodsucking mouths of the Tlic larvae—we learn that only men are "implanted." Human women are left to bear human children, especially sons for future Tlic usage and, at least superficially, human family bonding and happiness. Without such bonding, both species fear humans would become little more than pets or breeding stock.

One of the primary ways in which "Bloodchild" encourages a view of the Tlic power structure as a metaphor for human gender relations under patriarchy is through its depiction of men suffering the pains of childbearing (and when "birth" means removing grubs from around your internal organs, the pain can be intense). Even more powerful, however, is the suggestive complication of traditional gender roles during intercourse. Consider a description near the end of the story, as the young human male Gan recounts being drugged and "implanted" with T'Gatoi's eggs:

> . . . I undressed and lay down beside her. I knew what to do, what to expect. I had been told all my life. I felt the familiar sting, narcotic, mildly pleasant. Then the blind probing of the ovipositor. The puncture was painless, easy. So easy going in. She undulated slowly against me, her muscles forcing the egg from her body into mine.

The image of the female penetrating the male and impregnating him clearly complicates the traditional gendering of sexual imagery. The undulating body of T'Gatoi, forcing the egg into Gan's body, recalls human intercourse from both female and male positions: T'Gatoi's action embodies both possession of the female egg and male penetration

One of the primary ways in which 'Bloodchild' encourages a view of the Tlic power structure as a metaphor for human gender relations under patriarchy is through its depiction of men suffering the pains of childbearing. . . ."

and ejaculation. To this is added a representation of acquaintance rape in Gan's passivity, despite his agreement to be implanted. This example of popular cultural *gynesis* invites consideration of the gender complexity of the "pregnant man" and the "impregnating woman."

My argument that representation can destabilize the reencoding process, thereby providing readers with images (if not language) to reject limiting and misleading categories of identification, necessitates more intensive examination of these figures. For the metaphoric sex scene in "Bloodchild," the question of destabilization vs. replication becomes whether the "pregnant man" and "impregnating woman" enable readers to reach beyond shock value to consider the scene a complication rather than a simple reversal of traditional gender types.

The image can be read as destabilizing primarily because neither character is clearly identifiable in terms of gender. When we look closely at the figure of the alien T'Gatoi, we see more than a reversal of gender roles. The Tlic's insect-like reproductive cycle (which I will also discuss in terms of species) complicates the gender absolutes of human culture. Tlic eggs are fertilized by the shortlived male of the species, then implanted by the female in a host body, in the kind of reversed sexual act described above. The female raises the infants when they are old enough to exist outside the host. Thus, T'Gatoi can be seen metaphorically to fill all biological and social parenting roles—leaving the Tlic male a less clearly identifiable role—or to problematize the ease with which we ascribe gender roles in terms of parenting at all.

This destabilization of *gynesis* is limited, however, by an emphasis typical in Butler's fiction: Biological roles necessarily lead to the construction of social roles. T'Gatoi is both the government official in charge of the Preserve (filing a dominant and more traditionally "masculine" role, in terms of metaphoric reference to human culture) and caretaker of the humans against other Tlic who wish to return humans to the status of domesticated animals (the role of caretaker illustrating a more traditionally "feminine" role). It may seem merely logical to assign T'Gatoi both "masculine" and "feminine" social roles and personality traits to echo the gender implications of her reproductive functions. However, the emphasis on this parallel within the story evokes a problematic biological essentialism, for the problematization of gender roles seen in the complexity of the reproductive cycle becomes reduced to a simpler and more limiting role reversal when paired with biological determinism. That is, the depiction of reproduction we see in the scene between T'Gatoi and Gan cannot help us to destabilize the construction of gender if social roles reinforce a view of (biological) sex as determinant of subjectivity. Female Tlic dominate in this alien culture; males fill a passive, primarily reproductive function. Through this reversal of traditional human gender roles under Western patriarchy, we see a biologically determined matriarchy whose hierarchical nature limits its effectiveness as a creative textual response to patriarchy. Ultimately, destabilizing social roles would be more effective if biology were not destiny in Tlic culture, regardless of whether it resulted in a patriarchy or a matriarchy.

Source: Elyce Rae Helford, "'Would You Really Rather Die Than Bear My Young?': The Construction of Gender, Race, and Species in Octavia E. Butler's 'Bloodchild'," in *African American Review,* Vol. 28, No. 2, Summer, 1994, pp. 259–71.

Octavia Butler

In the afterword to her story "Bloodchild," Butler discusses the source of her inspiration for the story and provides some valuable insight into its meaning.

It amazes me that some people have seen "Bloodchild" as a story of slavery. It isn't. It's a

number of other things, though. On one level, it's a love story between two very different beings. On another, it's a coming-of-age story in which a boy must absorb disturbing information and use it to make a decision that will affect the rest of his life.

On a third level, "Bloodchild" is my pregnant man story. I've always wanted to explore what it might be like for a man to be put in the most unlikely of all positions. Could I write a story in which a man chose to become pregnant *not* through some sort of misplaced competitiveness to prove that a man could do anything a woman could do, not because he was forced to, not even out of curiosity? I wanted to see whether I could write a dramatic story of a man becoming pregnant as an act of love—choosing pregnancy in spite of as well as because of surrounding difficulties.

Also, "Bloodchild" was my effort to ease an old fear of mine. I was going to travel to the Peruvian Amazon to do research for my Xenogenesis books (*Dawn, Adulthood Rites,* and *Imago*), and I worried about my possible reactions to some of the insect life of the area. In particular, I worried about the botfly—an insect with, what seemed to me then, horror-movie habits. There was no shortage of botflies in the part of Peru that I intended to visit.

The botfly lays its eggs in wounds left by the bites of other insects. I found the idea of a maggot living and growing under my skin, eating my flesh as it grew, to be so intolerable, so terrifying that I didn't know how I could stand it if it happened to me. To make matters worse, all that I heard and read advised botfly victims not to try to get rid of their maggot passengers until they got back home to the United States and were able to go to a doctor—or until the fly finished the larval part of its growth cycle, crawled out of its host, and flew away.

The problem was to do what would seem to be the normal thing, to squeeze out the maggot and throw it away, was to invite infection. The maggot becomes literally attached to its host and leaves part of itself behind, broken off, if it's squeezed or cut out. Of course, the part left behind dies and rots, causing infection. Lovely.

When I have to deal with something that disturbs me as much as the botfly did, I write about it. I sort out my problems by writing about them. In a high school classroom on November 22, 1963, I remember grabbing a notebook and beginning to write my response to news of John Kennedy's assassination. Whether I write journal pages, an essay, a short story, or weave my problems into a novel, I find the writing helps me get through the trouble and get on with my life. Writing "Bloodchild" didn't make me like botflies, but for a while, it made them seem more interesting than horrifying.

There's one more thing I tried to do in "Bloodchild." I tried to write a story about paying the rent—a story about an isolated colony of human beings on an inhabited, extrasolar world. At best, they would be a lifetime away from reinforcements. It wouldn't be the British Empire in space, and it wouldn't be *Star Trek.* Sooner or later, the humans would have to make some kind of accommodation with their um . . . their hosts. Chances are this would be an unusual accommodation. Who knows what we humans have that others might be willing to take in trade for a livable space on a world not our own?

Source: Octavia Butler, Afterword to "Bloodchild" in *Bloodchild and Other Stories,* Four Walls Eight Windows, 1985, pp. 30-32.

Sources

Butler, Octavia. *Bloodchild and Other Stories,* New York: Four Walls Eight Windows, 1995.

Jonas, Gerald. Review of *Bloodchild and Other Stories. The New York Times,* October 15, 1995, p. 33.

Raffel, Burton. "Genre to the Rear, Race and Gender to the Fore: The Novels of Octavia E. Butler." *Literary Review,* Vol. 38, No. 3, Spring, 1995, pp. 454-58.

Sargent, Pamela, editor. *Women of Wonder: The Contemporary Years,* San Diego: Harcourt Brace, 1995.

Smith, Frances Foster. "Octavia Butler's Black Female Fiction." *Extrapolation,* Vol. 23, No. 1, Spring, 1982, pp. 37-49.

Williams, Sherley Anne. "Sherley Anne Williams on Octavia E. Butler." *Ms.,* March, 1986, pp. 70-71.

Further Reading

Donawerth, Jane. *Frankenstein's Daughters: Women Writing Science Fiction,* Syracuse University Press, 1997.
    An inquiry into female science fiction writers and the characters they create, focusing on utopian explorations of sex roles, the figure of the beautiful alien monster-woman, and stories written by women but narrated by male characters.

Lublin, Nancy. *Pandora's Box: Feminism Confronts Reproductive Technology,* Lanham, MD: Rowman and Littlefield, 1998.
    A sophisticated approach to the cultural and political dilemmas raised by the host of new reproductive technologies of the last decades, including surrogate parents, infertility treatments, and fetal surgery. Readers interested in the relationship between technology, reproduction, and sex roles will find challenging food for thought.

McCafferty, Larry, editor. *Across the Wounded Galaxies,* University of Illinois Press, 1990.
    A collection of in-depth interviews with many of the major figures in the science fiction world, along with informative introductions. An interview with Butler is included.

Sheehan, William. *Worlds in the Sky: Planetary Discovery from the Earliest Times through Voyager and Magellan,* University of Arizona Press, 1992.
    A lively study combining science history with anecdotes about human's long fascination with the real and hypothesized worlds in outer space.

Cathedral

Raymond Carver

1981

The first publication of the short story "Cathedral" was in the March, 1981, issue of *Atlantic Monthly*. It was selected to appear in *The Best American Short Stories, 1982,* and became the title story in the 1983 collection, *Cathedral*. This volume was very well-received by critics and readers alike, receiving nominations for the National Book Critics Circle Award and the Pulitzer Prize.

Many critics note a shift in Carver's work between the publication of *What We Talk About When We Talk About Love* and *Cathedral,* and many believe that Carver reached the zenith of his career with this collection. Adam Meyer, in his book, *Raymond Carver,* argues that "Carver is at the height of his powers here, having arrived at his full maturity, and *Cathedral* as a whole is certainly the most impressive of his collections."

"Cathedral," like many of Carver's other stories, portrays individuals isolated from each other for a variety of reasons. The narrator drinks too much and seems unable to adequately communicate with his wife. The wife has earlier tried to commit suicide because of loneliness. Only the blind man, Robert, seems able to form lasting human connections. Unlike Carver's other stories, however, "Cathedral" ends with hope; although there is no proof that the narrator will overcome his isolation, for the moment, he is in communion with himself and another human being.

Author Biography

Carver was born in Clatskanie, Oregon, on May 25, 1938, to laborer Clevie Raymond Carver and home-maker Ella Beatrice Carver. At an early age, Carver moved with his family to the working-class town of Yakima, Washington. Throughout his life, he drew on his experiences in the Pacific Northwest as settings for his stories.

Carver graduated from high school in 1956 and took a job working at a sawmill. In 1957, he married Maryann Burk, who was pregnant with their first child. By the time he was twenty, Carver was the father of two children. He and his wife worked menial jobs in order to pay their bills. Like many of the couples in Carver's short stories, he and his wife lived a hand-to-mouth existence, always in fear of some catastrophe that would upset their fragile solvency.

Carver, who wanted to write, studied under novelist John Gardner at Chico State in California. Still working low-paying jobs to support the family, he managed to take enough classes to graduate from Humboldt State University in 1963. After briefly attending the Iowa Writers' Workshop, he moved to Sacramento, California, where he became a hospital custodian for three years. During this time, he began writing seriously and publishing his stories.

Carver suffered personal turmoil in 1967, both losing his father and filing for bankruptcy. However, in the same year, his story "Will You Please Be Quiet, Please?" was chosen for *The Best American Short Stories, 1967.* Carver met with increasing success publishing his stories during the next few years. As a result, he was offered a number of teaching positions at universities. At the same time, alcohol increasingly began to affect his life. In 1976, unemployed and bankrupt, he began to drink very heavily. Carver and his wife separated and he underwent repeated hospitalizations for alcoholism.

In 1977, Carver met poet Tess Gallagher, and by 1979, the two were living together and teaching creative writing at Syracuse University. Carver's well-received collection *What We Talk About When We Talk About Love* appeared in 1981. With his writing flourishing and his personal life with Gallagher happy, Carver brought his drinking under control. He and his wife Maryann finally divorced in 1983.

In September of 1983, Carver published the collection *Cathedral.* The book marked a shift in Carver's fiction away from the bare minimalist prose of his earlier work toward a fuller, more detailed style. Critics hailed the book as a transition in Carver's work, singling out several stories, including the title story, "Cathedral," for praise.

Carver began battling cancer in 1987. Nevertheless, he continued to write, publishing his last major collection, *Where I'm Calling From,* in 1988. He married Gallagher in June, 1988, and died at their home in Port Angeles, Washington, on August 2, 1988.

Plot Summary

"Cathedral" opens with the narrator telling the reader in a conversational tone that a blind friend of his wife's is coming to visit them. The narrator is clearly unhappy about the upcoming visit. He then flashes back to the story of how his wife met the blind man when she worked for him as a reader. At the time, she was engaged to marry an officer in the Air Force. When she tells the blind man goodbye, he asks if he can touch her face. The touch of his fingers on her face is a pivotal moment in her life, something the narrator does not understand.

Although his wife has maintained contact with the blind man for ten years, this will be the first time she has seen him since her marriage, subsequent divorce, and remarriage. Robert, the blind man, has just lost his wife and will be traveling to Connecticut to visit with her family. Along the way he will spend the night at the home of the narrator and his wife. His wife tells the narrator that Robert and his wife, Beulah, were inseparable. The narrator further denigrates the blind man by considering how dreadful it must have been for Beulah not to have been seen by the man she loved.

When Robert arrives, he visits with the narrator's wife; the narrator observes them, but only occasionally joins in on the conversation. They all drink heavily and eat a large dinner, complete with strawberry pie. After dinner, they drink more, and the narrator continues to observe. Finally deciding that the blind man is "beginning to run down," the narrator turns on the television set, much to his wife's dismay. She leaves the room to get on a robe, and Robert and the narrator share a marijuana cigarette, again much to his wife's dismay.

The narrator's wife falls asleep and the narrator is left with Robert and the television. The narrator

Raymond Carver

attempts to describe what he sees on the television; however, when a cathedral appears in a documentary, the narrator is unable to find the words to describe it.

Robert asks the narrator to get some paper and a pen so that they can draw a cathedral together. The narrator does as he is asked. When he returns, he gives the paper to Robert who feels the size of the paper. Then Robert places his hand on the hand of the narrator that holds the pen. "'Go ahead, bub, draw,' he said. 'Draw. You'll see. I'll follow along with you. It'll be okay. Just begin now like I'm telling you.'"

The drawing goes on and on. Finally, Robert tells the narrator to close his eyes, and continue to draw. At this moment, something strange happens to the narrator. "It was like nothing else in my life up to now," he tells the reader. Even when Robert tells him to open his eyes, he keeps them closed. Something has happened to him that has changed his understanding of life. "My eyes were still closed. I was in my house. I knew that. But I didn't feel like I was inside anything." No longer hostile to Robert, no longer aware of Robert's blindness, the narrator experiences the possibility of change in his life.

Characters

Bub

See Narrator

Narrator

The unnamed male narrator, called "Bub" by Robert, the blind man, is the protagonist of the story. The story unfolds through the narrator's point of view. "This blind man, an old friend of my wife's, he was on his way to spend the night," announces the narrator conversationally in the first line of the story. The narrator is jealous of his wife's friendship with the blind man. He is unhappy in his work and isolated from others. According to his wife, he has no friends.

The narrator is unhappy about the blind man's visit. He seems to be uncomfortable with the notion of blindness, with his wife's connection to the man, and with his own inability to relate to other human beings.

After an evening of heavy drinking and pot smoking, the narrator turns on the television and begins to describe what he sees to the blind man. When clips of a cathedral appear on the screen, the narrator, ever inarticulate, is unable to describe a cathedral. The blind man teaches the narrator to "see" the cathedral through drawing.

Narrator's wife

Although she is never given a name in this story, the narrator's wife is an important character. It is her earlier friendship with Robert that provides the catalyst for the story. As a much younger woman, she went to work as a reader for Robert in order to earn money so that she and her childhood sweetheart could be married. As an airforce officer's wife, she moved frequently and lived in difficult conditions. Over the years she kept in touch with Robert; the connection between the two seems to be an important constant in her life. At one point after her marriage to the airforce officer and before her marriage to the narrator, she tried to commit suicide because she felt lonely and isolated. Her correspondence with Robert through the exchange of tapes continues into the present and appears to be her only outlet for her feelings.

The visit from Robert is important to her and she requests that her husband be polite. Although the woman falls asleep before the climatic moment of the story, her earlier encounter with Robert makes possible a life-changing epiphany in her husband's life.

Robert

Robert is the blind friend of the narrator's wife. He is well-traveled and well-educated. Some years before, the narrator's wife worked for him as a reader and they became good friends. As the story opens, Robert has just lost his wife and is traveling across the country to see his wife's family. He arranges to spend the night with the narrator and his wife. While at the narrator's house, Robert reveals himself to be a patient, kind man, someone who cares deeply for the narrator's wife. Even when the narrator is rude to him, Robert continues to be pleasant and outgoing.

Robert and the narrator share many drinks and smoke marijuana together. After the narrator's wife falls asleep and the narrator turns on the television set, Robert asks the narrator to describe a cathedral to him. When the narrator is unable to do so, Robert asks him to draw one for him. Robert places his hand on the narrator's hand as he draws, and in so doing, teaches the narrator how to experience a cathedral. By so doing, Robert facilitates growth in the narrator.

Themes

Alienation and Loneliness

Like the characters in many of Carver's works, the main characters experience, or have experienced, alienation and loneliness. The narrator is unhappy in his work, jealous of his wife, and unconnected to other human beings. In addition to not being connected to others himself, he seems to resent his wife's connections to other people as well. When he speaks of the impending visit by the blind man he states, "I wasn't enthusiastic about his visit. . . . A blind man in my house was not something I looked forward to." Further, once Robert arrives at the narrator's home, the narrator makes no special effort to engage him in conversation. He prefers to remain isolated and observe. Indeed, as

the conversation lags, the narrator turns on the television, an act that is not only rude, but one that provides evidence of the narrator's complete disengagement with his wife and her friend.

The narrator's behavior can be judged not only through his own responses to his wife, but also through the responses he reports his wife makes to him. For example, when the narrator says to his wife that he doesn't have any blind friends, she snaps at him, "'You don't have *any* friends. . . . Period.'"

It also seems clear that the narrator's wife has suffered through long periods of isolation and loneliness in the past, before her current marriage to the narrator. In the days just after she worked for Robert as his reader, she was married to an Air Force officer and was forced to move from base to base as he followed his career. At one point, she tried to commit suicide because, as the narrator reports, ". . . she got to feeling lonely and cut off from people she kept losing in that moving around life. She got to feeling she couldn't go on another step." Her correspondence with Robert via tape recordings seems to have provided her with healing. Nevertheless, there is little evidence that her current marriage to the narrator provides her with the human contact she so obviously yearns for. As she tries to prepare the narrator for the impending visit she pleads, "'If you love me . . . you can do this for me. If you don't love me, okay.'" There seems to be little certainty that she feels loved or needed by the narrator.

Of the three characters in the story, Robert, the blind man, seems to be the only one who does not suffer from alienation and isolation. This is ironic because not only is he blind, something which Carver seems to imply could stand in the way of forming human relationships, he has just lost his beloved wife. Certainly, one would assume that such a loss could engender great loneliness. However, there is no evidence for this in the story. Robert is out-going, polite, and interested in others. Although his journey is one of sadness and mourning, he nevertheless reaches out to both the narrator and his wife in an altruistic gesture of human kindness.

Change and Transformation

Both the narrator and his wife undergo change and transformation through their direct contact with Robert. Some years before the story opens, as the narrator's wife left the employ of Robert, he asked if

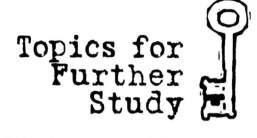

Topics for Further Study

- Critics often comment on the influence Ernest Hemingway had on Raymond Carver. Read several stories by each writer. How are their works alike? How are they different? Consider such items as dialogue, detail, characterization, and plot.

- Find several pictures of different cathedrals and study them carefully. Then shut your eyes and try to draw one of the cathedrals. How close is your rendition? How is the idea of the cathedral you have in your mind different or like the drawing you make? What did you "see" when you had your eyes closed?

- Try to find several accounts written by blind people about how they "see" the world. If possible, conduct an interview with a blind person and try to describe something that you see. Does doing this change the way you see the object? If so, why do you think the change occurred?

- Raymond Carver's work seems to change between the stories found in *Will You Please Be Quiet, Please?* and those found in *Cathedral*. Read several stories from each. What differences do you detect? What might account for the change in Carver's style?

---

he could touch her face. The narrator's wife tries to tell the narrator the importance of this event, and even shows him the poem that she has written. Even the fact that she has written a poem about the event suggests the transformative power of the touch; the narrator says, "She wrote a poem or two every year, usually after something really important had happened to her." The narrator, however, is unable to understand the importance of the event to his wife; he rejects her poetry, saying, "I didn't think much of the poem. . . . Maybe I just don't understand poetry."

During Robert's visit to the narrator and his wife, however, a similar circumstance seems to break through the narrator's isolation and at least open the possibility of change and transformation in his life. The moment occurs as the blind man asks the narrator to draw a cathedral for him. Robert places his hand on top of the narrator's as the narrator draws, and Robert encourages him every step. Finally he asks the narrator to close his eyes, and tells him to continue drawing. The narrator reports, "It was like nothing else in my life up to now." The narrator is not an articulate man; yet his final words, "It's really something," at least suggest that the world has suddenly opened for him.

Creativity and Imagination

In "Cathedral," Carver explores the role that creativity and imagination can play in the reduction of isolation and alienation in a character's life. Early in the story, the narrator reveals his own creativity. He imaginatively describes his wife's employment with the blind man, his wife's attempted suicide, even the relationship between Robert and Beulah, Robert's wife. However, although imaginative, this monologue is only shared with the reader, not with the other characters who people the story.

The narrator's wife reveals that she values creativity and imagination as she tries to write her one or two poems a year. She has, however, found an appreciative audience for her work. She reaches out to Robert and sends him her poetry. It is as if through the figurative language of poetry, she is able to reveal to him some important truths about the life she lives.

In the final, climatic scene of the story, Robert asks the narrator to employ his creativity and imagination in drawing a cathedral. By complying with Robert's wishes, the narrator finds himself in physical, intellectual, and emotional touch with the blind man. Through their shared imagination, the cathedral grows under their hands and behind their closed eyes.

Style

Narration and Point of View

One of the most interesting features of "Cathedral" is Carver's construction of the narrative point of view. The story is told by the unnamed, middle-aged, white male narrator, and the point of view is limited to him. The reader learns of the blind man's upcoming visit, the narrator's wife's previous life, and the course of the visit through the senses of the narrator. The narrator is not an articulate man; consequently, the narration is filled with gaps that the reader must fill in. In spite of the fact that the narrator controls what information the reader has, Carver provides plenty of clues to the personality of the narrator. That is, by carefully reading the story, the reader can discern things about the narrator that remain hidden even to himself. For example, although the narrator never mentions loving his wife, his jealousy is clear; he does not even want to name her first husband. In addition, it is possible to surmise that the narrator is uncomfortable with the whole notion of blindness, although he never states this directly. Finally, the use of a first-person, limited narrator allows the story to focus on the change in the narrator that occurs in the last few lines. This story is not only told by the narrator, it is also about the narrator. The change occurs almost without warning; certainly the narrator does not anticipate the epiphany that ends the story. Readers, too, are caught by surprise. Such surprise is only possible in a story where the narrative and the point of view are both tightly controlled.

Imagery

In literature, an image is a device which provides a concrete, sensory description of an idea, object or character. It is also possible for an image to become symbolic in a story. In "Cathedral," the controlling image is the cathedral. The cathedral moves from the title of the collection, to the title of the story, to the flickering image on the narrator's television, to the brown paper bag on which the narrator draws a cathedral, to finally, the wide screen of the narrator's imagination. A cathedral is a human construction, but a construction designed to provide a space for communion between humans and the sacred. While Carver never goes so far as to make this connection explicitly, it seems clear that his selection of a cathedral as the controlling image at least points to some religious significance. At the very least, a cathedral is an image that invites awe in viewers and readers. At the most, the image of the cathedral suggests the transformative powers that such a structure holds.

Epiphany

William Harmon and C. Hugh Holman in *A Handbook to Literature* define epiphany as "Literally a manifestation or showing-forth, usually of some divine being." They further explain that the word "epiphany" was first used as a term in literary criticism by James Joyce, "who used it to designate an event in which the essential nature of something . . . was suddenly perceived. It was thus an intuitive grasp of reality achieved in a quick flash of recognition in which something, usually simple and commonplace, is seen in a new light. . . ."

In "Cathedral" the narrator experiences such a flash of insight in the last few lines of the story. With his eyes closed and with the blind man's hand on his own, he suddenly "sees" the cathedral he has been attempting to draw. What he sees, however, is far greater than the image under his hand. Rather, the cathedral opens the possibility of transformation in the narrator's life. The epiphany in the story is indeed a small one; and the narrator seems unable to articulate it well. However, Carver's style is also spare, and lean, and the epiphany he offers is in keeping with this style. Further, one of the characteristic responses to an encounter with the sacred is speechlessness, the inability to adequately put into words the reality of the experience. Consequently, the narrator's final utterance, "It's really something," while nonspecific and general, points to some larger and greater intuitive leap. It is as if the narrator suddenly realizes that through contact with another person, he somehow encounters the divine.

Historical Context

Economic Climate

The characters who people Carver's short stories, including "Cathedral," find themselves in times of diminishing expectations. In 1978, only

Compare
&
Contrast

- **1980s:** Marijuana use, reaching a high point in the late 1970s, begins a decade long decline. Reported use among high school students in 1989 is half that reported in 1979.

  1990s: Marijuana use appears to once again be on the rise, as does the cultivation of marijuana in the United States. The long term effects of marijuana use are still not known.

- **1980s:** In the first year of the decade, Ronald Reagan is elected president. A Republican, Reagan institutes tax-cuts and increases military spending.

  1990s: In 1992, Bill Clinton is elected president. Clinton is a moderate Democrat interested in social reform. However, personal indiscretions lead to his impeachment.

- **1980s:** Television use increases. It is estimated that by 1980, over 100,000,000 television receivers are in use in the United States. Approximately 82 percent of American households have at least one color television at the beginning of the decade.

  1990s: Television use expands greatly. Cable stations multiply, and direct link satellite receivers are not uncommon. By 1995, 98 percent of American households have television sets. This averages to a set for every 1.2 persons in population.

- **1980s:** Although the rampant inflation of the 1970s is brought under control, the trade deficit continues and the national debt grows quickly. Some industries come out of the recession of the previous decade, but others stagnate. Although there are tax cuts, they benefit the wealthier members of the society much more than the less wealthy. The gap between the rich and the poor grows, with an ever greater percentage of the nation's wealth being held in the hands of an ever decreasing percent of the population.

  1990s: The decade of the bull market, the 1990s witness the nation's economy take an upswing, and the economy enjoys steady growth through the decade's end. The unemployment rate is at an all time low by the end of the decade. Real earning power, however, has decreased, and the gap between the rich and the poor continues to grow.

---

about 11.7 percent of the United States population was considered ''poor'' by government standards. The rate had steadily fallen since 1960. However, in the decade beginning in 1978, poverty once again increased. Further, in the early years of the Reagan administration, high inflation, high interest rates, and high unemployment reflected the recession that slowed American economic hopes. The unemployment rate in 1982, for example, was 10.8 percent. Ironically, the wealthy became wealthier during this period, while the gap between rich and poor steadily widened.

Even more disturbing, during this period those workers who were employed often earned wages that were not sufficient to raise them out of the poverty level. These people became known as ''the working poor.'' In 1988, 40 percent of all poor people worked without raising themselves above the poverty line. Consequently, for large numbers of Americans, the 1980s were a time of fear and trepidation: problems such as sickness, lack of transportation, or other hardship could knock an entire family into extreme economic difficulty.

Carver and his family were members of the working poor themselves. Married with two children by the time he was twenty in 1958, Carver continually found himself in poor-paying, low-status jobs. Although both he and his wife worked, their joint income barely kept the family afloat. Their problems exacerbated by Carver's alcoholism, the family twice had to declare bankruptcy and start over.

Likewise, the characters in Carver's short stories lead lives of near-panic. If they have work, the are generally unhappy with their jobs. Many critics describe Carver as a "blue-collar realist." In other words, Carver's characters are often modeled after people like himself, struggling to make relationships, break through isolation, and find hope in times of despair.

Social Climate

In times of recession and falling expectations, stress levels rise, alcoholism increases, and marriages falter. In Carver's stories, disaster always seems to be just outside the pages of the book. His characters generally have jobs, although they are jobs that do not contribute to their emotional or intellectual well-being. The characters seem to float in existential despair through their lives, unable to identify why the American Dream seems to have passed them by. Certainly, alcohol and alcoholism play important roles in Carver's stories. Like Carver himself, his characters often use alcohol as a means of escape from the stresses of their lives. Like Carver, his characters often find that alcohol renders them inarticulate and speechless.

In addition, although Carver does not generally refer to the social class of his characters, the lives they lead suggest that they are not wealthy people. Indeed, Carver has often been referred to as a "spokesperson" for blue-collar, working class people. Certainly, this is the milieu in which he himself grew to adulthood. As blue-collar, working class people, Carver's characters often lack both financial and emotional resources. They are also people who often lack the resources to express their feelings. As Lorna Sage points out in a discussion of Carver's prose, "Brevity was the name of his game: the people he spoke for, the white working-class Americans whose voices come over on the page haven't got too many words, or too much of anything else." They struggle with the minutia of daily life, trying to maintain their precarious hold on their lower middle class existence. Often their marriages are troubled. Certainly, in the United States of the 1980s, many marriages ended in divorce as a result of an easing of divorce laws in many states. In addition, the extra tension placed on individuals by recession and high unemployment rates also contributed to a rising divorce rate among the lower middle class during the time Carver was writing.

Critical Overview

The short story "Cathedral" first appeared in the *Atlantic Monthly* in 1981. The story was very well-received and was selected for inclusion in *The Best American Short Stories, 1982* before appearing as the title story in the 1983 collection, *Cathedral.* The story became the most widely anthologized story by Carver, and critics continued to find reasons to discuss its merits during the years following its publication.

Early reviewers of the collection singled out "Cathedral" as a story that broke new ground for Carver. Bruce Allen, for example, in a review for *The Christian Science Monitor* argued that the story was "the best example so far of the way Raymond Carver's accomplished miniaturist art is stretching itself, exploring new territories." Likewise, Josh Rubins in *The New York Review of Books* found, that unlike many of Carver's earlier stories, "'Fever' and 'Cathedral' are tales of salvation, uplift wrested from the most unpromising human materials."

Not all reviewers found Carver's spare style to be appealing, however, in spite of the shifts they noted in *Cathedral.* Anatole Broyard, for example, gave the volume faint praise while identifying the "problem" with Carver's style: "The trouble with this school of writing . . . is that it obliges the reader to be something of a semiologist, an interpreter of the faded signs of culture. The drama is always offstage, beyond the characters."

Carver himself viewed "Cathedral" to be different from his earlier work. In a 1983 interview with Mona Simpson and Lewis Buzbee, he told his interviewers about not writing for six months after *What We Talk About When We Talk About Love.* He continued, "And then the first story I wrote was 'Cathedral,' which I feel is totally different in conception and execution from any stories that have come before. I suppose it reflects a change in my life as much as it does in my way of writing. When I wrote 'Cathedral' I experienced this rush and I felt, 'This is what it's all about, this is the reason we do this.'" Indeed, reviewers and critics alike found that Carver's style deepened and enlarged in the stories collected in *Cathedral.*

In the months and years that followed the publication of "Cathedral," the story took on ever-greater importance with academic scholars and critics and generated a variety of critical readings.

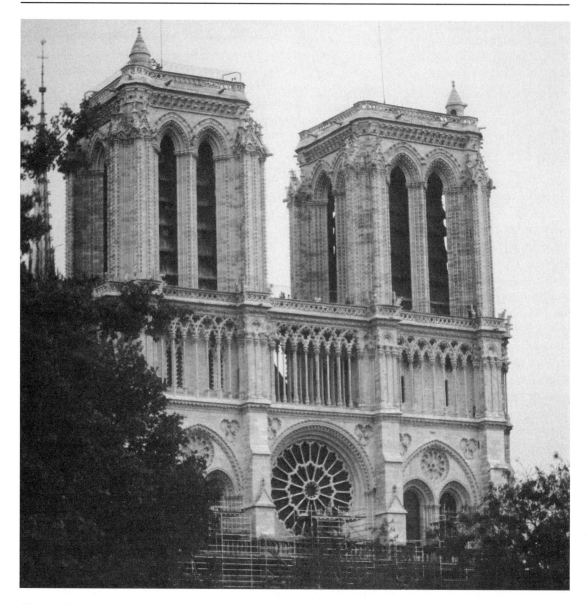

Notre Dame cathedral, often referred to as the ''World Ambassador of Gothic Cathedrals,'' was constructed over an 87-year period, 1163 - 1250.

Ewing Campbell, for example, agreed with earlier reviewers that ''Cathedral'' represented a ''new'' Carver. In a book-length study of Carver's fiction, Campbell argued that in ''Cathedral,'' Carver used a ''rarely seen opposite of an archetypal pattern.'' He further maintained that ''Cathedral'' ''provides the rare opposite of this familiar type: a narrator who discovers a life-affirming truth without the pain.''

Kirk Nesset, in a 1994 article appearing in *Essays in Literature* also read ''Cathedral'' as the story of a man who undergoes a change. In an expanded and revised version of this essay appearing in 1995, Nesset continued to explore the way the narrator breaks through his self-isolation through the shared, non-verbal collaboration with the blind man. As Nesset argued, ''It is through our collaboration with others, Carver implies, that we free ourselves from the slavery of self-absorption.''

Some critics, such as Jon Powell, focused on the hint of menace in Carver's short stories, the sense that everything is about to fall apart from some unknown and unnamed threat. Still others found Carver's style worthy of close study; Michael

Trussler, for example, examined Raymond Carver's stories in the light of a larger discussion of minimalism. Finally, in a 1998 article, Bill Mullen emphasized the role that television played in the short stories of Raymond Carver. He argued that criticism of Carver's work tends to fall into two camps: one that concentrates on Carver's minimalism, and another that "emphasizes the social and economic milieu of Carver's stories." Mullen argued in his article that "a bridge may be built between the two prevailing critical views of Carver by concentrating on the ways television may be read as both a subject of and an influence on his stories."

Criticism

Diane Andrews Henningfeld

Henningfeld is an associate professor of English at Adrian College who regularly writes and publishes critical essays for a variety of educational publishers. In the essay below, she uses reader response theory to demonstrate how readers use their imaginations to "see" the short story, "Cathedral," just as the narrator learns to "see" a cathedral through his collaboration with the blind man.

"Cathedral" first appeared in *The Atlantic Monthly* in 1981, before Carver chose to make it the title story of his 1983 collection, *Cathedral*. The collection, and most notably the story, was well-received by both readers and reviewers. Subsequently, the story has become one of the most frequently anthologized and most frequently taught short stories of Carver's body of work.

The success of the story can be accounted for in several ways. A number of reviewers (and Carver himself) identify the story as a transitional moment in Carver's career. As Adam Meyer suggests, " The notion that Carver's writing underwent a shift between *What We Talk About When We Talk About Love* and *Cathedral* has become a critical commonplace in Carver studies." The bleak, bare-boned minimalist prose of his earlier work gives way to a fuller, slightly more hopeful outlook. Carver attributes the change to a change in his life. Further, virtually all reviewers laud the shift.

Anatole Broyard, who suggests that a reader must be "something of a semiologist" to understand Carver, also links him with "strong American literary traditions." Carver's stories, he argues, "summon remembrances of Hemingway and perhaps Stephen Crane, masters of tightly packed fiction." Broyard, while not a fan of minimalist prose, nonetheless offers a clue as to how a reader could approach the short story, "Cathedral."

"Cathedral" can be called an "open text." That is, the story is a text that encourages its readers to actively participate in meaning-making; in other words, readers must act as semiologists, reading the signs that Carver leaves. The meaning of the story is not explicitly put before the reader, but rather is often hidden in the gaps of a story. The reader, by working collaboratively with the text, arrives at understanding through a cyclic process of reading and rereading the signs, trying to fill in the open spaces that are at the heart of such fiction. This kind of approach is sometimes called "reader response criticism."

The use of a first person limited narrator is one of the ways that Carver opens the text to multiple interpretation. Although the narrator speaks conversationally to the reader, his monologue clearly is constructed through both inclusion and exclusion of details. For example, the narrator tells the reader about his wife's past; through his inclusion of certain details, such as her suicide attempt, and the exclusion of others, such as his own feelings for her, the narrator constructs the character of his wife for the reader. However, the reader actively participates in the construction of the narrator's wife by "reading between the lines." Although the narrator never explicitly states that his wife is exasperated and angry with him, he gives enough details so that the reader can make that assumption. "My wife finally took her eyes off the blind man and looked at me. I had the feeling she didn't like what she saw," he reports.

A second way that Carver works collaboratively with the reader in building the text is through his parallel rendering of Robert, the blind man, and the narrator, a sighted man. The rendering is, of course, ironic. Robert clearly is a man who is educated and who has traveled extensively. He has friends all over the world. In addition, he has had a deep and meaningful relationship with his wife. Although he is blind, he "sees" how to get along with others in profound and important ways. By contrast, the narrator, although sighted, does not see how his isolation damages himself, his wife, and their relationship. He is metaphorically blind to his own human relationships. When his wife drives up with

What Do I Read Next?

- *Where I'm Calling From: New and Selected Stories* (1988), is the last collection published by Carver during his lifetime. The collection offers readers the chance to compare early and late Carver.

- Bobbie Ann Mason's collection of short stories, *Shiloh and Other Stories* (1982), is another example of well-written short stories. Mason, like Carver, has been labeled a ''K-mart realist'' by a number of critics.

- *The American Short Story: Short Stories from the Rea Award* (1993), edited by Michael Rea, provides students with a fine collection of short stories and minimalist prose. Rea has selected stories by Anne Beattie, Charles Baxter, Raymond Carver, and Grace Paley, among others.

- *Conversations with Raymond Carver,* edited by Marshall Bruce Gentry and William L. Stull (1990), offers twenty-five interviews with the writer, conducted during the years from 1977 to just before his death in 1988.

- *Ultramarine* (1986), is Carver's final volume of poetry, offering students a chance to see Carver the poet in addition to Carver the short story writer.

- The important Carver essay, ''On Writing,'' appears in a notable collection of Carver's short stories, poetry and essays, *Fires: Essays, Poems, Stories* (1983).

---

the blind man, the narrator reports, ''I got up from the sofa with my drink and went to the window to have a look. I saw my wife laughing as she parked the car. I saw her get out of the car and shut the door. She was still wearing a smile. Just amazing.'' In spite of the repeated references to sight in these lines, the narrator obviously is unable to see his wife in any other than the most basic, physical sense of the word. This is particularly ironic in that the narrator has just provided a long passage describing how sad it must have been for Beulah, Robert's wife, that her husband never saw her. ''. . . I found myself thinking what a pitiful life this woman must have led. Imagine a woman who could never see herself as she was seen in the eyes of her loved one. A woman who could go on day after day and never receive the smallest compliment from her beloved.'' Although the narrator believes that he is describing the relationship he imagines existed between Robert and Beulah, the reader knows that the description more accurately describes the relationship between the narrator and his wife.

Further, later in the evening when the three characters are having conversation, the narrator

decides that the blind man is ''beginning to run down,'' so he turns on the television. Television, of course, does not demand active participation in the same way that face-to-face communication does. The narrator prefers passively to receive impersonal visible information from a television screen than actively to participate in the two-way communication his wife and Robert share. While the narrator's wife and Robert enjoy a rich, interpersonal relationship, the narrator excludes himself from any such relationship. He is not a willing collaborator in the human project unfolding in his living room.

The limited point of view and the ironic parallels between the blind man and the narrator set up the final scene, the moment when the narrator, Robert, and the reader work together to create a moment of meaning. The phrase, ''The blind leading the blind,'' seems to best describe the action of this scene. When a television documentary begins showing pictures of cathedrals, Robert asks the narrator to describe them to him. Because the narrator is unable to adequately use language to create meaning, Robert asks him to draw a picture of the cathedral on a large piece of paper. Robert places his hand over the narrator's as he draws. Significantly, while the narrator draws, the television goes off the air. At this moment, perhaps for the first time in his life, the narrator is actively participating in meaning-making. As Robert tells him, "'Never thought anything like this could happen in your lifetime, did you, bub? Well, it's a strange life, we all know that. Go on now. Keep it up.''

With Robert's encouragement, the narrator continues to draw, finally adding people to his drawing at Robert's insistence. "What's a cathedral without people?'' the blind man asks him. And then, surprisingly, the blind man tells the narrator to close his eyes as he completes the drawing. "It was like nothing else in my life up to now," the narrator reports. Even when Robert proclaims the cathedral completed, the narrator keeps his eyes closed. It is as if in the darkness created by his closed eyelids that he finally "sees" the essence of the cathedral, and by extension, the essence of human life. In a moment of quiet epiphany, the narrator appears to make a shift toward active participation in life, made possible by the sightless communication he shared with Robert.

In this moment of epiphany, the reader's experience of reading "Cathedral" suddenly seems to parallel the narrator's experience of drawing the cathedral. Although the narrator has limited what the reader knows, the reader nonetheless actively uses imagination to construct the meaning of the story by filling in the gaps of information left out by the narrator. The details of the story such as the dinner menu, the wife's background, and Robert's beard, parallel the details of the cathedral such as flying buttresses, great doors, and windows with arches. And just as a cathedral becomes more than the sum of its parts, the story "Cathedral" becomes more than the sum of its details. The collaborative imaginative effort undertaken by the reader, the text, and Carver himself produces a moment of human understanding, a moment when options and possibilities open suddenly before the narrator, and before the reader as well.

"Cathedral" is a story that can be read and read again. Subsequent readings will never produce the same effect as the initial, naive reading; however, the act of rereading the text over time is much the same as the long, slow process of cathedral building. Each layer of bricks contributes to the transformation of hard marble to glorious transcendence. Each reading makes possible the rediscovery of the

> The use of a first person limited narrator is one of the ways that Carver opens the text to multiple interpretation. Although the narrator speaks conversationally to the reader, his monologue clearly is constructed through both inclusion and exclusion of details."

divine in the everyday world of Carver's working-class characters.

Source: Diane Andrews Henningfeld, for *Short Stories for Students*, The Gale Group, 1999.

Chris J. Bullock

In the following essay, Bullock argues that many of Carver's protagonists are concerned with dilemmas of masculine identity, most notably the narrator in "Cathedral."

In "The Castle of the Self," a chapter of his popular psychoanalytic study of the myths of masculinity, *What a Man's Gotta Do,* Antony Easthope (1990) explores the way that "in the dominant myth the masculine ego is generally imaged as a military fortification, especially in the last four hundred years of Western culture." Easthope argues that the view of ego as castle is comforting to men, because it fosters the belief that the ego can "*master* every threat." Defending the castle is not the satisfactory solution it seems, though, for, from a psychoanalytic perspective, the ego is an empty place, constructed only from the "continual effort" of defending "against hostile troops and treacherous members of the garrison."

It may seem strange to link the English cultural critic Easthope with the contemporary American short story writer Raymond Carver, who is most often discussed not in terms of sexual politics but in

> " The narrator's fear of blindness, then, suggests that control through vision is an important part of the functioning of the masculine ego."

terms of the virtues or vices of his allegedly "minimalist" style of writing, his "flatness of narrative tone, extreme spareness of story . . . [and] general avoidance of extensive rumination on the page." However, when we shift the focus from Carver's style to his characterization, we notice, I would argue, that many of his heroes are concerned with dilemmas of masculine identity readily illuminated by the psychoanalytic perspective that Easthope employs. Nowhere is this more apparent than in "Cathedral," his best-known story, published in a volume with the same title in 1984.

"Cathedral" is a story in three sections. In the long first section, the unnamed male narrator describes awaiting a visit from Robert, a blind male friend of his wife's; Robert's arrival; and the progress of an evening's eating and TV watching, up to the point at which the wife goes upstairs to change into her robe. In the brief second and longer third sections of the story, the narrator goes on to describe the development of an unexpected *rapprochement* between himself and the blind man, a *rapprochement* that concludes with the narrator drawing a cathedral on a shopping bag, with Robert's hand riding his. The particular interest of "Cathedral" is that Carver, like Easthope in "Castle," is portraying the masculine ego through the metaphor of architecture. Three architectural metaphors illuminate the action of the story: in the first section, the metaphors are the masculine ego as castle and as the less familiar Panopticon; in the second and third sections, the metaphor is the masculine self as cathedral. The first two metaphors I take to be *implied;* they seem to inform the story's detail even though they are not explicitly used in the way that the third metaphor is. In this article I will examine the use of each of these metaphors, and then bring together the understanding of masculinity and its possibilities that they convey.

If "a man's house is his castle," as the popular saying goes, then in "Cathedral" the narrator's castle is his living room, where he spends all his non-working time watching television and smoking marijuana. To understand his life there, let us return to Easthope and note his argument that

> The castle of the [masculine] ego is defined by its perimeter and the line drawn between what is inside and what outside. To maintain its identity it must not only repel external attack but also suppress treason within. It will not be surprising . . . if the enemy within the masculine individual turns out to be his own femininity.

Each of the features of ego as castle mentioned here can be found in the "living room" of the narrator's psyche.

First, the narrator's powerful need to draw the line "between what is inside and what outside" is revealed by the anxiety and aggression the narrator displays about having a "blind man in [his] house," a "blind man . . . coming to sleep in [his] house." The narrator's readiness to "repel external attack," to make himself the sole occupant of his "living room," has left him friendless, as we learn from his wife's riposte when he asserts that he doesn't have any blind friends: "'You don't have *any* friends,' she said. 'Period.'"

The narrator's lack of relationship extends to the relationship with his wife, as is evident not only in their sparring in the narrative present, but also in the remoteness of perspective as he tells the story of her attempted suicide a few years before:

> . . . one night she got to feeling lonely and cut off from people she kept losing in that moving-around life. She got to feeling she couldn't go it another step. She went in and swallowed all the pills and capsules in the medicine chest and washed them down with a bottle of gin. Then she got into a hot bath and passed out.

> But instead of dying she got sick. She threw up. Her officer—why should he have a name? he was the childhood sweetheart and what more does he want?—came home from somewhere, found her and called the ambulance. In time, she put it all on a tape and sent the tape to the blind man. . . . Next to writing a poem every year, I think it was her chief means of recreation.

This is an account written without relationship and without feeling, an account that dismisses poetry—a form of writing likely to contain feeling—as a trivial feminine recreation. In light of Easthope's comments on the castle, it seems plausible to read this account as a defense against "treason within," the feminine side of the narrator.

The peculiar irony of all this defensiveness is that only emptiness is being defended. As Easthope, following Freud, puts it, ''The ego has no energy or libido of its own and so must draw it from its reservoir in the unconscious, the id.'' In consequence

> The castle of the ego depends on what is other than itself, not vice versa. Although the castle meets attacks, its only aim is to do that, so it is in the end defined by what attacks it.

The emptiness of the narrator's living room is evident in his description of his life in it:

> Every night I smoked dope and stayed up as long as I could before I fell asleep. My wife and I hardly ever went to bed at the same time. When I did go to sleep I had these dreams. Sometimes I'd wake up from one of them, my heart going crazy.

Suppressing ''treason within,'' the narrator will have no relation with the unconscious, so that its energy can only find an outlet in his terrifying dreams.

Through the implied metaphor of the castle, then, ''Cathedral'' portrays what we might sum up as the *isolation* of the masculine ego, its pushing away of relationship with others and with other parts of the psyche. This portrayal of isolation is extended, qualified, and enriched by the second implied architectural metaphor in the story, a metaphor evoked by the story's emphasis on sight and vision.

For the ego as castle, any visitor may be a potential assailant, but a *blind* visitor seems to pose a particularly intense threat. The narrator goes to such lengths to dissociate himself from knowledge of or acquaintance with the blind that we must suspect the presence of what psychoanalysis calls *denial,* the attempt to push away things that feel like ''threats from the inner world.'' What is it that the narrator fears about the condition of blindness? We receive an important clue when he records his failure to understand how Robert and his recently deceased wife Beulah can have been ''inseparable . . . my wife's word, *inseparable*''

> They'd married, lived and worked together, slept together—had sex, sure—and then the blind man had to bury her. All this without his having ever seen what the goddamned woman looked like. It was beyond my understanding. . . . Imagine a woman who could never see herself as she was seen in the eyes of her loved one. . . . She could, if she wanted, wear green eye shadow around one eye, a straight pin in her nostril, yellow slacks and purple shoes, no matter.

In this passage the narrator is claiming sympathy with the blind man's wife, but more evident is the unconscious fear that a woman unseen has escaped control and can express herself in whatever way she pleases.

The narrator's fear of blindness, then, suggests that control through vision is an important part of the functioning of the masculine ego. The architectural metaphor that perhaps best expresses this kind of control is the Panopticon, or ''inspection house'' prison, proposed by Jeremy Bentham. Bentham's proposed Panopticon consisted of a circular building with many separate rooms, all of which could be surveyed continuously by the inhabitants of a tower in the middle of the circle. Michel Foucault (1979) describes the working of the building in the following way: ''in the peripheric ring, one is totally seen without ever seeing; in the tower one sees everything without ever being seen.'' To me the Panopticon is a wonderful metaphor for the position from which the narrator provides the account of his wife's attempted suicide. The figures in the story—the wife, the officer, the blind man—seem a long distance away, tiny separated figures, observed by a detached, all-seeing eye. They might as well be figures on the screen of the television, which is the narrator's own ''chief means of recreation.''

As implied metaphor for the masculine ego, the Panopticon, like the castle, suggests the isolating tendency of that ego, here represented by the distance between observer and observed. The Panopticon suggests even more powerfully than the castle does the problematic nature of the power achieved by living in this masculine ''building.'' Foucault describes the Panopticon as a machine, a ''mechanism of power reduced to its ideal form.'' The tower is part of the machine, part of the prison, and the mechanism ''also enables everyone to come and observe any of the observers.'' As implied metaphor in the story, the Panopticon suggests the *imprisoning* quality of the masculine attempt at control through vision. The tiny figures on the television may seem at the narrator's beck and call, but he spends every evening observing them, trapped in a mechanism of which he is unaware.

If the first section of ''Cathedral'' develops a portrayal of the isolating tendency of the masculine ego and its attempt at a power that is really more an imprisonment, the remainder of the story signals a shift in direction. The narrator, apparently reassured by Robert's failure to fit his stereotypes of the blind, admits that he is ''. . . glad for the company'' of the man. Late at night, the only entertainment the television offers is a program on cathedrals, and when the narrator tries to explain what a cathedral looks like, Robert suggests the narrator draw a cathedral and he will follow the narrator's hand with his own. The narrator is reluctant at first but eventually draws with an energy leading him to acknowledge that "I was in my house. I knew that. But I didn't feel like I was inside anything." Our earlier discussion of the narrator's house and living room as metaphors for the masculine ego makes it clear that here, at the end of the story, the narrator is acknowledging a moment of release from living according to the dictates of the isolating ego. Drawing a cathedral, then, becomes a metaphor for building, or at least designing, a kind of masculinity different from the masculinity of the castle or the Panopticon. As we follow the unfolding of the third section of the story, we can see each element required in the design of this piece of Utopian architecture.

The first thing that the two men see on the television at the start of the third section is

> a group of men wearing cowls . . . being set upon and tormented by men dressed in skeleton costumes and men dressed as devils. The men dressed as devils wore devil masks, horns and long tails. This pageant was part of a procession.

This procession is itself a very rich metaphor. For one thing, it picks up the repeated emphasis that on the outside of the cathedral there are "Gargoyles. Little statues carved to look like monsters" and that "Sometimes the cathedrals have devils and such carved into the front. Sometimes lords and ladies." The struggle between the "men wearing cowls" and the "men dressed as devils" depicts the struggle between light and dark, conscious and unconscious. The cathedral's gargoyles and devils act as reminders that the building of a valid masculinity cannot go on without the acknowledgment of the dark, of the unconscious. This is a necessary reminder to a narrator whose unconscious can only try to break through in terrifying dreams.

It may not simply be the unconscious that the narrator is denying however. The "men dressed in skeleton costumes" suggest that denial of death may also be part of the ego as castle; thus, acknowledging death may be a necessary part of the new building, the new masculinity, which the men will design. This interpretation is supported by the blind man's response to the scene the narrator describes to him: "'Skeletons,' he said. 'I know about skeletons.'" Because Robert has recently experienced the death of his wife, he can be seen as bringing an awareness and experience of death that the new building requires.

If a connection with the unconscious and an awareness of death imply the need for the narrator to connect with rather than defend against his inner life

and the physical world, the movement beyond the castle also involves regarding others as more than sources of potential assaults on the ego's stronghold. That the narrator is making this movement is indicated by the moment of empathy when he, for the first time, betrays an interest in what is in someone else's head. He asks the blind man

> Do you have any idea what a cathedral is? What they look like, that is? If someone says cathedral to you, do you have any notion what they're talking about?

The blind man responds by telling him what he has just heard on television: that "generations of the same families worked on a cathedral" and that the "men who began their life's work on them . . . never lived to see the completion of their work." Both the narrator's empathy and Robert's response indicate the obverse of the ego ideal of tightly defended, self-sufficient masculinity that Easthope criticizes so effectively; they indicate a communal and historical project. To put the point in its simplest form, the very fact that the narrator needs the blind man as a catalyst for his development proves that men, like cathedrals, "have to have these supports. To help hold them up, so to speak. These supports are called buttresses."

Why do men and cathedrals need supports? Because, as the narrator puts it, "They reach way up. Up and up. Toward the sky." And they reach "toward the sky" because "In those olden days, when they built cathedrals, men wanted to be close to God. In those olden days, God was an important part of everyone's life." Presenting the designing of an alternative masculinity through the metaphor of a religious building indicates the need for a religious or spiritual dimension to this design. But the presentation of this need is non-doctrinal; we are merely aware that the blind man is ready to bow his head when he expects grace and that he agreed to a church wedding with his wife.

Before the drawing, the designing of an alternative masculinity, can begin, the narrator must change his isolating orientation by finding, metaphorically of course, his connection to his inner life, to mortality and the physical world, to others, and to a spiritual dimension. For the drawing itself one more thing is required: a relation to the feminine. I noted earlier, following Easthope, that the narrator's suppression of inner life was also a suppression of femininity and poetic expression, regarded as feminine. To speak of the drawing in relation to the feminine may seem curious, since Carver makes a point of indicating that the narrator's wife is asleep as the process of drawing begins. However, he also notes that the narrator has no pen of his own to draw with and thus must use his wife's pen, found "in a little basket on her table." This is a marvelous image of finding expressive potency in the "little basket" of the feminine; furthermore, this image is not incompatible with that of the sleeping wife. The idea seems to be that the narrator must rely on his own access to the feminine rather than have his wife carry out the expressive and feeling side of life.

The conditions for the drawing are, as I have shown, extensive. Finally, in the last two pages of the story, it does begin. The drawing soon acquires a wonderful momentum of its own: "I put in windows. I drew flying buttresses. I hung great doors. I couldn't stop. The TV station went off the air." The narrator then pauses. The blind man feels the picture with his hand, then finds the narrator's hand again. The drawing continues. In its final stage the blind man asks the narrator to close his eyes and continue drawing; at the end of the process, the narrator, feeling he is no longer "inside anything," thinks he will keep his eyes closed "for a little longer."

It seems clear from this ending, in which the narrator refuses both enclosure and panoptical vision, that Carver is using the metaphor of the cathedral to present a possibility beyond the confines of the conventional socialization of the masculine ego. The message is that by moving towards the unconscious, the recognition of death, empathy with others, acknowledgment of the value of the dimension of spirit, and acceptance of the aid of the feminine, it seems possible to glimpse a masculinity that is based neither on enclosure nor on control by continual vigilance.

How attainable is the new masculinity imaged in the cathedral? Treating masculinity as architecture emphasizes the importance of socialization, of that which is *built* rather than simply given. In both Easthope and Foucault, the constraining aspect of the metaphor predominates; there seems little chance of breaching the modern fortress-prison. Carver offers a more optimistic vision. His narrator, initially presented as firmly under the constraint of castle and Panopticon, receives the help of a mentor and is able to take one of the mechanisms of constraint—the television—as the source of an image of alternatives. Carver's point seems to be that what is built can be differently built, however constrained the conditions. Thus "Cathedral" offers an encouraging lesson for modern men struggling themselves with the architecture of masculinity.

Source: Chris J. Bullock, "From Castle to Cathedral: The Architecture of Masculinity in Raymond Carver's 'Cathedral'," in *The Journal of Men's Studies,* Vol. 2, No. 4, May, 1994, pp. 343–51.

Keith Cushman

In the following excerpt, Cushman compares "Cathedral" to D. H. Lawrence's "The Blind Man," discussing the manner in which Carver's work is influenced by Lawrence and how Carver "rewrites" the ending of "The Blind Man," allowing a "communion" between the blind and the sighted to take place.

Anyone who reads Raymond Carver's "Cathedral," the title-story of his 1983 collection, with a knowledge of D. H. Lawrence's short stories might easily conclude that "Cathedral" is a shrewd, intriguing rewriting of "The Blind Man." Carver's tale presents a scrambled reprise of the crucial elements of Lawrence's great story. Lawrence's triangle of characters consists of a blind husband (Maurice Pervin), his wife (Isabel), and the wife's sighted friend (Bertie Reid). In "Cathedral," the unnamed husband and wife are sighted, but the wife's visiting friend (Robert) is blind. The interplay of husband, wife, and visitor comprises the slight action of both stories. Both "The Blind Man" and "Cathedral" conclude with a potentially transforming act of ritual communion between the two men. The husband in "Cathedral" genuinely enters Robert's world of blindness; Maurice Pervin does not realize how badly his attempted communion with Bertie has failed. The evidence seems clear: Carver uses Lawrence's story as the scaffolding for his own.

"Cathedral" is typical of Carver's stories in presenting trapped characters leading lives at once banal and nightmarish. As in W. H. Auden's "As I Walked Out One Evening," "the crack in the teacup opens / A lane to the land of the dead." Carver is a master at presenting what Gary L. Fisketjon has called the "terrifying implications of Normal Life." As Joe David Bellamy has put it, "[b]eneath the surface conventionality of [Carver's] salesmen, waitresses, bookkeepers, or hopeless middle-class 'occupants' lies a morass of inarticulated [sic] yearnings and unexamined horrors; repressed violence, the creeping certainty that nothing matters, perverse sexual wishes, the inadmissible evidence of inadequacy." With failed communication and missed connections so ubiquitous in Carver's stories, the mysterious but unmistakable oneness experienced by the husband and Robert at the end of "Cathedral" has a powerful impact,

> **'Cathedral' is typical of Carver's stories in presenting trapped characters leading lives at once banal and nightmarish."**

especially since the story concludes the collection. Indeed, beginning with ''Cathedral,'' Carver's work became somewhat less bleak and chilly.

In ''Cathedral,'' Carver enigmatically dramatizes the possibility of human change and redemption. This element of ''Cathedral'' is made all the more compelling by the awareness that Carver is rewriting the end of Lawrence's story, where no real communion takes place. One story resonates against the other. ''Cathedral'' offers a complex critique of ''The Blind Man'' even as it draws upon it. Chalk up one more striking example of Lawrence's influence on contemporary fiction writers.

This argument is vitiated by one major flaw. Raymond Carver wrote me in autumn 1987 that though he ''had read those three or four stories of [Lawrence's] that are always anthologized — 'The Horse Dealer's Daughter' and 'Tickets, Please' and one or two others,'' he had not read ''The Blind Man'' when he wrote ''Cathedral.'' Carver does acknowledge that when he read ''The Blind Man,'' not long after writing ''Cathedral,'' he liked Lawrence's story ''a good deal.'' He even had his students at Syracuse read ''The Blind Man'' ''in the fall term of 1982 (when [he] first read the story).'' Still, he does not ''*recall* noticing any, or many, similarities'' to his own story when he read ''The Blind Man.'' He also supplies a fascinating account of the genesis of ''Cathedral'':

> The thing that sparked the story was the visit of a blind man to our house! It's true. Well, stories have to come from someplace, yes? Anyway, this blind man did pay us a visit and even spent the night. But there all similarities end. The rest of the story was cobbled up from this and that, naturally. . . .

Though Carver had not read ''The Blind Man'' when he wrote ''Cathedral,'' he nevertheless produced a story that resides within the intertextual orbit of ''The Blind Man.'' The stories speak to and illuminate one another. Fredric Jameson, comment-

ing on Lawrence Kasdan's movie *Body Heat* (which he sees as a new version of James M. Cain's *The Postman Always Rings Twice*), notes that ''our awareness of the pre-existence of other versions, previous films of the novel as well as the novel itself, is now a constitutive and essential part of the film's structure.'' ''The Blind Man'' is similarly present in our response to ''Cathedral''—and vice versa.

Both ''The Blind Man'' and ''Cathedral'' associate blindness with a greater depth of being than is possible in the rational, limited sighted world. Over the centuries, the blindness trope has importantly signified the distinction between sight and insight. In classical mythology, the blind seer Tiresias perfectly embodies this tradition. When Oedipus gouges out his eyes, he is violently dramatizing his hard-won knowledge that all along he had been ''blind.'' His decision literally to blind himself contains a triumphant element, for the deeper understanding associated with blindness is to be preferred to the superficial grasp of reality associated with sight. The blinding of Gloucester in *King Lear* follows the same paradigm: paradoxically, Gloucester can ''see'' only after being blinded. Mr. Rochester is temporarily blinded at the end of *Jane Eyre* while selflessly trying to rescue his mad wife from the burning Thornfield Hall. Again blindness is associated with greater insight.

''The Blind Man'' and ''Cathedral,'' each in its own way, draw on this blindness trope, for Lawrence's blind Maurice and Carver's blind Robert see more deeply than their sighted counterparts. In ''The Blind Man,'' blindness is associated with instinct and the unconscious; in ''Cathedral,'' it finally represents an experience of self-abnegation and shared transcendence. Both tales rewrite a story central to the Western tradition. Both are rooted in the same cultural and literary heritage. . . .

''The Blind Man'' is actually a parable of unintegrated being, of the impossibility of bringing together body and mind, darkness and light.

Carver's ''Cathedral'' lacks such allegorical resonances, but it reads like a dream-image of Lawrence's story. As in ''The Blind Man,'' the intrusion of a visiting outsider breaks an imperfect marital equilibrium. As in Lawrence's story, Carver's characters eat together and talk inconsequentially while the husband grows jealous and uneasy. The husband is insecure; the wife feels that something is lacking in her marriage. The tension generated by "Cathedral," like that in "The Blind Man," is resolved by a surprising ending. Carver's story is also like Lawrence's in developing a fundamental dialectic between sight and blindness.

The husband narrates "Cathedral," providing the story with the off-hand, colloquial texture characteristic of Carver's fiction. Robert, the blind man who is an old friend of the narrator's wife, does not conform to stereotypes of blindness. He has a beard and a booming voice, his clothes are "spiffy"; he does not use a cane or wear dark glasses; he owns two television sets. Like Bertie Reid, the husband is uncomfortable with the other man's blindness: "his being blind bothered me." The narrator perceives the visitor as a threat.

The three people drink lots of scotch, they eat dinner, they smoke marijuana, they watch television (though of course the blind man cannot see). The wife falls asleep on the sofa as her husband and the blind man watch a late-night television program about medieval cathedrals. Robert asks the narrator to describe a cathedral to him—not an easy task. The narrator soon gives up, remarking that "cathedrals don't mean anything special to me. Nothing." Robert then suggests that they "draw [a cathedral] together": "He found my hand, the hand with the pen. He closed his hand over my hand. 'Go ahead, bub, draw,' he said." Though the narrator is "no artist," he starts drawing and can't stop. "You got it, bub," encourages the blind man. The wife awakens, but the husband continues to draw. Robert asks him to close his eyes, and he does. The blind man's "fingers rode my fingers as my hand went over the paper. It was like nothing else in my life up to now." The story ends enigmatically:

> I was in my house. I knew that. But I didn't feel like I was inside anything.
>
> "It's really something," I said.

The submerged erotic tension of Lawrence's story is closer to the surface in "Cathedral." The narrator, emotionally estranged from his wife, is unable to make human contact with anyone. He conceals his self-pity behind cynical humor, meanwhile keeping everyone at a distance. Jealous of his wife's first husband, the "man who'd first enjoyed her favors," he is also jealous of her blind friend, who years ago had said goodbye to her by touching "his fingers to every part of her face, her nose— even her neck!" The husband's jealous feelings are probably not misplaced: "My wife finally took her eyes off the blind man and looked at me. I had the feeling she didn't like what she saw."

The husband attempts to deaden his inner pain by pursuing various forms of sensory oblivion with his wife: the heavy drinking, marijuana smoking, and "serious eating": "We ate everything there was to eat on the table. We ate like there was no tomorrow. We didn't talk. We ate. We scarfed. We grazed that table." Bertie Reid is effete and intellectual, the husband in "Cathedral" is crude and unintellectual, but both reveal the limitations of sightedness.

The wife also seeks oblivion, for she too finds herself in a bad way emotionally. Like Isabel in "The Blind Man," she is an in-between character. This different woman suffers from aimlessness and anomie. Her suicide attempt at the breakup of her first marriage tells us that, unlike her husband, she at least does not hide from her emotions. She also writes poetry in order to confront and examine her life. (In contrast, the husband remarks sourly that poetry is not "the first thing I reach for when I pick up something to read.") Her happiness over her old friend's visit also demonstrates her openness to human contact. The husband notices that she is "wearing a smile" when she returns from the train depot with the blind man. "Just amazing," he says. She is one of the walking wounded, whereas her husband is one of the living dead. . . .

Raymond Carver has said that "Cathedral" is "totally different in conception and execution from any stories that have come before." When he wrote the story, he "experienced this rush and I felt, 'This is what it's all about, this is the reason we do this'." The "opening up" Carver experienced in writing the story is most strikingly reflected in the conclusion, which, as I have shown, powerfully rewrites the communion scene in "The Blind Man."

The details of touch in the two stories are similar. Maurice Pervin covers Bertie Reid's hand with his own, pressing the "fingers of the other man upon his disfigured eye-sockets," and Bertie stands "as if in a swoon, unconscious, imprisoned." In contrast, in "Cathedral" when Robert's fingers "rode my fingers as my hand went over the paper," "[i]t was like nothing else in my life up to now." Though the end of Carver's story is cryptic, there is no denying the oneness experienced by the two men in their community of touch and darkness.

It is no accident that the narrator and Robert draw a cathedral—a fact beautifully underscored by Carver's choice of title—for the implications of the story are somehow religious. Tellingly, the blind man asks if the husband is "in any way religious."

He responds, ''I guess I don't believe in it. In anything. Sometimes it's hard.'' Yet the shared experience at the end of the story offers a glimpse of religious belief. When the two men draw together, making physical contact, one blind and the other with his eyes closed, the narrator experiences transcendence, an experience ''like nothing else in my life,'' an experience in which he does not ''feel like I was inside anything.'' The story even conjures up a vision of lost religious community when the blind man tells the narrator: ''Put some people in there now. What's a cathedral without people?''

Lawrence's world of darkness is sacred but insufficient, for the darkness cannot be reconciled with its necessary antithesis. When Maurice forces the sighted Bertie to enter his all-encompassing darkness, he destroys him. In contrast, the narrator of ''Cathedral'' truly enters Robert's darkness, and that darkness is redemptive.

''The Blind Man'' communicates the unavoidable separateness between people. Sixty-five years later, Carver reimagines the story and finds a way to dramatize the possibility of renewed, revitalized human contact, to suggest that the barriers between self and self can be broken down. The story perfectly embodies Carver's remark that though he was not religious, he had to ''believe in miracles and the possibility of resurrection.'' At the end of ''Cathedral,'' the bruised, strung-out, cynical narrator has reentered the human community. Lawrence may have considered himself a ''passionately religious man,'' but he believed in struggle and commitment, not miracles. Resurrection never comes easily in Lawrence's works.

No doubt ''Cathedral'' had a personal dimension for Raymond Carver. He had much to overcome en route to becoming one of America's best, most influential short story writers: estrangement from wife and children, long years of dreary jobs, difficulty in getting established as a writer, a terrible history of alcoholism, before lung cancer finally killed him at the age of 50. The haunting affirmations of ''Cathedral'' reflect the hopeful upswing in the last decade of Carver's life as much as the change in his way of writing. These affirmations connect with the sense of moral certitude he articulated in 1981, proclaiming that ''in the best novels and short stories, goodness is recognized as such. Loyalty, love, fortitude, courage, integrity may not always be rewarded, but they are recognized as good or noble. . . . There *are* a few absolutes in this life, some verities, if you will, and we would do well

not to forget them.'' Such absolutes and verities were unavailable to the author of ''The Blind Man'' two generations earlier, no matter how strenuously he sought them. ''Cathedral,'' which yearns for absolutes, contains ''The Blind Man,'' which denies that absolutes are possible.

Both ''The Blind Man'' and ''Cathedral'' are spun out of one of the hoariest clichés of our culture: love is blind. In ''The Blind Man,'' Maurice Pervin's blindness finally convinces us of our irredeemable loneliness. But to love in ''Cathedral'' is to become blind: to enter the darkness, to respond instinctively, to abnegate self. Though Carver had not read ''The Blind Man'' when he composed ''Cathedral,'' how brilliantly he has rewritten Lawrence's story.

Source: Keith Cushman, ''Blind, Intertextual Love: 'The Blind Man' and Raymond Carver's 'Cathedral','' in *D. H. Lawrence's Literary Inheritors,* edited by Keith Cushman and Dennis Jackson, Macmillan, 1991, pp. 155–66.

Arthur M. Saltzman
In the following excerpt, Saltzman discusses the development of the narrator in ''Cathedral.''

[''Cathedral''] opens with the narrator explaining his consternation at learning that, following the death of his wife, a blind man is coming to stay at his home. His resistance to the idea is partly due to the awkwardness he anticipates—he has never known a blind person, and ''in the movies, the blind moved slowly and never laughed''—and partly due to the fact that the man, an old friend of the narrator's wife and with whom she has conducted a longstanding relationship of mailed tape recordings, represents a part of his wife's life that excludes him. She had been a reader for the blind man during the time of her relationship with her childhood sweetheart, a United States Air Force officer-in-training, which ended in his departure and her bungled suicide attempt. Both her lover and Robert, the blind man, were incorporated into poems that her husband cannot appreciate. Now the narrator is reluctant to endure the intrusion of a man who represents a competitive part of his own wife's life—a man who ''took liberties'' with her by reading her face with his hands! The awakening of his own selfishness makes the narrator sullen. He tries in vain to imagine how Robert's wife could have stood living with a man who could never see her, and in doing so exposes his own rather repellant insularity and lack of compassion.

However, Robert turns out to be a natural-born confounder of stereotypes. He is a robust, broad-gestured man who easily gets his bearings in new surroundings: he ravages his dinner, readily accepts his host's offer to smoke some pot, and even proves quite comfortable "watching" television. The combined influence of these activities inspires unaccustomed ease in the narrator; when his wife's robe falls open after she falls asleep, he cavalierly reasons that the blind man is unaware, of course, and does not bother to cover her up again.

As the two men turn their attention to a television documentary about cathedrals, the narrator tries to approximate what they are like for the sake of his guest, but "It just isn't in me to do it. I can't do any more than I've done. . . . The truth is, cathedrals don't mean anything special to me. Nothing. Cathedrals. They're something to look at on late-night TV." At Robert's suggestion the narrator gets pen and paper and together, and with Robert's hand riding on top of the narrator's they begin drawing a cathedral. In this way the amenities of keeping company evolve into a communal ceremony comparable to that which closes "A Small, Good Thing." With Robert's encouragement—"Never thought anything like this could happen in your lifetime, did you, bub? Well, it's a strange life, we all know that. Go on now. Keep it up"—the narrator is able to let go of his inhibitions and collaborate in an expressive vision. "It was like nothing else in my life up to now," he confesses to himself.

Eyes closed now, the narrator surrenders himself to Robert's gentle guidance, much as Carlyle gave himself over to Mrs. Webster's care in "Fever." Both stories, along with "A Small, Good Thing " and "Where I'm Calling From," emphasize the abundant compensations of shared experience. The protagonists of these stories are not necessarily more articulate than their precursors—the narrator of "Cathedral" can only come up with "It's really something" to appreciate the spiritual climax of the story—but they are available to depths of feeling they need not name to justify. If the images that conclude the richest stories in *Cathedral* are gestures by heavy hands—the breaking of bread against suffering or the unblinding of the blind—they begin to establish a basis for conduct beyond the limits set by stylistic austerity or introversion clung to like some ethical stance. A blind man whose wife has died and a man who admits that he does not believe in anything join together to create a cathedral. It is neither perfect nor complete, but the process is encouraging and adequate for now. Robert's belief in the concluding story is known throughout the volume: it *is* a strange life.

The most sympathetic, most human of Carver's characters "keep it up" anyway.

Source: Arthur M. Saltzman, *Understanding Raymond Carver,* University of South Carolina Press, 1988 , pp. 152–54.

Sources

Allen, Bruce. A review of *Cathedral. The Christian Science Monitor,* November 4, 1983, p. B4.

Broyard, Anatole. A review of *Cathedral. The New York Times,* September 5, 1983, p. 27.

Howe, Irving. A review of *Cathedral. The New York Times Book Review,* September 11, 1983, pp. 42-3.

Meyer, Adam. *Raymond Carver,* New York: Twayne Publishers, 1995, pp. 182-183.

Mullin, Bill. "A Subtle Spectacle: Television Culture in the Short Stories of Raymond Carver." *Critique,* Vol. 39, No. 1, Winter, 1998, pp. 99-114.

Nesset, Kirk. "Insularity and Self-Enlargement in Raymond Carver's *Cathedral." Essays in Literature,* Volume 21, No. 1, Spring, 1994, pp. 116-29.

Nesset, Kirk. *The Stories of Raymond Carver: A Critical Study,* Ohio University Press, 1995, p. 71.

Powell, Jon. "The Stories of Raymond Carver: The Menace of Perpetual Uncertainty." *Studies in Short Fiction,* Vol. 31, No. 3, Fall, 1994, pp. 647-56.

Rubins, Josh. A review of *Cathedral. The New York Review of Books,* November 24, 1983, p. 40-2.

Sage, Lorna. A review of *Elephant. The Observer,* August 14, 1988, p. 41.

Simpson, Mona, and Lewis Buzbee. An interview with Raymond Carver. In *Conversations with Raymond Carver,* Marshall Bruce Gentry and William L. Stull, editors, University of Mississippi Press, 1990, pp. 31-52.

Trussler, Michael. "The Narrowed Voice: Minimalism and Raymond Carver." *Studies in Short Fiction,* Vol. 31, No. 1, Winter, 1994, pp. 23-37.

Further Reading

Barth, John. "A Few Words About Minimalism." *The New York Times Book Review,* December 28, 1986, pp. 1-2, 25.

In this brief article, Barth offers a definition for minimalism and attempts to place it within a social and cultural context.

Runyon, Randolph Paul. *Reading Raymond Carver,* Syracuse University Press, 1992.
    A chapter-length discussion of the collection, *Cathedral,* with a section dedicated to the short story ''Cathedral.'' Runyon argues that the stories of *Ca-thedral* need to be read together, as a whole, because they ''create together what they could not have done by themselves.''

Saltzman, Arthur M. *Understanding Raymond Carver.* University of South Carolina Press, 1988.
    A good introductory critical survey of Carver's work; contains a chapter-length discussion of *Cathedral* as well as a useful annotated bibliography.

The Chrysanthemums

John Steinbeck

1937

First published in the October, 1937 issue of *Harper's,* "The Chrysanthemums" was included in John Steinbeck's 1938 short story collection, *The Long Valley.* In several significant ways, this story of an unhappy marriage is typical of Steinbeck's fiction. It takes place in the Salinas Valley of California, the "Long Valley" named in the title of his first short story collection. It concerns a married couple and examines the psychology of the unhappiness their marriage causes. Finally, it contains many vivid images of the seasons, weather, plants, and animals, all of which fascinated the writer his entire life.

One of Steinbeck's biographers, Jackson J. Bennett, has suggested that the character of the protagonist, Elisa Allen, was based on Steinbeck's first wife, a bright and energetic woman who gave up her career to follow her husband. Whatever her origins, Elisa is a woman who loves her husband, but whose life is narrow and unexciting, limited in what she can become by geography and opportunity. When a strange man passes through, a wanderer who travels up and down the coast sharpening scissors and repairing pots, her conversation with him leaves her feeling frustrated and dissatisfied.

From the beginning, this story has been regarded as one of Steinbeck's finest pieces of fiction — indeed, some have called it one of the best short stories ever written. More than sixty years later, it is still the author's most widely anthologized story, and one of his most debated. Critics are divided, for

example, over whether Elisa is sympathetic or unsympathetic, powerful or powerless. Few modern short stories have built up such a body of criticism as "The Chrysanthemums," as readers have tried to establish Elisa's reasons for her dissatisfaction with married life.

Author Biography

John Ernst Steinbeck was born on February 27, 1902, in Salinas, California, the setting for many of his early stories, including "The Chrysanthemums." The Salinas Valley was then, as it is now, largely rural and agricultural, a place of small towns and small farms. As a boy Steinbeck was a devoted reader. He wrote for his high school newspaper and attended college as an English major. Summers, he worked along the Salinas River harvesting beets. In 1925 he left home for New York City and took a job with a newspaper.

Though Steinbeck found reporting unsatisfying, he was determined to become a writer. He returned to California and published a novel about the Caribbean, *Cup of Gold,* just before the 1929 stock market crash. As the Great Depression unfolded, Steinbeck married the first of his three wives, met his closest friend, found his lifelong literary agents, and began writing about the California locations that he would feature in much of his work.

Within a few years he created some of his best work, including *The Red Pony,* (1933) *Tortilla Flat,* (1935), and *Of Mice and Men* (1937). He won awards, he was earning money, and in 1937 he was named one of Ten Outstanding Young Men of the Year. Finding celebrity distracting, Steinbeck took a tour of Europe and returned to work in seclusion. In 1930, he published a collection of short stories, *The Long Valley,* which was comprised of several previously published stories, including "The Chrysanthemums."

For years, Steinbeck visited migrant farm workers' camps, originally on assignment for the *San Francisco News.* The conditions the workers faced as they struggled to provide for their families angered and saddened him, prompting him to write his greatest novel, *The Grapes of Wrath* (1939). This novel cemented Steinbeck's reputation as a social critic. The success of *The Grapes of Wrath* and the 1940 film version ultimately separated him from the rural landscape and the rural people that had in-

formed his writing. He returned to New York City and continued to produce well-regarded and best-selling work for nearly thirty more years. He died of heart failure on December 20, 1968, at the age of sixty-four.

Steinbeck was one of the most famous and successful writers of his day. He won the Pulitzer Prize for *The Grapes of Wrath* (1940), the Nobel Prize for literature in 1962, and the United States Medal of Freedom in 1964. Three decades after his death, he continues to be one of a handful of writers whom nearly every American high school graduate has read.

Plot Summary

The story opens with a panoramic view of the Salinas Valley in winter, shrouded in fog. The focus narrows and finally settles on Elisa Allen, cutting down the spent stalks of chrysanthemums in the garden on her husband's ranch. Elisa is thirty-five, lean and strong, and she approaches her gardening with great energy. Her husband Henry comes from across the yard, where he has been arranging the sale of thirty steer, and offers to take Elisa to town for dinner and movie to celebrate the sale. He praises her skill with flowers, and she congratulates him on doing well in the negotiations for the steer. They seem a well-matched couple, though their way of talking together is formal and serious. Henry heads off to finish some chores, and Elisa decides to finish her transplanting before they get ready to leave for town.

Soon Elisa hears "a squeak of wheels and a plod of hoofs," and a man drives up in an old wagon. (He is never named; the narrator calls him simply "the man.") The man is large and dirty, and clearly used to being alone. He earns a meager living fixing pots and sharpening scissors and knives, traveling from San Diego, California, to Seattle, Washington, and back every year. The man chats and jokes with Elisa, who answers his bantering tone but has no work for him to do. When he presses for a small job, she becomes annoyed and tries to send him away.

Suddenly the man's attention is caught by the chrysanthemum stalks and seedlings. When he asks about them, Elisa's annoyance vanishes, and she becomes friendly again. The man remembers seeing chrysanthemums before, and describes them: "Kind of a long-stemmed flower? Looks like a quick puff of colored smoke?" Elisa is delighted with his description. The man tells her about one of his regular customers who also gardens, and who always has work for him when he comes by. She has asked him to keep his eyes open in his travels, and to bring her some chrysanthemum seeds if he ever finds some. Now Elisa is captivated. She invites the man into the yard, prepares a pot of chrysanthemum cuttings for the woman's garden, and gives him full instructions for tending them. Clearly, Elisa envies the man's life on the road and is attracted to him because he understands her love of flowers. In a moment of extreme emotion she nearly reaches for him, but snatches her hand back before she touches him. Instead, she finds him two pots to mend, and he drives away with fifty cents and the cuttings, promising to take care of the plants until he can deliver them to the other woman.

Elisa goes into the house to get dressed for dinner. She scrubs herself vigorously and examines her naked body in the mirror before putting on her dress and makeup. When Henry finds her, he compliments her, telling her she looks "different, strong and happy." "I'm strong," she boasts. "I never knew before how strong." As Henry and Elisa drive into town, she sees a dark speck ahead on the road. It turns out to be the cuttings the man has tossed out of his wagon. She does not mention them to Henry, who has not seen them, and she turns her head so he cannot see her crying.

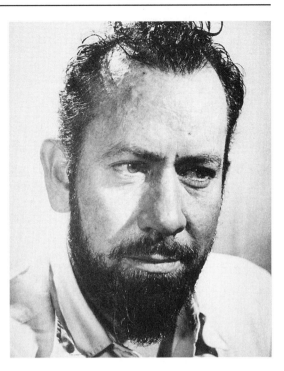

John Steinbeck

Characters

Elisa Allen

Elisa Allen is the story's protagonist, a thirty-five-year-old woman who lives on a ranch in the Salinas Valley with her husband Henry. She is lean and strong, and wears shapeless, functional clothes. The couple have no children, no pets, no near neighbors, and Henry is busy doing chores on the ranch throughout the day. Elisa fills her hours by vigorously cleaning the "hard-swept looking little house, with hard-polished windows," and by tending her flower garden. She has "a gift" for growing things, and she is proud of it. For the most part, Elisa seems satisfied with her life. When the traveling tinker comes along and talks about his wandering habits, she begins to think about how limited her life is, and she longs for adventure. The idea that her chrysanthemums will be shared with a stranger who will appreciate them gratifies her, makes her think that in a small way she is part of a larger world. When the man betrays her by throwing away the chrysanthemums, he makes it clear that her world extends only as far as the boundaries of the ranch.

Henry Allen

Henry Allen is Elisa's husband, a hard-working and successful small-scale rancher. As the story opens, he has completed the sale of thirty steer, and he wants to celebrate with Elisa. He suggests an evening in town, with dinner and a movie, and compliments her on her gardening skills. But there is no intimacy in his talk; the two are serious and formal with each other, and when Henry attempts a bit of humor Elisa does not understand it. As the couple prepare to leave for town, Henry can see that something is bothering his wife, but he cannot guess what it is and everything he says is wrong. In the face of her strange mood he "blunders," he is "bewildered" and speaks "helplessly." He is a good man, and he wants to make her happy, but he does not know what she needs.

"Autumn Days" chrysanthemums.

The man

The man is a tinker who travels up and down the coast every year with a horse-drawn wagon bearing the legend "Pots, pans, knives, sisors, lawn mores, Fixed." He is large, with careworn face and hands and a dirty suit. Because he depends on his salesmanship to earn his living, he is skillful at bantering small talk, but his friendly laughter is only superficial. Elisa has no work for him and is about to send him away when he notices the chrysanthemums and gets her to talk about them. Instantly her tone changes. She becomes enthusiastic, and she finds some work for him to do. When she finds her discarded chrysanthemums on the road that evening, Elisa realizes that his interest in the flowers was insincere, simply a way to win her over.

Themes

Limitations and Opportunities

The most discussed theme in "The Chrysanthemums" is limitations—the limitations under which a married woman lives. The idea of limitation

or confinement is presented as the story opens: "The high gray-flannel fog of winter closed off the Salinas Valley from the sky and from all the rest of the world. On every side it sat like a lid on the mountains and made of the great valley a closed pot." Within this closed pot, Elisa operates within even narrower confines. The house she shares with Henry is enclosed "with red geraniums close-banked around it as high as the windows," and the garden where she grows her flowers is surrounded by a wire fence. From these enclosures Elisa watches men come and go, the cattle buyers in their Ford coupe, Henry and the hired man Scotty on their horses, and the tinker in his wagon drawn by a horse and a burro.

Elisa does not express any regret at staying put while the men move about. She clearly is not always confined to the ranch, since she has enough knowledge of the roads to give the man advice. She knows that the dirt road to the ranch "winds around and then fords the river" in sand, and suggests, "I think you'll save time if you go back to the Salinas road and pick up the highway there." Does she know how to drive the family roadster? Perhaps she stays at home because she chooses to, or because she has nowhere to go. However, when the tinker describes his journey ("from Seattle to San Diego and back every year. Takes all my time. About six months each way. I aim to follow nice weather'') she replies, ''That sounds like a nice way to live.''

After she talks with the man and gives him some chrysanthemum cuttings, she asks him more about his life. ''You sleep right in the wagon?'' she asks, and he answers affirmatively. ''It must be nice,'' she replies. ''It must be very nice. I wish women could do such things.'' Of course, as the man points out, women cannot do such things, but just the thought of it gives her courage and strength. One day, she says, she might give the man some competition. ''I could show you what a woman might do.'' Again, he tells her that it would be an unsuitable job for a woman, too lonely and frightening. But she does not believe him. When Henry sees her a bit later she glows and boasts, ''I'm strong. I never knew before how strong.''

Her sense of strength comes from her encounter with the man, from the sexually charged moment they shared over their appreciation of the chrysanthemums and the wandering life. This connection enlarges her, takes her out of her confined self. When she sees she has been betrayed, by the man and by her romantic ideas, she feels limited again. Eagerly, desperately, she looks for some small way to break out of her confines. Henry senses her feelings, and observes, ''I ought to take you in to dinner oftener. It would be good for both of us. We get so heavy out on the ranch.'' He means well, but after Elisa's disappointment she needs more. Still, she does not have the strength or the power to take what she needs, just as she would never leave the ranch and pursue a different life. She asks permission: ''Henry, could we have wine at dinner?'' A bit later she asks, ''Do any women ever go to the fights?'' But the feeling passes. Although the narrator, Henry, and Elisa have all praised her for her strength, she is not strong enough to overcome her limitations, and she breaks down in weak tears ''like an old woman.''

Beauty and Aesthetics

Although there are other ways to describe it, the tension between Elisa and Henry, the reason they cannot communicate with each other or satisfy each other, is that they do not share an aesthetic sense. Elisa needs to experience beautiful things, but Henry values things because they are functional. He appreciates Elisa's ''gift with things,'' her ''plant-

Media Adaptations

- ''The Chrysanthemums'' was adapted as a twenty-three-minute film by Pyramid Film and Video in 1990. It is available from Pyramid as a 1/2-inch VHS videocassette.

- The making of the film adaptation has itself been captured on film, in the ''Behind the Camera'' segment of *Fiction to Film*. The forty-minute program, which shows the mechanics of producing a film, was produced by Mac and Ava Motion Picture Productions and is distributed on videocassette by the Indiana Department of Education, Instructional Video Services.

er's hands,'' and he praises her for this gift. But the quality he admires in the chrysanthemums is their size: ''Some of those yellow chrysanthemums you had this year were ten inches across.'' He would place more value on Elisa's gift if she could use it for production, to ''work out in the orchard and raise some apples that big.''

By contrast, the tinker appears to share Elisa's aesthetic sense. Although Elisa mentions the flowers' size, the man describes their beauty: ''Kind of a long-stemmed flower? Looks like a quick puff of smoke?'' His aesthetic appreciation brings out a response in Elisa that her husband is unable to evoke. Her eyes shine, she shakes out her hair, she runs excitedly and talks rapidly. Her breast swells passionately, her voice grows husky, and she talks about passion in language Henry would never understand: ''When the night is dark—why, the stars are sharp-pointed, and there's quiet. Why, you rise up and up! Every pointed star gets driven into your body. It's like that. Hot and sharp and—lovely.''

After the man leaves, Elisa dresses for her evening out with Henry, and tries to get an aesthetic response from him. She puts on her nicest clothes, ''the symbol of her prettiness,'' and waits for him to see her. But Henry fails the test. He notices at once

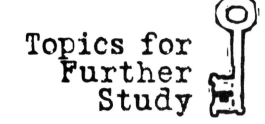

Topics for Further Study

- Many critics have found it useful to compare ''The Chrysanthemums'' with another Steinbeck short story from the same collection, ''The White Quail.'' Read both stories. Do you agree, as some have suggested, that Elisa Allen and Mary Teller are similar characters in different situations? Or do you agree with other critics, who believe the two women are opposites?

- Steinbeck was interested in plants and knew quite a lot about propagating them. Learn what you can about pollination, and about producing new plants by transplanting cuttings, as Elisa Allen does. What might Elisa's choice of methods say about her, in the context of the rest of the story?

- Find out what you can about steer. What exactly are they? How are they created? What are they used for? How does the fact that Henry raises steer connect with important issues in the story?

- Is Elisa Allen a victim of her circumstances? How might her situation be improved or made worse if she lived in our modern technological world?

that Elisa looks ''so nice,'' but he is unable to explain what he means. He knows he is being tested, and comments, ''You're playing some kind of a game.'' But he tries again to say the right thing. ''You look strong enough to break a calf over your knee, happy enough to eat it like a watermelon.'' There is no unkindness in Henry's evaluations. He is a good man who admires and respects his wife. But he does not appreciate beauty as she does.

Neither, as it turns out, does the tinker. Apparently, all of his words of appreciation were false, calculated to gain Elisa's confidence. Like Henry, he values what is practical. He has saved the flowerpot, but tossed the flowers into the road. As important as beauty is to her, Elisa has no one in her life who shares her feelings.

Style

Imagery

As is typical of Steinbeck's fiction, ''The Chrysanthemums'' uses clusters of images to subtly reinforce important themes and ideas. For example, imagery of seasons and weather reinforces the contrast between Elisa's life and the tinker's. Elisa's life is confined, closed in, as described in the story's opening line: ''The high gray-flannel fog of winter closed off the Salinas Valley from the sky and from all the rest of the world.'' The atmosphere in Elisa's world is grim; there is ''no sunshine in the valley now'' and the air is ''cold and tender.'' The tinker, however, moves about freely, and he is free ''to follow nice weather.'' He is not confined to this closed off place, and when he drives away Elisa notices, ''That's a bright direction. There's a glowing there.'' Later, as she again looks off in the direction he has taken, she notices that ''under the high gray fog'' the willows look like ''a thin band of sunshine.'' For Elisa there is ''no sunshine in the valley,'' but for a man who can travel, the horizon holds promise.

The story contains other image clusters that function in much the same way. As Ernest W. Sullivan, II, observes in *Studies in Short Fiction,* ''The correspondences between people and dogs elucidate the social and sexual relationships of the three humans, as well as foreshadow and explain Elisa's failure at the end of the story to escape from her sterile and unproductive lifestyle.'' R. S. Hughes examines the color yellow, in the ''yellow stubble fields'' and the willows' ''positive yellow leaves,'' and finds ''These bright sunny yellows (including Elisa's chrysanthemums) in the midst of winter suggest Elisa's hope, rekindled by the tinker, for a more fulfilling life.'' Images of hands, animals, enclosures and, of course, the chrysanthemums themselves, may be profitably lifted from the text and examined side-by-side for clues to Steinbeck's and the characters' intentions.

Point of View

''The Chrysanthemums'' is told by a third-person narrator who reports clearly about the actions of the characters, but who cannot read their thoughts or their motivations. This limited third person narrator helps establish the mood of the story by recreating for the reader the experience of Elisa and Henry hearing each others' words but having to guess at their meanings. When the tinker praises the beauty of the chrysanthemums, the narrator does not step forward to explain that he is being insincere; the reader must discover his deceit as Elisa discovers it. And when Henry tries to find the words to please Elisa and explain himself, the reader shares Elisa's frustration at not being able to read his thoughts.

But the third person narrator does not reveal Elisa's heart, either, and this contributes greatly to the air of mystery surrounding the story. Although Elisa is the protagonist and the reader feels closest to her, she too is revealed only through her actions and words. Why does Elisa "start" at the sound of her husband's voice? Why does she attack the weeds with such fury? What does she think about during those long hours in the garden? The reader never learns. After the tinker has gone away, Elisa gets dressed for her evening out. The narrator describes her preparations in fascinating detail: "she scrubbed herself with a little block of pumice, legs and thighs, loins and chest and arms, until her skin was scratched and red. When she had dried herself she stood in front of a mirror in her bedroom and looked at her body. She tightened her stomach and threw out her chest. She turned and looked over her shoulder at her back." Clearly these strange actions signal moments of contemplation for Elisa, continued when she sits on the porch and looks toward the river, "unmoving for a long time." Steinbeck calls attention to these strong emotional responses, but refuses to fill in the blanks. The result has been a large body of criticism of "The Chrysanthemums," each essay revealing perhaps as much about the critic as about Elisa Allen.

Historical Context

The Great Depression
Steinbeck wrote "The Chrysanthemums" in 1934, as the United States was just beginning to recover from the Great Depression. The Depression began with the collapse of the New York Stock Market in October 1929, and eventually affected employment and productivity around the world. Banks collapsed and businesses folded. Millions of people lost their jobs, and with less money to spend they bought fewer goods, leading to factory closings

and more unemployment. There was no federal "safety net" at that time, so poor and hungry people had to rely on individual states for assistance beyond what their families could provide. In many states, there was no help available. In 1932 President Franklin Delano Roosevelt initiated a series of programs, called the New Deal, to get the country back on its feet. He reformed the banking and stock market systems to make them more stable, created the Public Works Administration to create jobs, and gave new protection to labor unions to help workers get fair wages and decent working conditions.

The Depression did not affect all Americans equally, and many people even grew wealthier during the 1930s. With prices lowered by the Depression, it was possible to live well on less money. Necessities like food and housing, and luxuries like restaurant meals and fashionable clothing, were actually cheaper, because so few people worldwide could buy them at all. Some areas not directly affected by coal-mining, cotton-growing, and other devastated industries—California among them—continued to thrive. Elisa and Henry Allen seem to be among those who were not much affected by the Depression. They have a tractor and a car, and do not seem to be in desperate need of the money Henry brings in by selling his steers.

Steinbeck, too, lived relatively comfortably if simply through the early 1930s, even before he started to earn large sums for his writing. His wife Carol earned a small salary as a typist, while he devoted all his time to writing. They were able to supplement their diet with fish they caught in the ocean and with cheap local produce. But Steinbeck was not oblivious to those who were less well off. His novel *In Dubious Battle* (1936) is about migrant workers who go on strike in the California apple fields. Investigative newspaper stories that he wrote about migrant worker camps in 1936 led to his greatest work, *The Grapes of Wrath* (1939).

Forgetting Their Troubles
Even in stable and productive pockets of the country, the mood was grim during the depression. To escape their troubles for a short time, Americans turned their attention to the movies and to sports as never before. For its part, the movie industry tried to provide a refuge by erecting lavishly ornamented movie theatres where worried people could watch elaborate musical comedies, fantasy horror films,

Compare & Contrast

- **1930s:** The Great Depression swept across the United States and abroad, creating massive unemployment and poverty. Soup kitchens and bread lines were familiar sights. In the early 1930s, however, California still prospered because of the motion picture, oil, and fruit industries.

  1990s: The worldwide economy is relatively solid and stable, and the economy of the United States is strong, with low unemployment and high productivity. Some economists believe that rapid fluctuations in Asian economies could spell trouble for the United States.

- **1930s:** Popular movies included *King Kong* (1933), *Anna Karenina* (1935), and the movies of Shirley Temple, Fred Astaire, and the Marx Brothers. They tended to be glamorous and optimistic, providing audiences a refuge from economic and political troubles. Movies were mostly black-and-white, and a ticket cost about twenty-five cents. Roughly a third of Americans went to the movies at least once a week.

  1990s: Popular movies showcase special effects and science fiction, and are almost exclusively in color. Many present a grim view of human problems. A ticket costs six to eight dollars.

Fewer Americans go to the movies, but many watch movies at home on videocassette.

- **1930s:** Although newly built homes were wired for electricity, most older homes did not have it. Housework was done by hand, without electric appliances, and keeping a house clean was hard work. The first electric washing machine for home use was manufactured in 1937.

  1990s: Most families in the United States have either washing machines in their homes or inexpensive laundromats nearby. Typical homes have electric lights, vacuum cleaners, refrigerators, and other tools to make housework easier.

- **1930s:** Many farmers in the United States still used animals to pull plows and other equipment, but some, like Henry Allen, had tractors and other machines to help do their work. The sight of a horse-drawn wagon used for long-distance travel was uncommon, but not startling.

  1990s: Except for communities which have rejected modern technology, like the Amish, American farmers use gas-powered tractors and technologically advanced equipment. Most roads do not permit horse-drawn vehicles.

---

and sentimental family films like those starring Shirley Temple. Movie tickets were inexpensive, and about forty percent of the population of the United States went to the movie theatre every week. One in four people went at least twice each week. With the new technology for making talking pictures, Hollywood, California, became world's most important center for filmmaking. The year 1931 saw the first television broadcast, but the days of commercial networks and televisions in most people's homes were still years away.

Sports provided other diversions for a gloomy population. The 1932 Summer Olympic Games were held in Los Angeles, and the Winter Games in

Lake Placid, New York, the first time the Winter Games were held in the United States. Football and baseball drew large crowds. Boxing was a popular spectator sport, as Americans Jack Sharkey, Max Baer and Joe Louis held world heavyweight titles.

Critical Overview

Steinbeck knew as soon as he finished writing ''The Chrysanthemums'' that he had created something special. In a letter to his friend George Albee he wrote, ''I shall be interested to know what you think of the story, 'The Chrysanthemums.' It is entirely different and is designed to strike without the reader's knowledge. I mean he reads it casually and after it is finished feels that something profound has happened to him although he does not know what or how. It has had that effect on several people here.'' Over the next six decades, enough critics have attempted to pin down that ''something profound'' to create what has been called a ''small critical industry'' devoted to this one story.

Immediate response to the story, and to *The Long Valley,* the collection in which it appeared, was positive. Elmer Davis, in *The Saturday Review of Literature,* called the collection ''certainly some of the best writing of the past decade.'' The great French author André Gide, like Steinbeck a winner of the Nobel Prize for Literature, commented that the stories were as fine as those of the nineteenth-century Russian writer Anton Chekhov. In 1941, Joseph Warren Beach included Steinbeck among the eight American writers ''most worth our thoughtful consideration'' in *American Fiction, 1920-1940,* and singled out ''The Chrysanthemums'' for praise because ''the author does not waste words and insult his reader with . . . explanation.'' In the same study Beach penned what has become a frequently repeated line, calling Elisa Allen ''one of the most delicious characters ever transferred from life to the pages of a book.'' For Beach and others of his generation, the marriage between Elisa and Henry appeared to be ''one of confidence and mutual respect,'' and Elisa's grief at the tinker's betrayal was ''no tragic grief,'' but simply a reluctance we all feel if we ''let someone get the best of us.''

With the rekindling of the women's movement in the 1960s and 1970s, more critical attention was given to the roles of women in literature. New works by and about women appeared, and older works were examined for clues as to the relative status of women in society. Mordecai Marcus, in 1965, began a debate carried out in *Modern Fiction Studies* over the meaning of Elisa's dissatisfaction. Marcus, who considered ''The Chrysanthemums'' to be ''one of the world's great short stories,'' believed that Elisa's greatest desire is to become a mother, and ''her devotion to her chrysanthemum bed is at least partly an attempt to make flowers take the place of a child. . . . Denied a child, a wider world of experience, and that projection of oneself

into the world of fresh and broad experiences which possessing a child fosters, she finds a substitute in her flowers.'' Elizabeth E. McMahan, writing four years later, disagreed: ''Elisa's need is definitely sexual, but it does not necessarily have anything to do with a longing for children.'' In 1974 Charles A. Sweet found in Elisa ''an embryonic feminist,'' and read the story as ''Steinbeck's response to feminism.'' Elisa, he claimed, was ''the representative of the feminist ideal of equality and its inevitable defeat.'' All three writers express sympathy for Elisa, and see the source of her frustration as related to sex and gender, and to the limitations marriage imposes on a woman.

Robert Benton, in a chapter of *A Study Guide to Steinbeck,* also sympathizes with Elisa, but does not find sex to be the cause of her frustration. Rather, ''Henry does not fulfill her need for aesthetic companionship.'' William Osborne also rejects sex as the focus in an article in *Interpretations,* and recalls a common Steinbeck theme, ''the effect of a utilitarian society on the sensitive and romantic individual. At the root of Elisa's frustration is her uncertainty of who she is and what her relationship to her society should be.'' John H. Timmerman agrees, explicating a ''story about artistic sensibility'' in *John Steinbeck's Fiction.* He believes the story deals symbolically with ''the dream of the artist, the artist's freedom of expression, and the constraints of society upon that freedom.''

Stanley Renner is unusual in finding Elisa unsympathetic, and in rejecting the feminist interpretations of the story that abounded in the 1970s and 1980s. He believes that Elisa is ''less a woman imprisoned by men than one who secures herself within a fortress of sexual reticence and self-with-holding defensiveness,'' as he explains in *Modern Fiction Studies.* Thus Elisa is not frustrated by her husband, but continually frustrates him by rejecting reality for a romantic fantasy.

Criticism

Cynthia Bily

Bily is an instructor of English at Adrian College in Adrian, Michigan. In the following essay she

Salinas Valley, California, John Steinbeck's home and the setting for many of his stories, including "The Chrysanthemums."

explores connections between "The Chrysanthemums" and ecofeminism.

The many critics who have debated for decades over the reason for Elisa Allen's frustrations in "The Chrysanthemums" have focused on two ideas: that Elisa is oppressed, either by a male-dominated society or by a practical-minded one, and that her flowers are for her some sort of compensation for what is missing in her life. The chrysanthemums have been interpreted as symbols of Elisa's sexuality, or childlessness, or artistic sensibility, and all of

these connections make sense when looking at Elisa's connections to her husband or to society. It is also possible, I believe, and useful, to look at the flowers as literal flowers, as signs of Elisa's connection with the natural world.

Since the rekindling of the feminist movement in the 1960s and 1970s, and the rise of the environmental movement in the same years, writers including Annie Dillard, Alice Walker and Starhawk have wondered in writing whether the same impulses that lead men to conquer new land and dominate the environment also lead them to dominate women. In

What Do I Read Next?

- *The Grapes of Wrath* (1939), Steinbeck's Pulitzer Prize winning novel about migrant farm workers pursuing a happy life that is always just out of reach. During the Great Depression, the Joad family leaves dustbowl Oklahoma for California, where they hope to find a better life.

- "The White Quail" (1935) by John Steinbeck, collected in *The Long Valley* (1938) alongside "The Chrysanthemums." Mary Teller's dream of the perfect garden has such a firm hold on her that she gives all her devotion to it, ignoring even her lonely husband.

- "The Snake" (1935), a strange story by Steinbeck, collected in *The Long Valley* (1938). A woman enters an animal laboratory, buys a male snake, and asks to see it eat a rat. Though critics have interpreted the character differently, Steinbeck claimed "I wrote it just as it happened. I don't know what it means."

- *Winesburg, Ohio* (1919), a novel by Sherwood Anderson made up of thematically related stories. A young reporter encounters and learns the secrets of several of the inhabitants of his small town. Anderson's way of exploring people's secret lives influenced Steinbeck.

- *The Awakening* (1899), by Kate Chopin. A woman feels bored and unfulfilled with marriage and attempts to find her true self by having an extramarital affair. A century ago, this novel caused a furor.

- *Their Eyes Were Watching God* (1937), by Steinbeck's contemporary, Zora Neale Hurston. An African-American woman in rural Florida learns, through her relationships with three men, to rely upon herself and her own definition of herself to become a whole person.

1974, the French writer Françoise d'Eaubonne applied the term *ecofeminism* to the philosophy that women have a spiritual connection with nature that is stronger than men's, that women and nature are dominated by men in similar ways, and that women's connections to nature can be a source of strength. Carol J. Adams explains in the introduction to her anthology *Ecofeminism and the Sacred,* "Ecofeminism identifies the twin domination of women and the rest of nature. To the issues of sexism, racism, classism, and heterosexism that concern feminists, ecofeminists add naturism—the oppression of the rest of nature. Ecofeminism argues that connections between the oppression of women and the rest of nature must be recognized to understand adequately both oppressions."

"Oppression" seems too strong a word for the ways in which Elisa is subdued by her life as Henry's wife, yet clearly she is limited in ways that frustrate her. She is proud of her garden, but must fence it off to protect it from the domesticated animals, the "cattle and dogs and chickens." She feels she must ask Henry's permission to enjoy a glass of wine. Even the tinker, who seems to understand her at least a little bit, keeps telling her what she cannot do. "It ain't the right kind of life for a woman," he says. "It would be a lonely life for a woman."

Elisa already leads a lonely life, in terms of her connections with other human beings. Her only passion is for her garden, and when she is alone in the garden she is her truest self. As Henry says, she has "a gift with things." Her mother, too, had the gift. "She could stick anything in the ground and make it grow. She said it was having planters' hands that knew how to do it." Her connection with the garden, with nature, is something she feels but cannot explain. She tells the tinker, "I can only tell you what it feels like. It's when you're picking off the buds you don't want. Everything goes right down into your fingertips. You watch your fingers work. They do it themselves. You can feel how it is.

"Elisa already leads a lonely life, in terms of her connections with other human beings. Her only passion is for her garden, and when she is alone in the garden she is her truest self."

They pick and pick the buds. They never make a mistake. They're with the plant. Do you see? Your fingers and the plant. You can feel that, right up your arm. They know.'' It isn't just plant life that can call up this response. For Elisa, just being outside on a dark night sends her soaring: ''When the night is dark—why, the stars are sharp-pointed, and there's quiet. Why, you rise up and up! Every pointed star gets driven into your body. It's like that. Hot and sharp and—lovely.''

This gift, this oneness with the plant, is a source of strength. Several times throughout the story, Steinbeck comments on her strength. As she works in the garden, her face is ''lean and strong,'' she uses ''strong fingers,'' her work is ''over-powerful. The chrysanthemum stems seemed too small and easy for her energy.'' She feels at her most powerful when she is using her planter's hands, which ''never make a mistake. You can feel it. When you're like that you can't do anything wrong.'' The thought of sharing this connection to nature with another person—the ''lady down the road a piece'' who ''has got the nicest garden you ever seen''—makes Elisa giddy. Her eyes shine, her breast swells, her voice grows husky. And when she has done it, when she has reached past all the men in the story across the bridge of nature to another woman, she finds her greatest strength. ''I'm strong,'' she tells Henry. ''I never knew before how strong.''

What Elisa would like to do is get out of the Valley and see the world, to break her bonds with Henry and strengthen her bonds with the land. She is fascinated with the tinker's life, traveling back and forth trying ''to follow nice weather.'' ''That sounds like a nice kind of a way to live,'' she says. The word *nice* comes up again and again in her conversation with the tinker. The woman down the road has the ''nicest garden you ever seen,'' but she would like to have some ''nice chrysanthemums.'' ''It must be nice'' to sleep in the wagon, Elisa comments. ''It must be very nice. I wish women could do such things.'' For Elisa, the word is an expression of deep and mysterious feelings, of an essential connection. But both the men in her life reveal that they do not understand, that the word is one they can use casually. When Elisa describes the feeling of being under the stars, and comes close to reaching for the man, he replies, ''It's nice, just like you say. Only when you don't have no dinner, it ain't.'' His response makes her ashamed. She has been about to reach for a kindred spirit, and he has just brought the conversation down from spiritual fulfillment to material comfort. Henry, too, fails the test. He walks in when she is at her most artificial, when she is penciled and rouged and the least like her natural self, and declares, ''You look so nice!'' Her reply is swift and terrible: ''Nice? You think I look nice! What do you mean by nice?''

However kindly he may be, however hard he tries, Henry just doesn't get it. For him, nature is something to be subdued, brought under control. It's how he makes his living. When Elisa is disturbed, after Henry returns from his chores, she looks down toward the river road ''where the willow-line was still yellow with frosted leaves so that under the high gray fog they seemed a thin band of sunshine.'' When Henry is disturbed by his failure to say the right thing, he looks ''down toward the tractor shed.'' He acknowledges Elisa's ''gift with things,'' but he sees the flowers only in terms of their size, not their beauty. ''Some of those yellow chrysanthemums you had this year were ten inches across.'' (Elisa knows that for men, size is all that matters when it comes to flowers, and at first she brags about her chrysanthemums in those terms with the tinker.) Henry does not understand growing things only because they are beautiful. Instead, he wishes she would ''work out in the orchard and raise some apples that big.'' The tinker, even when he is trying to establish himself as a sensitive soul, makes a slip and betrays his own lack of comprehension. Just after describing their appearance he comments, ''They smell kind of nasty till you get used to them.'' ''It's a good bitter smell,'' Elisa retorts, ''not nasty at all.''

In ''The Chrysanthemums'' men are constantly at odds with nature. The first hint of human activity in the story is an image of farming: ''On the broad level land floor the gang plows bit deep and left the black earth shining like metal.'' Henry and the men from the Western Meat Company make a deal for steers, or castrated cattle. Henry's roadster bounces along the road disturbing animals, ''raising the birds and driving the rabbits into the brush. Two cranes flapped heavily over the willow-line and dropped into the river-bed.'' No wonder the narrator refers to the ranch as ''Henry Allen's foothill ranch.'' These activities are not Elisa's; she literally has no ownership of them. The ultimate betrayal of nature is the tinker's, the deliberate destruction of the chrysanthemums for the sake of fifty cents and a red pot.

Stanley Renner rightly points out that Steinbeck himself was not a feminist. In *Modern Fiction Studies* he writes, ''although, of course, biography need not inevitably determine a writer's perspective, Steinbeck's feelings about his marriage at the time the story was written were far from those of the implied author who would have written the essentially feminist version of the story.'' It is not at all required, however, that Steinbeck be a feminist himself, much less an ecofeminist, for the body of thought called ''ecofeminism'' to have something interesting to say about Steinbeck's fiction. This is a case, then, of the story standing as an example of something that is true and important—the different ways men and women might respond to nature—that the author was not aware of revealing.

Source: Cynthia Bily, Overview of ''The Chrysanthemums,'' for *Short Stories for Students*, The Gale Group, 1999.

John Ditsky

In the following essay, Ditsky likens ''The Chrysanthemums'' to a stage drama, exploring in detail many of its dramatic elements.

The longstanding critical assumption, routinely delivered and seldom questioned, that John Steinbeck represented an odd late flourishing of literary naturalism—rather than, as now seems increasingly clear, an innovative sort of romanticism—has had the predictable effect of retarding appreciation of his accomplishments. Among the latter are the ways in which Steinbeck's language emerges from his contexts: arises organically but not necessarily with ''real-life'' verisimilitude from situations which must therefore be seen as having demanded, and in a sense therefore also created, a discourse of a sometimes patent artificiality—of a rhetorical loftiness appropriate to the dramatic seriousness of the given

subject matter, but unlikely as an instance of ''observed'' intercourse in English, American variety. For only from such a vantage point can we hope to make sense of many of the exchanges which animate such diverse works as *Cup of Gold, To a God Unknown, The Moons Is Down,* and *Burning Bright.* Yet the sorts of usage I am referring to must necessarily give pause to the reader of even *In Dubious Battle, The Grapes of Wrath,* and *East of Eden.* Recently, however, Steinbeck criticism has increasingly begun to accept the writer on his own terms, a process no more complicated than the reading closely of what heretofore has been often subjected to a routinely and callously applied imposition of extraneous critical assumptions. I think that the ways in which situation creates language—and action—can be seen in such a famously ''naturalistic'' piece as that famous short story which leads off Steinbeck's single lifetime collection of short fiction, *The Long Valley* (1938): ''The Chrysanthemums.''

''The Chrysanthemums'' occupies its keynote position in *The Long Valley* with good reason. Not only does it serve as a striking introduction to a number of Steinbeck's attainments and prepossessions, but it also achieves an astonishingly eloquent statement of Lawrentian values that is valuable in its own right. The story is usually perceived—quite rightly—as a study in psychological interconnection and revelation, and I have no wish to alter such assumptions. Rather, I would like to direct some further attention to the ways in which Steinbeck allows text to flow from context: that is, shows speech and gesture being spontaneously brought into being by means of the rigors, the labor, of interpersonal drama. It is in short, the dramatist Steinbeck who concerns me here, though it is no one of his works created for the stage that I will use as my example.

In dramatic terms, ''The Chrysanthemums'' involves but three main characters: a ranch couple, Elisa and Henry Allen; and an unnamed tinker. It is December in the Salinas Valley. The Valley is shut off from the rest of the world by fog, and the weather anticipates change: ''It was a time of quiet and of waiting.'' The imminence of change is reflected in Nature herself, then: something is about to happen. Elisa Allen is already at work in her flower garden; she is a dramatic ''giver,'' her present quantity clearly laid out by the narrator:

> . . . She was thirty-five. Her face was lean and strong and her eyes were as clear as water. Her figure looked

> " Elisa and the stranger work through their temporary relationship through dialogue that has nothing to do ostensibly, with the struggle for power that is going on."

blocked and heavy in her gardening costume, a man's black hat pulled low down over her eyes, clod-hopper shoes, a figured print dress almost completely covered by a big corduroy apron with four big pockets to hold the snips, the trowel and scratcher, the seeds and the knife she worked with. She wore heavy leather gloves to protect her hands while she worked.

Steinbeck's list of *dramatic personae* is thus fleshed out by being given the additional accoutrements of sexual misidentification: Elisa wears men's clothing, and carries tools meant to prod and poke. She is also at a stage that later would be taken for granted as constituting "mid-life crisis." Moreover, the constricted world that Elisa inhabits is further limited by being divided—as more notably, later on, the world of *The Wayward Bus* is divided—into male and female precincts, domains of activity into which the members of the opposite sex shall not intrude. Elisa's world, of course, is that of her garden; at work within it, her femininity takes on a fullness it does not possess, apparently, inside her "hard-swept looking little house, with [its] hard-polished windows." She is mistress of her chrysanthemum milieu; indeed, "The chrysanthemum stems seemed too small and easy for her energy," and the flowers' insect enemies are no match for her "terrier fingers." As she looks towards where her husband is completing a deal to sell cattle to two other men—a deal he has not informed her of beforehand—"her face was eager and mature and handsome" in the enjoyment of indulgence in the creativity of helping beautiful things grow.

When her husband finally reports on his business transaction, Elisa is described as having "started" at the sound of his voice as he leaned "over the wire fence that protected her flower garden from

cattle and dogs and chickens" and, presumably, husbands. When he praises her prowess with growing things, we are told that "her eyes sharpened" at the notion that she might move over into the affairs of the ranch proper by raising apples as comparably big; she has "a gift with things," she confesses—something called "planter's hands." Her husband then suggests that they celebrate his successful transaction by going into Salinas for dinner and a movie; or, he jokes, they might attend "the fights." But she "breathlessly" admits that she "wouldn't like fights." When her husband goes off to locate the cattle he has sold, she resumes her work with her flowers; the language here suggests a woman in total control of her surroundings: "square," "turned the soil over and over," "smoothed it and patted it firm," "ten parallel trenches," "pulled out the little crisp shoots, trimmed off the leaves of each one with her scissors and laid it on a small orderly pile."

Again, one must not perhaps make too much of these patently theatrical stage directions, but we are in fact being prepared for the sudden appearance of that oldest of dramatic devices—the Arrival of the Stranger. He comes on in the form of a "big stubble-bearded man" driving a wagon which advertises his prowess at fixing just about anything—anything metallic, that is. When the man's dog is faced down by the ranch shepherds, flirtation begins immediately between Elisa and the stranger; it takes the form of an admission that the latter's dog's aggressiveness may be not all that responsive to need. Easy in his masculinity, the stranger jokes about the dog's dubious ferocity meanwhile, "The horse and the donkey [pulling the wagon] drooped like unwatered flowers." But here is a woman adept at making flowers thrive; and here is also a man with skills at fixing sharp tools. The banter falters, then continues: the man is off course; his animals, like his dog, are surprisingly vigorous "when they get started."

I should make note here of the alterations the stranger's arrival makes in the language of Steinbeck's narrative. When the husband reports his sale of cattle to his wife, her response is a tepid "Good." Indeed, she uses the same word four times in two lines, to react both to the cattle sale and to the prospect of dinner and the movies. "Good for you": it is his fine fortune and has little to do with her. But the bland textures of Elisa's existence are disturbed by the arrival of the "curious vehicle curiously drawn," and its driver. The driver's eyes are "full of the brooding that gets in the eyes of teamsters and of sailors," and if this perception is meant to be Elisa's as well, it marks her recognition of the appeal of the man's way of life—his ability to live with the simple "aim to follow nice weather." Her response is in the form of body language: she removes her gloves and hides them away with her scissors; and "She touched the under edge of her man's hat, searching for fugitive hairs." In short, she acknowledges his attractiveness by means of classic dramatic gestures.

The man's authority is equal to Elisa's within his own kingdom. "Fixed," his wagon proclaims, at the end of a listing of metallic objects which—no nonsense about it—he claims to be able to repair. No matter that the lettering is "clumsy, crooked," or the words misspelled; Steinbeck's story is a drama that relies on subtext—the unspoken—throughout. But when she is asked if she has anything needing repair or sharpening, "Her eyes hardened with resistance"; she becomes a bit metallic herself in the process of making it clear that she is not so easily won as all that. In the process of telling the man—four times—that she has no work for him to do, she manages to make him play the role of dependent inferior. "His face fell to an exaggerated sadness. His voice took on a whining undertone." The man's demeanor becomes dog-like; like an actor he uses expression and delivery to emphasize the import of his words: he is without a bit of work; he is off his usual road; he may not eat that day. Elisa is unmoved—is irritated, even.

Yet "irritation and resistance" melt from her face as soon as the man, resourceful, notices her chrysanthemums and asks about them. Hers, she avers, are "bigger than anybody around here" can raise; and since she has been pouring her private emotional existence into the raising of chrysanthemums, her boasting has a nice kind of sexual irony about it. He responds to his cue with spontaneous poetry: the flowers look "like a quick puff of colored smoke." A brief confrontation over the flowers' smell is quickly resolved; the aroma is a "good bitter" one, "not nasty at all," and the man likes it. Fine, then; for hers, Elisa claims, have produced "ten-inch blooms this year." Ah, then, returns the fellow (the dialogue by now quite strongly resembles Pinter's), there is this "lady down the road a piece" who, though she does find difficult work for him to do, has no chrysanthemums in her otherwise splendid garden. Can Elisa help this unfortunate out?

> " Whether or not 'The Chrysanthemums' is what I would call it, one of the finest American short stories ever written, surely its craft is such as to reward reader attention and require critical inquiry."

She can; she will. Assuring the man that she can send along flowers for transplanting by the other woman—"Beautiful . . . Oh, beautiful" ones—she tears off her hat; she shakes out "her dark pretty hair"; and with her eyes shining, she admits the stranger into her yard. She strips off her protective gloves after running "excitedly" after a flower pot, and with her bare hands prepares a selection of her flowers for the man—who is described as standing over her as she kneels to work—to take. She indulges herself in the revelation of her private craft as she gives him instructions to transmit to the other woman; she looks "deep into his eyes, searchingly," as if trying to measure the degree of their mutual sympathy. As she does, "Her mouth opened a little, and she seemed to be listening." Mouth and eyes and ears are open to this stranger as perhaps they have been to no one before as she explains her doctrine of "planting hands," the possessors of which can do nothing wrong. Her earnestness carries her away: "She was kneeling on the ground looking up at him. Her breast swelled passionately."

Again, the psychological underpinnings of this story, so Lawrence-like, have been commented on before this; what I am attempting to do for perhaps the first time is draw attention to the ways in which Steinbeck's text moves along according to imperatives which can only be termed *dramatic*. In other words, can the standard definitions of literary naturalism adequately account for the rising action and intensity of "The Chrysanthemums," its quasi-musical climaxing? This is fairly far from *The Jungle,* from *Studs Lonigan,* this passage; it is closer surely to *Brief Encounter.* Now the man's eyes are said to narrow as he averts his gaze "self-consciously'' and begins to make a comparison to his own life; "Sometimes in the night in the wagon there —'', he starts. But she interrupts, carried away by her own unexpectedly-piqued emotional empathy:

> Elisa's voice grew husky. She broke in on him, "I've never lived as you do, but I know what you mean. When the night is dark—why, the stars are sharp-pointed, and there's quiet. Why, you rise up and up! Every pointed star gets driven into your body. It's like that. Hot and sharp and—lovely.''

But Elisa's mystical attainment—her fusion of the psychosexual and the poetical—also has its natural and physical concomitant. The next paragraph says:

> Kneeling there, her hand went out toward his legs in the greasy black trousers. Her hesitant fingers almost touched the cloth. Then her hand dropped to the ground. She crouched low like a fawning dog.

She has opened herself to a stranger, and shown him a part of herself which presumably no one has seen before; and in the process, she has made herself as vulnerable to him as one of his subservient animals might be. Remarkably, for its time, the story also has Elisa adumbrating a world in which male and female experience might meld in an ecstasy of shared sensitivity—so unlike the one she has known on her husband's ranch.

But the stranger refuses this gambit. He reminds her that hunger is its own setter of standards; and so Elisa rises, "ashamed," and goes off to find the man some busy-work to do so that he can maintain his independence a bit longer. In the process, he reaffirms the radical dissimilarity of their two existences: when she speaks about a woman's being able to live such a life as his, he emphasizes its loneliness and frightfulness, wholly refusing to consider the implicit offer she is making. (Or is she?) Though they share body-language during this discussion—he concentratedly sucking his under-lip, she raising her upper lip and showing her teeth; both feral—he determinedly completes his routine repair work without deigning to consider her appeal for consideration of their shared romanticism. Indeed, when he finishes his job and accepts his pay and turns to go, he has already almost forgotten the pretext of the chrysanthemums to be delivered to that other woman down the road.

As the man and his animals depart, Elisa watches them off, silently mouthing "Good-bye" after him. "Then she whispered, 'That's a bright direction. There's a glowing there'"; and the sound of

her whispering startles her, though only her dogs had heard. This passage might seem extraordinary or simply inexplicable were it not for the consistent identification in Steinbeck's writing of "brightness" and "shining" with the quasi-divine power of absolute nature in the universe (as Blake's "Tyger" yields Steinbeck's title *Burning Bright*); and for that matter, the name "Elisa" and its variants are fairly commonly identified with idealized femininity in Steinbeck, from *Cup of Gold* onward. Elisa's next action is a sort of ritual purification followed by a donning of vestments: she tears off "her soiled clothes and flung them into the corner" of the bathroom. "And then she scrubbed herself with a little block of pumice, legs and thighs, loins and chest and arms, until her skin was scratched and red. When she had dried herself she stood in front of a mirror in her bedroom and looked at her body. She tightened her stomach and threw out her chest. She turned and looked over her shoulder at her back.'' Interestingly, Steinbeck's writing does not seek to titillate; the description of Elisa's *mikvah,* if I can call it that, is asexual, as though the operation were one which could be performed on any body as part of a ritual irrespective of gender. Yet Elisa's actions are also clearly narcissistic, her self-admiration clearly premised on a sense of having finally achieved, at her life's mid-point, some kind of summit of self-worth.

But now the naked Elisa begins to dress, again using makeup and costuming for theatrical effect—rather like Nora in Ibsen's *A Doll's House,* with the context of her presumably-imminent death giving abnormal beauty to what subsists of life. She begins with "her newest underclothing and her nicest stockings and the dress which was the symbol of her prettiness. She worked carefully on her hair, penciled her eyebrows and rouged her lips.'' One dresses—or divests oneself of clothing—this attentively, this ceremonially, only with an implicit or explicit awareness of preparing for one of the ritual events of life (including, of course, one's death). It is interesting that Elisa retreats from the world of her mannish exercises in the garden, wearing men's attire, to what is described as "her bedroom"; the two do not share a single sleeping-place. In this sort of dressing-room, then, Elisa prepares herself for a theatrical entry (or re-entry?) into life, an event in which she means to include her husband—who if he were but aware of the fact has been awarded this boon on the strength of a surrogate's efforts. Elisa neatly lays out her Henry's best clothes, so that he may do as she has finished doing, and then she goes out to the porch and sits "primly and stiffly" waiting for him, "unmoving," her eyes seldom blinking as they pursue the last of that bright glowing that she associates with the events of the afternoon, now disappearing beneath a "high grey fog."

When Henry finally appears, he is so taken aback at the appearance she has created for herself that he clumsily compliments her for looking "nice"—as though she seldom did. This reaction on his part comes in spite of the fact that her own self-assurance has made her "stiffen" at his approach, her face growing "tight" as she does. Henry compounds his error by defining "niceness" as looking "different, strong and happy"—again as if these were unfamiliar aspects of Elisa's demeanour. Indeed, Henry is so flabbergasted at the change in his wife's image that he unconsciously describes it as the theatricalization it actually is: "He looked bewildered. 'You're playing some kind of a game,' he said helplessly. 'It's a kind of a play. You look strong enough to break a calf over your knee, happy enough to eat it like a watermelon.'" Henry's flight of poetic utterance is a worshipful reaction to the irruption in his presence of the extraordinary in the ordinary, of the divine—the heroic, the Junoesque, if you will—into the human. At his tribute, her "rigidity" buckles briefly; she tells him that his venture into the domain of the ineffable was beyond his comprehension (instinctual?), and settles for the admission that "'I'm strong,' she boasted. 'I never knew before how strong.'" She sends him for the car, deliberately fussing over the set of her hat until his turning off the engine signals an admission that a new sort of patience is now called for.

But Elisa's short happy life—the effects of her dramatic transfiguration, her irradiation—is destined for an abrupt conclusion. When she and Henry set off for dinner in Salinas, it is not all that long until she sees "a dark speck" on the road ahead. Steinbeck has told this story, as was his initial habit, largely from the outside of his characters, from close observation of their gestures and speech. In a sense, he violates that practice now, giving the reader in two words what would in the theatre be expressed through a reaction of the face and body: "She knew." It is as if Elisa had always possessed, deep down, the certainty that her self-assurance was built upon a deception. Now, she cannot even avoid following the discarded chrysanthemum shoots with her eyes as they pass, recognizing as she ponders the tinker's apparent cruelty the fact that he left the flowers along the road because he couldn't afford to

throw away the bright red flower pot she had so carefully planted the flowers in—because it was the pot that had value in his world, and not—except as conversational pretexts—the flowers. She is able, however, to turn away from the sight of the tinker's wagon when their car overtakes it moments later.

"In a moment it was over. The thing was done. She did not look back," Steinbeck tells us. But her level of discourse, having fallen to the prospect of dinner, marks a change palpable enough for Henry to note it. "Now you've changed again" is his assessment; and the manner of his delivery is authorially noted as "complained" had Henry himself been buoyed by the brief brightening of Elisa? Now normality returns: she pats her knee; he makes small talk. Elisa has one last attempt at escape of the life-force within her. She makes what is apparently an unusual request, one that will make small ceremony out of the coming dinner out, itself a minor sacrament of sorts: ". . . could we have wine with dinner?" Henry agrees, and after a time of silence, she surprises her husband by an even more uncharacteristic question: do the boxers at prize fights "hurt each other very much?" (by which she means broken noses, she explains, with enough blood running down chests to get their gloves "heavy and soggy with blood"). Henry is startled, as are we; are these Elisa's Dionysiac propensities suddenly revealing themselves, or has her experience with the tinker taken an imaginative turn towards retribution, a perverse expression of the flowering of femininity he had seemed to foster? We are not told; but Elisa asks one more question: "Do any women ever go to the fights?" Some, yes, Henry answers, as if he cannot imagine his wife among them; not having been able to imagine her, a moment ago, as even having read about such things, he now offers to take her against his better judgment.

But Elisa's questioning has subsided, whether because of the unsuitability of her attending the fights or because of the torpor induced by the thought of attending them with a partner such as Henry. Withdrawing her face—on which tears have begun to show—she states that it will be enough to settle for "wine. It will be plenty." If the blood of Dionysiac sacrifice is not to be hers, she will settle for a conventional symbolism. Steinbeck alludes so obliquely to the Christian and the pagan at his ending that one is distracted, if at all, by the thought of how his final line—showing Elisa "crying weakly—like an old woman"—might have been ruined by claiming the strength of a metaphorical connection instead of making do with the subtlety of the simile. Elisa is, after all, only "like an old woman"; if she has nonetheless crossed a certain line in her life, it will take years, perhaps, for that fact to assert itself fully. Yet, as if she were one of the many animals mentioned throughout the story, she has made her sudden lunge towards a kind of life she may not have known she needed—only to have the constraints of her existence reassert themselves almost at once.

Whether or not "The Chrysanthemums" is what I would call it, one of the finest American short stories ever written, surely its craft is such as to reward reader attention and require critical inquiry. That craft, as I have suggested, is in great part a matter of introducing the materials of a naturalistic sort of fiction—the details of the occupations of tinker and gardener and the like—only to rise above them as a dramatist would: by raising the ante of artifice until the characters seem self-conscious of themselves as creative artists spontaneously creating a dialogue in a most poetic sort of drama, one in which the late flowers of a season of the human spirit can seem for a moment to be able to transcend their rootedness, to move farther down the road than just the town of Salinas. It is, finally, a craft by which seemingly ordinary individuals are made to see themselves as characters—persons moving in a world of "roles" and "symbols"—in search of an author who seems scarcely present at all. In the end, it is enough to make plausible a singular sort of epiphany: a bland sort of husband, likely one who has never been in a theatre in his life, being so astonished at the sight of his taken-for-granted wife suddenly appearing in "a kind of play" that he speaks, on the spot, his spontaneous rancher's ode.

Source: John Ditsky, "A Kind of Play: Dramatic Elements in Steinbeck's 'The Chrysanthemums'," in *Wascana Review*, Vol. 21, No. 1, Spring, 1986, pp. 62–72.

Ernest W. Sullivan, II

In the following essay, Sullivan explores the comparisons drawn between the characters and the dogs in "The Chrysanthemums" and the light this sheds on the social and sexual relationships within the story.

Anyone reading John Steinbeck's "The Chrysanthemums" cannot help being struck by the repeated association of unpleasant canine characteristics with the otherwise attractive Elisa Allen. These associa-

tions identify her with the visiting tinker's mongrel dog, further suggesting a parallel between the Allen's two ranch shepherds and the tinker and Elisa's husband, Henry. The correspondences between people and dogs elucidate the social and sexual relationships of the three humans, as well as foreshadow and explain Elisa's failure at the end of the story to escape from her unproductive and sterile lifestyle.

The dog imagery related to Elisa is uncomplimentary. In her garden, she destroys unpleasant creatures such as "aphids," "bugs," "snails," "cutworms," and similar "pests" with her "terrier fingers." When aroused by the tinker, she "crouched low like a fawning dog." Finally, in response to the tinker's assertion that his life of freedom "ain't the right kind of life for a woman," she bares her teeth in hostile fashion: "Her upper lip raised a little, showing her teeth." Burrowing in flower gardens, fawning, snarling—not a very pleasant picture of man's best friend.

The last two images directly link Elisa to the tinker's mongrel, and their physical descriptions clearly parallel these two unfortunates. She kneels before the tinker like a dog would to shake hands: "Kneeling there, her hand went out toward his legs in the greasy black trousers. Her hesitant fingers almost touched the cloth. Then her hand dropped to the ground. She crouched low like a fawning dog." As Elisa bared her teeth in resistance to the tinker, so his mongrel resisted the two Allen ranch shepherds "with raised hackles and bared teeth." Additionally, the cur is "lean and rangy"; Elisa is "lean and strong." Finally, of course, the tinker's mongrel, unlike the ranch shepherds, contains a mixture of dog breeds, and Elisa's personality mixes masculine and feminine elements.

Whereas Elisa shares several characteristics with the cur, the tinker and Henry resemble the two ranch shepherds. The two shepherds were born to their jobs, which they perform instinctively. Confident that "Pots, pans, knives, sisors, lawn mores" can all be "Fixed," the tinker feels at home in his occupation and world: "I ain't in any hurry, ma'am. I go from Seattle to San Diego and back every year. Takes all my time. About six months each way. I aim to follow nice weather." Henry Allen is also successful at his job and derives satisfaction from it: "I sold those thirty head of three-year-old steers. Got nearly my own price, too." On the other hand, Elisa, like the mongrel, does not participate in the main work on which her livelihood depends, even

John Steinbeck's house in Salinas, California.

though her husband suggests that she should become useful: "I wish you'd work out in the orchard and raise some apples that big." Both Elisa and the cur are merely companions for their respective breadwinners, their subservient position suggested by Elisa's kneeling before the tinker: "She was kneeling on the ground looking up at him."

The interaction of the three dogs closely parallels that of the three people and foreshadows Elisa's eventual failure to escape her confined lifestyle. When the mongrel darts from its accustomed position beneath the tinker's wagon, the two ranch dogs shepherd it back. The mongrel considers fighting,

but, aware that it could not overcome the two dogs secure on their home ground, retreats angrily back under the wagon and protection of its owner: "The rangy dog darted from between the wheels and ran ahead. Instantly the two ranch shepherds flew out at him. Then all three stopped, and with stiff and quivering tails, with taut straight legs, with ambassadorial dignity, they slowly circled, sniffing daintily. . . . The newcomer dog, feeling out-numbered, lowered his tail and retired under the wagon with raised hackles and bared teeth."

Elisa, in the course of the story, moves out of her accustomed role to challenge Henry and the

> "The interaction of the three dogs closely parallels that of the three people and foreshadows Elisa's eventual failure to escape her confined lifestyle."

tinker on their home ground, their occupations and sexuality. In response to Henry's comment that she could put her skills to productive use in the orchards, "Elisa's eyes sharpened. 'Maybe I could do it, too.'" But she never does. Her challenge to his sexuality is equally unfulfilled; in response to her appearance in "the dress which was the symbol of her prettiness," Henry observes that "You look strong enough to break a calf over your knee, happy enough to eat it like a watermelon" and goes to turn on the car. Elisa directly expresses an urge to compete in the tinker's occupation: "You might be surprised to have a rival some time. I can sharpen scissors, too. And I can beat the dents out of little pots. I could show you what a woman might do." The tinker rebuts her challenge: "It ain't the right kind of a life for a woman," and her career as a tinker never gets started. The tinker's feigned interest in the chrysanthemums clearly arouses Elisa's sexual instincts: "Her breast swelled passionately," and she does her unconscious best to arouse his: "Elisa's voice grew husky. . . . 'When the night is dark—why, the stars are sharp-pointed, and there's quiet. Why, you rise up and up! Every pointed star gets driven into your body. It's like that. Hot and sharp and—lovely'." And, as had her husband, the tinker deflects the conversation to one involving a less carnal appetite: "It's nice, just like you say. Only when you don't have no dinner, it ain't."

In each case, when Elisa threatened to encroach upon male territory, she was rebuffed and shepherded back to the refuge of her submissive and unproductive place. Elisa, like the cur, might be "a bad dog in a fight when he gets started," but, like the cur, she rarely, if ever, gets started: "sometimes [he does] not [get started] for weeks and weeks." The positions of the dogs after the meeting between Elisa and the tinker foreshadow her final defeat. The cur "took his place between the back wheels," and,

with Elisa's occupational and sexual challenge to the tinker rebuffed, the ranch shepherds could cease their watchfulness: "Only the dogs had heard. They lifted their heads toward her from their sleeping in the dust, and then stretched out their chins and settled asleep again."

Interestingly, neither the mongrel nor Elisa gives up until "out-numbered." Any previous challenges to her husband's role as breadwinner and sexual aggressor have apparently been frustrated: the story offers no evidence of her doing farm work; they have no children; and Henry responds unromantically to Elisa's effort to make herself sexually attractive. Yet her occupational and sexual challenges to the tinker show that she has not given up. After the tinker also rejects her by discarding the chrysanthemums that she had given him, Elisa, like the out-numbered cur baring his teeth at the two shepherds, vents her anger and frustration over her defeat through her description of the pain inflicted upon men in fights: "I've read how they break noses, and blood runs down their chests. I've read how the fighting gloves get heavy and soggy with blood." Overcome by the two men, Elisa never gets started in the fight to escape her role; she even decides against vicarious participation in the fight: "I don't want to go [to the fights]. I'm sure I don't." She retreats to the safety of her accustomed unproductive and sexless role, "crying weakly—like an old woman."

Source: Ernest W. Sullivan, II, "The Cur in 'The Chrysanthemums'," in *Studies in Short Fiction,* Vol. 16, No. 3, Summer, 1979, pp. 215–17.

Elizabeth E. McMahan

In the following essay, McMahan explores Elisa's sexual / romantic frustration in "The Chrysanthemums."

Virtually every critic who has considered John Steinbeck's short story "The Chrysanthemums" has agreed that its basic theme is a woman's frustration, but none has yet adequately explained the emotional reasons underlying that frustration. In fact, Kenneth Kempton would consider such an explanation impossible. He professes his inability to find any consistent motivation for Elisa's behavior, and declares the work "annoyingly arty, muddy, and unreal." But most critics who have examined "The Chrysanthemums" admire the story and find it meaningful. Warren French, after identifying the theme of the story as frustration, suggests that the central action concerns "the manipulation of people's dreams for selfish purposes''—an interesting and valid idea but one which fails to incorporate the obvious sexual overtones of the story. Another critic who overlooks the sexuality is Joseph Warren Beach. He sees the conflict in the story as a contest of wits between Elisa and the pot mender; frustration results from damage to her pride when she is outwitted. Ray B. West sees the story as ''based on the assumed relationship between the fertile growth of plant life and physical violence and sexuality in human beings.'' Peter Lisca explains Elisa's frustration as stemming from an unsuccessful ''silent rebellion against the passive role required of her as a woman''—an excellent idea but his treatment is too brief to account for all the elements of the story. F. W. Watt is on exactly the right track when he states that the story concerns Elisa's ''struggle to express and fulfill desires which are ambiguously sexual and spiritual.'' Unfortunately Watt, like Lisca, has not sufficient space in his book to give this story the thorough discussion that it deserves. The only such examination thus far is that of Mordecai Marcus. But his interesting and persuasive argument that Elisa's frustration results essentially from a longing for childbirth is not entirely satisfactory. Marcus encounters difficulties with the story which I think disappear if we do not equate sexual fulfillment with a yearning for motherhood. Elisa's need is definitely sexual, but it does not necessarily have anything to do with a longing for children.

In order to understand Elisa's emotions, we first should look closely at the relationship between her and her husband. Beach, somewhat surprisingly, observes that ''Nothing is said about the relationship of this married pair, but everything shows that it is one of confidence and mutual respect.'' Partially true, certainly, but confidence and mutual respect are not the only qualities that Elisa Allen desires in her marriage. The evidence points to an outwardly passive, comfortable relationship between the two which satisfies Henry completely but leaves Elisa indefinably restless with excessive energy which she sublimates into the ''over-eager'' cultivation of her chrysanthemums, and the care of her ''hard-swept looking little house with hard-polished windows.'' Henry is a good provider, we can be sure; he has just received a good price for thirty head of cattle. He is also thoughtful; he invites his wife to go into town that evening to celebrate the sale. A good provider, a thoughtful husband. But what else? There is a distinct lack of rapport between these two, despite all that mutual respect. And the confidence which Beach observes is an

> This symbolic rejection produces a need for female revenge in Elisa. The idea of attending a prize fight which was repugnant to her a few hours earlier has its appeal now."

assurance of each other's capability; it is not a warm mutual confidence of things shared.

We see this lack of rapport demonstrated early in the story as Henry makes a suggestion for their evening's entertainment:

Henry put on his joking tone. ''There's fights tonight. How'd you like to go to the fights?''

''Oh, no,'' she said breathlessly. ''No, I wouldn't like fights.''

''Just fooling, Elisa. We'll go to a movie.''

The fact that husband and wife do not share an interest in sports is not remarkable, but the fact that Elisa responds seriously to Henry's ''joking tone'' suggests either that she lacks a sense of humor or that for some reason she is not amused by Henry's teasing. We discover later that she has a ready sense of humor when talking to someone other than Henry. Unmistakably, Henry has no gift with words. When he compliments his wife on her chrysanthemums, he praises their size not their beauty and does so in the most prosaic terms. When he wants to compliment his wife on her appearance, he stammers, as if in surprise—and Elisa is hardly elated by the banal adjective:

''Why—why, Elisa. You look so nice!''

''Nice? You think I look nice? What do you mean by *nice?*''

Henry blundered on. ''I don't know. I mean you look different, strong and happy.''

Henry's word choice here is particularly unfortunate since his wife has just devoted her entire attention to heightening her femininity. She has put on her ''newest underclothing and her nicest stockings and the dress which was the symbol of her prettiness.'' ''Strong'' is the way she least wants to appear. But Henry manages to make matters even worse. Bewildered by Elisa's sharp retort, he is inspired to his only attempt at figurative language in hopes of making himself clear: "You look strong enough to break a calf over your knee, happy enough to eat it like a watermelon." It is hard to fancy the woman who would be pleased by Henry's agricultural comparison. Elisa is not amused.

We begin to sense the source of Elisa's discontent. She is a woman bored by her husband, bored by her isolated life on the farm. When the itinerant tinker arrives at Elisa's gate, we see that she is a woman who longs for what women's magazines vaguely call "romance." She wants, among other things, to be admired as a woman. The chrysanthemums that she cultivates so energetically produce great soft blossoms shaped like a woman's breasts. If one wishes to see the flowers as a symbol, they suggest the voluptuous softness of a sexually mature woman. There is no evidence to suggest that Elisa is a sex-starved female, that her husband is perhaps impotent, as Kempton suggests. Henry's placidity would seem to indicate the contrary. But neither is Elisa a sexually satisfied woman. Something is lacking in her relationship with Henry, and this something has a great deal to do with sex, but it is not as simple as a need for the sex act alone. This undefined longing becomes more clear as we examine her reaction to the tinker.

Unlike Henry, who has trouble finding the right words to please his wife, the tinker seems to know them intuitively. His greeting to Elisa is a mildly humorous remark about his cowardly mongrel dog: "That's a bad dog in a fight when he gets started." Elisa gives no dead-pan response as she did to Henry's feeble joke. Instead, "Elisa laughed. 'I see he is. How soon does he generally get started?' The man caught up her laughter and echoed it heartily. 'Sometimes not for weeks and weeks,' he said." In contrast with Henry's uninspired comment on the size of her flowers, the tinker remembers that chrysanthemum blooms look "like a quick puff of colored smoke." Elisa is obviously pleased. "That's it. What a nice way to describe them," she says.

The man's physical appearance has little about it to warrant such a friendly response: "Elisa saw that he was a very big man. Although his hair and beard were greying, he did not look old." His clothes are grease-stained and disheveled, his hands are cracked and dirty. But there is one physical characteristic which would make the man appealing to Elisa: "His eyes were dark, and they were full of the brooding that gets in the eyes of teamsters and sailors." Obviously he lacks the honest, dependable virtues of Henry, the virtues a woman should cherish in a husband. But the important thing he has that Henry lacks is an aura of freedom, unpredictability, perhaps adventure, maybe even poetry, which his gypsy life produces. It has got to be this element of the man that attracts Elisa to him. His first reference to his wandering, carefree existence produces an unconscious feminine response from her. The tinker says, "I ain't in no hurry ma'am. I go from Seattle to San Diego and back every year. Takes all my time. About six months each way. I aim to follow nice weather." Elisa removes her unfeminine heavy leather gloves and "touched the under edge of her man's hat, searching for fugitive hairs. 'That sounds like a nice kind of a way to live,' she said." But instead of continuing to talk about his roving existence, the tinker begins giving her his sales pitch about mending pots and sharpening knives and scissors. Elisa becomes suddenly distant: "Her eyes hardened with resistance." She is fast losing patience with him when, in an inspired move, he inquires about her chrysanthemums. She warms towards him again almost at once: "The irritation and resistance melted from Elisa's face." After the man shrewdly asks her if he can take some sprouts to a customer down the road, she becomes enthusiastic. "Her eyes shone. She tore off the battered hat and shook out her dark pretty hair"—a movement entirely feminine and essentially seductive. She immediately invites him into the yard.

Elisa is now clearly excited. She scoops up the soil into a flower pot, presses the tender shoots into the damp sand, and describes for him how the plants must be cared for. "She looked deep into his eyes, searchingly. Her mouth opened a little, and she seemed to be listening." She tells him about her "planting hands," which pluck buds instinctively and unerringly. But the reader is aware that such emotion could scarcely be generated solely by an enthusiasm for the care and clipping of chrysanthemums. Elisa, kneeling now before the man, "looking up at him," appears to be experiencing sexual excitement. "Her breasts swelled passionately." Not breast, but breasts. Not heaved, but swelled. The man is suspicious of her strange behavior, perhaps embarrassed: his "eyes narrowed. He looked away self-consciously." She has asked him if he understands her feelings, and he begins a response so in keeping with Elisa's mood that she quite forgets herself.

"Maybe I know," he said. "Sometimes in the night in the wagon there—"

Elisa's voice grew husky. She broke in on him. "I've never lived as you do, but I know what you mean. When the night is dark—why, the stars are sharp-pointed, and there's quiet. Why, you rise up and up! Every pointed star gets driven into your body. It's like that. Hot and sharp and—lovely."

The sexual implications of her last four sentences are unmistakable, yet the sexual impact lies just beneath the surface level of meaning in the phallic imagery. Elisa is, more than likely, unaware of the sexual nature of her outburst, but her next action, while probably still unconsciously motivated, is quite overt. "Kneeling there, her hand went out toward his legs in the greasy black trousers. Her hesitant fingers almost touched the cloth. Then her hand dropped to the ground. She crouched low like a fawning dog." The tinker's matter-of-fact comment jolts her at once back to her state of natural reserve: "It's nice, just like you say. Only when you don't have no dinner it ain't." She is aware that he does not understand after all the feeling of erotic mysticism that she is trying to communicate. "She stood up then, very straight, and her face was ashamed. She held the flower pot out to him and placed it gently in his arms." To avoid further embarrassment, she goes at once to find some old saucepans for him to fix. After regaining her composure, she returns with the battered pots and chats with him as he works. She pays him for the repairs, and as he is leaving, calls out a reminder to keep the plants watered. She stands watching him go. "Her shoulders were straight, her head thrown back, her eyes half-closed, so that the scene came vaguely into them. Her lips moved silently, forming the words 'Good-bye—good-bye.' Then she whispered, 'That's a bright direction. There's a glowing there.' The sound of the whisper startled her. She shook herself free and looked about to see whether anyone had been listening. Only the dogs had heard."

After this the story returns to the portrayal of the relationship between Elisa and her husband, and in the final scenes her feelings toward Henry are clearly revealed. As the tinker's wagon moves out of sight, Elisa quickly returns to the house. The next scene portrays Elisa performing a purification ritual. She felt shame after her display of passion before the stranger. Now she cleanses herself before returning to her husband, the man to whom she should lawfully reach out in desire. "In the bathroom she tore off her soiled clothes and flung them into the corner. And then she scrubbed herself with a little block of pumice, legs and thighs, loins and chest and arms, until her skin was scratched and red." The abrasive action of the pumice suggests expiation for

her imagined infidelity. Elisa then studies her naked body in a mirror: "She tightened her stomach and threw out her chest"—movements of a woman who wants to see her figure at its best, but also of it woman gathering resolution. The ceremonial preparation for her evening with Henry also has about it an element of resolve: "After a while she began to dress slowly. . . . She worked carefully on her hair, pencilled her eyebrows and rouged her lips." She is steeling herself for the coming evening. "She heard the gate bang shut and *set* herself for Henry's arrival" (Italics mine). Elisa, ready early, goes out onto the porch and sits "primly and stiffly down" to wait for her husband. "Henry came banging out of the door, shoving his tie inside his vest as he came. Elisa stiffened and her face grew tight." There follows the passage examined earlier in which Elisa bridles at each of Henry's inept attempts to compliment her. The scene culminates in his ill-chosen simile describing her in her carefully chosen finery as looking strong enough to break a calf over her knee. "For a second she lost her rigidity. 'Henry! Don't talk like that. You didn't know what you said.'" She seems to lose heart, to wonder if she can abide this insensitive man, but her resolution returns: "She grew complete again. 'I'm strong,' she boasted. 'I never knew before how strong.'"

In the final scene we see this strength tested to the breaking point, finally giving way and dissolving into despair. As the two are driving into town for their festive evening of dinner and a movie, "far ahead on the road Elisa saw a dark speck. She knew." The tinker has discarded her chrysanthemums, symbol of the femininity which she hopes will inspire the excitement she longs for. But he has kept the pot—an insult on any level of interpretation, to discard her treasure and keep its utilitarian container.

This symbolic rejection produces a need for female revenge in Elisa. The idea of attending a prize fight which was repugnant to her a few hours earlier has its appeal now. She asks Henry whether "the men hurt each other very much" and speculates on "how they break noses, and blood runs down their chests." But as her anger cools, she realizes the futility of vicarious vengeance. It can do little to salve her damaged ego or save her dying dream. Henry has promised her wine with dinner, and she tries to console herself with this small romantic touch. "It will be enough if we can have wine. It will be plenty," she tells Henry. But she knows it will not really be enough. She knows that she will always have good, dull, dependable Henry, but how will she keep her mind from whispering, "There has got to be something more exciting, more beautiful in life than this"? No, wine will not be plenty. "She turned up her coat collar so he could not see that she was crying weakly—like an old woman"—like an old woman for whom all hope of romance is a thing of the past.

Source: Elizabeth E. McMahan, "'The Chrysanthemums': Study of A Woman's Sexuality," in *Modern Fiction Studies,* Vol. XIV, No. 4, Winter, 1968, pp. 453–58.

Sources

Adams, Carol J. Introduction to *Ecofeminism and the Sacred,* New York: Continuum, 1993, p. 1.

Beach, Joseph Warren. *American Fiction, 1920-1940,* New York: Macmillan, 1941; reprinted New York: Russell & Russell, 1960, pp. 3, 311-14.

Benton, Robert M. "Steinbeck's *The Long Valley.*" In *A Study Guide to Steinbeck: A Handbook to His Major Works,* edited by Tetsumaro Hayashi, Metuchen, N.J.: Scarecrow Press, 1974, p. 71.

Davis, Elmer. Review of *The Long Valley. The Saturday Review of Literature,* September 24, 1938, p. 11.

Gide, Andre. *The Journals of Andre Gide,* translated by Juston O'Brien, London: Secker and Warburg, 1951, Vol. 4, p. 79.

Hughes, R. S. *John Steinbeck: A Study of the Short Fiction,* Boston: Twayne, 1989, p. 26.

Marcus, Mordecai. "The Lost Dream of Sex and Childbirth in ' The Chrysanthemums.'" *Modern Fiction Studies,* 1965, Vol. 11, p. 55.

Osborne, William. "The Education of Elisa Allen: Another Reading of John Steinbeck's 'The Chrysanthemums'." *Interpretations,* 1976, Vol. 8, p. 11.

Renner, Stanley. "The Real Woman Inside the Fence in 'The Chrysanthemums'." *Modern Fiction Studies,* 1985, Vol. 31, pp. 306, 313.

Steinbeck, John. *Steinbeck: A Life in Letters,* edited by John Steinbeck and Elaine and Robert Wallsten, New York: Viking, 1975, p. 91.

Sweet, Charles A. "Ms. Elisa Allen and Steinbeck's 'The Chrysanthemums'." *Modern Fiction Studies,* 1974, Vol. 20, p. 211, 213.

Timmerman, John H. *John Steinbeck's Fiction: The Aesthetics of the Road Taken,* University of Oklahoma Press, 1986, pp. 63, 67.

Further Reading

Benson, Jackson J. *The True Adventures of John Steinbeck, Writer: A Biography,* New York: Viking, 1984.
At over one thousand pages, the most complete of the Steinbeck biographies, and the one that explores most thoroughly Steinbeck's writing process. Includes many photographs.

Burg, David F. *The Great Depression: An Eyewitness History,* New York: Facts on File, 1996.
Over one hundred first-hand accounts of life in the 1930s, including newspaper stories, interviews, letters, memoirs, photographs and documents from leaders and from common people, give the reader a strong sense of what it was like to live during this period.

French, Warren. *John Steinbeck,* Boston: Twayne, 1975.
An overview of Steinbeck's life and works, intended for the general reader. The volume includes a chronology, an annotated bibliography, and an indexed discussion of all of Steinbeck's major writings in chronological order.

Ockenga, Starr. *Earth on Her Hands: The American Woman in Her Garden,* Clarkson Potter, 1998.
Interviews with eighteen women master gardeners, who discuss horticulture and the affect gardening has had on their lives. Lavishly illustrated with color photographs.

The Dead

James Joyce

1914

James Joyce wrote ''The Dead'' in 1907, three years after writing the fourteen other stories that were eventually published with it in his collection entitled *Dubliners* (1914). ''The Dead'' is the last story in the collection, and it unites the themes found in the earlier stories. In his book, Joyce wanted to give the history of Ireland. The prominent characteristic he saw in Ireland, and particularly in Dublin, was the spiritual paralysis of its people. The plot of ''The Dead'' presents the thoughts and actions of one man, Gabriel Conroy, on a night he and his wife attend a party given by his two aunts. With its meticulous detail, the story is realistic in style, focusing less on great events than on subtle symbolism. Conroy is presented as a rather awkward, condescending, and self-absorbed man, but he later has a moment of self-realization when his wife tells him about a relationship she had as a young girl with a youth who loved her passionately. Joyce does not make it clear, however, what kind of change Gabriel's revelation, or epiphany, brings in him. Critics disagree as to whether this change involves an acceptance of his own self-consciousness or whether he has a moment of spiritual growth, becoming a more compassionate and humane person. The story has many characters and a number of references to the dead, and many of the characters are based on people Joyce knew—his friends and family members. A great deal of critical attention has been given to the story over the years since it was published.

Author Biography

James Augustine Aloysius Joyce was born the oldest of eight children on February 2, 1882, in Rathgar, a suburb of Dublin, Ireland. His parents were John Stanislaus Joyce and Mary Jane Murray Joyce. From both parents Joyce inherited musical talent and, particularly from his father, a talent for playing with words and telling stories. Unfortunately, John Joyce liked to drink and spend money, which caused the family's gradual descent into poverty and forced them to move many times. Having lived in so many different addresses in and around Dublin (nearly twenty) allowed Joyce to gain an intimate knowledge of the city. Joyce dedicated his life to writing about the city and its people.

Despite the family's poverty, Joyce managed to get a good education at a series of Jesuit schools, where he was always an outstanding student. His academic career culminated in a degree in modern languages from University College, Dublin. While at the university he published an article about the Norwegian playwright Henrik Ibsen. This article launched his career as a writer and gave him the opportunity to meet other Irish writers, such as W. B. Yeats. Convinced that the best way to write objectively about his city was to exile himself from it, Joyce moved to Paris to study medicine upon graduation. While in Paris, with the help of Yeats and others, he began publishing reviews in the Dublin *Daily Express,* as Gabriel Conroy does in the short story ''The Dead.'' Joyce temporarily discontinued his exile and moved back to Dublin when his mother was dying. Mary Jane Murray Joyce died in August of 1903 at the young age of forty-four. For two years Joyce stayed in Dublin, where he continued to write and attempted to support himself by singing and teaching at a boys' school. During this period he met Nora Barnacle, a young woman from the rural region of Galway, Ireland. Shortly thereafter, Joyce and Nora moved to Trieste, Italy, where Joyce was employed as a language teacher. For the remainder of his life Joyce lived in Europe, returning to Ireland only twice— once in a failed attempt to start a cinema in Dublin and again to visit Galway.

After publishing *Chamber Music* (1907), a book of poems, Joyce made his first attempt to depict the people of Dublin in the short story collection *Dubliners,* in which ''The Dead'' appears. Joyce wrote most of the stories in 1904 and finished ''The Dead'' in 1907. Because publishers objected to the profane language in some of the stories and to Joyce's use of real names and places, *Dubliners* did not see publication until 1914. Meanwhile Joyce wrote a piece called *Stephen Hero,* which he later revised into the autobiographical novel *A Portrait of the Artist as a Young Man* (1916). From then on Joyce's works became even more ambitious and complex. From 1914 to 1921 he wrote *Ulysses,* which was published in 1922. He devoted the next seventeen years to his last book, *Finnegans Wake,* which he published in 1939. When Germany invaded France in 1940, Joyce and his family moved to Zurich, where he died in 1941.

Plot Summary

Gabriel's Arrival

Sisters Julia and Kate Morkan are hosting their annual holiday party and anxiously awaiting the arrival of their nephew Gabriel Conroy, who is the son of their late sister Ellen. It is after 10 p.m., and so far he has not come. When Gabriel and his wife, Gretta, arrive, Gabriel tries to engage in small talk with Lily, the housekeeper, who meets them at the door. He asks whether he will be going to her wedding with her ''young man,'' and Lily bitterly replies, ''The men that is now is only all palaver and what they can get out of you.'' Her reply flusters Gabriel, and he feels that he has made some sort of mistake. In an effort to make up for it, he gives Lily a coin, saying that it is a Christmas present. She tries to refuse it, but he is already running up the stairs to where the music and dancing are taking place.

Before entering the room where the guests are dancing and socializing, Gabriel waits for a waltz to finish and looks over the speech that he will give after dinner. He considers cutting a Robert Browning quotation from it because it might go over the heads of his audience, making him look as if he were ''airing his superior education.'' He fears that he will fail with them just as he did moments before with Lily. His aunts and his wife good-naturedly tease Gabriel about how he fusses over his family's health, and Gabriel laughs nervously. When the waltz finishes, Freddy Malins arrives. Aunt Kate asks Gabriel to go downstairs to make sure their friend Freddy is not drunk. She is relieved to have Gabriel present. Another guest, Mr. Browne, flirts with several of the women, who ignore him. When everyone begins to dance again, Mary Jane pairs Miss Daly with Bartell D'Arcy, the tenor. Gabriel guides Freddy up into the back room where the refreshments are being served. Freddy laughs at his own stories and is soon given lemonade instead of whiskey.

Confrontation with Molly Ivors

In a later dance, Gabriel is partnered with Miss Molly Ivors, a longtime friend and fellow teacher. Molly has a ''crow to pluck'' with him because she saw a review of his in the *Daily Express,* a conservative newspaper supporting British rule in Ireland. Molly, an Irish nationalist, accuses Gabriel of being a ''West Briton''—an Irish person who is loyal to England. Gabriel is taken aback by her accusation and feels uncomfortable responding to her in such a public place. Miss Ivors invites him to go on an excursion to the Aran Isles, a group of islands off of Galway in the western part of Ireland. She asks if Gretta is from there, to which Gabriel replies coldly, ''Her people are.'' Gabriel tells her that he likes to go cycling in Belgium or France. When Molly asks why, he says that it is to keep in touch with the language and for a change in atmosphere. Molly accusingly asks why he doesn't keep in touch with his own language, Irish. Gabriel replies that Irish is not his language, and he grows increasingly nervous. Molly presses the point, asking whether he doesn't have his own land to visit and his own people, whom he knows nothing about. Gabriel says that he is sick of his country. After dancing with Molly, Gabriel dwells on what she said as he visits with Freddy Malins's mother. Gretta comes over asking him to carve the goose, as he usually does. She asks what words he had with Molly, and he says that she invited him to go to western Ireland. Being from that region, Gretta excitedly encourages him to go because she would love to see Galway again. He curtly tells her that she can go alone if she'd like. He continues to dwell on Molly, wondering whether she has a life beyond her politics. He decides that in his speech he might contrast his aunt's generation with the current generation of Miss Ivors, which lacks the hospitality, humor, and humanity of the older.

The Dinner

To Gabriel's relief, Molly leaves before dinner begins. Gabriel carves the goose and serves everyone before himself sitting down to eat. The conversation turns to the opera, particularly to tenors past

James Joyce

and present, Irish and Italian. The time finally comes for Gabriel to give his speech. In his speech he praises his hostesses, Aunt Kate, Aunt Julia, and Mary Jane, as the three Graces. He notes that their hospitality is like Ireland's own, unique among modern nations, and that while some would consider this trait a failing, he would call it a princely failing. The generation of his two aunts still has the hospitable trait, but he fears that the new ''hypereducated'' generation coming up and present in Ireland lacks it. Alluding to the earlier conversation about great tenors of the past, he encourages his audience to hail and regard the great people of the past. He cautions, however, that one can always dwell on the unpleasant thoughts of the past—past youth, changes, and absent friends—but one should concentrate on the living and one's current duties and affections. In that context he speaks again of his regard for his hostesses, and all the guests begin singing ''for they are jolly gay fellows.''

After midnight, people begin putting on their coats to leave for home. While arranging cab rides and waiting for his wife to come downstairs, Gabriel tells the story of his grandfather Patrick Morkan, who once drove his mill horse into town for a military parade. The horse was used to walking around in a circle in order to run a machine that ground starch, and when Patrick took the horse to the park, it started walking in circles around a statue of King William III of England. Gabriel imitates the action by walking around in a circle himself. As Freddy and Mr. Browne are leaving, Gabriel notices the figure of a woman standing at the top of the stairway listening to an air being sung. It is his wife. She seems pensive and dignified to Gabriel, and he imagines that if he were a painter and painted the scene, he would call it *Distant Music*. After the singing stops, Gretta asks Mr. D'Arcy what he was singing, and he replies, ''The Lass of Aughrim.'' This vision of his wife arouses Gabriel's passion for her. On the ride home he admires her appearance and thinks about the early days of their courtship. When they get to the hotel, he is in an intense state of lust and passion, but Gretta seems distant and preoccupied. She finally walks over and kisses him. When they embrace he asks her what is the matter. She breaks down, falls on the bed, and cries. She tells him that the song Mr. D'Arcy sang reminded her of a young man she knew who also used to sing that song. His name was Michael Furey, and she feels that he died for her. They had courted, but one winter Gretta decided to move to a convent in Dublin. The night before she left, Michael, already sickly, came to her house in the cold rain and threw gravel against her window. When she went outside to him and told him he should go so as not to become even more dangerously ill, he told her that he did not want to live because she was leaving.

The Epiphany

As Gretta sleeps, Gabriel thinks about what she has told him. He now sees his wife differently, and he watches her sleep as though he and she had never lived together. Remembering watching his Aunt Julia singing and the look on her aging face, he knows that very soon he will be going to her funeral. Everyone slowly fades away, ''becoming shades.'' He thinks that perhaps it is best to boldly and passionately pass into the next world than to slowly wither away with age. Thinking of Michael Furey, Gabriel realizes that he could never love a person the way Michael loved Gretta. He feels his soul has reached the place of the dead and that the living world is becoming nonexistent, as if he is outside his body. He hears the snow tapping on the window pane and knows that it is time to begin ''his journey westward.'' The snow falls on everything all over Ireland, on the living and the dead.

Characters

Mr. Bergin

Mr. Bergin is one of the young men attending the Morkans' party. Mr. Browne turns to talk to him after having been ignored by Miss Furlong and Miss Daly. He dances a dance called ''quadrilles'' with Miss Furlong.

Bessie

Bessie is Gabriel and Gretta Conroy's housekeeper.

Mr. Browne

One of the guests at the Morkans' party, Mr. Browne likes to drink whiskey and flirt with the ladies. People do not seem to take to him as well as he would like to think—Kate Morkan, for example, walks away when he begins to explain why women are so fond of him. Some critics see him as symbolizing English rule over Ireland. Aunt Kate says of him in an irritable tone, ''Browne is everywhere,'' just as the presence of Britain is ominously everywhere in Ireland. Also, he is the only Protestant in the story, while the rest of the people are Irish Catholic. In Ireland it was and still is characteristic of Protestants to favor British rule, while Catholics tend to favor independence. He seems to be condescending toward other people. He continually mispronounces Freddy Malins's name as ''Teddy,'' and after Miss Julia sings, he mockingly says she is his latest discovery, then ''laughs heartily'' at his comment. When Freddy tells him that he might make a worse discovery, Browne keeps his condescension, saying, ''I think her voice has greatly improved.'' At one point, Kate signals to him to make sure that Freddy Malins drinks no more whiskey, as if Browne serves some authoritative function, like a policeman.

Constantine Conroy

Constantine is Gabriel Conroy's brother and a senior curate.

Ellen Conroy

Gabriel's mother, Ellen, was Julia and Kate's older sister. She has been dead some time. Gabriel remembers that she opposed his marriage to Gretta and that she called Gretta, in a derogatory way, "country cute." Unlike her sisters, she was not very musical, but her sisters considered her more intelligent. Her sisters have described her as "serious" and "matronly." Gabriel credits her with seeing that her sons got an education that allowed them to have a higher rank in life.

Eva Conroy

Eva is the daughter of Gabriel and Gretta Conroy. She is mentioned in passing when Gretta says that Gabriel forces Ellen to eat her "stirabout," or Irish porridge.

Gabriel Conroy

Gabriel, the nephew of Julia and Kate Morkan and cousin of Mary Jane, is the main character of the story. He is a young man, married and the father of two. Critics point out that Gabriel is the name of one of the archangels in the Bible, the messenger who announced the coming births of John the Baptist to Zechariah and the Messiah to Mary. The other archangel, Michael, is portrayed in the Bible as a warrior. In "The Dead" Gabriel is a more passive character than the dead Michael Furey. Critics note parallels between Gabriel and Joyce, surmising that Gabriel might be Joyce's portrait of his future self had he not left Ireland. Like Joyce, Gabriel lost his mother when he was younger; he writes reviews for the *Daily Express;* he is a literary person and an English professor; and he is less provincial than his contemporaries, seeing importance in absorbing European as well as Irish culture. Kate and Julia are both anxious for him to arrive at the party, give him the honor of carving the goose, and have him give a dinner speech every year. However, to some he comes across as condescending, for he smiles at the way Lily pronounces his surname, and when he inadvertently arouses her anger, he gives her money to appease her rather than making up for his carelessness in a more personal manner. He believes that if he quotes poetry by Robert Browning in his dinner speech, his audience will not understand his "superior education." Finally, he thinks his aunts are "two ignorant old women." Yet at the same time he is a sensitive, self-conscious, and timid person who is shaken by Lily's retort to his attempt at casual conversation. He does not know how to react to Molly Ivors when she accuses him of being a West Briton and thus sympathetic to English rule. He is afraid of "risking a grandiose phrase with her" in a public forum. Some believe that although he clearly loves and cares about Gretta, Gabriel

Media Adaptations

- *The Dead* is a 1987 film version of Joyce's story directed by John Huston. It stars Anjelica Huston as Gretta Conroy and Donald McCann as Gabriel Conroy.

- *The Dead and Other Stories* (1993) is an audiocassette published by Penguin. It is read by the actor Gerard McSorley.

- *"The Dead" and Other Stories from Dubliners* (1989) is an audiocassette by The Audio Partners. It is performed by Danny Huston and Kate Mulgrew.

treats his wife as more a prize than a human being. He fusses over her as if she were a child, making her wear galoshes although he knows she doesn't mind the snow. He jokes that she takes three "mortal hours" to get ready to go somewhere. When she becomes excited at the prospect of going back to Galway, where she grew up, his annoyance with Molly makes him curt with Gretta, and he tells her that she can go alone if she wants. For most of the story Gabriel takes Gretta for granted, beaming at her with pride and, later, lust. Not until after she tells him about Michael Furey does he see his relationship with her differently. Gabriel is the one character who seems to go through a change at the end of the story, where he has a sudden realization about his relationship with his wife as well as a realization about himself and the human condition.

Gretta Conroy

Gretta is the wife of Gabriel Conroy. Like Joyce's wife, Nora, Gretta comes from Galway, a rural region of western Ireland. She seems to love Gabriel and playfully teases him about his solicitous manner toward herself and their children. Gabriel is not, however, the first person she has loved. After hearing Bartell D'Arcy sing "The Lass of Aughrim," she is reminded of a former love, Michael Furey, who she says "died for her." According to Gretta,

Michael was passionately in love with her when she was a young woman. Knowing that she was going to a convent, Michael stood outside her window at the end of the garden in the rain the night before her departure. He told her that he didn't want to live, and he died after she had been in the convent only a week.

T. J. Conroy

Gabriel Conroy's father.

Tom Conroy

Tom is the son of Gabriel and Gretta Conroy. Gabriel makes him wear green eye shades at night and work out with dumbbells.

Miss Daly

Miss Daly is one of the young women attending the Morkans' party. She plays a waltz and is one of the women with whom Mr. Browne flirts.

Mr. Bartell D'Arcy

D'Arcy, a tenor, is one of the guests at the party. Though he is self-conscious about his voice because he has a cold, he sings the song "The Lass of Aughrim," which reminds Gretta Conroy of her old lover, Michael Furey.

Michael Furey

Michael is the love of Gretta Conroy's past, a gentle and delicate youth, mentioned only near the end of the story. Critics point out that Michael is the name of one of the biblical archangels, who is portrayed as a warrior as opposed to the archangel Gabriel, who has a more passive role as a messenger. Even Michael's last name connotes passion. Michael is an example of living life passionately, where Gabriel Conroy lives it more timidly and passively. Gabriel realizes that he has never loved anyone the way Michael loved Gretta. Gretta tells Gabriel that Michael was an excellent singer and wanted to study music, but he had poor health and worked at the gasworks. When Gretta was a young woman, she left Galway to spend the winter at a convent in Dublin. At the time she had a relationship with Michael, who was seventeen. He came outside her home on the cold, rainy night before she left, told her that he did not want to live, and died a week after she reached the convent. Gretta believes he died for her.

Miss Furlong

One of the young women at the Morkans' party, Miss Furlong is a student of Mary Jane.

Miss Molly Ivors

Molly Ivors, a friend of Gabriel's with whom he shares a dance, functions in the story as a contrast to Gabriel's politics. Gabriel notes that their lives are parallel: they went to the university together and they both teach. A passionate Irish nationalist, she feels that it is important to know the Irish culture; Gabriel feels that one should also cultivate the European culture and languages. He tells her that Irish isn't his language, implying that English is what people speak. Molly accuses Gabriel of being a "West Briton" because he writes for the *Daily Express*—"West Briton" being a derogatory term denoting someone loyal to British rule in Ireland, and the *Daily Express* a newspaper with the political stance favorable to the British. Molly wears a brooch with an Irish design and uses an Irish good-bye, "beannacht libh," when she leaves the party before dinner.

Mr. Kerrigan

Mr. Kerrigan is one of the young men attending the Morkans' party. Mr. Browne turns to talk to him after having been ignored by Miss Furlong and Miss Daly. He dances a dance called "quadrilles" with Miss Power.

Lily

Lily is the first character introduced in the story. She is the caretaker's daughter, the caretaker being a fellow tenant in the building where the Morkans live. She works as the Morkans' housekeeper, and at the beginning of the story she is busy meeting the guests at the door. Lily makes Gabriel feel uncomfortable after she responds curtly when he asks her if he might be going to her wedding in the future. She says, "The men that is now is only all palaver and what they can get out of you." Kate says that she does not know what has come over Lily and that "she's not the girl she was at all."

Freddy Malins

A friend of the Morkans' and a guest at their party. Freddy has a drinking problem—Julia and Kate are concerned that he will come to the party "screwed." Some critics think Freddy is Gabriel's counterpart because he comes to the party at almost the same time and they are physically similar. Freddy calls Mr. Browne on a sarcastic remark about "discovering" Julia's singing, defending her with the words, "Well, Browne, if you're serious you might make a worse discovery. All I can say is I never heard her sing half as well as long as I am coming here. And that's the honest truth."

Mrs. Malins

The mother of Freddy Malins.

Mary Jane Morkan

Mary Jane is Gabriel Conroy's cousin. She is the daughter of the now deceased Pat Morkan, who was the brother of Kate and Julia. Mary Jane moved in with her two aunts after her father died. She plays the organ on "Haddington Road," which is the conversational name for a Roman Catholic church. She is a graduate of the Royal Academy of Music and teaches children from upper-class families.

Julia Morkan

Julia is Gabriel Conroy's aunt and one of the hostesses of the party. Julia sings lead soprano at Adam and Eve's, a Catholic church in Dublin. The narrator says her face gives the appearance of a "woman who does not know where she is going."

Kate Morkan

Kate is Gabriel Conroy's aunt and one of the hostesses of the party. She is too feeble to go out much, so she gives music lessons to children at home. Though feeble, she is described as the more vivacious of the two sisters and gets rather passionate about the way she feels the Catholic church is unjust to women with Julia's talent.

Pat Morkan

Pat was the brother of Ellen, Julia, and Kate, and father of Mary Jane Morkan.

Patrick Morkan

Patrick was Ellen, Julia, Kate, and Pat's father and Gabriel's grandfather. Gabriel tells a story about him bringing a horse to a military parade in the park. The horse worked in a starch mill and was used to walking around in a circle in order to run a machine that ground the starch, so when Patrick took the horse to the park, it started walking in circles around a statue of King William III of England. Some critics note that the horse walking around the statue represents the state of Ireland beat into submission by Britain.

Miss O'Callaghan

Miss O'Callaghan is one of the young women attending the Morkans' party. While she, Gabriel, Gretta, and Mr. D'Arcy are crossing O'Connell bridge on the cab ride home, she points out an old saying that one never crosses the bridge without seeing a white horse. Gabriel says he sees a white man—the snow-covered statue of Daniel O'Connell, who was an Irish Catholic civil rights leader in the early 18th century.

Miss Power

A young woman attending the Morkans' party, Miss Power dances with Mr. Kerrigan.

Themes

Paralysis

When describing his intentions in writing *Dubliners,* Joyce said that the city of Dublin seemed to him the center of paralysis. By paralysis Joyce meant the inability to act, move, or grow beyond where one is spiritually and emotionally—the inability to live fully. In "The Dead," Gabriel is paralyzed by his self-consciousness. He is self-conscious about Lily's bitter remarks on marriage and about what he should say in his after-dinner speech. When Miss Ivors accuses him of being loyal to the British, he tries to avoid confrontation. He doesn't want to risk a "grandiose phrase" toward her in a room full of people. He fantasizes about using his speech to criticize Miss Ivors, but by the time he gives it she is gone, and he gives a speech that only serves to please his audience. The story Gabriel tells about Patrick Morkan's horse walking in circles around the statue of King William III suggests Ireland's spiritual paralysis, and Gabriel shows his own paralysis by walking in a circle himself while telling it. Finally, as he and Gretta are walking down the street to find a cab, he imagines himself making various romantic overtures to her, but he actually makes none of them.

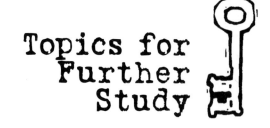

Topics for Further Study

- Do some research about contemporary Ireland, particularly the conflict in Northern Ireland. How does the political climate compare to the Ireland in Joyce's time?

- What does Joyce mean by paralysis? Do you find any examples of paralysis in American society?

- Readers disagree about the result of Gabriel's epiphany. Do you think he will change as a result of it, or will he remain as he was?

- How do you think women are portrayed in "The Dead." How would you compare their social status to women today?

British Rule vs. Irish Nationalism

For much of its history, Ireland has been dominated by British rule, and the debate between independence and allegiance to Britain appears in "The Dead." For instance, Molly Ivors confronts Gabriel about writing reviews for the *Daily Express,* a newspaper that supports British rule. Generally, those who supported Irish independence were Catholic, while those who allied themselves with the British were Protestant. Gabriel's family is Catholic. Some critics conclude that Mr. Browne, a Protestant, symbolizes British rule because most people dislike him and his nature is overbearing. Aunt Kate says of him, "Browne is everywhere," just as the oppressive rule of England is everywhere in Ireland.

Death and the Dead

Dead people play an important role in "The Dead." Gabriel honors them in his after-dinner speech, and several dead characters are mentioned during the story: Ellen (Gabriel's mother), Pat Morkan (his uncle), Patrick Morkan (his grandfather), and Michael Furey. Michael Furey particularly inspires Gabriel to a fuller self-awareness. Gabriel realizes after Gretta tells him of Michael's love for her that inevitably he and everyone he knows is going to die. Hence it is better to live life fully rather

than passively. Another reminder of death comes in the dinnertime discussion of a monastery whose monks sleep in coffins. The "dead" of the title are both those who are literally deceased and those who are merely going through the motions of living but who are spiritually dead.

Provincial Culture vs. European Culture

The setting of "The Dead" coincides with a period of revival of Irish culture. People wanted to revive Irish music, art, and language. The representative of this in "The Dead" is Molly Ivors. She wears an Irish brooch and advocates learning the Irish language. The guests discuss the talents of tenors past and present, but they also note whether they are Irish or European. Gabriel values traveling to Europe and learning the European languages. Joyce himself favored absorbing European culture and rejected the purely provincial beliefs of many of his contemporaries. Gabriel says to Molly that Irish is not after all his language—many people of that time indeed did not know or speak Irish fluently, but rather used English.

Self-Realization

Through most of "The Dead," Gabriel is a self-absorbed person who mostly cares about how he comes across to others. He doesn't care about the feelings of others so much as he cares about how he looks. For instance, when Lily angrily tells him that all young men are "palaver and what they can get out of you," Gabriel feels that he made a mistake with her. Instead of apologizing, however, he condescendingly and impersonally gives her money—calling it a Christmas present. Later in the story, after Gretta tells him about Michael Furey, Gabriel is able to suddenly step back and look at himself and his relationship to his wife and others.

Style

Point of View

Point of view is the perspective from which the writer tells the story. "The Dead" is told in the third person limited point of view. Although the narrator describes the action of many of the characters and even depicts some events Gabriel does not witness, only Gabriel's thoughts are given. Joyce's writing style is also relevant when discussing point of view. Joyce was one of the first writers to practice the mimetic style. Mimetic style—a style that mimics or imitates—does not report thoughts using objective language but shows the character's thoughts by using the character's language. In "The Dead," the first sentence is an example of mimetic style: "Lily, the caretaker's daughter, was literally run off her feet." The last phrase of that sentence, "literally run off her feet," is actually mimicking what Lily would say. Another example is when Gabriel looks over his speech and is worried that he "would fail with them just as he had failed with the girl in the pantry." The phrase is more akin to Gabriel's dialogue than to the words of an objective narrator, and it shows his frustration over his earlier encounter with Lily. This device has become common in fiction, but Joyce was one of the first to use it.

Realism

"The Dead" can be categorized with stories that are in the realist tradition. A realistic writer will simply try to present life as it is without making a sensational plot or interpreting events. A reader might say that nothing eventful really happens, as is so often the case in real life. In "The Dead" Joyce, for the most part, shows but does not tell. He simply presents the characters' thoughts and actions without comment. Even at the end, when Gabriel has his revelation, the reader is left not knowing exactly what his revelation means. Presentation without comment forces the reader to interpret the events for him- or herself.

Setting

Setting is simply when and where the action of the story happens. As with the rest of *Dubliners,* "The Dead" is set in Dublin, Ireland, in the early twentieth century. Joyce said that he wanted to write "a chapter in the moral history" of his country and that Dublin seemed the appropriate place because it seemed to him the center of paralysis. The action takes place in two specific places: at Kate, Julia, and Mary Jane's house in Usher Island, which is an actual section of Dublin, and at the Gresham, a fashionable hotel in Dublin. Critics conclude that it takes place on January 5th, which is the eve of Epiphany.

Epiphany

Epiphany is from a Greek word meaning *manifestation.* Christianity celebrates the feast of Epiphany on January 6, honoring the manifestation of the baby Jesus to the wise men from the East, and the term generally refers to the manifestation of God's presence in the world. Joyce, however, made the word into a literary term. He described it as a spiritual manifestation that reveals the true essence of an object or character, and he used it as the climax of many of his stories. In "The Dead" Gabriel has such a spiritual manifestation after Gretta tells him about Michael Furey, in the early morning hours of Epiphany.

Symbolism

A symbol is an object, person, or place that stands for something else, usually an abstract idea. For example, critics have said that Mr. Browne is a symbol for British rule in Ireland. The most debated symbol in "The Dead" is the snow which covers "all the living and the dead." Critics disagree over whether it stands for Gabriel's new ability to transcend his own self-absorption or whether it is a symbol of the paralysis that he still has and cannot overcome.

Historical Context

Imagism

Imagism was a movement in poetry founded around 1912 by the American exile poet Ezra Pound, along with Hilda Doolittle (H.D.) and Richard Aldington. Some tenets of imagism were to make a "direct treatment of the thing whether subjective or objective" and "to use no word or phrase that does not contribute to the presentation." The goal of the imagist was to present an image directly without any excess use of sentimental feeling or even metaphor. Although the movement focused on poetry, writers such as Ezra Pound have seen similarities to imagism in Joyce's style. Joyce directly presents Gabriel's thoughts (subjective) and the action of the story (objective) with little or no comment. In a review of *Dubliners,* Pound wrote, "Mr. Joyce's merit . . . is that he carefully avoids telling you a lot that you don't want to know. He presents his people swiftly and vividly, he does not sentimentalise over them, he does not weave convolutions." Pound valued Joyce for the ways in which Joyce was similar to him. Joyce treats the thing directly. Although Joyce knew and might have been influenced

Compare & Contrast

- **1900s:** In 1905 Arthur Griffith formed the Sinn Fein movement. The name stands for "we ourselves" or "ourselves alone." The organization's goals were to practice civil disobedience and passive resistance to British rule.

  1990s: Since aligning itself with the Irish Republican Army (IRA) with the advent of the civil war in the 1920s, Sinn Fein has acted as the IRA's political wing and plays a significant role in negotiating peace settlements in Northern Ireland.

- **1900s:** There was a revival of Irish culture and language in the early 1900s, led in part by the Gaelic League. Artists collected Irish music and stories, and it was popular to wear Celtic symbols.

  1990s: An Irish revival is happening again through the popularity of Irish stage shows such as "Riverdance." For the first time, numbers of Protestants are taking up Irish dancing, formerly practiced primarily by Catholics.

- **1900s:** In 1907 Britain granted dominion status to New Zealand, a former colony. This gave New Zealand the right to govern itself, even though the British monarch was still considered the head of state. Britain maintained rule over Ireland, however.

  1990s: British occupation of Hong Kong ended in 1998. Although a cease-fire exists in Northern Ireland, it is still under British rule.

- **1900s:** At the turn of the century, Protestants tended to favor British rule while Catholics supported independence or home rule. A small but influential minority of Catholics advocated radical nationalism.

  1990s: Protestant and Catholic loyalties essentially remain the same, particularly in Northern Ireland, where relations between the two groups are volatile. Militant organizations representing both groups have committed numerous acts of violence.

---

by Pound, he wrote "The Dead" five years before imagism came into vogue as a movement.

Philosophical and Social Mind-set

Even at the beginning of the twentieth century, people were starting to see the world differently, particularly artists and thinkers. The three thinkers who most shaped the mind-set of the early twentieth century were Friedrich Nietzsche, Karl Marx, and Sigmund Freud. Freud asserted that mental illness is a result of repressed unconscious sexual desires. Marx challenged the assumptions of the capitalist economic system, and Nietzsche challenged the values and assumptions of Christianity, asserting that God is dead. The writings of these men changed the intellectual climate in the early twentieth century. Artists and writers could no longer take for granted the structures and values that people used to rely on. Joyce himself questioned the authority of the Catholic church and later rejected it. He also questioned middle-class morality and institutions such as marriage. Because the old values were not as stable, artists were in a sense liberated to find new forms to represent reality, and they created works that questioned the usual ways people perceive reality.

Irish Cultural Revival

Around the turn of the century there was a movement to revive Irish culture and language. The Gaelic League was founded in 1893, and it still exists to preserve Irish culture and promote Gaelic as a spoken everyday language. Molly Ivors is sympathetic to the ideas of the Gaelic League. She chides Gabriel for not wanting to learn Irish but instead going to Europe to speak European languages. She says that Irish is his own language, but Gabriel denies this. The spoken language of Ireland was in fact English, and Joyce too felt that trying to revive Gaelic was like trying to impose something artificial on the culture. There was also a literary renaissance that concentrated on Irish folklore. This movement was led by such writers as William Butler Yeats and Lady Gregory—both contemporaries of Joyce. They collected Irish folk stories and wrote poems and plays based on Irish folklore. Joyce was not sympathetic with this movement either.

Critical Overview

"The Dead" was first published in 1914 as part of Joyce's short story collection called *Dubliners.* Joyce had actually written all the stories by 1907, when he finished "The Dead," but he struggled for seven years to get the collection published. The publishers were in a sense its first critics, refusing to publish the collection because some of the stories had mildly profane language and because they refer to real people and places in and around Dublin.

When *Dubliners* was finally published, the first critics were struck by Joyce's meticulous concentration on the ordinary and drab details of life. Joyce's subject matter, which avoids any attempt at the sensational, was noticeably different to them. A 1914 review in the *Times Literary Supplement* said that *Dubliners* "may be recommended to the large class of readers to whom the drab makes an appeal, for it is admirably written." Gerald Gould, writing for the *New Statesman,* had similar comments. He wrote that Joyce "dares to let people speak for themselves with awkward meticulousness, the persistent incompetent repetition of actual human intercourse." Although he thought Joyce a genius, Gould deemed it a pity that a man could write as Joyce does while insisting upon "aspects of life which are not ordinarily mentioned." But other critics approved of Joyce's examination of the mundane and ordinary. Ezra Pound praised Joyce for being a realist and not sentimentalizing over his characters, and in 1922 John Macy saw Joyce's work as superior to the usual stories of that time. Having little regard for the sentimental and genteel style found in most magazines of the period, Macy noted, Joyce's kinds of stories were "almost unknown to American magazines, if not to American writers." Macy called "The Dead" a masterpiece, but argued that it would never be popular because it is about living people.

As Joyce's popularity grew, his stories became overshadowed by his longer and more complex works, such as *A Portrait of the Artist as a Young Man* and *Ulysses.* By the 1940s, critics looked back to "The Dead" and saw it as an important work. Much critical attention has been given to it over the years, and critics have looked at the story in various ways. "The Dead" started getting more critical attention from academic critics in the 1940s and 1950s. These critics tended to be formalists, focusing on the story's shape and structure and the manner in which it was made. In 1950 Allen Tate wrote an essay which examines Joyce's method of presenting details in a way that goes beyond description to the level of symbol. His main example is how the snow appears in the story first as a physical detail on Gabriel's galoshes then gradually encompasses the whole story when it is the central symbol in Gabriel's epiphany. Kenneth Burke writes in his "Stages of 'The Dead' " that the story is structured in stages. The first is one of expectancy, where all are preparing for the party and waiting for Gabriel. The second is the party itself, and the third is leaving the party. Finally, the fourth stage, when Gabriel and Gretta are alone, has many stages of its own, building up to Gabriel's final moment of revelation.

In 1959, Richard Ellmann wrote an important essay that examines "The Dead" from the vantage point of Joyce's biography. In "The Backgrounds of 'The Dead'" Ellmann compares episodes in Joyce's life to similar ones in the story. Nora Barnacle, Joyce's lifelong companion and eventual wife, courted a man named Michael who was dying of tuberculosis when Nora decided to move from Galway to Dublin. This real-life Michael left his bed to visit Nora on a rainy night before she left for Dublin. Later, while she was in Dublin, she learned of his death. Ellmann also pointed out that Gabriel is similar to Joyce, as Gretta is similar to Nora. In fact, all the characters in the story seem to have real-life counterparts.

Another popular approach is a psychological reading of "The Dead." Michael Shurgot sees the paralysis of the characters in terms of Freud's theory of the death wish. Shurgot argues that characters in the story follow what Freud said was the aim in life, to go toward a state of inactivity or death. Daniel R. Schwarz examines Gabriel's psyche in relation to the author's and in a cultural and historical context. Still other critics approach the story in relation to the works of the psychologist Jacques

View overlooking the River Liffey and Usher's Island, the setting for "The Dead."

Lacan, who believed that the unconscious is structured as a language.

Critics have disagreed about the two most important aspects of the story: the meaning of Gabriel's epiphany and of the snow symbolism. The interpretation of Gabriel's epiphany falls into two camps: Some critics argue that Gabriel transcends his paralysis and will likely go on to live a different, less self-absorbed life; others think that Gabriel comes to understand himself, but this understanding is a reconciliation of who he actually is rather than a beginning for growth. The snow seems to many critics a symbol of death or paralysis, while to others it is a symbol of Gabriel's transcending his own self-consciousness to see things more compassionately and be sympathetic to the state of humanity. Robert Billingheimer considers the snow a more ambivalent symbol. Ice, he argues, usually symbolizes death, while water symbolizes life. Therefore snow symbolizes a state of death in life or life in death.

Beneath the story's surface of meticulous realistic detail, critics have found in "The Dead" many levels of meaning. Consequently the work has produced a large body of criticism treating the story from a variety of approaches.

Criticism

Eric Rapp

Rapp, who has taught English composition, has a master's degree and is a Ph.D. candidate in English literature at the University of Toledo. In the following essay, he argues that Gabriel's epiphany allows him to overcome paralysis by giving him a deeper understanding of his own mortality.

A major point of contention for critics of "The Dead" has been whether Gabriel overcomes his paralysis through his epiphany. Many critics, such as Kenneth Burke, feel that Gabriel does transcend his own paralytic self-consciousness. Others argue that he does not transcend his condition but rather, in a way, gives up any such notion and simply accepts that he is one of the spiritually dead. Michael Shurgot sees Gabriel being motivated by what Freud called a death wish. That is, he desires to avoid the problems and pressures of life and hopes to escape them by turning to some unfeeling state which would be ultimately similar to death. I would argue, like Shurgot, that death does play a role in Gabriel's epiphany; however, Gabriel's epiphany allows him to overcome his paralysis. Rather than achieving a death wish, Gabriel becomes aware of what philosophers and other twentieth-century writers call the subjective truth of death. This philosophical concept asserts that one must be aware of the possibility of one's own death to live an authentic existence. A person truly aware of his or her own death can concentrate on life as it is lived, not regretting the past or fearing the future, but living fully in the present.

Throughout most of the story it is clear that Gabriel is trapped in his own self-consciousness. It is interesting that many of the characters in the story are in fact dead. There is Gabriel's uncle Pat Morkan, his mother, the tenors of the past, Patrick Morkan his grandfather, and of course Michael Furey, among others. These figures from the past show up to subtly remind Gabriel of his own mortality.

A need to be more aware of one's mortality is hinted at while the guests of the party are eating the Christmas pudding. Mrs. Malins informs the rest of the dinner party that her son Freddy will be visiting the monastery in Mount Melleray. The rules of the religious order are mentioned—that the monks never speak, they get up at two in the morning, and they sleep in their own coffins. Mr. Browne shows his materialist tendencies by questioning why anyone would want to live as the monks do. A Protestant, he seems unable to understand the deeper spiritual meaning inherent in the monastic lifestyle. The Catholics, however, do not seem to understand the spiritual meaning either, for Aunt Julia simply says that it was the rule, as one would say who simply lives an unexamined life, by rote. But Mary Jane offers an explanation for why the monks sleep in their coffins that is one of the keys to the whole story: "The coffin . . . is to remind them of their last end."

Another place where the dead exert their influence on Gabriel is in his speech. In it he speaks of Ireland's tradition of genuine, courteous, warm-hearted hospitality. He looks at the current "hypereducated" generation and fears that they will lose the humanity, hospitality, and kindly good humor of the past generation. Ironically, such things as humanity and kindly good humor are precisely what Gabriel lacks. One sees this when examining the symptoms of Gabriel's paralysis.

Perhaps the first symptom of Gabriel's paralysis that is apparent is his condescending attitude toward others. With this attitude he tends to limit people to his own conceptions of them rather than seeing them with the complexity of human beings. He smiles at Lily for the apparently uneducated way she pronounces his name. He seems to see her still as the child he knew who sat on the front steps with a rag doll. When he attempts a conversation with her, he asks her if she still goes to school—the same sort of question one would ask a child. Judging from her answer, Lily has been out of school for some time, for she says, "I'm done schooling this year and more." So Gabriel modifies his question to one geared playfully toward a naive, lovestruck young girl: "I suppose we'll be going to your wedding one of these fine days with your young man, eh?" Lily's response indicates that she isn't as naive as Gabriel would suppose: "The men that is now is only all palaver and what they can get out of you." With this answer, Lily isn't responding with the same friendly tone that Gabriel tries to use. Instead she glances back at him over her shoulder and says it "with great bitterness." The reason for this bitterness isn't explained, but I suspect one can interpret it in two ways. The common and quite likely interpretation is that she is thinking of a man who has taken advantage of her in some way, and the recollection causes the angry response. One could also conclude that she is frustrated with the condescending level of Gabriel's questions. His questions are those that one might ask a child or teenager rather than a sophisti-

What Do I Read Next?

- *Dubliners* (1914) by James Joyce. The short story collection in which ''The Dead'' appears provides context for a better understanding of the story as part of a unified whole, with themes and characters interwoven throughout.

- *A Portrait of the Artist as a Young Man* (1916) by James Joyce. Joyce's autobiographical novel features Joyce's alter-ego Stephen Dedalus. Although technically a work of fiction, this work gives insight to Joyce's character and his aesthetic theories.

- *In Our Time* (1914) by Ernest Hemingway. This is Hemingway's first collection of short stories. He writes in a style similar to Joyce's, presenting the action with little or no comment.

- *The Stranger* (1942) by Albert Camus. Originally published in French as *L'entranger,* this novel's main character, Mersault, is much like the people in ''The Dead.'' Charged with the crime of murder, Mersault has an epiphany as he sits awaiting his death by guillotine.

- *Existentialism* (1974) edited by Robert C. Solomon. This book is an anthology of works by writers who are considered part of the philosophical movement of the title. The writers include Soren Kierkegaard, Albert Camus, and Friedrich Nietzsche, among others.

---

cated adult. Gabriel's condescension is shown in other instances as well. Shortly after his encounter with Lily, he goes upstairs, where he is reminded that the men dancing are of a different grade of culture by the sound of the ''indelicate clacking'' of their heels and the ''shuffling'' of the soles of their shoes. Also he is undecided about using a Robert Browning quote in his after-dinner speech because the lines might be above the heads of his listeners.

The concern about the Browning quote reveals another facet of Gabriel's paralysis. At the same time he is condescending, he is concerned about what others think about him:

> He would only make himself ridiculous by quoting poetry to them which they could not understand. They would think that he was airing his superior education. He would fail with them just as he had failed with the girl in the pantry.

Gabriel seems like a man who feels awkward because he is out of his element of university professors and is instead among a bunch of what he would probably call working-class brutes. Although he considers himself superior to them, he is frightened that they will reject him. This is why he is flustered after Lily's quick-tempered retort to his question about marriage. This fear of rejection occurs also when he is around someone he considers his equal. Molly Ivors has been a longtime friend of his, and they have had parallel careers. Both went to the same university, and both have become teachers. But when Miss Ivors confronts him about writing for the *Daily Express* he becomes tongue-tied and nervous. He answers her questions awkwardly because he wishes to flee from the confrontation altogether, and he can barely muster the strength to defend himself because he might displease her. Because she is a fellow teacher and of equal education, ''he could not risk a grandiose phrase with her.'' Still he manages to be condescending to her as he privately denounces her in his own thoughts afterwards: ''Of course the girl or woman, or whatever she was, was an enthusiast but there was a time for all things.'' By referring to her as a girl, Gabriel is slightly degrading Molly by reducing her to a child as he does earlier with Lily.

Another symptom of Gabriel's paralysis is his need to control reality. His solicitude has been a long-running joke between his two aunts. Although care and concern can be good character traits, Gabriel seems overly fussy when it comes to his wife and children. He makes his son wear green shades at night and lift dumbbells, forces his daughter to eat her "stirabout" (Irish porridge), and frets about his wife. He decides not to travel all the way back to his suburb of Monkstown after the party because he fears Gretta will catch cold as she did last year, and he insists that she wear galoshes. This insistence has other motives as well. Aside from protecting her feet from the wet and cold, it is apparent that they are the new trend—Gabriel is concerned about appearances.

The story reveals the symptoms of Gabriel's paralysis, which are condescension, concern about what others think, and a need to be in control. But through his own memories and the memories of others, he encounters figures of the past. His memories of the dead slowly enable him to have his epiphany and cure him of his paralysis. Gabriel's first encounter with the dead is when he reminisces about his dead mother, Ellen Conroy. She gave Gabriel and his brother Constantine their names because she was concerned about the dignity of the family. Gabriel has her to thank for his position, for though she and her husband were of modest means, her efforts made sure that Gabriel and his brother Constantine moved beyond her position in society to become professionals: Gabriel is a teacher and Constantine a priest. It is evident, then, that Ellen had a desire for her children to escape the position in which she found herself.

Another person from the realm of the dead who influences Gabriel this night is his grandfather Patrick Morkan. Gabriel tells the story of how his grandfather once drove his mill horse into town for a military parade. He became indignant when the workhorse began circling a statue of King William III of England the way he would circle in the mill harness. As many critics have pointed out, the action of the horse symbolizes the paralysis of Ireland, and Gabriel's imitation of it as he tells the story represents his own paralysis.

That person from the realm of the dead who finally manages to make Gabriel aware of his own mortality and thus have more compassion for his fellow human beings is Michael Furey. When Gretta tells him about her relationship for Michael and the way in which he passionately loved her, dying for her, as she says, Gabriel seems to look at himself differently:

> A shameful consciousness of his own person assailed him. He saw himself as a ludicrous figure, acting as a pennyboy for his aunts, a nervous well-meaning sentimentalist, orating to vulgarians and idealising his own

> " Gabriel seems like a man who feels awkward because he is out of his element of university professors and is instead among a bunch of what he would probably call working-class brutes."

clownish lusts, the pitiable fatuous fellow he had caught a glimpse of in the mirror.

This is just the beginning of his change. He feels the influence of the dead Michael Furey as an "impalpable and vindictive being . . . coming against him, gathering forces against him in its vague world."

After Gretta falls asleep, Gabriel has his epiphany, and it seems clear that what this epiphany involves is a new, deeply felt awareness of his own mortality. The beginning of this awareness is when he remembers Aunt Julia's haggard face as she was singing earlier that evening. He thinks to himself that she will soon be "a shade with the shade of Patrick Morkan and his horse." Then he realizes not only that Aunt Julia is becoming a shade, but that everyone will eventually die, and that it is better to live passionately like Michael Furey. Because of his own self-consciousness, he had never felt for a woman in the way Michael Furey had for Gretta, but he knows that such a feeling must be love.

At the height of Gabriel's epiphany comes the most curious passage in the story:

> The tears gathered more thickly in his eyes and in the partial darkness he imagined he saw the form of a young man standing under a dripping tree. Other forms were near. His soul had approached that region where dwell the vast hosts of the dead. He was conscious of, but could not apprehend, their wayward and flickering existence. His own identity was fading out into a grey impalpable world: the solid world itself which these dead had one time reared and lived in was dissolving and dwindling.

Kenneth Burke finds this passage to be the moment where Gabriel transcends the world of conditions. According to Burke, since the world of conditions is the world of the living, then the world of the dead would be the place where one has transcended those conditions and reaches the divine. But I would hesitate to make such a mystical reading. By being in the region of the dead, Gabriel has reached that state of consciousness where one has an inward awareness of death. If one were to actually lose the ability to feel and live in the "solid world" as the dead have lost the ability, he would come to have a greater appreciation for existence. As another twentieth-century writer, Wallace Stevens, said, "The greatest poverty is not to live in the physical world." Even the story's much-quoted last passage reiterates the importance of the awareness of one's own death:

> His soul swooned slowly as he heard the snow falling faintly through the universe and faintly falling, like the descent of their last end, upon all the living and the dead.

Some readers see the snow symbolizing paralysis, while others see it symbolizing transcendence. I would argue that the snow does symbolize death, but more specifically the awareness of death. The phrase "like the descent of their last end" echoes Mary Jane's earlier observation of the monks sleeping in their coffins: "The coffin is to remind them of their last end." Gabriel is able to see beyond his own self-consciousness to a broader perspective. He is now profoundly aware of his own mortality and is in a state of consciousness where he can live to the fullest what Martin Heidegger called being-toward-death.

In "The Dead" Joyce examines an issue common among twentieth-century writers: the need to live with an awareness of one's own death. Such an awareness is not easy to achieve, but with it, knowing that life will soon be gone, one can appreciate life to its fullest. Wallace Stevens put it almost as well as Joyce when writing about the dead:

> They were those that would have wept to step
>   barefoot into reality,
> That would have wept and been happy, have
>   shivered in the frost
> And cried out to feel it again, have run fingers
>   over leaves
> And against the most coiled thorn, have seized on
>   what was ugly.
> And laughed . . .

Source: Eric Rapp, Overview of "The Dead," for *Short Stories for Students,* The Gale Group, 1999.

Roland Garrett

In the following essay, Garrett offers six perspectives on "The Dead" by applying the principles of six different literary theories.

BIOGRAPHY. Joyce once said of one section of *Ulysses,* "I've put in so many enigmas and puzzles that it will keep the professors busy for centuries arguing over what I meant." Similarly, he inserted in his writings remnants of his own life and environment, so that scholars scour the details of his experience, and the people and places that he knew, for clues to the meaning of his work.

The most famous example in "The Dead" is the tragic love that Nora Barnacle knew in Galway when she was not quite sixteen years old, before she moved to Dublin, met Joyce, and ran off with him. Joyce was jealous of his dead rival, but Nora remembered the love fondly. In a conversation years later she spoke on the subject of "first love": "There's nothing like it. I remember when I was a girl, and a young man fell in love with me, and he came and sang in the rain under an apple-tree outside my window, and he caught tuberculosis and died." The dead boy had worked for the local gas company in Galway where Nora then lived. Joyce not only used that part of Nora's life as a model, but saw Nora as Gretta. He once wrote to Nora: "Do you remember the three adjectives I have used in "The Dead" in speaking of your body. They are these: 'musical and strange and perfumed.'" And the bedroom scene in "The Dead" captures Nora's character. Ellman says that "these final pages compose one of Joyce's several tributes to his wife's artless integrity"; she was "independent, unself-conscious, instinctively right."

Do we understand "The Dead" better when we know these things? Why not? It seems a narrow and exclusive sense of understanding to deny this. Joyce put in the story his wife, his dead rival, his city, his language, and elements of his national history. You could construct an interpretation of the text that ignored his wife, just as you could construct an interpretation that ignored Dublin, say, or even the English language (could the series of written marks that we call "The Dead" actually be a secret code that can be used by an Italian-speaking accountant in Trieste to record debits and credits?). But why should we want to be so unkind to the Joyces, or to isolate a literary work from the context of its creation? Joyce himself once said, "Imagination is memory." It would seem unreasonable for me to take my own imaginative interpretation of a literary work seriously without anchoring the interpretation at least in my own memory, and therefore setting it (unless I turn solipsist) in a larger history.

One great difficulty with biographical approaches to art is that we often know so little about the genesis of the work, so little that it is frequently counterproductive to look for personal sources. And our understanding of the work often seems still strangely incomplete even when we think we have found the personal sources. So we often make do with the little that we know, such as that a story is in English, is set in Dublin, and was written in 1907 by a man brought up as a Catholic. There often seems to be a kind of incompleteness to any finite summary of any particular meaning, anyway. And perhaps, given our interests, we do not really need to know too many details from the artist's life or environment.

DECONSTRUCTION. However, since our needs and interests often respond to and build on incompleteness, we might want to focus on a theory that stresses the phenomenon of incompleteness in the meaning of a text. In what way is a deconstructive approach to "The Dead" useful? Are we helped in understanding the story if we take seriously the principles that meaning is endless signification, that all interpretation is misinterpretation, or that all texts say also the opposite of what they seem to say?

Gabriel thinks: "Better pass boldly into that other world, in the full glory of some passion, than fade and wither dismally with age." Every word here except "wither" occurs elsewhere in *Dubliners,* and a recent detailed study of the occurrences of the words led to the following conclusion: "in fact, practically every word of Gabriel's maxim-like sentence is directly or indirectly contradicted by the rest of the text." The therapy implied in the maxim is thus "purely hypothetical," a "belated insight" that is "clearly shown to rest on delusive hopes." Perhaps we do not need an extensive word study like this to sense such a contradiction in the end of the story, but just a glance at the history of interpretation, where some critics have seen death and others rebirth; some mutuality, others personal isolation; some a dissolution of the subject, others a deeply personal reverie. Shifting, incompatible voices have been found in the narrative, like the "wayward and flickering" spirits that haunt Gabriel's vision. Allen Tate once said that "the snow is the story." But it has also been suggested that snow is a suitable symbol for the inclusiveness in the story precisely because the color white encompasses all the contrasting colors of the spectrum. Long ago the *Dubliners* expert Florence Walzl called Gabriel's prospective westward journey "one of the most remarkable ambiguities in literature, a conclusion that offers almost opposite meanings, each of which

> " At the turn of the twentieth century, Ireland had already for decades had the lowest marriage rate in the civilized world, and therefore the highest rate of unmarried men and women."

can be logically argued," although in those days before deconstruction it was felt appropriate to say that the ambiguity at the end of the story "was deliberate on Joyce's part."

The ambiguity is also found in reactions to the poetry of the concluding paragraphs of the story. What some see as musical or lyrical beauty, others see as a "highly rhetorical" manner with "narcotic verbal effects" in a passage that fulfills the image of paralysis with which *Dubliners* begins. Or even possibly as "exaggerated alliteration" in "an overwritten passage that conveys emotional deadness taking its last refuge in sentimentality," with repetition and syntactical reversal at the end that "are disturbing and create discord, at the very climax of the rising hymn."

When you survey in the bedroom scene alone the muttering, mumbling, noises, and silences, the interruptions and failures of communication, the immense distances between thought and speech, his "false voice" and her "veiled" voice, "the quaintness of her phrase" and "the failure of his irony," the "lame and useless" words and the now communicative sound of the snow at the window—it is not hard to see here a meditation on language that would be dear to deconstruction. In hindsight it is possible to see too the maid Lily at the outset of the story taking a step toward the theme of the world as text. "The men that is now," she said, "is only all palaver and what they can get out of you." Even Derrida felt "resentment," although an admiring resentment, at the generalized equivocality of writing in Joyce; "the endless plunge throws you back onto the river-bank, on the brink of another possible immersion, *ad infinitum.*" Derrida added: "every time I write, and even in the most academic pieces of work, Joyce's ghost is always coming on board."

> In the ballad of 'The Lass of Aughrim,' suffering is turned into ambiguity and the pleasure of music. Likewise, Gretta's tragic young love becomes a romantic story for the book reviewer and critic Gabriel."

Deconstruction is, like authorial biography, a productive spirit in which to approach "The Dead."

There is a peculiar logical problem in its stance, however. Since no one can list the endless number of separate immersions, we have at any moment a finite list, in which each item is distinguished somewhat from the others. Deconstruction, insofar as it is warranted, thus rests on some distinction, definiteness of description, and discovered pattern. What structure of language, image, or narrative in "The Dead" lead to the identification of ambiguity? Presumably we do not assume that all of these are themselves ambiguous in every way, or we could not build an argument on them. We could hardly conclude that the story says also the opposite of what it seems to say unless we are able to identify what it actually does seem to say. And if we conclude that, say, the snow is ambiguous, we presuppose not only definite evidence for that but a recognizable nature to the ambiguity. To describe the snow as ambiguous is not the same as to describe it as both-ambiguous-and-non-ambiguous. I think therefore that deconstruction, as a reasoned method, rests on discovery of structure.

STRUCTURALISM. How would structuralism work in an interpretation of "The Dead?" We might start, as Lévi-Strauss typically does, with familiar binary contrasts, such as, in this case, old and young, east and west, up and down, silence and sound, cold and warm, and see how these contrasts develop and connect in the course of the story. Connections are sometimes concrete, as when the window relates inside and outside, or the mirror relates the face to its mirror image. Or, we might look at a division based on some principle of

sequence or relational context, such as the breaks Joyce inserted between sections of the text, or the dominance of certain characters in different parts of the story. In the bedroom scene we can construct a variation on these approaches which abstracts temporarily from other themes in order to explore what the physical motion of Gabriel and Gretta contributes to the sense of the story.

When Gretta and Gabriel enter the hotel room, she stops before the mirror while he crosses the room to the window, looks out, and turns toward her, leaning on a chest of drawers. She then turns away from the mirror, walks toward him, exchanges a few words with him, and walks beyond him to the window. While she looks out the window, there is another exchange of words; then she comes unnoticed from the window to Gabriel and gives him a kiss. "Perhaps," he falsely surmises, "her thoughts had been running with his." He embraces her, but shortly she breaks loose and runs away from him to the bed. Gabriel follows her toward the bed, stopping a few paces away from her. He listens to her story of young Michael Furey and is close enough to her to caress one of her hands. Then he walks back to the window. An hour later Gretta is lying in bed asleep and Gabriel is observing and meditating, first leaning on his elbow, then lying down beside her.

What happened here? She followed him, and passed him; then she passed him again, and he followed her; then he walked away and returned. The structure of movement is that of two separate entities, moving in a single time and space, and in similar, connected patterns, almost chasing one another; but not moving together. When Gretta recalls her early love, she says: "He was very fond of me and he was such a gentle boy. We used to go out together, walking, you know, Gabriel, like the way they do in the country." Gabriel and Gretta do not walk together, just as their thoughts in fact do not "run" together. At the end she is "fast" asleep, while he swoons "slowly." The theme of miscommunication is thus reflected in the structure of movement.

"The Dead" is fertile ground for structuralism, of which this analysis of walking in the hotel room is one small example. Structuralism, although not necessarily in the familiar forms of binary contrasts or analysis of movement, typically contributes in some form or other to the range and utility of other methodologies in literary criticism.

Structuralism floundered, however, on questions of perceptibility and importance. Which structures count in literature, and why? Only those we are able to perceive? Only those that reflect what we do or ought to value? Are not some "binary contrasts," for example, just more important than others, given who we are and how we relate to one another? So one important binary contrast that structuralists utilize has taken on a critical life of some independent interest: the contrast of male and female.

FEMINISM. There are varieties of feminist approaches to Joyce, variously focused on background or works and mixing various levels of ethical judgment. Some critics, of course, like the statement attributed to Joyce that "the emancipation of women" "has caused the greatest revolution in our time in the most important relationship there is—that between men and women; the revolt of women against the idea that they are the mere instruments of men." At the turn of the twentieth century, Ireland had already for decades had the lowest marriage rate in the civilized world, and therefore the highest rate of unmarried men and women. Marriage before or at the age of twenty-five was rare, with most men marrying when they were between thirty-five and forty-five years old, and tending to marry women ten years or more younger than themselves. Florence Walzl presents this data and adds: "The results [for men] of abnormally delayed marriages, of sexual abstinence or guilt over illicit sex, and of long years of primarily male company led many to take a cold-blooded, unromantic view of marriage. . . . The results for women were often most unhappy. Girls, generally reared with a ladylike abhorrence of sex and with their emotions channeled into a frustrated romanticism, were ill prepared for the realities of marriage." In "The Dead" Gretta and Gabriel seem to be the only married couple at the party, and, in a general way (disregarding specifics in Walzl's description), their marriage seems colored by such cold-bloodedness and frustration. The story is in fact sometimes seen as a sequence of troubling encounters between Gabriel and a series of women—first Lily, then Miss Ivors, then Gretta.

The song "The Lass of Aughrim," which young Michael sang to Gretta, and which Joyce had heard from Nora, is a dialogue between a young woman standing in the rain with a baby, asking to be let in, and Gregory, whom she accuses of being the child's father but who refuses to recognize her as "the lass of Aughrim." Gregory demands "tokens" of proof and the young woman provides details. Since the woman sings that "we swapped rings off each other's hands, / Sorely against my will," and "you had your will of me," some feminists have introduced in interpretation the phrase "date rape." Similarly, a threat of "mate rape" is seen in Gabriel's angry, sexual desire to "crush" Gretta's body against his own, "to overmaster her." It has been said that "The Dead" is tailor-made for feminist interpretation.

As with other literary theories, though, a single heuristic can be misleading as well as suggestive. In "The Lass of Aughrim" the sequence of verses alternates with accusation and doubt, and Gregory interestingly does not challenge the general sexual accusation; he simply doubts that this is the woman. Is "date rape," or leaving the woman to stand in the rain, of greater interpretive importance for this song than the momentousness of ambiguity? Some interpretations of "The Dead" have actually omitted from quotation the first clause of Joyce's sentence reflecting Gabriel's thinking: "He longed to cry to her from his soul, to crush her body against his, to overmaster her." And few critics are bold enough nowadays to even raise the question whether Gretta shares the responsibility for her suffering because she chose to lock her secret in her heart for so many years, to say nothing of the degree to which, if Gabriel is determined by his maleness, that ought to affect judgment of him. Some recent ethics-oriented criticism thus in some ways seems to resemble the older religious criticism, which is, like the feminist, insightful and fruitful, although similarly "thought-tormented." ("So it is that snow is the perfect symbol for the Christian dead. It is the waters of life in a state of suspension.")

In any case, feminist approaches do often seem to recognize that they undercut their own success if they neglect or simply stand in conflict with other approaches. The lass of Aughrim could hardly be a wealthy aristocrat struggling for admission to a poor man's home. Not all "binary contrasts" are equally important, but it hardly seems reasonable in life or art to emphasize just one. And of course, as Walzl points out, the famine and poverty of nineteenth-century Ireland contributed to the suffering of women such as those Joyce describes.

MARXISM. What leads Gabriel to want to cry out to Gretta and "overmaster" her? Talk about money, that he cannot help taking; in fact, it is talk about a "sovereign," which is both money and politics. That is what gets Gabriel the "generous" kiss. It is Christmas time, but Christmas is mentioned in the hotel room only as an occasion for a shop that sells cards. The hotel setting is a similar commercialization of the marital bedroom; Gabriel realizes he is a ''pennyboy'' for his aunts and reflects how ''poor'' a part he has played in Gretta's life. Michael Furey worked for the gas company; perhaps, it has been suggested, in the young man's job of shoveling coal for coal-gas, which could contribute to the illness that kept him from a singing career and brought his early death. Presumably there was something in his experience that led him to tell Gretta that ''he did not want to live.'' In the ballad of ''The Lass of Aughrim,'' suffering is turned into ambiguity and the pleasure of music. Likewise, Gretta's tragic young love becomes a romantic story for the book reviewer and critic Gabriel. ''So she had had that romance in her life,'' he thinks, ''a man had died for her sake.'' In view of the reverie that follows, in which, as in the ballad, suffering seems to be assimilated to aestheticism, there is something to be said for the need to ''decode the bourgeois agenda of the narrative voice,'' and even for the claim that ''Joyce dramatizes in 'The Dead' the politics of art's determination to conceal its own politically oppressive functions.''

A logical difficulty with this view, however, is suggested by the question of how art can effectively dramatize what it is determined to conceal. If the story is perceived as a drama of this sort, it seems the story then has no such concealing function. The problem is similar to the one we noticed in deconstruction, when taken as a reasoned general theory; the theory is undermined by its own evidence. The critical methods and insights of Marxism are often shrewd and valuable, as in the case of deconstruction, despite epistemological difficulties of this sort. But there is an obvious danger in one easy, elitist solution to the logical problem—the solution that claims that there really is concealment in art because the ignorant masses do not realize they are duped, so that a few capable people (presumably exempt from superstructural self-deception) must elect themselves to educate the rest. It is well to remember that Gabriel's reverie, in which suffering is assimilated to aestheticism, is that of a literary critic, not an artist. There seems paradoxically to be such an aestheticism in the Marxist critic's play with political language that is diverted from the effort and risk of serious political conflict, and that, by its conceptual abstraction, in fact floats at a distance from the artistic work. Self-criticism is not Marxism's strong suit.

Consider the point in ''The Dead'' when Gabriel sees himself as a ''pitiable fatuous fellow.'' A Marxist response is as follows: ''The moment is one when false consciousness gives way to a potentially revolutionary insight, when the masks of ideology are lowered.'' In view of the multiple, shifting perspectives in Joyce, is it really so obvious which ones are ''true'' and which ones are ''false''? Does everyone get to vote on where to draw the line, including people like those in the story who find Gabriel helpful and appreciate his speech at the party? Are perspectives or ideologies really like ''masks,'' that can all be removed at once to reveal the true face? The certainty about truth and falsehood, which is introduced into literary criticism from external sources, has the unfortunate consequence that Marxism, by its own reasoning, often becomes one more ideology that art is not allowed to test or challenge. Thus it imposes on itself a separation from art.

The logic of this situation can be illustrated by the fact that ''The Lass of Aughrim'' has a version that does not speak of ''Lord Gregory'' but simply of ''Gregory.'' Is that version of the song devoid of class consciousness, to a fault? Or is it rather evidence that significant conflicts between men and women are sometimes unexplained by Marxist concepts of class structure, and that these concepts are therefore of limited value? One thing that seems needed is a psychology of concealment that recognizes its immense human and social complexity.

PSYCHOANALYSIS. It is easy to tack psychoanalysis on to this list of literary theories, since we have been talking about many of its interests: the author's background; miscommunication and psychic repression; walking around and talking instead of sex in a bedroom; concealment and sublimation; a dream-like reverie and a death-wish. Walzl describes the ''maternal domination of both daughters and sons'' in Irish society. She quotes a statement that the ''Irishman is the world's prime example of the Oedipus complex,'' and adds: ''Joyce knew this type well.'' We do learn in ''The Dead'' that Gabriel's mother was considered by one of her sisters to be the ''brains carrier'' of the Morkan family, that she is the one who gave Gabriel and his brother Constantine their distinctive names, and that some of her sons' professional achievements were realized ''thanks to her.'' Perhaps she is the one who taught her sons to read, for there is a picture Gabriel notices at the party that shows her pointing out something to young Constantine in an open book, a photograph that critics have noticed is a cropped version of a family photograph that includes Joyce and his own mother in the same pose. Presumably there is some psychological source or mechanism for the artist's selection of elements from the environment, for one's fascination with language, for the structures one identifies, and for the oppressions one creates or suffers; and Joyce seems to have thought of these issues along some psychoanalytic lines. Gabriel also is made to remember at the party his dead mother's "sullen opposition" to his marriage with Gretta. Is it reasonable to say that "with 'The Dead,' Joyce breaks with his need to identify with the father and authoritatively fix the meaning of the mother?" Or that Gabriel has an "oppressive superego," i.e., is "a thrall to the ghosts of his parents?" Psychoanalysis is another fruitful approach to "The Dead," although, as with some of the other approaches, the technical external terminology often adds little to perception and in fact, as illustrated by the abstract conclusions I have quoted, introduces another unfortunate dimension of critical self-assurance.

GENERAL REFLECTIONS. This sample of critical approaches is sketchy and incomplete, but perhaps useful still for some broader reflections.

First, each of these approaches has its strengths and each, taken in isolation, seems about as good and as bad as the others in accommodating "The Dead." This should not be surprising, since I have deliberately chosen one useful story for illustration, and a complex, much-studied story at that. There are also insightful interpretations of this story that utilize very different perspectives, from Irish mythology to the effect of structure and pace on the reader's response. Perhaps the critical history of the story would now permit an equally successful historical hermeneutics, in which the various approaches could be seen and evaluated as links between Joyce and the various social or moral cultures of his readers. There is a detailed recent study of the story which finds "all major film techniques" in it, such as varying focal lengths, flashbacks, soft focus, dissolves, zooms, backlighting, and the rest. "The Dead" (the story, not the movie) contains "six sequences, fourteen scenes, and one hundred and eighty-four shots," with a certain pattern in the "Average Number of Words per Shot." One earlier reading referred to a "dialectical form" in the story, like that of Plato's *Theaetetus,* and suggested that you might call "The Dead" "the narrative equivalent of a Platonic dialogue." Well, why not? Perhaps not *the* equivalent. But there is something to the comparison with Platonic dialogue.

Second, the utility of diverse theories in interpretation does not imply the simultaneous truth of all the claims in the theoretical inventory. One critic says "the central question of the text" is "whether or not art serves a political function"; another that "the story's major commitment is to noise, to noise as social disturbance and cosmic disorder, the two functions performed by D'Arcy's singing"; and a third that the "irreverence of Joyce's depiction of Epiphany Day nineteen centuries later is the crucial element of 'The Dead.'" It seems to me that there is not a clear enough conception of evidence or a clear enough formulation of principles to warrant any of these conclusions. The same applies to several other interpretive claims we have encountered, partly because they are often influenced by ideas uncritically imported from other fields of interest or inquiry. Even apart from the exclusivist claims of some critics there is a conflict of emphasis among the different approaches, versions of each often needing some puncturing of rhetorical pretension. It was a rare pleasure to read in John Kelleher's brilliant and groundbreaking study of "The Dead" the following qualification: "I consider almost nothing of what I have spoken of today as primary to the story. It is all atmospherics. . . ." In any description or interpretation, emphasis occurs in some context and for some purpose, and need not be construed to assert its own priority for all other contexts. Whether one theory is better than another depends in part on one's interpretive goals, which have not been, and probably cannot be, managed into a single universal goal.

Third, the different approaches, even taken as heuristics rather than universal theory, often mix with and depend on one another far more than I have indicated. The structuralist can quote documents from Joyce's biography, the Marxist may draw insights from psychoanalysis, the feminist could study the impact of incompleteness of meaning on the status of women. Moreover, in some contexts it seems futile to claim discovery of fundamental intentions or causes, not only because of individual, social, or artistic complexity, but because the very notion of "cause" is a relative and interpretive concept, an agency for construing recognizable situations in a manageable way, or perhaps for changing them. The same event may have many "causes," none intrinsically more fundamental than the others. It may not even be heuristically useful to modulate the various competing interpretations of "The Dead" into one consistent, umbrella interpretation, except to deflate the pretensions of the individual theories. For the interpretive competition is productive; even the logical inconsistencies found in a single theory, may help it to be suggestive and fruitful in construing art. It is a familiar notion that teaching students of literature to read and understand could well use all of the critical approaches we have glanced at, and more. The complexity of "The Dead" can help us appreciate why. Since my own view of the individual theoretical approaches to literature is pragmatic and skeptical, I am personally taken by Gretta's honest recognition of limitation in knowledge, regarding something as important in her life as Michael's illness: "He was in decline, they said, or something like that. I never knew rightly."

Source: Roland Garrett, "Six Theories in the Bedroom of 'The Dead'," in *Philosophy and Literature,* Vol. 16, No. 1, April, 1992, pp. 115–27.

L. J. Morrissey

In the following essay, Morrissey explores the conflict Joyce's characters experience when their "romantic inner perceptions" encounter "squalid outer reality."

In his short stories, Joyce's conspicuous symbols usually grow out of a disparity between a character's romantic inner perception and squalid outer reality. This disparity creates the strange sense of displacement common to so many characters in *Dubliners.* In some like "The Sister," "Counterparts," "Two Gallants," "Ivy Day in the Committee Room," "Clay," and "A Painful Case," the inner image is held only briefly. It may be no more than a nightmare glimpse of "some pleasant and vicious region" of the soul with its "long velvet curtains and a swinging lamp of antique fashion" as it is in "The Sisters." Or it may be no more than the romantic images of a song/poem, as it is in "Clay" ("I Dreamt that I Dwelt"), "Ivy Day. . ." ("The Death of Parnell") and "Two Gallants" ("Silent, O Moyle"). Even as corrupt a perceiver as Farrington, in "Counterparts," has a glimpse of the foreign, the romantically unattainable, as his "eyes wandered at every moment in the direction of one of the young women . . . [with her] immense scarf of peacock-blue muslin . . . wound round her hat . . . [her] bright yellow gloves, reaching to the elbow . . . [her] plump arm which she moved very often and with much grace . . . [and her] London accent." This image may be vulgar, but for Farrington, it is radically at odds with his squalid life of work, pub

and home, and it helps create sympathy in the reader for this displaced man.

In at least two of his short stories, Joyce intensifies and extends this disparity. In "Araby," for instance, the romantic image of the girl, with "her figure defined by the light from the half-opened door. . . . Her dress sw[inging] as she moved her body and the soft rope of her hair toss[ing] from side to side," is aggressively tested against Dublin reality. The boy tests her "image . . . in places the most hostile to romance," carrying it like a "chalice" "through the flaring streets, jostled by drunken men and bargaining women, amid the curses of labourers, the shrill litanies of shop boys who stood on guard by barrels of pigs cheeks." One "dark rainy evening" he tests the image in the squalid "back drawing-room in which the priest had died" and again on the Saturday night of the bazaar in "the high cold empty gloomy rooms" of "the upper part of the house." Through it all he sees "nothing but the brown-clad figure cast by [his] imagination." It isn't until he acts on *her* inner imagining ("She asked me was I going to *Araby*. . . . It would be a splendid bazaar, she said; she would love to go") rather than his own and goes to the squalid bazaar with its closed stalls and darkened hall, its money counters and flirtatious stall girl that his image of the girl fails him. Acting out her inadequate romantic imagining, which he has taken over ("The syllables of the word *Araby* were called to me through the silence in which my soul luxuriated and cast an Eastern enchantment over me"), he loses his own inner image of the girl and can only "remember with difficulty why I had come." All his pseudo-religious imagery surrounding the girl fails in this "silence like that which pervades a church after a service," and he sees himself "as a creature driven and derided by vanity."

By merging two disparate patterns of imagery, Joyce further intensifies this same disillusionment and loss of self in "The Dead." One set, those images of Gabriel's wife Gretta, are a complex version of the boy's image of the girl in "Araby"; the other those images of snow in the story. Each should be examined separately before seeing how they merge.

Gabriel is not an innocent like the boy. Instead, from the beginning of the story, he feels alienated from his culture and insecure as a result of his alienation. That is, he feels superior because "the indelicate clacking of the men's heels and the shuffling of their soles reminded him that their grade of culture differed from his.'' Yet he feels inadequate before them. ''He would only make himself ridiculous. . . . He would fail with them. . . .'' His inner image of his wife is comprised of a similar vacillation. He is delighted by her exterior image at the opening of the party; his ''admiring and happy eyes had been wandering from her dress to her face and her hair.'' Yet his attained ideal is corrupted by a nagging doubt, by a fear that, as his Mother said, she is only ''country cute.'' When she gently mocks Gabriel's continental affectation about goloshes with her Irish phrasing—''Tonight even he wanted me to put them on,'' ''Guttapercha things''—he reminds her of her ''grade of culture'': ''Gabriel knitted his brows and said, as if he were slightly angered: It's nothing very wonderful but Gretta thinks it very funny because she says the word reminds her of Christy Minstrels.'' Put in her place, Gretta falls silent. His ideal woman will no longer break into vulgar ''peal[s] of laughter.''

Nearly the same pattern is repeated at the end of the party. First Gabriel sees Gretta as a romantic image from a painting. Distanced and silenced by Bartell D'Arcy's singing of ''The Lass of Aughrim,'' she has been so self-effaced, so ''unaware of the talk about her,'' that Aunt Julia nearly misses her when the good-nights are said: ''O, good-night, Gretta, I didn't see you.'' Because she is so silent, Gabriel can continue his romantic revery despite the ''murky air'' of Dublin. He can nearly ignore that with ''her shoes in a brown parcel tucked under one arm and her hands holding her skirt up from the slush [s]he had no longer any grace of attitude.'' Like the boy in ''Araby'' he can take his romantic image into the squalid Dublin night and yet keep the romance alive. By editing the ''[m]oments of their secret life together [which] burst like stars upon his memory,'' he can ''forget the years of their dull existence together and remember only their moments of ecstasy.'' Again, like ''Araby,'' this inner romantic image of the male is brought down by the inner yearning of a simple Irish female. In ''The Dead'' Gretta's romantic imagining—''a boy in the gasworks'' ''died for me''—may not be quite as inadequate as Mangan's sister's interest in the bazaar; but Gretta's sentimental Irish love story, the memory of which is appropriately triggered by the melodramatic ''Lass of Aughrim,'' just as surely triumphs over her male's secret imaginings as the girl's does in ''Araby.'' Once again, when the male takes over the romantic imaginings of the female (''he imagined he saw the form of a young man standing under a dripping tree,'' he is left with

> Rather than recognize the disparity between his inner imaginings about the snow and the reality of the snow when confronted by it, Gabriel plunges into his sensual romantic revery about his 'secret life' with Gretta.''

squalid reality (''His eyes moved to the chair over which she had thrown some of her clothes. A petticoat string dangled to the floor. . . .'') and despair (''He had never felt like that himself towards any woman. . . .'').

At the same time that Joyce is developing this pattern of disparate images around the woman in ''The Dead,'' he is also developing another pattern of snow images. Like so many of Joyce's symbols, snow begins as a naturalistic detail of setting. It simply seems to be there to establish the time of year, as do the overcoats of the guests and Gabriel and Gretta's goloshes. When Gabriel enters ''scraping his feet vigorously . . . [with] a light fringe of snow lay[ing] like a cape on the shoulders of his overcoat and like toecaps on the toes of his goloshes,'' it is clearly winter. But Gabriel soon appropriates this outer reality as a romantic inner longing.

Gabriel has two reveries about snow while he is at the party. The first occurs after the first hiatus in the text and well into the party. Gabriel's general irritation with the vulgar dance has been exacerbated by Mary Jane's inappropriate ''Academy piece,'' by his ''rankl[ing] . . . memory'' of his mother's disapproval of Gretta, by Miss Ivors' challenge to Gabriel's cosmopolitan affectation and her allusion to Gretta's country background, and by an irritating few minutes beside Freddy Malins' tiresome mother. As he hears the ''clatter of plates and knives'' from the other room, Gabriel ''began to think again about his speech and about the quotation'' from Robert Browning. He retreats to the ''embrasure of the window'' and begins nervously tapping the cold windowpane with ''warm trembling fingers.'' ''How cool it must be outside! How pleasant it would be to

> "All of Gabriel's reveries about Gretta and snow . . . reveal that he is a conventional Dubliner."

walk out alone, first along by the river and then through the park! The snow would be lying on the branches of the trees and forming a bright cap on the top of the Wellington Monument. How much more pleasant it would be there than at the supper table!'' He next thinks of the snow moments before his after-dinner speech. He has risen, ''leaned his ten trembling fingers on the tablecloth and smiled nervously at the company.'' Unable to meet the eyes of the ''upturned faces he raised his eyes to the chandelier'' and drifts into another revery about snow. ''People, perhaps, were standing in the snow on the quay outside, gazing up at the lighted windows and listening to the waltz music. The air was pure there. In the distance lay the park where the trees were weighted with snow. The Wellington Monument wore a gleaming cap of snow that flashed westward over the white field of Fifteen Acres.''

Again Joyce sets up the inner/outer contrast simply by putting these reveries in the context of this genteel Dublin party where Freddy Malins' drunkenness, Miss Ivors' political discord, disagreements about music and religion, and Bartell D'Arcy's simple bad temper are covered over by euphemism, sentiment, and trivia. In addition to this contrast, Joyce establishes yet another. In the early morning after Gabriel's two reveries are over, and after some talk weather in the hallway (''we haven't had snow like it for thirty years''), we follow Gabriel and Gretta outside into the squalid reality of a Dublin snow. Rather than the ''gleaming cap of snow,'' it is ''slushy'' ''streaks and patches . . . on the roofs, on the parapets . . . and on the area railings.'' Rather than the ''pure'' air Gabriel imagines, we are told that ''a dull yellow light brooded over the houses and the river,'' that ''the sky seemed to be descending.'' The air is ''murky'' and ''the palace of the Four Courts stood out menacingly against the heavy sky.'' Even the horse is part of this brooding Dublin atmosphere as he ''galloped along wearily under the murky morning sky, dragging his old rattling box after his heels.''

Obviously, both of Gabriel's inner reveries about snow are in sharp contrast to the snow we see here. Once we experience the real Dublin scene of murk, slush, and menace, Gabriel's imagined scenes— ''cool,'' ''pleasant,'' ''bright,'' ''pure,'' ''gleaming,'' full of snow that ''flashed westward''— seem excessively idealized. His cozy winter park scene which he twice imagines, and his image of a jolly Christmas party seen from without (''People, perhaps, were standing in the snow. . . .''), are like Christmas cards from Freddy Malins' shop.

Joyce has also begun a wonderful overlapping of his two image patterns during this walk and ride through the Dublin streets to ''the Gresham.'' Rather than recognize the disparity between his inner imaginings about the snow and the reality of the snow when confronted by it, Gabriel plunges into his sensual romantic revery about his ''secret life'' with Gretta (''A heliotrope envelope,'' ''the warm palm of her glove,'' ''[h]er face, fragrant in the cold air''). The reader is made acutely aware of the way Gabriel escapes squalid reality through revery in this passage. Not only is the imagined snow very different from the real snow, but we also hear Gabriel consciously modifying the outer truth about the cold night and Gretta (''She had no longer any grace of attitude''; ''He longed to recall to her those moments, to make her forget the years of their dull existence together'') with images of fire borrowed from romantic poetry (''Moments of their secret life together burst like stars upon his memory,'' ''Like the tender fires of stars moments of their life together''; ''all their souls' tender fire''). Throughout this scene the text juxtaposes the reality of Gretta amidst slush with Gabriel's poetically imagined wife amidst fire.

Even more clearly than in ''Araby,'' this image disparity sets out the central problem in the story and in *Dubliners*. How can one have an imaginative inner life when one's imaginative ''vocabulary'' is limited? The boy's is limited by the church and by nineteenth-century notions of chivalric romance. Gabriel's imaginings about snow are the limited Christmas card reveries of an urban man. His prettily snow-covered trees and river are those of Dublin. The limit of his imagined escape is a walk in the park. It is also significant that in both of these reveries the ''West Briton,'' Gabriel, will think of the monument to the Irishman who had become an English hero, Wellington. Monuments of Anglo-Irish heroes are very much on Gabriel's mind this night. He will tell a comic story at the expense of his grandfather Patrick Morkan and his horse Johnny, who went ''round and round . . . King Billy's statue.'' The reader is surely to connect Gabriel's mimed ''pac[ing] in a circle round'' King Billy—a hero to Orangemen and villain to Catholics—with Gabriel's return in revery to Wellington's monument. In the same way, his reveries about his wife, while more poetically intense, are limited. When Gabriel sees Gretta descending the stairs, he sees that she is ''a symbol of something.'' Here Gabriel is the active, if unsuccessful, symbol searcher; he perceives his very flesh and blood wife as an aesthetic object. Although he asks what she is a symbol of, we know that he doesn't know the answer; he doesn't really know what spiritual quality is embodied in her attitude of ''grace and mystery.'' Specifically, he is blind to the love flooding her at that moment. All he can do when he glimpses Gretta on the stairs is see her as a sentimental romantic painter would and find an intriguing literal title for his picture (she is listening to distant music), which is unwittingly ironic. Once again Gabriel reduces experience to a conventional image that suggests to him comforting but unspecified symbolic meanings, as have his Christmas card images of Dublin. Finally, his perceptions are those of a husband ''happy that she was his, proud of her grace and wifely carriage.'' Even when his poetic ''fires of stars'' have ''kindl[ed] again . . . a keen pang of lust,'' he is too conventionally genteel to reach out to Gretta as the simple boy from the gasworks has. As he later realizes, his gentility has not been a yearning for some unattainable ideal; he has only been ''idealising his own clownish lusts.''

Gabriel's third, and final, revery about snow closes the story. As Gabriel leans and then lies on the bed beside Gretta, and before this final revery, we know that he has again been searching, consciously and then half-consciously, for a conventional means of embodying the deeply-felt experience of Gretta's revelation. Now the symbol he finds appropriate is that of sentimental death. He thinks of Aunt Julia dying, that is, of her euphemistically becoming a ''shade,'' the material for a comic after-dinner story like ''the shade of Patrick Morkan and his horse.'' He ''imagine[s]'' Michael Furey, ''the form of a young man standing under a dripping tree.'' Struggling for an appropriate yet comfortable image to enclose all of these ''shades,'' he has made a surprising euphemistic leap for a Catholic. Alive he has a soul: ''pity for her entered his soul''; ''his soul had approached. . . .'' Once he is dead he will be a ''shade'': ''One by one they were all becoming shades.'' Clearly, Gabriel's es-

chatology is an odd combination of Christian language (''soul'') and nineteenth-century euphemism (''shade''). Although Gabriel's brother is a ''senior curate,'' Gabriel's own image of death is tinged with non-Christian, nineteenth-century, heroic romanticism (''Better pass boldly into that other world, in the full glory of some passion . . .''). For him, the afterlife is Byronically vague: ''that region where dwell the vast hosts of the dead''; ''[h]is own identity was fading out into a grey impalpable world.'' Finally, there are the conventional sentimental tears, as much a part of Irish life as drink. Gabriel's are ''generous,'' but not so different from Little Chandler's ''tears of remorse'' at the end of ''A Little Cloud'' or Joe's comic tears at the end of ''Clay.''

As he is about to drift into sleep, comforted by his tears and his romantic eschatology (''the solid world itself which these dead had one time reared and lived in was dissolving and dwindling''), the two patterns of images merge for the final time. He is snapped into half wakefulness by a ''few light taps upon the pane [which] made him turn to the window.'' He watches the flakes fall against the lamplight. This snow has both the beautiful qualities of Gabriel's earlier reveries and the forbidding qualities of the real snow in the Dublin streets; ''the flakes'' are both ''silver and dark.'' But the snow in Gabriel's last revery is no more real than in his first two. This is not the streaky and patchy slush that has fallen on Ireland this night; it is an imagined heavy blanket, falling, annihilating and thickly drifting over everything. Although the snow is not real, Gabriel does sense the ambivalent nature of real snow, and this is appropriate to his imaginative sweep across Ireland. Thus the mood in the revery is partly that of the murky Dublin streets. The central plain is ''dark,'' the hills ''treeless,'' the waves ''dark mutinous,'' and finally we end in a ''lonely churchyard.''

Obviously, Gabriel's imagination has been forced beyond the bounds of urban Dublin. Now he flashes ''westward'' over all of Ireland, not simply over the ''Fifteen Acres'' of Phoenix Park. The park had imaginatively reassured him, with its pretty, snow-capped monument and its trees ''weighted with snow''; this last revery, however, gives him no easy escape from Gretta's revelation. Even the comic pedantry of remembered details from the party (''Yes, the newspapers were right, . . .'') cannot bring back Gabriel's reveries of comforting snow; the monument his imagination conjures up this time is not a gesture of Anglo-Irish urban patriotism. Instead, it is the simple grave of Michael Furey, whom he would rather forget. This monument to a West of Ireland hero who died for love is an accidental conglomeration of the iconography of a Christian hero ("crooked crosses," "spears," "barren thorns") rather than the planned iconography of English nationalism. At least imaginatively, Gabriel has left the safety of his urban, Anglo-Irish setting with its riverside quay, booksellers, and park, and he has taken the trip Miss Ivors challenged him to take: "The time had come for him to set out on his journey westward." The trip has become symbolic and nightmarish for Gabriel.

The snow drifts down, covering the Irish landscape, thickly drifting over the lonely graveyard. In this modern day *Night Thoughts,* the images of snow and death coalesce in the churchyard where Michael Furey lies buried. With these images in place, the narrator intervenes again, and begins to report Gabriel's sensations. Gabriel's drifting mind near sleep plays with the word pairs "falling faintly," "faintly falling," intensifying the oppressiveness of the snow in the repeated "falling" (repeated 7 times in 147 words) and reintroducing its delicacy in "faintly." He feels his soul swoon; he actually hears the inaudible snow falling "through the universe"; then in a simile ("like the descent . . .") he compares the snow with the fall of the last judgement. Although sentimental and melodramatic, Gabriel's final reported sensations give the reader a strong sense of ending, not of the ending of sleep but of death (to "go west" has been an English euphemism for death since the 16th century). Snow has thus undergone a symbolic change in Gabriel's mind, from a way of representing his desire for escape into an idealized urban landscape to a representation of the ultimate escape of death. Although by the end of the story he is at one with the dead, it is a oneness of limited terror because of his restricted imaginative "vocabulary."

All of Gabriel's reveries about Gretta and snow, even this final one, reveal that he is a conventional Dubliner. After Gretta's revelation he recognizes some of his emotional limits, just as he senses the ambivalent nature of snow. But even in his leap "westward," he cannot escape the limits of his confining "vocabulary." He is unaware of how completely his urban, Anglo-Irish culture has altered his religion, his perception of heroism and his private passion by restricting his imagination.

The strength of this story comes from the way these patterns of disparate images merge and rein-force each other in order to symbolically define and limit the reader's sympathy for Gabriel. Here is a sensitive and intelligent Irishman who is part of the conventionality, the petty squalor, the paralysis and death of Dublin. Both cliché-ridden and "hypereducated," he embodies the deadness of that culture, with its sentimentality, its third-rate opera singers and its musical evenings. Caught between European and Gaelic culture, like Miss Ivors, he can embrace neither, except timidly on summer holidays. We can have sympathy with such a displaced man who has so little sense of self but not with "that hemiplegia or paralysis which many consider a city" that created him.

Source: L. J. Morrissey, "Inner and Outer Perceptions in Joyce's 'The Dead'," in *Studies in Short Fiction,* Vol. 25, No. 1, Winter, 1988, pp. 21–29.

Rachel V. Billigheimer

In the following essay, Billigheimer discusses Joyce's use of contrasting images, such as cold and warmth; blindness and perception; and society and the individual experience.

In his short story "The Dead," James Joyce symbolically presents his critical view of Dublin society. The theme of the story is that of a spiritual paralysis which has seized a lifeless or "dead" society and of the vital effect in paradoxical contrast that the dead may have upon the living in urging them to a fuller self-awareness. In this juxtaposition of the symbolically living and the symbolically dead, the author works with the contrasting images of darkness and light, blindness and perception, cold and warmth, society at large and the individual experience, upper middle-class sterility and the fullness of a peasant's passion, and motion and stillness, all of which are united through the overall image of snow—the snow that falls upon the living and the dead.

The story opens when Gabriel enters a party given by his rich aunts in Dublin and comes in with his galoshes covered with snow. The guests participate in a musicale and in dancing. After some minor frustrations Gabriel longs to be outside with the refreshing snow. The guests gather round a plentifully laden dinner table. There is no meaningful communication or action until Gabriel delivers a speech honouring the noteworthy achievements of the deceased. The applause of the table guests is followed by laughter and singing. The guests leave, and their merry chatter in the hallway is silenced while the piano is heard accompanying the singing of Bartell D'Arcy. Gabriel sees his wife Gretta standing at the top of the stairs in the shadows listening to the music, and she appears to him like a picture which he would name *Distant Music.* As they drive westwards in their cab towards their hotel room, Gabriel becomes increasingly overwhelmed by his desire for Gretta. He discovers that since Bartell's singing, Gretta has been preoccupied. She reveals to Gabriel that Bartell's singing of "The Lass of Aughrim" recalled to her memory a former lover, Michael Furey, who used to sing that song. All her married years Gretta had held secret from Gabriel her love for Michael Furey, the tubercular lad who worked at the gasworks and died at seventeen burning with passion for her after he struggled through the rain to visit her. Gabriel stands motionless and silent in the dimly lit room as he comes to the realization of the dead boy's triumph over him in Gretta's love. He looks out of the window into the darkness, westwards onto the churchyard with the snow falling on Michael Furey's grave—the snow that falls upon the living and dead alike.

Although all the critics agree that the snow vision plays a significant role, they differ in their final interpretation. To some it is seen as the symbol of death. Others see the snow as symbolizing Gabriel's escape from his own ego to a vision of all humanity. To Kenneth Burke and Allen Tate the snow symbolizes rebirth through inner perception. In others again the snow has ambivalent connotations of life and death. While all these interpretations help to create a deeper insight into the story, we agree with Florence L. Walzl that a central theme in James Joyce is a preoccupation with the spiritually paralyzed—the spiritually dead—who will ultimately achieve spiritual rebirth.

This reversal of meaning in the main symbol of the story, snow, is typical of the dual or ambivalent aspects of the other major symbols in "The Dead," all of which relate to the living, the dead, the symbolically living, and the symbolically dead. The author begins with the symbolic setting of an upper middle-class party in the city of Dublin in the early 1900s. Amidst the frippery of the dancing, the display of fine clothes, elegant manners, affectation of speech, and an elaborately laden dinner table with food of the best quality, we have a lively spectacle of physical movement in contrast to the stultifying atmosphere. The constant bustle of action is frivolous and trifling. After the party Gabriel and Gretta drive eastward to their hotel room,

> "All her married years Gretta had held secret from Gabriel her love for Michael Furey, the tubercular lad who worked at the gasworks and died at seventeen burning with passion for her after he struggled through the rain to visit her."

where, at the end of the story, we have in contrast Gabriel now feeling himself completely isolated in the dimly lit bedroom, stricken with immobility in the swoon of his epiphany, and he is brought to ultimate self-awareness and the realization that the true life of the spirit is the life of self-sacrifice. This the story moves from a fast-moving but diffuse picture into one narrowed to a keen but silent-and-still concentration of focus. This intense moment of Gabriel's discovery is precipitated by Gretta saying to him, "I think he died for me." Gabriel recalls the reflection he had had of himself in the mirror—which symbolically reveals to him reality through illusion—and discovers himself as "a ludicrous figure, acting as a pennyboy for his aunts, a nervous, well-meaning sentimentalist, orating to vulgarians and idealising his own clownish lusts, the pitiable fatuous fellow he had caught a glimpse of in the mirror." The meaning of the mirror image progresses from illusion to reality and to inner vision. After achieving this vision of reality of himself, Gabriel then looks out of the window onto the outside world with the snow and thus beholds a cosmic vision of communion between the living and the dead.

Gabriel's physical journey, from the house situated in the west of the city eastwards to the hotel in the center of the city, associates him symbolically in terms of space and direction with the doom of the inhabitants of Dublin. Conversely, his spiritual movement westward in his moment of illumination symbolizes his transcendence of human inertia by recognizing and accepting the truth of himself. His spiritual journey westward is realized as he looks

> After achieving this vision of reality of himself, Gabriel then looks out of the window onto the outside world with the snow and thus beholds a cosmic vision of communion between the living and the dead."

westward out of the window onto the snowfall—the waters that have frozen to stillness.

Symbolic blindness in perception is another ambivalent facet of the symbolism of paralysis. The party guests are blind to their own condition. Although the older people have suffered, they lack insight and are insensitive. Eyes, eyesight, mirrors, and windows appear in ambivalent meaning, depending upon their context. At the party Gabriel's eyes are restless. On his first appearance he is introduced to the reader as a tall, stout, reddish-complexioned man: "On his hairless face there scintillated restlessly the polished lenses and the bright gilt rims of the glasses which screened his delicate and restless eyes." Again we see him: "Gabriel's eyes, irritated by the floor, which glittered with beeswax under the heavy chandelier, wandered to the wall above the piano." Later in the evening before he delivers his speech his eyes are nervously raised to the chandelier. His moving to look out of the windows into the darkness indicates his psychological uncertainty of himself. In turn, people outside, united by a common fate, are imagined as gazing into the little world inside.

Images of darkness associated with cold and of light associated with warmth are also met in juxtaposition and develop a paradoxical meaning at the end of the story. On entering the house, Gabriel finds his galoshes covered with snow, symbolizing his protection from the outside world. His destination is the party with its light, warmth, people, and luxurious entertainment. The party, in the physical environment of light and warmth, is conversely dark and cold in its spiritual sterility. In the dazzling light of the chandelier we observe the trifling ac-

tions of laughter, singing, and drinking of those who are dead. Gabriel, in his psychological isolation, looks out of the window and longs for the peace and solitude in the cold and dark outside. At the end of the party, after numerous biddings of "good-night," which suggest the transition into another life or perhaps the approach of death, the scenery outside, alternately light and dark, is pictured as ominous. The mist suggests the limited vision or "death" of the Dublin city dwellers.

This journey, symbolical of death, anticipates the scene in the hotel room in which the images are closely associated with death—the corridor, the darkness, the small room, Gabriel's demand that the candle be removed in favour of the "ghostly light" from the street lamp outside, which shines into the room through the window, and Gretta falling asleep on the bed after recalling with sobs the memory of her dead lover. In his final epiphany, Gabriel, whose eyes are now filled with tears, turns to the light coming through the window. He imagines the eyes of the dead lover at the moment when he tells Gretta that he does not want to live. In the partial darkness he achieves spiritual illumination.

The snow falling and melting is pictured as silvery flakes flickering under the lighted lamp in the dark. Snow in warm air turns to water, and water exposed to cold turns to ice. While water is the archetypal symbol of life, ice symbolizes death. Thus snow, ever subject to the influences of light and warmth, cold and dark, unites as a symbol of both the living and the dead.

Gabriel discovers that his marriage has been a life of paralysis. Through lust and shallow pleasures he had missed a marriage of close communion and self-sacrifice based on a deep love. On the way home he had anticipated the joy of being alone with his wife in the hotel room. In the pursuit of pleasure his children had been left overnight to be cared for by others. Gretta's life had also been moving towards death. Immersed in the memory of the past all these years, she had distanced herself from Gabriel. Each had moved away from the other towards a deadening of the spirit, the prevalent disease of Dublin middle-class society.

The continuous round of daily activities of a stultifying life of seeking pleasure and selfish gain is symbolized by Gabriel's pacing in a circle round the hall and jokingly mimicking Johnny, the horse continually circling round the statue of King William as if it were a mill. Ironically he misses the application to himself. Just as a person does not achieve anything in meaningless activity, the horse endlessly turning around the same circle is in effect static in its perpetual circling. Again, just as the horse galloping uses much energy aimlessly, the party guests going home all shout directions, cross-directions, and contradictory instructions to the cab driver. In the cab there is much laughter, confused discussion, and commotion. Gabriel is symbolized both by the horse galloping blindly in the mist and by the statue covered with the snow, which represents death in life.

The symbolism of the horse steadily and ceaselessly operating the treadmill would have applied to Joyce himself, whose own writing career was beset with difficulties of poverty, semiblindedness, and public misunderstanding. Thus, apart from the meaning of psychic paralysis attributed to the "dead," the image of the horse circling the treadmill may also signify inurement to life's difficulties without achieving progressive movement. However, in Gabriel's final vision the circle of life achieves a new stage, the stage of rebirth. In this transcendent stage all trivialities are seen as fitting into a scheme of cosmic events. Thus the conclusion of "The Dead" no longer takes place in a hotel room in the center of Dublin but in a general location in the universe. In achieving inner vision the fragments of experience are seen as parts of a comprehensive order.

As an example we may take Mr. D'Arcy's singing of the song "The Lass of Aughrim." While Gretta listens to the singing and Gabriel studies her standing "under the dusty fanlight and the flame of gas" which lights up the rich bronze of her hair," the flush of her cheeks, and the radiance of her eyes, he wonders, "[w]hat is a woman standing on the stairs in the shadow, listening to distant music, a symbol of. . . . *Distant Music* he would call the picture if he were a painter." Mr. D'Arcy's singing, which Gretta connects to the memory of her dead lover, is the initial instrument of Gabriel's epiphany. It is from the moment that Gabriel sees Gretta as a symbol of distant music that his whole situation assumes a reverse pattern. Gabriel is not aware of the significance of this moment, and ironically enough, he does not suspect how distant Gretta really is from him. He is preoccupied with her physical beauty, but there is no meaningful communion with her. At the moment of his most intense desire for her, she reveals to him that Bartell D'Arcy's singing recalled to her the secret memory of Mi-

chael Furey. Under the crushing impact of this revelation, Gabriel is led to his vision of reality, after which there is a complete reversal in the ambivalent aspects of the symbolism.

From the moment Gretta hears the song, she becomes an object of grace, beauty, and mystery to Gabriel, whose passion becomes more and more aroused as he watches her and joyfully anticipates the ecstatic fulfillment of his honeymoon night. When the precise moment arrives, Gretta discloses her preoccupation with Michael, who used to sing that song. Gabriel is filled with humiliation and shame, and this is necessary for his own self-discovery. Ironically Joyce shows the overwhelming power of the spirit, which is stronger than death, when Gretta says that Michael died for her. Now Gabriel's concern moves towards Gretta. It is thus through the spirit of the dead boy that Gabriel transcends his own situation and reaches towards a true communion with Gretta. He disciplines himself to relinquish his claims upon her as specifically his, and through this act of will he transcends the world of conditions. When he had approached her in his passionate desire, she had kissed him and called him a generous person. Now "generous tears" are in his eyes. These different levels of meaning show how he has transcended his condition into that of an impalpable world.

The music of the past pervades the atmosphere of the evening. The guests refer to past singers in conversation. Gabriel refers to his aunts as "The Three Graces of the Dublin musical world." In his speech Gabriel pays tribute to the singers of bygone days. Ironically it is after this that Mr. D'Arcy sings the old Irish song "The Lass of Aughrim" in the key turning point of the story. In Joyce, Brewster Ghiselin states, "music symbolizes the motion of the soul toward life or the call of life to the soul." As soon as he pictures his wife as a symbol of music, Gabriel recalls the joyful moments of their past. Music recalls the memories of the past and urges communion with the dead. The distant, remembered singing of Michael Furey, recalling a love of self-sacrifice, is a powerful summons to communion.

Through the device of music Gabriel has a deeper communion with Gretta. He transcends his own condition and achieves the cosmic vision of all humanity, the communion of the living with the dead. In his epiphany the image of Michael Furey becomes transformed into a Christ-like figure, "the form of a young man standing under a dripping tree.'' Michael Furey lay buried under the falling snow which drifted ''on the crooked crosses and headstones, on the spears of the little gate, on the barren thorns.''

The characters Michael and Gabriel may be seen on three levels of meaning. At first they are rivals for Gretta's love. At the climax of the snow vision they rise to mythic figures and archetypes. On a third level their significance may be related to their angelic names. Gabriel moves from a condition of psychic blindness to illumination after Gretta tells him that Michael visited her in the rain when he was ill, sacrificing his life to be with her. He then realizes that he has never lived with such intense depth of feeling and understands why Michael's love for Gretta has triumphed over his. Ironically it is Michael who is alive to Gretta and Gabriel who is dead.

Michael as a symbol of sacrificial love is seen both as a hero and as a god. Gabriel, the middle-class Dubliner, is incapable of such action. If we see Michael as representing the soil of Ireland, the country which Gabriel spurns, we may see the symbolic implication that it is the Dubliner that betrays Ireland.

In their representation of contrasting archangels, Michael as an angel surpasses Gabriel in the hierarchy, just as again in Gretta's mind Michael occupies a stronger position than Gabriel. In Jewish and Christian occult tradition, the archangel Michael symbolizes water. He is called ''the prince of snow'' and is associated with silver. Snow is the primordial substance of which the earth was created. Gabriel symbolizes the heavenly element fire. He is called ''the prince of fire'' and is associated with gold. All these symbolic aspects are suggested in the story.

In line with the New Testament, there is the polarity between Michael as the angel of the Last Judgment and of Gabriel as the angel of the Annunciation. This dimension is clearly pertinent to the snow vision, where Gabriel is brought to a judgment of himself by Michael. Michael can be seen as bringing Gabriel the realization that he is dead or conversely bringing him illumination at the point of spiritual death. Michael, the angel of water and snow, is associated with rain and cold. Gretta remembers him as her lover, who died for her from rain and cold as she recalls the picture of how he stood shivering under a tree. Finally, in Gabriel's epiphany, a vision appears of Michael as a Christ figure, having died under a tree dripping with snow.

Water and snow are ambivalent symbols of life and death. To Gretta, Michael is associated with rain, symbolizing life and love. This association shifts from an individual to a cosmic dimension when Michael appears in Gabriel's final vision. To Gabriel, Michael is associated with snow, which is associated with death.

In Gabriel's symbolic association with the angel of fire, his love for Gretta is described as ''the tender fires of stars'' representing ''moments of their life together'' which broke upon and ''illumined his memory.'' Thus his love also has an element of life-giving fire apart from the deadening fire of lust. In Dante's *Paradiso* the lustful are purged in fire while fire as light symbolizes God's love. Joyce's ''fires of stars'' are suggestive of Dante's vision of the planetary heavens as circles of light and the angelic choirs as circles of fire. These ambivalent aspects of life and death in fire are constituent parts of Gabriel's character.

In distinction to the austerity of Michael as the angel of the Last Judgment in the Old Testament, Gabriel is God's messenger sent to Daniel to interpret the Messianic prophecy. In the New Testament it is the archangel Gabriel who brings the Annunciation to the Virgin Mary. Similarly, the angel Gabriel appears in a vision to Zacharias, whose wife Elizabeth is advanced in years, bringing the prophecy of a new life in the birth of John the Baptist. If we view Gabriel's vision in the light of these biblical references, we may see it as a symbol of his rebirth. Perhaps, on the other hand, it formulates the sudden realization of his moribund state and his powerlessness as a human being to transcend it. These ambiguities create a wide perspective for Joyce's symbolic structure throughout the story.

The ambivalence of the facets of snow and fire, light and dark, warmth and cold, motion and stasis, and blindness and perception, which are reversed in their implications at the conclusion of the story, constantly permeates the paradoxical theme of death-in-life and life-in-death. Both the ambivalences and the ambiguities in meaning which culminate in the snow vision as death and rebirth illustrate the author's ironic perception of the frustrations of the living dead. The perpetual treadmill of the human condition can only be transcended by the sound of ''distant music,'' which is generated by a psychological crisis, represented as death and rebirth.

While Gabriel represents everyman, Michael, through his death of self-sacrifice, is a god-like hero. Only when Gabriel achieves his full maturation, ending in death and rebirth, can he in his spiritual illumination perceive the Angel of Judgment. He now sees that the snow which falls on "barren thorns" falls on an insensible humanity. Realizing his condition of death, Gabriel symbolically annunciates the new life through the salvation of Michael:

> His soul swooned slowly as he heard the snow falling faintly through the universe and faintly falling, like the descent of their last end, upon all the living and the dead.

Source: Rachel V. Billigheimer, "The Living in Joyce's 'The Dead'," in *CLA Journal,* Vol. XXXI, No. 4, June, 1988, pp. 472–83.

Sources

Burke, Kenneth. "Stages in 'The Dead'." In *Dubliners: Text and Criticism,* Robert Scholes and A. Walton Litz, editors, New York: Penguin, 1996, pp. 395-401.

Ellmann, Richard. "The Backgrounds of 'The Dead'." In *Dubliners: Text and Criticism,* Robert Scholes and A. Walton Litz, editors, New York: Penguin, 1996, pp. 373-88.

Gould, Gerald. A review of *Dubliners. New Statesman,* June 27, 1914, pp. 374-75.

Macy, John. *The Critical Game,* New York: Boni and Liveright, 1922, pp. 317-22.

Pound, Ezra. "*Dubliners* and Mr. Joyce." In *James Joyce: The Critical Tradition,* Robert H. Deming, editor, New York: Barnes and Noble, 1970, pp. 66-68.

Schwarz, Daniel R. "Gabriel Conroy's Psyche: Character as Concept in Joyce's 'The Dead'." In *The Dead,* Daniel R. Schwarz, editor, New York: St. Martin's Press, 1994, pp. 102-24.

Shurgot, Michael W. "Windows of Escape and the Death Wish in Man." *Eire-Ireland,* Vol. 17, No. 4, 1982, pp. 58-71.

Tate, Allen. "The Dead." In *Dubliners: Text and Criticism,* Robert Scholes and A. Walton Litz, editors, New York: Penguin, 1996, pp. 389-94.

Times Literary Supplement. A review of *Dubliners,* June 18, 1914, p. 298.

Further Reading

Anderson, Chester G. *James Joyce,* London: Thames and Hudson, 1967.
> An easy-to-read and comprehensive biography of Joyce, with many illustrations of Joyce, his family, friends, and Dublin.

Burgess, Anthony. *Here Comes Everybody: An Introduction to James Joyce for the Ordinary Reader,* London: Faber and Faber, 1965.
> A helpful introduction to Joyce designed for those who, as Burgess says, have been scared off by the professors.

Garret, Peter K., editor. *Twentieth Century Interpretations of "Dubliners,"* Englewood Cliffs: Prentice Hall, Inc. 1968.
> A good collection of informative, accessible essays useful for gaining a better understanding of Joyce and *Dubliners.*

Gifford, Don. *Joyce Annotated,* University of California Press, 1982.
> A comprehensive annotation of *Dubliners* and *Portrait of the Artist as a Young Man.* This is a useful reference for understanding the cultural context of both works. Gifford has an introduction giving a history of Ireland, and the book explains many obscure allusions.

Fever

1989

Throughout his career, John Edgar Wideman has emerged as a prominent voice of the African-American consciousness. Yet, he does not narrow his field only to African-American issues. His work, demonstrating an understanding of the greater themes that affect people of all races, speaks a universal language.

Wideman has also shown a drive for literary exploration, constantly searching for new ways to tell his stories. These characteristics combine in the title story of his 1989 short story collection, *Fever*. The author calls the challenging and complex "Fever" a "meditation on history." Through its examination of Philadelphia's 1793 yellow fever epidemic, it explores the racial ambiguities that exist in society. Wideman draws on real-life events and people to give his story a more credible and human feel. As his narrators explore the problems brought on by the fever, they present a concrete picture of the devastation the epidemic leaves behind, both in physical and emotional terms. Readers and critics alike admire "Fever" for its literary risks as well the significance of Wideman's message. Critics have consistently noted that it is one of his most ambitious pieces of short fiction.

Author Biography

John Edgar Wideman was born on June 14, 1941, in Washington, D.C., but he spent the first 10 years of

114

his life in Homewood, a poor African-American neighborhood in Pittsburgh. As a child, Wideman had two loves: basketball and storytelling. When he was 12, Wideman and his family moved to a predominantly white neighborhood, where Wideman attended a racially integrated high school.

Wideman was very successful throughout high school. He was a basketball star, senior class president, and valedictorian. During high school, Wideman pursued intellectual self-development, but he found the white-dominated world of academia to be incompatible with the African-American experience. Wideman tried to keep these two worlds separate to such an extent that he spent his free time with other African-American students but his class time with white students. Because of these actions, Wideman often felt isolated from his own community.

Wideman was awarded a basketball scholarship to the University of Pittsburgh, where he studied psychology and English. He continued in his attempts to divide his white world from his black world, essentially setting aside his racial identity. Wideman felt he needed to do so in order to excel academically.

In 1963, Wideman became only the second African-American Rhodes Scholar, and he studied at Oxford University in England for three years. Wideman next was made a Kent Fellow in the creative writing program at the University of Iowa, after which he joined the faculty at the University of Pennsylvania. Although he was a member of the English Department, he also helped create the Afro-American Studies program, which he chaired from 1972 to 1973. During his first year at the university, in 1967, Wideman published his first novel, *A Glance Away.*

In the 1960s, Wideman began to read African-American literature for the first time, beginning the process of redefining himself as an African-American man and writer. However, he still felt isolated from other African Americans. This problem was exacerbated when he and his family moved to Wyoming, where Wideman had accepted a university job. In the early 1970s, after returning to Homewood to attend his grandmother's funeral, Wideman began to integrate African-American traditions and cultures with the intellectual world that he inhabited.

Wideman has enjoyed a productive and successful literary career. He has published numerous novels and short stories as well as autobiographical meditations, primarily based on personal misfortunes that have affected his family. He is a two-time winner of the PEN/Faulkner Award for fiction, in 1984 and 1991. He is currently a professor of English at the University of Massachusetts—Amherst.

Plot Summary

The story opens in Philadelphia in 1793. The city, one of the centers of commerce and culture of the early United States, is gripped in the throes of a yellow fever epidemic. Those people with the means have fled the infected city, while the poor have been forced to remain behind, most likely to die. The city has essentially closed down.

The story's primary narrator is an African-American man called Allen. Although Allen has a wife and daughter, he has chosen to stay in the city, where he works for Dr. Rush, a practitioner determined to treat the fever's victims and understand the cause of the disease. Allen, once the founder of an African-American church, now spends his days caring for the sick and dying and burying the dead.

According to white Philadelphians, the disease has been brought to the city by slaves from Santo Domingo (present-day Haiti). This belief is based, not on any scientific evidence, but merely on racist ideas. Since the fever first began to spread, African Americans have been treated as pariahs; however, their services as caregivers and cemetery workers are still in great demand. In order to secure the services of African Americans for the sick, whites even falsely claim that African Americans are immune to the disease.

Prior to the outbreak of the epidemic, however, such ingrained racism was not always apparent. African-American slaves had fled to the North, seeking freedom in this Quaker haven where Christians claimed to uphold ideas of equality. While this standard had not been adhered to everywhere—at church, African Americans were forced to worship at the back of the pews—African Americans and whites had previously gathered together to commemorate the foundation of Allen's new church. A few Philadelphians do not fall prey to this racist rhetoric, however; some view the fever as a physical

John Edgar Wideman

manifestation of problems inherent in present-day society, particularly slavery.

While working for Dr. Rush, Allen has the chance to observe the doctor's autopsies. The autopsies of both black and white victims of the disease are the same—that is, there is no difference in the effects of the fever on the human body. Rush hopes to use the results of these autopsies to prove that in order to prevent the disease, the body's toxic fluids must be drained away.

Throughout the story, a series of disjointed voices intrude on Allen's meditations. These voices represent people of different backgrounds, including a Jewish merchant, an African aboard a slave ship, a contemporary African-American hospital orderly, and flu victims. They fault Allen for helping Dr. Rush when he should be serving his own people, talk of racism and human suffering, discuss how African Americans view freedom, and point to the universality—over both time and place—of prejudice. The narration also talks about another tragedy that took place in Philadelphia: a firebombing that took the lives of 11 people, including several children.

The story, which does not follow a chronological plot line, has no definite end. Neither Allen's

fate nor that of many of the other characters is made clear. The final image is that of an autopsy in which the doctors will find the miniature hand of a child next to the dead person's heart.

Characters

Master Abraham

Master Abraham is a Jewish shopkeeper from Europe. He came to America only to experience the same prejudice that drove him from Antwerp, where his son was killed in a racial attack. By the time he speaks in the story, he has become afflicted with the fever.

Allen

Much of the story is told by an African-American man named Allen, both from the first-person point of view and the second-person point of view. Many critics have suggested that Allen is based on Richard Allen, the founder of the African Methodist Episcopal Church. Allen serves as an assistant to Dr. Rush; he helps care for the victims of yellow fever, and in some cases, helps bury them. He also has a wife and a daughter from whom he is separated for fear that he will infect them. Allen spends much time thinking about the cause of the fever and ruminating on his life and the lives of other African Americans, both free and enslaved.

Before the fever epidemic, Allen had been a preacher and founder of a church for African Americans. How he has come to aide Dr. Rush is not made clear in the story, but Allen expresses his devotion to remaining in Philadelphia to help the dying. He does so out of concern for the sick, but also because the fever has, perversely, made him freer than ever because it has given him the opportunity to learn the skills of the white doctor. Allen is joined in his ministrations by his brother, Thomas.

Dr. Rush

Alternately called a charlatan and a lifesaver, Dr. Rush has remained in the city to care for the sick and to conduct research on what causes the fever. Dr. Rush has been attacked by other members of the medical profession for his practice of purging and bleeding patients. The autopsies he has performed on the bodies have led him to believe that fever victims die from drowning in their own toxic bodily fluids, and he publishes literature to this effect.

Voices

About halfway through "Fever," Allen says, "I recite the story many, many times to myself, let many voices speak to me. . . ." Wideman includes a number of different voices in "Fever," and these voices and their narratives expand the story's themes from the deaths in Philadelphia and the white people's placement of blame on African Americans to racism and prejudice in general. The characters who speak include an African aboard a slave ship; a modern-day African-American hospital orderly; and an unidentified person who refers to a firebombing that killed 11 Philadelphians in the 1980s.

Wilcox

Wilcox serves as an undertaker, carting the dead to their burial plots. After two months of such work, he is infected by a body and soon falls fatally ill with the fever himself.

Themes

Prejudice and Racism

One of the prevailing themes found in "Fever" is that of prejudice. The white Philadelphians place all blame for the yellow fever that grips the city on slaves who have been sent from Santo Domingo to Philadelphia. Although there is no factual or medical evidence linking the slaves to the spread of the fever, this belief continues to prevail. African Americans are shunned throughout the city except for when their services are required, such as for caring for the sick and burying the dead.

Through the different voices, prejudice against people other than African Americans is explored. A Jewish character, Abraham, reports how he was hated by even his employees. He also explores the universality of racism in his recollection of how European Jews were often accused of bringing fever and disease that killed entire cities.

Racism is inherent in the way African Americans are treated, both during this time of crisis and prior to it. Allen remembers how African Americans were forced to remain at the back of the church, so he founded a church solely for the worship of African Americans. At the same time, however, the story points to a time when African Americans and whites came together on an equal level, such as at the founding of Allen's new church. The tenuous connection between white and black Philadelphians is demonstrated by the ease with which it is severed.

Slavery

Slavery is an underlying theme that affects almost all of the story's major narratives. The description of a slave ship makes clear the horrible conditions under which Africans were brought to the Americas. The story also equates the plight of free African Americans in Philadelphia with their brothers and sisters still in chains. Thus, the issue of slavery is present in all aspects of African–American life in the 1700s, whether the African Americans are free or enslaved. Ironically, many African Americans were drawn to Philadelphia because it was a predominately Quaker city; followers of the Quaker faith emerged as some of America's earliest opponents of slavery.

Allen, though a free man, lives in a sort of self-imposed slavery. One of the voices accuses him of following Dr. Rush like a "loyal puppy" and then proceeds with a litany of racist slurs to emphasize how Allen is not truly acting freely but instead buckling under and becoming what the whites expect of him. The voice makes the slavery analogy more explicit by comparing Allen to a potential Moses for his people. Instead of leading the Hebrews out of slavery in Egypt, the voice challenges Allen to lead African Americans from the drudgery of their Philadelphia lives and their "lapdogging" to white people to a place where they would be appreciated for their own talents and skills.

Yet another voice—that of an afflicted person—emerges to speak of what slavery means. This voice maintains that sick people are more enslaved than anyone, white or black, for those with the disease have no choice but to follow its bidding. This voice urges Allen to break the bonds of his slavery to Dr. Rush and return to his family.

Finally, voices from more contemporary times emerge to give their reflections on slavery and freedom. A former slave recalls what it was like to be at the beck and call of a master. Another thoroughly modern voice speaks out, telling of his unpleasant job in a nursing home, but ending with the words, "But me, I'm free. It ain't that bad, really."

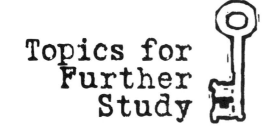

Topics for Further Study

- What insights can you draw about late 18th-century race relations from ''Fever''? Explain your answer.

- Investigate the 1793 yellow fever outbreak in Philadelphia. Try and find answers to such questions as how many people died; how people of different races were affected; how did the outbreak affect business and daily life; how and why did the outbreak end. After answering these and other questions, hypothesize how this epidemic affected the development of Philadelphia.

- In a 1996 interview, Wideman equated the 1793 yellow fever epidemic in Philadelphia with the present-day AIDS epidemic, which was not a serious medical factor at the time he wrote ''Fever.'' Do you find such a comparison apt? Why or why not? Conduct additional research as necessary to formulate your argument.

- Research the Black Plague, which devastated Europe in the 1300s, killing perhaps as much as 25 percent of the population. Draw comparisons between the Black Plague and the 1793 yellow fever epidemic of Philadelphia.

- Find an artistic representation of any plague period. Then compare the depiction of that plague with the one described by Allen in ''Fever.''

- How experimental a work of fiction do you find ''Fever''? How do the devices and narratives that Wideman employs affect your reading and your understanding of the story? Find other examples of experimental stories, and compare them to ''Fever.''

Illness and Death

In a story about a raging yellow fever epidemic, illness and death play a major part. The effects of yellow fever on the body are described in the autopsy reports, as are the maladies suffered by the afflicted people. However, the illness that holds Philadelphia in its grip is also reflected in the stillness of the streets and the stoppage of business. Philadelphia has become a place utterly transformed by the disease that decimates its inhabitants, and African Americans the scapegoat for the wrath and fear of the white inhabitants. Clearly, the yellow fever epidemic has affected not only its victims' physical bodies but also its victims' and soon-to-be victims' mental states.

The shadow of death pervades the story. Death manifests itself in the bodies piled high in the cemetery carts, in the cries of the orphans, in Allen's refusal to return to his wife and child, and in the almost-emptied city. However, death has the power to grab hold of everyone, as it captures Wilcox, who had been faithfully burying bodies for two months.

Style

Point of View

''Fever'' does not maintain any one consistent point of view. Much of the story is told from Allen's perspective, both from the first-person and third-person point of view; it is he who describes the dead bodies, the transformed city, and Dr. Rush's efforts and experiments. Allen is the character that readers most closely identify with. He appears to be knowledgeable and sincere in his desire to help fever victims and in his concern for chronicling life before and during the epidemic. Because he is a person of authority and respect in his community and because he shows such care for the victims of the disease, Allen's opinions and reflections are generally trusted.

However, many other voices, some of them not easily identifiable, emerge to give a more complete story and to broaden the story's field of inquiry. These other voices, which include persons who range throughout time, raise issues of slavery, prejudice, and racism. They allow the reader to see other perspectives on the way in which such evils can destroy a society and its people.

There is also the point of view of a detached narrator. This narrator gives historical background about the yellow fever epidemic, describes how it is blamed on African slaves, and explains the effects it has on its victims. Such inclusion helps ground the story more firmly in the reality of Philadelphia's 1793 yellow fever epidemic. The factual voice lends credibility to the story, making readers take its implications of racism inherent to American society more seriously.

Narrative

"Fever" utilizes a more complex narrative structure than many other short stories. It does not tell a complete story in the sense that the reader can read through and identify a clearly defined beginning, middle, and end. Instead, all the distinct sections of the story—some of which, however, do unfold chronologically and in a more ordered fashion—work together to make a composite picture of a specific time and place as well as to present more general themes about the human condition.

The story opens by firmly rooting the events about to unfold in their historical perspective by use of a quote and an address to a real person, Matthew Carey. From that point on, however, the story skips between Allen's narration, other voices, and factual presentation concerning yellow fever's origins and its effects on the human body. The end of the story returns the reader to contemporary times—when the story was written—with its discussion of a firebombing in Philadelphia.

Setting

The setting of the story is primarily late 18th-century Philadelphia. Wideman describes what the city was like before and during the epidemic period. He presents the complex society of Philadelphia in the interaction of its African-American and white inhabitants. Philadelphia's general racial progressivism is made clear through references to the Quakers; however, the delicate nature of such racial tolerance is also made clear in the abrupt change that the city undergoes as a result of the deadly fever.

However, the story has other settings as well. Voices of characters who live in Europe and in contemporary Philadelphia also emerge. This multitude of settings serves to demonstrate that some of the ills of 18th-century Philadelphia, such as racism, fear, and lack of communication, are prevalent facets of all societies, past and present.

Metaphor

The use of metaphor is an important aspect of "Fever." The fever becomes indicative of both suffering and injustice. Indeed, Wideman uses the yellow fever epidemic to demonstrate the insidious and destructive nature of racism. The same way that the fever has the power to destroy its victims, the racism of whites has the power to destroy goodwill and good relations between all people. The fever also represents the powerlessness that people hold over their own lives as it becomes the ultimate master of its victims, enslaving both whites and African Americans in its clutches.

Wideman makes use of other metaphors in the story. The attempts of doctors, or the holders of knowledge, to understand the cause of the disease becomes a metaphor for the attempts of humans to understand hate. Disease comes to represent not only a physical ailment but the manifestation of the sins of the unholy and unjust.

Historical Context

18th-Century Philadelphia

In 1682, colonial Pennsylvania's capital city Philadelphia was founded by Quakers, a Protestant sect that believed in the equality of men and women, religious tolerance, and nonviolence. Only a few years later Quakers in Pennsylvania lodged the first recorded colonial protests against slavery. Throughout the next several centuries, Philadelphia, and Pennsylvania, remained a capital of Quaker thought and ideology. Pennsylvania, a state that bordered the South, also was the destination of many fleeing slaves. However, the passage of the Fugitive Slave Act of 1793, which allowed slaveowners to capture runaway slaves without a warrant, led to the capture of many legally freed African Americans.

Despite such Quaker tolerance, true racial equality and lack of discrimination did not exist in Philadelphia. For instance, white Methodists favored the emancipation of the slaves, but they did not treat African Americans as equals.

Compare
&
Contrast

- **1790s:** African Americans in Pennsylvania number 10,274; the white population numbers 424,099.

  1990s: African Americans make up 1,157,000 of Pennsylvania's total population of 11,881,643.

- **1790s:** Slavery is practiced in many places around the world. The United States, Great Britain, the West Indies, South Africa, France, Denmark, Mexico, Holland, Puerto Rico, Cuba, Brazil, and Chile, as well as most parts of Central America and most Spanish colonies in South America make it legal to hold slaves.

  1990s: Most nations throughout the world have abolished slavery, although it is still practiced in some parts of Africa, Asia, and South America. The Anti-Slavery Society for the Protection of Human Rights in London estimates that forms of servitude affect more than 200 million poor people.

- **1790s:** Severe yellow fever epidemics occur in the West Indies, the United States, Spain, and parts of southern Europe, South America, and Central America.

  1990s: Populations in areas susceptible to yellow fever are generally vaccinated, but the sporadic appearance of the disease is reported in Africa and the Americas.

Richard Allen and the Yellow Fever Epidemic of 1793

In 1793, Philadelphia was hit by a yellow fever epidemic that decimated the city. The Black Plague, as it is known, took the lives of thousands of Philadelphians. While many people fled the city, others stayed behind to help care for the sick. The minister Richard Allen was one of these people. Although he had no medical training, Allen was a noted ''Bleeder,'' which is roughly the equivalent of a present-day surgeon. Along with his fellow African-American preacher Absalom Jones, Allen organized Philadelphia's African-American population to nurse the yellow fever victims. Dr. Benjamin Rush, a leading physician of the time and also a signer of the American Declaration of Independence, praised Allen for the service he gave to Philadelphia during this difficult time.

Allen was born into slavery, but through hard work he was able to buy his freedom from his owner. After heading North and becoming a Methodist preacher, Allen was appointed as assistant minister to a mixed congregation in Philadelphia. When church officials denied several African-American worshipers, including Allen, the right to pray at the front of the church and instead confined them to the rear, Allen decided to build an African-American owned church. In 1794, he and a group of 10 other African-American Methodists converted a blacksmith shop into the Bethel African Methodist Episcopal Church. In 1816, several other African-American congregations joined with Bethel to form the African Methodist Episcopal Church, and Allen was named its bishop.

Racial Issues in the 1980s

Throughout the 1980s, joblessness remained high among African Americans, especially unskilled workers in the inner cities. African Americans, who on the average had less education than whites, were, along with Hispanics, the last to be hired and the first to be fired. More than 30 percent of all African Americans, or nine million people, lived in poverty. Half of these families lived in a household headed by a woman.

African Americans, however, continued to rise to political power in the nation's cities. African–American leaders won or held the mayoral office in such prominent urban centers as Philadelphia, Chicago, New York, Los Angeles, Detroit, and Washington, D.C. On a federal level, the Reagan administration attacked and even reversed some civil rights legislation and policies. A 1988 *Newsweek* poll showed that 71 percent of the African-American respondents believed that the federal government was doing "too little" to help them. The Reverend Jesse Jackson, who ran for president in 1984 and 1988, became an important civil rights advocate.

Significant racial incidents also occurred in the 1980s. Riots took place in Miami, Florida after four white police officers were acquitted of beating an African-American man to death; young white men fatally shot an African American in Bensonhurst, New York; and neo-Nazis and members of the Ku Klux Klan attacked civil rights marchers who were celebrating the new Martin Luther King, Jr., holiday. Racial incidents on college campuses also rose, and many African-American students reported feeling greater hostility from whites.

The Bombing of MOVE
In May 1985 the Philadelphia police department bombed the residence of MOVE, a radical African-American group. The members had already resisted repeated orders to leave the premises, and the police force, knowing they were armed, decided that force was necessary to remove the group. The ensuing helicopter bombing of the MOVE house turned into a deadly fiasco. Police intended the bomb to open a hole in the house so officers could throw in tear gas canisters. Instead, the bomb caused a fire that killed 11 MOVE members, including 5 children. The fire soon raged out of control and burned down 53 houses located on the block, leaving an estimated 225 people without homes. This government intervention has since been called the bloodiest and the most aggressive action ever undertaken against an urban African-American community in the United States.

Critical Overview

Throughout his career, Wideman has been perceived as a serious, important interpreter of the African-American experience in America. He has examined issues ranging from the deterioration of African-American urban life, the meaning of being an African-American man, and the role that violence plays in American life. Many of these issues are raised in *Fever,* Wideman's second collection of short stories, which was published in 1989.

These stories all deal with suffering, death, the failure of communication, and the quest for redemp-

tion. Wideman, however, sees "Fever" as "the key story, the pivotal story." In an interview with Judith Rosen of *Publishers Weekly* in 1989 he explained: "I see the others as refractions of the material gathered there. All the stories are about a kind of illness or trouble in the air. People aren't talking to one another or are having a difficult time talking to one another. There's misunderstanding, not only on an individual level but on a cultural level."

Reviewers of *Fever* also single out the title story, noting its uniqueness, its range, and its message. Susan Fromberg Schaeffer, writing for *The New York Times,* calls "Fever" "almost majestic in its evocation of the goodness and evil of the human heart." She further notes the peculiar perspective used by Wideman in this collection, which she expresses as "not quite human but godlike, not limited by the conventions of ordinary storytelling." She finds that "Fever" makes use of this style of storytelling successfully, culminating in "an almost unbearably anguished meditation on human nature in plague time, the power and sadness of the story are enormous, its vision triumphant."

Wideman's career can be characterized by his search for new ways to explore themes and ideas and to express the African-American experience. "Fever" is a boldly experimental work, one that floats back and forth between time periods and narrators and thus defies easy labeling or analysis. Randall Kenan of *The Nation* forthrightly deals with Wideman's slipping back and forth in time; he presents his own reasoning: "It is as if Wideman is again playing games with us, forcing us to see the past and the present as one; how we are affected by what has gone before, not only in our thinking but in our acting and in our soul-deep believing." Despite the story's elusive nature and Wideman's claims to Rosen that the story "shouldn't be tied to any historical period," reviewers note his evocation of a specific period in American history. Other reviewers comment on the way Wideman collapses time to present a composite picture of a certain place and mindset. Cara Hood writing for the *Voice Literary Supplement* claims that present-day Philadelphia emerges as the protagonist of the story.

Reviewers do not overlook the significance of Wideman's message in examining his style. Herbert Mitgang in the *New York Times* finds that even after reading the story, he is left with the knowledge of Wideman's search for "some sort of universality" to the human condition. Some reviewers, however, do not care for the way in which Wideman attempts

A sketch of the New Market in Philadelphia, circa 1787.

to get his message to readers. For instance, Clarence Major of the *Washington Post* believes "Fever" to be the most ambitious if not the most artistically successful story of the collection. Mitgang recognizes the importance of what Wideman is saying when he writes that Wideman's "voice as a modern black writer with something to report comes through." Despite this praise, Mitgang does not believe that the rest of the stories are successful, asserting in his review of the collection that they add nothing to Wideman's reputation as a writer.

In Wideman's extensive and accomplished body of work, "Fever" occupies only a small spot. Yet, if it accomplishes nothing more, it demonstrates Wideman's careful exploration of relationships among people and the effects that these relationships have on society. Wideman's interest in the issues he raises in "Fever"—including racial relations, communication, personal freedom, and violence—is seen in the works that he has written later in his career. *Philadelphia Fire* picks up the final section of the story in its fictionalization of the 1985 MOVE bombing. *The Cattle Killing* explores the devastating effects of racial prejudice on the African Americans who remained behind in Philadelphia during the 1793 yellow fever epidemic in greater detail. The body of Wideman's work strength-

ens Robert Bones' assertion, made in 1978, that Wideman is "perhaps the most gifted black novelist of his generation."

Criticism

Rena Korb

Korb has a master's degree in English literature and creative writing and has written for a wide variety of educational publishers. In the following essay, she examines how Wideman presents themes of racism and equality in "Fever."

John Edgar Wideman's life could read as any of the dramatic, brooding novels and short stories that he has produced over the course of his long, successful career. Raised in a predominately African-American neighborhood in Pittsburgh, he nonetheless moved with fluidity in both the black and the white worlds. His talent at basketball led to a scholarship at the University of Pennsylvania in Philadelphia, where he proved himself a brilliant and diligent student. He won a Rhodes Scholarship in 1963, which brought him international attention because he was only the second African American to do so. Also that year, he was the subject of a maga-

What Do I Read Next?

- *Narrative* (1794) by Absalom Jones and Richard Allen is a personal memoir of Philadelphia's 1793 yellow fever epidemic.

- *Forging Freedom* (1988) by Gary B. Nash explores the formation and development of Philadelphia's African-American community from the 18th century and until the mid 19th century.

- *Bring Out Your Dead* (1949) by J. H. Powell chronicles the yellow fever epidemic that hit Philadelphia in 1793.

- *Burning Down the House* (1987) by John Anderson and Hilary Hevenor explores the establishment and development of MOVE and chronicles events surrounding the 1985 bombing.

- John Edgar Wideman's *Philadelphia Fire* (1990) presents a fictionalized account of the only survivor of the 1985 bombing of the MOVE house in Philadelphia.

- Jean Toomer's *Cane* (1923), a collection of short stories and poetry, explores life for southern and northern African Americans after slavery.

- Albert French's novel *Billy* (1993) explores how racial hatred in the South leads to a horrible crime perpetrated against a young boy.

- Also by Wideman, *The Cattle Killing* (1996) traces the path of an African-American preacher and other African Americans who nurse the victims of Philadelphia's 1793 yellow fever epidemic.

---

zine article in *Look* entitled "The Astonishing John Wideman."

Wideman saw his career as a writer take off in 1967, when he was only 26, with the publication of his first novel *A Glance Away.* While his writing brought him acclaim and contributed to a secondary career as a professor, his personal life was beset with difficulties. In 1976, his brother was convicted of murder and sentenced to life in prison after a man was killed by his accomplice in a burglary attempt. Then, in 1986, Wideman's teenage son stabbed and killed a classmate during a summer-camp trip; he was sentenced to life imprisonment. After this event, articles that appeared in *Vanity Fair* and *Esquire* characterized Wideman as filled with controlled racial anger.

Wideman, whose work often focuses on the unique experiences of African-American men, the deterioration of African-American urban life, and violence and criminal behavior in America, has used his writing to work through these devastating experiences. His memoir about his brother, *Brothers and Keepers,* was nominated for the National Book Award. *Philadelphia Fire* interweaves personal feelings about what happened to his son with a plot centering around the 1985 police bombing of the Philadelphia headquarters of the radical African-American group, MOVE.

These works do not follow a traditional storytelling style, using a much freer method for exploring issues raised by questions about suffering, race, and redemption. For instance, part II of *Philadelphia Fire* draws on literary, historical, and sociological commentary to broaden the scope of Wideman's narrative. The stories in *Fever,* Wideman's second collection published in 1989, also stretch the limits of the mainstream short story; his narrations play with historical time, style, voice, and sequence. Perhaps none of these stories do so to the extent of "Fever," which is in Wideman's opinion, the key story of the collection.

"Fever" centers around a deadly yellow fever epidemic that struck Philadelphia in 1793 and the effects it had on the city's African-American population, who were largely blamed for bringing the disease. The main figure in the story is a man named

> Wideman has truly produced a work that, while opening a door onto new ways of looking at issues, also shuts it in its complexity."

Allen, who Wideman leads the reader to believe is based on (or indeed is) the historical figure Richard Allen. The real-life Allen, like the fictional Allen, risked his own life to remain in Philadelphia to nurse the sick and dying. However, the story is truly much more than just the story of an epidemic and one man's role in it. It brings up significant issues of racism and prejudice and how these problems can destroy a community. In utilizing different voices and moving through time, Wideman makes clear that these problems are not tied merely to 18th-century America, but have existed throughout the world and throughout time and continue to the present day.

In discussing *Brothers and Keepers* Wideman had already presented his belief that telling stories in chronological order was pointless and even detracted from a truer meaning: "You never know exactly when something begins," he wrote. "The more you delve and backtrack and think, the clearer it becomes that nothing has a discrete, independent history; people and events take shape not in orderly, chronological sequence but in relation to other forces and events, tangled skeins of necessity and interdependence and chance that after all could have produced only one result: what is." In "Fever," some of the most startling innovations in the story are Wideman's use of a nonlinear time and multiple narrators, although these voices are often difficult to identify and distinguish. While such characteristics might make a cursory read of "Fever" confusing, these stylistic devices serve Wideman's greater purpose and message: that of the prevailing nature of racism and hatred among people.

The culminating force of the various voices point out the disharmony to which racism leads. While most white Philadelphians believe that African slaves from Santo Domingo have brought the affliction to their city, no scientific evidence exists to this effect. However, such racist thought is not to be dispelled, and African Americans in Philadelphia are shunned and treated as "evil incarnate." Allen notes, "A dark skin was seen not only as a badge of shame for its wearer, . . . It mattered not that some of us were born here and spoke no language but the English language, second-, even third-generation African Americans who knew no other country." Allen then compares African Americans to European immigrants who do not even speak English, making clear that prejudice against Philadelphia's African Americans is based merely on the color of their skin. The European immigrants exhibit more typically foreign traits, such as "clod-hopper shoes, strange costumes, . . . Lowlander gibberish that sounded like men coughing or dogs barking"; yet, these white people are not blamed for any disease. Perhaps even more indicative of the malignant nature of white Philadelphia's racism is the false charge that African Americans are immune to the disease, a story manufactured solely for the purpose of sending them out to the sick community as caregivers. In reality, the fever struck a severe blow to the city's African-American population. As Allen attests, "Among the city's poor and destitute the fever's ravages were most deadly and we are always the poorest of the poor."

Although Allen recognizes these falsehoods, expressing his anger against whites for their unfounded accusations—"My fellow countrymen searching everywhere but in their own hearts," he says, "the foulness upon which this city is erected"—he still remains within the disease-stricken community to help the sick, both white and African American. For this action, some of the story's other narrators chastise him: "Can you imagine yourself, Allen, as other than you are?" the voice of an afflicted person charges. Without his ties to Dr. Rush and the dying community, Allen would truly hold "the weight of your life in your hands," rather than the weight of others' lives. For Allen, this would be the harder task. "Tell me what sacred destiny, what nigger errand keeps you standing here at my filthy pallet?" asks the voice, implying that Allen, a free African American, is fulfilling the most common role of his race in America—that of a slave. Although a voice urges Allen to "dare be a Moses to your people and lead them out of this land," Allen resists the call and instead lingers in Philadelphia under the orders of Dr. Rush, a white man.

The story also makes clear, however, that captivity can exist in many forms. Allen identifies that former African-American slaves who had struggled to reach freedom in the North fell prey to a new form of slavery, the "chains of dissolute living." A fever victim speaks to Allen, claiming that he is "more slave than you've ever been," for he does the fever's "bidding absolutely." Even the city itself is held captive by "long fingers of river," and the city in turns holds many of its residents captive. One of the final voices of the story also affirms the precious gift of freedom. This voice belongs to an African-American hospital orderly who, although he complains about his job and the elderly people he cares for, ends his monologue with the words: "But me, I'm free. It ain't that bad, really."

The emphasis Wideman places on the various forms of slavery strengthens his thesis that the fever has not been brought by the Santo Domingan slaves but has been wrought by the evilness that lurks in human's hearts. "We have bred the affliction within our breasts. . . . Fever descends when the waters that connect us are clogged with filth. . . . Nothing is an accident. Fever grows in the secret places of our hearts, planted there when one of us decided to sell one of us to another." If fever is caused by slavery, slavery, he says, is caused by a failure to see beyond the color of a person's skin.

Yet, the fever also demonstrates that humans are all the same in their response to the disease. Autopsy reports confirm that the insides of the bodies of fever victims, both whites and African Americans, look alike. "When you open the dead," a narrator intones, "black or white, you find: . . ." The narrator then goes on to list the states of the various organs. The outer skin of the victims does, however, undergo a transformation. The skin of white people turn black, and one victim even acknowledges to Allen that "When I die, they say my skin will turn as black as yours." The fever is truly an equalizing force, for it makes everyone bow to its will.

Another device employed by Wideman to show the inherent, though often denied equality of humans is that of twinning. Literal and figurative twins abound in "Fever." People are paired: Dr. Rush and Deveze, Allen and his brother Thomas; the members of these two pairs perform the same function and are interchangeable. For each person, someone exists who is on the same level. The fever itself is seen as the twin to "Barbados's distemper" and is linked to epidemics in Europe. Allen also finds twin brown babies in a cellar where two Santo Domingan refugees have died. The twinning metaphor can be further drawn. For instance, Master

Abraham and Allen have very real similarities; both have left their wife and children behind to lose them forever. Further, Master Abraham's references to Palatine fever in Europe's cities, which many people claimed was brought by Jews, show that minority populations become the butt of racist fear at the hands of the majority. Such similarities further emphasize Wideman's thesis of racism as a universal feeling, one that has the ultimate power of destroying those who are its victims as well as those who perpetuate it.

In many ways, however, "Fever" resists comprehensive analysis. There are simply too many unexplained and unidentified persons, events, and references. Wideman has truly produced a work that, while opening a door onto new ways of looking at issues, also shuts it in its complexity. But with a writer of Wideman's stature and talent, clearly this confusion is intentional. Wideman may be seen as deliberately conflating characters and events in order to show that the themes of the story are so prevalent and so universal. His characters, as well as his narrative, defy labeling, even though the story actually challenges readers to do so. For instance, at times it is not even clear whether a speaker is African American or white, even though the story is so closely tied to racial issues. Wideman makes a reader ponder serious issues but allows for no real answers to any questions raised. In so doing, he opens a world of possibility for interpretation, which in turn, allows for greater personal understanding of the story.

Source: Rena Korb, Overview of "Fever," for *Short Stories for Students*, The Gale Group, 1999 .

Elisabeth Piedmont-Marton

In the following essay, Piedmont-Marton explores Wideman's use of the fever as a metaphor for racism.

Wideman calls "Fever" a meditation on history. Using the powerful and disturbing metaphor of plague or fever for racism and hatred, Wideman moves through history and brings together voices from the 18th to the late 20th centuries. He meditates on history, or past events, but also on history as the means by which human beings record and pass on knowledge. His commentary is as much about the process of history as it is about the events.

In the story's powerful opening paragraph, readers are introduced to the first of several unnamed characters. This paragraph is not located in

> Wideman's chilling conclusion to 'Fever' proves the narrator's claim in the beginning of the story that the fever's 'disappearance is as certain as the fact it will come again.'"

any particular historical moment, and its ominous imagery of dead trees and impending darkness is timeless. The narrative then veers sharply from the universal to the specific as Wideman piles on the details of a terrible fever epidemic in Philadelphia. He also distinguishes yellow fever from dengue and explains the symptoms of each as if preparing readers to enter the infected area or reminding them to check themselves for rashes or aching joints. Wideman imagines the epidemic's beginning in the hold of a slave ship and characterizes the mosquito that transmits the disease as a succubus, or evil female spirit. "In the darkness he can't see her, barely feels her light touch on his fevered skin. Sweat thick as oil but she doesn't mind, straddles him, settles down to do her work. She enters him and draws his blood up into her belly."

Back in Philadelphia the narrator seems to know about the origins and course of the disease, as if he has been present at its beginnings and during other epidemics. He says: "No one has asked my opinion. No one will. Yet I have seen this fever before, and though I can prescribe no cure, I could tell stories of other visitations, how it came and stayed and left us, the progress of disaster, its several stages, its horrors and mitigations." It's tempting to blame the newest outsider, the narrator says, the former slave refugees from the uprising in Santo Domingo, but "to explain the fever we need no boatloads of refugees, ragged and wracked with killing fevers, bringing death to our shores." He knows that "fever descends when the waters that connect us are clogged with filth," but he also advances a more metaphysical and moral cause, originating from the mosquito on the slave ship: "Fever grows in the secret places of our hearts, planted there when one of us decided to sell one of

us to another." Fever will come again and again so long as hatred and racism continue to exist.

The narrator's work with the dead and dying, then, can be seen as an attempt to treat both the symptoms and the real cause of the disease, to ease suffering and to combat racial hatred, but even his service to the sick must be understood in the context of racism itself. Even the devastation of the epidemic isn't enough to level the barriers between white and black. The narrator spends his days helping the prominent white Dr. Rush, but still tries to devote some energy to the poorest and most desperate of the city's black population in the caves and tunnels they live in on Water street, where they are especially vulnerable to the fever. As genuine as the narrator is in his attempts to heal the sick and comfort the dying, he knows he is being used: "The fiction of our immunity had been exposed as the vicious lie it was, a not so subtle device for wresting us from our homes, our loved ones, the afflicted among us, and sending us to aid strangers." When fever gripped the racially divided city, the narrator explains, "We were proclaimed carriers of the fever and treated as pariahs, but when it became expedient to command our services to nurse the sick and bury the dead, the previous allegations were no longer mentioned. Urged on by desperate counselors, the mayor granted us a blessed immunity. We were ordered to save the city." If the narrator is correct that the disease has a moral as well as a biological cause, if we have "bred the affliction within our breasts," then the mayor's despicable plan will only ensure fever's cyclical and inevitable return.

If the black population's immunity to the physical symptoms of the fever is a lie, then the narrator is also susceptible to the more insidious moral infection of the epidemic. When he enters the home of a rich white family to find everyone dead except one "loyal black maid, sick herself, who'd elected to stay when all others had deserted her masters," he wants to ask "why she did not fly out the door now, finally free of her burden, her lifelong enslavement to the whims of white people." Instead, he asks himself why he doesn't fly, why he "was following in the train on Rush and his assistants, a functionary, a lackey, insulted daily by those I risked my life to heal." That the narrator even has to consider the question demonstrates the horrible power of racism because it demands that he choose between freedom and life and asks him to give up his loved ones for the possibility of greater autonomy and material gain. The narrator explains: "Fever made me freer than I've ever been. Municipal government had collapsed. Anarchy ruled. As long as fever did not strike me I could come and go anywhere I pleased. Fortunes could be amassed in the streets.'' Finally, with words as clearly evident of fever's possession as the yellowed eyes of the dying, he says, ''I could sell myself to the highest bidder.''

As the grim prophecy of the disease's course predicts, the selling of human flesh—even yourself—demands a heavy price. The narrator's wife and children succumb to the fever and he never sees them again. Also, the narrator has not achieved the freedom and wealth that he was willing to trade all else for. In the story's final pages he is challenged, and called by name, by a elderly Jewish patient: ''Can you imagine yourself, Allen, as other than you are? A free man with no charlatan Rush to blame. The weight of your life in your hands.'' The narrator is trapped, enslaved, ''by an endless round of duty and obligation.'' The old man finally charges him: ''Your life, man. Tell me what sacred destiny, what nigger errand keeps you standing here at my filthy pallet? Fly, fly, fly away home.'' But the story of fever and its devastating consequences is a story that has ''no beginning or end, only the waters' flow, ebb, flood, trickle, tides emptying and returning.''

Wideman's chilling conclusion to ''Fever'' proves the narrator's claim in the beginning of the story that the fever's ''disappearance is as certain as the fact it will come again.'' As the story lurches forward into the late twentieth century, the familiar narrator's voice is interrupted by the distinctly modern voice of a hospital or nursing home attendant complaining about his job and about how badly the white people smell. Clearly the fever still grips Philadelphia. If readers doubted that, Wideman adds one more piece of evidence, ''almost an afterthought.'' The narrator describes the city recovering, returning ''to products, pleasures, and appetites denied during the quarantine months.'' But this is not aftermath of the fever epidemic that we've been reading about in some remote past. This is now, and the Mayor is referring to his decision to bomb a block of houses where poor blacks lived in an attempt to eradicate crime. ''A new century would soon be dawning. We must forget the horrors. The Mayor proclaims a new day. Says lets put the past behind us. Of the eleven who died in the fire he said extreme measures were necessary as we cleansed ourselves of disruptive influences.'' But like fever, history refuses to stay in the past. Hatred and racism will never be eradicated because they, like fever, thrive in darkness and filth, and because we guaran-

tee future outbreaks by not recognizing that we breed ''the affliction within our breasts,'' that ''fever descends when the waters that connect us are clogged with filth.''

Source: Elisabeth Piedmont-Marton, Overview of ''Fever,'' for *Short Stories for Students,* The Gale Group, 1999.

Barbara Kitt Seidman

In the following essay, Seidman provides a brief summary and analysis of ''Fever.''

''Fever,'' the title story in Wideman's 1989 collection of short fiction, provides an illuminating metaphor for the various episodes of racial antagonism depicted in the volume. As one of the story's narrative voices explains, ''Fever grows in the secret places of our hearts, planted there when one of us decided to sell one of us to another. The drum must pound ten thousand thousand years to drive that evil away.''

The narrative focus of the tale reflects Wideman's desire to correct the inaccurate historical record about the role of African Americans during the 1793 yellow fever epidemic that devastated Philadelphia; he dedicates the story to the author of one such fraudulent account and relies instead upon the eyewitness record left by black commentators. Among the chorus of voices in the text are those of two black men, one of them the historical Richard Allen and the other his fictionalized brother Thomas, whose differing perspectives on the disaster and its resultant hypocrisies work in counterpoint. Allen, a former slave, minister, and the founder of the African Methodist Episcopal Church, is a deeply spiritual man who identifies his vision of the mass emancipation of slaves with the promise of Christianity. Allen has been ordered to serve a Dr. Rush in his ministrations to and autopsies of plague victims. After performing exhausting labor among the whites, he turns to the destitute habitations of poor blacks whom the disease ravages with equal savagery and devotes himself to their spiritual and physical health despite their contempt.

Like many other elements of the narrative, Thomas' story further documents the presence of blacks in the public sphere of American history: Thomas fought with the rebels in the American Revolution and, as a prisoner of the British, recognized the degree to which he had been denied participation in the society whose ideals he championed. His embittered outlook on the situation now facing blacks in the plague-ridden city

> Rather than boasting a vigorous democratic climate, Wideman's Philadelphia festers in a stagnant environment whose waters breed contagion both literally and metaphorically."

stems from the opportunistic shifts of white opinion regarding blacks during the epidemic; while slaves were initially blamed for importing the disease following a bloody revolt in the Caribbean, blacks were later declared immune from its ravages and coerced to serve sick and dying whites. Each of these civic fictions exposes the denial of humanity underlying racism and responsible for the cultural pathology which is Wideman's principal target.

Philadelphia operates as symbolic setting for this story on religious as well as political grounds: Its Quaker egalitarianism does not preclude Allen's being refused a place at the communion table with white Christians, nor does the city's birthing of the young republic ensure that its African-American citizens will be accorded the same possibilities for prosperity available to the unending waves of European-born newcomers. Rather than boasting a vigorous democratic climate, Wideman's Philadelphia festers in a stagnant environment whose waters breed contagion both literally and metaphorically. Nor is water the only sinister natural element pervading the landscape; apocalyptic fire fills the streets of the city as a grim purgative for its soul-sickness.

The story evolves through a polyphonic orchestration of voices combining the points of view of slave and freedman, black and white, Christian and Jew, historian and eyewitness.

Wideman's characteristically fractured narrative jarringly shifts perspective to suggest that no one interpretation or "story" exists independent of the wider human drama playing itself out across time. Within his textual montage, Wideman melds such disparate elements as a newly enslaved African making the middle passage; a series of scientific

descriptions of the fever and its assumed insect carriers; and a report of autopsy results documenting the common physical devastation visited upon Black and white plague victims alike.

Added to the individualized voices of Richard and Thomas Allen is the combative monologue of a dying Jewish merchant who describes his own experiences with bigotry and aggressively challenges Allen's continued attentions to the white populace. This character, Abraham, alludes to the Lamed-Vov, or "Thirty Just Men" of Judaic tradition, designated by God "to suffer the reality humankind cannot bear" and bear witness to the bottomless misery and depravity of existence. Richard Allen is one such figure among many in these stories whose compassion in the face of unbearable injustice and grief offers the only hope for salvation that Wideman can envision.

To underline the timeliness of this meditation on so seemingly remote a historical episode, Wideman introduces toward the end of the story the voice of a contemporary black health-care worker contemptuous of his elderly white charges and the society that has discarded them. Finally, within a single paragraph, Wideman links the disease wasting Philadelphia's citizens in the late eighteenth century to the factual 1985 bombing of a black neighborhood ordered by the city's first black mayor, Wilson Goode, to eradicate the black radical group MOVE. Wideman claims that in "Fever" he "was teaching myself different ways of telling history"; with the publication of *Philadelphia Fire* in 1990, a novel that extends his analysis of the MOVE bombing, he returned to this later historical incident as evidence of the paradoxes of the United States' continuing racial self-destructiveness.

Source: Barbara Kitt Seidman, "Fever," in *Magill's Survey of American Literature,* edited by Frank N. Magill, Salem Press, 1991, pp. 2109–11.

Randall Kenan

In the following excerpt, Kenan discusses the manner in which Wideman manipulates time in "Fever."

Like present-day cosmologists, Wideman seems to have in mind not merely a blurring of the two concepts [Time and Space] but their elimination. He metajokes about our Western cultural bias toward "clock time, calendar time," to time "acting on us rather than through us" and "that tames space by manmade structures and with the *I* as center defines other people and other things by nature of their relationship to *I* rather than by the independent integrity of the order they may represent." Wideman's true mission appears to be to replace the *I* at the center of all his stories, to make it subject to an internal order of things rather than to external structures and limitations. Unlike Ishmael Reed, his humor does not slice to the bone to the truth; Wideman's humor is sparse if not (at times) nonexistent. And unlike Amiri Baraka, his rage is far from militant; it is sublimated, almost repressed.

Nowhere in this collection [*Fever*] is this more evident than in the title story. More a meditation than an eyewitness account, "Fever" centers around Philadelphia's yellow fever epidemic of the late eighteenth century. Snatching up bits and pieces of history here and there, he brilliantly creates an organism, like a New Age psychic channeler, that transports the sufferers from the 1700s to the present, and takes us back in time as well. Its scenes bring to mind images from Herzog's *Nosferatu* of a plague-ridden town debilitated, full of coffins, corpses, rats and decay: "A large woman, bloated into an even more cumbersome package by gases and liquids seething inside her body, had slipped from his grasp. . . . Catching against a rail, her body had slammed down and burst, spraying Wilcox like a fountain." Yet without warning the story shifts to the present, to the aftermath of the 1985 MOVE massacre, to the voice of a black hospital orderly. It is as if Wideman is again playing games with us, forcing us to see the past and the present as one; how we are affected by what has gone before, not only in our thinking but in our acting and in our soul-deep believing. Science (knowledge) becomes a metaphor for understanding hate; disease, a euphemism for the plague visited upon the wrongs of the unholy.

And the voices. Wideman leads us to believe the main character of "Fever" to be none other than Richard Allen, who founded the African Methodist Episcopal Church. His voice, initially eighteenth-century and pious, merges with a chorus of victims, singing of guilt, of racism, of ignorance. Ultimately the voices question Allen—a freedman—for staying in Philadelphia, abandoning his wife and children, risking his life by working with the virus-infected, practically enslaving himself to strange, clueless physicians. And Allen can articulate no reason for staying to combat the "unpleasantness from Egypt."

" . . . Unlike Amiri Baraka, his rage is far from militant; it is sublimated, almost repressed."

Source: Randall Kenan, "A Most Righteous Prayer," in *The Nation,* Vol. 250, No. 1, January 1, 1990 , pp. 25–7.

Sources

Mitgang, Herbert. A review of *Fever. The New York Times,* December 5, 1989, p. C21.

Rosen, Judith. An interview with John Edgar Wideman. *Publishers Weekly,* November 17, 1986, pp. 37-38.

Samuels, Wilfred D. Entry on John Edgar Wideman in *Dictionary of Literary Biography,* Vol. 33, Gale Research, Detroit, MI, 1984.

Schaeffer, Susan Fromberg. A review of *Fever. The New York Times Book Review,* December 10, 1989, pp. 1, 30-31.

Further Reading

Coleman, James W., *Blackness and Modernism,* University Press of Mississippi, 1989.
    Discusses Wideman's career in terms of his reorientation within the African-American community and cultural setting.

Mbalia, Dorothea Drummond. *John Edgar Wideman,* Susquehanna University Press, 1995.
    Analyzes the early works of Wideman's career as Eurocentric and the later works as indicative of his effort to reclaim the African personality.

TuSmith, Bonnie, editor. *Conversations with John Edgar Wideman,* University Press of Mississippi, 1998.
    A collection of interviews with Wideman.

A Guide to Berlin

Vladimir Nabokov

1925

Published in a Russian emigre newspaper in Berlin on Christmas Eve, 1925, "A Guide to Berlin" is among Vladimir Nabokov's earliest literary works and an unusual demonstration of his mastery of the storyteller's craft. Modeled loosely on a tourist's guide book to a foreign city, the story shows an unnamed narrator briefly observing and commenting on everyday aspects of Berlin life. Unburied utility pipes, an antiquated streetcar and its nimble conductor, glimpses of Berliners at work, a tour of the city's zoo, and an illuminating moment in a pub become a rumination on the power of memory and art to preserve and transform everyday life.

Although in 1930 Nabokov claimed that "A Guide to Berlin" was the best story in his collection *The Return of Chorb* (1929), it was not until he had established his reputation with such novels as *Lolita* (1955) and *Pale Fire* (1962)—and had translated, with his son, "A Guide to Berlin" into English (1976)—that the story began to receive critical attention. Since then critics have consistently found it among the best of Nabokov's early literary attempts and have praised, among other aspects, its "prose poem" style; its unusual and intricate structure; and its sophisticated integration of language and theme. Critics have also praised in particular Nabokov's handling of the theme of time, of the self's relationship to others, and of the literary artist's obligation to memorialize for future readers the details of ordinary life through acts of "proactive nostalgia." Some critics have argued that "A Guide to Berlin" resembles Russian novelist Ivan Turgenev's "careless sketch" style in his *A Sportsman's Sketches*, and others have pointed to the general influence of major Russian writers like Nikolai Gogol, Leo Tolstoy, Aleksander Pushkin, and Fedor Dostoevsky on Nabokov's early development. After Nabokov's statement in the mid-1970s that "A Guide to Berlin" was "one of my trickiest pieces," critics have paid closer attention to the story, and its reputation as perhaps the best of Nabokov's early Russian-language tales has grown.

Author Biography

Born to an aristocratic Russian family in St. Petersburg in 1899, Nabokov was raised in an environment of worldly achievement and educated liberal thought. In 1919, following Russia's Bolshevik Revolution, Nabokov's father, a leading democrat, was forced to flee to England, and, after enrolling Vladimir in Cambridge University in 1920, he joined the Russian emigre community in Berlin. In March, 1922, Nabokov's father was killed during an assassination attempt on a Russian political figure, and after taking his diploma in French and Russian literature, Nabokov himself moved to Berlin to work on the Russian-language newspaper his father had helped found. Nabokov married a fellow Russian exile in 1925 but because of his wife's Jewish ancestry was forced to flee Germany in 1937. In 1940 he moved to the United States, became a lecturer at Wellesley College, and was awarded U.S. citizenship in 1945. From 1948 to 1958 Nabokov was a professor of Russian literature at Cornell University, where he wrote his first widely popular work, *Lolita* (1955). In 1960, Nabokov moved to Switzerland, where he lived and wrote until his death in 1977.

Among Nabokov's major works, *Lolita, Pale Fire* (1962), and *Ada or Ardor* (1969) have received the warmest critical praise. One of the most controversial novels of the century, *Lolita* tells the story of a middle-aged European professor's sexual infatuation with a twelve-year-old American girl. Because of its treatment of the subject of pedophilia, the novel was the object of outrage and censorship, but critics then and since have consistently praised its literary quality and humor, as well as Nabokov's sympathetic though unsentimental depiction of Humbert Humbert, the novel's murderous antihero. In *Pale Fire,* Nabokov lampooned the tradition of

scholarly annotation of literary works by presenting the 999-line poem of a fictitious poet alongside the off-kilter commentary of a disturbed professor. Nabokov's longest and last major work, *Ada or Ardor,* is a widely praised exploration of the themes of time and memory in the story of a lifelong love affair between a brother and sister.

In a prolific and celebrated literary career, Nabokov published seventeen novels, around sixty short stories, seven plays, several books of poetry, a critical biography of Nikolai Gogol, an autobiography, numerous translations to and from Russian, and several volumes of essays, lectures, and correspondence. Throughout his life, he was also an avid lepidopterist, or butterfly specialist, and in his first years in the United States he worked as a research fellow in entomology at Harvard University's Museum of Comparative Zoology. In 1961 filmmaker Stanley Kubrick turned Nabokov's *Lolita* into a popular Hollywood movie, and it was filmed again in a more explicit version by director David Lynch in 1997. In 1995 virtually all of Nabokov's previously published short stories (including "A Guide to Berlin" and several never before translated from the original Russian) were collected as *The Stories of Vladimir Nabokov.*

Plot Summary

Part I: The Pipes
"A Guide to Berlin" begins with the narrator entering a Berlin pub with a drinking companion after a morning spent, he notes, observing "utility pipes, streetcars, and other important matters." The story's first section marks the beginning of the "guide to Berlin" that the narrator describes to his listener later that day. On his way to the Berlin Zoo, the narrator had encountered several utility pipes not yet installed beneath the asphalt of the street in front of his home. He describes how the pipes got there, the exploits of the neighborhood boys on them after they were unloaded, and their appearance that morning after receiving a fresh blanket of snow. As the section closes, he notes that someone has spelled out the name "Otto" on the snow covering one of the pipes, a name that strikes him as "beautifully" mirroring the shape of the pipes themselves.

Part II: The Streetcar
Boarding a streetcar that will eventually drop him off at the Berlin Zoo, the narrator is reminded of

Vladimir Nabokov

its resemblance to the now extinct horse-drawn trams of St. Petersburg, Russia. The narrator observes how efficiently the streetcar conductor takes change and gives out tickets despite his coarsened hands, and likens his dexterity to that of a pianist. He admires the conductor's flawless performance of his daily routine despite the swaying of the streetcar and the cold Berlin winter. When the streetcar reaches the end of the line, its two cars reverse positions: the first car is uncoupled and released onto a side track until it falls behind the second car and then joins up with it from the rear. The narrator suggests that the streetcar will soon go into a museum for technological antiques. As the narrator approaches the Berlin Zoo, he imagines a writer of the twenty-first century assembling the details of a vivid portrait of life in 1920s Berlin simply by studying a mothballed streetcar at some museum of the future. To the writer of the twenty-first century, the narrator's "yellow, uncouth" streetcar will be a historical treasure.

Part III: Work

In the story's third section, the narrator describes individual scenes of Berlin's commercial life visible from the windows of the streetcar. Workmen rhythmically drive iron stakes into the earth of a torn-up intersection; a flour-doused baker on a

tricycle shoots down the street, followed by a van collecting empty bottles from taverns; and a postman fills his mailbag from a stuffed letterbox. Of all these sights, the narrator's attention is arrested by the "fairest" sight of all, a meat merchant's truck piled high with skinned carcasses being delivered to Berlin butcher shops.

Part IV: Eden

In the story's fourth section, the narrator has arrived at the Berlin Zoo. He describes it as a "man-made Eden," a reminder of the "solemn, and tender," opening of the Old Testament, in which the tale of Adam and Eve and the Garden is first told. Although it is an imperfect paradise in that the animals are caged, it is the closest man can get to a utopia on earth, and thus the name of the hotel across from the Zoo—the Hotel Eden—strikes the narrator as particularly apt. Because it is winter, the narrator cannot view the Zoo's tropical animals, so instead he heads for the Zoo's amphibian, insect, and fish houses. The narrator likens the lighted windows of the aquarium to the portholes in Captain Nemo's submarine in the Jules Verne novel *20,000 Leagues under the Sea*. He then imagines that the red starfish he sees in one of the aquarium windows is the origin of the "notorious" red star emblem of the Soviet Union. By trying to establish a "topical utopia" like the legendary sunken city of Atlantis ("Atlantica"), the narrator notes, communist Russia only "cripples" the modern world with its ideological "inanities."

The narrator then makes a final guidebook-like recommendation: "do not omit to watch the giant tortoises being fed." Although the ancient tortoise dining on moist leaves is physically unprepossessing, its majestic "ageless" shell seems to the narrator to carry the "splendid burden of time."

Part V: The Pub

The story closes where it began, after the narrator's morning trek but with the narrator and his companion now seated within the pub some time after the narrator has left the zoo. The listener immediately objects that the guide to Berlin the narrator has just offered him is "very poor." The narrator does not answer but only peers into the room at the back of the bar where, on a table that sits in front of a couch below a mirror, the barkeep's son is being fed soup. The listener again demands that the narrator explain his peculiar guide to Berlin, a city that strikes him in any case as "boring," "foreign," and "expensive." Still receiving no answer, he follows the narrator's gaze toward the child in the back room, who now raises his eyes to look back out at the bar. The narrator describes what the child sees: the bar's pool table, the metal bar itself, two obese truckers seated at a table, and, at another, the narrator and his companion. Although the scene is a familiar one to the child, the narrator "knows" that whatever the child's future life may bring, he will always remember the view he had from this table: the billiard table, the bar's denizens, the hovering cigar smoke, the patrons's voices, and the narrator's "scarred face" and missing right arm. The listener complains that he "can't understand" what the narrator sees in the other room, to which the narrator silently replies "how can I demonstrate to him that I have glimpsed somebody's future recollection?"

Because of his apparent distaste for Russian communists ("topical utopias and other inanities"), the reader may infer that the narrator is also a Russian emigre living, as many of Nabokov's exiled countrymen did, in Berlin's Russian district south of the Berlin Zoo.

Unlike Nabokov, however, the narrator appears to have been terribly disfigured by war or some other tragic incident. The reader learns, for example, that he carries a "rubber heeled" walking stick; that women sympathetically give up their window seats for him when he boards streetcars, though they avoid looking at him; and that the child who regards him in the bar at the end of the story sees an "empty right sleeve and scarred face." Throughout the story, the narrator is quietly attentive, reflective, and sympathetic towards the world around him, and is acutely conscious of the passage of time.

Characters

Listener

After the narrator, the unnamed listener—the narrator's regular drinking partner—is the most important character in "A Guide to Berlin." The narrator introduces him in the story's first sentence as his friend, and it is to him that he narrates the odd guide to Berlin that comprises the bulk of the story. Although he is deemed "the listener," he, ironically, is the only character who speaks in the story. When the reader first hears him in the story's last section, he is scornfully rejecting the narrator's guide and complains that the city it purports to describe is, in any event, "boring," "foreign," and "expensive." One view of the listener's role in the story is that he represents the blinkered, unimaginative, ordinary world, trapped in its own present and unable to see the glimpses of the future that sustain the narrator's spirit.

Narrator

The unnamed narrator is the central figure in the story. His descriptions of the things he encounters during a morning's tram ride to the Berlin Zoo is the reader's only source of information about the city and its people. Although the narrator discloses little about himself, it appears that, like Nabokov, he is a writer who once lived in St. Petersburg, Russia.

Themes

Art and Experience

In "A Guide to Berlin" Nabokov presents a series of short vignettes of everyday life in the Berlin of the 1920s that illuminate the themes of time, memory, and the artist's response to experience. The artist's duty to record everyday experience is summed up in "The Streetcar" section, where the narrator declares, "I think that here lies the sense of literary creation: to portray ordinary objects as they will be reflected in the kindly mirrors of future times; to find in the objects around us the fragrant tenderness that only posterity will discern and appreciate in the far-off times when every trifle of our plain everyday life will become exquisite and festive in its own right." In the narrator's eyes, the artist's obligation to ordinary experience is not simply to *record* it, but to portray it with the same nostalgic generosity with which future generations will view it.

Throughout "A Guide to Berlin" Nabokov shows the narrator taking his idea of literary creation directly to heart. In the narrator's own creation—the guide he narrates to his drinking companion—he portrays the everyday life around him with "kindly" eyes, as the future, he imagines, will also

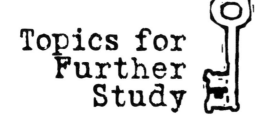

Topics for Further Study

- Research the history of Berlin and Germany's Weimar Republic in the 1920s and compare and contrast its political, cultural, and social climate with those of Berlin in the 1930s and 1940s under Adolf Hitler.

- Investigate the themes of memory and time in *Remembrance of Things Past* by Marcel Proust. Compare and contrast the ways Proust conceives of memory and time with Nabokov's use of them in "A Guide to Berlin."

- Investigate James Joyce's use of setting and realistic historical detail in *Ulysses* and compare and contrast it with Nabokov's use of them in "A Guide to Berlin."

- Research the history of the Russian emigrant community in Berlin in the 1920s through the 1940s.

view it. For example, he transforms the mute ordinariness of the sewer pipe into a linguistic object by noting its resemblance to the letters in the name "Otto." He compares the coarse, black-nailed hands of the streetcar conductor to the nimble hands of a pianist; he transforms the construction workers' brute pounding into a musical "iron carillon"; and he elevates a scurrying baker covered with flour into an "angelic" figure. Later, at the Berlin Zoo, the aquarium's ordinary windows become the portholes of Captain Nemo's submarine *Nautilus* in the Jules Verne novel *20,000 Leagues under the Sea*, and the ugly "ancient" tortoise messily eating its leaves is transformed into an "ageless" symbol of the "splendid burden of time."

The narrator of "A Guide to Berlin" not only asserts that the artist's duty to everyday experience is to "ennoble and justify" it as future generations will, he also actively memorializes it himself as he recounts the events of his morning trek through Berlin to his drinking companion.

Time

Although the timespan of the story "A Guide to Berlin" consists of the events of a single day (a December morning in Berlin in 1925), and primarily a single morning, Nabokov shows the past and future repeatedly invading the narrator's present. In addition to the everyday images that dominate the

narrator's trip to the Berlin Zoo, in "The Streetcar" section the historical past appears in the form of the narrator's memories of the St. Petersburg trams he rode eighteen years earlier. In the "Eden" section, however, the narrator also refers to a more distant, primordial past when he compares the Berlin Zoo to the Garden of Eden of the Old Testament. He reinforces this sense of the past as a profoundly remote and primal place through his images of the "ruins of Atlantis" or "sunken Atlantica" and of the "ancient . . . cupolas" (shells) of the Galapagos Islands tortoises. Although the tortoise is "ponderous" and "decrepit," for the narrator its very ancientness redeems it. By comparing its shell to the bronze dome of some architectural landmark, the narrator views the tortoise's old age and decrepitude as a "splendid burden." In "A Guide to Berlin," time is used to represent both the "antiquity" and "rickety" obsolescence of the everyday world, as well as its "old-fashioned charm" and "splendid" age.

Memory and Reminiscence

In his autobiography *Speak, Memory* Nabokov wrote, "How small the cosmos (a kangaroo's pouch would hold it), how paltry and puny in comparison to human consciousness, to a single individual recollection, and its expression in words!" In "A Guide to Berlin" human recollection is presented as the only antidote to the constant ''vanishing'' of the present into the past. The narrator asserts that the role of the artist is to portray the present in the heightened, nostalgic terms in which the future will see it. ''A Guide to Berlin'' is itself an example of the narrator's recollection preserving and elevating the ordinary objects of the present by recording them sympathetically for ''future times.''

In the story's last section, the narrator, seated with his friend at a Berlin bar, sees the barkeep's son facing them from the bar's back room. When the child lifts his eyes from his magazine to look out at the narrator and the listener, the narrator sees what the child sees through the mirror on the wall behind the child's table. ''Whatever happens to him in life,'' he thinks, ''he will always remember the picture he saw every day of his childhood from the little room where he was fed his soup. He will remember the billiard table and the coatless evening visitor who used to draw back his sharp white elbow and hit the ball with his cue, and the blue-gray cigar smoke, and the din of voices, and my empty sleeve and scarred face, and his father behind the bar, filling a mug for me from the tap.'' Like the Berlin of 1925 that will live on in the works of some writer of the twenty-first century, the child's gaze assures the narrator that he too will live on in the child's ''kindly'' memory.

Style

Point of View

In ''A Guide to Berlin'' Nabokov presents several short vignettes about ordinary life in Berlin in December, 1925, from the vantage point of an unnamed narrator who describes these scenes to a drinking companion later in the day. The point of view of the story is that of the narrator's first-person subjective ''I.'' In ''The Pub'' section, Nabokov introduces the voice of the listener—the story's second point of view (and its only use of spoken speech)—who complains that the ''guide'' he has just heard is dull and pointless. At the end of the story, the narrator sees himself as the barkeep's child views him by glimpsing his own reflection in the mirror that hangs on the wall behind the child. The story's third point of view is that of the silent child, whose field of vision and consciousness the narrator imagines as he views himself through the mirror.

Narration/Narrative/Narrator

The narrator of ''A Guide to Berlin'' is an unnamed Berliner who tells a drinking companion at a Berlin *Bierstube* about the events of his day in December, 1925. He narrates the entire story in the present tense but occasionally recalls or imagines events that occurred in the past or that could occur in the future. The narrator's narrative is subjective and personal: he idiosyncratically imagines, for example, that the shape of two utility pipes resembles the letters in the name ''Otto''; he declares that the street car will ''vanish'' in twenty years though he cannot actually know this; and he concludes that the red star of the Russian Bolshevists ''originated'' in the ''crimson five-pointed star'' of the starfish, though there is no evidence for his belief. The tone of his narrative about the city and its denizens is one of sympathy and beneficence: the women who give him their seats when he rides the streetcar are ''compassionate''; the conductor is like a ''pianist'' in his dexterity; the baker is ''angelic'' in his flour-covered clothes; and the pink and yellow animal carcasses on a butcher's truck are the ''fairest'' sight on Berlin's streets.

Setting

The setting of ''A Guide to Berlin'' is Berlin, Germany, shortly before Christmas in December, 1925. In this period Berlin and Germany were undergoing a significant transition. The economic hardship—notably runaway inflation, brought on by Germany's defeat in World War I—was disrupting German society and threatening its attempt to establish and nurture a democratic form of government after years of monarchical rule. The Berlin the reader encounters in ''A Guide to Berlin'' is viewed in small, sharply focused fragments. It is a busy, industrious place, a blend of obsolete technologies like the ''rickety,'' ''old-fashioned'' streetcar and the new energy of construction and economic change represented both by the soon-to-be-installed sewer pipes and the construction workers and other laborers the narrator glimpses through the streetcar's windows. Lurking in the shadow of this modern Berlin is the narrator's memory of St. Petersburg, Russia, the city of his youth, which is twice recalled by the image of the obsolete horse-drawn tram.

In the mid-1920s, Nabokov and the majority of his fellow Russian expatriates lived in central Berlin in the Schoneberg district, south of the Zoologischer Garten, the Berlin Zoo of Nabokov's story. In this same neighborhood forty years later U.S. president John F. Kennedy would give his famous ''Ich bin ein Berliner'' speech. In ''A Guide to Berlin'' the narrator concludes his tram ride by touring the Berlin Zoo, which reminds him of a man-made Garden of Eden and conjures up images of the legendary submerged kingdom of Atlantis and of the exotic Galapagos Islands. While the narrator's sympathy toward the city is clear throughout the story, in the last section Nabokov gives the reader another view of Berlin, that of the ill-natured listener, for whom the city is simply ''a boring, foreign city, and expensive to live in, too. . . .''

Structure

In describing ''A Guide to Berlin'' in 1976, Nabokov wrote that ''despite its simple appearance this Guide is one of my trickiest pieces.'' The simplicity Nabokov referred to is the story's apparently straightforward ''guidebook'' structure: its five seemingly cut-and-dried sections, each dealing with a different aspect of Berlin life, from sewer pipes and streetcars to working Berliners, the zoo, and a pub. As Nabokov hinted, this ''simple'' organization masks an unusual and complex structure. The story's opening paragraph and its closing section, for example, act as frames for the middle sections of the story by introducing the character (the unnamed listener) and the setting (a Berlin tavern) that the narrator will return to in the last section after his departure from the zoo.

After the opening frame, Nabokov presents five sections that begin with realistic, ''guidebook-like'' descriptions but that open or expand out into philosophical or impressionistic language. For example, the narrator's precise, realistic description of the unburied sewer pipes in ''The Pipes'' dissolves, by the end of the section, into an imaginative comparison of the pipes's shape to the letters in the name ''Otto.'' Similarly, ''The Streetcar'' begins with a narrow declarative assertion of fact about the future of the streetcar, but ends with an emotional artistic manifesto about the role of the literary artist. The ''Work'' section also opens by announcing the narrator's intent to give ''examples of various kinds of work,'' but the plain ''examples'' the narrative

presents are in fact colorful, cinematic images of human variety and activity.

Sections 1 through 4 of ''A Guide to Berlin'' all begin with simple declarative statements that are then followed by a series of long sentences often containing additional clauses. The subject of each of the story's sections also tends to expand in scope as the story progresses: the story begins with the four sewer pipes (section 1), broadens to encompass the activity in the streetcar (section 2), widens still further to the frenetic economic activity out on the street itself (section 3), and opens out yet again to the wide expanse of the zoo (section 4). Finally, although each vignette appears to be independent, each is subtly linked: the reflection of the streetcar's lights on the pipe in section 1 foreshadows the narrator's description of the streetcar in section 2, as well as the Berlin street scene he glimpses from the streetcar's window in section 3. And the image of the winking lion on the tavern sign at the story's opening, the horses pulling the St. Petersburg trams in ''The Streetcar,'' and the butchered sides of beef on the truck at the close of ''Work'' all anticipate the appearance of the animal world of the zoo in ''Eden.''

Images/Imagery

Because of the short length and everyday subject matter of ''A Guide to Berlin,'' the story's sharp and vivid imagery plays a central role in achieving its effects. At least one scholar has noted that the story's vignettes and images seem to be constructed cinematically, that is, like the visually arresting images of a movie. For example, Nabokov repeatedly uses color to create memorable imagery: the tavern's ''sky-blue'' Lowenbrau sign with its white lettering; the ''bright-orange heat lightning'' of the passing tram's lights reflected in the snow; the ''chrome yellow'' and ''pink'' beef carcasses hauled into the butcher's bloody ''red shop''; and the ''crimson'' starfish that reminds the narrator of the Soviet Union's national emblem.

In addition to color, Nabokov also emphasizes images that are sometimes constructed, as if by the black-and-white film of a camera, out of only light and darkness. In ''The Pipes,'' for example, the narrator describes a stark photographic contrast: ''an even stripe of fresh snow stretches along the upper side of each black pipe.'' In the climactic image of ''The Pub'' Nabokov creates a light-and-shadow effect through his description of the scene visible to the bar keep's son: "He will remember the billiard table and the coatless evening visitor who used to draw back his sharp white elbow and hit the ball with his cue, and the blue-gray cigar smoke, and the din of voices, and my empty right sleeve and scarred face, and his father behind the bar, filling a mug for me from the tap." In this intensely visual image, the narrator describes only parts of the things before him—an elbow, a pool cue, a sleeve, a face—because, like the film camera lens Nabokov may have used as his model here, the boy can only see what the light in the room exposes.

Symbols/Symbolism

Nabokov employs at least four major symbols in "A Guide to Berlin": the guide, the streetcar, the zoo, and the mirror. The story's conventional title prepares the reader to anticipate a factual, descriptive introduction to the major sights and locations of Berlin. Nabokov sustains this impression by dividing the story into brief, simply titled sections named like a tourist's guide after places and activities characteristic of urban life. As the narrator's idiosyncratic and subjective descriptions of Berlin soon make clear, however, his "city guide" is really a manual for *writers* in how to portray ordinary objects and people so as to ennoble and justify them for future generations. In the story's last scene Nabokov has the listener, who seems to represent a kind of insensitive everyman, underscore the fact that the story he has just heard is a "guide" altogether different than the one he had expected ("That's a very poor guide. . . . It's of no interest."). The narrator's true audience, however, seems not to be the listener, who utterly fails to see or understand what the narrator does, but rather some future sympathetic reader who may look with "kindly," comprehending eyes on the narrator's creation.

The streetcar explicitly unites the first three vignettes of the story. Its lights are reflected in the snow that covers the sewer pipes the narrator encounters in the first section. In the second section, the streetcar stands out as a symbol of a rapidly changing Berlin that in twenty years will replace the streetcar with a more efficient mode of transportation, just as the horse-drawn tram was replaced before it. "Everything about it is a little clumsy and rickety," the narrator observes, and though he admires the conductor's efficiency at taking change

and handing out tickets, the streetcar itself seems to represent the old ways of the narrator's distant St. Petersburg childhood: horse-drawn carriages, carriage boys in "long-skirted livery," and the "cobblestones" of a village street. The frenetic activity of the story's third section, "Work," seems only to assert the streetcar's obsolescence more pointedly: in a world quickly being transformed by construction workers and aswarm with motorized vans and trucks, the streetcar, like the "decrepit" tortoise of the "Eden" section, is an antique. And like the tortoise in the Berlin aquarium—and indeed like the crippled narrator himself—the streetcar is a symbol of a fading historical time that must wait hopefully for the "kindly mirrors of future times" to regain its past glory.

The zoo is the third major symbol of the story. From the opening sentence it is portrayed as the primary destination of the narrator's morning trip through Berlin, and all his encounters in the story's first three sections are preparations for his arrival there. The winking lion in the Lowenbrau sign in the opening paragraph, the horses pulling St. Petersburg's old trams in "The Streetcar" section, and the dead animal "carcasses" being carted into a butcher's shop in the scene before the narrator's arrival—all prepare the reader for the animal world described in "Eden." In that section, the narrator describes the zoo as a "man-made Eden on earth" that reminds "us of the solemn, and tender, beginning of the Old Testament." Although, the narrator admits, zoos cruelly confine animals behind metal bars, they represent "Eden nonetheless. Insofar as man is able to reproduce it." Like a writer's stories and other acts of "literary creation" or artistic reproduction, zoos are artificial things. They are human attempts to re-create what is unreal or lost, whether the biblical Garden of Eden of man's innocence and immortality or the original moments of past time that the writer can hope to portray and memorialize but can never relive. For the narrator the zoo symbolizes both the mortality that has been man's fate since his expulsion from the Garden and man's impulse to recapture "far-off times" through the act of literary creation.

The symbol of the mirror first appears in "The Streetcar" section, where the narrator describes the essence of "literary creation" as portraying "ordinary objects as they will be reflected in the kindly mirrors of future times." The Berlin writer of the twenty-first century, whom the narrator imagines re-creating the world of 1920s Berlin through a streetcar in a museum, will employ the "kindly mirror" of his future vantage point to transform the yellow streetcar. It will then become a "valuable and meaningful" object, ennobled and justified by its age into something "exquisite and festive in its own right." In the story's final vignette, the symbol of the mirror reappears again in the form of the mirror hanging on the wall behind the bar keep's son. From his vantage point in the bar the narrator sees his reflection in this mirror and thus can view himself as the child sees him. Once he is fixed by the child's gaze ("he is now looking our way"), the narrator, like the faded streetcar, can live on indefinitely in someone's memory.

Historical Context

Political Unrest

Vladimir Nabokov's life was profoundly and directly affected by many of the major political and social events of the twentieth century. As the grandson of a prominent Czarist government minister and the son of a minister of justice and leading Russian democrat, Nabokov grew up in an environment of material comfort and tolerant cosmopolitan liberalism. When the Bolshevists under V. I. Lenin launched their grasp for power following Russia's collapse in World War I, the Nabokovs, as quintessential members of the prewar Russian aristocracy, had no choice but to flee Russia for the West. In part because of his father's political background and in part because of his own talent and potential in languages and literature, Nabokov was admitted to Cambridge University from which he earned a degree in 1922. While he was at school, his father settled in the large community of expatriate Russian intellectuals in Berlin where he became the editor of a democratic daily newspaper named *The Rudder*. When his father was murdered in 1922 by reactionary Russians attempting to assassinate a prominent democratic Russian politician, Nabokov moved to Berlin and began contributing to his late father's paper while earning a living as a translator, writer, and instructor of English, Russian, and tennis. By 1925, the year "A Guide to Berlin" was published, the Bolshevists had all but secured their hold on

Russian society, and an ambitious Communist Party member named Josef Stalin had begun the ascent to power that by 1926 would give him dictatorial control over the Soviet Union.

Nabokov was naturally bitter about the communists' success in Russia, and although he rarely addressed political issues in his fiction, "A Guide to Berlin" provides a brief glimpse into his attitude toward the political movement that forced his family from their homeland. In the "Eden" section of the story, Nabokov's narrator sees a "crimson" starfish at the Berlin aquarium that reminds him of the red star emblem of the new Soviet regime. The narrator fancifully imagines that "this, then, is where the notorious emblem originated—at the very bottom of the ocean, in the murk of sunken Atlantica, which long ago lived through various upheavals while pottering about topical utopias and other inanities that cripple us today." In this brief aside, Nabokov imagines the "inanity" of communism as arising from the bottom of the sea to "cripple" modern life, an unreal and doomed "utopia" like the legendary sunken society of Atlantis.

Following its surrender to the Allies in 1918, Germany was forced to agree to armistice terms that required it to make substantial reparation payments to its former enemies. Whether because the German economy was too weak to bear these payments or because Germany's leaders were unenthusiastic about paying them, the German economy began to experience crippling hyperinflation in the mid-1920s, which eventually led to the financial ruin of the German middle class. Germany's economic chaos also fatally destabilized the young democratic government known as the Weimar Republic, which had been created after Germany's Kaiser Wilhelm II abdicated his throne in 1918. In 1925 the Locarno Treaty was signed in an attempt to stabilize Western Europe's postwar borders. But the Allies' uneasiness over Germany's geopolitical ambitions drove France in the same year to begin construction of the heavily fortified Maginot Line along the Franco-German border. Germany's continuing political and economic instability soon allowed Adolf Hitler and his National Socialist party to gain a foothold with the German electorate and eventually to seize power in 1933. Indeed, the same year "A Guide to Berlin" was published, the first part of Hitler's *Mein Kampf* reached Berlin bookstores, unambiguously announcing Hitler's nationalist and antisemitic philosophy to a receptive audience of disaffected Germans. Two decades later, Hitler's concentration camps would claim the life of Nabokov's younger brother, Sergey.

In the tolerant political climate of the Weimar regime, however, German culture briefly thrived, and Berlin became a mecca for avant-garde cultural and intellectual activity. Elsewhere in 1925, Franz Kafka's *Der Prozess* (The Trial), Boris Pasternak's *Detstvo Luvers* (Childhood), Virginia Woolf's *Mrs. Dalloway*, Ezra Pound's first installment of the poem *The Cantos*, and F. Scott Fitzgerald's *The Great Gatsby* all made their first appearance in print. It was also during the period of the early and mid-1920s that Nabokov began to experiment with the literary styles that would later establish him as one of the most stylistically inventive writers of the twentieth century. Critics agree that the short stories penned by Nabokov in Russian during the 1920s represent his stylistic apprenticeship, his attempt to discover the true voice that would characterize his later fiction. Despite his fifteen-year stay in the German capital, Nabokov always claimed to have never really learned the German language, and his social circle reflected his almost exclusive association with the other expatriate Russians who settled in Berlin's Russian district near the city's zoological gardens. Nabokov's at times insular life in Berlin (which he called "an odd but by no means unpleasant existence") is perhaps alluded to in "A Guide to Berlin." There, the narrator is shown interacting with only one other character, an unnamed drinking companion whose Russian nationality may be implied in his alienated description of Berlin as a "boring, foreign city, and expensive to live in, too. . . ."

Despite Nabokov's apparent aloofness toward his new German home, Berlin played a prominent role in much of his early fiction. Several of Nabokov's works from the 1920s take place in the German capital. In addition to the early Russian-language short stories "Blagost" ("Grace," 1924) and "Pis'mo v Rossiyu" ("A Letter that Never Reached Russia," 1925), Berlin is the setting for Nabokov's first novel, *Mashenka* (published a year after "A Guide to Berlin" and later translated as *Mary*): the story of a young Russian emigre living in a Berlin pension, or boardinghouse, who longs to be reunited with the lover he left behind in Russia. Similarly, in *Dar* (1937, later translated as *The Gift*), Nabokov

used Berlin as the setting for the story of a young Russian emigre writer whose romance and eventual marriage to a Russian woman is directed by a benevolent fate. Finally, in *Korol', dama, valet* (1928, translated as *King, Queen, Knave*), Nabokov identified the setting only as "Metropolis" but left little doubt about the city's true identity—Berlin: "In the very name of that still unfamiliar metropolis, in the weighty rumble of the first syllable and in the light ring of the second there was something exciting to him; the famous avenue, lined with gigantic ancient lindens; . . . luxuriantly grown out of the avenue's name."

Although Nabokov's closest ties were to Berlin's Russian emigre circle, he enthusiastically embraced the growing German film movement, which encompassed such prominent figures as Fritz Lang, Josef von Sternberg, and Erich von Stroheim. During the period in which Nabokov wrote "A Guide to Berlin," documentary films about Berlin (for example, Walter Ruttmann's *Berlin, Symphony of a City*) were an especially popular subject for German filmmakers, and Nabokov even served as an extra in a number of German films. Both Nabokov's fascination with the purely visual language of cinema and the popularity of these Berlin documentaries may well have played a part in the writing of "A Guide to Berlin." The documentary, "day-in-the-life" quality of the story's "guidebook" structure, for example, as well as Nabokov's use of brief, acutely visual vignettes and sharp images of color and light may hint at the influence of the German film movement on the story's development.

Critical Overview

The original publication of "A Guide to Berlin" (as "Putevoditel' po Berlinu") in a Russian-language newspaper for the Russian expatriate community in Berlin virtually guaranteed that Nabokov's fourteenth published story would receive little initial critical attention. By 1930, however, Nabokov's first three novels— *Mashenka, Korol', dama, valet,* and *Zashchita Luzhina*—had established Nabokov's literary reputation, and he decided to gather his early stories into the collection *Vozvrashchenie*

Chorba (1929, translated as *The Return of Chorb*). Writing to a friend in 1930, Nabokov described ''A Guide to Berlin'' as the best story in the collection, but contemporary reviewers preferred the title story, written in the same year as ''A Guide to Berlin,'' about the loss of a lover. As Nabokov's reputation grew with the publication of such works as *Priglashenie na Kazn'* (1938, *Invitation to a Beheading*) and *Lolita* (1955), critics continued to ignore ''A Guide to Berlin'' in favor of the contemporaneous ''The Return of Chorb.''

With Nabokov's reputation firmly established by the late 1960s, however, critics began to redress this imbalance, and ''A Guide to Berlin'' began to garner the attention Nabokov had always maintained it deserved. In his *Nabokov: His Life in Art,* critic Andrew Field devoted a page and half to the story, which he called a ''successful story of a purely descriptive sort.'' Field's insights included his assertion that the story comes close to achieving the form of the ''prose poem'' in some passages, his identification of the streetcar as a symbol of a passing Berlin, his noting of the Berlin Zoo's presence in the story as a ''dual metaphor of artistic form and human fate,'' his identification of a similarity between the story's style and that of Turgenev's ''careless sketches,'' and his assertion that the audience for the narrator's ''guidebook'' is primarily the literary artist. In her 1978 study of Nabokov's short stories of the 1920s, *Blue Evenings in Berlin,* Marina Turkevich Naumann echoed Field's observation that the ''guide'' Nabokov had in mind is a guidebook for literary artists writing for future generations. After noting that the things that populate the story—street scenes, trams, childhood memories—recur frequently in Nabokov's other works, Naumann discussed the story's ''compositional design,'' in which the opening and closing sections act as ''frames'' for the middle sections and the individual sections are linked by tone and subject matter. Characterizing ''A Guide to Berlin'' as a ''contemplative'' and ''philosophical'' piece, Naumann examined its literary influences, which include Turgenev and Gogol; its literary allusions (Jules Verne and the Old Testament); and its unusual grammatical structure.

D. Barton Johnson's ''A Guide to Nabokov's 'A Guide to Berlin''' (1979) placed the story in the context of Nabokov's early career and apprentice works. While noting the contributions of previous critics of the story, Johnson argued that none had satisfactorily explained why Nabokov had stated over the years that ''A Guide to Berlin'' was among his favorite and ''trickiest'' stories. After suggesting that ''in the most general terms, the story treats the favorite Nabokovian themes of time, memory, and their relationship to art and the artist,'' Johnson fastened on Nabokov's use of the mirror to explicate the story's ''tricky'' complexity. He noted that mirrors appear not only in ''The Streetcar'' and ''The Pub'' sections but that one of the characteristics of mirrors—image reversal (''left is right, right is left'')—occurs both in the narrator's descriptions of the coupling streetcars and on the level of the story's language itself, through Nabokov's use of palindromes and anagrams. According to Johnson, through the story's linguistic inventiveness Nabokov demonstrates the ''ingenious integration of theme and device that marks his mature work.''

In 1990, Brian Boyd discussed ''A Guide to Berlin'' in his biography of Nabokov's first forty years, *Vladimir Nabokov: The Russian Years.* Describing the story as ''the boldest advance yet in Nabokov's art,'' Boyd noted its ''disjointed structure,'' plotlessness, and Nabokov's mastery of arresting literary images and detail. Boyd viewed the story as organized not so much by the objects and locales of the physical Berlin—the pipes, the streetcar, the working Berliners, and the zoo—as by the ''different possible relations of time.'' For example, Boyd pointed out how the story's focus shifts between present, past, and future, moving from the narrator's vision of the near future, when he believes that the streetcar will have vanished, to the past of St. Petersburg and its horse-drawn trams, to the twenty-first century, when an ''eccentric'' writer will re-create 1920s Berlin, and finally, at the story's close, to the child's future recollections of the time in which the story takes place. For Boyd, Nabokov's principal subject in ''A Guide to Berlin'' is ''the absurdity of our inability to return to our past.''

In his 1992 study, *Nabokov's Early Fiction: Patterns of Self and Other,* Julian W. Connolly argued that ''A Guide to Berlin'' illustrates the theme of ''the value of remaining receptive to the everyday flow of life and of establishing channels of communication with external others.'' For Connolly, the ''other'' the narrator wishes to connect with is not the unseeing listener in the Berlin bar at the

A placid scene of a Berlin street in winter, before the destruction caused by World War II.

story's conclusion but the "future generations of curious readers" who offer the narrator the only hope of "empathic connection." The narrator demonstrates his ability to forge this bond with others by projecting himself into the inner life of the bar-keep's child. The narrator somehow knows, for example, that the child is "forbidden to touch" the billiard cue ball and is not "dismayed" by the scene in the bar he views from the back room. In his contribution ("The Future Perfect of the Mind: 'Time and Ebb' and 'A Guide to Berlin'") to a 1993 study of Nabokov's short fiction, Robert Grossmith

discussed "A Guide to Berlin" as an example of Nabokov's "fascination with the premonition of future memories and the attendant defamiliarizing power of such perceptions." For Grossmith, the story's final scene, in which the narrator "memori-alizes" the present moment by glimpsing the child's "future recollection," represents the "keystone of an entire aesthetic," in which realistic details and everyday "trivia" must be captured and preserved by the writer in order to ensure their survival into the future. The writer can achieve this, Goldsmith argued, only by "defamiliarizing" them, that is, by removing them from their ordinary contexts in order to render them strange and memorable.

Criticism

Paul Bodine

Bodine is a writer, editor, and researcher who has taught at the Milwaukee College of Business. In the following essay, he discusses the style of "A Guide to Berlin," focusing on Nabokov's description of the story as "tricky."

When the full extent of Nabokov's talent began to declare itself in the novels he wrote between 1940 and 1970, Nabokov's critical reputation began a steady ascent that by the time of his death had earned him, in the eyes of some critics, a place among the twentieth century's foremost literary masters. "As long as Western civilization survives," his obituary in the *New York Times* concluded, "his reputation is safe. Indeed, he will probably emerge as one of the greatest artists our century has produced." For many of his admiring critics Nabokov seemed an altogether unique literary presence laboring in a sphere all his own. One such critic called him "one of the most strikingly original novelists to emerge since Proust and Joyce," and *Time* magazine claimed that "he derived from no other writers and leaves no true imitators." Although Nabokov's genius was often attributed to his elegant and precise command of language (the English novelist Martin Amis, for example, called him "our greatest stylist"), for many critics the brilliance and erudition of his prose were secondary to his true gift: an ironic, haughty, but finally compassionate view of the world that was pervaded by a sense of exuberant, mischievous play. Nabokov was described by the *Sunday Times* of London, for example, as a "high-souled genius" who "communicated in every sentence his own playful and godlike bliss." And among the contemporary novelists who could perhaps claim to be among his peers, John Updike said of him, "Nabokov writes prose the only way it should be written, that is, ecstatically."

At the time of his death Nabokov's exalted reputation rested largely on his novels. From his first English translation of one of his early Russian-language novels, *Despair* (1937), to his celebrated master works—*Lolita, Pale Fire*, and *Ada*—Nabokov seemed to have left his Russian short stories of the 1920s decisively behind him. In the decade before his death, however, Nabokov, with the help of his son Dmitri, began systematically translating his 1920s Russian stories for publication in the 1976 collection *Details of a Sunset*. It was only then, a half-century after the original publication of "A Guide to Berlin," that the story Nabokov had more than once singled out for special praise become accessible to his English-language critics.

Most early critics of "A Guide to Berlin" contented themselves with explications of the story's odd "guidebook" format, its major images, and its apparent aesthetic message. The narrator's "guide to Berlin," these critics agreed, was in reality a guidebook or manual for literary artists, and its five seemingly independent sections were in fact subtly linked vignettes (brief sketches focusing on sharp detail), framed by the story's opening and closing sections and connected internally by the presence of the streetcar that carries the narrator from his home to the Berlin Zoo. Unable perhaps to make sense of the story's odd vignette structure, its apparent lack of plot or action, and its strange blend of detailed imagery and literary manifesto, these early critics described "A Guide to Berlin" in absolute terms as either a "philosophical" or "contemplative" piece, or as a kind of "realistic," "purely descriptive" work. In a 1979 essay on the story D. Barton Johnson argued that while these labels were helpful as far as they went, none managed to adequately explain why in 1930 Nabokov had called "A Guide to Berlin" his best story or why, forty-five years later, he was still talking about it as "one of my trickiest." In his essay, Johnson approached this putative "trickiness" head on, using the appearance of the mirrors in "The Streetcar" and "The Pub" sections of the story as clues to the story's hidden complexity.

As students of Nabokov's later works would have recognized, "The Eye," his 1930 novella about the artistic process and a poet's failed romance, had also employed the device of the mirror in a tale also set in Berlin, that combined elements of the love story, detective novel, and social commentary. In "A Guide to Berlin," Johnson showed, the mirrors were keys to the story's "tricky" meaning; Nabokov had deliberately "coded" the story, he argued, to emphasize the ideas of "reflection" and "image reversal" suggested by his use of the image of the mirror in two sections of the story. In "The Pipes," for example, Nabokov has a passing streetcar reflect its lights in the snow that covers a pipe in front of the narrator's home, and then has the

What Do I Read Next?

- *Lolita,* Nabokov's darkly comic 1955 bestseller about a European professor's sexual obsession with a precocious American twelve-year-old girl and the murder his passion for her drives him to commit.

- *Pale Fire,* the much-praised 1962 novel by Nabokov that consists of a 999 line poem by the late poet John Shade, together with the odd foreword and scholarly commentary of an unhinged Shade scholar.

- *Before the Deluge: A Portrait of Berlin in the 1920s* (1972) explores various social, cultural, and scientific developments in Berlin between World Wars I and II.

- *The Stories of Vladimir Nabokov,* a 1995 collection of fifty-four stories and sketches (including ''A Guide to Berlin'') previously published in earlier collections plus eleven stories translated from Russian for the first time.

- *Sally Bowles,* 1937, by Christopher Isherwood. Collection of well-known stories about bohemian life in Berlin in the 1930s. Source for the film ''Cabaret.''

- *Goodbye to Berlin,* 1939, by Christopher Isherwood. Sketches about Berlin just before the outset of World War II.

---

narrator discover that the name ''Otto,'' scrawled in the snow on the pipe, is mirrored in the very shape of the pipe itself, with its ''tw*o o*rifices'' (O—O) and its taci*t t*unnel'' (-tt-). Similarly, in the next section, ''The Streetcar,'' Nabokov twice uses the narrator's memory of the now ''vanished'' horse-drawn trams of St. Petersburg as reflections from the past, or as historical mirrors of the eventual fate of the ''old-fashioned'' streetcar in which the narrator rides. In the section's penultimate paragraph, Nabokov underscores this sense of historical ''mirroring'' by repeating the phrase ''the horse-drawn tram has vanished'' from the section's opening line. Then, in his manifesto for an art of ''proactive nostalgia'' (as Johnson calls it) at the end of ''The Streetcar,'' Nabokov employs the mirror image directly: ''I think that here lies the sense of literary creation: to portray ordinary objects as they will be *reflected* in the kindly *mirrors* of future times'' (emphasis added).

With the symbol of the mirror established as perhaps the key to the story's ''trickiness,'' it takes center stage in the story's final section, ''The Pub.'' The mirror behind the shoulders of the bar keep's son in the pub's back room enables the crippled narrator to see himself in the child's eyes, assuring

him that as long as the child survives, he, too, will be preserved through the child's ''future recollection.'' Nabokov makes clear, however, that only the narrator can see what the child sees; he has the narrator's disagreeable companion, the unnamed listener, flatly state, ''I can't understand what you see down there.'' What enables only the narrator to ''see'' the child's future memories? Throughout the story Nabokov has hinted that the narrator's crippled physique may account for his ability to empathetically see others's ''future recollections'': either as a result of war or misfortune, the narrator walks with a ''rubber heeled stick,'' his ''scarred'' features cause the women on the streetcar to try ''not to look too closely'' at him, and when the child views him from the bar's back room, he sees only the narrator's ''empty right sleeve and scarred face.'' The narrator's empty right sleeve in particular underscores his similarity to the aged, repulsive tortoise at the Berlin Zoo, whom the narrator describes as having, like himself, ''totally useless paws.''

By emphasizing the narrator's physical disability (and, as Marina Turkevich Naumann has shown, reinforcing it by adding a new reference to it in his English translation), Nabokov seems to suggest that only the crippled narrator can see others'

> Nabokov had deliberately 'coded' the story, he argued, to emphasize the ideas of 'reflection' and 'image reversal' suggested by his use of the image of the mirror in two sections of the story."

''future recollections'' because he most of all depends on the ''kindly mirrors of future times'' to transform his physical decrepitude into something noble and splendid. When the narrator's companion complains that he doesn't see what the narrator sees, the narrator's note of triumph or exultation (''What indeed!'') reflects his realization that—like the rickety streetcar, the ruins of Atlantis, or the decrepit tortoise—he, too, can be transfigured, despite his age and infirmity, into something ''valuable and meaningful'' through ''someone's future recollection.''

Since D. Barton Johnson's 1979 essay helped to unlock the ''trickiness'' of ''A Guide to Berlin,'' later critics have identified the story as perhaps the earliest example of the subtlety and complexity that characterize Nabokov's later masterpieces. For example, in 1990 the author of Nabokov's definitive biography, Brian Boyd, described ''A Guide to Berlin'' as ''the boldest advance yet in Nabokov's art'' and argued that the story's surface organization of five vignettes dealing with the physical or ''spatial'' Berlin of 1925 gives way to a deeper temporal structure involving the relationship between the past (St. Petersburg and its horse-drawn trams; the ancient past of Atlantis), the present (Berlin in December, 1925), and the future (the eccentric Berlin writer of the twenty-first century; the child's future recollection). According to a 1992 study of the story, the narrator's ability to project himself into the consciousness of the barkeep's child—his ability to somehow know, for example, that the child is ''forbidden to touch'' the cue ball or to understand that the child is not ''dismayed'' by the scene in the bar before him—suggests that as early as 1925 Nabokov was experimenting with the theme

of the relationship between the self and other. These themes would lead into his later themes of obsession and the merging of the self in another in such novels as *Lolita*, *Pale Fire,* and *Ada.*

Nabokov once remarked that ''art at its greatest is fantastically deceitful and complex.'' For the half-century between the original publication of ''A Guide to Berlin'' and the appearance of Nabokov's English translation, the story had been relegated to the heap of ''experimental'' tales in which Nabokov struggled, not always successfully, to find his own voice and themes. If it was read at all, it was seen as one of Nabokov's early ''straightforward'' apprentice works, lacking in ''the polish, intricacy and artifice'' of his later, more famous novels. But with Nabokov's English translation and his helpful hint to critics that the tale was as ''tricky'' as his mature work, ''A Guide to Berlin'' now stands as perhaps the first clear example of Nabokov's celebrated ability to interweave his favorite themes—memory, time, and their relationship to the literary artist—within a story of complex structure and ingenious imagery, of striking visual detail and playful verbal innuendo.

Source: Paul Bodine, Overview of ''A Guide to Berlin,'' for *Short Stories for Students,* The Gale Group, 1999.

Julian W. Connolly

Connolly is Professor of Slavic Language and Literature at the University of Virginia. In the following excerpt, he offers an interpretation of the theme of ''A Guide to Berlin,'' emphasizing Nabokov's development of imagery.

Nabokov's most comprehensive statement about the value of remaining receptive to the everyday flow of life and of establishing channels of communication with external others arises in the unusual sketch entitled ''A Guide to Berlin.'' Published in December 1925, this sketch is the only one of the period to have an overtly programmatic orientation. While most of the early works revolve around a protagonist's preoccupation with the absence of a beloved other, this work has a different focus: the relationship of the writer to the outside world and to his potential audience. Nabokov's treatment of the self-other relationship here establishes principles which remain in force throughout his literary career.

The sketch consists of an untitled introductory paragraph and five separate vignettes bearing the titles ''The Pipes,'' ''The Streetcar,'' ''Work,'' ''Eden,'' and ''The Pub.'' Much of the text presents the narrator's detailed observations of ordinary Berlin street scenes. In the second vignette, however, the narrator articulates the reason why he believes that such a record of observed detail is valuable. Stating that trolley cars will disappear some day, he declares that future writers will have to resort to museums to view the authentic remnants of the past. In those future days, every "trifle" (*meloch'*) from the past will be precious and meaningful. It is up to the writer, then, to take the interests of future generations into account. The narrator now introduces a key image—that of the mirror—to explain his view of the "sense" of literary creation. As he puts it, literary creation is meant to portray "ordinary objects *as they will be reflected in the kindly mirrors* of future times . . . when every trifle of our plain everyday life will become exquisite and festive in its own right." The implications of this mirror image will be discussed below. For the moment, however, one should recognize that the narrator's awareness of the inevitability of loss in life and of the role that verbal art may play in preserving life's transient experiences points to a basic concern of Nabokov's own art. His fiction is permeated both with a haunting recognition of the fragility of all that is precious in life and with a fervent desire to find a way to preserve treasured moments of experience. The narrator also reveals here his sensitivity to the needs of an unknown "other"—in this case, future generations of curious readers. He underscores this conviction in the last vignette.

Describing a pub in which he sits with a companion, the narrator observes that the pub consists of two rooms. He and his companion sit in one room, while in the other—part of the proprietor's apartment—he sees a couch, a mirror, and a table at which a child sits eating soup. This segment may seem at first glance to be a passage of neutral description, but two elements herald its special import. First, the reference to the mirror echoes the theme of the perception by future generations introduced earlier in the sketch. Moreover, as the narrator continues the description, he includes not only *his* view of the scene, but also that of the *child*: "he is now looking our way. From there he can see the inside of the tavern—the green island of the billiard table, the ivory ball he is forbidden to touch . . . a pair of fat truckers at one table and *the two of us* at another."

This incorporation of the child's perspective draws attention to an important feature of the narrator's approach to the outside world. As in the earlier

> " While most of the early works revolve around a protagonist's preoccupation with the absence of a beloved other, this work has a different focus: the relationship of the writer to the outside world and to his potential audience."

passage about the writer's responsibility to the future, he expresses an awareness of the perspective of an external other. He even speculates on the child's psychological attitude toward the scene he beholds, stating that the child has long grown accustomed to this scene and therefore is not "dismayed" by its proximity. The narrator's ability to imagine the inner world of another is a vital attribute of the artist in Nabokov's world, so long as this capacity does not cascade into massive personal projection, thereby obliterating the other's autonomy.

The narrator's comprehension of the other's viewpoint has a positive effect on him. Mentally responding to his companion's lack of appreciation for the import of this moment, he expresses his delight at having glimpsed "somebody's future recollection." Although the narrator's satisfaction in achieving a sense of empathic connection might be rewarding for any artist, this experience may have an additional benefit for him. Focusing on the fact that the child "will always remember" the view he had of the pub scene, and perceiving that an image of the narrator himself is included in the child's view, the narrator may have discovered here a possible means of transcending the personal limits of his own time and space. By envisioning himself as part of the scene that the boy will remember in the future, the narrator perceives that he will remain alive in the boy's memory, and therefore will not be consigned to oblivion as long as the child himself survives. A small emendation that Nabokov made when revising his story for translation supports this premise. In the original version, the items listed by the narrator in his description of the child's perspective included the billiard table, a billiard player, and the child's father. The English version, however, adduces a new item: ''my empty right sleeve and scarred face.'' An image of the narrator himself is now explicitly included among those things which the boy will recall in future years and which therefore will survive the passage of time.

At several points in the text, then, Nabokov's narrator indicates the importance of forging a connection to an external other, whether it be making an impression on the memory of a child or conveying the essence of things ''as they will be reflected in the kindly mirrors of future times.'' What makes ''A Guide to Berlin'' particularly distinctive, however, is that Nabokov not only articulates the premise within the narrator's discourse, he also illustrates it by manipulating the very building blocks of that discourse—the letters of the text itself. As D. Barton Johnson has pointed out, Nabokov carefully embedded in his text ''mirror image'' palindromes and anagrams of key words such as ''OTTO''; this mirroring technique ''pre-figures'' the central theme of ''future memories.'' At the same time, however, it reaffirms the narrator's fundamental concern— the importance of being aware of the perceptions of anonymous others. That is, while the narrator's discourse speaks *overtly* about a potential audience of future generations, the text of his discourse— composed by the authentic *auctor*—speaks *covertly* to just such an other: the presumed reader of the sketch itself.

It is worth noting that Nabokov's narrator does not find a receptive audience for his observations within his narrated world. Although the narrator shares his collected observations with his drinking companion, the latter remains unresponsive. He calls the narrator's guide ''very poor'' and suggests that no one cares about the narrator's experiences. Nor does the narrative mention any other addressee in the text. Yet while the other who is physically present within the narrator's world is not receptive to the narrator's vision, there exists a different type of other who is not physically present in that world but who may indeed be more receptive—the presumed reader of the text. Nabokov's works frequently focus on characters who find themselves surrounded by an unresponsive world and who look to an anonymous audience for understanding and acceptance.

The presence of encoded verbal material within the text of ''A Guide to Berlin'' thus discloses a seminal feature of Nabokov's art: the potential of his narratives to speak on two distinct levels simultaneously. In addition to the surface-level message which his fictional narrators intend their readers to absorb, one may perceive a second message from the implied author to the implied reader which may modify or contradict the first message. In ''A Guide to Berlin,'' the message of the secondary channel of communication opened by the embedded verbal material reinforces that of the surface level: both levels indicate the importance of establishing communicative links to external others. In later Nabokov texts, however, the two messages can diverge radically.

''A Guide to Berlin'' offers direct insight into the writer's concerns and convictions during his first years as a prose writer. Foremost among these is his belief in the importance of sensitivity to the potential perceptions of others. Not only does such sensitivity sharpen the observation and the description of life in art, it may provide a way to transcend the narrow spatial and temporal limitations of one's own life. The sensitivity to the perceptions of others which the narrator reveals in ''A Guide to Berlin'' is, however, not matched by most of the other protagonists in Nabokov's early fiction. While many of his protagonists express concern for the feelings of others, they often submerge that concern under their own needs and projections. In his first novel *Mary*, Nabokov provides his first detailed treatment of this problem.

All together, Nabokov's stories of the 1924-25 period lay down the foundations upon which the complex edifice of his subsequent fiction will be built. They highlight the dangers of obsession with an internal image of another, while signalling the benefits of establishing empathic bonds with others. They also disclose the first traces of the seminal bifurcation between the authorial and character dimensions of the self in Nabokov's fictional world, and they suggest the central role that projection and creation can play in the development of a character's identity. Although the early stories do not explore the implications of these processes in detail, they indicate the direction Nabokov's subsequent fiction will follow. . . .

Source: Julian W. Connolly, '''A Guide to Berlin','' in *Nabokov's Early Fiction: Patterns of Self and Other,* Cambridge University Press, 1992, pp. 27–31.

D. Barton Johnson

In the following excerpt, Johnson offers an interpretation of Nabokov's use of mirror images in

"A Guide to Berlin," noting connections between imagery and theme in the story.

The eight-page sketch "A Guide to Berlin" was Nabokov's fourteenth published story and was first published in the Russian emigre newspaper *Rul'* on Christmas Eve, 1925. At the opening of the story the nameless narrator, an emigre Russian writer, sits in a Berlin *Bierstube* and describes the sights of his wholly unremarkable day. This seven-line *mise en scène* is the first half of a frame which is completed at story end by a longer, present tense episode set in the same pub. The piece consists of five numbered vignettes which range in length from a single paragraph to slightly over two pages. The first, entitled "Truby" ("Pipes"), describes a row of large utility pipes lying along the curb awaiting burial in an as yet undug trench. As the narrator goes out in the morning after a night snowfall he notes with pleasure that someone has written the word "OTTO" in the fresh strip of snow atop the pipe. The narrator has planned a trip to the Berlin Zoo and boards a tram. The tram and its conductor form the subject matter of the second vignette which is called "Tramvaj" ("Streetcar"). This episode is conceived in the form of a nostalgia piece written in part from the viewpoint of a writer of the next century. The narrator-guide lovingly catalogues such inconsequentialities as the trolley pole jumping its overhead wire, the ceremony of the conductor at this job, and the ritual of the end-of-the-line decoupling of the two tram cars with their switch of position and subsequent recoupling—all reminiscent of the switching of the horses on the horse-drawn trams of Petersburg some eighteen years before. The vignette ends with an apotheosis in which the very "sense of literary creation" is said to be the recreation of the minutia of the present as they will be seen "in the kindly mirrors of future times ... when every trifle of our plain everyday life will become exquisite and festive in its own right." The guided tour continues in the third vignette, "Raboty" ("Work"), with the speaker enumerating various people seen at their daily tasks through the tram window: street repair men, a passing truck loaded with empty beer bottles, a postman emptying a corner mailbox, a man delivering fresh carcasses to a butcher shop. In the fourth section, entitled "Edem" ("Eden"), our guide arrives at the city zoo where he muses on the Atlantis-like aquarium exhibits. Of particular interest to him are the crimson starfish, which recall the "notorious emblem," that is, the Bolshevik Red Star, and the giant tortoises, whose domed shells resemble church cupolas. The cycle of sights comes to an end in the fifth section, "Pivnaja" ("The Pub"), where the narrator has been recounting his day's travels to his companion, who is bored by the mundane guided tour. The modest pub in which the two friends sit drinking is divided into two rooms, and the narrator can see through the passageway into the squalid back room where the publican's blowzy faded wife is serving her small son a bowl of soup. As the narrator watches him, the boy looks out into the bar where his gaze takes in the narrator and his companion. The narrator then reflects that the boy will always remember the sight of the barroom through the passageway, his father serving the customers, and so on. As the narrator muses, his friend irritably remarks that he cannot understand what is so interesting in the view. In the closing line the writer ponders "How can I demonstrate to him that I have glimpsed somebody's future recollections?"

There have been two rather extended discussions of this story. Field notes that in places the piece "comes extremely close to the form of the prose poem." The tram episode he views merely as a pretext for the above-cited passage in which Nabokov defines and justifies his conception of the writer's role. The zoo, an artificial paradise with bars, is seen as Nabokov's "dual metaphor of artistic form and human fate." Following his description of the pub scene, Field concludes that "A Guide to Berlin" is a "guide book written with a very restricted type of tourist in mind; it is a guidebook for the artist." Naumann provides a more detailed analysis. Although noting the poetic qualities of the sketch, the author includes it in her category of "realistic" (as opposed to "symbolist") stories. Noting with some puzzlement the odd assortment of sights included in the "Guidebook," Naumann views the story primarily as a collage of Nabokov's favorite Berlin motifs, pointing out their frequent occurrence in his other works. Like Field, she sees the story as an artist's credo but one "not written merely for art's sake, nor for a drinking companion, but for future generations." It is, she says, Nabokov's explicit statement of the *raison d'être* of minutia in literature. Both of these exegesis have some interesting insights and would doubtless seem satisfactory were it not for Nabokov's comments suggesting greater depths in the story. Certainly neither commentary gives sustenance to Nabokov's claim that the story is one of his trickiest.

In the most general terms, the story treats the favorite Nabokovian themes of time, memory, and their relationship to art and the artist. These themes

" In the most general terms, the story treats the favorite Nabokovian themes of time, memory, and their relationship to art and the artist."

are stated explicitly in two passages. The "Streetcar" vignette opens with the narrator's reflection on the obsolescent electric tram and its predecessor, the horse-drawn tram. In a hundred years, he thinks, a writer visiting a town museum in search of local color for his work will be enchanted by the 1920s tramcar and its appurtenances. It is this passage that leads to the formulation of the narrator's artistic credo: "to portray ordinary objects as they will be reflected in the kindly mirrors of future times; to find in the objects around us the fragrant tenderness that only posterity will discern and appreciate." In the concluding section, the narrator watches the boy in the back room and muses that the scene viewed by the lad is the stuff of the boy's "future recollections." In addition to their common theme the two passages are linked by a common structural device. We have remarked the metaphoric "kindly mirrors of future times." The final pub scene contains a vital but unobtrusive real mirror which is the actual source of the narrator's image of the boy's future recollections. Looking through the passageway from the bar into the apartment the narrator's eye is greeted by "a cramped little room with a green couch under a mirror, out of which an oval table . . . topples and takes up its solid position in front of the couch." A few lines later it is mentioned that the narrator "can make out very distinctly the couch, the mirror, and the table in the background beyond the passage." These mirror references occur in both the Russian and the English texts. In the translation, however, yet a third reference (not found in the original text) calls attention to the device: while the Russian text reads "Tam, v glubine, rebenok ostalsja na divane," the English has been altered to "There, under the mirror, the child still sits alone," with the critical mirror replacing "v glubine." This sentence introduces the description of what the boy sees in the barroom. A close reading reveals that the de-

scription of the boy's view is actually the view seen by the narrator in the mirror above and behind the boy. By virtue of the mirror the narrator is seeing himself, his friend, and the interior of the barroom as it appears to the boy whose future memories the narrator is thus observing. This is the mirror of future recollections. Further supporting this interpretation of the role of the wall mirror is that in contrast to the other vignettes the physical layout of the barroom and its furnishings, the passageway, and the living quarters in the rear are all carefully detailed. The lines of sight are clearly drawn and the crucial position of the mirror is emphasized and reemphasized.

This embodiment of theme in structural device is characteristic of much of Nabokov's best later work and may in some measure account for his particular affection for the story. It would, however, scarcely qualify the story as one of his "trickiest." This interpretation also leaves aside the role of the material in the other vignettes. One possibility is that the episodes treating the utility pipes, the jobs, and the zoo might serve as exemplification of the "pro-active nostalgia" theme that the narrator sees as the meaning of literary creation. This view, while plausible to an extent, would not seem to justify Nabokov's high opinion of the piece, for these remaining vignettes seemingly fail to display the cunning integration of allusion and motif with theme which synthesizes Nabokov's best work. As examples we might cite the numerous Poe allusions which form a persistent and peculiarly appropriate subtext to *Lolita*, or the pervasive motif of the iconic Old Church Slavic alphabetic characters betokening the linguistic (and physical) imprisonment of the artist-protagonist in *Invitation to a Beheading*.

The mirror image motif which dominates the final scene and which reflects the earlier thematic statement is obviously central to the story's meaning but appears to be restricted to those sections and, hence, does not seem to qualify as an integrative device joining the various vignettes into a unified whole. Before discarding the possibility, however, it might be well to consider that mirrors have other properties in addition to reflection. Just as Nabokov neglects to mention that the narrator is viewing the boy's future memories via a mirror, he also leaves to the reader's imagination a second quality of mirrors. Mirrors reverse their images: left is right, right is left. Mirror image reversals play an important role in Nabokov's repertory of literary devices both on the level of thematic metaphor and of microstylistics. . . .

Various kinds of mirror image inversion, albeit without benefit of mirrors, permeate all of the remaining sections of "A Guide to Berlin." Perhaps the most evident of these reversals occurs in the "Streetcar" section. After his inventory of the activities of the conductor at work, the narrator continues: "At the end of the line the front car uncouples, enters a siding, runs around the remaining one and approaches it from behind . . . I am reminded of how . . . the horses used to be unhitched and led around the potbellied blue tram." Left and right, or depending on your point of view, front and back, are reversed.

The foregoing represents a mirror image reversal on the level of narrative event. Another, and more important type of reversal is to be found on the word and phrase level. Before considering this second type of inversion, however, we must ponder the question, what is the written language's equivalent to mirror image reversal? The answer is—palindromes. On rereading the individual vignettes we find that all contain mirror image palindromes and, in addition, anagrams—some of which are also palindromic. At the end of the first vignette, "Pipes," the narrator, seeing the word "OTTO" traced in the snow atop the pipe thinks how appropriate the name with its "dvumja belymi 'o' po bokam i cetoj tixix soglasnyx poseredke" is to the pipe with its "dvumja otverstviem i tainstvennoj glubinoj." Not only is the name "OTTO" a mirror image palindrome, but its reversible physical shape bears an obvious resemblance to the large utility pipe with its "O" at each end. Also noteworthy is the descriptive phrase "OTverstviem i TainstvennOj glubinoj" which anagrammatically contains the iconic key word "OTTO." Nabokov's Englishing of the passage shows some modification of the wording in order to obtain the requisite effect: ". . . that pipe with its two Orifices and its Tacit Tunnel." It might further be noted that the open pipe permits reciprocal vision and that the older Russian expression for 'telescope' is *opticeskaja truba* . The "Streetcar" section, in addition to the reversal of narrative image already described, also includes an "OTTO" anagram in its opening lines. Commenting on the decline of the streetcar as a mode of transport, the narrator remarks pointedly "Ja uze cuvstvuju v nem cto-to OTzivsee, kakuju-TO staromodnuju prelest'." It is perhaps forced to see the *to-to* of *cto-to* as a reversal of the syllables of the following anagrammatic "OTTO," but it nonetheless rather neatly prefigures the subsequent reversal of the tram cars at the end of the line.

> A close reading reveals that the description of the boy's view is actually the view seen by the narrator in the mirror above and behind the boy."

The mirror image palindrome "OTTO" also occurs in an anagram in the first line of the third vignette, "Raboty": "Vot obrazy raznyx rabOT, koTOrye ja nabljudaju iz tramvajnogo okna." The device of letter transposition is also used here: *OBRAzy . . . RABOt* perhaps echoing the *to-to/ot-to* inversion. It would be possible to attribute such matters to chance were it not for the fact that the corresponding English passage in the translation has been markedly expanded in order to incorporate equivalent anagrammatic elements. In the Russian original the above quoted sentence is the entire first paragraph. This sentence-paragraph has been augmented in the English as follows: "Here are examples of various kinds of work that I observe from the cRAMmed tRAM in which a compassionate woman can always be relied upon to CEde me her window SEat—while trying nOT TO LoOK too CLOsely at me." The "cRAMmed tRAM" obviously mimics *obRAZy RAZnyx*; "nOT TO," *rabOT, koTOrye*, and perhaps, the, metathesized "LoOK . . . CLOsely" deliberately parallels the transposed *OBRAz . . . RABOt*. These syllable doublings and inversions iconically evoke the dual nature of the streetcar with its two, reversible, cars in tandem. Even were it not for its divergence from the Russian text the new material in the English might well call attention to itself simply by its Baroque and gratuitous nature.

"Eden," the fourth vignette, is perhaps the most intricate in its inversions. Looking through the portholes of the Berlin Zoo aquarium, the narrator sees a crimson, five-pointed starfish. This, he thinks, is the source of the "preslovutaja emblema:—samogo dna okeana—iz temnoty poTOPlennyx Atlantid, davnym-davno perezivsix vsjakie smUTy,—OPyty gluPOvaTyx UTOPij—i vse to, cto trevozit nas." This passage on the origin of the Bolshevik Red Star contains two notable

incidences: the usual anagrammatic "OTTO"—
temnOTy poTOplennyx, and the first of a series of
plays on the root sequence *(u)top-ija* and *pot(u)* in
which the root of *uTOPija* turns to *pot* 'sweat.'
There is a further pun involving *uTOPija* and
poTOPlennyj 'drown.' The English text, again with
some adjustment, succeeds in capturing both of
these bits of word play: "The notorious emblem
originated . . . at the very bOTTOm of the sea, in the
murk of sunken Atlantica, which long ago lived
through various upheavals while pOTTering abOuT
TOPical uTOPias and OThter inanities that cripple
us TOday." The following paragraph of both texts
continues the plays on the palindromic "OTTO"
and the inverted utopias. The final vignette also
contains its own encoded anagrammatic "OTTO"
and, moreover, at a particularly appropriate point.
In the passage containing the narrator's description
of the scene which he, the narrator, sees indirectly in
the mirror and which the boy sees directly, the
introductory expression is "OTTuda vidnO." The
boy and the narrator are looking through the telescope, the *opticeskaja truba*, of time. It is also of
note that the physical layout of the pub building
with its two openings connected by the passageway
through which the characters regard the scene resembles the pipe-telescope with its inscription.

Nabokov's theme of "future memories," the
true artist's creative goal, which is cleverly captured
in the tacit mirror imagery of the final section, is
consistently and cunningly prefigured in all of the
preceding guidebook vignettes by means of the
various technical devices illustrated above. "A Guide
to Berlin," despite its seeming artlessness, is thus
the first of Nabokov's writings to show the ingenious integration of theme and device that marks his
mature work. Perhaps this accounts for Nabokov's
special affection for the story over a period of half a
century.

Source: D. Barton Johnson, "A Guide to Nabokov's 'A
Guide to Berlin'," in *Slavic and East European Journal*,
Vol. 23, No. 3, Fall, 1979, pp. 353–61.

Marina Turkevich Naumann

*Turkevich Naumann is a professor at Douglas
College, Rutgers University. In the following excerpt, she offers her interpretation of the significance of the imagery in "A Guide to Berlin."*

Berlin is the city that is almost always a background
theme in Nabokov's early stories. For him Berlin
did not have the special, personal, social, or political
connotation that Paris had for Balzac or London had

for Dickens. It assumed importance because it actually surrounded him as he wrote. Apropos of this,
Nabokov said: "I have always been indifferent to
social problems, merely using the material that
happened to be near, as a voluble diner pencils a
street corner on the table cloth or arranges a crumb
and two olives in a diagrammatic position between
menu and salt cellar." Berlin is the setting for his
novels *Mashen'ka* and *Korol' dama valet*, for instance. In *Dar*, Fedor's peregrinations through Berlin are pages long. Berlin is the prominent backdrop
in "Blagost'" and "Pis'mo v Rossiiu"; and it is the
central theme of one of Nabokov's earliest stories,
"Putevoditel' po Berlinu" ("A Guide to Berlin").

Ostensibly this story is a standard guide to
Berlin's sights and scenery, but not the type of red
guidebook that Nabokov depicted on the old woman's stool in "Blagost." This is a special guide to
some of the "important" sights and aspects of the
city: the pipes, the trams, the jobs, the Hotel Eden,
the beer hall.

One is struck first by the narrator's opening
comment that these disparate and seemingly trifling
things are "important" features of Berlin and,
secondly, by the odd combination they represent.
However, as the narrator describes them, it becomes
clear that this is a writer's guide and that this writer
has a definite purpose. He has not written it merely
for art's sake, nor for a drinking companion, but for
future generations: . . .

> I think that here lies the sense of literary creation: to
> portray ordinary objects as they will be reflected in the
> kindly mirrors of future times; to find in the objects
> around us the fragrant tenderness that only posterity
> will discern and appreciate in the far-off times when
> every trifle of our plain everyday life will become
> exquisite and festive in its own right: the times when a
> man who might put on the most ordinary jacket of
> today will be dressed up for an elegant masquerade.

Actually the aspects of Berlin he has chosen are
not as disparate as they appear to be initially. They
are all facets that particularly interested Nabokov.
The Berlin street life, trams, childhood memories
that dip into the past or project into the future, and
even the fascinating letter combinations considered
in this story are recurrent motifs in many of his
other works.

The entire story is told in the present tense, and
the hero-narrator is the subjective "I." Its tone is
marked by the narrator's reiteration of his subjectivity and by his positive reaction to Berlin, which is
in turn rejected by the writer's drinking companion
in the final frame of this piece. Only then does the

narrative move into dialogue. However, this dialogue is one-sided. The drinking companion speaks, but the narrator continues his straight narrative. Thus two methods are employed simultaneously.

Seemingly "Putevoditel' po Berlinu" follows a guidebook format and therefore does not have the traditional short-story structure. It does, however, have a compositional design. There is a definite frame. The narrator, after a morning trip to the zoo, goes into a beer hall with a drinking companion. Thus the storyteller and listener are immediately presented. Within the frame are vignettes of various spots in Berlin: I. "Pipes"; II. "Tram"; III. "Jobs"; IV. "Eden"; and V. "Beerhall." The last scene ties the conclusion structurally to the introductory frame. All of these short pieces, although clearly divided by Roman numerals, are intricately linked by subject matter and by the general tone of beauty and philosophy that colors the realistic descriptions. An introductory comment to the effect that the narrator will speak of "pipes and trams" brings the reader to the first sketch, so brief and poetic that it appears to be a poem. The trams, which have left their orange reflection on those pipes, are the subject of the second vignette. Here he speaks of fashions and passing fads. In "Pis'mo v Rossiiu" he had noted modish fluctuations in various dances; now he turns to the fate of diligences and horse trams and sadly reflects that the electric trams will soon be replaced as well. The narrator focuses in particular on the tram conductor, whom Nabokov has already depicted in "Pis'mo v Rossiiu." He observes how nimbly the man goes about his duties: . . .

> The conductor who gives out tickets has very unusual hands. They work as nimbly as those of a pianist, but, instead of being limp, sweaty and soft-nailed, the ticketman's hands are so coarse that when you are pouring change into his palm and happen to touch that palm which seems to have developed a harsh chitinous crust, you feel a kind of moral discomfort. They are extraordinarily agile and efficient hands, despite their roughness and the thickness of the fingers.

In "Putevoditel' po Berlinu," Nabokov's narrator regards the details of Berlin's daily life with sympathy. To him, it seems that in the future this trivial material will be of museum caliber. The rickety yellow tram and the conductor's uniform will be found in display cases and some twenty-first-century writer will see them as curious aspects of the past. This observation brings the narrator to [a] momentary reflection upon the duty of the writer. . . . For him, however, all of these everyday details are not only valuable for history but are meaningful and beautiful in themselves. For in-

> **Indictments of the Soviet regime by Nabokov are rare. When he focuses on his homeland, it is usually the Russia of his past, not the Soviet Union of his present (1925)."**

stance, the Christmas trees at the tram stop not only reflect the holiday publication date of this story (24 December 1925) but are poetically shown as a part of the Berlin scene: . . .

> . . . at the stop, at the edge of the pavement, crowd the Christmas trees.

In Part III, "Jobs," life is—not too surprisingly—described from the tram window. The tram is still the structural link. The observer's field of vision is limited by the window and is perpetually moving. First the narrator sees the asphalt and the street itself. Men are working on it, as in "Vozvrashchenie Chorba." Compare the two following sentences: . . .

> She attempted to catch it on the wing by means of a child's spade found near a heap of pink bricks at a spot where the street was under repair. A little way off the funnel of a workers's van emitted gray-blue smoke which drifted aslant and dissolved between the branches—and a resting workman, one hand on his hip, contemplated the young lady, as light as a dead leaf, dancing about with that little spade in her raised hand.

> At an intersection the pavement has been torn up next to the track; by turns, four workmen are pounding an iron stake with mallets; the first one strikes, and the second is already lowering his mallet with a sweeping, accurate swing; the second mallet crashes down and is rising skyward as the third and then the fourth bang down in rhythmical succession.

This last image recalls the contented stoking sailors in "Port," for there is a live rhythm and music to their tasks akin to bell chimes: . . .

> I listen to their unhurried peal, the cast-iron chiming, four repeating notes.

In *Pnin* Nabokov repeats this image of street repairs: ". . . workmen came and started to drill holes in the street—Brainpan Street, Pningrad—and patch them up again, and this went on and on, in fits of shivering black zigzags and stunned pauses, for weeks.''

In ''Putevoditel' po Berlinu '' the writer continues to observe other elements of Berlin street life, and with positive adjectives and editorial comments he describes the angelic baker, the emerald bottles on the truck, the graceful larch on the sleigh, the postman with his big black bag, and the most vivid scene, the butcher carrying the meat on his back: . . .

> But perhaps fairest of all are the carcasses, chrome yellow, with pink blotches, and arabesques, piled on a truck, and the man in apron and leather hood with a long neck flap who heaves each carcass onto his back and, hunched over, carries it across the sidewalk into the butcher's red shop.

Having turned his attention thus, the narrator not unexpectedly moves to Part IV, ''Eden.'' In this vignette he becomes increasingly philosophical, reflecting first on the city zoo as an earthly paradise created by man. In the frame to this story, the narrator had noted that he had visited the zoo in the morning. According to him, the zoological gardens tell us about the beginning of the world. Although he laments that all the animals are in cages, he concedes that the lion, if loose, would eat the doe. Nonetheless, it is a paradise to the extent that man can make it so. Appropriately, the Hotel Eden stands opposite the zoo. The writer moves figuratively into the zoo, where now in the winter he finds the amphibians, fish, and insects the most interesting. Jules Verne's Captain Nemo and the mythological submerged continent of Atlantis color his description of his visit to the aquarium. He sees fish and marine flora and focuses on a live, deep red, five-pointed starfish lying on the sandy bottom.

This star evokes one of Nabokov's rare, although oblique, political comments: . . .

> This, then, is where the notorious emblem originated—at the very bottom of the ocean, in the murk of sunken Atlantica, which long ago lived through various upheavals while pottering about topical utopias and other inanities that cripple us today.

The upheavals caused by utopian experiments such as Atlantis are still troubling the world today. In ''Pis'mo v Rossiiu'' these perturbations had been alluded to even more indirectly. Indictments of the Soviet regime by Nabokov are rare. When he focuses on his homeland, it is usually the Russia of his past, not the Soviet Union of his present (1925).

The fifth section of this story, ''The Beerhall,'' represents the other side of the frame but describes the interior, not the exterior, of the beer hall. The narrator notes the bar, the billiard table, the little

tavern tables, and presents a scene similar to the restaurant in ''Port.'' However, his description has an interesting twist. It picks out the divan, mirror, and table in the adjoining room belonging to the beer-hall owner. There the narrator observes the owner's child being fed soup and then looking at an illustrated newspaper. Suddenly the narrator inverts the picture and shows what the child sees and how he views the narrator and his fellow drinker. Finally, the writer moves into the future: . . .

> Yet there is one thing I know. Whatever happens to him in life, he will always remember the picture he saw every day of his childhood from the little room where he was fed his soup.

In this concluding fragment, the drinking companion repeatedly raises questions that indicate he has missed the point of the narrator's guide, thus accentuating and emphasizing by omission what the writer has described. For him the guide and Berlin are boring and dull. For the narrator, on the other hand, all that he has noted is important. Even the future memories of the beer-hall keeper's child hold significance for him. Thus the concluding remarks of the story aptly point to the future: . . .

> How can I demonstrate to him that I have glimpsed somebody's future recollection?

The structure of this story is rather unusual. Not only are the short sections unobtrusively joined, but each section has a realistic description supplemented by a philosophical reflection on some aspect of the scene. Furthermore, the topics enlarge in scope as the story progresses. The reader moves from pipes to trams, to street life in general, to the zoo and animal life, and finally to the child whose life still lies ahead of him. The pervading sense of this story is that life in Berlin is gratifying and meaningful to the artist in all its aspects.

''Putevoditel' po Berlinu'' has been compared with Turgenev's *Sportsman's Sketches* by Field. He notes that this story ''has some of the air of a carefully arranged 'careless sketch'.'' These vignettes are in the narrative style and the language is realistic. This realism, as I indicated above, is acknowledged by the narrator. There are only ten or so ''made-strange'' adjective-noun combinations. Longer metaphoric phrases are more numerous. For example, the street pipes are the iron hoses or intestines (*kishki*) of the street. This image brings to mind Nabokov's later anatomical image in *Dar*, where a poplar resembles the nervous system of a giant. Other extended metaphors deal with the conductor's agile hands, the music of the street workers, and a turtle whose shell is both a bronze cupola and the burden of time. These metaphors are not intended to convey any symbolic dimension in the way that the zoo denotes an earthly paradise. Instead, they serve to revivify ordinary objects that have dulled.

It is crucial here to consider Nabokov's training as a writer. In *Speak, Memory*, he recalled his tutor: "He made me depict from memory, in the greatest possible detail, objects I had certainly seen thousands of times without visualizing them properly: a street lamp, a postbox, the tulip design on the stained glass of our own front door. He tried to teach me to find the geometrical coordinations between the slender twigs of a leafless boulevard tree, a system of visual give-and-takes, requiring a precision of linear expression, which I failed to achieve in my youth, but applied gratefully, in my adult instar . . . to certain camera lucida needs of literary composition."

Nabokov's literary training also owed much to Gogol. Significantly, in his study of Gogol Nabokov cited the following passage from *Dead Souls*: "But a different lot and another fate await the writer who has dared to evoke all such things that are constantly before one's eyes but which idle eyes do not see—the shocking morass of trifles that has tied up our lives, and the essence of cold, crumbling, humdrum characters with whom our earthly way, now bitter, now dull, fairly swarms; has dared to make them prominently and brightly visible to the eyes of all men by means of the vigorous strength of his pitiless chisel."

Nabokov's observations are enlivened not only by metaphoric expressions but by the use of a variety of stylistic devices. Above I have noted his interest in letter shapes and sounds. In the frame of "Putevoditel' po Berlinu" Nabokov focuses on the blue beer-hall sign with white lettering and a picture of a winking lion. Part I concludes on a contemplative note about the letters etched into the snow on the pipes, which read "Otto": . . .

> Today someone wrote "Otto" with his finger on the strip of virgin snow and I thought how beautifully that name, with its two soft o's flanking the pair of gentle consonants, suited the silent layer of snow upon that pipe with its two orifices and its tacit tunnel.

In Part III literary allusions are made not only to Jules Verne and mythology but to the Gospels and the Old Testament. Colors, which quickly convey an impression, occur throughout these sketches, and with particular frequency in the street scene in Part III where realistic vignettes predominate. These are almost fleeting, cinematic shots. Color is singular in its application in Part IV, "Eden." Crimson (*purpurnyi*) is the only color mentioned and qualifies a star. This emphasis on the red hue of the star poetically expresses Nabokov's idea of the "notorious emblem," the Red Star of communism.

The grammatical structure of the sentences in "Putevoditel' po Berlinu" is singular. The sentences are very long, with many secondary clauses. Brief sentences are conspicuous by their infrequency. Parts II, III, and IV open with factual statements that give way immediately to sentences a paragraph long. In Part V Nabokov used *v glubine* (in the depths) three times within a single page. I noted this recurrent phrase in "Port"; here it is used strictly with reference to the child whom the narrator sees sitting in the back room. The phrase accentuates not only the writer's spatial detachment from this child but the depth with which the author considers the child and his future memories. It also emphasizes a narrowing or a focusing of Nabokov's artistic lens. Nabokov often coalesced his images. In this instance the mirror, table, divan, and child are brought together linguistically. With the aide of *v glubine*, Nabokov moves from a large image to a small one. I point to the focusing-in found in the following three excerpts. In the final excerpt only the common denominators of the first remain: *v glubine, divan, rebenok* (child). The translation and italics are mine. . . .

> (1) "*In the depths* is a wide passageway, and there one can see a cramped little room with a green *divan* along the wall, under a mirror from which flows, a semicircular table covered with a checked oilcloth, and firmly stands in front of the *divan*. This room relates to the squalid little apartment of the owner. There, his wife, a faded German, feeds her towheaded *child* soup.

> (2) From our corner, beside the counter, one very clearly sees *in the depths*, in the passageway—the *divan*, the mirror, the table. The mistress clears the dishes off of the table. The *child*, leaning on his elbows, is attentively examining the illustrated magazine.

> (3) There, *in the depths*, the *child* remained on the *divan* alone.

"Putevoditel' po Berlinu" is thus another contemplative story that focuses on the "important" facets of the hero's surroundings. Once again the narrator is an artist—a writer—who concerns himself with the everyday sights of Berlin. However, this story, like "Pis'mo v Rossiiu," has a philosophical note. Nabokov projected into the future and observed that the child of the beer-hall keeper will someday recall the very minutiae of the present scene. Thus, trivial aspects of daily life not only assume value as past memories but have their place in the creation of new and future ones. The hero concludes that the significance of a writer's creation lies in the depiction of these commonplace things. This was Nabokov's explicit statement of the raison d'être of minutiae in literature. . . .

Source: Marina Turkevich Naumann, in *Blue Evenings in Berlin: Nabokov's Short Stories of the 1920s,* New York University Press, 1978, pp. 56–67.

Sources

Boyd, Brian. *Vladimir Nabokov: The Russian Years,* Princeton University Press, 1990, pp. 250-53.

Field, Andrew. *Nabokov: His Life in Art,* Boston: Little, Brown and Co., 1967, pp. 141-42.

Grossmith, Robert. ''The Future Perfect of the Mind: 'Time and Ebb' and 'A Guide to Berlin'.'' In *A Small Alpine Form: Studies in Nabokov's Short Fiction,* edited by Charles Nicol and Gennady Barabtarlo, Garland Publishing Co., 1993, pp. 149-53.

Further Reading

Field, Andrew. *VN: The Life and Art of Vladimir Nabokov,* Crown Publishers, 1986.
   In a biographical study of Nabokov's life and work, Field provides a detailed treatment of Nabokov's life among the Russian emigres of Berlin in the 1920s.

Nabokov, Vladimir. *Speak, Memory: An Autobiography Revisited,* Vintage International, 1967.
   Published when Nabokov was in his late sixties, this autobiography has been called ''the finest autobiography written in our time.''

Hills Like White Elephants

Ernest Hemingway
1927

First published in *transition* in August of 1927, "Hills Like White Elephants" became an important piece in Hemingway's second collection of short stories, *Men Without Women.* Hemingway wrote the story soon after the publication of his 1926 novel, *The Sun Also Rises,* while living in Paris. *Men Without Women* was well-received, as were Hemingway's other early works. He was embraced by the expatriate literary community in Paris and received strong reviews on his work in the United States and abroad. Although he continued to write novels and stories throughout his career, the early short stories are often considered to be among his finest works. "Hills Like White Elephants," a widely-anthologized and much-discussed story, offers a glimpse at the spare prose and understated dialogue that represents Hemingway's mastery of style.

The story, told nearly in its entirety through dialogue, is a conversation between a young woman and a man waiting for a train in Spain. As they talk, it becomes clear that the young woman is pregnant and that the man wants her to have an abortion. Through their tight, brittle conversation, much is revealed about their personalities. At the same time, much about their relationship remains hidden. At the end of the story it is still unclear as to what decision has or has not been made, or what will happen to these two characters waiting for a train on a platform in Spain.

Author Biography

Ernest Hemingway was born in Oak Park, Illinois, on July 21, 1899, to Clarence and Grace Hemingway. His father was a doctor and his mother a musician who had given up her career to care for the couple's six children.

Hemingway's early life was an upper-middle class, comfortable existence. He and his family spent summers at their cottage in northern Michigan. He graduated from high school and went to work as a reporter, a career he continued on and off for the rest of his life.

The comfortable life ended, however, in 1918, when Hemingway volunteered as a Red Cross ambulance driver to do service on the front lines of World War I in Europe. While in Italy, just before his nineteenth birthday, he was severely wounded while helping to rescue another wounded man. The experiences that Hemingway had in the war and during his recuperation stayed with him for the rest of his life, impacting his work greatly.

After the war, Hemingway returned to his work as a reporter. He married Hadley Richardson in 1921 and the couple moved to Paris. There he developed connections with other expatriate writers, including Ezra Pound and Gertrude Stein, among others. He also met and established a friendship with James Joyce. Throughout this period, he continued to work as a correspondent while launching his own literary career.

In 1926, Hemingway published *The Sun Also Rises,* his first novel, which generated considerable critical attention. The novel firmly established Hemingway as the voice of his generation, which is sometimes referred to as the ''lost generation.'' He continued to meet with success in publishing his short stories. In 1927, he and his first wife divorced and he married Pauline Pfeiffer. In that same year, he published the well-received collection of short stories, *Men Without Women,* a collection that included the short story, ''Hills Like White Elephants.''

In the years that followed, the Hemingways established a household in Key West, Florida. In 1929, Hemingway's novel *A Farewell to Arms* was published. Hemingway's fame continued to grow, but not only for his literary skill—his ''extracurricular'' activities placed him squarely in the public eye. He hunted big game in Africa in the 1930s and German submarines in the Caribbean in the 1940s, and after covering the Spanish Civil War as a reporter, he memorialized the Loyalist cause in *For Whom the Bell Tolls* (1940).

By 1940, Hemingway had moved to Cuba and married his third wife, Martha Gellhorn. He subsequently divorced Gellhorn and married Mary Welsh in 1946. In 1952, he published *The Old Man and the Sea,* for which he was awarded the 1953 Pulitzer Prize. In 1954, Hemingway won the Nobel Prize in Literature.

Hemingway's final years were filled with growing physical and mental pain. In 1961, at his home in Ketchum, Idaho, he took his own life with a shotgun blast, ending a decades-long literary career and a life filled with both the highest adventure and the deepest depression. His work continues to generate immense critical and popular interest.

Plot Summary

The story opens with the description of distant hills across a river in Spain. An American and his girlfriend sit outside a train station in the heat. No other details about their relationship are provided at the beginning of the story. They decide to order beer, and the woman who works at the bar brings the drinks to their table. The girl remarks that the distant hills look like white elephants, but the man discounts her remark.

The story continues to unfold through dialogue, and it becomes clear that the girl, Jig, does not understand Spanish while the American does. In addition, it begins to become apparent that the two are having some sort of disagreement. The subject of the disagreement, however, is hidden, until the man says, ''It's really an awfully simple operation, Jig. . . . It's not really an operation at all.'' When Jig fails to respond, the man tries several more times to tell her that the ''operation'' is all ''perfectly natural.'' His description of the operation implies that Jig is pregnant and he is trying to talk her into having an abortion.

Jig wants reassurance that if she has the operation the American will still love her and that life will go back to the way it was before the pregnancy. However, even as she asks for reassurance, it becomes clear that she does not want to have the abortion. Further, it also becomes clear that she understands that nothing will ever be the same again.

Although the man continues to assert that he does not want her to have the abortion unless she wants to, he obviously does not mean this. Jig stands, and looks out across the valley. She seems to contemplate what is at stake in their relationship and in her life. When she says that they "could have everything," the man agrees. For Jig, "everything" seems to include the baby. For the American, it means carefree life without the baby. Jig finally becomes frustrated with the conversation and asks the man to be quiet. Rather than listen to her, he continues to tell her how she ought to feel, and what she ought to realize. In addition, he continues to tell her that he knows exactly what the operation will be like. Finally, she quietly explodes: "Will you please please please please please please please stop talking?"

The man tries once more, but Jig tells him she will scream. He takes the bags to the other side of the station and quickly has a drink at the bar as he passes through. He observes that many people are "reasonably" waiting for the train, supposedly in contrast to what he sees as unreasonable behavior from Jig. He returns to the table and Jig smiles at him. He asks if she is better, and she replies that she feels fine. The story ends before the train arrives and with little indication of what the final decision will be or what the state of the relationship will be in the future.

Ernest Hemingway

Characters

The American

The American is one of two characters in Hemingway's story. He sits at a table with a girl at a train station in Spain. Through his conversation, it becomes clear that the girl with him is his lover. Throughout the story, the American tries to convince the girl that she should have an abortion. He tries to make himself sound perfectly reasonable and rational, but as the dialogue continues, it becomes clear that he is both selfish and hypocritical. He says, "You've got to realize . . . that I don't want you to do it if you don't want to. I'm perfectly willing to go through with it if it means anything to you." He does not mean, however, that he wants the girl to have the baby, although he says that he'll "go through with it." By the end of the story, the American has revealed himself to be self-centered and lacking in feeling for the girl, Jig, despite his protestations of love.

The girl
See Jig

Jig

The second character is called "Jig" by the American; however, Hemingway refers to her as "the girl" throughout the story. This is in contrast to Hemingway's naming of the other character as "the American" or "the man." Jig is a young woman who finds herself pregnant with her lover's child. She and her lover have been traveling in Europe; the labels on their suitcases name the hotels where they have spent nights together. At the time of the story, she is sitting at a table with the American, drinking beer and anise liqueur, waiting for a train. It slowly becomes clear that the man is trying to talk her into aborting the child she carries. Although the subject is never mentioned directly, the pregnancy is at the heart of the conversation. It is not clear what decision Jig reaches by the end of the story, or if she has reached any decision at all. It does seem clear, however, that she is unhappy with both choices in front of her: keep the baby and lose the American, or abort the baby and keep the American. She seems unconvinced that either scenario will develop as the American promises it will.

Media Adaptations

- ''Hills Like White Elephants'' is one of three short stories filmed as a cable television movie. The other two stories on the film include ''The Man in the Brooks Brother Shirt'' by Mary McCarthy, and ''Dusk Before Fireworks'' by Dorothy Parker. The ninety minute film aired on HBO entertainment network in 1990 as *Men and Women*. The video version of the film is titled *Women and Men: Three Tales of Seduction* and is a 1996 Front Row Entertainment production. David Brown and William S. Gilmore are the producers. The film stars Beau Bridges, Melanie Griffith, Elizabeth McGovern, Molly Ringwald, Peter Weller, and James Woods.

As the story closes, Jig asserts that she is ''just fine.'' Under the circumstances, however, it is clear that this is not the case.

Themes

Choices and Consequences

''Hills Like White Elephants'' presents a couple in the midst of a crisis. Although unmarried, the girl is pregnant and the man who has made her pregnant wants her to have an abortion. His belief is that the choice for abortion will free them to return to the lives they had lived before the pregnancy. He does not want to share the girl with anyone, particularly not a baby. He believes that the consequences of having the baby will lead to the breakup of the relationship.

Jig, however, seems to have a more realistic assessment of the choices and consequences in front of her. She knows that she is the one who must make the choice about the child she carries. Although she

asks for reassurance, and wants the man's love, she also knows that the chances of them finding long term happiness are remote, regardless of the decision she makes. For her, the choice to abort or not to abort will, in all likelihood, render the same consequences: life without the American.

Doubt and Ambiguity

The story of Jig and the American is a story of doubt and ambiguity for the American, for Jig, and for the reader. While the American speaks in the language of certainty, he may or may not mean what he says. In addition, he can have little knowledge of what it would mean to the girl to have the abortion he so desperately wants her to have.

Although she seems unconvinced that the abortion is the best plan, Jig nonetheless wants reassurance from the man that she is with that he will stay with her. ''And if I do it you'll be happy and things will be like they were and you'll love me?'' she asks the man. His reassurances seem to fall flat, however. For Jig, the path ahead is unclear. If she chooses to have the abortion, she may be unhappy with the loss. The American may leave her anyway. She may not survive the operation, in spite of the American's reassurances that it is ''perfectly simple.'' If she chooses not to have the abortion, she may be left alone in Spain, without support, in a country where she does not even speak the language.

Even at the very end of the story, there seems to be no resolution. What does Jig decide? Does she get on the train or not? Does the couple stay together or separate? The clues in the story are sparse, and can be read either way. Thus, the doubt and ambiguity facing the characters are mirrored by the story itself.

Men and Women

In ''Hills Like White Elephants,'' Hemingway explores the way that men and women relate to each other. Hemingway's stories are often heavily masculine, and his protagonists are often patriarchal and sexist. As Peter Messent argues, however, in this story, Hemingway ''foregrounds a woman's point of view.'' The more the American speaks, the more ridiculous he becomes. For example, he tells Jig, ''It's really an awfully simple operation, Jig. . . . It's not really an operation at all.'' Jig does not respond to this statement for several reasons. First, she knows what an abortion is and how it will be performed. It is, after all, her body. In addition, it is not simple: abortions are not legal at this time and place (abortion was not legalized in Spain until 1985), and sometimes women die. Jig knows this, and the man's denial of the complexity of what he is asking the woman to do only serves to highlight his own selfishness.

In addition, throughout the opening part of the story, the American tries to talk Jig into the abortion by telling her how simple it is. He claims superior knowledge and wants her to acquiesce. The moment, however, that she says she will have the abortion because *he* wants her to have it, the man says, "I don't want you to do it if you don't want to. I'm perfectly willing to go through with it if it means anything to you." The use of "it" in this line is revealing: it refers not only to the abortion, but to the baby as well. And although the American wants Jig to have the abortion, he does not want to assume the responsibility for it. Not only must she have the abortion to keep him, she must also agree to the abortion on his terms, as something she wants. In this story, Hemingway suggests that sometimes a man wants to control not only the situation he finds himself in, but also the reactions a woman has to the situation as well.

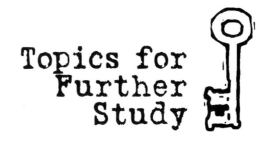

Topics for Further Study

- Read *The Sun Also Rises* and the other stories in *Men Without Women*. How do you characterize the human relationships portrayed by Hemingway in the books? What different kinds of relationships does Hemingway explore?

- Investigate the American expatriate community in Paris during the years 1920 through 1929. Who are the members of the community? What is their relationship to each other? How did their close affiliation affect their writing?

- The Treaty of Versailles ended the hostilities of the First World War. However, many historians argue that the terms of the treaty made the Second World War inevitable. Investigate the treaty and the years between the wars. Describe the connections between the Treaty of Versailles and movement toward World War II.

- The role and status of women changed dramatically during the years from 1920-1929. Investigate this shift by looking at representations of women in art, music, and literature. What does this investigation reveal about the relationship between the sexes at this time?

- Visit an art gallery, or check out books on art from your library. Examine art produced during the years between 1920 and 1929. How is this work different from the work produced during the last half of the nineteenth century? What might account for the dramatic shifts?

Style

Setting

In "Hills Like White Elephants" the setting serves both to locate the story in space and time and to function as an important symbol. The story is set in Spain, in the valley of the Ebro River. More immediately, the setting is a railway station "between two lines of rails in the sun." The American and the girl sit at a table. On one side of the station, the land is parched and desolate. A number of critics have noted the similarity between this landscape and that of T. S. Eliot's *The Wasteland.* On the other side of the station, there are trees and grain. By dividing the setting in half, with one side sterile and the other fertile, Hemingway uses the setting to reinforce the division between the couple. They can choose sterility through the abortion, or fertility through the pregnancy. The landscape outside the couple's conversation reflects the inner landscapes of the relationship.

Dialogue

The most striking feature of this story is that it is constructed almost entirely of dialogue. There are only seven short descriptive paragraphs that are not part of the dialogue itself. Further, there is very little action in the story: the girl walks from one side of the station to the other, they drink beer, and the man moves the luggage. By controlling the narrative so tightly, Hemingway forces the reader to participate in the scene almost as an eavesdropper. The reader ''hears'' the dialogue, but cannot break into the characters' inner thoughts. With so little else present, the weight and the meaning of the story depend on the reader's ability to decipher the cryptic comments the two characters make to each other. Hemingway himself once suggested that a short story is like the tip of an iceberg, the meaning of the story submerged beneath the written text. Certainly in ''Hills Like White Elephants,'' only the smallest portion of the story's subject is apparent, and the reader must guess at the rest.

Lost Generation

The term ''Lost Generation'' has come to apply to a group of young writers, most born around 1900, who fought in the First World War. As a group, the Lost Generation found that their understanding of life had been severely affected by their experiences during the war. Many of the Lost Generation lived in Europe, notably in Paris, during the post-War period. The term came from a comment that Gertrude Stein made to Hemingway, ''You are all a lost generation.'' Hemingway used the comment as a epigraph in his novel, *The Sun Also Rises.* Other writers included in this group are F. Scott Fitzgerald, Hart Crane, Louis Bromfield, and Malcolm Cowley.

The aimlessness of the characters in ''Hills Like White Elephants'' is one of the characteristics of the fiction of the Lost Generation. Jig and the Americans are expatriates, moving from place to place to ''look at things and try new drinks.'' They are people who live in hotels, out of luggage, rather than being rooted in one place. The lack of rootedness, then, becomes an important motif in the literature of this generation.

Historical Context

Europe Between the Wars

Hemingway wrote ''Hills Like White Elephants'' in 1926 while living in Paris. Europe between the First and Second World Wars provided the historical and cultural context for the story. Hemingway was twenty-two, newly married and ready to begin a career as a serious writer when he arrived in Paris in 1921. His experiences as an ambulance driver during World War I continued to affect him, and the sense of alienation and isolation characteristic of modernist writing can be found in the writing he produced during these years.

Europe was in the process of recovering from the war; however, it was a time of political and economic upheaval for most of the nations. Many nations suffered political struggles as right and left wing factions attempted to wrest control of their particular countries. In Italy, for example, strikes, violence, and political unrest led to the 1922 Fascist March on Rome. Mussolini established himself as dictator in that country. In Germany, the heavy reparations called for in the Treaty of Versailles that ended WWI caused economic chaos. The German mark steadily lost ground as the rate of inflation spiraled upward. Germans would rush to buy goods the moment they received cash because the value of their cash would decrease by the end of the day. The other nations of Europe, their countryside scarred and their young men dead or wounded, reeled under a deep and severe recession.

The Lost Generation

In the United States, however, the economy boomed. The stock market reached dizzying heights and the dollar enjoyed an extremely favorable rate of exchange with most European currencies. In addition, many young Americans had been in Europe during the War, allowing them to feel more comfortable in the different cultures. Armed with the strong American dollar and the familiarity with the language and culture, many writers found Paris a very attractive milieu—collectively, these writers became known as the ''Lost Generation.'' According to Michael Reynolds, some six thousand Americans lived in Paris at the end of 1921; by ''September 1924, the city's permanent American population was thirty thousand and rising.'' Hemingway brushed shoulders with many notable writers and literary figures while in Paris, including Ezra Pound, Gertrude Stein, Alice B. Toklas, F. Scott Fitzgerald, and James Joyce, among others.

Hemingway himself popularized the idea of a lost generation through his first novel, *The Sun Also Rises.* In his later memoir of the Paris years, *A Moveable Feast,* Hemingway writes of a conversation he had with the writer Gertrude Stein in which she called all young people who had been in the war ''a lost generation.'' Subsequently, Hemingway used Stein's comment as one of two epigraphs that open the book. Hemingway, perhaps better than any

Compare
&
Contrast

- **1920s:** Post-war American economy roars, fueled by a growing stock market. Credit is easy, and fortunes are made and lost in a day. The culture becomes increasingly consumer-oriented as new technology puts desirable products into the hands of the middle classes.

  1990s: The United States enjoys a period of nearly unprecedented prosperity. Credit is easy, and the stock market spirals upward. The growth of technology has made computers, video games, digital cameras, and cell phones affordable for the middle classes.

- **1920s:** Women finally receive the right to vote in the United States. They use their new-found voting power to make the consumption of alcohol illegal in the United States through a Constitutional Amendment prohibiting the making or sale of alcohol. Women work outside the home, and the ''flapper'' becomes the symbol for a generation of young women.

  1990s: Women hold elected offices, serve on the Unites States Supreme Court, and manage large corporations. Nevertheless, the earning power of women still lags behind that of men. Sexual discrimination and harassment laws protect women from being fired or demoted because of their gender.

- **1920s:** Abortions are illegal in most countries in Europe and in the United States. Nevertheless, many women have abortions, and many die from poorly performed illegal abortions. Because there is no reliable means of birth control, and because of the great social stigma against unmarried mothers, women endanger their own lives rather than endure social censure.

  1990s: Abortions are legal in the United States. In Spain, abortions have been legal since 1985. In the United States, a growing segment of the population believes that abortion is wrong, with some anti-abortion activists turning to violence. Abortion doctors are murdered and abortion clinics subject to bombings and violent demonstrations.

- **1920s:** Modernism, the sense that the old ways of doing things no longer apply, takes hold of art, literature, and culture in Europe and the United States. Artists experiment with new forms and subject matter. In spite of disillusionment with human enterprise, the modernists still believe that art and literature can say something important about reality.

  1990s: Postmodernism grows in response to modernism, now deemed worn out and old. Literature becomes self-reflective and meta-fictional. Reality seems to splinter into ever smaller fragments; truth becomes increasingly contingent.

---

other writer of his generation, captured the sense of waste and loss and the resulting aimlessness that the War engendered in the young people of his era.

Social Change

The years between the war were ones of rapid social change. In the United States, the economic boom caused by easy credit and technology allowed people to own products as never before. Middle class people were able to own cars, radios, and telephones.

Social change was reflected in other important ways as well. Perhaps most important, women received the right to vote in 1920 and entered the work force in growing numbers. Women bared their legs, lit up cigarettes, and cut their hair. Such expressions of emancipation threatened traditional male values, and the clash between the genders figured in many of the literary works of the day.

Many writers left the United States, preferring the less restrictive morality of Europe. Disillusioned with civilized society, alienated from traditional values, and shell-shocked from a brutal War, these writers experimented with literary form, content, and style.

Critical Overview

Hemingway's ''Hills Like White Elephants'' first appeared in the magazine *transition* in August, 1927, and within a few months appeared again in the collection *Men Without Women. The Sun Also Rises,* Hemingway's 1926 novel of life in Paris and Pamplona, had already secured the author's reputation as the spokesperson for his generation. *Men Without Women* further solidified critical approval of his early work. ''Hills Like White Elephants'' was singled out for special attention from reviewers. For example, Dorothy Parker, enamored with Hemingway and his prose, called the story in an early review ''delicate and tragic.'' She further added, ''I do not know where a greater collection of stories can be found.''

Virginia Woolf, on the other hand, did not seem appreciate Hemingway or his prose. Her review, contemporary with the publication of the story, was filled with what could be termed ''left-handed compliments.'' For example, she wrote, ''There are . . . many stories which, if life were longer, one would wish to read again. Most of them indeed are so competent, so efficient, and so bare of superfluity that one wonders why they do not make a deeper dent in the mind than they do.'' She criticized Hemingway for ''excessive'' dialogue and ''lack of proportion.''

A final contemporary reviewer, Cyril Connolly, offered a more balanced critique of *Men Without Women.* He wrote that the volume ''is a collection of grim little stories told in admirable colloquial dialogue with no point, no moral and no ornamentation.'' Although he called Hemingway's work ''irritating,'' he also found the stories ''readable and full of . . . power and freshness.''

In the years after the initial publication of the story, an increasing number of critics have offered readings of ''Hills Like White Elephants.'' Indeed, as the story began to appear ever more frequently in anthologies of short stories and American literature textbooks, it also generated many critical articles. Criticism of the story most generally focuses on

structural issues, such as the use of dialogue and/or figurative language; examines the sources, analogues, and biographical material used in the story; or discusses Hemingway's construction of gender and language.

Robert Paul Lamb, for example, has studied Hemingway's role in the development of twentieth-century literary dialogue. He argues that in ''Hills Like White Elephants,'' Hemingway ''blurred the line between fiction and drama, allowing dialogue an unprecedented constructive role in a story's composition.'' He demonstrates the way that the dialogue simultaneously reveals and hides the subject of the story.

Other critics such as Howard L. Hannum concentrate on the symbolism of the story, exploring the many meanings of the term ''white elephant'' and the contrast between the fertility and sterility of each side of the railway station. He also noted the story's connection to T. S. Eliot's *The Waste Land* in his discussion.

An important way of reading the story for many critics has been to examine gender and communication. Pamela Smiley, for example, in a 1990 article, discusses the story in terms of gender marked language, basing her analysis on the gender communication theory of Deborah Tannen. Peter Messent includes a chapter called ''Gender Role and Sexuality'' in his book-length study of Hemingway. He argues that ''Hemingway's texts show divided attitudes to matters of sexual politics.'' Further, Messent writes, while many of Hemingway's stories privilege the male protagonists, ''Hills Like White Elephants'' is a story in which ''''women's sensibilities' are certainly not ignored but rather highlighted in an extremely sensitive manner.'' Messent points out that it may be for this reason that the story has become more frequently anthologized in recent years. Finally, critic Stanley Renner in a 1995 article argues that a close analysis of the language reveals that the story's ending is not as ambiguous as most readers have thought. He believes that Jig's final words reveal that she has decided to keep the baby. For Renner, the story ''side[s] with its female character's values'' and ''understands and sensitively dramatizes her struggle to take charge of her own arena, to have a say about the direction of her own life.''

In addition to this sampling of critical approaches, many other critics have undertaken readings of the story. Such variety and diversity in

La Casa Verda visitors' center, Ebro delta National Park, Spain. The hills seen in the background are part of the same range as in "Hills Like White Elephants."

approach suggest that "Hills Like White Elephants" is a rich and open story, one that will continue to engender multiple readings from its many readers.

Criticism

Diane Andrews Henningfeld

Henningfeld is an Associate Professor of English at Adrian College, in Adrian, Michigan. She writes widely on literature and history for a variety of academic and educational publishers. In the following essay, she discusses the tragic and comic elements of "Hills Like White Elephants," placing these elements within the context of modernism.

In 1927, Ernest Hemingway completed and published his collection of short stories, *Men Without Women*. The collection included several important stories, stories that have been closely examined by critics almost since the day of their publication. Among the stories in the collection, however, "Hills

What Do I Read Next?

- *The Sun Also Rises* (1926) is a semi-autobiographical account of Hemingway's post-World War I experience as an expatriate. The well-received novel earned Hemingway the title of spokesperson for his generation.

- *Where I'm Calling From: New and Selected Stories,* (1988) is a collection by short story writer Raymond Carver. Most critics agree that Carver's style was influenced by Hemingway's early stories.

- Michael Reynolds's *Hemingway: The Paris Years* (1989) is a careful examination of Hemingway's expatriate period in Paris as a member of the "Lost Generation." The time period covered includes the years when Hemingway wrote and published "Hills Like White Elephants."

- *A Moveable Feast* (1964) is Hemingway's memoir of his years as a young writer in Paris. Hemingway worked on the manuscript during 1957 and 1958, and the volume was published after his death in 1961.

Like White Elephants'' has become the most widely anthologized and the most frequently taught. The story continues to generate scholarly interest and heated debate among students.

"Hills Like White Elephants" is a very short story. Only about one thousand words, the story itself is comprised almost entirely of dialogue. Although there is a situation, there is no plot; although there are words spoken between the main characters, there is no resolution. The topic of their conversation, an abortion, is never even mentioned by name by either of the characters. In spite of the brevity of the story, and in spite of the absences created by the dialogue, scholars continue to produce pages and pages of critical commentary. Such critical interest at least suggests that the story is a rich, open text, one that invites reader participation in the process of meaning-making.

The story appears deceptively simple. A man and a woman sit at a table at a Spanish railway station, waiting for a train. They engage in a conversation, Hemingway seems to suggest, that has been going on for some time. The reader is dropped in the middle of the conversation without context and must glean what information he or she can from the words the characters say. The setting of the story is contemporary with its writing; that is, although there is no definite mention of the date, it seems to be set sometime during the years after the First World War, but before the Spanish Civil War. In addition, the setting is narrowly limited both in time and space. The story is framed by the narrative announcement in the first paragraph that the "express from Barcelona would come in forty minutes" and by the Spanish woman's announcement near the end of the story, "The train comes in five minutes." Thus, all of the story takes place within the thirty-five minutes. In addition, the characters never leave the train station itself.

There are several important ways that critics have read "Hills Like White Elephants." Some concentrate on the structure of the story, noting the use of dialogue and the placement of the few short descriptive passages. John Hollander, for example, suggests that the story develops the way a film or play might develop and that the short descriptive passages read almost like stage directions. Other critics develop careful and complicated readings of the story based on word level analysis, examining the way that Hemingway uses allusion, simile, imagery, and symbolism. Some of these critics also include an examination of Hemingway's sources, connecting the story to T. S. Eliot's modernist masterpiece, *The Wasteland.* A more recent group of scholars concentrates on the use of gender-marked language in the story, looking closely at the different ways the American and Jig use language to communicate. Still others try to use Hemingway's autobiographical manuscripts and letters to read parts of Hemingway's life into the story. However, the fact that so many critics read this story in so many ways does not mean that the story is flawed; it means, rather, that it is a text that invites participation. As Paul Smith argues, Hemingway does not tell the reader "how the characters arrived at their present condition, or how they will resolve their conflict; we do not need to be told, for the answers are embedded in what we so briefly do see and hear." Although Smith seems to suggest in this statement that the "answers" are there for the reading, it is possible to arrive at a multiplicity of answers, using the same lines of text.

In an early review of the story, Dorothy Parker described the story as "delicate and tragic." Although it is unlikely that Parker meant to suggest that "Hills Like White Elephants" is a tragedy in the classical Greek sense of the word, it is possible to use her statement as an entry point into the story. An examination of both the comic and the tragic elements reveals how these ideas function in the story, and how modernism has transformed the ideas themselves.

To begin, it is important to make clear that the term "comic" here does not imply humor, or laughter. In this discussion, "comedy" does not refer to a television situation comedy that is designed to be funny. Rather, for the purpose of this discussion comedy is a shape that fiction can take. Comedy has its roots in the fertility rituals of spring. It celebrates marriage, sexual union, birth, and the perpetuation of society. Comedy is not always light-hearted, however; it frequently carries with it pain, frustration, and near-catastrophe. The threat of death is always located in the underside of comedy. Ultimately, however, it is the triumph over death that gives comedy its characteristic shape.

Tragedy, on the other hand, has its roots in death and sterility. It announces the end of the line, the end of a family, the end of society. Its characteristic images are winter and wasteland. Modernism, the period of literature generally placed as beginning during World War I, reflects the culture's loss of history, tradition, and certainty in the face of the War's carnage, made possible by human-made technology. Modernism reduces the scope of the tragic in literature, focusing on smaller characters in more limited settings. Unlike the tragedies of the past, they no longer need to be about larger than life characters, trapped by their own tragic flaws. Rath-

> "Hemingway leaves his characters as he found them, in the middle of something larger, outside the margins of the story."

er, tragic movement can be seen in the alienation and isolation of contemporary life. Modernist tragedy tends to emphasize ironic detachment and T. S. Eliot's quiet, "not with a bang but a whimper" ending.

Close examination of "Hills Like White Elephants" reveals that Jig and the American are in a moment that teeters on the border between the comic and the tragic. They are at a moment of decision, one that will push them one way or the other. The landscape around them reflects both possible futures. On the one side of the station, the land is fertile and green. The water from the river nourishes new life. This is the comic landscape, the landscape of regeneration. On the other side of the station, the land is bleak and dusty, lacking in sustenance and life. The American, an essentially flawed character, fails to note the dichotomy of the landscape. His vision is limited by his own needs and desires. He lives in the perpetual "now," wanting only momentary pleasure, not lasting growth. The girl's pregnancy, a state that necessarily points toward the future, has upset his equilibrium in the moment. Acknowledging the pregnancy itself forces him to acknowledge the future. Strikingly, he never mentions the word "pregnancy" in the entire story, as if the mere mention of the word will both implicate and complicate his life.

Jig, on the other hand, seems highly aware of the precipice on which she stands. What she wishes for is the comic resolution, one in which the American will marry her, they will return home, and they will establish a family. She will participate in the birth of the next generation, and will focus her attention forward. However, she also realizes that what she wishes for is not likely what she will get. When she stands and walks to the end of the station, she observes the fertile valley of the Ebro in front of her, and she understands the connection between that landscape and the future she desires. As Barry Stampfl argues, ''Jig indicates the truth about her relation with the American and about her feelings for her unborn baby by talking about landscapes.''

In some ways, this is a choric moment, that is, a moment when a detached observer makes a judgement about the characters and their actions. In this tiny story, Jig must play the part of her own chorus. At this moment, Jig stands outside herself and sees the larger situation. Looking out over the valley she says, ''And we could have all this. . . . And we could have everything and every day we make it more impossible.'' It is as if she realizes that the comic ending is slipping away from her. She may be about to play a role in a modernist tragedy, a tragedy in which she finds herself, at best, isolated and alone, keenly aware of the absence of life in her womb. At its worst, she may find herself dying in an abortion clinic, surrounded by people who do not speak her language.

Unlike traditional comedies and tragedies, however, ''Hills Like White Elephants'' does not offer a recognizable resolution. Rather, the end of the story is inconclusive, the possible endings fragmented. For Jig, the longing for the fertile valley is both a longing for an Edenic past and the longing for progeny to carry on into the future. Neither of her choices offers the fulfillment of that longing, and she knows it. The American's glance at their suitcases covered with hotel labels signals his desire to remain in the permanent present, a present without past or future. Again, regardless of their choice, the man's desire will remain unfulfilled.

The story ends, the train still five minutes down the track. Frozen in the space between comic and tragic resolution, the characters remain, Jig and the American, the conversation ended. Although critics, academics, readers, and students may argue about what will ''happen next,'' the truth is that nothing happens to the characters after the story ends. Hemingway leaves his characters as he found them, in the middle of something larger, outside the margins of the story. Jig and the American truly come to represent the lost generation at this moment. Without resolution, each isolated and alienated from the other, they remain in the no man's land of inconclusivity, the possibility of tradition and continuity represented by the fertile valley just outside of their reach.

Source: Diane Andrews Henningfeld, Overview of ''Hills Like White Elephants,'' for *Short Stories for Students*, The Gale Group, 1999.

Kenneth G. Johnston

In the following essay, Johnston examines Hemingway's ''theory of omission'' and its effect on his prose style.

His stories came back in the mail, slipped through the slit in the saw-mill door where he lived, ''with notes of rejection that would never call them stories, but always anecdotes, sketches, contes, etc. They did not want them, and we lived on poireaux and drank cahors and water.'' Those were the early, lean years in Paris when Ernest Hemingway was submitting to the discipline of hunger and to the discipline of his new theory of fiction: ''That you could omit anything if you knew that you omitted and the omitted part would strengthen the story and make people feel something more than they understood'':

> Well, I thought, now I have them so they do not understand them. There cannot be much doubt about that. There is most certainly no demand for them. But they will understand the same way they always do in painting. It only takes time and it only needs confidence.

Time has proven Hemingway right, although his short fiction based on the theory of ''omission'' is not universally admired, or fully understood, not even by some of his fellow craftsmen. Frank O'Connor, for instance, complains that ''Hills Like White Elephants'' does not provide the reader with enough information to make the necessary moral judgments. ''The light is admirably focused,'' admits O'Connor, ''but it is too blinding; we cannot see into the shadows.''

One does not take lightly criticism by a short story writer of O'Connor's stature and talent, but O'Connor is wrong. The reader can see, clearly and deeply, into the shadows if he submits to the discipline of close reading and fleshes out the implications of this lean story. A rich pattern of dialogue, setting, action, and allusion is carefully woven into ''Hills Like White Elephants.'' With swift, sure strokes, without a wasted word or motion, Hemingway creates a taut, tense story of conflict in a moral wasteland.

''Hills Like White Elephants'' opens quietly. The day is hot, and a young couple, who are waiting for the train from Barcelona, are relaxing in the shade of the station and discussing the small matter of ordering a cool drink. When the girl remarks that the hills across the valley look like white elephants, an argument flares, but is quickly extinguished by the girl. But moments later it flares again, this time sparked by references to licorice and absinthe. These small clashes, one gradually realizes, are part of a larger conflict that centers on the question of abortion. Hemingway makes no mention of that key word, nor does he explicitly state that the conflict has been smoldering and flaring for weeks. But since nearly every topic of conversation rekindles the argument, it is quite apparent that this is not the first time that this vital issue has been discussed. The unborn child is dominating the couple's thoughts and emotions and has been for some time. The man's impatience with the girl is attributable in part to his anger at discovering, with the bags all packed, and apparently with the final decision made, that the issue is not settled at all. Now, once again, they resume their intense dialogue, with the unborn child's life hanging in the balance. . . .

Hemingway has skillfully used the setting in "Hills Like White Elephants" to help reveal and reinforce situation, characterization, and theme. The Spanish setting contributes to the ironic tone of the story, for the moral drama takes place in a predominantly Catholic country where the church stands in firm opposition to abortion. However, the girl does not understand Spanish, a fact which helps to reveal her essential helplessness and dependency. She is a stranger in a foreign land where her male companion is her only interpreter and guide. Their rootless existence is symbolized by the train station and by their baggage, with "labels on them from all the hotels where they spent nights." The station sits between two lines of rails to suggest the two directions in which the couple may go—toward Madrid and the abortion or away from Madrid toward a settled, family life. The description of the Ebro valley embodies the poles of the conflict too: It is both barren and fruitful. On the side which they sit facing, there are no trees and no shade, and in the distance the country is brown and dry; on the other side of the valley, there are "fields of grain and trees along the banks of the Ebro." Only the girl looks at the fruitful side of the valley where she glimpses the life-giving water through the trees. But as she watches the scene, "the shadow of a cloud moved across the field of grain," foreshadowing the death of her unborn child. (This shadow line is one of several important revisions that Hemingway made in a titled pencil manuscript of "Hills Like White Elephants": He changed "The girl looked away" to "The girl looked at the ground the table legs rested on"; He inserted "The girl looked at the bead curtain, put her hand out and took hold of two of the strings of beads"; He inserted "The shadow of a

> "The reader can see, clearly and deeply, into the shadows if he submits to the discipline of close reading and fleshes out the implications of this lean story. A rich pattern of dialogue, setting, action, and allusion is carefully woven into 'Hills Like White Elephants.'"

cloud moved across the field of grain and she saw the river through the trees.")

The hills like white elephants also serve to remind one of the couple's conflicting views on abortion. A white elephant, in one meaning of the term, is anything rare, expensive, and difficult to keep; any burdensome possession; an object no longer esteemed by its owner though not without value to others. This is basically how the man feels about the unwanted child. On the other hand, a white elephant is also a rare pale-gray variety of Asian elephant held sacred by the Burmese and Siamese. The girl's reverence for life is captured by this meaning of the phrase. Her reluctance to have the abortion and the enormity of her sacrifice when she finally capitulates to the man's insistent demands are clearly suggested by her revealing gesture involving the beaded bamboo curtain. The curtain hangs across the open door to the bar to keep out the flies, and it is repeatedly called to the reader's attention during the story. It is the girl who first comments on the curtain because she is curious about the Spanish words painted on it. A short time later, when her companion is pressuring her to submit to the operation, "the girl looked at the bead curtain, put her hand out and took hold of two of the strings of beads," as though clutching the beads of a rosary to give her the moral courage to resist. One need not argue that she is a Catholic, but this scene makes it quite clear that she is calling upon her moral and religious strength in her moment of crisis.

On the other hand, the man brushes aside such considerations; at story's end, "he went out through the bead curtain."

The girl is sympathetically portrayed in "Hills Like White Elephants." She is the man's superior in imagination, sensitivity, and capacity for love. She has the imagination to see white elephants, whereas the earthbound man can see only long white hills. No doubt she is thinking of her swelling pregnancy as she gazes at the swollen mounds of earth. "'They're lovely hills,' she said, 'They don't really look like white elephants. I just meant the coloring of their skin through the trees'." She senses truly the nature of her dilemma. Her instincts tell her that their relationship will be radically altered, perhaps destroyed, if she goes through with the abortion. But if she refuses, she knows full well that he will leave her: "I'd do anything for you," he declares, yet he refuses to respond to her silent and sounded pleas for child and family or to take seriously her premonitions of future unhappiness and irreparable loss. His pledge is an empty gesture: "I'm perfectly willing to go through with it if it means anything to you," he insists, revealing his appalling insincerity and insensitivity. As the girl looks out across the grain fields toward the river, she remarks prophetically, "We could have everything and every day we make it more impossible." "What did you say?" he asks. He is not even listening. Finally, against her better judgment, her instincts, and her moral principles, she agrees to "do it," because "I don't care about me." The man does not understand. But her reason is a simple one: she cares about him; she loves him. The man is puzzled because he is incapable of such an act of selflessness, which is the truest expression of love.

The man, identified only as an American, is the villain of the piece. He is a selfish, insensitive, emotional bully, the eternal adolescent who refuses to put down roots or to shoulder the responsibilities which are rightfully his. His empty, barren life style is summed up by the girl: "That's all we do, isn't it—look at things and try new drinks." But he will not be baited into a review of the past. The girl is well aware that the intrusion of a child will send the man packing, for he will not tolerate any hindrance to his vagabond, hedonistic life style. He makes no secret of the fact that the "thing" definitely "bothers" him and makes him "unhappy." One even detects a veiled threat of abandonment beneath his "if-you-don't-want-to-you-don't-have-to" declarations. He makes his position very clear: "I don't want anybody but you. I don't want any one else." And there are no bonds of legal marriage to hold him if he should tire of their arrangement.

One of the drinks that apparently reminds them both of their passionate past is absinthe, the highly potent (140 to 160 proof), green alcoholic drink. It is the "forbidden" drink, outlawed in France, Switzerland, the United States, and other countries, but still legal in Spain. It was banned because it acts powerfully on the nervous system and is thought to cause sterility. However, it is also popularly believed to be an aphrodisiac and, thus, held in high esteem by pleasure seekers. The taste of Anis del Toro reminds the girl of the licorice taste of absinthe, but her remark irritates the man: "Oh, cut it out," he snaps. Very likely he introduced her to absinthe, too, in hopes that she would become sexually aroused. Now he wishes to be rid of the unwanted by-product of that passion. He is not amused by such ironic references. But it is doubtful that he has the wit to perceive the further irony of linking absinthe, with its connotations of forbidden fruit, to sterility and abortion. Quite obviously he does not appreciate the irony of his own remarks when he refers to the abortion as "an awfully simple operation," "perfectly natural," and "perfectly simple."

At story's end, with the train due in five minutes, the man leaves the girl to take the baggage to the other side of the station. He then stops off at the bar inside to have a drink alone. The people there, he observes, "were all waiting reasonably for the train." As he sees it, he is the calm voice of reason, the rational man who must convince the emotional, irrational girl that "the best thing" for him is "the best thing" for her. (The titled pencil manuscript of "Hills Like White Elephants" at the Kennedy Library exhibits Hemingway's talent for honing a scene. Hemingway originally wrote: "He drank an anis at the bar and looked at the people. There must be some actual world[.] There must be some place you could touch where people were calm and reasonable. Once it had all been as simple as this bar." He changed this to read: "He drank an anis at the bar and looked at the people. They were all waiting reasonably for the train.") The signs of the man's discontent are quite ominous. His implicit criticism of the unreasonable girl and, more important, his seeking a moment of pleasure apart from her, tend to confirm the girl's dark premonitions and to hint at some future dissolution of their relationship, some later permanent abandonment. Meanwhile, the emotionally drained girl looks out toward the dry side of the valley and waits for the train that will speed her toward the irreversible moment.

Source: Kenneth G. Johnston, "'Hills Like White Elephants': Lean, Vintage Hemingway," in *Studies in American Fiction,* Vol. 10, No. 2, Autumn, 1982, pp. 233–38.

Lewis E. Weeks, Jr.

In the following essay, Weeks discusses the imagery and symbolism in "Hills Like White Elephants," focusing specifically on the image suggested by the title.

Although subject, setting, point of view, characterization, dialog, irony, and compression all make "Hills Like White Elephants" one of Hemingway's most brilliant short stories, the symbolism implicit in the title and developed in the story contributes more than any other single quality to the powerful impact.

Emphasis by position and repetition clearly suggests the importance Hemingway attached to the comparison. Besides the reference in the title, there are, within this very short three-page story, two references to the whiteness of the hills and four to them as white elephants, although one of these suggests that the hills do not look like white elephants but only have their coloring.

On first reading the title, one assumes the comparison may merely be to the color and to the rounded contour of the hills that constitute part of the setting, a quite literal reference. This impression is reinforced by the first sentence, the subject of which is "long and white" hills. The second time they are mentioned, they are contrasted with the countryside, which is brown and dry, suggestive of the limitations and aridity of the relationship of the man and woman, which begins to unfold and which is the basis of the conflict and the meaning of the story.

Then only twenty lines into the story, the young woman remarks for the first time that the hills look like white elephants; and the first hint of tension between her and the man appears in his ironic reply, "I've never seen one," and her retaliation, "No, you wouldn't have." Although they seem to talk of trivia in the next four lines of dialog, the tension increases; and it is apparent that an argument is about to erupt or re-erupt. Talk of the drink Anis del Toro, that they have just tried and that tasted like licorice, leads her to say, "Everything tastes of licorice, especially all the things you've waited so

> The richness, complexity, and irony of the white elephant symbol increases as we see the conflict over the unborn child develop and as we recall that the actual white elephant is a rarity in nature, is considered sacred and precious, and is revered and protected."

long for, like absinthe." The implication as to the casualness and triviality of their lives, in which drinks are of such importance, and the further ironic implication in the bitterness of absinthe, with its wormwood basis, is made apparent. In addition, the belief in absinthe as an aphrodisiac adds another ironic twist to its mention. Color symbolism involving the blackness of licorice and the whiteness of the hills suggests the contrast between sorrow and joy as has the already mentioned contrast between the white hills and the brown, dry countryside. The living green color of absinthe also suggests a contrast with the dry drabness of the countryside.

As the tension increases between the couple, he tries to smooth things over by saying, "Well, let's try to have a fine time." She replies, "All right, I was trying. I said the mountains looked like white elephants. Wasn't that bright?" He agrees, and she continues, making explicit her opinion of the shallowness of their life together, "That's all we do, isn't it—look at things and try new drinks?" He tentatively acquiesces; and she looks across at the hills, saying, "They're lovely hills. They don't really look like white elephants. I just meant the coloring of their skin through the trees." His unconsciously ironic reply is to offer her another drink. Immediately afterwards and for the first time, we learn what the problem is through his reference to an "awfully simple operation . . . not really an operation at all . . . just to let the air in." She is pregnant, and he wants her to have an abortion.

Immediately the symbolic significance of the title and the reason for the frequent mention of the hills becomes apparent. A number of images and emotional reactions flood the reader's mind as the dialog swiftly makes clear that the girl wants the baby, not the abortion, which he says will make no difference in their relationship and which hypocritically he persists in assuring her he does not want if she objects to it.

The final reference to the hills occurs about halfway through the story in the girl's plaintive but skeptical appeal that, if she does go through with the abortion, "it will be nice again if I say things are like white elephants, and you'll like it?" Our immediate understanding of the white elephant reference when we learn that the story's conflict revolves around an unwanted pregnancy is probably that associated with the ubiquitous white elephant sale. These sales raise money for worthwhile causes by providing an opportunity for people to donate unwanted objects, white elephants, which will be sold at low prices to people who can find some use for them or think they can. To the man, the child is a white elephant that, in his selfishness, he wants to get rid of. To the girl, the child is a white elephant only insofar as its father rejects it; she would like to bear the child.

Another association and image surely comes to mind in terms of the comparison and is encouraged by the third reference, involving the skin of the hills. This image is of the fully pregnant woman, nude and probably lying on her back with her distended belly virtually bursting with life and with her breasts, engorged by the approaching birth, making a trinity of white hills. However, this image, stimulating as it does, the sense of wonder at the miraculous process of pregnancy and the remarkable elasticity and resiliency of the human body is one that will not blossom into birth for this couple. The man will not permit it; and the woman will be denied the fulfillment of motherhood, the loving support of the child's co-creator throughout the period of pregnancy, the shared joy of the birth, and the care and nurture of the child.

The richness, complexity, and irony of the white elephant symbol increases as we see the conflict over the unborn child develop and as we recall that the actual white elephant is a rarity in nature, is considered sacred and precious, and is revered and protected. Moreover, we may remember that Buddha's mother, Mahamaya, before his birth, dreamed of a beautiful silvery white elephant that entered her womb through her side. The priestly interpretation of this dream was, of course, that she would give birth to a son who would become either a universal ruler or a Buddha.

However, like the story's white elephant child, the actual white elephant is also paradoxical in its nature. On the one hand, it is rare and valuable, associated with potentates, the royal elephant, and has sacred attributes and spiritual powers. On the other hand, the figurative use of the term as a gift or possession that is worthless, a burden, even harmful, or overwhelmingly troublesome is said to derive from the fact that the white elephant has an enormous appetite and, being sacred, can neither be disposed of nor used as a beast of burden but must be cared for and treated with care, respect, and concern until it dies. Consequently, if a king or potentate had an enemy to whom he wished ill, he could present him with a white elephant, ostensibly a mark of singular favor but in reality a burden whose expensive upkeep might bring ruin and would certainly confer hardship.

Hemingway's use of the white elephant symbol in his title and throughout the story has immeasurably enriched this poignant episode, with its insight into the complexities, the disappointments, and the sadness of life's "might-have-beens." It is a particularly significant story for our times when radical changes in traditional sexual morality and the issue of legalized abortion seem to emphasize the age-old problem presented in "Hills Like White Elephants."

Source: Lewis E. Weeks, Jr., "Hemingway Hills: Symbolism in 'Hills Like White Elephants'," in *Studies in Short Fiction*, Vol. 17, No. 1, Winter, 1980, pp. 75–77.

Reid Maynard

In the following essay, Maynard explores the ironic manner in which symbols of unity operate in "Hills Like White Elephants."

Ernest Hemingway's short story "Hills Like White Elephants" is about a selfish man who wants his girl friend to have an abortion so that they can continue to have fun and be unencumbered by a child. The man's callousness and sterile view are contrasted with the girl's sensitive, sensuous response to life. As an ironic contrast to their present disunified relationship, a leitmotif of oneness, or unity, threads through the story. This leitmotif takes the form of the repetition, with variation, of the word *two*.

Before considering scenic irony and the leitmotif of unity, we should first observe the general features of the scene. The first paragraph creates the stage on which all of the action, what little there is, and dialogue take place (the leitmotif is also unobtrusively introduced in this description—but more about it later):

> The hills across the valley of the Ebro were long and white. On this side there was no shade and no trees and the station was between two lines of rails in the sun. Close against the side of the station there was the warm shadow of the building and a curtain, made of strings of bamboo beads, hung across the open door into the bar, to keep out flies. The American and the girl with him sat at a table in the shade, outside the building. It was very hot and the express from Barcelona would come in forty minutes. It stopped at this junction for two minutes and went on to Madrid.

The man and the girl are appropriately positioned on a sterile, wasteland plain with "no shade and no trees." In the distance are objects that are symbolic of a sensuous, fertile, pure, natural life: "Across, on the other side, were fields of grain and trees along the banks of the Ebro. Far away, beyond the river, were mountains." The mountains and the river and the fields of grain are as far removed from the railway station café as the man's and girl's present strained relationship is removed from their past close relationship. When the girl wistfully views the distant scene, "the shadow of a cloud" moves "across the field of grain" and distorts the purity of her nostalgic vision, bringing her thoughts back to the sordid present. The "hills like white elephants" and other objects in the distance suggest to the girl the sensuous beauty of a love relation that is quickly deteriorating, now that she has become conscious of her lover's selfishness.

Since these images suggest the man's and the girl's past experience, they are appropriately in the background of the story's canvas. In the center of this prose painting is the railway station, where the Barcelona express stops for two minutes on its way to Madrid. The description of the station's position between the two railway lines subtly introduces the leitmotif of "two," to be reiterated in the story, but in this single instance "two" appears in an image of division or separation and suggests the actual state of the lovers; i.e., it is not an ironic "two." "Two" in "two minutes" is unobtrusively reiterated and prepares the way for the oneness, or unity, images of "two" which follow. All of these oneness or unity images operate ironically in the story, for they suggest a kind of life (symbolized by the river, mountains, and fields) which is the direct opposite of the life now being experienced by the couple. These images are of course integrated smoothly into

> " The 'hills like white elephants' and other objects in the distance suggest to the girl the sensuous beauty of a love relation that is quickly deteriorating, now that she has become conscious of her lover's selfishness."

the literal level of the story, as such symbolic images are in all of Hemingway's works. Symbols should not stand out like raisins in raisin bread, Hemingway felt.

So far, I have mentioned only two appearances of "two," both of them in the first paragraph. More such images are needed if a leitmotif strand is to be established. And they are present: "Dos cervezas," "two glasses of beer," "two felt pads," and "two anis del Toro" are images of paired objects in which the two entities of each pair are alike and, as it were, unified. These images serve as ironic contrasts to the divided couple sitting at the table, who, because of their quite different responses to life, are so unlike each other that they cannot in any sense be considered a unified pair. Not one of these "two" images would be construed as a symbol if it were seen only in terms of its literal function in an isolated context. But, collectively, the piling-up of "two" images suggests that their connotative meanings are of more significance in the story than their literal functions.

When the man callously tells the girl that her pregnancy is the only thing which has made them unhappy, the girl, deeply hurt, looks at the bead curtain and takes "hold of two of the strings of beads." Since she knows that what they once had together can never again be the same, she subconsciously reaches out to take hold of that which is lost to them. Here again their former union is suggested to the reader by the reiterated "two" motif, which at this point in the story has been established and which is now emphatically objectified, or made tangible, by the two strings of beads. And the repetition of "two" is continued in the images of "two heavy bags" and in the reappearance of "two glasses" and two "damp felt pads."

One aspect of the girl's sensitive, sensuous response to life is her fertile imagination. For example, she imagines that the hills have the skin of white elephants. "They look like white elephants," she says to the man. "I've never seen one," he replies. "No, you wouldn't have," she says, realizing that he is incapable of sharing her fancy. Since elephants, which are herbivorous animals, live in areas of vegetation, perhaps the girl associates them with such images of fertility as the grain fields and the river. Or maybe their largeness and shape suggest a pregnant woman. Or perhaps their whiteness marks them as unnatural elephants—sports—and suggests the unnatural aspects of the abortion the girl fears so much. These are only conjectures. The point is that in looking at the hills she can respond imaginatively, while the man cannot.

Later, her imagination subdued by the man's flat replies, the girl says, "They don't really look like white elephants. I just meant the coloring of their skin through the trees." But the hills still look like white elephants to the girl. The title, "Hills Like White Elephants," and the oneness motif both represent her attitude, which is an imaginative, sensuous, warm appreciation of life.

No matter what the girl and the man do now, the man's selfish desire to avoid complications has hurt them beyond repair. Their present state has a tragic aura that pervades the scene, and their pathetic condition is largely manifested by the ironic contrast provided by the leitmotif of oneness.

Source: Reid Maynard, "Leitmotif and Irony in Hemingway's 'Hills Like White Elephants'," in *The University Review,* Vol. XXXVII, No. 4, Summer, 1971, pp. 273–5.

Sources

Connolly, Cyril. A review of *Men Without Women. New Statesman,* November 26, 1927, p. 208.

Hannum, Howard L. "'Jig Jig to dirty ears': White Elephants to Let." *The Hemingway Review,* Vol. 11, No. 1, Fall, 1991, pp. 46-54.

Hollander, John. "Hemingway's Extraordinary Reality." *Ernest Hemingway,* edited and with an introduction by Harold Bloom, New York: Chelsea House Publishers, 1985, pp. 211-6.

Lamb, Robert Paul. "Hemingway and the Creation of Twentieth Century Dialogue." *Twentieth Century Literature,* Vol. 42, Winter, 1996, pp. 453-80.

Messent, Peter. *Ernest Hemingway,* New York: St. Martin's Press, 1992, pp. 90-92.

Parker, Dorothy. A review of *Men Without Women. New Yorker,* October 29, 1927, pp. 92-4.

Renner, Stanley. "Moving to the Girl's Side of 'Hills Like White Elephants'." *The Hemingway Review,* Vol. 15, No. 1, Fall, 1995, pp. 27-41.

Reynolds, Michael. *Hemingway: The Paris Years,* Oxford: Basil Blackwell, 1989.

Smiley, Pamela. "Gender-Linked Miscommunication in 'Hills Like White Elephants'." In *New Critical Approaches to the Short Stories of Ernest Hemingway,* edited by Jackson J. Benson, Duke University Press, 1990, pp. 288-99.

Smith, Paul. "Introduction: Hemingway and the Practical Reader." In *New Essays on Hemingway's Short Fiction,* Cambridge University Press, 1998, pp. 1-18.

Stampfl, Barry. "Similes as Thematic Clues in Three Hemingway Short Stories." *The Hemingway Review,* Vol. 10, No. 2, Spring 1991, pp. 30-8.

Woolf, Virginia. A review of *Men Without Women. New York Herald Tribune Books,* October 9, 1927, pp. 1, 8.

Further Reading

Meyers, Jeffrey, editor. *Hemingway: The Critical Heritage,* London: Routledge and Kegan Paul, 1982.
    Contains many important contemporary reviews of Hemingway's books, including reviews of *Men Without Women* by Virginia Woolf, Dorothy Parker, and Edmund Wilson, among others.

Reynolds, Michael. *The Young Hemingway,* Oxford: Blackwell, 1986.
    A thorough and readable biography of Hemingway's early days by a notable Hemingway biographer.

Rovit, Earl, and Gerry Brenner. *Ernest Hemingway,* Boston: Twayne, 1986.
    An excellent introduction to Hemingway studies. Includes biographical material, criticism of many of Hemingway's works, and a useful bibliography.

Smith, Paul, editor. *New Essays on Hemingway's Short Fiction,* Cambridge University Press, 1998.
    A collection of recent critical essays on Hemingway's short stories. Contains a useful introduction by editor Paul Smith, "Hemingway and the Practical Reader."

Wagner, Linda W., editor. *Ernest Hemingway: Six Decades of Criticism,* Michigan State University Press, 1987.
    A collection of important reviews and critical articles on Hemingway, spanning his entire career.

Lost in the Funhouse

The first thing John Barth asks the reader to do when opening the cover of the book that contains his story "Lost in the Funhouse" is cut out a little strip of paper on which the words "Once upon a time" appear on one side and "There was a story that began" on the other. If the reader follows Barth's directions for connecting the opposite corners to each other, he will have made a Moebius strip, a continuous loop about stories about stories, a visual demonstration of the theory behind the stories in the collection.

The title story is the centerpiece of the book. First published in the *Atlantic Monthly* in 1967, "Lost in the Funhouse" has become not just one of Barth's most famous pieces, but one of the most critically acclaimed short stories of the latter half of the twentieth century. While some readers are baffled or put-off by Barth's interrupting and self-conscious narrator, others have been dazzled by his virtuosity and humor. Most agree, however, that he succeeds in his declared intent to present old material in new ways. In the words of critic Charles Harris, "Barth's fiction reflects the grim if often comic—at times noble—determination to find new ways to express the old (which is to say *fundamental, essential*) significances."

John Barth
1967

Author Biography

John Simmons Barth was born on May, 27, 1930, to John Jacob and Georgia Barth in Cambridge, Maryland. After graduating from public high school in 1947, he enrolled in the prestigious Julliard School of music with dreams of becoming an arranger, or orchestrator. He soon shifted his interest, however, and enrolled in Johns Hopkins University in Baltimore and began his lifelong involvement with literature and writing. By the time he had received his B.A. from Johns Hopkins in 1951, he was married and the father of a daughter.

Barth continued at Johns Hopkins and received his M.A. in creative writing in 1952. After the birth of his second child, he was forced for financial reasons to discontinue his doctoral work and accept a teaching position at Pennsylvania State University. After his first novel, *The Floating Opera,* was nominated for the National Book Award, he was promoted to the rank of assistant professor. Three novels later, in 1960, he was promoted to associate professor. He moved to Buffalo to become professor of English at the State University of New York in 1965, was divorced in 1969, and remarried in 1970. Finally, in 1973, Barth returned to his Maryland roots and became a professor of English and creative writing at Johns Hopkins. In 1990 he retired with the rank of Professor Emeritus, but has remained an active and productive writer. His latest novel, *The Tidewater Tales,* was published in 1997.

Three aspects of Barth's life have shaped and colored his remarkable literary career. The first is his early and sustained interest in music. Although he discontinued his formal study at Julliard, Barth has remained fascinated with playing the role of the arranger in his fiction. The second aspect of his life reflected in his work is the landscape and history of his native Maryland where he has lived for nearly all of his life and where much of his fiction is set. Finally, Barth's work is also informed by his long career in academia, where he was immersed in the influence of literary criticism and theory.

Plot Summary

On the surface, "Lost in the Funhouse" is the story of a thirteen-year-old boy's trip to the beach with his family on the fourth of July during World War II. With Ambrose are his older brother Peter, their mother and father, their Uncle Karl, and a fourteen-year-old neighbor girl, Magda, to whom both Ambrose and Peter are attracted. Having learned that the beach is covered in oil and tar from the fleet off-shore, the group decides to go through the funhouse instead. Both boys fantasize about going through the maze with Magda, but it suddenly becomes clear to Ambrose that he has misunderstood the meaning of the funhouse, has failed to see "that to get through expeditiously was not the point." He realizes that he is too young to understand or engage in the sexual play associated with the funhouse's dark corners. More profoundly, however, he also realizes that he is constitutionally different from his bother and Magda: he is not the type of person for whom funhouses are fun. Confused and separated from the others, Ambrose takes a wrong turn and loses his way. During the process of finding his way out of the dark corridors and back hallways, he comes to some realizations about himself and about funhouses. Specifically, he understands that his crippling self-consciousness also comes with a gift, an extraordinary imagination. Recognizing that the artistic life brings alienation as well as satisfaction he resolves to "construct funhouses for others and be their secret operator—though he would rather be among the lovers for whom funhouses are constructed."

Ambrose's ill-fated visit to the funhouse, however, is only part of the story. A third person omniscient narrator, sometimes identified with Ambrose or with the author himself, constantly interrupts the story of Ambrose and his family's visit to the beach to comment on the story's own construction and to call the reader's attention to the way literary devices make meaning. The story itself becomes a funhouse of language through which the reader must find his or her way, but the narrative intrusions also point out what's real and what's reflection—or more accurately, that everything is a reflection—and how the hidden levers work behind the scenes.

Characters

Ambrose

Ambrose is the main character in the story and serves as the author's alter ego, or other self. At thirteen, he is "at that awkward age," and in addition to the usual adolescent gawkiness, he is exceptionally introspective and self-conscious. Ambrose is not only just becoming aware of his sexuality, he is experiencing the first inklings of his artistic temperament. In the narrator's words, "There was some simple, radical difference about him; he hoped it was genius, feared it was madness, devoted himself to amiability and inconspicuousness."

Father

That Ambrose's father wears glasses and is a principal at a grade school is essentially all the description the story provides. Later in the story, the narrator describes the boys' father as "tall and thin, balding, fair-complexioned." At times he betrays a disgruntled nostalgia for the old days.

Fat May

Not technically a character, Fat May the Laughing Lady is a mechanical sign at the entrance to the funhouse whose laughter and bawdy gestures Ambrose feels are directed toward him.

Magda

At fourteen, Magda, a girl from the boys' neighborhood, is "very well developed for her age." When she goes through the funhouse with Ambrose's older brother, Ambrose realizes how different he is from the "lovers" for whom the funhouse is fun. On an earlier occasion, she is the girl who provides Ambrose with his first (and unsatisfying) sexual experience as part of a game. She is the object of Ambrose's desire, and he likes to imagine himself married to her someday.

Mother

Ambrose and Peter's mother is a cheerful woman whom the narrator describes as "pretty," but any additional details are withheld. She does not share Ambrose's brooding qualities. In fact, she likes to tease her sons because of their attention to Magda.

Peter

Peter, Ambrose's fifteen-year-old brother, possesses the physical grace and uncomplicated view of life that Ambrose lacks. Although Ambrose knows that his older brother is not as smart as he is (he won't be able to grasp the secret to being the first to spot the landmark Towers on the way to Ocean City, for example), he envies Peter's ability to understand the purpose of the funhouse and to find his way through it.

John Barth

Uncle Karl

Though the story never reveals whose brother Karl is, in physical appearance he is the father's opposite. Both Peter and Karl have "dark hair and eyes, short, husky statures, deep voices." He works as a masonry contractor and likes to tease the boys and their mother.

Themes

Sex

Just as the funhouse poses mirrors in front of mirrors, tempting the viewer to mistake image for substance, "Lost in the Funhouse" seduces readers into believing the familiar literary truism that sex is a metaphor for language. What Ambrose learns in his journey through the three dimensional funhouse in Ocean City and the narrative funhouse of the story is that the opposite is true: language is just a metaphor for sex. Sex, in fact, is the "whole point . . . Of the entire funhouse!" Everywhere Ambrose hears the sound of sex, "The shluppish whisper, continuous as seawash round the globe, tidelike falls and rises with the circuit of dawn and dusk." He imagines if he had "X-ray eyes" he would see that "all that normally *showed,* like restaurants and

Topics for Further Study

- Although Barth abandoned his early formal study of music, he remains interested in it. In fact he said in an interview that as a writer he still thinks of himself as an arranger, "a kind of re-orchestrator." What about "Lost in the Funhouse" strikes you as musical and why?

- Investigate the effects World War II had on the social and economic lives of Americans. How is the wartime setting significant to the story?

- What other characters from literature you have read remind you of Ambrose? How has Barth presented the old story in new ways?

- Barth has said that he believes that "Lost in the Funhouse" "would lose part of [its] point in any except print form." Nevertheless, can you imagine a way that the story could be told on film, video, or the stage? What about a hypertext version for the computer?

---

dance halls and clothing and test-your strength machines was merely preparation and intermission."

Ambrose's fascination with and fear of sex derives not just from his age, but also from his special temperament. He knows that the funhouse is fun for lovers and that he's not one of the lovers. Recalling the time when Magda initiated him into the world of sex during a childhood game, he remembers most poignantly not the passion or the physical pleasure, but the cognitive dimensions of the experience. Unable to "forget the least detail of his life," Ambrose remembers "standing beside himself with awed impersonality," cataloging the details of the scene in the woodshed, like the design of the label of a cigar box. Later he describes his "odd detachment" at that moment: "Strive as he might to be transported, he heard his mind take notes upon the scene: *This is what they call* passion. *I am experiencing it.*"

Consciousness

One of the key elements in any funhouse is the hall of mirrors where visitors see images of images of themselves in strange and unfamiliar shapes. Of course, this awareness of self, or consciousness, is one of the distinguishing and most problematic features of humanness. Ambrose and his narrator alter ego are both marked by their exceptionally keen awareness of self. This is why they are drawn to the hidden levers of funhouses and are resigned to take pleasure in manipulating them rather than enjoying them.

Unlike lovers like Peter and Magda, Ambrose and the narrator are not capable of losing themselves in the play of reflection: "In the funhouse mirror-room you can't see yourself go on forever, because not matter how you stand, your head gets in the way." The problem with consciousness, the story suggests, is not just the paralysis and alienation it engenders, but that one never knows which self is the real one and even if there is a real one. As Ambrose says, "You think you're yourself, but there are other persons in you." After finally making his way back to the main part of the funhouse, Ambrose finds himself in the mirror-room, where ironically, surrounded by his own distorted reflections he sees "more clearly than ever, how readily he deceived himself into supposing he was a person."

Storytelling

Barth said in an interview in 1994 that "Fiction has always been about fiction." Objecting to the critical term *metafiction* because he believes it has negative connotations, Barth explained: "Fiction about fiction, stories about storytelling, have an ancient history, so much so that I am convinced that if the first story ever told began with the words 'Once upon a time,' probably the second story ever told began with the words 'Once upon a time there was a story that began Once upon a time.'"

"Lost in the Funhouse" is one of those stories about stories. The narrator tries to tell the story of Ambrose's coming of age, but constantly interrupts the narrative to comment on its effectiveness and to call attention to the various literary devices he has in his tool box. Barth's point, however, is not to diminish the art of storytelling or to suggest that, in the words of critic Eric Walkiewicz, "the possibilities of fiction have been exhausted and that he [Barth] has been reduced to making the most of what some . . . [critics] find to be an annoying self-indulgent brand of self-consciousness." Rather, the deliberate exposure of the usually hidden works of fiction is a form of play. The story is a funhouse for readers, and the narrator is the same kind of "secret operator" that Ambrose aspires to become in the story's last paragraph.

Style

Metaphor

Barth's use of metaphor in "Lost in the Funhouse" is anything but subtle. On several occasions the self-conscious narrator comments on the metaphoric and symbolic elements in the story. In the opening lines, for example, the narrator announces that Ambrose "has come to the seashore with his family for the holiday, *the occasion of their visit is Independence Day, the most important secular holiday of the United States of America.*" This is an invitation to consider Ambrose's adolescent struggles as a move toward independence, from his family, from his paralyzing self-consciousness.

The dominant use of metaphor in the story, however, is the funhouse itself, an exceptionally rich and fertile device for Barth. According to critic Gerhard Joseph, "The funhouse becomes the excruciatingly self-conscious symbol for the many distorted perspectives from which he [Ambrose] views his troubled psyche, a barely disguised reflection of the authorial narrator's own disintegrating self." Just as Ambrose envies Peter and Magda's unconscious ability to "find the right exit" the narrator laments his inability to lead us through the maze: "We should be much farther along than we are: something has gone wrong; not much of this preliminary rambling seems relevant. Yet everyone begins in the same place; how is it that most go along without difficulty but a few lose their way?" The narrator, like Ambrose, is lost in the funhouse. His sentences betray him and his plot "winds upon itself, digresses, retreats, hesitates, sighs, collapses, expires." The power of the funhouse as symbol for narrative is that it celebrates the playfulness and inventiveness of language while also acknowledging that everything is (just) representation, that storytelling is not a clear lens through which readers view reality, but one of many mirrors in which we see the play of a multitude of images.

Postmodernism

The term *postmodernism* on its most basic level defines the literary period that follows modernism. But this definition is also the least helpful. The term, which literary and cultural studies borrowed from the field of architecture, has come to dominate scholarly discussions about contemporary literature and culture since the 1980s. Some of the ambiguity of the term comes from a dispute about whether it signifies the end of modernism or modernism in a new phase. *The Oxford Concise Dictionary of Literary Terms* says that postmodernism "may be seen as a continuation of modernism's alienated mood and disorienting techniques and at the same as an abandonment of its determined quest for artistic coherence in a fragmented world." In other words, the postmodern writer no longer expects a coherent pattern of images and meanings in the world, nor does he or she strive to give shape and meaning to the confusion. Instead, a writer such as Barth self-consciously plays with the disconnectedness that he inherits.

In addition to contributing many novels and short stories to the genre of postmodern fiction, Barth is also one of the movement's most articulate spokespersons. Even at the time he was writing "Lost in the Funhouse," he had already begun to clarify his thoughts about the state of literature and published them in 1967 in a now famous essay called "The Literature of Exhaustion." As he told an interviewer in 1994, he and some other writers of his generation "share a feeling that the great project of modernism, the art and literature of the first half of the century, while an honorable project, has essentially done its job." He is interested, he goes on to explain, in "shaking up bourgeois notions of linearity and consecutivity and ordinary, realistic description of character, ordinary psychological cause and effect." In a remarkably clear explanation of the practice of postmodern literature, Barth explains in the same interview that he and writers like him "begin with the assumption that art is an artifice, that it has an element of artifice in it. And so far as wanting our reader to forget that they are reading a novel, we are more inclined ... to remind them from time to time that this is a story, not that this is only a story, but whatever else it is, it is a story. You're enthralled, you're spellbound, if we are doing our work right, by a storyteller, and do not confuse this with reality. Art ain't life.''

Historical Context

Literature of Exhaustion

In 1967, Barth published a now famous essay describing what he believed to be the state of literature at the time and sketching out some theories that he finished developing in a 1980 essay called ''The Literature of Replenishment.'' Because the essay was written at approximately the same time Barth was working on the volume that included ''Lost in the Funhouse,'' readers can assume a close relationship with the major theoretical points of the essay and the experimental form of the story.

The essay's main argument, according to critic Charles Harris, is that contemporary writers, facing what Barth called the ''used-upness of certain [narrative] forms and or possibilities,'' must (in Harris's words) ''successfully combine moral seriousness and technical virtuosity.'' What Harris calls ''passionate virtuosity,'' Barth had defined as the duty of the modern writer to use all his or her technical abilities, all the techniques, but still ''manage nonetheless to speak eloquently and memorably to our still human hearts and conditions, as the great artists have always done.''

Social Change

The year that ''Lost in the Funhouse'' was published, 1967, was an especially tumultuous period in American social history, and Barth, as a writer and an intellectual with a faculty position, was right in the thick of it. As the Vietnam War escalated and domestic resistance to it stiffened, colleges and universities were often the site of angry student protest. These protests were primarily aimed at the nation's leaders, but students also had other revolutionary causes to fight for.

Many students were involved in, or were at least sympathetic to, the civil rights movement, which was galvanized after the assassination of its leader, Martin Luther King, Jr., in 1968. The profound injustices and inequalities that the movement exposed inspired many young students to question their relatively privileged positions in the social order and to demand more relevance and accountability out of the educational institutions where they were enrolled.

These revolutionary impulses were certainly political, but they were also cultural and artistic. Young artists and writers sought new ways of expressing their ideas, ways that would reflect the fragmented and fraught world they lived in. Modernism's quest for order seemed to miss the point, as Barth argued in ''The Literature of Exhaustion,'' and much of the literature and art of the period reflects the writers' and artists' giddy sense that they could make-up new rules for themselves. As both a university professor and a writer of new kinds of fiction like ''Lost in the Funhouse,'' Barth could participate in the new kinds of creativity around him; but as a trained scholar, he also took on the more arduous task of analyzing the moment and laying down the beginnings of its theoretical foundation.

Critical Overview

The stories in the volume *Lost in the Funhouse* received mixed reviews when they appeared in 1968. This is not to suggest that individual reviewers were ambivalent or undecided about their assessment of the book. Early reviewers either loved it or hated it. Since then the book and its title story have taken their places in American literary history and are widely regarded as among the best of the genre. ''Lost in the Funhouse'' is frequently anthologized and still offers fresh challenges to readers and critics thirty years after its initial publication.

Writing in the *New York Times Book Review* in October 1968, Guy Davenport called Barth's book ''thoroughly confusing,'' and not ''quite like anything for which we have a name handy.'' By the end of the review, however, he recognizes what Barth is up to in writing about writing and says that he ''has served his readers as handsomely as the best of storytellers.'' R. V. Cassill, another early reviewer calls the book ''pure folly'' and ''blitheringly sophomoric,'' except for the final story, ''Anonymiad,''

The Ocean City Amusement Park, setting for "Lost in the Funhouse."

which he calls "dazzling." On the other side of the critical divide, Walter Harding says the book's title story and a few others "are outstanding . . . [and] have all the verve and hilarity" of Barth's novels.

Several book-length studies of Barth's work appeared in the 1970s and 1980s, which raised his critical profile and gave readers some needed explanation. Two of these works, David Morell's *John Barth: An Introduction* and Charles Harris's *Passionate Virtuosity: The Fiction of John Barth,* remain essential reading today for any student of Barth's work. In general the critics of this period focused on careful explication of the texts. They helped connect Barth's scholarly and theoretical writings with his experiments in fiction. Morell, Harris and others from this period also identified other works in literature that were similar to the stories in *Lost in the Funhouse,* such as James Joyce's classic modernist novel, *A Portrait of the Artist as a Young Man.*

As postmodernism gains more currency in both critical and popular circles, Barth's famous story about the funhouse of language remains at the center of serious literary debate. "Lost in the Funhouse" has given another generation of readers and scholars the opportunity to work out their theories of language and storytelling.

Criticism

Elisabeth Piedmont-Marton

Elisabeth Piedmont-Marton teaches American literature and writing classes at the University of Texas. She writes frequently about the modern short story. In this essay she suggests that readers can enjoy the funhouse even if they are privy to its hidden works.

The narrator of Lost in the Funhouse asks a straightforward question in its opening lines: "For whom is the funhouse fun?" and then suggests a possible answer: "Perhaps for lovers." One of the things the story will go on to do is test that hypothesis. Will it always be *a place of fear and confusion* for Ambrose, or will he learn to appreciate the pleasure of its apparent pointlessness? Are lovers the only ones who find it fun? The narrator is, like Ambrose, one who would "rather be among the lovers for whom funhouses are designed," but will settle for the more cerebral pleasure of being their "secret operator." Readers, then, who enter Barth's funhouse of a story will have to answer the same question for themselves: lover or behind-the-scenes operator of the levers and trap doors that make Magda and Peter and the others squeal with delight? I argue that the

What Do I Read Next?

- *A Portrait of the Artist as a Young Man* (1964) by Irish writer James Joyce is a classic coming of age story about a young man and is considered one of the benchmarks of modernism as well as one of the inspirations for Barth's Ambrose.

- "The School," (1976) by Donald Barthelme, is a postmodern story in which dim-witted teachers are completely unable to understand reality while third graders speak like eloquent college professors.

- *Pale Fire* (1962) by Vladimir Nabokov is a unique work of satire about literary scholarship. The novel, an interesting experiment in narrative technique, includes a 999-line poem with accompanying exegesis.

- *Love in the Time of Cholera* (1988) by Gabriel Garcia Marquez. Latin American magic realism by one of Barth's favorite writers.

---

brilliance of Barth's justifiably famous story is that it imagines—even creates—a reader who can be both, who can find the funhouse fun even if he or she understands that it is all based on illusion.

Writers employ certain techniques to enhance the effect of their writing, the narrator explains, but "as with other aspects of realism, it is an *illusion* that is being enhanced, by purely artificial means." Barth's narrator is like a magician who wants us to be amazed at his dexterity even if we can see the strings and wires. "Description of physical appearance and mannerisms," he says, "is one of the standard methods of characterization used by writers of fiction." After explaining how "It is also important to 'keep the senses operating'," by appealing to the reader's imagination, the narrator goes on to fail in his attempts to use this very technique: "The brown hair on Ambrose's mother's forearms gleamed in the sun like," and "The smell of Uncle Karl's cigar smoke reminded one of." These two aborted similes are forecasted by the narrator's lecture on the means of literary description, but the imagery is strangely effective anyway because our awareness is heightened. Having called attention to the "used-upness" of these kinds of narrative techniques, the narrator occasionally abandons his cynicism and offers stunningly precise and evocative descriptions. Here's how he describes Ambrose's view of Magda's back as she leans forward in the back seat of the car: "Two sets of straps were discernible through the shoulders of her sun dress; the inside right one, a brassiere strap, was fastened or shortened with a small safety pin. The right armpit of her dress, presumably the left as well, was damp with perspiration." At moments like these in the text, readers experience the funhouse like lovers—they can simply enjoy the pleasures of it—but their pleasure is not diminished by knowing how the funhouse works. If anything, Barth is suggesting that for the right kind of reader the pleasures of the funhouse can be enhanced by having special knowledge of its inner works.

The narrator might also ask, "For whom is the funhouse fun again and again?" Certainly lovers like Peter and Magda understand that the point is not to remain upright in the tumbling barrel, is not, as Ambrose says, "to go through expeditiously." But once they know how to "find the right exits," will the funhouse be fun on repeat visits? Both Peter and Magda had been through it before, the narrator says, but perhaps they are seeking just to repeat the experience, not to have a new one. This will be Ambrose's first time through, and after getting lost behind the scenes he is resigned never to experience the real sensory delights of the funhouse. Barth's narrative funhouse, however, may offer another choice by presuming multiple readings, or visits.

Barth has crafted the narrative structure in "Lost in the Funhouse" to be deliberately recursive, or designed to be repeated. Just like the Moebius strip, the story invites, even compels, re-reading. At one point, the narrator even gives readers a hint. Describing the scene in which Ambrose is exploring beneath the boardwalk and hears his family laughing above him, the narrator comments: "If the joke had been beyond his understanding, he could have said: *'The laughter was over his head.'* And let the reader see the serious wordplay on the second reading." And later, the narrator interrupts Ambrose's musings about his life to comment on the stuttering progress of the story: "And it's all too long and rambling, as if the author. For all a person knows the first time through, the end could he just around any corner; perhaps, *not impossibly,* it's been within reach any number of times. On the other hand he may be scarcely past the start, with everything yet to get through, an intolerable idea." On the first reading, this could be a comment on the literal funhouse on the boardwalk, the figurative funhouse of the story, or on the progress of Ambrose's adolescence itself. Unlike visitors to the "real" funhouse, however, Barth's readers don't have to chose correctly or risk the consequences by wandering off into the dark back hallways like Ambrose does.

All three of the possible interpretations of the passage will lead somewhere, and, Barth seems to suggest, visitors will be rewarded for exploring all the possibilities. After all, the "point is not to go through expeditiously." Nor does Barth seem to endorse visitors/readers who, like the crude sailor and his girlfriends, "get the point" of the funhouse after the first time through and thus pay no more attention to its subtleties and reduce the experience to its basest level. While lost Ambrose says that "In a perfect funhouse you'd be able to go only one way, like the divers off the highboard; getting lost would be impossible; the doors and halls would work like minnow traps or the valves in veins." But his own mind betrays him as he spins out several possible exit scenarios. Maybe he will find his way and meet his family just as the police arrive; maybe he'll meet up with another person in the dark and have heroic adventures. Maybe he even "died telling stories to himself in the dark; years later, when that vast unsuspected area of the funhouse came to light, the first expedition found his skeleton in one of its labyrinthine corridors and mistook it for part of the entertainment." In this version of his story, Ambrose imagines a secret door in the narrative. Although he "died of starvation telling himself stories in the dark," the story survives for readers today because "unbeknownst unbeknownst to him, an assistant operator of the funhouse, happening to

> **Barth's narrator is like a magician who wants us to be amazed at his dexterity even if we can see the strings and wires."**

overhear him, crouched just behind the plywood partition and wrote down every word." But then Ambrose gets a better idea for his story—since he is its "secret operator"—the transcriber is not the assistant, but "the operator's daughter, an exquisite young woman with a figure unusually well developed for her age," who, naturally falls in love with him through the partition and whose tears stain the page on which she has written his heroic story.

The story ends by answering the question posed by its beginning. Yes, the funhouse is fun for lovers, but it is also less a "place of fear and confusion" for Ambrose than it had seemed in the beginning. For readers the story has become a funhouse with almost infinite possibilites. Unlike lovers, readers' pleasure does not depend on willfully ignoring the artifice and machinery of the funhouse. On the contrary, the dark hallways and gears and levers through which Ambrose wanders, and their narrative equivalent, the narrator's asides and intrusions, are part of the funhouse, not its frightening and confusing opposite.

Source: Elisabeth Piedmont-Marton, Overview of "Lost in the Funhouse," for *Short Stories for Students*, The Gale Group, 1999.

Thom Seymour

In the following excerpt, Seymour praises Barth's technical mastery of narration in "Lost in the Funhouse."

One of the most puzzling things about the John Barth short story "Lost in the Funhouse" is its apparent neglect. It has not been neglected by the reading public, presumably; after all, the story first appeared in a mass-market magazine and has since been included in a volume of Barth's short fiction (available in a paperback edition from a mass-market publisher), not to mention the current edition of *The American Tradition in Literature.* I mean, rather, the neglect, in recent years, of commentators. When it first appeared, in 1968, the volume that contains "Lost in the Funhouse," *Lost in the Funhouse,* received generally unfavorable reviews. Though perforce hastily conceived, these reviews were not entirely wrong, for there are a number of pieces in the book that strike us today, as they did then, as mere baubles, toys for and of an exhausted imagination. Indeed, this is the line of attack most reviewers took toward the work: you have circled back so fully on your own self-awareness, Mr. Barth, where can you go from here? But what the reviewers failed to see is that this question is largely answered by the book itself. For the two stories that were most frequently praised were "Menelaid" and "Anonymiad," Barth's retelling of Greek myths, in which the telling not the tale is updated. Thus, these stories anticipate the brilliant novellas of *Chimera,* which in turn anticipate God-knows-what. It seems that Barth, if he wanted to, could go on in this vein forever.

Still, as good as "Menelaid" and "Anonymiad" are, the finest piece in *Lost in the Funhouse* must be the title story. Even admitting, as Gerhard Joseph does of *Giles Goatboy,* that "one reader's imaginative profundity [may be] another's puerile shallowness and irresponsible navel-gazing," "Lost in the Funhouse" is still extraordinary, if only because of its perfect technical integration. From the baldest "reality" to the subtlest distortion to the most labored pedantry—the cutbacks, false turns, dead ends, and mirror images all reinforce each other on every level of the narrative. The story is extraordinary as well because it is what it says it is, a *fun*house. What sets this story apart from the sterility of so much "experimental" fiction, what makes it (and, indeed, most of Barth's writing) such a delight, is the sense of play, of pure fun-ness, that pervades it. For something which in outline is so serious, even sentimental, the tale is riddled with howlers, puns, silliness, and simple, small jokes, in all of which we too become lost, and like Fat May, the mechanical laugher on the boardwalk, are left wheezing and clutching our sides.

The Joke—

One of the smallest jokes in "Lost in the Funhouse" is an even smaller mystery. The joke is a throwaway, really, but one that involves both craftiness and craft. In the mode of phony *roman à clef* of preceding centuries, Barth refuses to give us either the last names of his characters or the year (even decade) of the story's events. Hard on the heels of

this refusal, however, comes Barth's pedantic explanation that this is nothing more than a gimmick of fiction used to heighten the illusion of fact. Of course, by making such an admission, Barth obviously destroys any illusion of factuality in his own piece of fiction.

Yet the joke is just beginning. For imbedded in the matrix of the narrative are all the clues we need to come up with the exact date (more accurately, the exact day in one of two possible years) on which the events of the story take place. Early on, we are told that it is "*Independence Day, the most important secular holiday of the United States of America,*" in the year 19__. July fourth it is, but what of the decade? The principals travel to Ocean City in a "black 1936 LaSalle sedan," so it is at least the late thirties. But we know further, from numerous small references, that it is wartime. There are references to matchbook covers advertising "U.S. War Bonds and Stamps" or "warning that A Slip of the Lip Can Sink a Ship"; there is a scarcity of tobacco; there is talk of "tankers torpedoed offshore"; there are the prizes in the digger machines in the penny arcade, prizes "made now in USA"; there is mention of a "brown-out": "on account of German U-boats, . . . streetlights were shaded on the seaward side." The examples go on and on. So we know that it is World War II—July 4th, 1942, at the earliest; the U.S. was not in the war on any Independence Day before that. On the other hand, because of the fear of German U-boats, it cannot be as late as 1945; the war in Europe was over before July of that year. The story must take place on July 4th, 1942, 43, or 44. Yet even one of these years can be eliminated. Nineteen forty-two is out once we are told that "some of the [digger] machines wouldn't work on white pennies." During the war, to save precious copper, the U.S. government minted a penny with a greatly reduced copper content. This coin, with its zinc and steel coating, was called a gray or white penny. However, this penny was minted only in 1943. So, granting even that white pennies were in wide circulation in Maryland by July of that year, the events of the story could have happened only on July 4th of 1943 or (more likely) 1944.

But what is the point of all this? There isn't any. That's the point. Needless to say, the exact date of the story's events matters not at all. And that, of course, is part of the joke; that Barth would go to such trouble to conceal from us, yet provide all the clues to the discovery of, an essentially meaningless fact. After all our careful groping down this one dark passage in the funhouse of this fiction, we come upon just one more dead end, and must turn around and stumble back and start over again.

The Paragraph—

Gerhard Joseph has said that "*Lost in the Funhouse* provides ample evidence that, aside from all questions of aesthetic success, [Barth] is one of the two or three most aware, most technically experimental writers of acknowledged power at work in America today." As goes the book, so goes the story. "Lost in the Funhouse" is a technical *tour de force*. Barth molds together in this tale so many aspects of the technique of fiction, and yet does it so brilliantly and with such seeming ease, that all questions of aesthetic success are definitely not aside. Barth can crack jokes, offer asides, rewrite, question the validity of his characters, question the worth of his story, question the worth of himself as a storyteller, while at the same time he can keep what narrative there is going, and keep the reader interested in it and in the jokes, asides, etc. And this is to say nothing of Barth's dazzling manipulation of language itself.

"Trust the tale not the teller" is, with "Lost in the Funhouse," a foolish admonition, for the tale amounts to little more than this: a pubescent boy, his family and would-be girlfriend, take the family's usual Independence Day outing to Ocean City, Maryland's answer to Atlantic City. After one or two minor adventures on and under the boardwalk, the boy gets lost in the funhouse, from which he presumably escapes or gets rescued, though we never find out (another of the story's small jokes). All the while, he attempts to come to terms with his budding, befuddling sexual cravings and his increasing sense of alienation from those around him and from the world in general. It is, in short, one version of the classic modern tale of the outsider, the sensitive, grown-up child with powerful gifts of observation and rumination who must inevitably settle for the oyster of art since the pearl of love apparently will forever elude him. The character is, of course, cliché and sentimental, as is the whole story. But this is hardly a concern. There is so much else going on here that the shabbiness of the story's impetus is neither readily apparent, nor, once discerned, of any import. As with much contemporary fiction, we are not really expected to learn of "life" from the story, to be instructed by the author in the ways of the world. The "message," we know now, is not the enduring quality of any piece of fiction. More important, many contemporary writers know it as well. Therefore they (and Barth is a good

" It is, in short, one version of the classic modern tale of the outsider, the sensitive, grown-up child with powerful gifts of observation and rumination who must inevitably settle for the oyster of art since the pearl of love apparently will forever elude him."

example) have become increasingly uninterested in preaching at the reader or in convincing him that that which he is reading is "real." They have become, in other words, story*tellers* instead of *story*teller. "Lost in the Funhouse" is a product of this shift in emphasis; the tale itself counts for very little, so the telling—if not the teller—is all.

It is not possible to get at, briefly, all or even most of the ways in which "Lost in the Funhouse" works. Nor does such an analysis seem quite appropriate. A close textual analysis of the entire story would prove most boring, and for that reason, if for no other, would violate both the "beingness" of the story and its appeal. But "Lost in the Funhouse" clearly merits careful consideration, and to that end the synecdochic approach should suffice, with one paragraph selected to stand for the whole.

But though he had breathed heavily, groaned as if ecstatic, what he'd really felt throughout was an odd detachment, as though someone else were Master. Strive as he might to be transported, he heard his mind take notes upon the scene: *This is what they call passion. I am experiencing it.* Many of the digger machines were out of order in the penny arcades and could not be repaired or replaced for the duration. Moreover the prizes, made now in USA, were less interesting than formerly, pasteboard items for the most part, and some of the machines wouldn't work on white pennies. The gypsy fortuneteller machine might have provided a foreshadowing of the climax of this story if Ambrose had operated it. It was even dilapidateder than most: the silver coating was worn off the brown metal handles, the glass windows around the dummy were cracked and taped, her kerchiefs and silks long-faded. If a man lived by himself, he could take a department-story mannequin with flexible joints and modify her in certain ways. *However*: by the time he was that old he'd have a real woman. There was a machine that stamped your name around a white-metal coin with a star in the middle: A_____. His son would be the second, and when the lad reached thirteen or so he would put a strong arm around his shoulder and tell him calmly: "It is perfectly normal. We have all been through it. It will not last forever." Nobody knew how to be what they were right. He'd smoke a pipe, teach his son how to fish and softcrab, assure him he needn't worry about himself. Magda would certainly give, Magda would certainly yield a great deal of milk, although guilty of occasional solecisms. It don't taste so bad. What if the lights came on now!

Apart from the simple story line, there are at least four major aspects to the narrative of "Lost in the Funhouse," all of which, in varying degrees, are evidenced in this paragraph. One of the most obvious aspects involves comments by the author on the story in progress, comments directed sometimes to the reader, sometimes to himself, frequently to both. The sixth sentence, the one that begins, "The gypsy fortuneteller machine, . . ." is obviously an example of this. These comments are inserted not just for humor, but also to push the reader back from the story. They keep him reminded of the fact that the story is indeed a fiction, an artifact, a creation from experience, not experience itself.

Aligned with this is the second major aspect, the sense of the story as unfinished, a rough draft, perhaps, full of uncompleted thoughts, false starts, and options expressed but not exercised. This has much the same effect as the author's running commentary, for it too forces the reader to remember that a fiction is a made object, that regardless of how inevitable a story seems when finished, it is shaped and directed from the outset. The third from last sentence is a perfect example of the literal "rough draftness" of the story: whether Magda "gives" or "yields" her milk will have to be decided during a later revision.

Related to this, but somewhat more subtle, is the third major aspect, the illogicality of the narration. Throughout the story, and clearly in this paragraph, sentence frequently follows sentence as a total *non sequitur*. How exactly, for example, we get from the experiencing of sexual passion to a discussion of the condition of the digger machines in the penny arcades is not at all clear. What we have here is a form of stream-of-consciousness. However, it is not a character's stream flowing by, but the author's. In other words, we are taken back to an earlier stage in the manufacture of a story, back to

the point before the story itself and the author's fabrication of it have been separated.

Finally, one of the most intriguing of these narrative aspects is Barth's handling of the distinction between author/narrator and protagonist. Barth cunningly refuses either to maintain the distinction steadfastly or to collapse it entirely. At one point he even asks (who? the reader? himself?), "Is there really such a person as Ambrose, or is he a figment of the author's imagination?" And in the paragraph quoted above, for example, we begin inside the protagonist's thoughts: "he heard his mind take notes upon the scene: *This is what they call* passion. *I am experiencing it.*" The comments that follow on digger machines and their worsening prizes are clearly those of the narrator. So far so good. But what of this: "If a man lived by himself, he could take a department-store mannequin with flexible joints and modify her in certain ways"? Or this: "Suppose the lights came on now"? Whose notions are these, and how can we tell? The point is, of course, that not only can we not tell, but that it does not matter. More properly, it matters that we *not* be able to distinguish here between the narrator and the protagonist. For by blurring the distinction between the two, Barth is able, subtly, to raise questions about the relationship between biography and fiction, reality and imagination—questions important not only to this particular story, but to much contemporary fiction, if not, indeed, to all fiction of all times everywhere.

In sum, the whole of "Lost in the Funhouse," on every level, from title to tag, is very, very artfully managed. The apparent off-handed handling of the story's immense technical problems is in itself simply stunning. But to approach the story on that level alone—technical problems invented, technical problems solved—is surely a mistake, for that takes much of the fun out of the funhouse. Barth himself insists that technique is the means not the ends. On the dust jacket of *Lost in the Funhouse,* he is quoted as saying, "My feeling about technique in art is that it has about the same value as technique in love-making. That is to say, heartfelt ineptitude has its appeal and so does heartless skill; but what you want is passionate virtuosity." Still, the story's concerns with technical questions cannot and should not be avoided. "Lost in the Funhouse" does seem to be more of an artifact than, say, something by I. B. Singer. And the major thrust of its technical investigation comes in the area of authorial self-awareness. One hates to use the inverted logic of some modern criticism (more in the plastic arts than in literature) which suggest that a difficult and obscure work is in fact a simplification, a return to basics. But that is really what we have here: a case of new being old, complication simplicity, and obfuscation ingenuousness. For the question of the writer's self-awareness—and the reader's consequent awareness of him as well—so integral a part of "Lost in the Funhouse," emphasizes the (generally unacknowledged) *sine qua non* of any piece of fiction: the author and the words. We have always discussed plot and theme, mood and character as if they existed on their own, as if their creation existed independent of their creator. If Barth does nothing else in "Lost in the Funhouse," at least he moves us a step closer to a realization of this error in our ways. And if we can thank Barth for nothing else, we can thank him for having the honesty to report, on his return from the literary wars, that he has met the enemy and found, as did Pogo, that it is he.

Source: Thom Seymour, "One Small Joke and a Packed Paragraph in John Barth's 'Lost in the Funhouse'," in *Studies in Short Fiction,* Vol. 16, No. 3, Summer, 1979 , pp. 189-194.

Edgar H. Knapp

In the following essay Knapp examines Barth's story in light of its use of "myth, masque, cinema, and symposium."

Nor is there singing school but studying
Monuments of its own magnificence
—W. B. Yeats

After John Barth's "Lost in the Funhouse" appeared in *The Atlantic* of November, 1967, common men had a taste of terror, the mad felt a twinge of sympathy, and a faint and tweedy generation of English professors found themselves in the mirror maze of a new fiction.

Warning. You cannot read "Lost in the Funhouse" simply for the fun of it. Read it three times: once, to get knocked off your feet; again to regain your balance; and then to be knocked down again. Perhaps a fourth time . . . for the fun of it.

The story adheres to the archetypal pattern of passage through difficult ways, and the hero seems to be a thirteen-year-old boy on a family outing to Ocean City, Maryland, during World War II. The story line is straight. It's the how of the tale that upends one. Its mixture of myth, masque, cinema, and

> Warning. You cannot read 'Lost in the Funhouse' simply for the fun of it. Read it three times: once, to get knocked off your feet; again to regain your balance; and then to be knocked down again. Perhaps a fourth time . . . for the fun of it."

symposium makes "Lost in the Funhouse" one of the oldest and freshest of stories.

Myth

The setting of Barth's story is intensely true to the texture of life in tidewater Maryland, 1943. Lucky Strike's green has gone to war; V——— (Vienna) is the halfway point of the trip to the shore; at the end of the boardwalk is an inlet the Hurricane of '33 had cut to Sinepuxent Bay (which the author can't bear to leave as Assawoman). Nevertheless, the setting has another dimension: it is an ironic garden. At the Ocean City amusement park the roller coaster, rumored to be condemned in 1916, still runs; many machines are broken and the prizes are made of pasteboard (in the USA). Everyone except Ambrose M——— and his father exudes and ingests the carnival spirit—on Independence Day in a time of national crisis. Barth ruminates: "In a short-story about Ocean City, Maryland, during World War II the author could make use of the image of sailors on leave in the penny arcades and shooting-galleries, sighting through the cross hairs of toy machine-guns at swastika'd subs, while out in the black Atlantic a U-boat skipper squints through his periscope at real ships outlined by the glow of penny arcades." In a slight variation on the independence theme, Ambrose recalls that, five years before, the kids played "Niggers and Masters" in the backyard. And on the day of the story, even the sensitive hero is uncomfortable to think that a colored boy might help him through the funhouse. The boardwalk is a begrimed paradise to which there is no return: "Already quaint and seedy: the draperied ladies on the frieze of the carousel are his father's father's mooncheeked dreams; if he thinks of it more he will vomit his apple-on-a-stick.''

Ambrose at thirteen suffers from undescended identity. He has experienced two initiation ceremonies which left him cold: one sexual, in a tool shed at the age of eight; another religious, at his own belated baptism during the year of the story. (Each involved kneeling and the forgiveness of a master.) Ideally, such acts as these betoken man's communion with his own kind and with his God, but to the aggravation of his sense of loss, Ambrose "felt nothing." He feigned passion, he feigned tears. From time to time he even pretends to be a real person. And so it is his identity he seeks in a funhouse world where nothing is as it seems.

The dark passageways of the funhouse increase his sense of isolation. Still he must find his way out himself. Peeping through a crack in a plywood wall, Ambrose sees the lonely, old funhouse operator (God?) asleep at the switch. An ironic epiphany. Especially as we interpret the funhouse as world (and the world as funhouse), the mythic structure becomes more visible. Ambrose's adventures are like heroic suffering, death, and resurrection (if indeed one sees him as out of the funhouse at the story's end). The witchlike ticket-seller calls him a marked man. And we recall the tumble of unconscious formulation which follows his brush with life in the raw (''*an astonishing coincidence*'') under the boardwalk: ''Magda clung to his trouserleg; he alone knew the maze's secret. 'He gave his life that we might live,' said Uncle Karl with a scowl of pain, as he.'' These words relate to a subsequent dream scene in the funhouse when a Magda-like assistant operator transcribes the hero's inspirational message, the more beautiful for his ''lone dark dying.'' Mention of the Ambrose Lightship, beacon to lost seafarers, and the meaning of *Ambrose* (divine) and echoes of *ambrosia* (that bee-belabored stuff of immortality) reinforce the mythic overtones of his characterization.

Masque

This Ambrose seems clearly to be the protagonist but in another sense he is not. The ''quaint and seedy'' sextet may be the hero—each aspects of generalized man. Ambrose and father, both thin, fair-skinned, and bespectacled, combine as soulful tenors; brother Peter and Uncle Karl, both squat and swarthy, thump out a basso counterpoint, with which the two women harmonize as one voice—a sexy alto, limited in range. (They complement each other, appearing to be an at-once-sinister-and-dexterous female unit, the reflections of one another.)

Perceived as aspects of the same personality, Ambrose and his father represent acute awareness of experience and artistic intuition. Unlike his lustful, mesomorphic brother and uncle, Ambrose is seized by ''terrifying transports'': ''The grass was alive! The town, the river, himself, were not imaginary; time roared in his ears like wind; the world was *going on!*'' Peter and Uncle Karl represent ''the withness of the body,'' Whitehead's phrase, which Delmore Schwartz uses as an epigraph to his poem ''The Heavy Bear.''

> That heavy bear who sleeps with me
> Howls in his sleep for a world of sugar,
>
> *   *   *   *
>
> Stretches to embrace the very dear
> With whom I would walk without him near,
> Touches her grossly, although a word
> Would bare my heart and make me clear.

Womankind is the honey that keeps the heavy bear ''lumbering.'' (The women held the syrup-coated popcorn.) Also, the naming within the party of the flesh is symbolic: *Magda* for Mary Magdalene, sinful woman; *Peter,* meaning rock; *Karl,* man of the common people, who is coincidentally a stone mason and an inveterate cigar smoker. (He kept his stone-cutting chisels in an empty cigar box.)

The sextet enacts a masque-like drama symbolic of the inner transactions which result in human behavior. Members of the ''heavy bear'' quartet communicate by tactile and kinaesthetic means—playful shoves, tugs, punches, and slaps. Prufrock-like, Ambrose recoils from physical contact: the brown hair on his mother's forearms gleams in the sun; he sees perspiration patches at Magda's armpits. (He even gets to play the crab scuttling across the turning funhouse floors.) In the car he removes his hand ''in the nick of time,'' and later in the funhouse he fails to embrace Magda in keeping with his vision.

Additional support to the sextet theory: the two males of each generation, although their actions contrast, share the same woman without deceit or suspicion. Nor is there conflict between corresponding members of the different generations. Although communication is strained between the separate selves, still they gravitate toward one another in artificial ways. For instance, at poolside Ambrose feigns interest in the diving; Magda, disinterest. ("'He's a *master* diver,' Ambrose said. . . . 'You really have to *slave* away at it to get that good.'" [Italics mine]). These oscillations toward and away from members of the same generation create what may be termed *synchronic resonance.* Given the anachronistic setting, the mirrored manners and adherence to the same routines from one generation to the next have special implications in this Barth story. And particularly the reveries in which Ambrose sees himself, standing before Fat May, with Ambrose the Third. ("Magda would yield a great deal of milk although guilty of occasional solecisms.") By flicking images of generation-to-generation resemblance on the reader's screen, Barth effects a *diachronic resonance.*

Cinema

Whereas the action of the story is mythic and its characterization is related to archetypal masque, its scenic values—its choreography—derive from cinematic techniques. The scenic splicing is suggestive—and not only in a ribald sense. The interstitching of dream and action supports the basic theme of the merging of illusion and reality. Other splices create abrupt switches, with utter absence of transition, from narrative flow to textbook exposition, reminding us that not even the story is real. The action is suspended—reminiscent of the lights dimming and the actors freezing at intervals in Samuel Beckett's play *Waiting for Godot*—and then the motion picture resumes. Another and more conventional sort of juxtaposition is used, as when Fat May's canned laughter sounds ironically over images of war and death.

Perhaps the most intriguing aspect of Barth's scenic art is his use of symbolic ballet. Reinforcing the masque-like characterization, the physical interrelationships in the "blocking" of particular scenes are allegorical. For instance, the story opens and closes with the thematically loaded formation of the older generation in the front seat—the woman between the competing interests of the spirit and the flesh—reflected by the younger generation behind. Barth avoids perfect symmetry by contrasting the arm position of the sexually mature mother with that of the sexually maturing Magda (from B——— Street), who has her arms down, but "at the ready."

The theme is only slightly varied as the *sex*tet swings down the boardwalk to the swimming pool, the heavy bears next to the syrup-coated popcorn.

The mirror motif is intensified at the pool: Peter grasps one ankle of the squirming Magda; Uncle Karl goes for the other ankle. Had either looked up he would have seen his reflection! The communion motif, as well, is reflected in the choreography, being subtly varied from the sexual to the religious: first by the child kneeling in sin in the tool shed and later by the fallen woman clutching her savior in supplication in the funhouse.

Not only scenic arrangement but also the varied sensory appeals of Barth's imagery support the illusion-reality theme. Paint peels from the hotels—themselves facades, within which lovers may pretend passion. Not only do the mirrors within the funhouse distort and confuse but also the sounds of fumbling bees and lapping wavelets re-echo in Amby's ears. He suffers from vertigo, if not labyrinthitis. And "candied apples-on-a-stick, delicious-looking, [were] disappointing to eat."

Symposium

And so we have a significant human experience imaginatively presented in structure and textures organically related to the whole. But the story has one more funhouse dimension which is most puzzling—its point of view. Although Barth's story is spun from the consciousness of the protagonist, a precocious adolescent, in the telling at least six distinct bands of mental formulation seem to be randomly mixed: (1) report of the action proper, (2) recollection of past experience, (3) conscious contrivance of a reasonable future, (4) uncontrolled swings into a fantastic future, (5) consciousness of problems of composition, and (6) recollection of sections from a handbook for creative writers. (After a while the reader can visualize the author seated before a console, gleefully pushing buttons according to the sprung rhythm of his whim.) The first four bands on the list qualify as spritely narrative; the last two, as the conscience of an author not completely free from the shackles of conventional fiction. The relationship which is generated between these technical obtrusions and the rest of the story is that of a symposium. We have a running Platonic dialogue between the experimental Barth and the tradition out of which his work has grown. The dialectic is undeniable, but what is the artistic reason for it? It obtrudes upon the illusion of reality. And it has to be Barth's strategy—similar to Pirandello's and Wilder's experiments in the theatre—to remind the reader continually of the contrivance of literature, the fact that a story is the semblance of lived-experience, not experience. The frequent italicized phrases are likewise reminders of the artificiality of fiction. One purpose could be to wean us from the particular in time and place so that we will appreciate the universality of Amby's fate, that he is also ourselves, and that we have our opportunities for heroism.

But wait; we're not out of the funhouse yet. Could it be that Barth's story, and not Barth himself, is playing the bright, young heterosexual Phaedrus to a tired, old Socrates, who is in fact the 19th century short story? (Peruse Barth's essay "The Literature of Exhaustion" in *The Atlantic* of August, 1967, and you have to believe it.) This doesn't vitiate other interpretations of the story-within-the-story; it is merely an additional crown to the apple-within-an-apple nest of "Lost in the Funhouse."

Granted this detachment and accepting the universality of the human experience represented by the M——— family's journey, an allegory of the flesh and the spirit, we are in position to appreciate one more tantalizing suggestion: that one generation of the M——— family is symbolic not only of essential M-a-n but also of essential M-y-t-h—the attempt in story form to help man find his way in the non-human world. The earliest of these fictions portrayed gods as the main strugglers. Hence, the divine characteristics of Ambrose, which set him apart from the common man; his wanderings in a strange dark underworld; his yearning to discover his identity.

When we see a generation of the M——— family as a story, the reappearance of the old structure and dynamics in later generations takes on fresh significance. As every man is like his father, every story bears a likeness to its archetype. The diachronic resonance in the characterization suggests the relationships within literary genres. As Northrop Frye points out, individual works of literature reveal "family likenesses resembling the species, genera, and phyla of biology."

Fiction as we have known it, Barth implies, is at the water's edge. The myth-carrying vehicles have not changed radically (train, car, autogiro), and these recurring outings of the monomyth are distastefully decked with anachronistic trappings. Mention of "the draperied ladies on the frieze of the carousel [seen as] his father's father's mooncheeked dreams" is a comment on "the literature of exhausted possibility," as critic John Barth has labeled it.

And so in a central room of the funhouse, the maze of mirrors, we have the eye. We trust it, as we have learned to, and its imperfect perception goes to a bleary brain: a flickering of self-knowledge (Ambrose did find his name coin there—symbolic of himself.) But with it the *awful* chain of reflection cast backward and forward, in space and time. Outside is the funhouse of a lifetime. Beyond that, the history of humanity and the extension of its possibilities. And encompassing that, the marvelous funhouse of imaginative conception, which can project images, construct funhouses, *et cetera et cetera et cetera*. And we can come to the chimerical conclusion that the eye in the funhouse—yours and mine—is at once that of reader, author, character, god, and story. (The hero is amb——— "O brightening glance . . ." Could six characters be in search of an author?) Selfhood is not easy. Best be a common man and not think about it.

But I'm still worried about Ambrose. Did he make it out of the funhouse? If I can still be worried about him after peering down and up these other echoing funhouse corridors, then I consider the story to be a really good one. I tend to believe the dissembling narrator when he says, "The family's going home. Mother sits between Father and Uncle Karl who tease him [Ambrose] . . ." and I say he's out of the Ocean City funhouse, though still in his funhouse world, as much "a place of fear and confusion" as it was. The voice of convention, nevertheless, has reminded us that the climax will be reached when the protagonist is out. But Ambrose doesn't have climaxes and he will expire in his funhouse world. Lost as he is, he can find purpose in life—at least make "a stay against confusion" (and have a fighting chance for one sort of immortality)—through imaginative design. The Whiffenpoofs are lost too, but "the magic of their singing" makes it a joy to be lost with them. And from another angle, we know that when the operator of our funhouse sets the tumbling-barrel turning, struggle for equilibrium does beget fresh intellectual and/or intuitive formulation. And so the funhouse for *man thinking* is a womb of possibility from which he may be reborn. I ruminate: if in one house of fiction we discover that we are lost and toppled and we regain our equilibrium, even to our knees, the author will have found us and so saved himself, according to the terrible and wonderful necessity which only he can know.

Source: Edgar H. Knapp, "Found in the Barthhouse: Novelist As Savior," in *Modern Fiction Studies,* Vol. XIV, No. 4, Winter, 1968-1969, pp. 446-51.

Sources

Cassill, R. V. Review of *Lost in the Funhouse. Book World,* Sept. 15, 1968, p. 16.

The Concise Oxford Dictionary of Literary Terms, Oxford University Press, 1990

Davenport, Guy. Review *Lost in the Funhouse. New York Times Book Review,* Oct. 20, 1968, p. 4.

Harding, Walter. Review of *Lost in the Funhouse. Library Journal,* Sept. 15, 1968.

Harris, Charles B. *Passionate Virtuosity: The Fiction of John Barth,* University of Illinois Press, 1983.

Joseph, Gerhard. "John Barth." In *American Writers: A Collection of Literary Biographies,* Charles Scribner's Sons, 1974.

Morrell, David. *John Barth: An Introduction,* Pennsylvania State University Press, 1972.

Plumley, William. An interview with John Barth. In *Chicago Review,* Fall, 1994, Vol. 40, p. 6.

Walkiewicz, Eric. *John Barth,* Boston: Twayne Publishers, 1986

Further Reading

Bowen, Zack. *A Reader's Guide to John Barth,* Greenwood Press, 1994.
This excellent and up-to-date introduction to Barth's work provides background, context, biographical and critical information

Fogel, Stanley. *Understanding John Barth,* University of South Carolina Press, 1990.
Another updated introductory critical text that contains an excellent bibliography and index.

Odour of Chrysanthemums

D. H. Lawrence

1911

"Odour of Chrysanthemums," regarded as one of D. H. Lawrence's most accomplished stories, was written in 1909 and published in Ford Madox Hueffer's *English Review* in June, 1911. A different version, which transformed and expanded the concluding section in which Elizabeth Bates reflects on her married life in the presence of the body of her husband, was published in 1914 in *The Prussian Officer and Other Stories*. The story's controlled analysis of the harsh industrial setting and of Elizabeth Bates's psychological transformation has been widely admired. H. E. Bates has even argued that Lawrence's greatest achievement is his short fiction.

The story's evolution in its three major versions has been examined by a number of critics. The final version's unsentimental and highly judgmental condemnation of Elizabeth Bates for the failure of her marriage has been related to Lawrence's liberation from the influence of his beloved mother upon her death in 1910. The story is frequently compared to *Sons and Lovers,* a largely autobiographical novel, in which Lawrence explores his parents' conflicted relationship. As in "Odour of Chrysanthemums," an inarticulate, drink-obsessed miner in *Sons and Lovers* is disparaged by his wife who longs for a more genteel life. The harsh, bleak mining villages of Nottinghamshire, which Lawrence knew so well, are powerfully evoked in "Odour of Chrysanthemums" and contrasted with the unfettered beauties of the natural world.

When Lawrence's editor at the *English Review,* Ford Madox Hueffer, first read "Odour of Chrysanthemums," he considered it a work of genius, but it did not prevent him from demanding a cut of five pages. The story was one of Lawrence's first and it underwent two major revisions before it appeared in its final form in *The Prussian Officer and Other Stories.*

Hueffer (a distinguished author in his own right, who is better known as Ford Madox Ford) was immediately struck by Lawrence's title, which he describes as "at once a challenge and an indication. The author seems to say: Take it or leave it. You know at once that you are not going to read a comic story about someone's butler's omniscience. The man who sent you this has, then, character, the courage of his convictions, a power of observation. All these presumptions flit through your mind."

Author Biography

The fourth child of Arthur John Lawrence, an illiterate coal miner, and Lydia Beardsall Lawrence, a former school teacher, David Herbert Lawrence was born in 1885 and raised in the mining village of Eastwood, Nottinghamshire. From boyhood he shared a close relationship with his mother and grew to hate the debilitating mine work he considered responsible for his father's debased condition. Later in his life, however, he acquired a genuine sympathy for his father's plight. Lawrence attended local grammar and secondary schools and later, from 1906 to 1908, studied at Nottingham University College, where he began writing short stories. In 1908, he moved to Croyden, just south of London, to teach school. While there he discovered the works of such writers as Thomas Hardy and Joseph Conrad. He also came to the attention of novelist Ford Madox Hueffer (later known as Ford Madox Ford), who was editor of the *English Review.* Hueffer published some of Lawrence's early poetry and stories, including an early version of "Odour of Chrysanthemums," which was written in 1909 and published in 1911—the same year that the onset of tuberculosis forced Lawrence to resign from teaching. Also in 1911, Lawrence published his first novel, *The White Peacock,* which was well received by critics. When he was twenty-seven, Lawrence eloped to Germany with Frieda von Richthofen Weekley, the wife of one of his college professors, and the two were married in 1914.

In 1913, Lawrence published his first major work, the largely autobiographical novel *Sons and Lovers,* and also wrote "The Prussian Officer," the title story in a volume which also contained a substantially revised version of "Odour of Chrysanthemums." Just before the outbreak of World War I, Lawrence returned to England, where he and Frieda endured continual harassment by the English government because of her German ancestry and his objections to the war. Lawrence's next novel, *The Rainbow* (1915), a complex narrative focusing on relationships between men and women and particularly on the nature of marriage, was judged obscene for its explicit discussion of sexuality and was suppressed in England. These events intensified Lawrence's bitter struggle with social orthodoxy and the forces of modern civilization, which he came to believe were arrayed against him and most certainly influenced his decision to leave England. "The Rocking-Horse Winner," a short story written in 1926, also deals with a strained marriage and the dangers of materialism. Lawrence's last major novel, *Lady Chatterley's Lover* (1928), met with similar resistance and was available only in an expurgated version until 1959 in the United States, and 1960 in England, when a landmark obscenity trial vindicated the book as a work of literature. After the war, the Lawrences lived briefly in Germany, Austria, Italy, Sicily, England, France, Australia, Mexico, and in the southwestern United States, where Lawrence hoped someday to establish a utopian community. These varied locales provided settings for many of the novels and stories Lawrence wrote during the 1920s and also inspired four books of admired travel sketches. In 1930 Lawrence entered a sanatorium in Vence, France, in an attempt to cure the tuberculosis that afflicted him throughout his life. He died that same year.

Plot Summary

"Odour of Chrysanthemums" focuses on a dramatic moment in the life of Mrs. Elizabeth Bates, the accidental death of her husband, Walter Bates. The story develops in three major stages.

Part I—Waiting

The story begins with a description of the sights and sounds of a bleak mining village at the end of the mine's afternoon shift. Mrs. Bates calls her son, John, in for the evening meal and provides a light snack for her father, a train driver, while chiding her

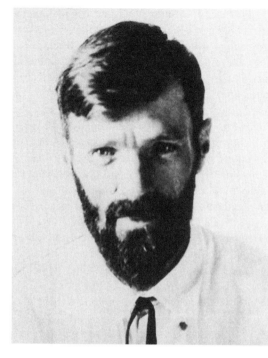

D. H. Lawrence

daughter, Annie, about being late from school. She is also upset because her husband is not home from work yet, and she has a feeling he is drunk at the pub again. Mrs. Bates's daughter directs her to begin the evening meal without their father and appreciates the flowers her mother wears in her apron. Mrs. Bates can only criticize her husband before her children and lament the misery and neglect in her life. She is a fretful, nagging mother, but clearly one who wants a better life for her children, and she doesn't hide her outrage at her husband's recklessness.

Part II—The Search

In the second part of the story, Mrs. Bates, now worried and no longer angry, goes out to search for her husband. Tension builds as she asks her neighbors for news about Walter's whereabouts, and Mr. Riley goes in search of his missing partner. Everyone knows that while Mr. Bates may simply be drunk in one of the village's many pubs, he may also be seriously injured, though their fears are unspoken. When Walter's mother arrives to comfort Elizabeth, at Mr. Rigby's suggestion, we know something is amiss and rapidly the disaster is revealed, but not until the two women display their very different views of Walter. The elder Mrs. Bates recalls a lively boy and suggests his wife should be

more forgiving and generous to him. Elizabeth muses to herself that if her husband is merely wounded, she may be able to nurse him to better physical and moral health. She quickly realizes how sentimental these thoughts are, indicating, along with her memory of Walter's gifts of flowers, and Mrs. Bates's memories of his youthful liveliness, the mixture of fond delusion and unspoken sexual desire which first made Walter attractive to her.

Part III—Death

The story's pace accelerates with the speed of disaster. The men from the mine arrive with Walter's body, and now Elizabeth knows for certain that he has died. She shows almost more concern for her carpet and a smashed vase than she does for the body of her husband, but she goes and kindly comforts her daughter woken by the sounds in the house. After the men leave, depositing the body in the parlor, but safely away from the carpet, Elizabeth Bates and her mother-in-law begin to wash the body. Rinsing the dirt from the unmarked body, Elizabeth comes to reevaluate her husband's worth and their life together, realizing that they never really knew each other and that she might have been to blame for the failure their marriage had become.

Characters

Annie Bates

Annie Bates is the daughter of Elizabeth and Walter Bates and the sister of John Bates. She is a schoolgirl with curly hair that is changing from her father's blonde color. Annie is chided by her mother for returning late from school, an assessment Annie disputes. The mother and daughter consider Walter Bates's late arrival, and they both understand the signs which indicate that he may have stopped at a pub on his way home. Annie feels pity for her mother and at Annie's suggestion they all begin supper without her father. Annie is sensitive to her surroundings and speaks imaginatively of the caves she sees within the fire, though she is chided by her brother for playing with and inadvertently suppressing the fire. After supper, Annie enters an imaginative "play-world" with her brother. Annie clearly loves her mother and wants to comfort and delight her, and she shares in her mother's concerns for Walter Bates, though she perhaps is more prepared to distance herself from her father's bad habits and lack of consideration. She admires the scent of the chrysanthemums in her mother's apron and tries to make her mother keep the flowers there. She awakens when the men bring in the body of the dead Walter Bates, but she takes comfort in the soothing words of her mother.

Elizabeth Bates

Elizabeth Bates is the wife of Walter Bates, a miner, and the mother of two children, John and Annie. The story's central character, Elizabeth is shown awaiting the arrival of her husband, who may have stopped off at a pub on his way home. She calls in her young son, who is playing outside and gives tea to her father, the driver of a mine train, who briefly drops in to see his daughter and tell her of his upcoming marriage. When her daughter arrives, Elizabeth scolds her for being late. After Elizabeth and her children eat their supper, she searches for her husband. A neighbor sends her mother-in-law, Mrs. Bates, to comfort her when it appears that Walter Bates has been injured in the mine. After the men from the mine bring home the body of Walter Bates, the two women lay out the corpse.

Elizabeth is a proud, even "imperious," woman. She resents her husband, who drinks irresponsibly. She feels that he undermines her efforts to provide a respectable home for their children. However, the sentimental musings she entertains about possible outcomes from the accident suggest that she had romantic illusions in the past about what marriage to the handsome and jolly Walter Bates might bring. She blames herself for her folly. She clearly considers herself to be in a higher social class than her neighbors, as indicated by her use of standard English and her disdain for any displays of impropriety, whether it be her father's hasty marriage, her son's dirty clothes, or her neighbor's unkempt household. At the end of the story, encountering the dead body of her husband, she recognizes that she has never really understood Walter Bates and has been largely responsible for the failure of her marriage.

John Bates

John Bates is the five-year-old son of Elizabeth and Walter Bates and the brother of Annie Bates. At the beginning of the story, he is called in from playing outside. He is resentful and defiant towards his mother, who wants to keep him from playing at the brook and from doing things that she considers "nasty," like destroying flowers. John wears a "cut down" version of men's clothes and his mother wishes to make him into a more respectable adult than his father. Inside the house John works at a piece of wood with a knife, and his mother "saw the father in her child's indifference to all but himself." Like his father, John is associated with darkness and shadow; moreover, the "invisible" John complains that his sister's handling of the fire has reduced his ability to see. His mother complains that he is "as bad as your father if it's a bit dusk!" She lights a lamp for him, and after supper he plays under the sofa "like a frog," emerging with a dirty shirt, after which he says his prayers and goes to bed. He does not wake up when the men bring home the body of his father.

Mrs. Bates

Mrs. Bates is the mother of Walter Bates, the miner whose death is at the heart of this story. A somewhat naive and irritable, self-pitying woman of about sixty, Mrs. Bates is asked by a neighbor to go and sit with her daughter-in-law when it is discovered that Walter has had an accident in the mine. She sits with Elizabeth, voicing her fears about the fate of her son and recalling memories of his early life. When Walter's dead body is brought into the house, she begins to weep and lament, and she has to be quieted so that she doesn't wake her grandchildren. She finally assists Elizabeth in washing and laying out the body of her beloved son, and she has vivid memories of his liveliness and beauty when he was a boy and a young man. In conversation with Elizabeth, she suggests that Elizabeth contributed to Walter's decline of recent years because of her critical attitude to his excesses. She says that Elizabeth should have made "allowances" for him. She laments and weeps for her son, her behavior contrasting with the seemingly cold efficiency of Elizabeth.

Walter Bates

Walter Bates, a miner, is the husband of Elizabeth Bates and the father of John and Annie. He is probably dead from the time the story begins, and he is present in the story only in the words and thoughts of his wife, his children, his mother, and his neighbors. He is a handsome and energetic young man who it seems wooed Elizabeth with his charm. Even in death, he retains his "handsome body," "fine limbs," and blond good looks. The history of his marriage is a sad one; he has become increasingly reckless and irresponsible and is prone to heavy drinking and other forms of excess. He works in the mine and finds his joy in drinking in the genteel-sounding "Prince of Wales" pub. He is a man associated with the darkness and warmth of the mine and with the energy and vigor of attractive youth.

He dies at the end of his work shift in the mine when he decides to stay behind after the other miners have left the area. There is a rock fall and he is suffocated. His body, covered with the grime of the mine, is carried to Mrs. Bates's parlor by other miners, and his wife and mother wash and lay out his body, which, surprisingly, is still warm from the mine and, due to the circumstances of his death, unmarked on the surface by the fatal accident. His body, which retains its youthful beauty, shocks Elizabeth Bates and makes her realize that she has never really known her husband.

Mother
See Mrs. Bates

Themes

Light and Darkness

The theme of light and darkness is of significance since most of the story takes place late in the afternoon and at night, and the narrative focuses on the relationship of life and death. Elizabeth Bates awaits her husband as shadows lengthen, her son emerges from dark undergrowth, and her daughter returns late from school. The family huddles in the house where the light is insufficient for Elizabeth's son John, who, like his father, always craves more brightness and warmth than his home provides. The boy is even dissatisfied with his sister's tending of the fire as if he may lose that light. When Mrs. Bates goes out to her neighbors to seek her husband, "there was no trace of light," and even the helpful neighbors ominously suggest that their children, if unattended, may "set theirselves afire." Elizabeth has said earlier that her daughter's reaction to the chrysanthemums she wears in her apron is so extreme that "One would think the house was afire." Fire which should bring light and warmth, and which is trapped in the coal the workers seek in the mine, is here insufficiently bright and even conveys a sense of danger. Awaiting her husband back in her own home, Elizabeth is unable to make a fire in the parlor where there is no fireplace. When the men arrive with the body of Walter Bates, Elizabeth carries an unlighted candle, and after the men leave, Elizabeth and her mother-in-law clean the body in the dim light cast by a single candle.

Only when Elizabeth is confronted with the naked reality of her husband does she realize that she never knew him: "they had met in the dark and fought in the dark." The darkness signifies their inability to really comprehend and appreciate the separation. Now that she has gained an insight into this separation and now that the darkness of death, a death occurring in a mine's darkness, is plainly before her, she sees clearly. The unrecognized gulf between herself and her husband has been as wide as that between light and darkness, life and death, and now she is left to wonder if she and her husband were to meet in the "next world" whether he would recognize her.

Appearances and Reality

Just as the darkness has obscured her vision, so Elizabeth's anger has distorted her perception of her husband and she has failed to recognize the reality of his essential difference. Similarly, her sense of smell has been deluded by illusory associations. She has associated the odor of the beautiful, though disheveled, chrysanthemums, a sign of beauty even in the rat-infested, mining village, with the main stages of her life with her husband, in which, as she tells her children, she has been a "fool." Only after the breath of her husband is smothered in the mine does she recognize that the smell of the chrysanthemums is really the smell of death. She has been more concerned with maintaining respectable appearances, such as when she ignores the body of her husband to clean up the dropped vase of chrysanthemums, than with facing concrete realities. Finally, after she has cleared the dirt from her husband's body, she sees the reality of his masculine beauty and his difference from herself, and the vast gap which has always existed between them.

Sex Roles

The story stresses the essential separation of all people, particularly the separation of men and women. This is indicated by Elizabeth Bates's emotional distance from all those around her, with the exception of her daughter, Annie, and with the way in which characters talk at, rather than engage in dialogue with, each other. Recognition of the separation of all people and particularly of men and women, for Lawrence, must take place in the dark, through the sensual channels of dimmed sight, muffled odors, and touch rather than through intellectual understanding. Elizabeth Bates recognizes the apartness of her husband by gazing on and touching his still-warm body. She recognizes that

Topics for Further Study

- Investigate the condition of mines in England at the turn of the century. To what extent does the mine in "Odour of Chrysanthemums" function as a silent but forceful character?

- Research the position of women in England in the early twentieth century. Is Elizabeth Bates's life-style common to those of other women at that time?

- What references to the effects of environmentally unfriendly industrial practices can you find in the story?

- Elizabeth Bates thinks her husband drinks too much. What kind of medical, social, psychologi-

cal, or economic effects of alcohol abuse are revealed in the story?

- In what ways is the death of Walter Bates foreshadowed in the story? What are the indications that a disaster is looming?

- Examine the portrayal of the two children, John and Annie, in the story. How are they psychologically affected by the family situation in which they are raised? To what extent do they reproduce their parents's attitudes? In what ways do you think Elizabeth Bates might treat the new child differently than she has treated her other two children up to this point?

---

he is now apart from her in the world of death, just as during his life he was apart from her in his sexual difference, his masculinity. Similarly, his son John, who resembles his father, is described as being separate from his mother in his shadowy darkness and even in his "play-world." Finally aware of the "infinite" separation between herself and her husband whom "she had known falsely," Elizabeth will submit to life, her new "master," as she had not submitted to her husband by acknowledging his essential otherness.

Death

While the centrality of death in the story's conclusion is anticipated in its first paragraph, the arrival of Walter Bates's dead body at the Bates's home introduces the story's climactic final phase. This phase addresses the relationship between death and life, in light of a consideration of the relationship between men and women. From the beginning, darkness and gloom permeate the story's atmosphere, and a sense of dread oppresses Elizabeth Bates. In the story's first paragraph, the mine and its train are presented as life-destroying forces which startle animals, blight the natural setting, and cramp human lives. Given the dangers of underground work, Elizabeth Bates and her neighbors seem aware

that Walter Bates may have died in the mine. In addition to the sense of melancholy fatalism which pervades the beginning of the story, readers learn that in the recent past, Elizabeth Bates's father has been widowed. These different elements foreshadow the focus on death at the conclusion of the story and the way it will inform the future life of Elizabeth Bates.

While Walter Bates has probably been dead for the first part of the story, a period coinciding with Elizabeth Bates's anxious anticipation of his arrival, the story shifts into a mythic dimension with the stark presence of his half-naked body. The two women kneeling by the miraculously untouched and still beautiful body conjure up images of the *pieta,* the scene of the Virgin Mary holding the body of the crucified Christ. In the story, however, there is another mythic dimension evoking the Egyptian story of Isis and Osiris. This mythic story concerns the care of Isis for her husband Osiris who becomes a lord in the realm of the dead. In Lawrence's story, Elizabeth Bates nearly worships her husband's corpse and imagines a possible meeting with him in the afterlife. Encountering the dignity and finality of death, she realizes that she has been misguided in her futile attempts to criticize and change her husband. The story implies that she will spend the rest of her life attempting to incorporate this realization, achieved through an encounter with death, into her life. She will live, the story implies, anticipating a meeting with her husband in the realm of the dead.

Social Class

"Odour of Chrysanthemums" is set in a rural mining village, and there are strong indications that Elizabeth Bates considers herself socially superior to her husband and his fellow working-class colleagues who labor underground; however, by the end of the story, through her mythic encounter with his dead body, she comes to value her husband, and by implication, to ignore his class position. Elizabeth Bates is described as a woman of "imperious mien," who chides her son's destruction of flowers because it looks "nasty" and appears to censure her father's decision to remarry soon after being widowed because it violates social propriety. Unlike her neighbors, she does not use the local dialect, an indication of class position, but she is not above criticizing one neighbor's unkempt house. Unlike other miners' wives in the community, she refuses to demean herself by entering the local pubs to entice her husband home. She is distressed when her children mimic their father's habits and preferences.

Most significantly, however, Elizabeth Bates indicates her disdain for the social position of her community by fighting against her husband and his values. Probably lulled into marrying him by his good looks and his lust for life, she now resents him for making her feel like a "fool" living in "this dirty hole." She seems to despise the manual nature of her husband's work, indicated by her unwillingness to wash the residue of pit-dirt from his body when he emerges from his shift in the mine. Awaiting his return, she angrily says she will force him to sleep on the floor. However, her attitude dramatically shifts when she learns about the accident. She even entertains a fleeting, deluded notion that she may transform her husband morally while nursing him back to health, but her illusions disappear when the dead body of her husband is carried into her home by miners supervised by the pit manager. Viewing the body "lying in the naive dignity of death," she is appalled and humbled at what appears to be her husband's new distance from her, but she slowly comprehends that their former connection was based solely on an unnamed attraction above and beyond the conditioning of social class, and the lure of compatible personality, common interest, or shared experience. She now acknowl-

edges that their relationship was part of a different order of experience, which belonged to a mythic dimension. It is a dimension which includes the physical work of the dark mine, the sexual attraction of the body, and the mysterious world of the dead. The story ends with the laws of this new mythic dimension overriding Elizabeth Bates's former concerns about social class.

Style

Setting

"Odour of Chrysanthemums" is a story about Elizabeth Bates and the recognition she gains, upon her husband's death, concerning the gap between them. The style of "Odour of Chrysanthemums" is highly poetic and is characterized by a profusion of descriptive adjectives and adverbs. The story's first paragraph juxtaposes the hard, inhuman machine-world of the mine and the beautiful, vulnerable, natural world. This description introduces the gap between people and nature which will widen at the end of the story to reveal an absolute division between men and women, and life and death. In the story's first sentence, the mine's locomotive engine startles a colt and traps a woman walking on the track, and its smoke coats the grass. The mine's pit-bank is powerfully described as having "flames like red sores licking its ashy sides," as if the slag heap is a wounded animal. In this setting where the oak is "withered," the cabbages "ragged," and the chrysanthemums "dishevelled," the miners pass "like shadows" and even Elizabeth Bates's son is associated with the darkness. The "invisible" John is "almost hidden in the shadow" and "almost lost in the darkness." This is a world where neglected dinners get heated "to a cinder" and women fear their children being burned in house fires. The flames which should bring light and comfort to the fearful dark world are insufficient or bring only a threat of danger.

Point of View

The point of view used in the story is third-person omniscient. The invisible narrator, however, stays very close to the central character, Elizabeth Bates, and readers are presented with her thoughts. She is revealed fully from without and within. She is the center of consciousness, and the narrative follows her movements, so that, for example, when she goes to search for her husband, the narrative focus shifts to the Riley's home and does not return to Elizabeth's children left behind. Readers are also given access to her thoughts, which are revealed in the form of free indirect speech in which a report is given of a character's thoughts. This bears a clear impression of the narrator's mediating involvement. For example, ''What a fool she had been to imagine that anything had happened to him! He was merely drinking over there at the 'Prince of Wales.''' In this passage we are presented with Elizabeth's uncertain thoughts, but the third person pronoun ''she'' and not the first person ''I'' is used, indicating the omniscient narrator's invisible presence.

Imagery

The story contains patterns of imagery associated with darkness and fire, but its most obvious pattern relates to the flowers of its title. Elizabeth Bates is described, and the progress of her marriage is presented, in relation to chrysanthemums. She unconsciously picks some of the flowers at the beginning of the story, placing them in her apron where they attract her daughter Annie's attention. The flowers represent Elizabeth's struggle to maintain a sense of grace and beauty amid the dreariness of her world. Later, she explains to her children the flowers' association with her wedding, the arrival of her children, and ominously with her first sight of her husband's drunkenness. Now her illusions are tarnished, just as the flowers fighting the mine dust outside the home are ''dishevelled.'' Soon, while awaiting the arrival of her husband's body, she notices that the odor of the flowers she has picked is ''cold'' and ''deathly.'' The men arriving with the corpse knock over a vase holding the chrysanthemums, signifying her smashed illusions concerning her marriage.

Historical Context

The British Empire and Industrialism

''Odour of Chrysanthemums'' was written between the end of the Victorian period in 1901, and the beginning of World War I in 1914. It was a time when England was still a powerful international force, and the head of a huge empire that extended from India to Nigeria, which demonstrated England's political power and also provided a vast market for its manufactured goods. During the nineteenth century, England's industrial machine had developed the factory system, which produced surplus goods for export. The colonies provided a captive market for such products and the powerful factories, located mostly in England's north, distributed their goods through a complex transportation system of canals, railways, and ships.

One of the major sources for the energy which drove this industrial machine was coal. However, as Lawrence shows in this story, the sites where coal was extracted were dreary and the people involved in this labor often led bleak, despairing lives. Like their living quarters located near the coal pits, people's personal lives were coated with the dust and grime of mineral extraction. Human labor was needed for this work and the exhaustion it produced coupled with the anxiety of working in life-threatening conditions was often relieved in pubs, a type of working men's social club. Unfortunately, as Lawrence shows, the comforts of the pub were paid for at a high price in alcoholism and the disruption of home life.

The comforts of the pubs numbed the miners' awareness of the injustices of the laborers' lot, and their wives were burdened with the care of large, unregulated families on their husband's meager wages. At the same time, the writings of Karl Marx and the socialist Fabians were encouraging many to re-examine their political and social rights. In just eight years, such dissatisfactions with a much more oppressive imperial system would lead to violent revolution in Russia. Early twentieth-century class divisions were largely established in England as a result of the division of industrial labor during the Victorian period, and working-class men and women, such as the miners in ''Odour of Chrysanthemums,'' were almost a different species from the manager Matthews who supervises the delivery of Walter's body. There are a number of hints in the story that Elizabeth Bates has reluctantly come into this working class world and regards herself as being more refined than her husband and her surroundings.

One of the solaces to many downtrodden people in circumstances like those of Elizabeth Bates was Christian faith, located for many in industrial England in denominations other than the national Church of England. However, the early twentieth century saw the results of the Victorian crisis of

Compare & Contrast

- **1911:** Massive labor protests take place throughout England, with many turning violent. The British government stations more than 50,000 armed troops in London where the nationwide transportation workers' strike is threatening a nationwide famine.

  1999: Labor disputes in the past year have crippled the economic gains of major corporations, including General Motors and Northwest Airlines.

- **1911:** The National Insurance Bill, which provides for unemployment and sickness insurance, is passed in England.

  1999: Many European nations utilize a system of socialized medicine. The United States continues to try to address the rising cost of healthcare through legislation aimed at reform.

- **1911:** The first cable message is sent around the world by telegraph from New York City.

  1999: Over 3.5 billion international telephone calls are made from the United States each year.

faith, which followed the mid-nineteenth-century religious revival. The crisis was caused in part by intellectual forces, such as the historical criticism of the Bible and the challenges of evolution, and partly by disillusionment with the conservatism and sometimes the corruption of the state Church. The widespread decline in Christian belief was noted by English chaplains during World War I. In intellectual circles in England, the questioning of Christian beliefs coincided with a fascination for non-European and non-Christian beliefs and myth systems.

This period in history was also a tumultuous one for relations between the sexes. Lawrence looked partly to non-European mythology for a new way of exploring the relationship between men and women. With the rejection of Victorian religious enthusiasm in this period, there was a more general rejection of patriarchal Victorian social norms and particularly a reevaluation of women's roles in

society. What the Victorians called ''The Woman Question,'' the consideration of women's social and political rights, became a more organized political force in the early twentieth century, though it would be some years before all women gained the right to vote (1928). Significantly, the Education Act of 1870, which provided education to all children up to the age of twelve, increased the need for teachers, and provided a career and independence for many working-class women. The revolution in women's social roles was influenced, especially in intellectual circles in this period, by the writings of Austrian psychologist Sigmund Freud. Lawrence learned about Freudian notions from his German wife in the years before this story's final version was published (1914), and he was an advocate of distinct gender roles and male supremacy. These forces are present in ''Odour of Chrysanthemums,'' though they are only distantly suggested rather than explicitly discussed. The very lack of awareness of the social and cultural contexts in which the story's characters are bound is one of its striking features. The story ends with Elizabeth Bates's realization about the nature of her husband and their relationship. It is a quasi-spiritual revelation about the nature of gender roles, which discounts the economic, social, and political forces which place such pressures on their lives.

Critical Overview

Early reviews of *The Prussian Officer and Other Stories,* R. P. Draper notes, while highly critical of the collection's title story, afforded ''Odour of Chrysanthemums'' high praise. More recent responses to the short story, such as those of Keith Cushman, Nora Foster Stovel, and John Worthen, have also stressed its technical brilliance, by examining the differences between its three versions, and the ways in which it slowly reveals its theme. Weldon Thornton, for example, writes that ''What Lawrence wrestled with in his successive revisions of the story was not the philosophical/ideational challenge of what that situation means, but the exploratory/artistic challenge of how to be faithful to the powerful and complex emotional structure of such an experience as it unfolds for the character.'' The way the story skillfully conceals and yet also foreshadows its final revelation is examined in an essay by Michael Black, who notes that Elizabeth "is jolted out of that judgement [that Walter is away from the home getting drunk], and we are jolted with her." Comparative analyses of this story and Lawrence's other work have also been popular. Consideration of the relationship between Lawrence's handling of reactions to a beloved's death in texts such as *The White Peacock* and *The Rainbow* has revealed the way in which Lawrence works, reworks, and even worries a single theme again and again. The conflict between Elizabeth and Walter has also been regarded in terms of Lawrence's treatment of this relationship in *Sons and Lovers.*

Criticism

Oliver Lovesey

Lovesey currently teaches at Okanagan University College in Kelowna, British Columbia. In the following essay, he offers an in-depth analysis of the imagery in Lawrence's "Odour of Chrysanthemums."

Early criticism of Lawrence's work focused on what was considered to be his sex-obsession. His novels, stories, poems, and paintings were all subjected to various degrees of censorship. While his novels have attracted the lion's share of critical interest, Lawrence was one of the twentieth century's most accomplished poets and short story writers. Most critical material on "Odour of Chrysanthemums" concerns either its relationship to other writings by Lawrence, such as *Sons and Lovers,* or the revisions of the story, made between 1909 and 1914. Mired in "this dirty hole, rats and all," of a rough mining village, Elizabeth Bates has perhaps begun to regard her husband as just another of the area's rodents. Even the doctor refers to the method of Walter Bates's accidental death, a rock fall in the mine tunnel which cuts off his air supply, as being like the action of a mousetrap. However, by the end of the story, when the grime and dirt from the mine are washed off Walter Bates's handsome body, his natural beauty emerges and he is again the innocent "lamb" his mother remembers from his boyhood. The story concerns his transformation from an irresponsible, hurtful, and selfish man into a symbol of masculine beauty and life itself. More importantly, it concerns the metamorphosis of Elizabeth Bates. By the end of the story, she has recognized the true, abstract worth of her husband, and the "otherness" of another world, which he represents. She is humbled by this revelation and will be a chastened and more reverential woman in future. The story accomplishes the transformation of the two characters through the manipulation of a variety of symbols, and through the representation of Elizabeth Bates as an intrusive reader and interpreter of grand symbolic occurrences in her own life.

The story uses a variety of symbols and achieves its effects through suggestion and nuance. First, the story employs a traditional catalogue of symbolic contrasts, such as the natural world's separation from the dark, satanic mine. Second, the story employs biblical symbolism, particularly associated with Walter's dead body. Third, the closure of the story implies a parallel with the Egyptian myth of Osiris and Isis, and fourth, the story draws on the symbolism in Lawrence's personal mytho-poetic philosophy, associated with the relationship of the sexes.

The story makes reference to a range of traditional symbols. Like much of Lawrence's work, it draws extensively on nature imagery. In this way, Lawrence belongs to a line of prose writers in the pastoral narrative tradition of Charlotte Brontë, George Eliot, and Thomas Hardy, who celebrated rural life, discovering in nature something of profound spiritual significance. Their sympathy with nature also indicates a nostalgia for a mythic English past, which probably never existed in the idealized form they presented. Certainly, however, the rural environment was being transformed from the mid-eighteenth century up to the time of Lawrence by industrialization, which blights the environment of the Bates's family home at the beginning of "Odour of Chrysanthemums." The story opens with the image of an awkward, stumbling train startling a young colt, which can still outrun it, and frightening away birds. The engine's smoke clings to the grass just as the effects of the mine's pollution have caused the oak tree to wither. Unlike many Victorian novels, such as George Eliot's *Felix Holt,* in which the train represents progress, here it merely destroys. In this environment, a vine clutches at a cottage as if it wants to pull the structure down, and even the chrysanthemums are "dishevelled." The war between the organic world and the hard, machine world of the mine reflects the conflict between the characters in the story. Walter is associated until the end with the murderous, mechanical domain of the mine, and Elizabeth with the chrysan-

Miners standing on the tracks near the opening of a mine in Wales.

themums, now disheveled, which have appeared at significant moments of her life, and which she now views with disillusionment.

Another natural image is introduced in the story's first paragraph when the burning pit-bank is described as having "flames like red sores licking its ashy sides." Fire and flame, which can both purify and destroy, are here linked with disease. The Bates's kitchen, however, has the warmth and comfort of a coal fire, and its light illuminates the cups prepared for tea, an occasion for communal sharing. The kitchen's warmth forms a stark contrast with the bleak, cold world outside the home, though

Elizabeth knows that the local pub attracts her husband not just with its fellowship, but its physical warmth. She soon learns that her husband was smothered, like a flame, in the mine. When his body, still warm, arrives, it must be set down on the floor, though covered with a red tablecloth, in a cold and damp room without a fireplace. Even the pink chrysanthemums in the room have a cold, deathly smell now. The reddish color of the chrysanthemums and the cloth, like the "smoky burning" of Walter's life, are both now cold. The story takes place during late afternoon and night, and all of its events are illuminated faintly by fire light. As such,

What Do I Read Next?

- "The Woman Who Rode Away," D. H. Lawrence's short story from 1928, contains a mythological and apocalyptic conclusion which may be anticipated in "Odour of Chrysanthemums."

- *Sons and Lovers,* D. H. Lawrence's autobiographical novel from 1913, involves a very similar relationship between a miner and his wife as that portrayed in "Odour of Chrysanthemums."

- D. H. Lawrence's essay "Cocksure Women and Hensure Men," in *Phoenix II: Uncollected, Unpublished, and Other Prose Works by D. H. Lawrence,* published in 1968, is a brief and stark statement of Lawrence's view of problems in relations between the sexes.

- *Modern Times: Reflections on a Century of English Modernity,* edited by Mica Nava and Alan O'Shea and published in 1996, is a valuable introduction to many of the major social and cultural movements of the early twentieth century.

- *The Twentieth-Century Mind: History, Ideas, and Literature in Britain,* written by C. B. Cox and A. E. Dyson and published in 1972. Volumes I and II provide a general introduction to the historical and cultural contexts in which Lawrence was writing.

Elizabeth's world comes more and more to resemble the underground mine world of her husband, a place of male comradery and sweaty physical work, symbolically associated with dark passions, and possibly, the demonic. The darkness, associated with Walter Bates in his underground work and in what his mother calls "his hateful ways," also belongs to his son who is hidden in shadow, lost in darkness, and even invisible in the dark family room. The dark also represents the mysterious and the unnameable, which Elizabeth finally confronts in the form of her husband's corpse which she gazes at and interprets, acknowledging the hidden, dark forces she has ignored.

The story's use of darkness in light may also be interpreted as belonging to its Christian frame of reference. This is an implied level of meaning indicated by various references: darkness and light; women weeping over a man's body, which one refers to as a "lamb"; a projected meeting in the "next world" after death; and the opening words of the final paragraph, "At last it was finished," recalling Christ's last words on the cross. These references immediately suggest biblical parallels, which would have been obvious to most English readers of Lawrence's day. Significantly, however,

Lawrence transforms these biblical references to make them part of his own mythological system. Though raised in a Christian home, and though his writing is suffused with Christian imagery, Lawrence felt that Christianity was partially responsible for much of the hypocrisy and superficiality he despised in England. As a result, while the story incorporates a Christian range of reference, it does so in a way which partly reverses the usually understood meaning of certain symbols. For example, in the story, darkness is associated with blindness, human separation, and perhaps even the demonic, but it is also linked with passion and with access to a deeper, mysterious, more meaningful life. Moreover, the body of Walter Bates has, like the body of Christ, been wept over by the women surrounding him. However, here, the wife of the dead man weeps from shame that she has "denied" her husband. Elizabeth recognizes in his dead body something powerful and essential, which is both the masculine principle and the concentration of dark, passionate forces, as well as all which is "other." The beauty of the body and what she feels to be her husband's absolute integrity makes Elizabeth conscious of a gap between herself and him, life and death, male and female, and between the forces of

> The acknowledgment of an essential separation of men and women was one of the central tenets of Lawrence's philosophy, and its elucidation in his personal mythic system is the fourth main pattern of symbolism in the story."

conventional, middle-class respectability which she aspires to, and the dark, physical, working-class values he symbolically embodies.

The third major symbolic frame of reference belongs to the pre-Christian myth of Osiris and Isis. This Egyptian myth allows ''Odour of Chrysanthemums'' to deal with the forces of darkness, death, and renewal in a positive way, and it also intermingles with the Christian frame of reference. Osiris is the Egyptian god of vegetation, but he is dead and reigns over the realm of the dead, though he is green and lifelike. The myth of Osiris and Isis is the story of the jealousy of Osiris's brother over his goodness as a sovereign god. Osiris's brother plots to kill Osiris, by making a wooden chest the precise size of Osiris's body, which Osiris enters in response to a challenge. Once inside, Osiris is imprisoned and the chest dropped into the ocean, from where it is later recovered after an extended search by Isis. The corpse is then abducted by Osiris's brother, dismembered and scattered over Egypt. Once again Isis recovers the sections of the body, washing and embalming the body so artfully that it looks as if it were alive. Isis even conceives a child, Horus, with the body of Osiris. The cult of Osiris is associated with fertility, the rotation of the seasons, and with the preservation of the ruling monarch. Some of the parallels with Lawrence's story are obvious. The body of Walter Bates is recovered from the mine, as Osiris's body is dredged up from the ocean. The miracle of the body's being intact and unmarked by the calamity is noted by everyone, and is almost as magical as the assembling of the dispersed body of Osiris. Similarly, once the dirt which covers Wal-

ter's body is washed off, he looks as if he is living again, and his body is even warm and his face flushed. Furthermore, Elizabeth is pregnant with Walter's child. Seeing his dead body, she is overwhelmed with her husband's apartness, his detachment from herself which she never recognized before. The implication is that her life will be transformed by her awareness of the infinite gap which separates, and always has separated, them. This knowledge will probably now influence her raising of her children, particularly her male children, representatives of the separateness of her husband.

The acknowledgment of an essential separation of men and women was one of the central tenets of Lawrence's philosophy, and its elucidation in his personal mythic system is the fourth main pattern of symbolism in the story. Lawrence developed an elaborate mythic view of history which held that in Europe and especially England, as the result of a variety of forces, men and women had lost the sense of their fundamental difference, and this loss unleashed a myriad of evils. Lawrence attempted to correct this imbalance by incorporating into his own personal mythology figures from various non-European myth systems such as Osiris. The characters in ''Odour of Chrysanthemums'' represent much larger unconscious forces. In a sense, Elizabeth and Walter represent all English men and women who have lost a sense of their deep differences and also a respect for one another's apartness. At the end of the story, there is a sense that Elizabeth is washing the body of a god of the underworld which she has no right to touch—an act which previously she refused to perform—and that in future she will be the guardian of this experience and a kind of priestess to her dead husband. Elizabeth, first introduced as ''imperious,'' is at the conclusion of the story reduced and chastened. Walter's mother suggests that Elizabeth's failure to make allowances for the lively energy of her beloved son contributed to his decline into drink and dissipation. Elizabeth's recognition of her husband's separateness seems to acknowledge the correctness of this judgement. Like Walter's mother who is now jealous of her daughter-in-law's natural right to claim and wash the body, Elizabeth has been jealous, it is implied, of her husband's natural, masculine ''mastery'' and has tried to rule him.

The close of the story strongly suggests that Elizabeth will be ruled in the future by the mastery of life—represented symbolically by her son—and by the mastery of death—symbolically, her deceased husband. No real access to rebirth and renewal is offered Elizabeth at the end of the story, except through a kind of worship of the principles she has discovered embodied in her departed Osiris. Rebirth in the story is offered exclusively to Walter Bates, a common man, who carries within him a portion of the god Osiris, and who will be reborn in the realms of death. Often in Lawrence's work, renewal and rebirth are associated with either an impending departure or with religious eros, the investing of spiritual meaning in sex. Here, the renewed and youthful body of Walter Bates is resexualized in death, and like Osiris, associated with fertility. The dark world of the dead which Walter enters is the true place for sexual passion, which for Lawrence lies at the center of creation and ensures its fertility and renewal. Elizabeth will remain a chaste devotee of her husband's memory, with the possibility that if she perfects her recognition of his exclusive separation, he will not be a stranger to her in the next world.

"Lawrence spent his life writing guidebooks for women," noted Simone de Beauvoir, cited in Kate Millett's *Sexual Politics,* and again and again women in his fiction must become subject to men's views of their true nature, true sexuality, and true social role. In "Odour of Chrysanthemums," Elizabeth learns to interpret the symbolism in the body of her husband, shorn of the distracting, seemingly familiar trappings of habit and personality. Washing his body, an act of love, devotion, and servitude, she sees its wondrous strangeness and its erotic power. This non-intellectual, almost reverential action of washing and weeping, a corollary to her previous, somewhat fretful action of sewing to distract herself, and her mother-in-law's keening and mindless rocking, is a tactile reading of the mysterious body of her husband. In this reading of the body, she unconsciously comes to recognize her much despised, degraded husband as a Christ-like figure, but transformed into a god of the underworld. The remainder of her life will be an extended interpretation of this encounter with the mythic unknown, and she will "submit" to her "masters," both in life and in death.

Source: Oliver Lovesey, Overview of "Odour of Chrysanthemums," for *Short Stories for Students,* The Gale Group, 1999.

Michael Black

In the following excerpt from commentary on "Odour of Chrysanthemums," Black suggests some meanings that the reader may be intended to draw from the story's portrayal of Elizabeth Bates's series of thoughts, moods, and emotions as she first angrily, then fearfully, awaits her husband's return, and then strips, washes, and lays out his dead body.

The two great masterpieces among the stories begun in the period 1909–11 are "Daughters of the Vicar" and "Odour of Chrysanthemums." Neither reached its present version easily; it was in drastic revision in the period from 1911 until 1913 and 1914 that they reached the form in which we have them, and the changes that Lawrence made in revising them were crucial. Their completion takes us into the first period of his maturity, so that they represent a substantial advance on *Sons and Lovers,* in his own grasp of what he wanted to say, and his ability to express it. Yet they are related to the material of that novel, as well as to the stories already considered.

They do a final justice to the mining community of Eastwood, to the men and women of that life; and they provide a comment also on the relationship of Walter and Gertrude Morel. The dead miner in "Odour of Chrysanthemums" is called Walter; like Morel he is a drunkard, or in danger of becoming one; his wife Elizabeth is becoming estranged from him. . . .

"Odour of Chrysanthemums" is widely accepted as among Lawrence's masterpieces. We are back in another cottage by the railway-side; the story is shorter, very concentrated, and "dramatic" in that the events take place in a few hours and have the weight and inevitability of those climactic moments in which a fate is worked out. There is a sense of years being summed up and given a meaning; but no eventful "plot," and only one central character—the miner's wife. All others are mere attendants. The mature embittered woman is shown awaiting her husband's return at the end of the day, at first in anger, then in dread. The anger is because she thinks he is getting drunk at the pub. But he is brought in dead, smothered by a fall of rock at the coal face. The wife and his mother lay out and wash the body in the greatest of all Lawrence's ritual lavings: and in the course of this Elizabeth . . . seeing the body before her, comes, too late, upon an essential truth, a revelation about the otherness of the man—what he was.

In the page or two in which the laying-out is described—like a Deposition or a Pietá by a great artist—the simple language is again both Biblical and peculiarly Lawrentian. These paragraphs are

> "That gesture of the woman 'claiming' the man, as if she owned him, became peculiarly hateful to Lawrence. . . ."

one of the great set-pieces in the language. The passage begins:

> When they arose, saw him lying in the naive dignity of death, the women stood arrested in fear and respect. For a few moments they remained still, looking down, the old mother whimpering. Elizabeth felt countermanded. She saw him, how utterly inviolable he lay in himself. She had nothing to do with him. She could not accept it. Stooping, she laid her hands on him, in claim. . . .

It is a movement of the ego, in response to a feared loss. That gesture of the woman "claiming" the man, as if she owned him, became peculiarly hateful to Lawrence, as we grasp from the poem "She said as well to me" in *Look! We Have Come Through*. So this is an initial hubris, provoked by the implicit denial the body seems to offer. But Elizabeth is embarked on the process which will lead her to "see," in the same way as Louisa comes to "see" Alfred, though the two situations are polar opposites, since in the one case Alfred is alive, and coming more alive, while Walter is dead, and even his life with Elizabeth is being denied its previous significance.

She continues her anxious exploration; pursuing her claim, but still refused:

> . . . Elizabeth embraced the body of her husband, with cheek and lips. She seemed to be listening, inquiring, trying to get some connection. But she could not. She was driven away. He was impregnable.

Partly because she must do it anyway, and partly because it induces a different attitude to laying her hand on the body "in claim," she prepares to wash him. The Biblical element in the syntax and language ("When they arose. . .," "She had nothing to do with him") begins to stir:

> She rose, went into the kitchen, where she poured warm water into a bowl, brought soap and flannel and a soft towel.

> "I must wash him," she said. Then the old mother rose stiffly, and watched Elizabeth as she carefully

washed his face, carefully brushing the big blonde moustache from his mouth with the flannel. She was afraid with a bottomless fear, so she ministered to him.

There is the word. The act is now one of service, performed in awe:

> At last it was finished. He was a man of handsome body, and his face showed no traces of drink. He was blonde, full-fleshed, with fine limbs. But he was dead.

The word "fleshed" generates, a few lines later, sentences in which both the Biblical doctrine and the physical reality lie side by side: again her attempt to reach him is repulsed:

> Elizabeth sank down again to the floor, and put her face against his neck, and trembled and shuddered. But she had to draw away again. He was dead, and her living flesh had no place against his.

The old mother breaks out into a lament, and her words remind us of Alfred Durant's living body, and of Miss Mary's baby son. Underneath the words (and she calls the man a lamb, twice) there may be a reference also to the other Mary's baby; immaculate:

> "White as milk he is, clear as a twelve-month baby, bless him, the darling!" the old mother murmured to herself. "Not a mark on him, clear and clean and white, as beautiful as ever a child was made."

Elizabeth then has her tragic recognition, accepting the dead man as unreachably other, as unknown:

> Life with its smoky burning gone from him, had left him apart and utterly alien to her. And she knew what a stranger he was to her. In her womb was ice of fear, because of this separate stranger with whom she had been living as one flesh. Was this what it all meant— utter, intact separateness, obscured by heat of living? In dread she turned her face away. The fact was too deadly. There had been nothing between them, and yet they had come together, exchanging their nakedness repeatedly. Each time he had taken her, they had been two isolated beings, far apart as now. He was no more responsible than she. The child was like ice in her womb. For as she looked at the dead man, her mind, cold and detached, said clearly: "Who am I? What have I been doing? I have been fighting a husband who did not exist. *He* existed all the time. What wrong have I done? What was that I have been living with? There lies the reality, this man."—And her soul died in her for fear: she knew she had never seen him, he had never seen her, they had met in the dark and had fought in the dark, not knowing whom they had met nor whom they fought. And now she saw, and turned silent in seeing. For she had been wrong. She had said he was something he was not; she had felt familiar with him. Whereas he was apart all the while, living as she never lived, feeling as she never felt.

The "smoky burning" we have met before. The word "womb," used several times, both of the mother and of Elizabeth, is distinctly Biblical. Here the striking phrase ''in her womb was ice of fear'' reminds us that Elizabeth is pregnant; so that her Annunciation, unlike Louisa's, is a negation of joyful prophecy. It is an annihilating negation that she faces; but her grief is not egoistic: she feels pity as well as awe and shame:

> She looked at his naked body and was ashamed, as if she had denied it. After all, it was itself. It seemed awful to her. She looked at his face, and she turned her own face to the wall. For his look was other than hers, his way was not her way. She had denied him what he was—she saw it now. She had refused him as himself.—And this had been her life and his life.—She was grateful to death, which restored the truth. And she knew she was not dead.

> And all the while her heart was bursting with grief and pity for him. What had he suffered? What stretch of horror for this helpless man! She was rigid with agony. She had not been able to help him. He had been cruelly injured, this naked man, this other being, and she could make no reparation. There were the children—but the children belonged to life. This dead man had nothing to do with them. He and she were only channels through which life had flowed to issue in the children. She was a mother —but how awful she knew it now to have been a wife. And he, dead now, how awful he must have felt it to be a husband. She felt that in the next world he would be a stranger to her. If they met there, in the beyond, they would only be ashamed of what had been before. The children had come, for some mysterious reason, out of both of them. But the children did not unite them. Now he was dead, she knew how eternally he was apart from her, how eternally he had nothing more to do with her. She saw this episode of her life closed. They had denied each other in life. Now he had withdrawn. An anguish came over her. It was finished then. . . .

The Biblical phrase hints a kinship with the dead Christ. And the phrase about this episode of her life being closed is a comment on Cyril Mersham's cheerful wish to be done with this part of his life in ''A Modern Lover.'' Her earlier gesture is now corrected:

> She was almost ashamed to handle him; what right had she or anyone to lay hands on him; but her touch was humble on his body.

The final sentences are again both Biblical (the repetition of ''it was finished'' is deliberate) and characteristically Lawrentian:

> At last it was finished. They covered him with a sheet and left him lying, with his face bound. And she fastened the door of the little parlour, lest the children should see what was lying there. Then, with peace sunk heavy on her heart, she went about making tidy the kitchen. She knew she submitted to life, which was her immediate master. But from death, her ultimate master, she winced with fear and shame.

That last cryptic judgement yields its meaning slowly. It had been made more immediately comprehensible in the cancelled reading in the page-proofs: ''For in death she would have no life, for she had never loved. She had life on earth with her children, that was all.'' But it is a niggling explanation, and Lawrence did well to take it out.

The story, first drafted in 1909, has its origins in the period of *The White Peacock*. But it was rewritten more than once, and there are two published versions—one in the *English Review* of June 1911 and one in the collection *The Prussian Officer* of 1914. These differ greatly from each other, and from the first manuscript versions. The most important changes come at the end, in the long sequence describing the washing of the body. Some decisive change took place in Lawrence between 1909 and 1914. His attitudes had changed, so that the story quite alters its point. In the very first version, when the two women strip the body, they feel an access of love, and it is comforting, almost euphoric. There is nothing of the later significance, the withering self-recognition which falls upon Elizabeth. It is hard to tell how much Lawrence himself in 1909 was feeling the warm gush that passes through the women. It is a maternal emotion: motherly pride and dominating complacency; and it leads the wife to handle the body in a spirit which later seemed sacrilegious to Lawrence:

> When they rose and looked at him lying naked in the grandeur of death, the women experienced suddenly the same feeling: the sense of motherhood. Elizabeth knelt and put her cheek against him and put her arms around him; the mother took his hand . . . and held it, sobbing, whispering ''My son!—Oh my son!'' . . . Elizabeth kissed him again and again, and touched him with her hands and her face.

There is more to this effect, reinforcing the idea of the two women acting as if they shared a sleeping child. Elizabeth handles the body very freely, smoothing his yellow hair from his forehead, and kissing him ''on the smooth clear ripples just below the breasts. She loved him very much now —and she was content. Her tears were all for the pity of it— and for the pity of him. Ah, the pity of it! . . . Ah, she loved him, how she loved him now!'' The story ends ''Poor dear, he was more helpless than a baby—and so beautiful.''

All this easy emotion, and the easy manipulation of the body, might have been noted with savage irony: a satire on an assumed tendency of women to turn their loss into an indulgence of maternal self-satisfaction. It is hard to be sure; it seems possible that Lawrence is divided here: part of him is reacting against what in another part of him flows very freely. But his intelligence would not let him rest there, nor would his developing experience. Between 1909 and 1914 he rejected that reaching-out of the mother to claim her child, and the wife reaching out to claim her husband as if he too were a child. If we turn to the story as we now have it, certain key words have a new resonance. The corpse lies "inviolable." It is not open to claims for emotional satisfaction, still less dominance or possession. The wife still, at first, lays her hand on the body "in claim," but already she is "listening, inquiring. But she could not. She was driven away. He was impregnable." She is "unavailing" and "countermanded."

The sense that he is "apart and utterly alien" then leads to her bitter discovery about the meaninglessness of their life together: the futility, the error of their struggle. What she now feels is a just emotion, since it does retrospective justice to the man and is a judgement on herself. J. C. F. Littlewood has pointed out that it is very like a comment on the struggle between Gertrude and Walter Morel in *Sons and Lovers*, and therefore like a step towards a just account of Lawrence's father. That is true, but is not all: Lawrence is not only shifting his emotional balance away from his mother, but from all women who "claim" men—the betraying gesture is her laying her hand on his body in the wrong spirit.

Source: Michael Black, "Short Stories II," in *D. H. Lawrence: The Early Fiction,* Cambridge University Press, 1986, pp. 188–210.

Robert N. Hudspeth

In the following excerpt, Hudspeth discusses ways that Lawrence presents a history of the Bates's married life through depicting Elizabeth Bates's state of mind as she waits for her husband, not knowing he has been killed.

"Odour of Chrysanthemums" develops from an apparently simple, recurring conflict between a young collier and his wife, now pregnant with their third child. The husband is given to regular drunken sprees, which the wife bitterly resents. Through the narrative, Lawrence reveals the complexity in their lives: the husband's drunkenness is a result of intense frustrations that the wife has never understood; these frustrations emerge as basic, ineluctable human realities for Lawrence. The story is formally divided into two sections, each reinforcing

and clarifying the other. The first section dramatizes the woman's anger and frustration as she waits for her husband to return from the mine. From her resentful anticipation of the evening's inevitable end, Lawrence creates the tension that has long existed between the two. Then, in part two, the dominant emotion shifts from anger to fear as the husband arrives home—dead, not drunk. Only with his death does the wife understand the meaning of isolation: pain and horror are life's defining characteristics.

The story opens with a precise evocation of an appropriate mood: "The fields were dreary and forsaken, and in the marshy strip that led to the whimsey, a reedy pit-pond, the fowls had already abandoned their run among the alders, to roost in the tarred fowl-house. The pit-bank loomed up beyond the pond, flames like red sores licking its ashy sides, in the afternoon's stagnant light." The dreary land, lit only by the demonic glare of the mine, is an embodiment of the psychic lives of the couple who stand at the center of the story. The grimness, the desolation, the connotations of waste and ruin are all appropriate to the lives of Walter and Elizabeth Bates. In the midst of this landscape is a richly symbolic image: a woman stands trapped between the evening ore train and the highway hedge. Caught by nature on one side and by man's machine on the other, the woman prefigures Elizabeth's isolation and Walter's suffocation in the mine. The wife has been trapped by nature's inescapable reality as surely as the husband has been trapped by the accident. The apparently minor detail of an ordinary scene creates more connotations of isolation and frustration for Lawrence to exploit.

From this general setting, the narration narrows to a specific figure in a specific yard. Lawrence retains the sombre connotations of the opening paragraph by the image of a "large bony vine [which] clutched at the house, as if to claw down the tiled roof." Dishevelled chrysanthemums, the central image of the story, adorn the bleak yard, adding not beauty but pathos to the scene by their bedraggled look and their incongruous presence in so blighted a place. All the forebodings inherent in the original description of the scene are implicit in Elizabeth's first speech. Her sharp words reveal her tension as she releases her exasperation on her son. Lawrence makes everything in the general atmosphere appropriate to Elizabeth's character. He quickly heightens the careful, muted introduction of conflict in the story by the encounter with her father, a widower, now planning remarriage. The older man's defensive question, "'Well, what's a man to do? It's no sort of life for a man of my years, to sit at my own hearth like a stranger'," appropriately brings to the story the theme of isolation, for, as one critic accurately notes, "what becomes evident, through detail after detail, is that everyone in Mrs. Bates's household does sit by the hearth a stranger" [George H. Ford, *Double Measure: A Study of the Novels and Stories of D. H. Lawrence*, 1965].

One of Lawrence's brilliant accomplishments in "Odour of Chrysanthemums" is to create the crackling tension between husband and wife without the man appearing. First in her sharp words to her son, then in the father's sympathetic report of the husband's drunken bragging, Lawrence indirectly creates the antagonism that dominates Elizabeth's life. The scene ends with the shrill wail of the winding-engine raising and lowering the elevator in the mine shaft. This mechanical chorus to the domestic tragedy reminds the reader of the mechanical rounds of work and frustration that have added to Elizabeth's anxiety. Like the image of the trapped woman, the recurring wail of the winding-engine contrasts the human and the mechanical worlds.

From this careful introduction of mood, image, and character, the scene moves indoors to the darkened kitchen where the mother and children sit, appropriately shrouded in darkness, unable to see each other. They are present, yet separated; their lives seem defined by darkness. The growing sense of isolation reinforces Elizabeth's frustration at her husband's absence. At teatime, the hour of some family fellowship, he is (supposedly) drinking in the tavern. The scene continues the gloomy suggestions of the opening paragraph and the conversation between Elizabeth and her father. Whatever might be creative is blighted; whatever could exist has died of hostility and frustration. At this moment, Lawrence expands the flower imagery that he began in the description of the yard. Elizabeth has stuck a handful of the tattered chrysanthemums in her waistband. When the daughter remarks on their aroma, the mother replies, "It was chrysanthemums when I married him, and chrysanthemums when you were born, and the first time they ever brought him home drunk, he'd got brown chrysanthemums in his button-hole."

The flowers for her have marked moments of heightened passion: marriage, birth, outrage; tonight, they mark the moment of death. Both the title of the story and the girl's response emphasize the sensory quality of the flowers. The image conveys

> As she stands and looks at Walter's body, she sees the absolute separateness of their existence. He had a life; she has one, but the life of each has been foreign to the other."

the *contact*, concrete and definite, with the moments of intense reality. Through the image, Lawrence attempts to circumvent the abstractions "birth," "anger," and "death," by closely associating these states with concrete, precise sensory data. The recurring use of the flowers also introduces a bitter irony into the story, for ordinarily they are delightful, beautiful objects. Here their beauty must exist with bitterness and hostility.

The first part of the story ends with a pair of grotesquely ironic statements that reinforce the reader's awareness of Elizabeth's isolation. In thinking of the impending drunken arrival of Walter, she says, "Eh, he'll not come now till they bring him. There he'll stick! But he needn't come rolling in here in his pit-dirt, for *I* won't wash him. He can lie on the floor." "They'll bring him when he does come—like a log. . . . And he may sleep on the floor till he wakes himself. I know he'll not go to work tomorrow after this!" These outbursts are chillingly fulfilled as townsmen bring Walter's body home like a log; he does lie on the floor, but she *does* indeed wash him. The point of this ironic foreshadowing is not to make Elizabeth into an unwittingly callous woman but to emphasize the fact that Walter is no more removed from her in death than he was in life. He has not been a true part of her life any more than he will be from now on. The irony heightens the blindness; the horror of the accurate predictions reflects the lack of understanding between the husband and wife.

In this first part of "Odour of Chrysanthemums," Lawrence has relied on compression and indirection to convey the appropriate emotional reality in Elizabeth Bates. The desolate scenery, the anger, the frustration, the flowers combine with the symbolically arranged kitchen scene with its dark-

> Lawrence's vision is demanding, but he consistently refuses to sentimentalize his story."

ened faces and gloomy shade to convey the wasted life in Elizabeth's existence. As in Chekhov, whom Lawrence admired, we infer the quality of life from the quality of the scene. Lawrence has created the static reality of blight and futility that dominate Elizabeth's life. Unlike a longer narrative, which would focus on the growth of the crisis or probe the various reasons for the tension, this short story conveys an accomplished fact. "Odour of Chrysanthemums" does well what short fiction does best: it illuminates a moment of reality. To prepare for the coming understanding, Lawrence devotes the first part of the story to a careful presentation of Elizabeth's ordinary life: everything in the scene and action persuades the reader that this night is quite like many in the past. Nothing seems unusual; the details are as ordinary as they are precise, but with the shift in part two from anger to fear, the story moves to a new level.

With increasing alarm, Elizabeth goes to the neighbors seeking news of her indifferent mate. The winding-engine, previously only a detail of the familiar background, becomes more ominous, "She was startled by the rapid chuff of the winding-engine at the pit, and the sharp whirr of the brake on the rope as it descended." Her turbulent emotions come to an awful pitch as the miners bring her husband in—dead of suffocation, a victim of an all-too-common industrial accident. In a chilly room, pervaded with the odour of chrysanthemums, Elizabeth and her mother prepare the body for burial.

Now anger has changed to horror; frustration has become despair. The ordinary, bitter wait for the drunken man has become an extraordinary facing of death. The whole fabric of desolate commonness Lawrence so carefully built in Part 1 now contrasts with a moment so powerfully charged that the old blinders of familiarity are lost; Elizabeth, for the first time, enters into a rich but devastating perceptiveness of her husband's world.

As she stands and looks at Walter's body, she sees the absolute separateness of their existence. He had a life; she has one, but the life of each has been foreign to the other. They are no more able to communicate now than they were when he lived. "Elizabeth felt countermanded. She saw him, how utterly inviolable he lay in himself. She had nothing to do with him. She could not accept it." ". . . She knew she had never seen him, he had never seen her, they had met in the dark and had fought in the dark, not knowing whom they met nor whom they fought. And now she saw, and turned silent in seeing. For she had been wrong. She had said he was something he was not; she had felt familiar with him. Whereas he was apart all the while, living as she never lived, feeling as she never felt." This sudden knowledge is a climactic moment. The tension so precisely created earlier in the story now gains its *full* meaning. Lawrence brings to bear the careful details, the ordinariness of the evening on the truth of life for Elizabeth. Walter's action has incalculably deeper meaning than she had suspected. Lawrence has prepared her (and the reader) for this moment; the image that dominates the scene—darkness—is appropriate for the meaning and consistent with the connotations of the previous images.

Suddenly, painfully, she can feel awe, grief, and pity for Walter. "What had he suffered? What stretch of horror for this helpless man! She was rigid with agony. She had not been able to help him. He had been cruelly injured, this naked man, this other being, and she could make no reparation." With tragic irony, Lawrence shows the chasm separating his characters; only in death, only in the most traumatic moment does isolation give way to pity. "Life with its smoky burning gone from him, had left him apart and utterly alien to her. And she knew what a stranger he was to her. In her womb was ice of fear, because of this separate stranger with whom she had been living as one flesh. Was this what it all meant—utter, intact separateness, obscured by heat of living?"

To Lawrence, man is denied the luxury of having both comfort and knowledge. Like Emily Dickinson, who proclaimed "Success is counted sweetest / By those who ne'er succeed," Lawrence accepts the reality of deprivation: death and truth are grim partners.

From the pain of her ignorance, Elizabeth has come into the pain of understanding. For Lawrence, the absoluteness of their isolation is mirrored in technique of organization. He has emphasized her loneliness and pain by creating the tension between her and the absent husband. In the story, man and woman live without essential contact. The lurid light of the opening scene, the trapped woman, the darkened kitchen, the ironic foreshadowing all heighten the connotations of pain, loneliness, and despair. Lawrence embodies the thematic abstractions in the precise, concrete details of the narrative.

Both method and theme emphasize the disparity between the necessary human life force (copulation and procreation) and the equally necessary human psychic existence. To be a mother is necessary and good, but to be a wife is a terrible thing to Elizabeth (and to Lawrence). "He and she were only channels through which life had flowed to issue to the children. She was a mother—but how awful she knew it now to have been a wife. And he, dead now, how awful he must have felt it to be a husband." Using Elizabeth's pregnancy, Lawrence creates a tension between the static blight of their psychic lives and their parental fecundity. The cycle of birth and death is incompatible with the static hostility of their roles as husband and wife. Like the pain that must accompany Elizabeth's understanding of their isolation, the pain of her knowledge of this horrible paradox of human life is ineluctable. Merely to know, to rise above the daily blindness of life is not to free oneself from pain. Lawrence's vision is demanding, but he consistently refuses to sentimentalize his story.

The story focuses on the present state of pain and frustration by relying, in part, on the careful, precise evocation of the continuity of blight in the Bates's lives. Through the image of the chrysanthemums, the reader accepts the prior existence of a wasted life and so is compelled to accept its extension into Elizabeth's future, because the aesthetic logic works for both past and future. Past and future collapse upon the present moment of pain to define life's salient qualities. Lawrence extends the incompatibility of male and female existence as Elizabeth envisions her life with her next two "husbands," life and death. "She knew she submitted to life, which was her immediate master. But from death, her ultimate master, she winced with fear and shame." Lawrence's use of *master*, the colloquial British term for husband, re-enforces the sense of paradox in Elizabeth's life. Just as she has been required to be both mother and wife, so is she required to be a consort to both life and death. The paradox of being a wife and mother is mirrored in this final image of life and death. We can escape neither paradox; the pain of frustration is a human

curse. The clarification Lawrence achieves through Elizabeth Bates precisely reveals what isolation is: the inevitable expression of the paradoxical human necessity to surrender yet remain inviolable.

Source: Robert N. Hudspeth, "Lawrence's 'Odour of Chrysanthemums': Isolation and Paradox," in *Studies in Short Fiction,* Vol. 6, No. 5, Fall, 1969, pp. 630–36.

Frank Amon

In the following excerpt, Amon briefly notes the principal themes and symbols in "Odour of Chrysanthemums" and comments on the story's characteristic autobiographical elements.

Lawrence, like Chekhov, stands for a distension in the form of the [short] story. Like Chekhov, he had the genius for portraying the intimate feeling of a place, a landscape, a conversation, or a character. Like Chekhov—but in a manner peculiar to his technique—he crystallized vacancy, frustration, inertia, and futile aspiration. We see that all of Lawrence's stories share one characteristic: all depend, as stories, upon subtle psychological changes of character.

With Lawrence's characters (as with Chekhov's) the subconscious seems to come to the surface and they communicate directly without the impediment of speech. Naturally the most interesting point for Lawrence is that at which the interplay of psychic forces is incomplete, where the adjustment is difficult, where the emphasis is on discord rather than on harmony. Consequently, Lawrence focused his attention, as Frederick Hoffman has said, "on the subtle complexity of an emotional state which a character assumes in a crisis."

The significance of this is that Lawrence has accomplished a transfiguration of experience. He lifts his characters from the surface experience of the concrete world onto new and immediate levels of psychic consciousness, and then returns them, sanctified and altered, to the concrete world in which they must continue. Inevitably this is the symbolic *rites de passage*, the ceremony or initiation or baptism, which ushers an individual into a new way of life; and in this, too, it is the spiritual death and rebirth motif of Lawrence's chosen symbol, the Phoenix.

If we take, for example, "The Odour of Chrysanthemums," one of Lawrence's earliest stories, ... this *rites de passage* aspect comes out quite clearly.

> **"**Naturally the most interesting point for Lawrence is that at which the interplay of psychic forces is incomplete, where the adjustment is difficult, where the emphasis is on discord rather than on harmony."

The autobiographical setting of Lawrence's youth—the lower-class colliery family—is of course common to many of his early stories and novels. But the theme, too, is central to Lawrence: the inviolable isolation of the individual psyche, the utter separateness of those with whom we share physical intimacy.

The revelation of the theme (of which for us the entire story is the qualifying and modifying symbol) comes to the wife through the death of her husband. Revelation through death then is the means of objectifying the theme. However, it is the *moment* of revelation with which we are concerned here and with the peculiar means of objectifying that moment.

Gradually, as the story unfolds, our interest in the chrysanthemums increases. At first, they hang dishevelled, "like pink cloths." A little later, Elizabeth's small son tears at the "ragged wisps of chrysanthemums" and drops the petals in handfuls along the path: "'Don't do that—it does look nasty,' said his mother. He refrained, and she, suddenly pitiful, broke off a twig with three or four wan flowers and held them against her face." . . . [Later] Elizabeth's daughter wants to smell the flowers:

"Don't they smell beautiful!"

Her mother gave a short laugh.

"No," she said, "not to me. It was chrysanthemums when I married him, and chrysanthemums when you were born, and the first time they ever brought him home drunk, he'd got brown chrysanthemums in his button-hole."

Here then is their significance: they are talismans of change, transition into a new way of life—a

tragic way of life. They are markers of marriage, birth, and—inevitably—death. The chrysanthemums, we might say, are the omens, and it is through them that a great part of our interest is aroused and focalized; and it is through them (but not through them alone) that the father's death is foreshadowed.

[Lawrence was able to] thoroughly incorporate into his art the most appropriate action—literal and symbolic—to objectify his theme.

We find incipient in this story such other patterns and motifs as the *Mater Dolorata*, possessive motherhood, lack of rapport between the sexes, and father-hatred-envy, which were to occupy Lawrence the rest of his life. . . .

Source: Frank Amon, "D. H. Lawrence and the Short Story," in *The Achievement of D. H. Lawrence,* edited by Frederick J. Hoffman and Harry T. Moore, University of Oklahoma Press, 1953, pp. 222–34.

Sources

Cushman, Keith. "Odour of Chrysanthemums." In his *D. H. Lawrence at Work: The Emergence of the Prussian Officer Stories,* Harvester, 1978. pp. 47-76.

Draper, R. P. Introduction to his *D. H. Lawrence: The Critical Heritage,* Barnes and Noble, 1970, pp. 1-29.

Millett, Kate. *Sexual Politics,* New York: Doubleday, 1970, 393 p.

Stovel, Nora Foster. "D. H. Lawrence and 'The Dignity of Death': Tragic Recognition in 'Odour of Chrysanthemums,' 'The Widowing of Mrs. Holroyd,' and *Sons and Lovers.*" *The D. H. Lawrence Review,* Vol. 16, No. 1, Spring, 1983, pp. 59-82.

Thornton, Weldon. "Odour of Chrysanthemums." In his *D. H. Lawrence: A Study of the Short Fiction,* Twayne, 1993, pp. 29-35.

Worthen, John. *D. H. Lawrence,* London: Edward Arnold, 1991, 136 p.

Further Reading

Boulton, James T. "D. H. Lawrence's Odour of Chrysanthemums: An Early Version," *Renaissance and Modern Studies,* Vol. 13, 1969, pp. 4-48.

An edition of the printer's proofs of the story, with editorial comment on variations between the proofs, Lawrence's revisions, and the published version of 1911.

Fernihough, Anne. *D. H. Lawrence: Aesthetics and Ideology,* Oxford: Oxford University Press, 1993, 211 p.
In this book, Fernihough discusses Lawrences use of aesthetics and ideology.

Ford, Ford Madox. "D. H. Lawrence." In *Portraits from Life*, pp. 70–89. Boston: Houghton Mifflin Co., 1937.
Ford tells about his first reading of a D. H. Lawrence story, "Odour of Chrysanthemums," and lists some of the qualities that convinced him Lawrence was an author of genius.

Kinkead-Weekes, Mark. *D. H. Lawrence: Triumph To Exile, 1912-1922,* Cambridge University Press, 1996, 943 p.
In a comprehensive account of Lawrence's life, Kinkead-Weekes investigates many of the themes which arise in the story.

McCabe, T. H. "The Otherness of D. H. Lawrence's 'Odour of Chrysanthemums'." *The D. H. Lawrence Review,* Vol. 19, no. 2, Summer, 1987, pp. 149-56.
McCabe traces how an intuitive awareness of otherness in the story, associated with gender and death, leads to self-discovery.

Nash, Walter. "On a Passage from Lawrence's 'Odour of Chrysanthemums'." *Language and Literature: An Introductory Reader in Stylistics,* edited by Ronald Carter, George Allen and Unwin, 1982, pp. 101-20.
Nash provides a detailed stylistic analysis of the first paragraph of Lawrence's story, showing how it reveals the theme of alienation.

Schulz, Volker. "D. H. Lawrence's Early Masterpiece of Short Fiction: 'Odour of Chrysanthemums'." *Studies in Short Fiction,* Vol. 28, No. 3, Summer, 1991, pp. 363-70.
Schulz's general reading of the story explores its realistic setting and the progress to the final revelation.

Wulff, Ute-Christel. "Hebel, Hofmnannsthal and Lawrence's 'Odour of Chrysanthemums'." *The D. H. Lawrence Review,* Vol. 20, No. 3, Fall, 1988, pp. 287-96.
Wulff explores Lawrence's knowledge of German literature and the parallels between this story and tales by Johann Peter Hebel and Hugo von Hofmannsthal.

Pomegranate Seed

Edith Wharton

1931

Edith Wharton composed the ghost story, "Pomegranate Seed," near the end of 1930, and saw it published by the *Ladies' Home Journal* in 1931. The tale was subsequently included in Wharton's collection of short fiction, *The World Over* (1936), and then in her collection, *Ghosts,* published in 1937, the last year of the author's life. Readers of that collection admired Wharton's skill in writing tales of the supernatural, but several reviewers believed the ghost story to be a less important genre than the novels of social observation by which Wharton had made her reputation over the previous decades. While Wharton's novels remain at the center of her achievements, her ghost stories have gained critical acknowledgment over the years. "Pomegranate Seed" is admired for the relentless pacing of its suspenseful plot, for the particularity with which its principal characters are rendered, and for the chilling evocation of the supernatural achieved by the story's ending. "Pomegranate Seed" surely possesses the "thermometrical quality" cited by Wharton as the hallmark of good ghost stories; she believed a well-crafted ghost story should send a cold shiver down the reader's spine. The story's title is derived from the Greco-Roman myth of Persephone, which Wharton is likely to have read in Ovid's *Metamorphoses*. Abducted by Pluto, the Lord of the Dead, Persephone is not permitted to leave the underworld permanently because she has eaten six pomegranate seeds in the gardens of death. Contemporary critical debate on Wharton's story

has focused, in large degree, upon establishing correspondences between Wharton's characters and their predecessors in the Persephone myth. Striking in its mythological resonances, ''Pomegranate Seed'' is also a powerful meditation on the supernatural, on the conflict between flesh and spirit, and on the constant risk of alienation in human life.

Author Biography

Born Edith Newbold Jones in 1862, Edith Wharton was a member of the New York leisure class that would become the subject of much of her fiction. Few American women obtained university educations in the decades when Wharton was coming of age; her schooling was conducted by private tutors employed by her parents.

As a child, this future practitioner of the supernatural tale had a terrible fear of ghosts and ghost stories. In an essay entitled ''Life and I'' Wharton reminisced that ''till I was twenty seven or eight, I could not sleep in the room with a book containing a ghost story, and I have frequently had to burn books of this kind, because it frightened me to know that they were downstairs in the library!'' Still, the young woman discovered a talent for literature, privately publishing a volume of poetry at the age of sixteen and placing her first short story in *Scribner's* magazine at twenty-eight.

In 1885 she married Edward Wharton, a wealthy Bostonian sportsman. The marriage ended in divorce in 1912, by which time Wharton was well established as a writer. Important friendships of Wharton's middle and later years included one with Bernard Berenson, connoisseur and art historian, and Henry James, master of the international novel of manners and author of short stories, including the supernatural classic *The Turn of the Screw.*

Wharton's fiction has often been compared to that of James, whom she met in 1904. Indeed, in her critical volume *The Writing of Fiction,* Wharton speaks of her craft as derived from James, who felt, she said, ''every great novel must be based on a profound sense of moral values, and then constructed with a classical unity and economy of means.'' In Wharton's work that ''sense of moral values'' involves scrutiny of the ethical corruption of the American leisure class, and of the role of women in that class. In her greatest novels, *The House of Mirth* and *The Age of Innocence,* Wharton indicts the wealthy families of New York as hypocritical, exclusionary, and materialistic.

After her marriage ended, Wharton took up permanent residence in France. During World War I, she organized relief efforts in France and worked to help Belgian orphans, work for which she was decorated with the Legion of Honor by the French government. In 1921 Wharton became the first female winner of the Pulitzer Prize in literature for *The Age of Innocence.* She died in 1937 at St. Brice-sous-Forêt in France.

Plot Summary

Part I

''Pomegranate Seed'' opens as Charlotte Ashby enters the vestibule to her New York home and pauses before entering the house. She has paused to remember the course of her brief marriage to Kenneth Ashby, and to consider the mysterious events that have clouded their recent months together. Kenneth Ashby, a lawyer, is a widower whose marriage to Charlotte has apparently healed the grief he felt at the death of his first wife, Elsie Ashby. Charlotte has moved into the house Kenneth had shared with Elsie, and come to feel at home there. Kenneth has even moved the portrait of Elsie that had hung in his library up to the nursery of his two children, in order that Charlotte might feel herself to be the mistress of the house. When they returned from their honeymoon, however, Kenneth found waiting for him a mysterious letter in a gray envelope. Charlotte never learned the contents of the letter, addressed to Kenneth in a woman's handwriting, but from its effects on her husband—withdrawal, sadness, and perhaps a touch of fear—suspects it is from a former lover. Several similar letters have arrived for him since the honeymoon, each one deepening Kenneth's withdrawal and Charlotte's suspicion. Charlotte enters the house at last and finds that yet another letter is waiting for her husband.

Part II

Troubled by the most recent letter's arrival, Charlotte decides to spy on Kenneth when he comes home. Positioning herself behind the door to the entry hall, Charlotte watches as Kenneth opens the letter, reads it with an expression of great sadness and, to her dismay, kisses the paper on which his mysterious correspondent has sent the unknown

Edith Wharton

message. Charlotte comes out of her hiding place and accuses Kenneth of maintaining a correspondence with a former lover. Kenneth denies this, maintaining that the letters are about business. When Charlotte confronts him with his having kissed the letter, Kenneth continues to evade her questions and finally ends the conversation without having shown Charlotte the letter's contents.

Part III

Alone now, Charlotte reflects upon the former happiness of her brief marriage and resolves to help Kenneth in any way she can. She considers seeking Kenneth's mother's assistance. Mrs. Ashby is a forthright, practical person with whom Charlotte has always felt a bond. To go to his mother about the letters, however, would be a violation of Kenneth's privacy, and Charlotte rejects the idea. At dinner Charlotte suggests to Kenneth that they go away together for a vacation to relax Kenneth's nerves. Kenneth declines the offer, putting Charlotte off with vague explanations of his inability to travel. It occurs to Charlotte that Kenneth won't leave New York because his mysterious correspondent will not let him go. Kenneth weeps when his wife challenges him with this suspicion, and then agrees to leave town with her.

Part IV

When Charlotte wakes up the next morning she finds that Kenneth has already left the house, telling the maid to inform her that he plans for them to begin their vacation that very day. Charlotte is to expect news of when they will sail. When Charlotte telephones Kenneth's office, however, the secretary tells her that Kenneth has gone out of town. Hours pass with no word from Kenneth, and when evening comes Charlotte is worried and visits Kenneth's mother in hopes of an explanation. Mrs. Ashby has heard nothing from her son and is surprised to learn of their sudden plans for a holiday. Together the two women return to Charlotte's house only to discover that another gray letter has arrived in their absence. Charlotte is resolved to open the letter and get to the bottom of things.

Once out of its envelope the letter proves to be almost illegible, its letters pale and faint. Charlotte is able to make out only the words ''mine'' and ''come.'' She remarks: ''I suppose everything's pale about a ghost.'' This is the first time the story uses the word ''ghost,'' but it is an appropriate term, for as Mrs. Ashby reaches for the phone to call the police, the impression is given that Kenneth has answered the call of Elsie, his first wife, and gone to join her in the other world.

Characters

Charlotte Ashby

Charlotte Ashby, the second wife of widower Kenneth Ashby, is dismayed to discover a series of mysterious letters to her husband. At first she suspects that Kenneth is corresponding with a former lover. As the story unfolds, however, Charlotte comes to believe that the letters are from the ghost of Kenneth's first wife, Elsie. Her increasing certainty about the ghostly source of the letters illustrates the story's theme of alienation as she discovers an unknown side of her husband's character.

Elsie Ashby

Elsie Ashby was the first wife of Kenneth Ashby and now her ghost haunts the house of her former husband and his new wife, Charlotte. It is Elsie who sends the mysteriously delivered letters that causes Kenneth and Charlotte such dismay. A controlling and rigid woman in life, Elsie seeks to remain in control of Kenneth even from beyond the grave. Her message to Kenneth can be summarized by the only two intelligible words Charlotte can make out in Elsie's last letter: "mine" and "come."

Kenneth Ashby

Kenneth Ashby, a newly remarried widower, begins to receive a series of letters from the ghost of his first wife, Elsie. He tries to keep the letters and their sender a secret from his second wife, Charlotte, but she gradually comes to understand his secret. The letters and his efforts to conceal their nature alienate Kenneth from his new wife. Kenneth, however, is a model of marital fidelity. As he tries to be faithful both to the ghost of his dead wife and to his living one, Kenneth succumbs to a terrible nervous strain. The end of the story gives the impression that Kenneth has gone to join Elsie in death.

Mrs. Ashby

Mrs. Ashby is the mother of Kenneth Ashby. Kenneth's second wife, Charlotte, seeks out the guidance of Mrs. Ashby once Kenneth has disappeared near the end of the story. Mrs. Ashby is present when Charlotte opens the last of the mysterious letters.

Ghost

See Elsie Ashby

Themes

The Supernatural

In Edith Wharton's "Pomegranate Seed," the newly remarried widower, Kenneth Ashby, begins to receive letters from the ghost of his first wife, Elsie. Charlotte Ashby, Kenneth's second wife, believes at first that the letters are from a former lover of Kenneth's. When she realizes the truth about the letters, it is too late; Kenneth has gone to join Elsie, his first wife, in the afterworld. In the preface to her collection *Ghosts,* Wharton wrote that "the more one thinks the question over, the more one perceives the impossibility of defining the effect of the supernatural." In the absence of such a clear definition, she believed the ghost story "must depend for its effect solely on what one might call

its thermometrical quality; if it sends a cold shiver down one's spine, it has done its job and done it well."

Flesh vs. Spirit

Tales of the supernatural inevitably involve a contest between the flesh and the spirit. The many forms this contest can take explain the wonderful diversity of supernatural fiction. Consider the many versions of the vampire story, in which the triumph of the spirit over the flesh results in a cursed and agonized immortality. In Mary Shelley's *Frankenstein* the theme of flesh vs. spirit supports an essentially didactic account of man's corruption of nature.

In Wharton's "Pomegranate Seed" the contest is won by the spirit. Elsie Ashby comes back from death to reassert her claim to her house and her husband, Kenneth Ashby. The force of Elsie's will is so great that she persuades Kenneth to free his spirit from his own body and join her in death. Moreover, Elsie's spirit is apparently strong enough to permit her to take actions not normally thought of as being within the ability of a ghost, such as writing and delivering letters. Experienced readers of ghost stories recognize this victory of the spirit over the physical.

Alienation

Perhaps the most interesting ghost stories are those in which a supernatural element acts to reveal some characteristic or circumstance of the people in the story that might not otherwise have become evident. This is the case in "Pomegranate Seed," as Elsie's ghost reveals a quality of alienation within Kenneth and Charlotte's marriage. When Charlotte first confronts Kenneth about the mysterious letters: "A line of anger she had never seen before came out between his eyes, and she said to herself: 'The upper part of his face is too narrow; this is the first time I ever noticed it?'" As the tale continues, the distance between husband and wife grows as Charlotte comes closer to understanding the truth about the letters Kenneth has been receiving. Pleading with her husband for an explanation of the mystery, Charlotte comes to see her husband as "a stranger, a mysterious incomprehensible being whom no argument or entreaty of hers could reach." Kenneth has been a passionate and attentive husband to his second wife, but Elsie's ghost reveals a reserve and a privacy in Kenneth that Charlotte cannot touch.

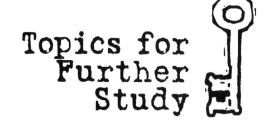

Topics for Further Study

- Read a selection of Grimms' fairy tales and make note of what features any of them have in common with Wharton's ''Pomegranate Seed.''

- Research the effects of the Great Depression in New York City, and compare the Ashbys' experience of the 1930s with others you might discover in your investigation.

- Read the myth of Aphrodite and Adonis in Ovid's *Metamorphoses,* and consider what it has in common with the myth of Demeter and Persephone. Consider what sort of ghost story might be made out of the Adonis myth. Write a ghost story based on the myth of Adonis and Aphrodite.

Style

Point of View

The narrative point of view in Wharton's ''Pomegranate Seed'' is third-person limited. In a work of fiction related from a third-person limited point of view, the narrator is not a character in the story, but someone outside of it who refers to the characters as ''he,'' ''she,'' and ''they.'' This outside narrator, however, is not omniscient (or all-knowing), but is *limited* in knowledge to the perceptions of one or more of the characters in the story. The narrator of ''Pomegranate Seed,'' and therefore its reader, sees the events of the story through the eyes of Charlotte Ashby, even though it is not Charlotte herself who tells the story. The story's readers never have more information than Charlotte does at any point in the narrative, and are thus more fully involved in the story's mystery than they might have been if it were told by an omniscient narrator.

Setting

''Pomegranate Seed'' takes place in two locations in 1930s New York City: Kenneth Ashby's house and the nearby residence of his mother. Wharton makes clear that the Ashbys' neighborhood is a relatively quiet one; theirs is a ''street long since deserted by business and fashion.'' Even from this quiet street, however, ''the soulless roar of New York'' is apparent to Charlotte's ears. ''Pomegranate Seed'' is the only one of Wharton's ghost stories to have an urban setting, and Wharton may have placed the story there as a sort of challenge to herself as a writer.

Allusion

An allusion is an indirect reference by one literary text to another text, or to a historical event, a myth or legend. The title, ''Pomegranate Seed,'' is an allusion to the Greek myth of Persephone. Daughter of Zeus and Demeter, the goddess of the harvest, Persephone is abducted by Hades, the god of death, and carried off to the underworld. At Zeus's insistence, Hades agrees to release Persephone on the condition that she has eaten no food while in the underworld. Unfortunately Persephone has eaten six pomegranate seeds in Hades's garden, and for that reason is allowed to return to the world of the living for no more than six months at a time. This can be likened to Wharton's story, in that Kenneth is pulled between the underworld and the world above: between Elsie, who is dead—or in the underworld—and Charlotte, who is flesh and blood and belongs to the world familiar to Kenneth, the land of the living.

Gothicism

''Gothic'' has had many meanings throughout history. Originally describing a medieval Germanic tribe, the Goths, the term later named a style of European architecture of the late medieval and early renaissance periods. In Anglo-American literature since the eighteenth century, ''Gothic'' has described works of prose fiction characterized by the grotesque, violence, and supernatural apparitions.

Wharton's "Pomegranate Seed" may be considered a late work in the Gothic tradition.

Historical Context

Ghost Stories and History

In one important way, the historical considerations that readers bring to the interpretation of other kinds of fiction do not apply to ghost stories. Ghost stories deal with situations that are outside of nature and, for that reason, outside of history. Ghosts and the emotions with which audiences read stories about ghosts exist in a realm that is not much affected by history, politics, and economy. At the same time, of course, writers live and work inside history, and the media with which writers practice their craft—language and literary genre—are very much shaped by historical factors. For these reasons, and not because Elsie Ashby's ghost is in some recognizable way a ghost of the 1930s, Wharton's "Pomegranate Seed" is a story whose historical and cultural background may be profitably explored.

For one thing, "Pomegranate Seed" is a story that presents its setting and characters as being very much up to date. It is Wharton's only urban ghost story, taking place amid what she calls the "soulless roar of New York." Much of the story's action is presented as dialogue exchanged over the telephone—a work of technology that was still something of a novelty when the story was first published by the *Ladies' Home Journal* in 1931. Kenneth Ashby, the remarried widower who is haunted by his first wife's mysterious letters, is a lawyer with a bustling career in the metropolis. Clearly, much of the story's effect is derived from the intrusion of something so old-fashioned as a ghost upon the lives of the modern-day Ashbys.

The Ashbys, however, seem to be curiously exempt from what worried Americans most at the time of the story's first publication: the Great Depression. Beginning with the Stock Market Crash of 1929 and lasting until the early 1940s, the Depression left more than 16 million people unemployed and reduced the U.S. Gross National Product by almost fifty percent. For many Americans it was a time of lost hope, skepticism toward government, and brutal poverty. Wharton herself suffered some financial reverses after 1929 as the New York real estate in which her money was invested declined in value, and as the magazines to which she sold her

work were forced to reduce the sums they paid contributors.

The Depression does not figure in "Pomegranate Seed" in part because ghost stories do not typically concern themselves with economic history, and in part because, as with most of Wharton's fiction, the story is about people who are very secure financially. With the important exceptions of *Ethan Frome* (1911) and *Summer* (1917), most of Wharton's fiction is about members of America's most privileged leisure class. Specifically, Wharton's novels have chronicled the tension between persons of inherited wealth and their rivals, the newly wealthy entrepreneurial class who sought access to distinctions and pleasures that before had belonged exclusively to "old money." This rivalry is the backdrop to events in her two most acclaimed novels, *The House of Mirth* (1905) and *The Age of Innocence* (1920), both late examples of the novel of manners. A tradition of the Anglo-American novel since the eighteenth century, the novel of manners often presents class conflicts as it defines heroism through moral integrity and develops character through the practice of social norms or manners.

By 1931 when "Pomegranate Seed" was first published, and certainly by 1937 when it came out in Wharton's collection *Ghosts,* the novel of manners would have seemed quite old-fashioned. John Steinbeck's *Of Mice and Men* and Hemingway's *To Have and Have Not* were published in 1937; both are novels of gritty realism in which the economic dislocations of the Depression are given center stage, and in which heroism takes the form of bitter stoicism. Moreover, the conflict between old money and new money which occupied Wharton in her finest novels might also have seemed like old news in the Depression, which brought poverty or near-poverty to almost all social classes and robbed many Americans of the class status they had prized before 1929.

Critical Overview

Between 1930 and 1937, the year of her death, Edith Wharton published four original collections of short stories. The productions of a Pulitzer Prize-winning writer near the end of her career, these collections were almost universally praised, yet little detailed attention was given to individual stories in these collections. In the decades since Wharton's death, the ghost stories have received little critical com-

Compare
&
Contrast

- **1926:** Renowned magician and escape artist Harry Houdini dies. During his lifetime, Houdini devoted much of his energies to debunking spiritualists and mediums who claimed they could contact the dead. He claimed that if there were truly a way to contact the living after one's death, he would do so. He set up a code with his wife Bess, who faithfully attended seances and awaited his return for ten years, after which time she gave up.

  1990s: "Psychic hotlines," telephone numbers people can call to speak with someone who offers advice through various extra-sensory means, become extremely popular and are endorsed by various celebrities.

- **1929:** Wall Street's Dow Jones Industrial Average reaches 381, up from 88 in 1924. On October 29, 16.4 million shares of stock are traded,

prompting the Dow Jones to drop 30.57 points. Despite assurances by leading economists that no business depression is imminent, liquidation continues, prompting the Great Depression.

  1990s: The Dow Jones sets records annually, reaching 10,000 in early 1999.

- **1931:** New York's Empire State Building opens April 30th at Fifth Avenue and 34th Street. The 102-story skyscraper stands as the world's tallest building for more than 40 years.

  1998: The CN Tower, located in Toronto and completed in 1976, is the world's tallest building. Standing at just over 1,815 feet, the tower was built to improve the clarity of radio and television signals that were being obscured by the growing number of skyscrapers in downtown Toronto.

---

mentary. To a great extent, Wharton's short fiction has been less discussed than her novels, and her fiction of social observation has been of greater interest to scholars than her supernatural fiction.

Since the 1970s, however, as the women's movement has prompted a reevaluation of neglected works by female writers, Wharton's ghost stories have been the focus of some critical discussion. In 1970, writing in *Criticism* magazine, Margaret B. McDowell argues that the true focus of Wharton's ghost stories is on the living characters and how their contact with supernatural elements reveals what is central to them. Specifically of "Pomegranate Seed," McDowell argues that Elsie's ghost reveals moral weaknesses in Kenneth and Charlotte: "If Kenneth has not been altogether candid with her, Charlotte has helped him too little in his crisis. She loses him forever, as much by her moral flaccidity as by her rival's malevolence."

In a 1987 issue of *Literature and Psychology,* Virginia L. Blum presents the story as an analysis of man's conflicted understanding of women. As Ken-

neth Ashby chooses between his dead wife and his living one, he is also choosing between an idealized and sexless conception of woman, and one that is real, sexual, and demanding. Given these opposed ideas of women, Blum argues that Wharton's "Pomegranate Seed" reveals the impossibility of the sexes uniting in an understanding way in the real world. Annette Zilversmit presents an argument in *College Literature* magazine that contradicts Blum's: in her contest with Elsie, Charlotte is defeated not by the ghost but by her own fear that she is less sexually desirable than her rival.

In a 1991 issue of *Women's Studies,* Carol J. Singley and Susan Elizabeth Sweeney maintain that Wharton's "Pomegranate Seed" is a self-reflexive story; that is, one that comments on its own status as a work of verbal art. Singley and Sweeney argue that the story explores women's attitudes to the previously male-dominated activities of reading and writing. According to these critics, Charlotte is a reflection of the female reader, and Elsie is a version of the female writer. Both experience an ambivalence the critics call "anxious power" as they undertake these verbal activities. Moreover, Singley and Sweeney suggest that "Pomegranate Seed" offers a new model of reading as "the production of meaning rather than the discovery of truth."

Criticism

Benjamin Goluboff

Goluboff is an associate professor of English at Lake Forest College. In the following essay, he examines the influence of Greek mythology on Wharton's "Pomegranate Seed."

Edith Wharton's "Pomegranate Seed" is a remarkable story that has largely eluded modern anthologies of short fiction. Perhaps this is because anthologists don't consider ghost stories to be serious literature; more likely the omission is a result of how Wharton's ghost stories have been overshadowed by the fiction of social observation through which she made her reputation in the first decades of this century. Nevertheless, "Pomegranate Seed" is very much deserving of our attention both for the way it makes the conventions of the traditional ghost story work in a setting that is conspicuously modern, and for its deft use of Greek myth to lend classical resonance to the events in that modern setting.

When Wharton sent a revised manuscript of "Pomegranate Seed" to the *Ladies' Home Journal* in 1931, she complained in the accompanying letter that the editor of the magazine, Loring Schuyler, had failed to understand the allusion contained in the story's title: "As for the title, Mr. Schuyler must refresh his classical mythology. When Persephone left the underworld to re-visit her mother, Demeter, her husband, Hades, lord of the infernal regions, gave her a pomegranate seed to eat, because he knew that if he did so she would never be able to remain among the living, but would be drawn back to the company of the dead." It must have seemed to Wharton that the world had become an alien place by 1931 if the editor of a popular journal did not know his classical mythology. In the preface to her 1937 collection *Ghosts,* where the story was reprinted, Wharton remarked that ". . . in the dark ages of my childhood an acquaintance with classical fairy lore was as much a part of our stock of knowledge as Grimm and Andersen. . . ."

Sculpture entitled "The Rape of Proserpina," by Italian Baroque sculptor Gian Lorenzo Bernini. Proserpina is a variant spelling of "Persephone."

The summary of the Persephone myth that Wharton made for Loring lacks several important details. As the story is told in Ovid's *Metamorphoses,* a versified collection of Greco-Roman myths from the first century B.C., Hades is not Persephone's husband. He has abducted her and carried her off to the underworld against her will. Persephone's father, in Ovid's version, is Zeus, who at Demeter's insistence has tried to persuade Hades to release

What Do I Read Next?

- *The Turn of the Screw* (1898). Composed by Edith Wharton's friend and mentor, Henry James, this is considered to be one of the greatest ghost stories in the English language. A young governess who takes charge of two children on a British estate begins to see, or imagines she sees, the ghosts of former employees attempting to corrupt her two young charges.

- Ovid's *Metamorphoses*. Roman poetry written in the first century B.C., this is a relatively easy way for students to become familiar with the mythology of the Greco-Roman tradition.

- *Something Wicked This Way Comes* (1962), by Ray Bradbury, tells how the citizens of a small Midwestern town are tempted by their hidden, basest desires when a carnival comes to town, offering the townspeople, through its deadly attractions, the fulfillment of humanity's oldest dream: "Ye shall be as gods."

- "An Encounter by Mortstone Pond," included in Russell Kirk's story collection *Watchers at the Strait Gate* (1984), tells of a lonely boy's brief meeting with his older self, and, in later years, his encounter in old age with his boyhood self. The older man muses that he is in the presence of an indissoluble mystery, as "We are essences— but insubstantial really, such stuff as dreams are made of, not understanding death because we do not know what life is."

- "A Cautionary Note on the Ghostly Tale," also included in Kirk's *Watchers at the Strait Gate* (1984). Kirk addresses the question: "In an era of the decay of religious belief, can fiction of the supernatural or preternatural, with its roots in myth and transcendent perception, succeed in being anything better than playful or absurd?"

- Thomas Ligotti's essay, "In the Night, in the Dark: A Note on the Appreciation of Weird Fiction," which prefaces his collection of ghostly tales *Noctuary* (1994), is an informative general introduction to the characteristics of the supernatural tale.

---

their daughter. Moreover, Persephone has not eaten one pomegranate seed, but six. As the daughter of Demeter, goddess of the harvest, Persephone is the personification of vegetation. The six seeds from the underworld ensure that like the crops, Persephone will spend six of the year's months among the living, and the other six in the underworld.

How, then, does the Persephone myth function in Edith Wharton's short story? In what way may we better understand the story's characters and theme by using the myth as a guide? If we take Mrs. Ashby (Kenneth's mother) as the story's Demeter figure because, like the goddess of the harvest, she has had a child taken away by death, then Kenneth Ashby becomes Wharton's Persephone figure. Despite his male gender, Kenneth stands in nicely for Persephone as a figure torn between the world of the living and the "company of the dead." Elsie Ashby,

certainly then, becomes Hades, the beckoning representative of death. And Charlotte Ashby, Kenneth's second wife who seeks to persuade him back from the gates the underworld, plays the role of Zeus who tried to persuade Hades to let Persephone go free.

While these mythological parallels bring the identities of Wharton's characters into sharper focus, they also raise several baffling questions about "Pomegranate Seed." In classical mythology, for example, Hades is considered the second most powerful of the gods, yielding precedence only to Zeus himself. When Zeus and Hades come into conflict over Persephone in the original myth, their dispute is settled in something like a draw: Persephone must spend six months in the underworld and six months on earth. In Wharton's version of the myth it seems that the forces of death win out over those of life, that Elsie triumphs over Charlotte in claiming Kenneth as exclusively her own. Does Wharton, then, invert the order of the gods as established in Greco-Roman mythology, giving Hades precedence over Zeus?

Another way of asking the same question is to remember that the original myth suggests that nature undergoes cyclical renewal from year to year. As personification of crops and vegetation, Persephone divides the year between the upper and lower worlds, returning to earth every year with the return of the spring. In Wharton's story, is there any comparable hope for cyclical renewal? If Kenneth Ashby is the Persephone figure, is there reason to believe that he will eventually return to Charlotte and the world of the living? The final scene of "Pomegranate Seed" offers little hope in this regard. When they are finally convinced that Kenneth has in fact disappeared Mrs. Ashby picks up the phone to call the police, saying to Charlotte: "We must do everything—everything." To which Charlotte grimly replies: "Exactly as if we thought it would do any good to do anything?" The story's ending seems to foreclose any faith we might have that Kenneth will come back. Perhaps Wharton has given us a version of the myth in which death gains a definitive upper hand.

Finally, there is the question of just what is the "seed" to which the story's title refers? In her 1987 essay, "Edith Wharton's Erotic Other-World" (*Literature and Psychology*), Virginia L. Blum claims that "The 'seed' is simply sex itself in a story about a man's conflicting perceptions of woman." Blum argues that Elsie lures Kenneth away from his living wife because she offers relief from the demands of Charlotte, a living sexual being. But one could also argue that the "seed" is Kenneth's memory of his lost wife, his nostalgia for, as Wharton put it in her letter, "the company of the dead." Perhaps the "seed" is something like a death-wish on Kenneth's part, or a symbol of Kenneth's acknowledging, as Wharton seems to do in her manipulation of the Persephone myth, that Hades is a greater power than Zeus. Wharton's use of the Persephone myth, finally, lends perspective to the ghost story, even as it poses a series of rich interpretive questions.

Much of the effect of "Pomegranate Seed" comes from the way Wharton introduces these elements of classical mythology into a setting that is conspicuously modern. Indeed, Wharton may have set out in this story to invent a ghost that would "work" in those modern conditions that she saw as

> As personification of crops and vegetation, Persephone divides the year between the upper and lower worlds, returning to earth every year with the return of the spring."

antithetical to supernatural fiction. In her preface to the collection *Ghosts* Wharton wrote that "... deep within us as the ghost instinct lurks, I seem to see it being gradually atrophied by those two worldwide enemies of the imagination, the wireless [radio] and the cinema." Ghosts, or our willingness to believe in them, may be expected to vanish from an increasingly technological society because they "require two conditions abhorrent to the modern mind: silence and continuity." In the "roaring and discontinuous" world of the American twentieth century, ghosts will no longer find receptive imaginations to haunt.

It is striking, for this reason, that Wharton sets "Pomegranate Seed" in precisely those circumstances she has identified as least conducive to the supernatural. Charlotte Ashby is very much aware of this. As she stands upon the threshold of her house, preparing to go in and face another ghostly letter, she thinks, "Outside there ... skyscrapers, advertisements, telephones, wireless, airplanes, movies, motors [automobiles], and all the rest of the twentieth century; and on the other side of the door something I can't explain, can't relate to them. Something as old as the world, as mysterious as life. ..." Of the technological items in Charlotte's list, the story dwells particularly on the telephone. Early in Part III of "Pomegranate Seed" Kenneth tries to calm Charlotte's suspicions by making conversation about neutral topics. These include "... French painting, the health of an old aunt, and the installing of the automatic telephone." In the climactic fourth part of the story, nearly half of the narrative action takes the form of telephone calls, as Charlotte tries to trace Kenneth's whereabouts. And, of course, the final image of the story is that of Mrs. Ashby, picking up the receiver to call the police.

Clearly in Elsie Ashby, Wharton seeks to give her readers a ghost who can endure the technological discontinuities of the twentieth century, whose spell can't be broken even by the "soulless roar of New York." That Elsie also appears in the story as a figure traceable to Greco-Roman mythology lends her dimension and timelessness. Grounded in Wharton's contemporary moment, and articulating itself in a vocabulary derived from ancient myth, "Pomegranate Seed" is a story that very much deserves renewed attention.

Source: Benjamin Goluboff, Overview of "Pomegranate Seed," for *Short Stories for Students,* The Gale Group, 1999.

Carol J. Singley and Susan Elizabeth Sweeney

In the following excerpt, the critics explore the power of the written word over the characters, maintaining that Charlotte Ashby reflects the reader's ambivalence about reading while Elsie Ashby embodies the author's anxiety about writing. The critics also propose that the relationships between the women in the story is dependent upon their connection to Kenneth Ashby.

At the beginning of Edith Wharton's story "Pomegranate Seed," Charlotte Ashby pauses on the threshold of her house, half-afraid to enter because she wonders whether another "square grayish envelope" addressed to her husband lies on the hall table within. Such letters, which figure prominently in Wharton's fiction and especially in "Pomegranate Seed," have the distinct power to alter relationships between men and women and between characters of the same sex. Eager and fearful to discover the contents and author of these ambiguous letters, "so alike in appearance that they had . . . become one letter, become 'it'," Charlotte feels ambivalent about the letter and the opportunities for independent interpretation and expression that it represents. She experiences what we will call "anxious power": she covets the power of language and yet feels anxious about the trespass implied by a woman's appropriation of such power.

Charlotte wrestles with the choice between the power of written discourse—traditionally a male domain—and the power of romance—traditionally a female domain. The horror of the story is that on the one hand, Charlotte fears she cannot compete with the letter's uncanny power over her husband; on the other hand, she attempts to master that power by appropriating and reading the letter, but with ambiguous results (she gains a mother, but loses a husband). Charlotte's anxiety extends to her sense of herself as a typically passive woman and as a potential usurper of texts and the power that they represent. She is poised "on the threshold," suspended between two realms of gendered expectation, a fact underlined by the narrative construction of the tale itself—its supernatural *and* realistic tone, its multitude of indeterminacies, gaps, and absences.

Indeed, Wharton's story provides an excellent example of the ways in which ambivalence toward reading and writing—like that which Hester Lynch Thrale acknowledges—shapes narrative by women. . . . [In order to show how "Pomegranate Seed" exemplifies anxious power,] we show how the story's three female characters—Charlotte and Mrs. Ashby, who fearfully read a letter that does not belong to them, and Elsie, who writes illegible letters from beyond the threshold of the grave—represent the anxious power of female readers and writers. In other words, we propose to read "Pomegranate Seed" as a parable about women's ambivalence toward the power of reading and writing. . . .

Charlotte's forbidden reading is described as an act of transgression, in which she not only appropriates Kenneth's letter but interprets various blank spaces and missing parts: the space where Elsie's portrait hung, Kenneth's disappearance, and the text of the letter itself. Instead of standing on the doorstep, "shivering with the premonition of something inexplicable, intolerable, to be faced on the other side," or secretly watching her husband's correspondence with the letter, Charlotte crosses the threshold, usurping Kenneth's library, desk, and letter-opener as well as the letter itself. In this climactic act of reading the ninth and last letter, Kenneth's death is implied, the author of the letters is identified, and Charlotte's new relationship with Mrs. Ashby is established. Despite the certainty implied by these resolutions, however, the ending of "Pomegranate Seed" remains ambiguous, evoking ambivalent responses in both Charlotte and the reader.

By purloining not only Kenneth's letter, but also his possessions, Charlotte assumes in this scene the male role of reader, detective, and penetrator of secrets, a role emphasized by phallic imagery of authority and rape. Charlotte first stares at the letter "as if she could force her gaze to penetrate to what was within"; but the envelope is not only closed to her gaze, but "so tightly stuck that she had to hunt on her husband's writing table for his ivory letter-opener." In fact, opening the letter seems to confirm Kenneth's death: when she rummages through his desk, the items on it "sent through her the icy chill emanating from the little personal effects of someone newly dead," and when she opens the envelope, "the tearing of the paper . . . sounded like a human cry."

But what does Charlotte gain by appropriating Kenneth's letter? The sheet of paper inside the envelope is nearly blank, unreadable: "Her sight must be blurred, or else dazzled by the reflection of the lamplight on the smooth surface of the paper . . . she could discern only a few faint strokes, so faint and faltering as to be nearly undecipherable." This sentence ironically recalls Wharton's earlier description of the curtains on Charlotte's front door, which prevented her from seeing if a letter had arrived because they "softened the light within to a warm blur through which no details showed." Although Charlotte has now crossed the threshold and even read the letter, she is confronted with the same blurred, illegible surface as before.

In a series of triadic relationships, Charlotte had watched Kenneth read the eighth letter; she herself was "watched by Mrs. Ashby" as she tried to read the ninth; and now, unable to comprehend it, she watches her mother-in-law read it in turn. While Mrs. Ashby tries to decipher the almost invisible handwriting in the lamplight, Charlotte studies her face as if it were the letter, just as earlier she had tried to learn the eighth letter's contents by reading Kenneth's face. Indeed, Charlotte learns more about the letter's contents from her mother-in-law's face than from the letter itself: Mrs. Ashby's features, which usually express only "simple and sound emotions," now express more ambivalent ones: "a look of fear and hatred, of incredulous dismay and almost cringing defiance . . . as if the spirits warring within her had distorted her face to their own likeness."

Although the letter's contents remain mysterious, Charlotte does discover its author when she asks whether Mrs. Ashby recognizes the handwriting. Significantly, she learns the answer not through Mrs. Ashby's words, but through her gaze. Earlier, Charlotte watched her read the empty page; now she watches her gaze at the empty walls, as her "anxious eyes [steal] with a glance of apprehension around the quiet familiar room," hesitating to pronounce the name aloud. When Charlotte counters, "'You'd better say it out, mother! You knew at once it was *her* writing?' . . . Mrs. Ashby looked up; her eyes, travelling slowly past Charlotte, were lifted to the blank wall behind her son's writing

> Charlotte wrestles with the choice between the power of written discourse-- traditionally a male domain-- and the power of romance-- traditionally a female domain."

table." Elsie is thus named by her absence rather than her presence, just as the letter has meaning specifically because its contents are withheld. In fact, Elsie's signature is the "blank wall" —placed, appropriately enough, behind the writing table— which resembles her letter: as Charlotte tells Mrs. Ashby, "If even you can see her face on that blank wall, why shouldn't he read her writing on this blank paper?"

In "Pomegranate Seed" Wharton literally represents the act of reading as peering at an almost blank page, filling in gaps, absences, ellipses. "No one could possibly read that letter," Mrs. Ashby tells Charlotte, and after considerable effort, with the aid of a bright lamp and even a magnifying glass, Charlotte believes that she can decipher only two ambiguous words: "I can make out something like 'mine' —oh, and 'come.' It might be 'come'." As readers of "Pomegranate Seed," we must also fill in blanks. The words "come" and "mine" demand that we construct hypothetical sentences, such as a command addressed to Kenneth ("Come, you will always be mine, and you belong with me"), or a message addressed to Charlotte, who, after all, is the one who reads the letter and therefore, according to Lacan, its intended recipient ("He has come to me, he is mine"). In "Pomegranate Seed," then, Wharton defines reading as the production of meaning rather than the discovery of truth. As readers of the story, we, like Charlotte, must make our own decisions and recognize our ambivalence about them. . . .

Kenneth's disappearance is another mystery for which the reader must devise her own explanation. In fact, his absence, like other absences in the story, somehow suggests a presence: even after his apparent death, Kenneth continues to shape the

> Ironically, at the very moment that Charlotte claims her own power by appropriating and reading Elsie's letter, she is presumably willing to surrender it as evidence in a police investigation, an act which reinforces the letter's role as signifier."

women's relationships with one another. For example, we can read Elsie, Charlotte's predecessor, as her double, in the same way that Bertha Rochester is Jane Eyre's double. After all, Charlotte makes few changes in the house because Elsie's drawing-room is "exactly the drawing-room she would have liked for herself." As she attempts to discover the letter's contents, Charlotte resembles Elsie more and more, until, entering Kenneth's library and appropriating the final letter, it is, in [Annette] Zilversmit's phrase [in "Edith Wharton's Last Ghosts," *College Literature* 14, 1987], as if Charlotte "resurrected the ghost herself." Wharton expresses this relationship, too, in terms of the gaze: when Charlotte sits "singing at her image in the glass," imagining her triumph over the mysterious other woman, she is actually gazing at herself." The power of Elsie's letter—"something she can't explain"—unlocks Charlotte's own repressed desire for power and knowledge, helping her to reach a secret goal: "to feel herself the sovereign"—not just of Kenneth's past, but of her own future. Charlotte's romantic bid to rescue her husband fails, however, as does her attempt to read Elsie's letter, despite its apparent invitation—"come"—which may be addressed to her as well as to Kenneth. The story suggests, then, that a woman may gain power either through romance or language, but not both.

"Pomegranate Seed" also holds out a third possibility: a daughter may gain power through her connection with the maternal. When Charlotte and Mrs. Ashby read the letter together, their relationship is different from the competitive relationships

that the letter evokes among Charlotte, Kenneth and Elsie. Indeed, Charlotte's act of reading brings her closer to Mrs. Ashby, her "proxy mother," strengthening their "tacit bond" at the same time that confirms Kenneth's death—as if the price for intimacy were loss of the husband. All three women—each named "Mrs. Ashby," defined in relationship to Kenneth, and connected only through him—thus gain new relations with one another in his absence.

For help deciphering the barely legible script, then, Charlotte turns to the mother figure, who responds ambivalently with both caution and support. Charlotte senses that she knows the writer's identity; but Mrs. Ashby, "spirits warring within her," refuses to reveal the knowledge of Elsie's authorship which reading the letter would confirm. Instead, Mrs. Ashby's maternal instincts ultimately lead Charlotte back to a traditional feminine dependence on male authority, as she "resolutely" reaches for the telephone to call the police, advising Charlotte not to act but to wait for an explanation from Kenneth or the authorities.

This insertion into the text of another figure— the police—transforms Charlotte's intimate relationship with her mother-in-law into another triangle: Charlotte, Mrs. Ashby, and male authority. Thus "Pomegranate Seed," like the Persephone-Demeter myth, seeks to replace the conjugal relationship with the primacy of the mother-daughter bond, but succeeds only in reaffirming male power. . . . Ironically, at the very moment that Charlotte claims her own power by appropriating and reading Elsie's letter, she is presumably willing to surrender it as evidence in a police investigation, an act which reinforces the letter's role as signifier. As Shoshana Felman notes [in "On Reading Poetry: Reflections on the Limits and Possibilities of Psychoanalytic Approaches," *The Purloined Poe: Lacan, Derrida, and Psychoanalytic reading*, eds. John P. Muller and William J. Richardson, 1988], "the significance of the letter is situated in its *displacement,* that is, in its repetitive movements toward a *Different* place" rather than in its content (original emphasis).

As women reading "Pomegranate Seed," how do we respond to the proposition that bonding with other women depends upon the absence or death of a man—or that bonds between women ultimately yield to male authority? The story invites us to respond in ambivalent ways. We can conclude that Charlotte's traditional domestic power is no match for Elsie's masculine force, which can be read as either "malevolent" or constructive. We can also read Charlotte's appropriation of the letter as either reprehensible or admirable: as a violation of Kenneth's privacy, or as the justifiable acquisition of knowledge that she has been denied. Zilversmit blames Kenneth's disappearance on Charlotte's behavior and assumes that "the reader" does the same: "Charlotte thinks that her husband has perhaps gone to join her [Elsie]. The reader realizes that the second wife's guilt and insecurity have driven the husband away." [In "Edith Wharton's Ghost Stories," *Criticism* 12, No. 1, 1970, Margaret B.] McDowell blames Kenneth, Charlotte, and Elsie equally: "death and negation triumph in this marriage because of Charlotte's distrust, possessiveness, and cowardice; because of Kenneth's inertia, nostalgia, and resentment; and because of Elsie's craving for continued power over one whom she has supposedly cherished." And in her psychoanalytic study of Wharton's seductive female ghosts ["Edith Wharton's Erotic Other-World," *Literature and Psychology* 33, No. 2, 1987, Virginia L.] Blum reads the story not from Charlotte's but from Kenneth's point of view: "he at once yearns for the living and is drawn to the dead. We find here a very literal enactment of a man's inability to decide whether the woman is the Angel in the House or the Angel of Death."

We suggested earlier that Charlotte, poised expectantly on her doorstep, was a figure for Wharton's reader, poised on the threshold of "Pomegranate Seed." And when Charlotte finally crosses the literal and figurative thresholds of the story to read Elsie's letter, she evokes for female readers, in particular, divided allegiances that reveal our own ambivalence toward knowledge and power. In reading "Pomegranate Seed," we discover not answers to our questions, but new questions that we must answer—just as Charlotte, trying to find out when she and Kenneth will leave together, learns that he has left town and sits "blankly gazing into new darkness."

If Charlotte reflects our own ambivalence about reading, then her double, Elsie, reflects Wharton's anxiety about writing. Although feminist criticism may too quickly identify Wharton with her female characters, the parallels between Elsie Ashby and Wharton's sense of herself as a writer are obvious. The very ghostliness of Elsie's writing evokes Wharton's own literary creativity, which she describes as an alienating and mysterious process that occurs "in some secret region on the sheer edge of consciousness." It is also characteristic of Wharton

to express her anxiety about the writing process in a ghost story; as Zilversmit points out, she often used such tales "as a metaphor of internal fears."

Elsie Ashby can be read, then, as a ghost writer for Wharton herself; and her spectral letters suggest Wharton's internal fears about her own appropriation of the male role of writer, what [Sandra M.] Gilbert and [Susan] Gubar call [in *The Madwoman in The Attic: The Woman Writer and the Nineteenth-Century Literary Imagination*, 1979] the "anxiety of authorship." Not only does Elsie's writing take the traditionally feminine from of letters—the "forgotten genre," as [Patricia Meyer] Spacks calls it—but it is barely able to communicate. Excluded and repressed, "written as though there were not enough ink in the pen, or the writer's wrist were too weak to bear upon it," her letters are "so faint and faltering as to be nearly undecipherable."

If Elsie is represented primarily by her writing, then her death—an absence that cannot quite be repressed—also signals Wharton's ambivalence toward female art and authorship. If, as Susan Gubar suggests [In "'The Blank Page' and the Issues of Female Creativity," *The New Feminist Criticism: Essays on Women, Literature, and Theory*, ed. Elaine Showalter, 1985], "the creation of female art feels like the destruction of the female body," then in "Pomegranate Seed" the artist's body is dead and buried. Like Margaret Aubyn in *The Touchstone*, whom [Mary Suzanne] Schriber calls [in *Gender and the Writer's Imagination: From Cooper to Wharton*, 1987] "the only serious female artist figure whom Wharton dared to commit to paper," Elsie is dead before her story even begins. Living female artists in Wharton's fiction fare no better: although she often portrays artists of either gender with irony and ambivalence (Spacks, *Female Imagination* 249–54), she particularly satirizes female artists in such stories as "The Pelican," "April Showers," and "The Expiation." Schriber concludes that "the younger Edith Wharton was not secure enough in her vocation to draw out of her foundering self a female protagonist who is an artist; the older Edith Wharton, realizing that women novelists were ignored by the culture, purposely did not assign her own gender to an artist, choosing instead to satirize the state of the arts as governed by men." Wharton does, in fact, depict a successful female writer, Helen Dale, who refers to herself as "the greatest novelist . . . of the age," and has authored many best-sellers. But even Helen Dale's success is marred by her ambivalence: faithful readers are a poor substitute for the married lover she gave up years ago; and her debate with that lover about using their old love letters as "copy" for forthcoming memoirs implies that female artistic success comes only at the cost of emotional fulfillment.

The fact that Elsie's handwriting is so remarkably androgynous —"bold but faint," manifesting "masculine curves" and yet somehow "visibly feminine"—also reveals Wharton's anxious power. Indeed, Elsie's pen(man)ship implies that one alternative to the absence of the female artist is male disguise —as if for a woman authorship and authenticity were incompatible. Schriber wonders whether Wharton "imagined that a character confident in a vocation to art required a male identity for reasons of verisimilitude"; in fact, Wharton once appropriated a male identity for herself—the pseudonym "David Olivieri"—to publish her early novel *Fast and Loose*. In addition to granting legitimacy, masculine disguise provides protection from public exposure. For Wharton, "the author who circulates her name on a title page" is "as vulnerable as the lady of leisure who displays herself as an art object." Accordingly, Elsie Ashby's authorship, as represented by her handwriting, is ambiguous and contradictory, as if for a woman male disguise were necessary in order to write at all.

The empty sheet which constitutes Elsie's writing is itself an ambivalent figure, as Susan Gubar's essay on female authorship implies. In traditional metaphors of literary creativity, Gubar argues, woman is typically described as a blank page to be inscribed by the pen of the masculine author. Such metaphors—as well as the cultural attitudes that they represent—force the female writer to experience her own authorship as "a painful wounding," a "self-inflicted violence," in which she writes upon the blank page of her body with her own blood. The solution to this identification of women's art with physical suffering is to reappropriate the image of the blank page. In Isak Dinesen's story "The Blank Page," for example, that image "becomes radically subversive. . . . Not a sign of innocence or purity or passivity, this blank page is a mysterious but potent act of resistance." Elsie Ashby's page—an almost "absolute blank," which nevertheless bears traces of illegible writing—similarly represents in a single image both the suppression and the expression of her art. If death represents an internal and external restriction of Elsie's art, then the fact that her writing transcends death, by crossing the very threshold of the grave, suggests the strength of her need to express herself—as if writing were more important

than being. Her letter, then, is also "radically subversive." In keeping with Mary Jacobus's definition of feminist writing, Elsie's letter, "though necessarily working with 'male' discourse . . . work[s] ceaselessly to deconstruct it: to write what can't be written." In other words, it asserts the feminine, which [Julia] Kristeva describes [in "La Femme, ce n'est jamais ça," trans. Marilyn A. August, *New French Feminisms*, ed. Elaine Marks and Isabel de Courtivron, 1980] as "that which is not represented, that which is unspoken, that which is left out."

Thus Elsie's writing, when finally deciphered, spells out Wharton's own anxious power. "The conscious mind of Edith Wharton did not break free entirely from her culture's ideology of woman," Schriber explains; "Her imagination, however, the driving force behind her fiction, saw well into it and beyond." "Pomegranate Seed" is shaped by this difference between Wharton's imagination on the one hand, and her fearful acceptance of social convention on the other. In this ghost story, Edith Wharton purloins both the "letter" and the power it represents; but she also reflects her own ambivalence—and that of the female reader—toward the possession of such power.

Source: Carol J. Singley and Susan Elizabeth Sweeney, "Forbidden Reading and Ghostly Writing: Anxious Power in Wharton's 'Pomegranate Seed'," in *Women's Studies: An Interdisciplinary Journal,* Vol. 20, No. 2, 1991, pp. 177–203.

Annette Zilversmit

In the following excerpt, Zilversmit focuses on Charlotte Ashby's rivalry with the ghost of her husband's first wife, maintaining that she is overcome and eventually defeated by her fear that she is not as sexually desirable as her rival.

Near the end of her life, Wharton, like [Henry] James, wrote two of her best and most revealing stories of psychological terror, "Pomegranate Seed" (1931) and "All Souls'" (1937). In "The Jolly Corner" James finally exposes the true source of his isolation in the specter of the fingerless and maimed alter-ego his protagonist encounters. So Wharton, nearing her seventies, called up her most potent fears, the phantoms, not of men or society, but of other women, seemingly more attractive and deserving than herself or her heroines. These other women, like the rivals in many of her novels, seem so formidable as to be in touch with other-worldly powers that enhance them and allow them to defeat and destroy the seemingly helpless protagonists. The final brilliance of these last tales is that long before the external spectres are confirmed, the inner aberrations of the heroines are felt. The final presence of the supernatural only confirms the entrapment of these women in their own long-denied fears.

"Pomegranate Seed" recounts the rivalry between Charlotte Ashby and the ghost of her husband's first wife. Even before faintly written letters begin arriving and disturbing the apparently happy marriage, the competitiveness of Charlotte with Elsie Ashby had begun. Like most of the other women in the familiar triangles of Wharton's novels, the rival is acquainted with the heroine (this time they are casual friends). On the occasion of her only visit to the first Mrs. Ashby's home, Charlotte had already felt "it to be exactly the drawing room she would have liked for herself." When this wife of twelve years dies, the heroine marries Kenneth Ashby, and acquires the house, which becomes a "veiled sanctuary . . . in the soulless roar of New York."

But when barely legible letters addressed to her husband in a handwriting "visibly feminine" begin to arrive, Charlotte's confidence erodes. Her husband becomes upset, but Charlotte confirms that "he seemed to recover; she couldn't." With no thought of spectral possibilities, she imagines the letters are from an old or present mistress. When her husband tries to reassure her that they are "about business," she demands them as proof of his innocence. He refuses, declaring, "It is not easy to prove anything to a woman who's once taken an idea into her head," and yet he leaves to arrange their vacation together.

When he fails to return, Charlotte rushes the ninth and latest letter to her mother-in-law, who recognizes the handwriting of the deceased wife. Charlotte thinks that her husband has perhaps gone to join her. The reader realizes that the second wife's guilt and insecurity have driven the husband away. Despite all her momentary bravura, the seemingly successful woman concedes victory to her once toppled rival. As though she has resurrected the ghost herself, Charlotte believes her dead rival now exerts a greater hold, a greater attractiveness for the desired man than an alive and devoted wife. Like the moral and social imperatives other Wharton heroines (like Ellen Olenska and Mattie Silver)

> " The strange and seemingly irrelevant title Wharton gives this story, 'Pomegranate Seed,' offers clues to perhaps the deeper identity of the letter-writing phantom who haunts Wharton's heroine."

have raised when renouncing their victories, the forces that seem to lure the desired man away reside in powers that seem ghostly and supernatural. In relegating defeat to forces outside themselves, such women try to avoid pain and responsibility, and keep themselves forever from controlling their destinies. Ghosts are the final confession of one's self-pitying helplessness.

The strange and seemingly irrelevant title Wharton gives this story, "Pomegranate Seed," offers clues to perhaps the deeper identity of the letter-writing phantom who haunts Wharton's heroine. By alluding to one of the early sub-species of the supernatural tale, the Greek myth of Persephone, Wharton concedes that the fears of her heroines are rooted in the mesh of Western civilization even as Wharton's modern retelling yields new meaning.

R. W. Lewis's brief summation at the bottom of the title page suggests its significance to the author: "Persephone, daughter of Demeter, goddess of fertility, was abducted and taken to Hades by Pluto, the god of the underworld. Her mother begged Jupiter to intercede, and he did so. But Persephone had broken her vow of abstinence in Hades by eating some pomegranate seeds. She was therefore required to spend a certain number of months each year—essentially the winter months—with Pluto." Although now usually viewed as raped by Pluto, Persephone can also be viewed as initially only abducted. More importantly, her failure to return to her mother is attributed not to her imprisonment by her abductor nor his eventual ravishment of her, but to her own decision to forgo abstinence and to partake of the forbidden fruit of sexuality. Persephone, the myth suggests, has chosen to remain partially with Pluto. Compelled eventually by Demeter's threats of sterility, she returns to spend part of her life as dutiful daughter, but she has at least assured her return to the realm of husband and sexuality, even if that realm remains swathed in guilt and the shadows of death.

Wharton seems to be suggesting that this myth is a Greek and woman's version of the Hebraic and masculine Garden of Eden and, like the Biblical legend, dramatizes the conflicts of men and women to establish an independent and sexual life. Persephone's intimacy with Pluto is complicated by the fact that he is her father's brother and thus her desire is also both competitive and incestuous (a note Wharton sounded more and more clearly in her later work until, in "The Beatrice Palmato Fragment," a daughter sleeps with her father). Persephone's guilt, which the eating of the red fruit accents, is further compounded in that she not only feels she has usurped the mother but been more successful. Unlike the polygamous lover of her mother, Zeus, Pluto desires and achieves a lasting marriage with the conflicted daughter.

But, in Wharton's modern retelling of the story itself, Charlotte Ashby is doomed by more than the displaced Oedipal competition with her mother. True, she feels she has eaten the forbidden seeds of usurping another woman's husband, descending with him to the hot climes of the West Indies, and even making him happier. But it is the husband who returns finally to the underworld, leaving Charlotte with a proxy mother, Mrs. Ashby senior. Since sex is relegated to the realm of the dead, Kenneth Ashby's return there symbolizes Wharton's heroine's deepest and unacknowledged fear, the most potent spectre of all, the conviction that she is not as sexually desirable or legitimately deserving as her rival. After nine months of marriage and nine letters, instead of becoming a secure and fertile (child-

bearing) wife, Charlotte Ashby, through her self-fulfilling prophecy of guilt and inadequacy, has driven her husband into the arms of her rival, although the woman is a corpse. The last scene of Charlotte enclosed now in her dearly desired house with only her mother-in-law confirms what Charlotte has chosen: the less fulfilling, but more familiar role of defeated and lonely woman, forever wedded to a mother figure, a fate more limited than even Persephone's. . . .

Source: Annette Zilversmit, "Edith Wharton's Last Ghosts," in *College Literature,* Vol. XIV, No. 3, 1987, pp. 296–305.

Sources

Blum, Virginia. "Edith Wharton's Erotic Other-World." *Literature and Psychology,* Vol. 33, 1987, pp. 12–29.

McDowell, Margaret B. "Edith Wharton's Ghost Stories." *Criticism,* Vol. XII, No. 2, Spring, 1970, pp. 133–52.

Further Reading

Lewis, R. W. B. ed. *The Letters of Edith Wharton,* by Edith Wharton. New York: Scribner's, 1988.
    The standard collection of Wharton's correspondence, this volume traces the writer's career in her own words. Meticulously edited and annotated by Wharton's biographer.

Wharton, Edith. *The Ghost Stories of Edith Wharton,* New York: Scribner's, 1973.
    The definitive collection of Wharton's supernatural fiction, this volume contains eleven stories, plus the 1937 preface to Wharton's *Ghosts* and a fragment from her autobiography.

The Ring

Isak Dinesen
1958

The short story "The Ring" by Isak Dinesen (whose real name was Karen Blixen) can be seen both as typical of its author's literary art and as different from her most characteristic mode of expression. Its eighteenth-century Danish setting places it within the deliberate archaism of Dinesen's storytelling, and its concern with fundamentals such as identity, sexuality, and violence echo such concerns in her other tales. On the other hand, "The Ring" has a simplicity not found in some of Dinesen's other works. In its concise style, it resembles a folktale or an episode from a medieval saga. "The Ring," which appears in the 1958 collection called *Anecdotes of Destiny,* adheres to the classical styles of storytelling, the Aristotelian unities of character, setting, and temporal span, and explores the way in which violence both breaks and reforges character.

Although dismissed by some of her contemporaries as an archaist who manipulated devices of eighteenth-century storytelling in a manner irrelevant to the modern condition, Dinesen has since come to be valued as an incisive commentator on modernity. While "The Ring" deals with a group of people, rural Danes of a past century, quite alien to the American reader of the 1990s, the tale addresses a universal human condition: Like Lovisa, the young bride, readers can find themselves caught up in a world which they did not make but with which they must come to terms.

Author Biography

Like Oswald Spengler, Thomas Mann, Sigrid Undset, and Hermann Hesse, Isak Dinesen (1885-1962), whose real name was Karen Blixen, was born in the nineteenth century and to a great extent remained true to its Romantic ideals though she lived well into the twentieth century. They participated fully, if critically, in the great artistic, social, philosophical, and political phenomenon known as modernity. To mention Dinesen, a daughter of Danish nobility whose roots were traceable all the way back to the middle ages, in company with Spengler, Mann, Undset, and Hesse is to point out that her modernity, like theirs, was one of dissent which aimed at compensating for the modern flatness of life through the revival of an antique ethos. Like Spengler, whose *Decline of the West* (1919) colored the era, Dinesen saw European civilization as descended primarily from a Gothic, or what Spengler called a Faustian, vision of life: A sense of distance as something to be conquered, an urge toward exploration both of inner and outer space, a willingness to confront violence and to accept the tragic. Like Mann in *Doctor Faustus* (1944), Undset in *Kristin Lavransdatter* (1921-23), and Hesse in *Narcissus and Goldmund* (1940), Dinesen in her literary art often traveled back to a medieval or baroque setting, resurrected Gothic themes and motifs, and indeed exploited a lowering saga-like atmosphere for everything that it was worth.

Dinesen's life itself was like a saga or romance. There was her birthplace, Rungsted, in North Zealand, which in a radio-talk she described as ''one of the oldest houses—perhaps the oldest house—between Elsinore and Copenhagen,'' a country-seat of minor Danish nobility where time might well have stopped in the eighteenth century. Critics who complain that Dinesen's settings are falsely archaic fail to contend with the Gothic quality of Rungsted, to which many of her imaginary locales strongly correspond. The rural farmstead supplied a stock setting in traditional Danish storytelling as well, as in Steen Steensen Blicher's famous *Diary of a Parish Clerk* (1841).

Dinesen's saga was filled with both adventure and disappointment. Her father, to whom she was very close, committed suicide when she was ten. Dinesen entered the Royal Academie of Fine Arts in Copenhagen in 1903 to study painting but left a few years later to begin writing. She published her first stories in a Danish periodical in 1907, using the pen name Osceola. Dinesen fell in love with her second cousin, Hans von Blixen-Fienecke, who refused to marry her; she later married his twin brother, Bror. Dinesen and Blixen managed a six thousand acre coffee plantation in Kenya, East Africa. Together they socialized with British aristocrats, many of whom inspired characters in Dinesen's later stories. Soon after marrying, however, Dinesen contracted syphilis from her unfaithful husband, and the disease affected her for the rest of her life.

Dinesen eventually became sole manager of the plantation, and she was divorced from Blixen in 1925. In 1918 she had met Denys Finch Hatton, a British pilot with whom she had an affair until his death in 1931. The financial condition of the plantation deteriorated until Dinesen finally sold it, also in 1931. She returned to Denmark, where she began her writing career in earnest.

Dinesen published her earliest tales before World War One but fell silent as an author during the Kenya hiatus. In 1934 she published *Seven Gothic Tales,* a work which appeared in Danish but which, surprisingly, she composed in English, a second language, and then translated into her native Danish. The *Gothic Tales* were followed by *Winter's Tales* (1942), *Last Tales* (1957), and *Anecdotes of Destiny* (1958), all consisting of independent short stories and novellas unified by recurrent themes and the pervasive Dinesen atmosphere. Dinesen wrote two memoirs, *Out of Africa* (1937) and *Shadows on the Grass* (1960, English translation 1961). She also wrote a novel, *Ehrengard* (1963), and many essays on a wide variety of topics. At first slighted by critics, she gained a reputation as one of Denmark's greatest living authors by the time of her death in 1962. Competent in English and concerned with universal human conditions, Dinesen also attracted an international following.

Plot Summary

Dinesen, writing in the 1950s, sets the action of ''The Ring'' in rural Denmark ''on a summer morning one hundred and fifty years ago,'' which would correspond approximately to the year 1800. Sigismund and Lovisa, two newlyweds (twenty-four and nineteen years of age) whose love, after much tribulation, has prevailed over the reluctance of the bride's family, are out walking to observe the pasturage of Sigismund's farm and to inspect the Cotswold rams by which the farmer hopes to ''improve his Danish stock.'' Dinesen's narrator divulges Lovisa's reminiscences of their struggle against her parents' wishes (she is of higher station in life than he, and her family is wealthier than his) and her present sense of having been liberated into ''freedom'' by her marriage. Lovisa delights in the ''rustic atmosphere'' of the locale and experiences joy in the notion that she has no secret from her husband.

At the sheepfold, sheepmaster Mathias tells Sigismund that two of his English lambs are dead and two more sick. While two helpers go off to fetch the sick lambs for examination, Sigismund and Mathias converse about the sheep thief who has been plaguing the district. The thief drags off his prey ''like a wolf'' and three nights earlier killed a man and injured the man's son in order to escape capture after having been caught by them red-handed. Lovisa wants to know more and gets Mathias to tell the story in full for her benefit. Details of a bloody fight in a sheep house, during which the thief broke his arm, excite her: ''She felt a pleasant thrill running down her spine.'' Mathias says that the man should be hanged; Sigismund says ''poor devil.'' Lovisa wonders that her husband could pity such a violent and lawless man.

Sigismund sends Lovisa home, and she leaves her hat with him to carry back for her; she walks slowly, daydreaming and delighting in the landscape. She fondly imagines that soon Sigismund will return after her and decides to play a trick to show her husband how much she means to him. She hides in a glade that she had previously discovered so that Sigismund, not seeing her on the path, will wonder for awhile where she has taken herself. The glade is the main setting of the tale and the stage of its central incident.

In order to enter the glade, Lovisa must push aside stubborn underbrush and thickly entwined low branches of trees. At the center a clearing opens with room for three or four people, so shielded by the tangle surrounding it that it is perfectly isolated from the rest of the world; a green realm, a fine and private place. Entry proves difficult, and when she wins it, she finds herself face-to-face with a ragged, bloody stranger, ''about her own age,'' who is none other than the much-rumored sheep thief. They

Isak Dinesen

stare at each other. The narrator states that the confrontation immediately changed Lovisa from the innocent that she had been up until the moment into something else. But the change is not instantaneous; it is acted out in careful, ritual steps.

The thief, crouching, lets his right arm dangle between his legs, the hand grasping a bloody knife, which he points upward at Lovisa's throat by bending his wrist; the corners of his mouth nervously twitch. He puts the knife into its sheath. Lovisa nervously removes her wedding ring, offering it to the thief, as though to bargain for her life. She drops the ring on the ground before him, but he kicks it away into the brush. She also drops her handkerchief, and it is this that the thief picks up. He wraps his knife in the handkerchief and leaves. Lovisa has been spared. She leaves the glade.

Now, however, when she meets Sigismund on the trail, Lovisa can only stutter that she is missing her ring; she harbors a secret, and the whole world appears changed. Walking in front of Sigismund on the homeward path, she suddenly sees herself as destined to ''poverty, persecution, total loneliness.'' Sigismund kisses her hand, telling her not to worry about the ring, but the kiss feels cold. He asks if she has any idea where she was when she lost it. She has, she says, no idea at all.

Characters

Lise

See Lovisa

Lovisa

Lovisa, who is called Lise by her husband, is the main character in Dinesen's story. She is nineteen years old and has been blissfully married for only a week to Sigismund, whom she has planned to marry for ten years. She is from a family of greater rank and wealth than Sigismund's, and her parents originally objected to him. Lovisa is girlish in many respects: she was still playing with dolls until fairly recently; the story of the thief reminds her of a fairy-tale character, "Red Ridinghood's wolf"; she has "never in her life been exposed to danger"; and she plays a game of hide–and-seek on Sigismund to make him grieve her absence. Yet Lovisa considers herself much more mature than her twenty-four-year-old husband. She delights in the freedom of having no secrets from him. Though she wants "to obey him in everything," she is still willing to disagree with him, as when she objects to Sigismund's feeling that the thief should be pitied, agreeing instead with Mathias that he should be killed. Her accidental encounter with the thief arouses her empathy, and her gesture of offering him her wedding ring, which he spurns, makes her feel that she has thus wedded herself to "poverty, persecution, total loneliness." Her freedom disappears in the knowledge of the secret encounter she now keeps from her husband.

Mathias

Mathias, an older man, is the sheep master on Sigismund's farm. At the beginning of the story he tells Sigismund about the death of one of his English-bred lambs and the illness of two others. Eventually he also describes the sheep thief's activities, saying he would like to kill the thief for what he has done.

Sigismund

Sigismund is a twenty-four-year-old sheep farmer who has been married to his nineteen-year-old bride and childhood sweetheart for one week. He is determined to protect Lovisa from misfortune, promising himself that "from now there should be no stone in his bride's path, nor should any shadow fall across it." A modern farmer, Sigismund has traveled outside of Denmark to learn the latest methods of sheep breeding and has had sheep imported from England to improve his flock. He is so happy in his newly married life that he cannot join his wife and Mathias in condemning the thief but rather pities the man. On the other hand, he is preoccupied with his sheep at the expense of his wife: when Lovisa is distressed by the sick lambs, he advises her to go home—she is "turned away by an impatient husband to whom his sheep meant more than his wife." When near the end of the story Lovisa admits she has lost her ring, he asks, "What ring?"

Thief

The thief never speaks, and much of what is known of him is learned from the story of Mathias, the sheep master. Repeatedly likened to a wolf, the thief has been stealing sheep from local farmers for several weeks and recently killed a farmer who had caught him in the act. The thief is hiding in a grove on the farm of Sigismund and Lovisa and is covered with blood and surrounded by sheep bones when Lovisa unexpectedly enters the grove. He says nothing to her but points a bloody knife at her throat, his hand dangling between his legs. He refuses the wedding ring Lovisa offers him, choosing instead to wrap his knife in a handkerchief which she dropped. Once the knife is put back into its sheath, the thief disappears. The thief represents an intrusion of disturbing and deadly violence into the flat and pacific landscape of the Danish countryside as well as into the innocent, paradise-like world of Lovisa.

Themes

Identity

In the first paragraph of the story, Dinesen explains that the events happened one hundred and fifty years ago in the Danish countryside. The two young people at the center of the story are Sigismund, aged twenty-four, and Lovisa, aged nineteen, newlyweds who have been married only a week. In Dinesen's aesthetic—indeed in her view of the world—such facts are important because much of human identity comes from *milieu,* the particular place and time in which an individual finds himself. Sigismund, the story says, is a "squire," a propertied gentleman-farmer; that is his role. Lovisa's role is the gentleman-farmer's loving wife. It is a case not so much of individual but of traditional, even

Topics for Further Study

- Dinesen sets ''The Ring'' in a particular locale, rural Denmark, at a particular historical moment, the early nineteenth century. This setting is preindustrial, manorial (if not feudal) in its social arrangements, and highly custom-bound. In other words, it is hard to imagine a more parochial environment. Discuss why the story is universal in its implications despite its parochial setting.

- Analyze and discuss the imagery of the episode in the glade where Lovisa encounters the thief.

Pay close attention to Dinesen's diction and to the way she describes the state of consciousness of her point-of-view character, Lovisa.

- Much has been written about the sexual implications of ''The Ring.'' What clues in the story might tell us something about the erotic side of Lovisa and Sigismund's marriage? Do critics overemphasize or underemphasize the sexual element in the story? Explain why you think so.

---

geographic, identity. The two young people have not yet transcended their milieu to become fully individual; rather, they still bear the impress of the countryside where they were born and of the roles which circumstances have bestowed on them. Interestingly, Lovisa thinks that Sigismund's intentness on being a scientific sheep-farmer is boyish, a pose, but she does not see her own affectations or understand her own immaturity. Identity is something into which one grows.

More than this, however, identity—*healthy identity*—combines unique individual traits derived from experience with a deeply internalized relation to institutions and norms, like business and marriage, or moral and legal standards accepted by the majority of one's community. Identity, in Dinesen's understanding, consists of a balancing act that requires careful and fully conscious maintenance by every person. The relation of the individual to society, and to norms, is often conflicting, in that the individual must sacrifice much of his own will to the peace of the community, or to specific other persons within the community, just as a man and a woman concede much to each other in marriage.

Duty and responsibility

As Dinesen saw it, individuals enter a world which none have made, which exists prior to their birth, and which makes certain nonnegotiable demands. Some of these demands are simply physio-

logical: birth endows a person with the characteristics of one sex or another and with all of the organic limitations inherent in being a mortal creature. Tradition, too, imposes and coerces, with the norms and standards which constitute the prevailing moral consensus of a people. Arising from centuries of human existence, morality guards against behaviors that disrupt communal order and generate misery. Sigismund has a duty to succeed at sheep farming so he can keep his wife from poverty; he must devote himself to his role even if doing so entails paying less sentimental attention to his wife than she, for her part, might demand. The wedding ring binds them not only to each other but to centuries of custom and to the wisdom that custom contains.

The Meaning of Life

Before her encounter with the thief, Lovisa thinks she knows the meaning of life: it is to be loved by her husband and to love him in return. The encounter leaves her in grave doubt, and giving away her wedding ring in an attempt to barter for her life puts her in a new and unsettling relation with marriage, the one social institution on which she has founded her new life.

Consciousness

Consciousness, for Dinesen, is an external awareness of oneself and one's condition. Lovisa's passage from naive satisfaction with her life to anxious dissatisfaction with it is a passage from unconsciousness to consciousness, mediated by an encounter with violence. Sigismund, by contrast, remains absorbed in the pragmatics of squiredom. Lovisa claims to Sigismund that she has "no idea" what became of her ring, but she knows she is lying. At the same time, she grasps her life in a new and startling way, as though she were an observer looking at herself with cold objectivity. The thief, animal-like in his wild appearance and silence, evokes the danger of unconscious or animal urges, such as those associated with sexuality.

Sex

Dinesen tells the reader that Lovisa was quite recently still playing with dolls, a childish activity indicating a pre-sexual existence. Also like a child, Lovisa plots to draw her husband into a game of hide-and-seek. They have been married a week, but the reader does not know whether the newlyweds have consummated their union. Sigismund is too preoccupied with his farm during the course of the story to give his wife much of his attention, in contrast with Lovisa's musings on wedded bliss. Her entry into the glade has been taken by some as a metaphor for sexual penetration, and her encounter with the thief contains a variety of sexually suggestive elements, such as the unsheathing and resheathing of the bloody knife and the criminal's taking her handkerchief (a hymeneal symbol). Sigismund's plan to improve his stock through the importation of English stud-animals also has a sexual aspect.

Violence and cruelty

The farmers introduce the theme of violence in their discussion of the sheep-thief, and Lovisa encounters the source of that violence in the glade. In Dinesen's view, violence and cruelty are part of human nature, but however disagreeable in themselves, they also denote the presence of vitality, of something like the "will-to-power," as the German philosopher Friedrich Nietzsche termed it. Violence and cruelty therefore represent the energy that fuels creative endeavor, that awakens consciousness. The question for vital human beings is how to channel their vitality, their will-to-power, creatively rather than destructively. In Dinesen's Nietzschean view of things, art is the sublimation of violence, and every instance of beauty (as in Lovisa's glade) contains something violent.

Style

Style

Isak Dinesen faced the accusation throughout her career that she used an archaic style irrelevant to the social reality of the modern world. While less baroque and internally complicated than some of her other stories, "The Ring" nevertheless illustrates what critics mean when they accuse Dinesen of archaism. Here, Dinesen travels beyond the baroque, back to the style of medieval folktale and saga. For example, there is a moment, in *The Prose Edda*, one of the great mythological poems of the Scandinavian middle ages, when the god Thor fights the World Serpent. Thor will slay the Serpent, the poet says, and then stagger back nine paces—not a few paces, not eight, not ten, but precisely nine paces—and then die from the Serpent's poison. The ritualistic exactitude is reported matter-of-factly. Dinesen's style, in "The Ring," derives from the laconic, the ritualistic, precision of medieval narrative.

Dinesen narrates Lovisa's encounter with the thief in her glade step by step, with saga-like matter-of-factness and precision. When Lovisa finds the thief he stands precisely "two steps off" from her; their silent transaction requires exactly "four minutes"; and when she offers her wedding ring that the thief should take it and depart, "her young form had the grave authoritativeness of a priestess conjuring down some monstrous being by a sacred sign." Again, the thief's movements when he picks up Lovisa's handkerchief from where she has accidentally dropped it get a precise description. Dinesen calls the encounter a "pantomime," and in endowing each movement with visual precision so that the reader can imagine it perfectly, Dinesen also charges every gesture with significance.

Setting

Like the English countryside in the poetry of William Wordsworth or the novels of George Eliot, the Danish countryside tends to achieve the status of a character in the works of Isak Dinesen and of other Danish writers. But the Danish countryside is flatter, altogether less variegated, sparer, and at times bleak. It is settled in the form of farmsteads and associated small villages. Throughout the nineteenth century the rural areas of Denmark retained their isolated character; they were not in continuity with cities like Copenhagen or Aalborg, but they were in continuity with their own massive traditions. It is into such a milieu that Dinesen places

Lovisa and Sigismund, on a summery day around the year 1800. On Sigismund's sheep farm, footpaths lead through the gently rolling furze, and there are, here and there, stands of trees.

One such stand, or glade, serves as the principal setting of the tale. Lovisa's secret glade differs from the surrounding countryside. It consists of a thick tangle of underbrush and tree branches, which she must force apart in order to gain entry to the inner "alcove," as she calls it. The glade has the character of an inner sanctum, shut off from the rest of the world, an asylum of pure privacy—now violated, however, by the presence of the thief. The cinders of his fire, strewn about with gnawed bones from his rude feast, give the scene a primitive character.

Stream of consciousness

Although the story begins as a classic third-person narrative, the episode of Lovisa's encounter with the thief exhibits elements of stream-of-consciousness narration: during this event Dinesen lets the reader see, without interruption and with little comment, through Lovisa's perception. The shift in narrative technique emphasizes the paradoxical awakening of consciousness.

Realism

Despite the archaism and the distance of the setting, Dinesen charges "The Ring" with elements of her characteristic realism. This realism chiefly concerns the encounter with the thief, whose physical state Dinesen carefully describes. On the other hand, the thief's vanishing is so abrupt that it acquires a magical quality, which challenges the episode's concreteness, giving it a dreamlike quality.

Paradox

If one of the principal themes of "The Ring" is consciousness, one of the ways in which Dinesen conveys this theme is through the construction of a paradox. In Dinesen's vision, consciousness itself is paradoxical. The paradox consists of the fact that Lovisa's happiness turns out to be a delusion. Delusion is a state from which one would want to be delivered, if one knew about it, and yet the very deliverance from it, into objective knowledge, entails the dissolution of happiness. And happiness, seen from the perspective of the anxiety of doubt that comes with consciousness, can seem a refuge. Having come into consciousness—having, that is, understood something of the truth about her condition—Lovisa finds that she cannot speak the truth to

her husband, as when she ironically says that she has no idea where her wedding ring disappeared. Earlier, Lovisa expressed the thought that she was "a hundred years older than" Sigismund, but by the end of the story that delusion gives way to the truth that she is only now wiser than he. She thus understands the import of his words, when he argues that the loss of the ring means nothing, because both of them "are the same" as on their wedding day. He remains the same; she has become something different.

Structure

The structure of "The Ring" reflects the changing relationship between Lovisa and Sigismund. In the beginning, husband and wife are walking together, then they separate, leaving Lovisa on the trail home by herself. Next the story ushers Lovisa into the glade to confront the thief, who at last vanishes, whereupon Lovisa finds herself back on the path with Sigismund, walking this time not beside him but in front of him, with her back to him, so that their unity is heavily qualified.

Symbolism

The symbol of the wedding ring dominates the story, a purely conventional symbol upon which the meaning of the events depends. A wedding ring is the token of unity of a married couple, signifying their decision to make themselves one in the sight of God. Facing the thief, Lovisa's wedding ring becomes for her an amulet that has the power to chase away an apparition, and in removing the ring, although she does not think of herself as bartering for her life, she does devalue the symbol of her marriage. The reader cannot be sure whether the ring becomes, at that instant, merely a knickknack, quite replaceable, or whether the act of trying to give it to the thief in exchange for his departure possesses richer significance for Lovisa. The story does link the ring to a marriage which has been transformed, in her eyes, negatively, and the removing of the ring to Lovisa's "marriage" to a crueller understanding of life and fate—a philosophical marriage which becomes the transcendental context for the naive marriage to Sigismund. Another symbol is the thief's bloody knife, commonly endowed with phallic characteristics in the manner of a Freudian interpretation. But the knife can also symbolize violence in general, in addition to sexual violence. Commentators have identified the glade both as a sexual symbol and as a symbol of consciousness; it can be seen as the interior of Lovisa's mind.

Historical Context

Diminishing Danish Influence

Militarily, economically, and artistically, Denmark was a much more influential nation in the nineteenth century that it would be in the twentieth. This fact is significant for an understanding of Isak Dinesen (1885-1962), whose life straddles both centuries. When the nineteenth century began, Denmark controlled an empire: Iceland, Greenland, the Faeroe Islands, and the Danish Virgin Islands were all territories of the Danish crown, and so was the region of Slesvig-Holstein, a corner of the European continent which would, in the war of 1864, fall under the control of Prussia. Not only did Denmark begin the nineteenth century both as a power and with an empire, but in the middle of that century it suffered a humiliating defeat. One effect of the loss was to disabuse the Danes of further geopolitical ambitions and provoke them to seek status by cultural means. For a small country, Denmark could already, by mid-century, claim a good share of Europe's literary and artistic achievement, not least in the work of well-known and respected writers like Hans Christian Andersen, Adam Oehlenschlager, Meir Goldschmidt, Jens-Peter Jacobsen, Soren Kierkegaard, and Georg Brandes. Even the redoubtable Henrik Ibsen, though a Norwegian, wrote in Danish and could be considered part of Danish literature. As for Brandes, he was, in the last third of the nineteenth century, the most influential literary critic in Europe, a herald and explicator of the burgeoning, self-conscious movement of artistic modernity. In painting, Edvard Munch broke ground as an exponent of the expressionist school.

Dinesen came of age exactly at the turn of the century, an era of sophistication. She enrolled as a student in *Det Kongelige Akademi,* the Royal Academy of Fine Arts, in Copenhagen, aiming at making a career as a painter. It did not work out that way, but in Copenhagen Dinesen was exposed to the leading currents of contemporary thought and art. Under the influence of Brandes, for example, she made herself familiar with the work of Friedrich Nietzsche, the radical German thinker popularized by Brandes in a widely disseminated book called *Aristocratic Radicalism,* whose title in many ways describes Dinesen's own outlook. Nietzsche argued that all the inherited "values" of European civilization were exhausted of their relevancy and that a new breed of men was required to create new values to replace the dead ones. In Nietzsche's view, life was entirely "imma-

nent," that is, life was what people might make of it, and if their aims were heroic, then life itself would be heroic; but if their aims were those of shopkeepers and bureaucrats, the bourgeoisie, then life would be a paltry affair of routine and habit. In the absence of God, urged Nietzsche, the locus of all genuine values was art; under Nietzsche's dispensation, the justification of life lay in beauty, not in worship.

Just as the war with Prussia in 1864 chastened Denmark, so too did the World War of 1914 to 1918 chasten all of Europe. The traditionalists who thought that tradition itself formed a bulwark against catastrophe and the radicals who thought that the unleashing of the will would lead to a utopia of supermen—all found that humanity was a fragile thing that could collapse out of control if not supervised with the utmost vigilance. Although Denmark had kept out of the war, Dinesen herself, in Kenya at the time, was in it, for her farm lay in the skirmishing ground between British and German forces in East Africa. Dinesen returned to a Europe devastated by war, intoxicated by the "Roaring Twenties," headed for financial collapse in a worldwide depression (1929), and plunging into an era of fascism and nationalism. In the heady atmosphere of the 1920s, the leading lights in art and literature were self-proclaimed modernists, either experimentalists like James Joyce in England or social realists like Tom Kristensen in Denmark. Although a modernist in her outlook (she remained a Nietzschean, even after the war), Dinesen belonged to a group of Scandinavian writers who were severe critics of modernism, advocates of a type of Gothic or preindustrial ethos.

Two writers are important in this regard: Knut Hamsun and Sigrid Undset, both Norwegians. Hamsun's novels celebrate the world of the Norwegian coastal village, a world of fishermen and small farmers; Undset's look back to the medieval period, when Christianity was newly consolidated in Scandinavia and the fishing and farming communities described in Dinesen's tales had found their basic form. In her Gothicism, Undset is particularly close to Dinesen, and her trilogy *Kristin Lavransdatter* (1920-22) explores on an epic scale the same issues that are central for Dinesen. But Dinesen's earliest significant work, the *Seven Gothic Tales,* appeared only in 1937, much later than Undset's work; *Anecdotes of Destiny* belongs to the mid-1950s. Meanwhile, the heritage of English literature exerted some influence on Dinesen, who spoke the language well enough to write the *Seven Gothic Tales* in English. Shakespeare meant a great deal to her, and so did Edgar Allan Poe, an earlier critic of modern life and another expert teller of the short story.

The Europe of the height of Dinesen's career (1937-1957) saw even more tumult than the Europe of her youth. A second world war did not spare Denmark but engulfed it; the Nazis' professed admiration for Nietzsche and his concept of the "superman" tainted the Brandesian notion of aristocratic radicalism so dear to Dinesen. Unsullied by twentieth-century developments, however, and at last coming into his own as an important thinker was Kierkegaard, a Christian psychologist and aesthetician who became increasingly visible as a factor in Dinesen's outlook. For Kierkegaard, human life consisted of profoundly consequential choices, each one of them an "either-or" which admitted no compromise and demanded action. Before Nietzsche, before Freud, Kierkegaard had conducted a brilliant and disturbing analysis of human motives, and Dinesen was not the only one during the Second World War and after to turn to him in qualified preference to the now-suspect Nietzsche.

Dinesen's last decade (1952-1962) belonged to the Cold War and to the increasing possibility of nuclear destruction. The impulses of the would-be superman were now more dangerous than ever, but were the circumstances of eighteenth- and early nineteenth-century landed gentry more relevant to the modern condition than they had been before or only less relevant than ever? It was still an assertion of aristocratic radicalism to pay no attention to the critics, to depend on the discernment of sensitive readers, and to forge ahead according to one's own lights. In her last years, the facts of the contemporary world, of milieu, diminished in importance for Dinesen. She exerted her own influence rather than taking her cues from the present.

Critical Overview

By the time "The Ring" appeared in *Anecdotes of Destiny*, the critical judgment on Dinesen had long since fully registered, and whatever controversy her stubborn art had earlier generated had become the

mere expert background to her work. Critics who wrote about her did so mostly from a stance of approval, and those who disapproved—the ascendant Marxist school, for example—tended to ignore her. Judith Thurman in *Isak Dinesen: The Life of a Storyteller* (1982) summarizes the initial critical reaction in Denmark to Dinesen's fiction this way: "Many readers were offended by Karen Blixen's frank nostalgia for the *ancien regime* and by her flight from the grim realities of Danish life. There was also some resentment over the fact that she had written originally in English and had had her first success in America."

After the Second World War, Danish writers began to reassess their earlier commitments to social realism. A generation grew up whose work implicitly acknowledged the influence of Dinesen: both Martin A. Hansen and H. C. Branner looked to earlier centuries than the twentieth for settings which might foreground the essentials of the human condition, and both were, like Dinesen, critics of modernity. Appreciative accounts of Dinesen and her work began to appear by respected critics like Aage Hendriksen.

Critical response to *Anecdotes of Destiny* is perhaps best summed up by Thomas R. Wissen, who writes in *Isak Dinesen's Aesthetics* (1973) that this final volume amounted to a denouement in that it "contains stories . . . which do not contribute significantly to the illustration of points she has made previously." Nevertheless, says Wissen, "the tales will not disappoint . . . they conform to a fully realized aesthetic." And yet critics have responded with interest to individual tales in the *Anecdotes*. Bruce Bassoff recognizes "The Ring" as an instance of Dinesen's assertion that human beings respond to a native urge towards transcendence. Writing in 1990 in *Studies in Short Fiction*, Bassoff states that Lovisa "muses over her happiness" only to discover, through her encounter with the thief, that "life is both more and less than imagined promises." More than that, in Bassoff's reading, Lovisa's encounter leaves her with the sobering conviction that "she is no longer free," as she had earlier imagined herself. Robert Langbaum offers an interpretation in *The Gayety of Vision: A Study of Isak Dinesen's Art* (1964) that suggests for the tale an underlying vampire-aesthetic: "The sexual symbolism [in the encounter] suggests that there has been a union between [Lovisa and the thief], that he has taken her spiritual, as well as her physical,

Farmhouse in Faaborg, Fyn Island, Denmark.

virginity.'' Yet Langbaum also claims that only in the loss of the ring is Lovisa's ''marriage to [Sigismund] fully consummated.''

Janet Handler Burstein, writing in *Texas Studies in Language and Literature* (1978), avails herself of the contemporary critical idea of ''otherness'' to bring out what, for her, is the significance of ''The Ring.'' According to Burstein, it was Dinesen's conviction that individual identity included ''otherness'' essentially; that which is not one's self, which is different, as poverty is to wealth or cruelty to kindness, nevertheless forms a basic and non-negating part of every individual person. Thus

''although [Lovisa] is happily married to the man she loves,'' she nevertheless discovers, in her encounter with the thief, an opposite to her world which, in effect, completes that world. Lovisa's consciousness, says Burstein, ''is changed [and] henceforth, at the very heart of her secure and familiar world, [she] will know the 'other' whose alien eyes have met her own.'' Burstein's reading reveals an emergent trend in writing about Dinesen: feminist criticism. Yet while Dinesen was, to put it in terms of gender politics, a great *female* artist, she was not herself of any ''progressive'' persuasion and still less any kind of feminist.

Criticism

Thomas Bertonneau

Bertonneau is a Temporary Assistant Professor of English and the humanities at Central Michigan University and Senior Policy Analyst at the Mackinac Center for Public Policy. In the following essay, he maintains that Dinesen's story "The Ring" is an example of art describing tragedy.

Isak Dinesen, who owed much philosophically to the German philosopher and poet Friedrich Nietzsche, would certainly have agreed with Nietzsche's *Twilight of the Idols* (1888) that "whatever does not kill me makes me stronger." For this precept is simply a concise statement of the meaning of tragedy—that wisdom stems from pain and sorrow—and Dinesen's art always displayed an orientation towards the tragic. Just as Nietzsche's vision of tragedy can help readers to understand Dinesen's art, however, so can instances of Dinesen's art help readers to understand the basic structures—the human anthropological essence—of tragedy. To the extent that tragedy reflects life, it also reflects consciousness, the human perception and interpretation of life. And, as both Nietzsche and Dinesen powerfully reveal, violence has a relation, possibly generative, to consciousness. Thus if the cruelty at the heart of a Greek play like Sophocles's *Oedipus Rex* fascinates us, it is because the shock acted out on stage mirrors the shocks that have promoted each one of us from unconsciousness to consciousness. With this in mind, consider the case of the young bride, Lovisa, in Dinesen's brief but rich story "The Ring."

In the opening paragraphs of "The Ring," Dinesen stresses the youth and inexperience of the newlywed couple Sigismund and Lovisa: He is twenty-four and she is nineteen; they have been married only a week, and Lovisa in particular remains rapt in a girl's fantasy about the bliss of wedded life. "They were wonderfully happy," and after overcoming the resistance of Lovisa's parents to their union, "their distant paradise had descended to earth and had proved, surprisingly, to be filled with the things of everyday life." Dinesen's simple syntax, representative of Lovisa's as-yet rather simple thinking, tells us much. The "and" which links the idea of paradise with the idea of everyday things really ought to be a "but"; paradise and everyday things are normally incompatible. To the extent that one lives in the real world of the everyday, one does not live in paradise. And paradise, for its part,

implies the irrelevance of everyday things. Indeed, everyday things predominate in Sigismund and Lovisa's life together, especially Sigismund's preoccupations in his role as a gentleman-farmer of quality sheep. Sigismund's intentness on bettering his flock in fact distracts him from the marriage itself, as when he sends Lovisa home from the sheepfold. Even so, Lovisa feels that she "move[s] and breathe[s] in perfect freedom because she could never have any secret from her husband."

To emphasize her innocence, Dinesen dresses Lovisa up in "a white muslin frock and a large Italian straw hat," making her the image of girlishness:

> It was not a long time since she had played with dolls; as now she dressed her own hair, looked over her linen press and arranged her flowers she again lived through an enchanting and cherished experience: one was doing everything gravely and solicitously, and all the time one knew one was playing.

Thus attired, she walks with Sigismund to inspect the flocks, but arriving at the sheepfold, where sheepmaster Mathias is waiting, they are greeted with ominous news: one of the English-bred lambs is dead and two lambs are sick. As two assistants go to fetch the sick lambs, Sigismund and Mathias converse about a sheep thief who has been on the prowl in the district. "Three nights ago the shepherd and his son on an estate ten miles away had caught him in the act. The thief had killed the man and knocked the boy senseless." There had been a long fight, and the thief's arm was broken. Lovisa, listening to the story, feels "a pleasant little thrill running down her spine." This thrill seems to be connected, moreover, with the blush that had twice colored her face a few moments before when she was thinking her own thoughts as Sigismund and Mathias talked. What makes a young bride blush? Thoughts of the bed chamber seem probable. In that case, Lovisa's erotic musings have dovetailed with her contemplation of violence in Mathias's narrative about the thief and his bloody fight. Somehow the thrill of the two phenomena is related.

The glade within the grove where Lovisa seeks—all at once—solitude and adventure on her way home from the sheepfold, and where she will encounter the sheep thief, will serve as the scene in which the themes of violence and consciousness come together in Dinesen's story. There Lovisa will be jolted out of her childishness into a consciousness of life that deserves the name "tragic." To enter the inner sanctum, it is necessary for Lovisa "gently [to force] her way into the shrubbery," "to

What Do I Read Next?

- "Bjergtagen," or, in English, "Bewitched," by Meir Goldschmidt, a nineteenth-century Danish storyteller, makes use of the ancient folk-motif of the mortal woman seduced by a supernatural lover, a troll. Dinesen's story "The Ring" makes oblique reference to the motif and perhaps also to Goldschmidt's story, which is available in a number of translations in anthologies of Danish literature.

- "On Mottoes of My Life," by Dinesen, in *Daguerreotypes and Other Essays* (1979), a book of essays, is a concise summation of her world view.

- "The Dreamers," by Dinesen, in *Seven Gothic Tales* (1934), is a much longer narrative exploring the theme of "tragic wisdom" of the generative relation of loss and betrayal to consciousness.

- *A Severe Mercy,* by Sheldon Vanauken (1977), tells of the deep love the author shared with his wife, Jean Palmer Davis (nicknamed "Davy"), of how the "Shining Barrier" of their love was breached one day when Davy was threatened by a stranger in an urban park, and of how, in the Christian faith embraced by both, love is stronger than death.

divide the foliage and make a door to her sylvan closet." In the center of the glade Lovisa has previously discovered "a narrow space like a small alcove with hangings of thick green and golden brocade, big enough to hold two or three people in it." The imagery is undeniably sexual. Dinesen writes that "a little way into the grove, the soil became moist," and the locale is qualified by its emphatic "secretness." The glade within the grove also boasts the features of a fairy-tale wilderness, radically separate from the everyday world, but it is best characterized as a scene of heightened consciousness and self-awareness. Of course, as Lovisa enters it, to hide from her husband and provoke him into worrying about her that he might appreciate her the more, she finds an unexpected danger whose presence changes her playful attitude radically.

The thief himself suddenly "stood up erect, two steps off." His appearance is alarming: "His face was bruised and scratched, his hands and wrists stained with dark filth. He was dressed in rags, barefooted, with tatters wound round his naked ankles." Dinesen has arranged an interesting and undoubtedly meaningful symbolic sequence beginning with the whiteness of Lovisa's dress; continuing with her blushes (presumably red) and with Mathias's mention of the thief's bloody fight in the

sheephouse of the nearby estate; and culminating in the actual bloodiness of the thief himself. With his right hand, the thief "clasped the hilt of a knife." From the lack of awareness and girlish indifference betokened by the white dress, Dinesen has led us to the bloody criminal, blade in hand. The blade, threatening Lovisa from between the thief's legs, suggests the dreadful possibility of rape. The sexuality and the violence of these images are quite entangled, but the point is that together, whatever the formula of their mixture, they stimulate Lovisa into a new intensity of awareness. The last thing that one can say of that awareness is that it is girlish. Says Dinesen, "She beheld the man before her as she would have beheld a forest ghost: the apparition itself, not the sequels of it, changes the world to the human who faces it."

For one thing, the thief has altered the arboreal inner sanctum from Lovisa's place of private asylum into his own thief's den, from an alcove into a covert. As the thief stares at her in complete silence (he never speaks), Lovisa intuits that "he was wondering, trying to know" what her intentions might be towards him and what his, practically speaking, might be towards her. The situation exhibits a type of primitive symmetry, and Lovisa thinks that she can "see herself with the eyes of the wild animal at bay in his dark hiding-place: her silently approaching white figure, which might mean death.'' Now this might really be empathy. Dinesen's words do not preclude such an inference. But it is also projection, for, despite Lovisa's naivete, the thief ''might mean death'' to her in a very real sense. After all, he is wounded, but he is armed. At some level, she knows this, and even though the narrative imputes to her a ''fearless . . . nature'' and reports her as thinking that she is *not* bartering for her life, her pantomimed offer to buy-off danger amounts to the same thing. Lovisa draws off her wedding ring to offer it to the thief. The thief spurns the ring, but he does pick up her handkerchief, which she has inadvertently dropped. He wraps it around the blade and resheathes the knife. Injured, uncertain what Lovisa's presence means, the thief vanishes. Lovisa has the impression of having commanded him to do so. But this, readers need to remind themselves, is an *Anecdote of Destiny,* and Fate must be conceded its role in the affair.

Back on the path, she sees Sigismund, but the way ''was so narrow that he kept half behind her and did not touch her. He began to explain to her what had been the matter with the lambs. She walked a step before him and thought: All is over.''

Earlier, Lovisa imagined herself to be ''a hundred years older'' than Sigismund, a conceit which at the time was false. Now she is a step ahead of him, with her back to him, and he is following her from behind. In the tragic sense, Lovisa now could repeat her earlier conceit and it would be true. Sigismund notices Lovisa's distraction and inquires what is the matter. She reports having lost her ring. Sigismund's response indicates why his consciousness is no longer adequate from Lovisa's transformed point of view: ''What ring?'' In all probability, Sigismund is still preoccupied with problems of animal farming. Lovisa now understands that losing the ring marked a new marriage, not that of a girl to her childhood lover, but of a woman, a newly conscious woman, ''to poverty, persecution, total loneliness. To the sorrows and the sinfulness of this earth.'' The shock against the senses has opened her eyes to all this, but the invoice should not be interpreted as negative. It is, properly speaking, tragic, and it includes a type of moral development.

When Lovisa heard the story of the thief from Mathias, she agreed with him that the thief, if caught, should be killed. (Mathias had made a brutal pantomime of throttling the criminal with his bare hands.) To Sigismund's casually pitying sentiment

> Dinesen has arranged an interesting and undoubtedly meaningful symbolic sequence beginning with the whiteness of Lovisa's dress; continuing with her blushes (presumably red) and with Mathias's mention of the thief's bloody fight in the sheephouse of the nearby estate; and culminating in the actual bloodiness of the thief himself."

that the thief was a ''poor fellow,'' Lovisa objected. Now, however, Dinesen credits her with a sense of ''persecution and total loneliness,'' which sounds remarkably like a truly empathetic understanding of the thief's plight. Lovisa may still believe that the thief deserves to die, but a part of her now, at least in part, understands the thief's situation. Standing in judgment can include *identification* at some level. As despondent as the insight leaves her, then, the important thing is that it increases her awareness of the world, of the human inner dimension. The insight does not kill her. No, indeed, it makes her stronger, for an increase in consciousness, in Dinesen's world, is an increase of strength.

Source: Thomas Bertonneau, Overview of ''The Ring,'' for *Short Stories for Students,* The Gale Group, 1999.

Bruce Bassoff

Bassoff is Professor of English at the University of Colorado. In the following excerpt, he contends that Lovisa's (here called Lise) encounter with the thief—and the ''real world''—results in a dramatic change in her character.

Structuring [''The Diver''] are plot elements that we find also in ''The Ring'' and ''Babette's Feast'': a desire for transcendence (represented by the motifs of birds and angels); a fall (or its refusal) caused

by the ''real world'' in which ''dreams are tested'';
and either new knowledge or resignation, true art or
its simulacrum. In ''The Ring'' Lise, a young,
wealthy newlywed wife, muses over her happiness.
Unlike the Softa, who wants to transcend everyday
life through converse with an angel, Lise feels like
the angel herself: the ''distant paradise'' she shares
with her husband has ''descended to earth'' and is
''filled with the things of everyday life.'' If the
artist, as we are told in ''The Diver,'' seeks secrets
from the depths, our domestic angel finds freedom
in the fact that she has *no* secret from her husband,
whom she wants to obey in everything. Though she
does everything ''gravely and solicitously,'' she
knows that she is playing. Like the fish in ''The
Diver,'' who are ''upheld and supported on all
sides,'' Lise lacks gravity. Unlike the veiled dancer
in ''The Diver,'' who understands how the world
works, she has no interest in the real world. From
time to time, however, a blush—a version of the
''burning'' decried by the fish in ''The Diver''—
unveils her innermost being. When this diffusion of
blood occurs in the *outside* world, where it betokens
the need and mortality she has ignored, she is
humanized.

A thief, hungry and desperate, has killed and
taken a sheep and killed a man who tried to stop
him. When the sheepmaster compares the thief to a
wolf, Lise remembers pleasurably the wolf in ''Little Red Ridinghood,'' but she criticizes her husband
for sympathizing with the thief. Like those in power
in ''The Diver,'' she fears ''revolutionary'' ideas.
As she walks back to the house, she surveys a
landscape that for her is full of promise. Still playing at life, she decides to hide from her husband to
make him feel ''what a void'' life would be without
her. Hiding in a ''narrow space like a small alcove''
that she finds in the woods, she discovers, however,
someone very foreign to her make-believe world:
the beleaguered thief. During a silent exchange of
looks, she sees herself with his eyes and discovers
that life is both more and less than imagined promises.

The thief makes a gesture that is both threatening and sexual: ''He moved his right arm till it hung
down straight before him between his legs. Without
lifting the hand he bent the wrist and slowly raised
the point of the knife till it pointed at her throat.''
While she offers him her wedding ring—in the hope
he will disappear and allow her to pretend that he
never was—he takes her handkerchief and wraps it
round his knife, which he fits into its sheath. Then
he closes his eyes and frees her.

She is no longer free, however, as she was when
she had no secret and wanted only to obey her
doting husband. She loses her wedding ring, which
the thief discards in the woods, but finds in its loss
an emblem of life's limits: ''With this lost ring she
had wedded herself to something. To what? To
poverty, persecution, total loneliness. To the sorrows and the sinfulness of this earth.'' While ''The
Diver'' goes beyond the Softa's fall to his subsequent but premature equilibrium, ''The Ring'' ends
with the heroine's fall—into material scarcity, sexuality, and death.

Source: Bruce Bassoff, ''Babette Can Cook: Life and Art in
Three Stories by Isak Dinesen,'' in *Studies in Short Fiction,*
Vol. 27, No. 3, Summer, 1990, pp. 385-89.

Janet Handler Burstein

*In the following excerpt, Burstein suggests that
the conflict between self-identity and social stereotype is experienced by many of the female characters in Dinesen's works. She then explores Lovisa's
(here called Lise) struggle with her selfhood in
''The Ring.''*

Because the work of Isak Dinesen reflects her
patrician inclinations, her skeptical view of ''eman-
cipated'' women, and her high regard for the symbolic—rather than the sociological or psychological—value of art, her stories often appear fairly
remote from contemporary concerns; in a world
animated largely by individual striving for equality and self-realization, Dinesen seems to speak,
conservatively, for values that many of us have
learned to distrust. And yet, Dinesen's work is
deeply rooted in her abiding preoccupation with a
problem that is alive in our own time. Experienced
as a disjunction between identity and role, or between self-image and social stereotype, this problem has been formulated by Simone de Beauvoir
[in *The Second Sex*, 1952] as a conflict between
selfhood and ''otherness.'' In her analysis of the
social, psychological, and political implications of
''otherness'' for women, de Beauvoir has shown
that the role of ''other'' deprives one of autonomy,
of a sense of self based upon norms that are appropriately female, and ultimately of a valid personal
and generic identity. Quite simply, to be cast as the
''other'' is, for de Beauvoir, to lose one's sense of
oneself as a subject and to accept a peripheral,
passive role as object in a busy world dominated
largely by men. But for Dinesen, ''otherness,''
despite its dubious implications for individual autonomy, is a vital fragment of human identity that

must be acknowledged and accepted before selfhood can be achieved.

Dinesen's preoccupation with the idea of "otherness" appears in virtually all her published work; as a major theme, a source of metaphor, and a seed of dramatic situation, therefore, this idea bears looking at from a strictly literary point of view. But from another perspective, one might explore this idea in her work simply for its own sake, to consider possibilities that may be obscured by the tendency to conceive the roles of subject and object, self and "other," as mutually exclusive. If one has learned, in other words, to reject the role of "other" as threatening to the integrity of the self, Dinesen may reveal self and "other" as two states of being that can co-exist in fruitful tension. Like all the great antinomies which bracket human existence, self and "other" may be seen, in the words of one of her characters, as "two locked caskets, each of which contains the key to the other." And to achieve a sense of the relationship between them may be, as it is for the characters in Dinesen's work, to widen the range of one's own experience and to understand that experience more fully.

For Dinesen's characters, the need to conceive oneself as the "other" and also the quest to experience and understand life more fully are determined partly by the nature of her fictional "world." Whether she writes of twentieth-century Africa or nineteenth-century Europe, Dinesen's "world" is essentially realistic in one important respect: it never wholly yields to the individual will or conforms to the needs of men and women who live within it. Like our own world, it may allow individuals the brief illusion that they shape events according to their own desires, or the momentary pleasure of finding themselves in tune with a larger, cosmic harmony, but it is always, simply, itself: resistant, or at best indifferent, to the human desire for mastery. When locusts descend on a beloved coffee plantation, or a ledge of ice breaks under the weight of two young lovers, Dinesen's "world" seems to express its resistance to the individual will, and it is partly this resistance that illuminates the limits of individual autonomy and reveals the self as "other." In short, for Dinesen, the "other" in oneself seems called into being in response to experiential encounter with a will that is not one's own.

Experience alone, however, is not sufficient to the task of human understanding, for Dinesen's stories also demand that characters learn to appreciate the logic which governs the resistance of the

> The thief makes a gesture that is both threatening and sexual: 'He moved his right arm till it hung down straight before him between his legs. Without lifting the hand he bent the wrist and slowly raised the point of the knife till it pointed at her throat.'

world and limits the autonomy of the self. Thus, unlike our own world which is often opaque, bewildering, absurd, Dinesen's fictional "world" is always transparently symbolic: entirely coherent, wholly expressive, thoroughly meaningful. If, as [Donald Hannah] has observed [in *Isak Dinesen and Karen Blixen*, 1971], her characters "change colour vividly . . . grow rigid with rage or terror . . . shake with laughter . . . tremble with anger, fear or grief . . . [and] blush—in all hues of red," they do so partly because they are fulfilling their function as symbols; the self of each is entirely devoted to the task of symbolic revelation, of showing that meaning inheres in every gesture, word, wish, and response of every individual. Many of the tales also manifest a structural concern with the showing forth of meaning; the fine network of separate stories interpolated within single works can invariably be seen, in retrospect, as a deliberate design in which all the stories play small but mutually relevant parts. Images too, particularly images of masks, mosaics, and marionettes which abound in the tales, reflect Dinesen's apparently fundamental belief that the world and all within it are symbolic in their design; as one character puts it, "Life is a mosaic of the Lord's that he keeps filling in bit by bit," a vast and intricate design whose meaning becomes clear only when the pattern is complete and one's own role in the pattern is recognizable.

This conception of the world as mosaic has, of course, both religious and philosophical implications. Its human implications, however, are worth noting, for they account for the distinct emphasis on

> In Lise, then, who dares to risk discovery of both selfhood and otherness, one might see a paradigm of the quest that absorbs so many characters in Dinesen's short stories."

the importance of seeing oneself as both subject and object that seems so pervasive in Dinesen's work. Theoretically, if life is a mosaic, then the identity of individual tiles is never submerged; the color, shape, size, and texture of separate pieces will always remain distinct within the whole, for a mosaic is not an ill-defined blur of color, but, to use Dinesen's phrase, ''a homogeneous up-heaping of heterogeneous atoms''—a harmonious construct, if you will, whose ingredients retain their separate identities. But the identity of every tile, however remarkable in itself, is also part of a larger identity, for each tile participates with its near and distant neighbors in a larger image. And it is the need to perceive the self in both of these roles, as a subjective, autonomous individual and as an objective part of the whole, that seems to motivate many of Dinesen's characters.

For most characters in the stories, awareness of oneself as both self and ''other'' depends partly upon one's sensitivity to the symbolic meaning of experience, and partly upon one's openness and vulnerability to forces outside the self. And because these two human faculties are rarely balanced in individual characters, the stories allow one to recognize the differing virtues of both symbols and experience in the quest for selfhood and ''otherness. . . .''

Beyond the metaphor of young love, . . . Dinesen fully exploits the imagery of sexuality to suggest the more mature awareness that individuals belong not only to themselves and to each other, but also to a vast design that embraces God and the whole human community. In at least two fairly late stories, this highly abstract notion, as difficult to realize as it is easy to articulate, is embodied in the experiences of two women: Lady Flora Gordon, the gigantic, red-haired heroine of ''The Cardinal's Third Tale,'' and

Lise, a young woman, recently married, in ''The Ring.'' In part, Dinesen may have chosen female characters for central roles in both stories because of their vulnerability to sexual violation, for in both works the fact of human community shatters the illusion of self-sufficiency that Dinesen appears to associate with sexual innocence.

In both stories, sexual imagery is unusually emphatic and richly expressive of Dinesen's thematic concern. The white dress of the young wife suggests that, despite her marital status, her essential innocence is still intact; she may preside over the pleasures of her new domain, like a child with a new dollhouse, but in all important respects she is still virgin—her being as yet untouched, as the bright circle of her existence is still unruptured, by experience of the world. In the wedding band that she offers to the fugitive whose hiding place she stumbles upon, one sees a symbol not only of the sexual contract that binds wife to husband in mutual fidelity, but also of the secure but rigid self-enclosure in which this young woman exists. And in the fugitive's disinterest in the ring one sees the contempt of one who knows experience for the facile symbol of domestic security. . . .

It is important to note that even in these two stories, where the intactness of the self is shattered to allow for growth and where this experience is identified, both thematically and imagistically, with the violation of female innocence, Dinesen appears to insist that these women remain active subjects whose own initiative partly shapes their destinies. Lady Flora must offer the gift of her devotion to God before she can be shown the truth of her implication in humanity. And the young woman in ''The Ring'' must desire to break free of her domestic encirclement before she can encounter the ''other'' who reveals herself.

Indeed, ''The Ring,'' which Dinesen set at the end of her last collection of stories, probably offers the most complete illustration of her belief that ''otherness'' is an essential fragment of identity and does not negate, but rather enhances, the self. Lise, the young woman in this story, discovers the reality of her single self just moments before she is made aware of the ''other'' both within and beyond her. Although she is happily married to the man she loves, she discovers, like the sailor boy, the ''sweetness'' of her initiative when her husband, preoccupied with difficulties at the sheepfold, impatiently suggests that she walk home without him: ''just walk ahead slowly,'' he tells her, ''and I shall catch up with you.'' But as she walks, savoring the taste of her first moments alone, she imagines ''it would be sweeter still . . . to steal into the grove and to be gone, to have vanished from the surface of the earth from him when, tired of the sheep and longing for her company, he should turn the bend of the road to catch up with her.''

On impulse, then, and at her own initiative, like Lady Flora, she finds the grove of shrubbery that she has thought of earlier as ''the very heart of her new home,'' and walks toward it, her white dress shining in the sun and her straw hat dangling its blue ribbons in the grass. As she enters the shadowy grove, she discovers the man who has intruded himself into her existence, a fugitive whose

> face was bruised and scratched, his hands and wrists stained with dark filth. He was dressed in rags, barefooted, with tatters wound round his naked ankles. His arms hung down to his sides, his right hand clasped the hilt of a knife.

Although the physical images of the two characters fully articulate the contrast between self and ''other'' that Dinesen appears to emphasize, the last sentences of the paragraph bind the two images together, relating them in fruitful tension without fusing or unifying or reconciling them: ''He was about her own age. The man and the woman looked at each other.''

In this moment of silent looking, as so often in similar moments in Dinesen's work, Lise's perception of both herself and the world is changed; although nothing happens, the narrator observes that ''the apparition itself, not the sequels of it, changes the world to the human who faces it.'' Henceforth, at the very heart of her secure and familiar world, Lise will know the ''other'' whose alien eyes have met her own. And in those eyes, she will also discover an image of the ''other'' in herself:

> After a while she realized that he was observing her just as she was observing him. He was no longer just run to earth and crouching for a spring, but he was wondering, trying to know. At that she seemed to see herself with the eyes of the wild animal at bay in his dark hiding place: her silently approaching white figure which might mean death.

Although she has earlier believed that it is impossible to feel ''pity'' for such a man, when he releases her and she returns to her husband she keeps the secret of his hiding place. Having recognized the vulnerable ''self'' in him and the threatening ''other'' in herself, she has broken the sterile circle of her existence and discovered compassion.

In Lise, then, who dares to risk discovery of both selfhood and otherness, one might see a paradigm of the quest that absorbs so many characters in Dinesen's short stories. One might question the appropriateness of this quest in our own time, for it assumes a confidence in the logic of the world that has been deeply eroded by contemporary experience; if the mosaic of life is actually a heap of rubble, then the search for a meaningful cosmic design and for one's own contributory role in that design is clearly absurd. But other elements of Dinesen's quest remain viable and compelling to the contemporary imagination, for they suggest that the fully achieved self is not negated but enhanced by forces that seem to oppose it, and that by sustaining the tension between selfhood and ''otherness'' one may transform a sterile opposition into a creative opportunity.

Source: Janet Handler Burstein, ''Two Locked Caskets: Selfhood and 'Otherness' in the Work of Isak Dinesen,'' in *Texas Studies in Literature and Language,* Vol. 20, No. 4, Winter, 1978, pp. 615-32.

Robert Langbaum

In the following excerpt, Langbaum assesses the theme of the human condition as found in Dinesen's ''The Ring,'' particularly as it relates to the character of Lovisa. He also studies the sexual symbolism of the story.

The few brief notes sounded in ''The Ring'' make an interesting epilogue to the volume [*Anecdotes of Destiny*]. . . . epilogue reminds us of the contrary theme that has been dealt with for the most part negatively in *Anecdotes*—the theme of the richly ambiguous human way. Like Eve when she meets Satan, the newly married, inhumanly innocent wife encounters a young thief and murderer. To buy him off, she offers him her wedding ring, which he spurns so that it falls to the ground and he kicks it away. He picks up, instead, the handkerchief she has also let fall, wraps it around the blade of his knife and puts the knife back in its sheath before disappearing. The sexual symbolism suggests that there has been a union between them, that he has taken her spiritual, as her husband took her physical, virginity. When, lying to her husband, she tells him she has lost her wedding ring, she realizes that she has now married two men—that ''with this lost ring she had wedded herself to . . . poverty, persecution, total loneliness. To the sorrows and the sinfulness of this earth.'' Only now, we are to understand, when she has this secret from her husband, is her marriage to him fully consummated. . . .

In ending *Anecdotes* on a tragic note, Isak Dinesen shows the artist's instinct for a complex symmetry. Looking back from a vision that transcends tragedy, she says what she has implied throughout, that tragedy is our distinctively human glory. But she praises tragedy from a point of view that . . . makes it a part of comedy. . . .

Source: Robert Langbaum, ''The Redemption of Ariel: *Anecdotes of Destiny* and *Ehrengard*,'' in *The Gayety of Vision: A Study of Isak Dinesen's Art,* Random House, 1965, pp. 245-86.

Sources

Thurman, Judith *Isak Dinesen: The Life of a Storyteller,* New York: St. Martin's Press, 1982.

Wissen, Thomas R. *Isak Dinesen's Aesthetics,* Port Washington, N.Y.: Kennikat Press, 1973.

A Rose for Emily

William Faulkner
1930

William Faulkner's "A Rose for Emily" was originally published in the April 30, 1930, issue of *Forum*. It was his first short story published in a major magazine. A slightly revised version was published in two collections of his short fiction, *These 13* (1931) and *Collected Stories* (1950). It has been published in dozens of anthologies as well. "A Rose for Emily" is the story of an eccentric spinster, Emily Grierson. An unnamed narrator details the strange circumstances of Emily's life and her odd relationships with her father, her lover, and the town of Jefferson, and the horrible secret she hides. The story's subtle complexities continue to inspire critics while casual readers find it one of Faulkner's most accessible works. The popularity of the story is due in no small part to its gruesome ending.

Faulkner often used short stories to "flesh out" the fictional kingdom of Yoknapatawpha County, Mississippi, for his novels. In fact, he revised some of his short fiction to be used as chapters in those novels. "A Rose for Emily" takes place in Jefferson, the county seat of Yoknapatawpha. Jefferson is a critical setting in much of Faulkner's fiction. The character of Colonel Sartoris plays a role in the story; he is also an important character in the history of Yoknapatawpha. However, "A Rose for Emily" is a story that stands by itself. Faulkner himself modestly referred to it as a "ghost story," but many critics recognize it as an extraordinarily versatile work. As Frank A. Littler writes in *Notes on Mississippi Writers*, "A Rose for Emily" has been

"... read variously as a Gothic horror tale, a study in abnormal psychology, an allegory of the relations between North and South, a meditation on the nature of time, and a tragedy with Emily as a sort of tragic heroine."

Author Biography

William Faulkner was born in New Albany, Mississippi, on September 25, 1897. His family moved to Oxford, Mississippi, just before he was five. Faulkner belonged to a once-wealthy family of former plantation owners. He spent his boyhood hunting and fishing in and around Lafayette County. He grew up listening to the stories and myths of the region, and he was especially impressed by the legendary life of the great-grandfather who was his namesake. He was a high school dropout, but he nevertheless developed a passion for literature, originally planning to be a poet. After working briefly as a clerk for the Winchester Repeating Arms Company, he reported to a recruiting station to sign up for World War I. He hoped to become a pilot and fight the Germans in the skies over France; however, they rejected him for being too small. He later signed on with the Royal Canadian Air Force (RCAF) to train as a pilot, but the war ended before he saw any combat.

After the war ended, Faulkner worked in a bookstore in New York, where he met Elizabeth Prall Anderson, the wife of noted writer Sherwood Anderson. His apprenticeship as a serious writer began when he traveled to New Orleans and lived among a group of writers and artists, including Anderson, who encouraged Faulkner's vision. Although he originally dreamed of being a poet, he ultimately found his voice in fiction. His invention of the mythical Yoknapatawpha County, Mississippi, gave him an almost endless source of colorful characters and stories. His greatest novels and short stories are set in Yoknapatawpha.

Faulkner used pieces of his own life and family history in his fiction. His great-grandfather, William Clark Falkner (Faulkner added the ''u'' to the spelling of his name when he joined the RCAF so that it would appear ''more British'')—who was also known as the Old Colonel—served as the inspiration for Colonel Sartoris. Colonel Sartoris, who plays a small but important role in ''A Rose for Emily,'' is also a major character in the novel *Flags*

in the Dust. Faulkner based part of the character of Emily on a cousin, Mary Louise Neilson, who had married a Yankee street paver named Jack Barron. More importantly, the character of Miss Emily is the town eccentric—Faulkner certainly understood eccentricity, having made it a lifelong practice. For example, when he was in his twenties taking language classes at the University of Mississippi, he was known as ''Count No Count'' for what many considered to be an aloof, arrogant, and foppish manner (though his poetry, essays, and sketches were in all of the student publications of the time). Like Emily, Faulkner was often frowned upon in his own home town. He became a pariah in Oxford in the fifties when he spoke out publicly against racism and segregation.

Faulkner published almost twenty novels, several volumes of short fiction, and two volumes of poetry. He wrote many screenplays, essays, and articles for magazines and newspapers. He traveled widely, giving lectures at American colleges as well as foreign universities. He won two Pulitzer Prizes, a National Book Award, and the Nobel Prize for Literature. Faulkner died on July 6, 1962, the same day his great-grandfather, the Old Colonel, had been born on 137 years earlier.

Plot Summary

The story, told in five sections, opens in section one with an unnamed narrator describing the funeral of Miss Emily Grierson. (The narrator always refers to himself in collective pronouns; he is perceived as being the voice of the average citizen of the town of Jefferson.) He notes that while the men attend the funeral out of obligation, the women go primarily because no one has been inside Emily's house for years. The narrator describes what was once a grand house ''set on what had once been our most select street.'' Emily's origins are aristocratic, but both her house and the neighborhood it is in have deteriorated. The narrator notes that, prior to her death, Emily had been ''a sort of hereditary obligation upon the town.'' This is because Colonel Sartoris, the former mayor of the town, remitted Emily's taxes dating from the death of her father ''on into perpetuity.'' Apparently, Emily's father left her with nothing when he died. Colonel Sartoris invented a story explaining the remittance of Emily's taxes (it is the town's method of paying back a loan to her father) to save her from the embarrassment of accepting charity.

The narrator uses this opportunity to segue into the first of several flashbacks in the story. The first incident he describes takes place approximately a decade before Emily's death. A new generation of politicians takes over Jefferson's government. They are unmoved by Colonel Sartoris's grand gesture on Emily's behalf and they attempt to collect taxes from her. She ignores their notices and letters. Finally, the Board of Aldermen sends a deputation to discuss the situation with her. The men are led into a decrepit parlor by Emily's black manservant, Tobe. The first physical description of Emily is unflattering: she is "... a small, fat woman in black" who looks "bloated, like a body long submerged in motionless water, and of that pallid hue." After the spokesman awkwardly explains the reason for their visit, Emily repeatedly insists that she has no taxes in Jefferson and tells the men to see Colonel Sartoris. The narrator notes that Colonel Sartoris has been dead at that point for almost ten years. She sends the men away from her house with nothing.

Section two begins as the narrator segues into another flashback that takes place thirty years before the unsuccessful tax collection. In this episode, Emily's neighbors complain of an awful smell emanating from her home. The narrator reveals that Emily had a sweetheart who deserted her shortly before people began complaining about the smell. The ladies of the town attribute the stench to the poor housekeeping of Emily's manservant, Tobe. However, despite several complaints, Judge Stevens, the town's mayor during this era, is reluctant to do anything about it for fear of offending Emily ("Dammit, sir ... will you accuse a lady to her face of smelling bad?"). This forces a small contingent of men to take action. Four of them sneak around Emily's house after midnight, sprinkling lime around her house and in her cellar. When they are done, they see that "... a window that had been dark was lighted and Miss Emily sat in it, the light behind her, and her upright torso motionless as that of an idol."

The narrator notes the town's pity for Emily at this point in a discussion of her family's past. The narrator reveals that Emily once had a mad great-aunt, old lady Wyatt. He also notes that Emily is apparently a spinster because of her father's insistence that "none of the young men were good enough" for her. The narrator then describes the

William Faulkner

awful circumstances that follow Emily's father's death. Emily is at first in such deep denial she refuses to acknowledge that her father is dead. She finally breaks down after three days and allows the townspeople to remove his body.

The narrator begins to detail Emily's burgeoning relationship with Homer Barron, a Yankee construction foreman, in section three. The narrator seems sympathetic, but the ladies and many of the older people in town find Emily's behavior scandalous. They gossip about how pathetic Emily has become whenever she rides through the town in a buggy with Homer. However, the narrator notes that Emily still carries herself with pride, even when she purchases arsenic from the town's druggist. The druggist tells her that the law requires her to tell him how she plans to use the poison, but she simply stares at him until he backs away and wraps up the arsenic. He writes "for rats" on the box.

At the beginning of section four, the town believes that Emily may commit suicide with the poison she has purchased. The narrator backs up the story again by detailing the circumstances leading up to Emily's purchase of the arsenic. At first, the town believes that Emily will marry Homer Barron when she is seen with him, despite Homer's statements that he is not the marrying type. However, a marriage never takes place, and the boldness of their relationship upsets many of the town's ladies. They send a minister to talk to Emily, but the following Sunday she rides through town yet again in the buggy with Homer. The minister's wife sends away for Emily's two female cousins from Alabama in the hope that they will convince Emily to either marry Homer or end the affair. During their visit, Emily purchases a toilet set engraved with Homer's initials, as well as a complete set of men's clothing, including a nightshirt. This leads the town to believe that Emily will marry Homer and rid herself of the conceited cousins. Homer leaves Jefferson, apparently to give Emily the opportunity to chase the cousins off. The cousins leave a week later, and Homer is seen going into Emily's house three days after they leave. Homer is never seen again after that and the townspeople believe he has jilted Emily.

Emily is not seen in town for almost six months. When she is finally seen on the streets of Jefferson again, she is fat and her hair has turned gray. Her house remains closed to visitors, except for a period of six or seven years when she gives china-painting lessons. She doesn't allow the town to put an address on her house and she continues to ignore the tax notices they send her. Occasionally, she is seen in one of the downstairs windows; she has apparently closed the top floor of the house. Finally, she dies, alone except for her manservant, Tobe.

The narrator returns to his recollection of Emily's funeral at the beginning of section five. As soon as Tobe lets the ladies into the house, he leaves out the back door and is never seen again. The funeral is a morbid affair. Soon after Emily is buried, several of the men force the upstairs open. There they find what is evidently the rotten corpse of Homer Barron. Even more grotesque, they find a long strand of iron-gray hair on the pillow next to his remains.

Characters

Homer Barron

Homer Barron is the Yankee construction foreman who becomes Emily Grierson's first real beau. His relationship with Emily is considered scandalous because he is a Northerner and because it doesn't appear as if they will ever be married. In fact, it is known that he drinks with younger men in

the Elks' Club and he has remarked that he is not a marrying man. The lovers ignore the gossip of the town until Emily's two female cousins from Alabama arrive. Homer leaves town for several days until the cousins go back to Alabama. Meanwhile, Emily purchases arsenic, a monogrammed toilet set with the initials H.B., and men's clothing. Homer returns to Jefferson three days after Emily's cousins leave and he is seen entering her home. He is never seen (alive) again. However, what is presumably his corpse is discovered in a ghastly bridal suite on the top floor of the Grierson house after Emily's funeral.

Druggist

The druggist sells Emily arsenic while her two female cousins from Alabama are visiting her. Emily just stares at him when he tells her that the law requires her to tell him why she is buying it. He backs down without an answer and writes "for rats" on the box.

Miss Emily

See Emily Grierson

Emily's cousins

Emily's cousins arrive after receiving a letter from the Baptist minister's wife. Apparently, they visit to discourage Emily's relationship with Homer Barron. Homer leaves while they are in town, and then returns after they have been gone for three days. The narrator, speaking for many in the town, hopes that Emily can rid herself of the cousins because they are "... even more Grierson than Miss Emily had ever been."

Emily's father

Although there is only a brief description of Emily's father in section two of the story, he plays an important role in the development of her character. Certainly Emily learns her genteel ways from him. It is his influence that deprives her of a husband when she is young; the narrator says that the town pictured Emily and her father as a "... tableau, Miss Emily a slender figure in white in the background, her father a spraddled silhouette in the foreground, his back to her and clutching a horse-whip, the two of them framed by the backflung front door." Emily at first refuses to acknowledge his death. She doesn't allow anyone to remove her father's body; finally, after three days she breaks down and lets someone remove the cadaver. This foreshadows the town's discovery of Homer Barron's decomposed corpse on the top floor in Emily's house after her death.

Emily Grierson

Emily Grierson, referred to as Miss Emily throughout the story, is the main character of "A Rose for Emily." An unnamed narrator tells her strange story through a series of flashbacks. She is essentially the town eccentric. The narrator compares her to "an idol in a niche . . . dear, inescapable, impervious, tranquil, and perverse." Emily is born to a proud, aristocratic family sometime during the Civil War; her life in many ways reflects the disintegration of the Old South during the Reconstruction and the early twentieth century. Although her mother is never mentioned, her father plays an important part in shaping her character. He chases away Emily's potential suitors because none of them are "good enough" for his daughter. His death leaves Emily a tragic, penniless spinster. She may even be mad—she denies that her father is dead at first and she won't allow anyone to remove his corpse until she breaks down after three days. However, she later causes a scandal when she falls in love with Homer Barron, a Yankee construction foreman who is paving the streets in Jefferson. The narrator's various clues (Emily's purchase of arsenic; the awful smell coming from her home after Homer disappears) and the town's grotesque discovery at the end of the story suggest that Emily is driven to murder when she begins to fear that Homer may leave her.

Minister

The Baptist minister, under pressure from the ladies of the town, goes to Emily (although she is Episcopal) to discuss her relationship with Homer Barron. He never tells anyone what happens and he refuses to go back to her. The following Sunday, Emily and Homer are seen riding through the town in the buggy again.

Minister's wife

The minister's wife sends a letter to Emily's relations in Alabama after her husband calls upon Emily. The letter prompts a visit from two of Emily's female cousins.

Narrator

The unnamed narrator refers to himself in collective pronouns throughout the story. As Isaac

Media
Adaptations

- "A Rose for Emily" was adapted for film by Chubbuck Cinema Co. It was produced an directed by Lyndon Chubbuck and written by H. Kaye Dyal. Anjelica Huston plays the role of Miss Emily.

Rodman points out in *The Faulkner Journal,* "The critical consensus remains that the narrator of 'A Rose for Emily' speaks for his community." Although there are a few sub-groups to which the narrator refers to as separate (for example, the "ladies" and the "older people" of the town), readers assume that he speaks for the majority of the average people of Jefferson. He tells Emily's story in a series of flashbacks which culminates in the dreadful discovery of a decomposed corpse on the top floor of the Grierson home after her death. The narrator never directly claims that Emily murders her lover, Homer Barron, and keeps his corpse in a bed for more than forty years. However, the events he chooses to detail, including Emily's purchase of arsenic and the stench that comes from her house after Homer Barron's disappearance, lead readers to that perception.

The negro
See Tobe

Colonel Sartoris

Colonel Sartoris is the mayor of Jefferson when Emily's father dies. He remits Emily's taxes "into perpetuity" because he knows that her father was unable to leave her with anything but the house. Sartoris, being a prototypical southern gentleman, invents a story involving a loan that Emily's father had made to the town in order to spare Emily the embarrassment of accepting charity. The narrator contrasts this chivalrous act with another edict made by Sartoris stating that ". . . no Negro woman should appear on the streets without an apron.'' Colonel Sartoris appears in other works by Faulkner; he is a pivotal character in the history of Yoknapatawpha County.

Judge Stevens

Judge Stevens is the mayor of Jefferson when the townspeople begin to complain of the awful odor coming from the Grierson house. Like Colonel Sartoris, he is from a generation that believes an honorable man does not publicly confront a woman with an embarrassing situation. He refuses to allow anyone to discuss the smell with her. Instead, four men sneak onto the Grierson property after midnight and sprinkle lime around the house to rid the town of the disgusting stench.

Tobe

Tobe is Emily's black manservant and, for most of the story, her only companion. He is often the only sign of life about the Grierson house. The ladies find it shocking that Emily allows him to maintain her kitchen, and they blame his poor housekeeping for the development of the smell after Emily is ''deserted'' by Homer Barron. He rarely speaks to anyone. He is the only person present when Emily dies. He lets the townspeople into the Grierson house after her death, after which he promptly leaves, never to be seen again.

Old Lady Wyatt

Old lady Wyatt is Emily Grierson's great-aunt. The narrator makes reference to her as having gone ''. . . completely crazy at last,'' suggesting perhaps that madness runs in the Grierson family. The narrator also mentions that Emily's father had a falling out with their kin in Alabama over old lady Wyatt's estate.

Themes

Death

Death is prevalent, both literally and figuratively, in ''A Rose for Emily.'' Five actual deaths are discussed or mentioned in passing, and there are obvious references to death throughout the story. The story begins in section one with the narrator's recollections of Emily's funeral. He reminisces that

it is Emily's father's death that prompts Colonel Sartoris to remit her taxes ''into perpetuity.'' This leads to the story of the aldermen attempting to collect taxes from Emily. The narrator's description of Emily is that of a drowned woman: ''She looked bloated, like a body long submerged in motionless water, and of that pallid hue.'' One of the reasons the aldermen are bold enough to try to collect Emily's taxes is that Colonel Sartoris has been dead for a decade. Of course, this doesn't discourage Emily—she expects the men to discuss the matter with him anyway. When the narrator returns to the subject of the death of Emily's father, he reveals that Emily at first denies that he is dead. She keeps his body for three days before she finally breaks down and allows her father to be buried. This scene foreshadows the grisly discovery at the end of the story. The narrator also mentions the madness and death of old lady Wyatt, Emily's great-aunt. Finally, the discovery of a long strand of iron-gray hair lying on a pillow next to the moldy corpse entombed in Emily's boudoir suggests that Emily is a necrophiliac (literally, ''one who loves the dead'').

The Decline of the Old South

One of the major themes in Faulkner's fiction is the decline of the Old South after the Civil War. There are many examples of this theme in ''A Rose for Emily.'' Before the Civil War, Southern society was composed of landed gentry, merchants, tenant farmers, and slaves. The aristocratic men of this period had an unspoken code of chivalry, and women were the innocent, pure guardians of morality. For example, Colonel Sartoris concocts an elaborate story to spare Emily's feelings when he remits her taxes; the narrator states, ''Only a man of Colonel Sartoris's generation and thought could have invented [the story], and only a woman could have believed it.'' When the smell develops around the Grierson house, a younger man suggests that Emily should be confronted with it. Judge Stevens, who is from the same generation as the Colonel, asks him, ''Dammit, sir . . . will you accuse a lady to her face of smelling bad?'' It is also noted that Emily's father is from this same generation, an arrogant Southern aristocrat who believes that no man is good enough for his daughter.

However, post-Civil War society in the South was radically different. At one time, the Grierson home was in one of the finest neighborhoods in Jefferson; by the time of Emily's death, ''. . . garages and cotton gins had encroached and obliterated even the august names of that neighborhood.'' The generation that follows Colonel Sartoris is not swayed by his old Southern code of honor. This is why the twentieth-century Jefferson Board of Aldermen attempts to collect Emily's taxes a decade after the Colonel's death. The reaction to the Yankee, Homer Barron, also serves to delineate the difference between the generations. The younger generation finds it easier to accept Homer, while the older folks find his relationship with a woman born to old Southern gentility unacceptable. Emily's china-painting lessons also show the change in Southern society. Her pupils are the daughters and granddaughters of Colonel Sartoris's contemporaries. However, the narrator notes that ''. . . the painting pupils grew up and fell away and did not send their children to her with boxes of color and tedious brushes and pictures cut from the ladies' magazines.'' Finally, Emily's dark secret might serve as a metaphor for the general decadence of the Old South.

Community vs. Isolation

The odd relationship between the town of Jefferson and Emily is a recurrent theme in ''A Rose for Emily.'' At her funeral, the narrator notes that Emily has been ''. . . a tradition, a duty, and a care; a sort of hereditary obligation upon the town.'' However, Emily has very little to do with the townspeople during her life. Her father prevents her from dating anyone because he doesn't believe any of the men in Jefferson are good enough for her and, after his death, Emily continues to isolate herself from the rest of the community for the better part of her life. The only notable exceptions to her isolation are her Sunday rides with Homer Barron, her shopping trips for arsenic and men's clothing, and the china-painting lessons she gives to the young women of the town for a few years. These exceptions only serve to show how alienated Emily is from the rest of Jefferson.

Although Emily is indifferent to the town, the town seems to be almost obsessed with her. The reaction Jefferson has to her relationship with Homer Barron exemplifies this obsession. The ladies of Jefferson are mortified because they think the relationship is ''. . . a disgrace to the town and a bad example to the young people.'' The older people dislike the relationship because they think it is bad form for a Southern woman to associate with a Yankee. The narrator pities Emily and secretly hopes that she will outsmart her cousins and marry Homer. These various reactions demonstrate an interesting conflict. Even though Emily views her-

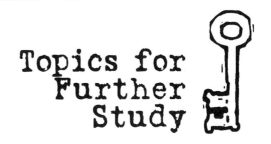

Topics for Further Study

- Except for the title, roses are never mentioned in the story. Why do you think Faulkner chose this title? Do you think the rose symbolizes anything in the story?

- As the narrator is telling the story of how Emily's taxes were remitted, he remarks that Colonel Sartoris is the father of an edict declaring that ''. . . no Negro woman should appear on the streets without an apron.'' Why do you think the narrator mentions this law? What does this remark tell us about the Colonel Sartoris and the narrator?

- Look up the definition of ''eccentric'' in the dictionary. Find examples of eccentric characters in literature and film. Compare your examples with Emily Grierson. What qualities do these characters share? What is there to admire or dislike about them?

- Only once in the story does the narrator place an event in a specific year. Find that event and year and see if you can put together a chronology. Does it seem consistent and realistic? Why or why not?

self as separate from the community, the community still embraces her. They view her as ''. . . an idol in a niche . . . passed from generation to generation—dear, inescapable, impervious, tranquil, and perverse.''

Style

Flashback and Foreshadowing

Flashback and foreshadowing are two often used literary devices that utilize time in order to produce a desired effect. Flashbacks are used to present action that occurs before the beginning of a story; foreshadowing creates expectation for action that has not yet happened. Faulkner uses both devices in "A Rose for Emily." The story is told by the narrator through a series of non-sequential flashbacks. The narrator begins the story by describing the scene of Emily's funeral; this description, however, is actually a flashback because the story ends with the narrator's memory of the town's discovery of the corpse in the Grierson home after Emily's funeral. Throughout the story, the narrator flashes back and forth through various events in the life and times of Emily Grierson and the town of Jefferson. Each piece of the story told by the narrator prompts another piece of the story, regardless of chronology. For example, the narrator recalls Emily's funeral, which leads him to remember when Colonel Sartoris relieved her of taxes. This of course leads to the story of the aldermen trying to collect Emily's taxes after the death of the Colonel. The narrative thus works much in the same haphazard manner as human memory does.

The narrator foreshadows the grisly discovery at the end of the story with several scenes. First, when the aldermen attempt to collect Emily's taxes, her house is described as decrepit, almost a mausoleum. Emily herself is compared to a drowned corpse. Then, in section two, the stench that emanates from the Grierson house is most certainly one of death. Another powerful example of foreshadowing comes when Emily refuses to let anyone take the body of her father after his death until she relents after three days. When Emily finally has access to another corpse, she jealously guards it for over forty years!

Point of View

The point of view in "A Rose for Emily" is unique. The story is told by an unnamed narrator in the first-person collective. One might even argue that the narrator is the main character. There are hints as to the age, race, gender, and class of the narrator, but an identity is never actually revealed. Isaac Rodman notes in *The Faulkner Journal* that the critical consensus remains that the narrator speaks for his community. (Rodman, however, goes on to present a convincing argument that the narrator may be a loner or eccentric of some kind speaking from "ironic detachment.") Regardless of identity, the narrator proves to be a clever, humorous, and sympathetic storyteller. He is clever because of the way he pieces the story together to build to a shocking climax. His humor is evident in his almost whimsical tone throughout what most would consider to be a morbid tale. Finally, the

narrator is sympathetic to both Emily and the town of Jefferson. This is demonstrated in his pity for Emily and in his understanding that the town's reactions are driven by circumstances beyond its control (". . . Miss Emily had been a tradition, a duty, and a care; a sort of hereditary obligation upon the town").

Setting

"A Rose for Emily" is set in Faulkner's mythical county, Yoknapatawpha, Mississippi. The town of Jefferson is the county seat of Yoknapatawpha. In *William Faulkner: His Life and Work,* David Minter writes, "More than any major American writer of our time, including Robert Frost, Faulkner is associated with a region. He is our great provincial." Jefferson and Yoknapatawpha County are based upon the real city of Oxford and Lafayette County in Mississippi, where Faulkner spent most of his life. Once he established this fictional, yet familiar, setting, he was able to tap his creativity to invent a history for Yoknapatawpha and populate the county with colorful characters like Emily Grierson and Colonel Sartoris. The land and its history exert a great influence over many of Faulkner's characters. Emily is no exception; she is trapped in Jefferson's past.

Structure

The best of Faulkner's fiction is characterized by the craftsmanship of its structure. *The Sound and the Fury* and *As I Lay Dying* are both examples of daring experimentation with point of view and time in the novel. He wrote "A Rose for Emily" during the same period he worked on those novels. The story moves seamlessly back and forth in time through almost fifty years in its five sections. Each episode in the life of Emily and the history of Jefferson is obviously interconnected, yet the clues aren't given in chronological order. Thus, the final scene is powerful because the narrator does not tell the story in a straightforward, beginning-to-end fashion. This is why the story is even more entertaining and enlightening when read for the second time.

Historical Context

The South after the Civil War

The Reconstruction after the Civil War had a profound and humbling effect on Southern society.

Compare & Contrast

- **1930s:** The 1929 collapse of the stock market in the U.S. leads to the Great Depression. Unemployment grows from 5 million in 1930 to 13 million in 1932 (24.9% of the population).

  1990s: The U.S. economy booms. The stock market climbs to unprecedented levels, while unemployment is at a quarter-century low.

- **1930s:** The thirties are part of a three-decade long golden age of radio. Families gather around the radio after dinner to listen to news, sports events, and dramas such as "The Shadow" and "Little Orphan Annie."

  1990s: Media is pervasive in late twentieth-century life. The choices seem endless; radio, television (with hundreds of channels), film, and the Internet provide people with information and entertainment twenty-four hours a day.

- **1930s:** Bruno Hauptmann is tried for the kidnapping and murder of the Lindbergh baby. (Charles Lindbergh was the first man to fly across the Atlantic Ocean on a solo voyage.) Although many believe that there is a rush to judgement in Hauptmann's conviction, he is executed in 1936 via the electric chair. The press dub the proceedings the "Trial of the Century."

  1990s: Former football star O.J. Simpson is arrested for the brutal murder of his ex-wife Nicole and her friend, Ron Goldman. The most incendiary topics of the time are involved: race, class, sex, gender, and fame. Simpson is acquitted (although a later jury finds him liable for the murders in a civil case). The press dub the proceedings the "Trial of the Century."

The South's outdated plantation economy, based so long upon slave labor, was devastated by emancipation. Northern opportunists, known as "carpetbaggers," came in droves to take advantage of the economic chaos. Some Southern aristocrats found themselves working the land alongside tenant farmers and former slaves. Faulkner came from a family that once owned a plantation. The history of his family and of the South in general inspired Faulkner's imagination.

The short stories and novels Faulkner wrote about Yoknapatawpha County combine to create an epic, mythical history of this era. David Minter, in his biography *William Faulkner: His Life and Work,* notes that as a teenager, Faulkner was known for being observational to the point of oddness: "Sometimes he joined the old men of Oxford on the town square . . . there he sat or stood motionless, quiet, as though held fast by some inner scene or some inner sense of himself." It was in this manner that Faulkner soaked up the legends of his region. He heard Civil War stories from the old veterans, hunting stories from his father, stories of his great-grandfather's

heroic exploits from his grandfather, and fables about the animals in the forest told by Mammy Caroline Barr, an ex-slave who watched over him when he was a small boy. The stories he heard, along with his experiences in Oxford during his own lifetime, greatly inform the scope of his work.

"A Rose for Emily," in a few pages, covers approximately three-quarters of a century. The birth of Emily Grierson takes place sometime around the Civil War. Her death takes place sometime in the late 1920s or early 1930s—that is, sometime around the year Faulkner wrote the story. Because Faulkner came from a family with an aristocratic bearing and associated with other similar families, he was familiar with the arrogance of characters like the Griersons. Some of these people continued to behave as if they were still privileged plantation owners although their wealth was gone. However, Faulkner spent much of his time observing ordinary townspeople as well, and this is why he was able to capture the voice of the common people of Jefferson in the character of the narrator.

The narrator in "A Rose for Emily" notes a change in the character of his town when Jefferson's Board of Aldermen attempts to collect Emily's taxes. Originally, the town was governed by men of the old South like Colonel Sartoris and Judge Stevens. Men like this operated under a code of chivalry that was extremely protective of white women. Thus, Colonel Sartoris is unable to allow the town to tax a poor spinster, and Judge Stevens is unable to confront Emily about the smell coming from her house. As each generation passes the torch, however, the newer generations are further and further away from the antiquated social mores of their forebears. The men who try to collect Emily's taxes don't operate under the same code of conduct as their grandfathers and great-grandfathers did. Emily is not a "damsel in distress" to these men; she is a nuisance, a hindrance to progress. Faulkner was very interested in this conflict between nineteenth and twentieth-century Southern society. The old Southern families of his novels, such as the Compsons in *The Sound and the Fury,* ultimately collapse under the weight of their histories. In "A Rose for Emily," Emily Grierson is certainly a character trapped in her genteel past, although she literally has a "skeleton in the closet."

Critical Overview

Faulkner is now regarded by most critics as one of the greatest American writers of the twentieth century. However, "A Rose for Emily," written in 1929, was actually rejected by *Scribner's* and other magazines before *Forum* published it in 1930. Although one of his greatest novels, *The Sound and the Fury,* was published just before "A Rose for Emily" in 1929, many American critics did not immediately recognize Faulkner as a groundbreaking writer. As is often the case with many challenging American authors, Faulkner was identified as a unique American voice in Europe long before he gained respect at home. In fact, as late as 1950, after he won the Nobel Prize for Literature, the *New York Times* (quoted in Robert Penn Warren's introduction to *Faulkner: A Collection of Critical Essays*) published an editorial claiming that his work was "too often vicious, depraved, decadent, [and] corrupt." "Americans most fervently hope," the *Times* continued, that neither the award given by Sweden nor the "enormous vogue of Faulkner's works" among foreigners meant that they associated American life with his fiction.

Interestingly enough, it is in *The New York Times* twenty years earlier that one can read an extremely favorable review of *These 13,* the first collection of Faulkner's short stories. "A Rose for Emily" is published in this edition. The reviewer notes that Faulkner was "hailed in England, before he was known here except to a small circle, as the latest star in the American literary firmament." He writes that "A Rose for Emily" is "one of the strongest, as it is certainly the most gruesome, tales in the volume." The story was also published in *Collected Stories* in 1950. The reviews for this volume were even more laudatory. In the *New York Herald Tribune,* Horace Gregory compares Faulkner to influential and brilliant writers such as Dostoevsky, Melville, James, and Joyce.

Presently, critics continue to write about "A Rose for Emily." The subjects of the story are timeless: love, death, community vs. individuality, and the nature of time. Some of the criticism written recently concentrates on possible literary references within the story. For example, Peter L. Hays, in an article published in *Studies in American Fiction,* suggests that Faulkner may have used Emily Dickinson as a model for Emily Grierson. In *Studies in Short Fiction,* John F. Birk draws analogies between the structure, theme, and imagery in "A Rose for Emily" to the poem "Ode on a Grecian Urn" by Keats. The story continues to resonate even after seventy years because so many of the story's themes are a part of everyone's experience.

Criticism

Donald Akers

Akers is a freelance writer and editor. In the following essay, he discusses the major critical interpretations of "A Rose for Emily."

William Faulkner is widely considered to be one of the great American authors of the twentieth century. Although his greatest works are identified with a particular region and time (Mississippi in the late nineteenth and early twentieth centuries), the themes he explores are universal. He was also an extremely accomplished writer in a technical sense. Novels such as *The Sound and the Fury* and *Absalom, Absalom!* feature bold experimentation with shifts in time and narrative. Several of his short stories are favorites of anthologists, including "A Rose for Emily." This strange story of love, obsession, and death is a favorite among both readers and critics. The narrator, speaking for the town of Jefferson in Faulkner's fictional Yoknapatawpha County, Mississippi, tells a series of stories about the town's reclusive spinster, Miss Emily Grierson. The stories build up to a gruesome revelation after Miss Emily's funeral. She apparently poisoned her lover, Homer Barron, and kept his corpse in an attic bedroom for over forty years. It is a common critical cliché to say that a story "exists on many levels," but in the case of "A Rose for Emily," this is the truth. Critic Frank A. Littler, in an essay published in *Notes on Mississippi Writers* regarding the chronology of the story, writes that "A Rose for Emily" has been read variously as "... a Gothic horror tale, a study in abnormal psychology, an allegory of the relations between North and South, a meditation on the nature of time, and a tragedy with Emily as a sort of tragic heroine." These various interpretations serve as a good starting point for discussion of the story.

The Gothic horror tale is a literary form dating back to 1764 with the first novel identified with the genre, Horace Walpole's *The Castle of Ontralto.* Gothicism features an atmosphere of terror and dread: gloomy castles or mansions, sinister characters, and unexplained phenomena. Gothic novels and stories also often include unnatural combinations of sex and death. In a lecture to students documented by Frederick L. Gwynn and Joseph L. Blotner in *Faulkner in the University: Class Conferences at the University of Virginia 1957-1958,* Faulkner himself claimed that "A Rose for Emily" is a "ghost story." In fact, Faulkner is considered by many to be the progenitor of a sub-genre, the Southern gothic. The Southern gothic style combines the elements of classic Gothicism with particular Southern archetypes (the reclusive spinster, for example) and puts them in a Southern milieu. Faulkner's novels and stories about the South include dark, taboo subjects such as murder, suicide, and incest.

James M. Mellard, in *The Faulkner Journal,* argues that "A Rose for Emily" is a "retrospective Gothic;" that is, the reader is unaware that the story is Gothic until the end when Homer Barron's corpse is discovered. He points out that the narrator's tone is almost whimsical. He also notes that because the narrator's flashbacks are not presented in an ordinary sequential order, readers who are truly unfamiliar with the story don't put all the pieces together until the end. However, a truly careful first reading should begin to reveal the Gothic elements early in the story. Emily is quickly established as a strange

A 19th century print of roses, showing various stages of bloom.

character when the aldermen enter her decrepit parlor in a futile attempt to collect her taxes. She is described as looking "... bloated, like a body long submerged in motionless water, and of that pallid hue." She insists that the aldermen discuss the tax situation with a man who has been dead for a decade. If she is not yet a sinister character, she is certainly weird. In section two of the story, the unexplained smell coming from her house, the odd relationship she has with her father, and the suggestion that madness may run in her family by the reference to her "crazy" great-aunt, old lady Wyatt,

What Do I Read Next?

- *Collected Stories* (1950) by William Faulkner is an exhaustive collection of his short fiction. The volume includes ''Barn Burning'' and many other stories about Yoknapatawpha County.

- *The Sound and the Fury* (1929) by William Faulkner is the novel that established his reputation as an important writer. This experimental novel concerns the decline of the once proud Compson family of Yoknapatawpha County. The story is told in four sections, each one detailing the disintegration of the Compsons from a different character's viewpoint. Faulkner used this technique in other novels as well, including *As I Lay Dying* (1930) and *Absalom, Absalom!* (1936).

- Many of the works of Flannery O'Connor are in the same Southern Gothic tradition as ''A Rose for Emily.'' Her short story ''A Good Man Is Hard to Find'' (1955) details a vacationing family's doomed encounter with an escaped criminal known as the Misfit.

- Southern playwright Tennessee Williams examined many of the same themes in his work as Faulkner. His play *A Streetcar Named Desire* (1947) is the story of aging, tarnished Southern belle Blanche DuBois and the tense relationship she has with her brutish brother-in-law, Stanley Kowalski.

- Some of Truman Capote's fiction concerns life in the South in the 1930s. His novel, *The Grass Harp* (1951), tells the story of a group of eccentrics who disrupt their community when they retreat to the woods and begin living in a treehouse.

- The 1996 film *Kissed,* directed by Lynne Stopkewich and written by Barbara Gowdy, Angus Fraser, and Stopkewich, is the story of a woman (Molly Parker) whose obsession with death as a young girl leads her to a job in a mortuary and necrophilia.

---

are elements that, at the very least, hint at the Gothic nature of the story. Emily's purchase of arsenic should leave no doubt at that point that the story is leading to a Gothic conclusion.

It is Emily's awful deed that continues to captivate readers. Why would she do something so ghastly? How could she kill a man and bed his corpse? This line of questioning leads to a psychological examination of Emily's character. David Minter, in *William Faulkner: His Life and Work,* notes in several different passages the significant influence that Sigmund Freud, the father of modern psychoanalysis, had on Faulkner's fiction. Freud theorized that repression, especially if it is sexual in nature, often results in psychological abnormality. In the story, Emily's overprotective, overbearing father denies her a normal relationship with the opposite sex by chasing away any potential mates. Because her father is the only man with whom she

has had a close relationship, she denies his death and keeps his corpse in her house until she breaks down three days later when the doctors insist she let them take the body. Later in the story, the ladies of the town and her two female cousins from Alabama work to sabotage her relationship with Homer Barron. Of course, the narrator suggests that Homer himself may not exactly be enthusiastic about marrying Emily. However, it is left to the reader to imagine the exact circumstances leading to Homer's denouement. Finally, Emily takes the offensive by poisoning Homer so he can't abandon her. The discovery of a strand of her hair on the pillow next to the rotting corpse suggests that she slept with the cadaver or, even worse, had sex with it. Emily's repressive life therefore contributes to her (rather severe) psychological abnormality: necrophilia.

Some readers have interpreted the story as an allegory of the relations between the North and the

South. This is apparently because the character of Homer Barron is a Yankee and Emily kills him. However, it would be difficult to argue that Emily's motivation in dating Homer is to kill him because he is a Northerner. The most obvious explanation for her willingness to date a man outside of her social caste would be that she is simply a very lonely woman. A less obvious, but nonetheless reasonable, explanation for her relationship with Homer would be that is her way of rebelling against her dead father. During his lifetime, her father prevented her from having an "acceptable" suitor. Thus, she rebels by associating with a man her father would have considered a pariah: a Yankee day-laborer. There is really little to suggest that the story is an allegory of the Civil War other than the fact that a Yankee is killed by a Southerner. Faulkner himself, in his lecture on the story at the University of Virginia, denies such an interpretation. He said that he believed that a writer is ". . . too busy trying to create flesh-and-blood people that will stand up and cast a shadow to have time to be conscious of all the symbolism that he may put into what he does or what people may read into it."

One can more confidently argue that "A Rose for Emily" is a meditation on the nature of time. Although the story is only a few pages long, it covers approximately three-quarters of a century. Faulkner cleverly constructed the story to show the elusive nature of time and memory. Several critics have written papers in attempts to devise a chronology for the story. It would surely please Faulkner that few of these chronologies are consistent with each other. In "A Rose for Emily," he is not concerned with actual dates. He is more interested in the conflict between time as a subjective experience and time as a force of physics. For example, in section five of the story, the narrator describes the very old men gathered at Emily's funeral. The old men, some who fought in the Civil War, mistakenly believe that Emily was a contemporary of theirs when in fact Emily was born sometime around the Civil War. The old men have confused ". . . time with its mathematical progression, as the old do, to whom all the past is not a diminishing road but, instead, a huge meadow which no winter ever quite touches, divided from them now by the narrow bottleneck of the most recent decade of years." Here, Faulkner profoundly and poetically comments on the human need to deny the passage of time and the astounding capacity of the human mind to use memory in that ultimately futile denial. Emily, of course, has other methods of denying time.

> " Faulkner despised slavery and racism, but he admired much of the chivalry and honor of the old South. Emily is a product of that society and she clings desperately to it as when she refuses to give up her father's body."

Since the denial of time is futile, it is also tragic. This is one reason the story can be read as a tragedy. But every tragedy needs a hero or heroine. Can Emily actually be considered a tragic heroine? At first glance, this is a tough sell. Many readers quite reasonably believe that Emily is some kind of monster, regardless of what Freud might have said. However, as many critics have noted, Faulkner's title suggests that he may think otherwise. "In his fiction," notes Minter in his biography of Faulkner, "he characteristically mingles compassion and judgement. Even his most terrible villains . . . he treats with considerable sympathy." Emily is such an example. In fact, the narrator twice describes Emily as an idol. Although she commits a foul crime, Faulkner views Emily as a victim of her circumstance. Faulkner despised slavery and racism, but he admired much of the chivalry and honor of the old South. Emily is a product of that society and she clings desperately to it as when she refuses to give up her father's body. She also becomes a victim of her old society. The one time in her life that she dares to let the past become a "diminishing road," that is, when she dates Homer, she is ridiculed, ostracized, shamed, and finally jilted. Her response is an effort to actually freeze time by poisoning Homer and keeping his corpse in her ghoulish boudoir.

Finally, it is a tribute to Faulkner's talent that this compact yet expansive story lends itself to so many interpretations. The discussion above briefly describes the most common interpretations made by readers and critics. However, there is a great deal of scholarship, entire volumes, written on "A Rose for

Emily.'' Several critics, including Isaac Rodman in *The Faulkner Journal* and Milinda Schwab in *Studies in Short Fiction,* have presented convincing arguments of the town's complicity in Homer's murder. Many critics have written interesting papers on literary allusions that they find in the story; alternately, many critics find allusions to "A Rose for Emily" in contemporary literature. (An interesting paper might be written comparing and contrasting Faulkner's Emily with the character of Norman Bates, the schizophrenic, homicidal hotel-keeper/amateur taxidermist of Alfred Hitchcock's 1963 film, *Psycho.*) "A Rose for Emily" remains a remarkable, provocative work regardless of the critical approach.

Source: Donald Akers, Overview of "A Rose for Emily," for *Short Stories for Students,* The Gale Group, 1999.

Michael L. Burduck

In the following article, Burduck argues that the narrator of "A Rose for Emily" could be female.

In a recent article, Hal Blythe discusses the central role played by the narrator in William Faulkner's gothic masterpiece "A Rose for Emily." Focusing on Miss Emily's bizarre affair and how it affronts the chivalric notions of the Old South, the narrator, according to Blythe, attempts to assuage the grief produced by Miss Emily's rejection of him by relating her story; telling her tale allows him to exact a measure of revenge. Faulkner's speaker, without doubt, serves as a pivotal player in this tale of grotesque love. Although Blythe grasps the significance of the narrator's place in the story, he bases his argument on a point that the story itself never makes completely clear. Blythe assumes that Faulkner's narrator is *male.* The possibility exists, however, that Faulkner intended his readers to view the tale-teller as being *female.*

Hints in the text suggest that Faulkner's speaker might be a woman. The narrative voice (the "we" in the story), a spokesperson for the town, appears very concerned with every detail of Emily's life. Faulkner provides us with an important clue concerning the gender of this narrator when he describes the townspeople's reaction to Emily's attachment to Homer Barron: "The men did not want to interfere, but at last the ladies forced the Baptist minister . . . to call upon her." Jefferson's male population seems apathetic regarding Emily's tryst; the men are not the least bit scandalized. The

females in town (the "we" in the tale) are so concerned with Emily's eccentricities that they force their men to act; one very interested female in particular, the narrator, sees to it that Emily's story is not forgotten.

This coterie of Jefferson's "finer" ladies (represented by the narrator) seems highly offended by Emily's actions. This resentment might stem from two primary causes. First, the ladies (the phrase "the ladies" appears throughout the tale and might refer to the "proper" Southern belles living in town) find Miss Emily's pre-marital relationship immoral. Second, they resent Emily's seeing a Yankee man. In the eyes of these flowers of Southern femininity, Emily Grierson becomes a stain on the white gown of Southern womanhood.

Despite their bitterness toward Emily, the ladies of Jefferson feel some degree of sympathy for her. After her father's death, the ladies reminisce: "We remembered all the young men her father had driven away. . . ." Later, Homer Barron disappears, prompting this response: "Then we knew that this was to be expected too, as if that quality of her father which had thwarted her woman's life so many times had been too virulent and furious to die." These intensely felt statements suggest how a woman might react to another woman's loneliness; the narrator seems to empathize with Miss Emily on a woman-to-woman basis. Faulkner himself sheds interesting light on this matter when he describes Miss Emily as a woman "that just wanted to be loved and to love and to have a husband and a family," The women of Jefferson know that Emily, a fellow woman, possessed these feelings, and as women they feel as if some sort of biological bond links them to "the last Grierson." Unlike the majority of the ladies in town, Miss Emily experienced neither the joys of marriage nor the fulfillment of child-bearing. If the ladies did not view Emily in a sympathetic way, would they have sent their daughters to her house for china-painting lessons?

Another possible reason exists for the speaker's sympathetic view of Emily. Our narrator knows (perhaps from the druggist) that Emily purchased poison, ostensibly to kill "rats." One slang use of the term "rat" applies to a man who has cheated on his lover. Perhaps Faulkner's tale-teller suspects that Emily feared that Homer would not remain faithful to her. In order to "keep" Homer by her side, Emily poisoned him. The speaker might sympathize with Emily somewhat because she believes that Emily did what she could to retain Homer's companionship and insure that he would not give her up for another woman. Faulkner's female narrator does not approve of Miss Emily's methods, but she understands what prompted them: Emily's weariness of being alone.

An additional clue regarding the narrator appears toward the end of "A Rose for Emily" when Faulkner's speaker emphasizes the first-person pronoun "they." Previously, our narrator has used "we" to indicate the town's collective female element. After Miss Emily is buried, the tale-teller relates how the residents of Jefferson learned of the gruesome secret lying upstairs in the long-closed bedroom. She makes one point very clear: " *They* waited until Miss Emily was decently in the ground before *they* opened it [my italics]." The "they" in this sentence are people strong enough to break down the door of this death chamber. Since most ladies in Jefferson would not be strong enough to force in a door, might not the reader assume that these initial intruders are men? The ladies follow the men into the room and make their ghastly discovery: "For a long while *we* [my italics] just stood there looking down at the profound and fleshless grin."

The reader is left with a very important question: why would a lady desire to repeat Miss Emily's story? The narrator's "dual vision" (as Blythe calls it) provides a clue. As a woman offended by Emily's actions, the speaker relates this tale of necrophilia in an attempt to vindicate Southern womanhood. She wants her listeners to understand that Emily was not representative of the typical "Southern Lady." Perhaps familiar with Caroline Bascomb Compson, Joanna Burden, and Rosa Coldfield, other infamous females living in the Jefferson vicinity, the narrator wants to convey to her audience that virtuous women (such as herself?) *do* still live in Jefferson. On the other hand, the speaker's sympathy for Emily, a woman lost in her own particularly lonely world, also prompts her to recall the tragic events of Emily's sterile life. As a woman, the tale-teller allows her heart to go out to "poor Emily."

Viewing the narrator of "A Rose for Emily" as a woman allows the reader to enjoy Faulkner's tale from a unique perspective. Indeed, such an interpretation offers an interesting alternative reading that emphasizes the important role women play in the fiction of Oxford, Mississippi's Nobel laureate.

Source: Michael L. Burduck, "Another View of Faulkner's Narrator in 'A Rose for Emily'," in *The University of Mississippi Studies in English,* Vol. VIII, 1990, pp. 209–11.

> " Despite their bitterness toward Emily, the ladies of Jefferson feel some degree of sympathy for her. After her father's death, the ladies reminisce: 'We remembered all the young men her father had driven away. . . .'"

William V. Davis

In the following essay, Davis discusses Faulkner's use of time and narrative structure in "A Rose for Emily," commenting that together they "provide some of the most lucid and meaningful understandings of Faulkner's fiction."

Nearly everyone familiar with the writings of William Faulkner is aware of the fracturings of time so common in his work. Many of his major characters spend much of their fictional lives trying to piece together their experiences and lives, to put them in some kind of chronological or existential order. Few of them succeed; and when they do, as is perhaps the case with Quentin Compson (*The Sound and the Fury* and *Absalom, Absalom!*), they most often find that to make sense of their lives is to create the necessity for self-destruction. But, most often, Faulkner's characters are like Charles Bon of *Absalom, Absalom!* who, when he leaves for college, is only on the periphery of an area of knowledge about himself and his world. Bon is described as "almost touching the answer lurking, just beyond his reach, inextricable, jumbled, and unrecognizable yet on the point of falling into a pattern which would reveal to him at once, like a flash of light, the meaning of his whole life."

But if Faulkner's characters are often at a loss with respect to the movements of their existences through time, his critics cannot be. Indeed, such detailings of temporal chronology, together with structural elaborations, provide some of the most lucid and meaningful understandings of Faulkner's fiction. Almost all of Faulkner's stories and novels can be better appreciated and more accurately un-

> " Thus, with respect to the relationships of time and structure in 'A Rose for Emily' Faulkner seems to be saying that although Miss Emily resists the passage of time, resists change, time ultimately fixes her in a rather perverse manner."

derstood and interpreted through a detailing of the interrelationships of time and structure. In Faulkner's world theme exists as the hyphen in the compound temporal-structure. Not the least of such cases is "A Rose for Emily."

"A Rose for Emily" is divided into five sections, the first and last section having to do with the present, the *now* of the narration, with the three middle sections detailing the past. The story begins and ends with the death of Miss Emily Grierson; the three middle sections move through Miss Emily's life from a time soon after her father's death and shortly after her beau, Homer Barron, "had deserted her," to the time of her death.

Late in the fourth section of the story, Faulkner writes of Miss Emily, "Thus she passed from generation to generation—dear, inescapable, impervious, tranquil, and perverse." On first reading, this series of adjectives appears to be only another catalogue so familiar in Faulkner. Often it seems that Faulkner simply lists such a series of adjectives as if to say, "Take your choice of these, I don't care." Not so in this instance. Rather, it would seem that Faulkner uses these five adjectives to describe Miss Emily with some care and for a specific purpose. It could be argued that they are intended to refer to the successive sections of the story, each becoming as it were a sort of metaphorical characterization of the differing states through which the townspeople of Jefferson (and the readers) pass in their evaluation of Miss Emily. Correlating the two present sections with the adjectives that fall to them, we see Miss Emily as the paradox she has become in death, "dear" and "perverse," while before her

death she was "inescapable, impervious, tranquil." Thus, during her life, the enigma of Miss Emily's personality, which kept her seemingly immortal, impenetrable, and almost inevitably inescapable, has been clarified and crystalized by her death. A woman who, alive, "had been a tradition, a duty, and a care," and thus "dear" in several senses of that word, is revealed, in death, to have been what for years she had been suspected of being, "perverse."

But indeed even in the first section of the story there are numerous hints at the final portrait of the Miss Emily of section five. The men go to her funeral "through a sort of respectful affection for a fallen monument." Her house is "an eyesore among eyesores," it symbolizing Miss Emily herself in its "coquettish decay"; inside there is a "tarnished gilt easel"; Miss Emily has an "ebony cane with a tarnished gold head"; and she herself looks "bloated, like a body long submerged in motionless water."

Section two details the inescapable smell which surrounded Miss Emily's house after the disappearance of her suitor, Homer Barron. Section three recounts Miss Emily's romance with Homer Barron and the imperviousness of her position even after the townspeople feel pity for her (four times in this section—and once in section four—she is referred to as "poor Emily"). "She carried her head high enough—even when we believed that she was fallen. It was as if she demanded more than even the recognition of her dignity as the last Grierson; as if it had wanted that touch of earthiness to reaffirm her imperviousness." And section four moves from the time Miss Emily bought the arsenic, through the departure, return, and final disappearance of Homer, to the time of her death.

Miss Emily, who had been idle most of her life, is looked upon as an idol by the people of Jefferson. The word "idol" occurs twice in the story: when the men are sprinkling lime around her house a window is lighted "and Miss Emily sat in it, the light behind her, and her upright torso motionless as that of an idol"; and in later years, on and off at intervals, "we would see her in one of the downstairs windows—she had evidently shut up the top floor of the house—like the carven torso of an idol in a niche, looking or not looking at us, we could never tell which." Miss Emily is indeed a kind of living avatar (she doesn't believe in death and refuses to admit that her father is dead until the townspeople "were about to resort to law and force") of the past of Jefferson. In the first section of the story she is described as a ''fallen monument.'' Often she is referred to as a kind of deity, or at least as a representative, if not of the religious at least the political and social hierarchy of Jefferson: ''the high and mighty Griersons.'' ''When we saw her again, her hair was cut short, making her look like a girl, with a vague resemblance to those angels in colored church windows—sort of tragic and serene.'' And at death, catching up the earlier detail of ''submerged in motionless water,'' Miss Emily is described as if she were in some sacred vault, ''She died in one of the downstairs rooms, in a heavy walnut bed with a curtain, her gray head propped on a pillow yellow and moldy with age and lack of sunlight.'' ''They held the funeral on the second day, with the town coming to look at Miss Emily beneath a mass of flowers.'' The townspeople ''waited until Miss Emily was decently in the ground'' before they opened the upstairs room. The room and the corpse are described as if they are the accouterments of an ancient tomb.

> The violence of breaking down the door seemed to fill this room with pervading dust. A thin, acrid pall as of the tomb seemed to lie everywhere upon this room decked and furnished as for a bridal: upon the valance curtains of faded rose color, upon the rose-shaded lights, upon the dressing table, upon the delicate array of crystal and the man's toilet things backed with tarnished silver, silver so tarnished that the monogram was obscured. . . . The man himself lay in the bed. For a long while we just stood there, looking down at the profound and fleshless grin. The body had apparently once lain in the attitude of an embrace, but now the long sleep that outlasts love, that conquers even the grimace of love, had cuckolded him. What was left of him, rotted beneath what was left of the nightshirt, had become inextricable from the bed in which he lay; and upon him and upon the pillow beside him lay that even coating of the patient and biding dust.

Thus, with respect to the relationships of time and structure in ''A Rose for Emily'' Faulkner seems to be saying that although Miss Emily resists the passage of time, resists change, time ultimately fixes her in a rather perverse manner. In terms of life and existence, Miss Emily's past and her passages through and within time are ''inescapable''; her struggles against time are of no avail. Time moves forward tranquilly, imperviously, and inescapably. Miss Emily is seen in the story, first and last, as she is in death. The struggle for existence and meaning in the *now* of every present is commendable, but to have too high a regard for the dearness of one's own life is ultimately to deny the possibility for its realization. To covet life too highly, thereby attempting to stop time, to freeze the flux of life, is to make of something ''dear'' a perversity.

Source: William V. Davis, ''Another Flower for Faulkner's Bouquet: Theme and Structure in 'A Rose for Emily','' in *Notes on Mississippi Writers,* Vol. VII, No. 2, Fall, 1974, pp. 34–8.

Ray B. West, Jr.

In the following essay, West discusses the contrast between the past and present in ''A Rose for Emily.''

The first clues to meaning in a short story usually arise from a detection of the principal contrasts which an author sets up. The most common, perhaps, are contrasts of character, but when characters are contrasted there is usually also a resultant contrast in terms of action. Since action reflects a moral or ethical state, contrasting action points to a contrast in ideological perspectives and hence toward the theme.

The principal contrast in William Faulkner's short story ''A Rose for Emily'' is between past time and present time: the past as represented in Emily herself, in Colonel Sartoris, in the old Negro servant, and in the Board of Aldermen who accepted the Colonel's attitude toward Emily and rescinded her taxes; the present is depicted through the unnamed narrator and is represented in the *new* Board of Aldermen, in Homer Barron (the representative or Yankee attitudes toward the Griersons and through them toward the entire South), and in what is called ''the next generation with its more modern ideas.''

Atmosphere is defined in the *Dictionary of World Literature* as ''The particular world in which the events of a story or a play occur: time, place, conditions, and the attendant mood.'' When, as in ''A Rose for Emily,'' the world depicted is a confusion between the past and the present, the atmosphere is one of distortion—of unreality. This unreal world results from the suspension of a natural time order. Normality consists in a decorous progression of the human being from birth, through youth, to age and finally death. Preciosity in children is as monstrous as idiocy in the adult, because both are *unnatural*. Monstrosity, however, is a sentimental subject for fiction unless it is the result of human action—the result of a willful attempt to circumvent time. When such circumvention produces acts of violence, as in ''A Rose for Emily,'' the atmosphere becomes one of horror.

Horror, however, represents only the extreme form of maladjusted nature. It is not produced in ''A Rose for Emily'' until the final act of violence has

> **Just as Emily refused to acknowledge the death of her father, she now refuses to recognize the death of Colonel Sartoris. He had given his word, and according to the traditional view, 'his word' knew no death."**

been disclosed. All that has gone before has prepared us by producing a general tone of mystery, foreboding, decay, etc., so that we may say the entire series of events that have gone before are "in key"—that is, they are depicted in a mood in which the final violence does not appear too shocking or horrible. We are inclined to say, "In such an atmosphere, anything may happen." Foreshadowing is often accomplished through atmosphere, and in this case the atmosphere prepares us for Emily's unnatural act at the end of the story. Actually, such preparation begins in the very first sentence:

> When Miss Emily Grierson died, our whole town went to her funeral: the men through a sort of respectful affection for a fallen monument, the women mostly out of curiosity to see the inside of her house, which no one save an old manservant—a combined gardener and cook—had seen in at least ten years.

Emily is portrayed as "a fallen monument," a *monument* for reasons which we shall examine later, *fallen* because she has shown herself susceptible to death (and decay) after all. In the mention of death, we are conditioned (as the psychologist says) for the more specific concern with it later on. The second paragraph depicts the essential ugliness of the contrast: the description of Miss Emily's house "lifting its stubborn and coquettish decay above the cotton wagons and the gasoline pumps—an eyesore among eyesores." (A juxtaposition of past and present.) We recognize this scene as an emblematic presentation of Miss Emily herself, suggested as it is through the words "stubborn and coquettish." The tone—and the contrast—is preserved in a description of the note which Miss Emily sent to the mayor, "a note on paper of an archaic shape, in a thin, flowing calligraphy in faded ink," and in the

description of the interior of the house when the deputation from the Board of Aldermen visit her: "They were admitted by the old Negro into a dim hall from which a stairway mounted into still more shadow. It smelled of dust and disuse—a close, dank smell." In the next paragraph a description of Emily discloses her similarity to the house: "She looked bloated, like a body long submerged in motionless water, and of that pallid hue."

Emily had not always looked like this. When she was young and part of the world with which she was contemporary, she was, we are told, "a slender figure in white," as contrasted with her father, who is described as "a spraddled silhouette." In the picture of Emily and her father together, framed by the door, she frail and apparently hungering to participate in the life of her time, we have a reversal of the contrast which has already been presented and which is to be developed later. Even after her father's death, Emily is not monstrous, but rather looked like a girl "with a vague resemblance to those angels in colored church windows—sort of tragic and serene." The suggestion is that she had already begun her entrance into that nether-world (a world which is depicted later as "rose-tinted"), but that she might even yet have been saved, had Homer Barron been another kind of man.

By the time the deputation from the new, progressive Board of Aldermen wait upon her concerning her delinquent taxes, however, she has completely retreated into her world of the past. There is no communication possible between her and them:

> Her voice was dry and cold. "I have no taxes in Jefferson. Colonel Sartoris explained it to me. Perhaps one of you can gain access to the city records and satisfy yourselves."
>
> "But we have. We are the city authorities, Miss Emily. Didn't you get a notice from the sheriff, signed by him?"
>
> "I received a paper, yes," Miss Emily said. "Perhaps he considers himself the sheriff. . . . I have no taxes in Jefferson."
>
> "But there is nothing on the books to show that, you see. We must go by the—"
>
> "See Colonel Sartoris. I have no taxes in Jefferson."
>
> "But Miss Emily—"
>
> "See Colonel Sartoris." [Colonel Sartoris had been dead almost ten years.] "I have no taxes in Jefferson. Tobe!" The Negro appeared. "Show these gentlemen out."

Just as Emily refused to acknowledge the death of her father, she now refuses to recognize the death of Colonel Sartoris. He had given his word, and according to the traditional view, "his word" knew no death. It is the Past pitted against the Present— the Past with its social decorum, the Present with everything set down in "the books." Emily dwells in the Past, always a world of unreality to us of the Present. Here are the facts which set the tone of the story and which create the atmosphere of unreality which surrounds it.

Such contrasts are used over and over again: the difference between the attitude of Judge Stevens (who is over eighty years old) and the attitude of the young man who comes to him about the "smell" at Emily's place. For the young man (who is a member of the "rising generation") it is easy. For him, Miss Emily's world has ceased to exist. The city's health regulations are on the books, "Dammit, sir," Judge Stevens replied, "will you accuse a lady to her face of smelling bad?" Emily had given in to social pressure when she allowed them to bury her father, but she triumphed over society in the matter of the smell. She had won already when she bought the poison, refusing to comply with the requirements of the law, because for her they did not exist.

Such incidents seem, however, mere preparation for the final, more important contrast between Emily and Homer Barron. Emily is the town's aristocrat; Homer is a day laborer. Homer is an active man dealing with machinery and workmen— a man's man. He is a Yankee—a Northerner. Emily is a "monument" of Southern gentility. As such she is common property of the town, but in a special way—as an ideal of *past* values. Here the author seems to be commenting upon the complex relationship between the Southerner and his past and between the Southerner of the present and the Yankee from the North. She is unreal to her compatriots, yet she impresses them with her station, even at a time when they considered her *fallen:* "as if [her dignity] had wanted that touch of earthiness to reaffirm her imperviousness." It appeared for a time that Homer had won her over, as though the demands of reality as depicted in him (earthiness) had triumphed over her withdrawal and seclusion. This is the conflict that is not resolved until the final scene. We can imagine, however, what the outcome might have been had Homer Barron, who was not a marrying man, succeeded, in the town's eyes, in seducing her (violating her world) and then deserted her. The view of Emily as a monument would have been destroyed. Emily might have become the object of continued gossip, but she would have become susceptible to the town's pity—therefore, human. Emily's world, however, continues to be the Past (in

its extreme form it is death), and when she is threatened with desertion and disgrace, she not only takes refuge in that world, but she also takes Homer with her, in the only manner possible.

It is important too, to realize that during the period of Emily's courtship, the town became Emily's allies in a contest between Emily and her Grierson cousins, "because the two female cousins were even more Grierson than Miss Emily had ever been." The cousins were protecting the general proprieties against which the town (and the times) was in gradual rebellion. Just as each succeeding generation rebels against its elders, so the town took sides with Emily against her relations. Had Homer Barron been the proper kind of man, it is implied, Miss Emily might have escaped both horns of the dilemma (her cousins' traditionalism and Homer's immorality) and become an accepted and respected member of the community. The town's attitude toward the Grierson cousins represents the usual ambiguous attitude of man toward the past: a mixture of veneration and rebelliousness. The unfaithfulness of Homer represents the final act in the drama of Emily's struggle to escape from the past. From the moment that she realizes that he will desert her, tradition becomes magnified out of all proportion to life and death, and she conducts herself as though Homer really had been faithful— as though this view represented reality.

Miss Emily's position in regard to the specific problem of time is suggested in the scene where the old soldiers appear at her funeral. There are, we are told, two views of time: (1) the world of the present, viewing time as a mechanical progression in which the past is a diminishing road, never to be encountered again; (2) the world of tradition, viewing the past as a huge meadow which no winter ever quite touches, divided from (us) now by the narrow bottleneck of the most recent decade of years. The first is the view of Homer Barron and the modern generation in Jefferson. The second is the view of the older members of the Board of Aldermen and of the confederate soldiers. Emily holds the second view, except that for her there is no bottleneck dividing her from the meadow of the past.

Emily's small room above stairs has become that timeless meadow. In it, the living Emily and the dead Homer have remained together as though not even death could separate them. It is the monstrousness of this view which creates the final atmosphere of horror, and the scene is intensified by the portrayal of the unchanged objects which have surrounded Homer in life. Here he lay in the roseate atmosphere of Emily's death-in-life: "What was left of him, rotted beneath what was left of the nightshirt, had become inextricable from the bed in which he lay; and upon him and upon the pillow beside him lay that even coating of the patient and biding dust." The symbols of Homer's life of action have become mute and silent. Contrariwise, Emily's world, though it had been inviolate while she was alive, has been invaded after her death—the whole gruesome and unlovely tale unfolded.

In its simplest sense, the story says that death conquers all. But what is death? Upon one level, death is the past, tradition, whatever is opposite to the present. In the specific setting of this story, it is the past of the South in which the retrospective survivors of the War deny changing customs and the passage of time. Homer Barron, the Yankee, lived in the present, ready to take his pleasure and depart, apparently unwilling to consider the possibility of defeat, either by tradition (the Griersons) or by time (death) itself. In a sense, Emily conquered time, but only briefly and by retreating into her rose-tinted world of the past, a world in which death was denied at the same time that it is shown to have existed. Such retreat, the story implies, is hopeless, since everyone (even Emily) is finally subjected to death and the invasion of his world by the clamorous and curious inhabitants of the world of the present.

In these terms, it might seem that the story is a comment upon tradition and upon those people who live in a dream world of the past. But is it not also a comment upon the present? There is some justification for Emily's actions. She is a tragic—and hero-ic—figure. In the first place, she has been frustrated by her father, prevented from participating in the life of her contemporaries. When she attempts to achieve freedom, she is betrayed by a man who represents the new morality, threatened by disclosure and humiliation. The grounds of the tragedy is depicted in the scene already referred to between Emily and the deputation from the Board of Aldermen: for the new generation, the word of Colonel Sartoris meant nothing. This was a new age, a different time; the present was not bound by the promises of the past. For Emily, however, the word of the Colonel was everything. The tax notice was but a scrap of paper.

Atmosphere, we might say, is nothing but the fictional reflection of man's attitude toward the state of the universe. The atmosphere of classic tragedy inveighed against the ethical dislocation of the Grecian world merely by portraying such dislocation and depicting man's tragic efforts to conform both to the will of the gods and to the demands of his own contemporary society. Such dislocation in the modern world is likely to be seen mirrored in the natural universe, with problems of death and time representing that flaw in the golden bowl of eighteenth and nineteenth-century natural philosophy which is the inheritance of our times. Perhaps our specific dilemma is the conflict of the pragmatic present against the set mores of the past. Homer Barron was an unheroic figure who put too much dependence upon his self-centered and rootless philosophy, a belief which suggested that he could take whatever he wanted without considering any obligation to the past (tradition) or to the future (death). Emily's resistance is heroic. Her tragic flaw is the conventional pride: she undertook to regulate the natural time-universe. She acted as though death did not exist, as though she could retain her unfaithful lover by poisoning him and holding his physical self prisoner in a world which had all of the appearances of reality except that most necessary of all things—life.

The extraction of a statement of theme from so complex a subject matter is dangerous and never wholly satisfactory. The subject, as we have seen, is concerned not alone with man's relationship to death, but with his relationship as it refers to all the facets of social intercourse. The theme is not one directed at presenting an attitude of Southerner to Yankee, or Yankee to Southerner, as has been hinted at in so many discussions of William Faulkner. The Southern Problem is one of the objective facts with which the theme is concerned, but the theme itself transcends it. Wallace Stevens is certainly right when he says that a theme may be emotive as well as intellectual and logical, and it is this recognition which explains why the extraction of a logical statement of theme is so delicate and dangerous an operation: the story *is* its theme as the life of the body *is* the body.

Nevertheless, in so far as a theme represents the *meaning* of a story, it can be observed in logical terms; indeed, these are the only terms in which it can be observed for those who, at a first or even a repeated reading, fail to recognize the implications of the total story. The logical statement, in other words, may be a clue to the total, emotive content. In these terms, "A Rose for Emily" would seem to be saying that man must come to terms both with the past and the present; for to ignore the first is to be guilty of a foolish innocence, to ignore the second is to become monstrous and inhuman, above all to betray an excessive pride (such as Emily Grierson's) before the humbling fact of death. The total story says what has been said in so much successful literature, that man's plight is tragic, but that there is heroism in an attempt to rise above it.

Source: Ray B. West, Jr., ''Atmosphere and Theme in Faulkner's 'A Rose for Emily','' in *William Faulkner: Four Decades of Criticism,* edited by Linda Welshimer Wagner, Michigan State University Press, 1973, pp.192–98.

Sources

Birk, John F. ''Tryst Beyond Time: Faulkner's Emily and Keats.'' *Studies in Short Fiction,* Vol. 28, No. 2, Spring 1991, pp. 203-13.

Gregory, Horace. A review of *The Collected Stories of William Faulkner. The New York Herald Tribune,* August 20, 1950, p. 1.

Gwynn, Frederick L. and Joseph Blotner. *Faulkner in the University: Class Conferences at the University of Virginia, 1957-1958,* University of Virginia Press, 1959, p. 26.

Hays, Peter L. ''Who Is Faulkner's Emily?'' *Studies in American Fiction,* Vol. 16, No. 1, Spring 1988, pp. 105-110.

Levitt, Paul. ''An Analogue for Faulkner's 'A Rose for Emily'.'' *Papers on Language and Literature,* Vol. 9, 1973, p. 91.

Littler, Frank A. ''The Tangled Thread of Time: Faulkner's 'A Rose for Emily'.'' *Notes on Mississippi Writers,* Vol. 14, No. 2, 1982, p. 80.

Mellard, James M. ''Faulkner's Miss Emily and Blake's Sick Rose: Invisible Worm, Nachtraglichkeit, and Retrospective Gothic.'' *The Faulkner Journal,* Vol. 2, No. 1, Fall, 1986, pp. 39-41.

Minter, David. *William Faulkner: His Life and Work,* The Johns Hopkins University Press, 1980, 1997, pp. 1, 14, 16.

Rodman, Isaac. ''Irony and Isolation: Narrative Distance in Faulkner's 'A Rose for Emily'.'' *The Faulkner Journal,* Vol. 8, No. 2, Spring, 1993, pp. 3, 7.

Schwab, Milinda. ''A Watch for Emily.'' *Studies in Short Fiction,* Vol. 29, No. 2, Spring 1992, p. 216.

Warren, Robert Penn. An introduction to *Faulkner: A Collection of Critical Essays,* Englewood Cliffs, NJ: Prentice-Hall, 1966, p. 9.

Further Reading

Allen, Dennis W. ''Horror and Perverse Delight: Faulkner's 'A Rose for Emily'.'' *Modern Fiction Studies,* Vol. 30, No. 4, Winter 1984, pp. 685-96.
A fine overview of the story, featuring an in-depth psychological analysis of the character of Emily.

Blotner, Joseph. *Faulkner: A Biography,* New York: Random House, 1974.
This exhaustive study written by one of Faulkner's colleagues at the University of Virginia is considered by most critics to be the definitive Faulkner biography.

Jacobs, John T. ''Ironic Allusions in A Rose for Emily'.'' *Notes on Mississippi Writers,* Vol. 14, No. 2, 1982, pp. 77-79.
Jacobs provides a critical analysis of the role that the character of Homer Barron plays in the story.

Wilson, G.R., Jr. ''The Chronology of Faulkner's 'A Rose for Emily' Again.'' *Notes on Mississippi Writers,* Vol. 5, No. 2, Fall, 1972, pp. 43-62.
Wilson devises a seemingly logical time-line for the story.

Winchell, Mark Royden. ''For All the Heart's Endeavor: Romantic Pathology in Browning and Faulkner.'' *Notes on Mississippi Writers,* Vol. 15, No. 2, 1983, pp. 57-63.
Winchell compares ''A Rose for Emily'' with Robert Browning's poem ''Porphyria's Lover.''

A Simple Heart

Gustave Flaubert

1877

"A Simple Heart" ("Un Coeur Simple"), by French writer Gustave Flaubert, is one of the stories in his *Three Tales* (*Trois Contes*), published in 1877. It received admiring reviews at the time and has continued to be second only to his novel *Madame Bovary* (1857) in recognition and acclaim.

Originally entitled "Le Perroquet" ("The Parrot"), "A Simple Heart" is the story of one woman's apparently fruitless existence. The protagonist, a hardworking, good-hearted, poor and uneducated woman named Félicité, is said to have been modeled after a maid employed by Flaubert's family during his childhood, a much beloved woman of tremendous character. The story is unusual among the author's writings because it is about goodness. In this story of a simple housemaid's life and death, the reader is invited to view a world of boundless, if not reciprocated, love and spirit. Félicité, a woman of simple mind and devoted heart, suffers tremendous loss but continues to her last breath to love unconditionally. Some critics have suggested that Félicité's apparently meaningless life and misplaced worship of the parrot, Loulou—whom she adores and whom she imagines, in her dying moment, to be an incarnation of the Holy Ghost—reflect Flaubert's melancholy and disillusionment with life and with organized religion, particularly the Roman Catholic Church. Most critics agree that this is a poignant account of a sweet, simple, and unrewarded life, one which may have been happy precisely because it was unexamined. It does not matter that Félicité

may have misinterpreted or simply not interpreted many of the events in her life: she dies smiling, and thus lives up to her name to the last.

Author Biography

Much has been made of the relationship between Flaubert's life and his depiction of the servant in "A Simple Heart." There are several notable parallels. During the time Flaubert was writing the story, he suffered some of the greatest loss and depression of his life. His friend and fellow writer George Sand, for whom he undertook the story, died before it was finished, and Flaubert's mistress, the poet Louise Colet, died in 1876. He was forced to sell off part of his family properties, a great and symbolic desolation. It is often said that the tone of this story represents a turning point in Flaubert's work, a point which signals a sympathy for the human spirit, a generosity simply not present in earlier works.

Gustave Flaubert was born in 1821 in Rouen, France, the second of three children of a provincial doctor. He was educated in Rouen and later studied law in Paris, where he began to write. During this time he suffered the first of a lifelong series of epileptic seizures.

Because of his illness, he gave up his studies and dedicated himself fully to his writing. In the next decade he composed several pieces of prose, including some memoirs, but he was in no hurry to publish. In fact, for all of his life, although he was employed solely as a writer, Flaubert appears to have felt no particular compulsion to publish his work. Success, he wrote in a letter to George Sand, is a result; it should not be a goal.

In 1851 he began work on *Madame Bovary,* the novel which would bring him lasting fame and notoriety. Its publication in 1857 caused a scandal; its depiction of adultery and suicide led to an obscenity trial in which the author was narrowly acquitted. Flaubert's realistic writing style contributed to the controversy. Unlike the romantic writers popular at the time, Flaubert did not believe in inspiration and muses; he believed in working very hard at reporting what he saw. He believed in observation and faithful reproduction. That life was closely reproduced in *Madame Bovary* came as a shock to its middle-class readers, and this bourgeois repugnance for self-examination showed even in the critical reviews. Thus George Saintsbury wrote

of Flaubert that "he has to a very remarkable degree the art of chaining the attention even when the subject is a distasteful one to the reader." Serious literary critics wrote well of the book, however, and the scandal in the end did nothing but promote Flaubert's literary reputation.

Flaubert never married; he spent most of his life close to home and in relative solitude. He kept a residence in Paris and a country house in Normandy, where he spent much of the year. He continued to write, his publications including the novels *Salammbô* and *L'Education Sentimentale* (*Sentimental Education*). Three years before his death he published his best-known and perhaps most exemplary works in *Three Tales* (*Trois Contes*), which contains the story "A Simple Heart." It was with these stories that Flaubert's mature genius finally produced what George Sand had once urged him to write, a "literature of consolation rather than desolation."

Plot Summary

Part I

"A Simple Heart" opens with a description of "Madame Aubain's servant Félicité as having been "the envy of the ladies of Pont-l'Évêque for half a century." As cook and general servant she does all the work of the household for a mere four pounds a year while remaining "faithful to her mistress, unamiable as the latter was."

Madame Aubain has been left a widow with many debts and two small children, but after selling most of her property she manages to make do. The family lives in a musty old house filled with dilapidated furniture. Félicité is described as scrupulously clean, thrifty, and energetic. She always wears the same clothes; she seems untouched by the passing years, always looking about forty; she is "like a woman made of wood, and going by clockwork."

Part II

Orphaned early, as a girl Félicité works on one farm as a cowherd, then on another as a dairymaid. When she is eighteen, she attends a dance in a nearby town where she is dazzled by the light and the noise. There she meets a young man, Theodore, who offers to walk her home, roughly tries to have sex with her, and leaves when she begins to protest. Later she encounters Theodore again and begins a romance involving his passionate overtures and her

Gustave Flaubert

consistent refusals; out of frustration or simply out of "artlessness," Theodore proposes marriage. One evening when she goes to meet him, however, she is met by one of his friends, who tells her Theodore has decided to marry a wealthy old woman, Madame Lehoussais, who can pay to keep him from being drafted into the army. Heartbroken, she leaves the farm and goes to Pont-l'Évêque, where she is hired by Madame Aubain.

Félicité soon becomes an exemplary housekeeper. She is especially enthralled with the children—Paul, who is seven, and Virginie, who is four—and Madame Aubain admonishes her for kissing them too much. Monsieur Bourais, a retired solicitor, handles Madame's affairs and visits frequently, at one point bringing a geography book to the children. Paul explains the pictures to Félicité: this is the sum of her formal education. The family sometimes visits the Geffosses Farm, part of the slight property Madame has managed to retain. One day Félicité saves the entire family from an angry bull, keeping it at bay by throwing clods of earth at it; the tale becomes a local legend, but Félicité does not see her actions as anything unusual.

As a result of her fright with the bull, Virginie develops a nervous ailment, and the family spends some weeks at Trouville on the coast. There Félicité

happens to meet one of her long-lost sisters. Madame Aubain becomes annoyed at the frequent visits of the sister and her children and at Félicité's habit of making them presents. When the family returns home, Paul is sent to a boys' school in Caen. Félicité is saddened but soon distracts herself with Virginie's catechism classes.

Part III

Accompanying Virginie to her catechism lessons, Félicité—who had had no religious education as a child—becomes profoundly caught up in the ritual and the emotional quality of Catholic observances. When Virginie makes her first communion, Félicité is as excited and nervous as if she herself were the communicant. Soon Virginie is sent off to a convent school, and Félicité mourns her absence deeply. To distract herself from her grief she asks and receives permission to have Sunday visits from her nephew, Victor. She soon comes to dote on him, making him dinner and mending his clothes, while he, at his parents' instructions, always tries "to get something out of her—a packet of moist sugar, it might be, a cake of soap, spirits, or even money at times." Victor, however, soon leaves her as well, bound by ship for Cuba. Félicité hurries to see him off, but his ship is leaving just as she arrives at the quay, and she merely glimpses him as the ship moves out. She worries about him constantly; when she has not heard from him for several months, she begs Monsieur Bourais to show her Havana on the map, asking him to point out the house where her nephew lives. Monsieur Bourais laughs at her simplemindedness. Soon afterward she receives a letter from her brother-in-law. Unable to read, she takes it to her mistress, who informs her that her nephew has died.

Virginie, in her convent school, now begins to grow weaker, suffering from a lung disease. The girl soon dies. Félicité keeps vigil by the body for two nights and prepares it for burial. In the weeks after the funeral Madame Aubain seems in danger of slipping into despair, but Félicité "lectured her gently," reminding her mistress of her duty to her remaining child and to her daughter's memory. The doctors forbid the mother to visit Virginie's grave, but Félicité visits it every day and tends it carefully, so that when Madame Aubain is finally allowed to visit it she is greatly comforted.

Several years go by, and many of Madame Aubain's acquaintances pass away. Paul becomes a drunkard who is constantly in debt, to his mother's grief. Madame Aubain and Félicité often take walks and talk about Virginie. Eventually Félicité helps her mistress sort out her dead daughter's things. Félicité asks for an old plush hat as a keepsake, and in the emotion of the moment the two women connect in a way they never have before:

> Their eyes met fixedly and filled with tears; at last the mistress opened her arms, the servant threw herself into them, and they embraced each other, satisfying their grief in a kiss that made them equal.

> It was the first time in their lives, Mme. Aubain's nature not being expansive. Félicité was as grateful as though she had received a favor, and cherished her mistress from that moment with the devotion of an animal and a religious worship. (Excerpt from ''A Simple Heart,'' translated by Arthur McDonnell)

Félicité's kindness blooms; she nurses cholera patients, assists Polish refugees, and cares for a homeless old man, father Colmiche, suspected of committing atrocities during the French Revolution. On the day the old man dies, an acquaintance who is moving out of town presents her pet parrot to Madame Aubain. Félicité has been fascinated with the parrot for some time; because it came from America, it reminds her of her dead nephew Victor.

Part IV

The parrot, whose name is Loulou, has such annoying habits that Madame Aubain turns him over to Félicité, who teaches him to speak and becomes extremely attached to him. One day, after Félicité leaves him on the grass for a moment, he disappears. Frantic, she looks for him all over town. Loulou returns, but Félicité suffers a chill and as a result loses some of her hearing. Three years later she is completely deaf, able to hear only the parrot. They have conversations together, he repeating his limited repertoire—phrases such as ''Nice boy!'' ''Your servant, sir!'' and ''Good morning, Marie!'' When Loulou dies, Félicité weeps so vigorously that Madame suggests she have him stuffed. Not trusting the mail system, she walks the dead parrot to Honfleur for stuffing. En route, she is knocked down by a wagon, whose driver lashes her with the whip; but she gets up and goes on.

Félicité installs the stuffed parrot in her room and treats it with reverence. Noticing a resemblance between the stuffed bird and depictions of the Holy Spirit in the form of a dove, she buys a cheap color print in which the similarity is particularly striking and hangs it in her room. In her prayers, the parrot becomes increasingly confused with the Holy Spirit.

Paul, now thirty-six, finally finds a niche in the Registrar's Office and becomes engaged to the inspector's daughter, who looks down on the provincialism of Pont-l'Évêque. Soon afterwards, Madame Aubain dies, mourned primarily by Félicité. The heirs remove most of the furniture and threaten Félicité with eviction. Since no one leases or buys the house, however, she continues to live there for several years on her small pension as the house gradually falls into complete disrepair. Finally she falls ill with pneumonia. After Easter; one of the public altars is set up in Madame Aubain's garden. Upset that she has nothing to contribute to the decorations on the altar, Félicité asks Mere Simon, who is nursing her, to put Loulou on the altar.

Part V

As Félicité lies dying, a religious procession comes to the garden, and she sees it as if she is there. Smelling the incense, she smiles. In her final moments, she thinks she sees the heavens open, and hovering above her head—like the Holy Spirit in a religious painting—a giant parrot.

Characters

Madame Aubain

Madame Aubain employs Félicité in her service for half a century. At the beginning of Félicité's employment Madame is the mother of Paul, seven, and Virginie, four, and the widow of a man who has left her with many debts. Although Madame Aubain rarely displays affection or appreciation for her servant, Félicité is deeply devoted to her and in many ways protects her. It is Félicité who bargains with tradespeople, who eases obnoxious visitors out of the house, who saves the family from an angry bull they encounter during an outing. When Virginie dies, it is Félicité who keeps vigil by the body and tends the grave, since Madame is too overcome to do so. Most of Félicité's possessions, including the parrot, Loulou, are Madame's castoffs. When Madame dies, few mourn her; she always kept people at a distance. Félicité, on the other hand, is devastated.

Félicité

Félicité is Madame Aubain's faithful servant and the central character of the story. She is a woman of simple mind and simple heart, a believer in the supernatural, clean living, and hard work. Orphaned early in her life, she is a cow-herder and dairy girl until a broken heart compels her to leave and seek work in a nearby town, Pont-l'Évêque. Thus, at eighteen, she is hired by Madame Aubain as a cook and housemaid. She soon takes over the running of the household while forming a succession of deep emotional attachments to Madame and her two children, to her own nephew, and ultimately to her parrot, Loulou. When the parrot dies, she has it stuffed and keeps it in her room.

Although Félicité's devotion is almost never reciprocated or appreciated, her need to love never flags. Despite a life of hard work, repeated disappointment, and the gradual loss of everyone dear to her, she is unwavering in her faith. As she grows older, she begins to confuse the stuffed parrot with images of the Holy Spirit in the form of a dove that she sees in religious paintings and stained-glass windows. As she lies dying of pneumonia, she has a vision of the heavens opening and the Holy Ghost descending upon her in the form of a giant parrot, and she dies smiling.

Loulou

Loulou the parrot is the final love of Félicité's life. He originally belongs to the wife of a government official whose family pays social calls on Madame Aubain. Because the bird comes from America, he reminds Félicité of her nephew, Victor, who died in Cuba. When the official is transferred to another district, the wife gives the parrot to Madame Aubain, but his habits so annoy her that she turns him over to Félicité. Félicité becomes very attached to him. When he goes missing one day Félicité searches for him all over town. The bird eventually returns on his own, but in searching for him Félicité has caught a chill, and the ensuing illness leaves her deaf. Subsequently the only sound she seems able to hear is that of the parrot repeating his meaningless phrases.

When Loulou dies, Félicité has him stuffed and puts him in her bedroom. Noting his resemblance to certain depictions of the Holy Spirit, she gradually begins to focus her prayers on the dead bird as a sort of religious icon. As she lies dying, she has a vision of the parrot as the Holy Spirit, and she dies smiling.

Madame

See Madame Aubain

Parrot

See Loulou

Paul

Madame Aubain's son and Virginie's brother, Paul is seven years old when Félicité enters the family's service. Félicité quickly becomes attached to both the boy and his sister and is saddened when he is sent away to school in Caen at a young age. As an adult, Paul passes from one unsuccessful career to another, spending his time in taverns and running up debts which his mother pays off. At the age of thirty-six, shortly before his mother's death, he finds apparent success at the Registrar's Office, where an inspector offers Paul his daughter's hand and a promotion.

Theodore

Félicité's first and only romantic interest, Theodore is a farmhand who meets Félicité at a fair when she is eighteen. A night after Félicité resists his passionate overtures, Theodore proposes marriage. One day, however, he fails to show up for one of their meetings, sending a friend to say that he has decided to marry a wealthy elderly woman, Madame Lehoussais, who he hopes will pay to protect him from conscription into the army. Félicité then leaves the farm and goes to the town of Pont-l'Évêque, where she is hired by Madame Aubain. Many years later Félicité overhears a comment that suggests Madame Lehoussais did not marry Theodore after all, but the matter is never resolved.

Victor

Victor is Félicité's nephew and one of her many profound and simple attachments. She first discovers his existence when she is visiting the seaside with the Aubain family and comes across one of her sisters—Victor's mother—whom she has not seen since she was a child. Félicité asks that Victor be allowed to visit her after Virginie is sent away to school. Félicité dotes on Victor, cooks him dinner, and mends his clothes. He, on the other hand, at the urging of his parents, never fails to ask her for food or money to take home. Eventually he signs on as a cabin boy on a ship sailing to America. Félicité walks the twelve miles to Honfleur to see him off, but the ship is leaving and she merely gets a glimpse of him as it pulls out. Months later she learns that he has died in Cuba: the doctors bled him too severely while treating him for yellow fever. Victor is one of the reasons for Félicité's attachment to the parrot, Loulou—Loulou reminds her of America, the place where Victor died.

Virginie

The daughter of Madame Aubain, Virginie is four when Félicité enters the household. A close call with an angry bull leaves the child suffering from a nervous complaint, and the whole family spends several weeks at the seaside in an attempt to cure her. Félicité accompanies her to her catechism classes, where the housemaid develops a fervent if simple religious faith; Félicité experiences Virginie's first communion as profoundly as if it were her own. Soon thereafter the child is sent away to a convent school, and Félicité is deeply grieved. When Virginie dies of a lung infection, Félicité keeps a vigil by the body, and later she visits Virginie's grave every day. Both Madame and Félicité mourn deeply for her, and their shared grief leads to Madame's one reported open display of affection towards her housemaid. A moth-eaten hat that belonged to Virginie is one of Félicité's most precious possessions.

Themes

God and Organized Religion

As in many of his earlier works, in "A Simple Heart" Flaubert dealt with notions of simplicity, sainthood, religious faith, and duty. Many critics have interpreted this story as a profound but veiled critique of organized religion—particularly the Roman Catholic church in nineteenth-century France—and of its unquestioning following among the bourgeoisie, or middle class. As a realist writer, Flaubert believed the artist must not express his opinions in his works. The story's reputed critique of the Church is not explicit—critics find it conveyed through such techniques as irony and symbolism. Félicité's vicarious devotion to the church through Virginie's first communion experience, while passionate and profound, is also arbitrary and circumstantial. She comes upon her faith by chance, by the simple accident of being required to accompany her young charge to her religion classes. Her devotion to the church is not based on an embrace of its beliefs: "Of doctrines she understood nothing—did not even try to understand." Rather, it stems from an emotional reaction to the stories told by the priest, full of familiar images of country life, and to the mystery and pomp of the communion ceremony. Moreover, Félicité's religious devotion eventually becomes

Topics for Further Study

- Gustave Flaubert has been called the master of "Art for Art's Sake." Research the literary school of realism and the idea of "art for art's sake" and discuss "A Simple Heart" in those terms. You might choose to draw parallels to realism in the visual arts and sciences.

- Flaubert, it is said, was attempting to write realistically, to report what he saw, and to write with the beautiful precision of the language of science. Discuss how a writer of literature can be said to resemble, in style, tone, rhythm, or diction, a composer of music or of a work of science.

- Read *Madame Bovary* and discuss the various parallels between that novel and "A Simple Heart." In particular, examine the similarities and differences in the worldviews expressed in the two works.

- "A Simple Heart" was originally entitled *Le Perroquet (The Parrot)*. Discuss how each title suggests a different approach or meaning to the story.

- Compare Félicité to the character Forrest Gump in the movie of the same name. Discuss some of the similarities and differences between the two works in terms of the points they make and how they make them.

indistinguishable in her mind from her devotion to her dead parrot.

Duty and Responsibility

A not-unrelated theme is that of duty and responsibility. In her simplicity, which makes possible her tremendous capacity to love, Félicité never questions her duty or her responsibility. Her determination in this respect is dogged, whether or not it is admirable. She works relentlessly for half a century for a ridiculously low wage, without complaint. When she rescues the family from the raging bull, she endangers her own life without a second thought. When she walks through the night to bid adieu to Victor, she does not question the wisdom of or reason for her task, and when she is knocked over while taking her dead parrot to be stuffed, she simply picks herself up and continues her journey. Her simplicity makes her virtually unstoppable, except by death. While Félicité herself is never portrayed in a negative light, her consistent history of disappointment, loss, and exploitation by others throws into question the value of such blind and unswerving devotion in the face of a thankless and unrewarding world.

Innocence and Ignorance

Félicité embodies innocence and Christian charity; she is virtuous and self-abnegating and good. At eighteen she does not at first seem to suspect that Theodore, the young man who befriends her at a dance, has any ulterior motive—when he makes sexual advances she is frightened and cries out. Later, the narrator remarks that "she was not innocent as young ladies are—she had learned knowledge from the animals—but her reason and the instinct of her honour would not let her fall." After saving her mistress's family from the bull, she has "not the barest suspicion that she had done anything heroic." She is ignorant in some ways—for example, "so stunted was her mind" that she thinks one can see a particular house on a map, and though she takes Virginie to catechism, she understands nothing about doctrine. She cannot read. When Virginie dies and Félicité keeps vigil, the narrator notes that if Virginie had revived during her watch Félicité "would not have been immensely surprised . . . to minds like hers the supernatural is quite simple."

Wealth, Poverty, and Exploitation

Simple, uneducated, and poor, Félicité is repeatedly exploited and victimized, from her early days as a farm worker to her relationship with Theodore to her service with Madame Aubain. She is used by everyone she loves; everyone leaves her; sadness repeatedly threatens to destroy her. Yet she is so unaware of evil, so accepting of good, that she is incorruptible. Her heart, as the title suggests, is simple enough to be pure, and her capacity to love is her wealth.

Death, Time, and Loss

While death is a recurring theme in "A Simple Heart," time and loss seem more important to the story as a whole. Death is ever-present, a product of

time and a vehicle of loss. Félicité is orphaned at an early age and separated from her siblings. When she does locate one of her sisters, the woman seems primarily interested in taking advantage of her. With the passage of time she suffers the loss of Theodore, her only human lover, of Virginie, Victor, Paul, and even of Madame Aubain. Always poor, she is threatened after her employer's death with eviction from her home. She seems to have no control over her losses. When her parrot disappears, her frantic efforts to find him prove fruitless, although the bird comes back on his own. Victor's ship disappears just as she arrives to see him off. She loses the chance to see Virginie before the girl dies, arriving too late because she stayed behind to lock the house out of duty to Madame Aubain's interests. Toward the end, she is physically diminishing, growing smaller, becoming deaf. She hears, literally and figuratively, only the voice of the parrot, and the parrot can only repeat empty phrases. "The little circle of her ideas grew narrower and narrower." Thus her small world becomes ever smaller, until it is reduced to a single vision of a dead parrot as the Holy Ghost. The related themes of time as erosive, of loss as inevitable, become one theme as her death approaches.

Style

Point of View

Critic Victor Brombert has said that Flaubert's great accomplishment in "A Simple Heart" was that he presented a protagonist, or central character, who is completely inarticulate and uneducated, and yet he made the reader view things as she does. The author allowed the reader to view Félicité's character from both the outside and the inside: from the outside, through the omniscient narrator's impassive and factual account of events and of the attitudes of other characters towards her; from the inside, through the narrator's reports of her thoughts, actions, and motives. The contrasts that are introduced between Félicité's generous acts and thoughts and the generally self-centered and callous reactions of the more sophisticated characters around her create sympathy for the main character and an implied critique of her supposed superiors. Since the narrative voice never offers a direct opinion of the action, however, the reader is left to form his or her own interpretation of the story's meaning.

Irony

Irony is a use of language in which the intended meaning appears to be different from what is directly stated. The narrative voice in ''A Simple Heart,'' for instance, may be seen as ironic because although it offers no direct commentary on the story, the evidence it reports builds sympathy for the main character and exposes the shallowness and egoism of those who exploit her.

The more subtle the irony, the more difficult it may be to determine exactly what is meant. Critics disagree about the extent and meaning of Flaubert's use of irony in ''A Simple Heart.'' Much of Félicité's behavior—such as her devotion to her parrot, which eventually approaches idolatry—is so simpleminded as to seem absurd. Yet Félicité herself is so selfless in her love and so unconquerable in her resistance to despair that to most readers she is a likable and sympathetic character; no matter how simple and naive her actions, she herself does not seem ridiculous.

Symbolism

Loulou is the most obvious symbol in the story, although there are many more. As a parrot, he can only repeat empty phrases, generally out of context, and thus he is a particularly ironic symbol as the vehicle through which Félicité should experience divinity. Félicité's deafness in her old age is symbolic of her inability to comprehend or interpret the world around her. Many of the names in the story also appear to have symbolic significance, often with ironic overtones. Félicité (whose name, like the English word ''felicity,'' implies both happiness and good fortune) lives a life of repeated misfortune and great sadness, but she dies smiling. Victor is certainly not victorious; Virginie dies before she lives, virginal by default, another life wasted; ''aubaine,'' in French, refers to a godsend or windfall, but while Félicité may see Madame Aubain in this light, one could argue that Félicité was less than fortunate in her choice of employers.

Realism

Flaubert was one of the leaders of the realist movement in French literature, which sought to portray life in a realistic manner primarily through the use of an objective narrative point of view and the accumulation of accurate details. He believed in meticulous observation and exact reporting of events. He also held firmly that the writer must not express his opinion through his art—that he must simply tell the story. Thus in ''A Simple Heart,'' the narrator reports the story of Félicité's life without commentary or reflection. The reader is thus obliged to draw his or her own conclusions—much as in real life.

Historical Context

Unlike the other two tales which make up the collection *Three Tales*, ''A Simple Heart'' is not a historical reconstruction. It is a story set in the time and the country of the author, and thus it reflects the attitudes and habits of France in the nineteenth century. Félicité represents a realistic picture of a woman living in the France that Flaubert knew and observed.

Romanticism and Realism in Nineteenth-Century France

Flaubert figures as one of the leading authors of the realist movement, and ''A Simple Heart'' is typical of his work in this regard. Realistic writers sought to represent life in its purest form, without exaggeration or embellishment. They considered themselves reporters, attempting to chronicle their worlds honestly and objectively. Conventional morality was not a concern: logic, common sense, and pragmatism informed their literary endeavors. Realism was in many ways a reaction to and a movement away from romanticism, which had dominated French literature in the earlier part of the century. The romantic movement, an artistic and literary tradition established in late eighteenth-century Europe, had been characterized by an interest in nature and an emphasis on individualism, imagination, and emotion. Ultimately, realism became the dominant literary style until the end of the century.

Political and Social Influences in Nineteenth-Century France

The school of realism took shape in French literature after the coup d'etat in 1851 that brought

Louis Napoleon to power. Louis Napoleon—the nephew of the Emperor Napoleon I (Napoleon Bonaparte), who had been forced to abdicate in 1815—had himself proclaimed emperor in 1852, and he ruled as Napoleon III until 1870. In many ways realism represented a reaction against the social climate of this period of the ''Second Empire.'' While many people made fortunes in this developing capitalist society, the gap between rich and poor seemed to be widening. Meanwhile, wealth ruled, and the bourgeoisie, or entrepreneurial middle class, dominated society and politics. There was a general sense of self-satisfaction, even self-righteousness, among the wealthy classes. Prosperity, respectability, conformity, and order were strong mandates, both politically and socially. At the same time, there was dissension among the lower class: workers were unhappy with their treatment, and social revolution and political anarchy were brewing just below the surface.

The Catholic Church in Nineteenth-Century France

Although the Roman Catholic Church enjoyed a strong position in France in the nineteenth century, its mandates were challenged by positivist philosophy. The invention of philosopher Auguste Comte, positivism rejected the romantic notions of dream, imagination, mysticism, and even God. Anything which could not be proved scientifically or seen with the eye was to be dismissed as whimsy; anything which was contingent upon faith was suspect. As a popular philosophy in French social and intellectual circles, positivism thus threw the mandates of the Church into question. Many critics writing about ''A Simple Heart'' have remarked on the significant religious symbolism and criticism of the church and its followers. Certainly many of Félicité's attitudes appear to be grounded in her religion, and, as a servant to all and a peasant herself, she may represent the simple, uneducated, and religiously-observant class in nineteenth-century France.

Critical Overview

Although *Three Tales* (*Trois Contes*), the collection which includes ''A Simple Heart,'' was written

more quickly than any of Flaubert's other known works, it is generally considered most exemplary of his mature style. Flaubert began writing the piece in 1875, attempting a more gentle and humanitarian literature, and he completed the three tales in 1877, just three years before his death. In 1878, in the *Fortnightly Review*, English critic George Saintsbury claimed that ''A Simple Heart'' ''displays exactly the same qualities of minute and exact observation, the same unlimited fidelity of draughtsmanship, which distinguish *Madame Bovary* and *L'Education Sentimentale* [*Sentimental Education*].'' Commenting on Flaubert's realism, Saintsbury remarked, ''There are few things more curious than the combination of such an imagination with the photographic clearness of observation and reproduction.''

The book's moral character, unlike that of *Madame Bovary*, has never been in question. The obscenity trial and notorious controversy surrounding the publication of *Madame Bovary* in 1857 had had much to do with the ''moral content'' of that book, of course. But that controversy had also to do with Flaubert's realistic writing style; he was not a man given to inspiration and muses—he believed in working very hard and reporting what he saw. He believed in observation and faithful reproduction. That life was closely reproduced in *Madame Bovary* came as a shock to readers, and this bourgeois repugnance for self-examination showed even in the critical reports. Thus Saintsbury also writes of Flaubert that ''he has to a very remarkable degree the art of chaining the attention even when the subject is a distasteful one to the reader.''

Furthermore, although some critics at the time suggested that ''A Simple Heart'' was purely a moral tale, it is generally thought that Flaubert's intentions were, as he said, to write of a simple life, a simple woman. He was writing a tale of consolation rather than desolation, a more humanitarian literature, in response to requests from his old friend and fellow writer George Sand and in light of his own losses and growing empathy for human beings. Albert Thibaudet (in his *Gustave Flaubert, sa vie, ses romans, son style*) claims that this story heralds a true turning point in Flaubert's life and worldview, a turn toward human pity. Flaubert himself remarked in a letter that perhaps now he would be called humane. Claims about the moral bent of ''A Simple Heart'' have been largely set aside as less than central. If, according to Brunetière, ''A Simple Heart'' was simply another attack on human stu-

On her deathbed, Félicité sees a giant parrot, which she believes is the manifestation of the Holy Spirit.

pidity and the bourgeoisie, how could a reader then explain Flaubert's mood of sympathy for Félicité?

These interpretations are not mutually exclusive. According to critic Ben Stoltzfus (1961), "Flaubert's treatment of Félicité does represent an increasing sympathy and tolerance towards man, [but] he consciously and artistically had to use symbolism in order to inject his criticism of the church. This criticism is not Félicité's but his." Stoltzfus suggests a dual point of view—that of Flaubert and Félicité—so that readers are able to accept Flaubert's subliminal criticism of organized

religion and the Roman Catholic Church because they become sympathetic to Félicité as victim. American critic Robert Denomme (in *Studies in Short Fiction*, 1970) agrees, saying that "whatever irony emerges from "Un Coeur Simple" stems from the respective positions and attitudes of Flaubert and his readers who will evaluate both Félicité and the environment in which she has been compelled to function."

Other views, of course, vary: the story has been called a direct attack on the Roman Catholic Church of nineteenth-century France, and it has been hailed as a simple tale of human compassion. It has recently been suggested that, through the elimination of that which is masculine and violent, Flaubert in *Three Tales* affords his reader a hopeful vision identified with feminine nature. In her *Flaubert's Straight and Suspect Saints: The Unity of "Trois Contes,"* Aimee Israel-Pelletier suggests that "Flaubert's 'swan song' is, ironically for a writer who has been so consistently characterized as a cynic and a hater of humanity, the most hopeful and, aesthetically, the most beautifully crafted of all his works." Whatever the differences, the critical and popular consensus has always held "A Simple Heart" as a profound and beautiful story.

Criticism

Jacqueline Perret

Perret teaches English at Lake Forest College, in Lake Forest, Illinois. In the following essay, she examines "A Simple Heart" in terms of its portrayal of what was expected from a woman of the lower class in nineteenth-century France.

When Gustave Flaubert wrote to Madame Roger des Genettes that his aim in "A Simple Heart" was "to move, to bring tears to the eyes of the tenderhearted," he was explaining his intention to create in Félicité a sympathetic character—a central persona with whom we could identify and empathize. He claimed that his story was in no way ironic but rather "serious and extremely sad." And even when he describes "A Simple Heart" as "just an account of an obscure life, the life of a poor country girl who is pious but mystical, faithful without fuss, and tender as new bread," he must certainly have been sincere. It is speculated that, though "A Simple Heart" was the second tale written in the trilogy *Three Tales* (*Trois Contes*), Flaubert chose to place it first in the collection because it was closest to his heart, most equal to his values at the time. Furthermore, some critics have suggested that the character of Félicité is modeled on a cherished maidservant, Julie, from Flaubert's childhood, although it is said that she was probably more intelligent and worldly than Félicité. He was also hoping to please his longtime friend George Sand, who had admonished him to create a literature of "consolation" rather than "desolation." In "A Simple Heart," then, Flaubert wished to compose a simple story about a good woman, and most critics agree that he did just that.

Still, there has been much controversy about the interpretation of the story. Ever since its publication and very fond reception in 1877, "A Simple Heart" has been variously interpreted. Some have seen it as a testimony to the futility of faith and religious dogma (witness Félicité's life of loss and exploitation despite her unquestioning love and devotion to all within her reach), particularly centering on the Roman Catholic church of nineteenth-century France. Others take it as a simple declaration of faith in the human spirit and its undying capacity to love (witness again Félicité's unquestioning love and devotion to all within her reach and her steadfast refusal to give in to despair). Both of these readings can apply; in fact, Flaubert has left the ending of his story open to varied and even contradictory interpretations. Many feel that Félicité dies, smiling and with the vision of a giant parrot as Holy Ghost, believing her troubled life is being rewarded at last. Others interpret the delusion of the parrot during her final moments as suggestive of the utter and final misperception of a useless life. Neither of these interpretations, however, or anything one can imagine in between them, fully explains the story. A more complete understanding can be reached if we recognize that on a very fundamental level, "A Simple Heart" is the story of women in nineteenth-century France. Viewed from this perspective, Félicité functions as a representative of female class and culture in a particular society. More universally, it can be argued, her character comprises traditional views and perceptions of female behavior and thought.

"She loves, simply and without second thoughts. The pattern of her life is therefore tragic, for she can neither stop herself from loving, nor ever be loved in return, since others see her as made of wood and functioning automatically," says Murray Sachs. That she can be viewed as nothing but wooden, that she is simple, that she functions automatically, that she loves without measure or boundary: all of these qualities suggest archetypal female qualities. To be sure, Félicité is a woman of relentless love and compassion and empathy. When she witnesses the communion of Virginie, the young daughter of her mistress, she is moved beyond sympathetic tendencies to pure empathy:

> When it was Virginie's turn, Félicité leant forward to see her, and in one of those imaginative flights born of real affection, it seemed to her that she herself was in the child's place. Virginie's face became her own, Virginie's dress clothed her, Virginie's heart was beating in her breast; and as she closed her eyes and opened her mouth, she almost fainted away.

What Do I Read Next?

- *The Awakening* is author Kate Chopin's turn-of-the-century masterpiece. Often compared to *Madame Bovary*, this short novel tackles some of the same issues that appear in Flaubert's work.

- *Candide* (1759), by the French author Voltaire, is an earlier example of a work in which the experiences and perceptions of a naive character are used to produce an ironic commentary on society.

- Winston Groom's 1986 novel *Forrest Gump* also uses the life of a naive and good-hearted protagonist to comment on the society of its time—in this case, that of the United States in the late twentieth century. The film adaptation, starring Tom Hanks, was released in 1994.

- *The Letters of Gustave Flaubert* is translator and critic Francis Steegmuller's collection of Flaubert's correspondence during the later years of his life. Entertaining and informative, these letters offer a fascinating look at the author's life and times.

- *Madame Bovary*, Gustave Flaubert's best known and most controversial novel, was the subject of an obscenity trial in 1857. The characters of Emma Bovary and Félicité make for interesting comparisons.

- *Three Tales*, the collection from which "A Simple Heart" is taken, also contains the stories "The Legend of St. Julien l'Hospitalier" and "Herodias." It was the last work published during Flaubert's lifetime, and it was the one most quickly written. It is also interesting as a trilogy, as each tale has a successive relationship to the others.

In fact, critic Victor Brombert suggests that "vicarious experience goes hand in hand here with utter generosity and lack of self-awareness." Here again we find the exemplary female: complete empathy, complete selflessness, complete and unquestioning servitude to others. This is the story of a truly simple heart, a predictable soul, a female life.

Here is the story of a woman who, not despite but because of her obedience to the rules, worked for next to nothing, had no children, worshipped a dead, stuffed parrot, and yet lived a full life and was fully equipped to deal with loss and tragedy. She died smiling because she lived lovingly. She had stayed, as it were, within the lines, lived well within the expectations and dictates of her class and culture and, particularly, her gender. Thus we can speculate that, consciously or unconsciously, Gustave Flaubert has given us a tale that tells us as much about the simple expectations and constraints of gender as it tells us about God and organized religion.

That many have suggested a relationship between "A Simple Heart" and Flaubert's first, notorious, and controversial success, *Madame Bovary,* is neither surprising nor inaccurate. But readers find Emma Bovary unlikable or unsympathetic for the most part, whereas Félicité is, though uncomplicated, a sympathetic character. Critic Enid Starkie suggests that Félicité "has nothing to fight against and could be nothing but good." That there exists no temptation to sin, that there is no struggle in her between good and evil explains her purity and suggests a sharp contrast to the character of Emma Bovary. And of course Félicité has all of the qualities of Christian virtue, as critics suggest when they read the story as a critique of organized religion. It is not surprising, then, that she also embodies characteristics, virtues, if you will, frequently attached to the archetypal female: goodness, a pure and loving heart, self-abnegation, charity, and a simple, unself-conscious mentality.

"It is not particularly clear," says Starkie, "why [Flaubert] should have thought of writing 'A Simple Heart' at that moment, except that he wanted to compose a tale which was entirely kind and

> On a very fundamental level, 'A Simple Heart' is the story of women in nineteenth-century France. Viewed from this perspective, Felicite functions as a representative of female class and culture in a particular society."

consoling, though it need not have dealt with a very unintelligent servant.'' The intimation that perhaps Flaubert could not make the equation of female goodness with intelligence also argues the contrast to Emma Bovary who, though stupid in action, is not unintelligent, and is also therefore not particularly "good" or sympathetic.

This, then, is key: the female characters in these stories exist on a sliding scale from good to evil which directly corresponds to their native intelligence and to their capacity for self-examination. By extrapolation, their "goodness" might also be said to correspond to their level of sexual experience. Virginie dies a virgin at a very young age, in a convent; Félicité dies innocent in almost every way; Madame Aubain, on the other hand, a widow with children, is cold and ungiving and unlikable. She even sends her children away, and, though this may have been the fashion, it contradicts maternal instinct. Emma Bovary, who is intelligent and imaginative, is also promiscuous, as well as expensive and dangerous to her husband and child; in fact, she finds her child ugly. ("It is strange," she thought, "how ugly that child is.") So innocence on any level (physical, sexual, intellectual or spiritual) corresponds to goodness in women, while knowledge—sexual or otherwise—corresponds to evil.

When Flaubert writes of "A Simple Heart" that it is not an ironic tale, rather "serious and extremely sad," he is suggesting a virtue in Félicité's innocence which exists exclusively because she is viewed, or misconstrued, as an ideal female. With no children or husband of her own, she is accessible and serviceable to all, and with no capacity for self-examination, she lives this way hap-

pily. In fact, she outlives everyone she cares for, which is as it should be: the ideal woman ever-present, ever-loving, everlasting. Nobody's mother, she can be everyone's mother, chaste and good.

So here is the story of a simple woman in nineteenth-century France who, by circumstance of her class and gender, lives an unexamined but pure and happy life. Viewed as such, Félicité's life, her reverence for the parrot Loulou, and her possibly blissful death are not so sad and serious. She is trapped by gender and she is a victim of circumstance, but she accepts her fate willingly. There is no contest between good and evil, no self-examination, and, in the end, no painful struggle with conscience or fear of death. Flaubert was indeed sincere when he said that this is not an ironic story, but rather "serious and extremely sad." For he intended no irony. But in order to create a perfectly sympathetic and, as he said, "good" woman, he found it necessary to make her simple and stupid. "Flaubert was so constituted that he was unable to see kindness and goodness in a sophisticated and intelligent human being," Enid Starkie concludes of Félicité's character. Nonetheless, this beautiful tale is profoundly moving and is considered one of Flaubert's most exemplary and heartfelt works. Félicité is, in spite of her representation as ideal female, never presented in a negative light, and she is thus an arguably sympathetic character.

In fact, even on a structural level, this story is the story of one woman and one woman only. We may call her stupid, but we like her, and this is Flaubert's tour de force. We like Félicité because she is good, but also because we understand why she sees the world as she does. We are allowed to see both inside and outside her character. This narrative device affords us a particularly poignant and comprehensive view of her life and her circumstances. We do not blame her, as we do Emma Bovary, for example, for her troubles. She is, after all, a good woman; who could blame her? Thus she is sympathetic to the end, when, as she dies, her beautiful female vitality ebbs and flows, "as a fountain sinks, an echo disappears." Perhaps her life was ridiculous; perhaps she was no more than a peripheral echo, like the utterances of her sacred parrot; but she was good and in the end, real or not, she believed she was being rewarded. So here the story ends and must end, with the end of her life, and the conclusion of her point of view. It is here, finally and completely, that Flaubert shows us—by ending the story where he does—that this is a story about one woman and that, most importantly, her story has been worth telling. (In obvious contrast, *Madame Bovary* does not end with the death of Emma Bovary; rather the novel continues for many pages and ends, ironically, with Homais receiving the cross of the Legion of Honor.) In "A Simple Heart," Flaubert ends his narration with the humble and even beautiful death of Félicité, and in so doing he emphasizes finally the breadth and depth of her spiritual and moral integrity.

Source: Jacqueline Perret, Overview of "A Simple Heart," for *Short Stories for Students,* The Gale Group, 1999.

Robert T. Denommé

In the following excerpt, Denommé argues that Flaubert's style in "A Simple Heart" leads the reader to feel sympathy with the main character despite her delusions.

Despite Flaubert's vigorous disclaimer to the contrary, a number of critics of recent vintage have been prompted to interpret " Un Coeur simple" as an ironic commentary on human stupidity and on stultifying bourgeois attitudes. Flaubert's writings prior to 1876, to be sure, virtually resound with pages of biting satire and bitter irony; *Madame Bovary, Salammbô* and *L'Education sentimentale* all attack virulently, at strategic intervals, the vacuity of many social, political and religious institutions. What distinguishes "Un Coeur simple" from the previously completed stories, however, is the discernible shift of tone and mood that the narrative assumes. Indeed, the remarkable fusion of tenderness with what Victor Brombert [in *The Novels of Flaubert: A Study of Themes and Techniques,* 1966] so aptly terms "refined irony" produces an effect hitherto alien to the majority of the novelist's better-known interpretations of humanity. This notable shift of emphasis may be at least partially explained by the series of unfortunate incidents that befell Flaubert from 1870 to 1876. The critical failures of *La Tentation de Saint-Antoine* and *Le Candidat,* the deaths of his mother and of such friends as Louis Bouihlet, Sainte-Beuve, Louise Colet, and George Sand, and the serious financial difficulties he encountered all doubtlessly contributed in some manner in altering his literary vision and modifying his personal attitude. The resulting attenuation in mood and tone, far from emerging as the fitful and short-lived personal reaction to unfavorable circumstances, resulted rather from Flaubert's scrupulous attention to relevant details and his painstaking effort to obtain specific effects; he wrote to his niece, Caroline, on 1 July 1876: "Je lutte comme un forcené contre les difficultés de mon *Coeur simple,* qui augmentent de jour en jour" ["I am struggling like a madman with the difficulties of my 'Simple Heart,' which increase from day to day"]. Flaubert's modified vision of humanity reaches its culminating point in the unfinished *Bouvard et Pécuchet,* which illustrates, ironically, the intellectual pursuits and failures of two friends without ruthlessly exploiting or condemning them for their folly. Like the two male protagonists, Bouvard and Pécuchet, Félicité in "Un Coeur simple" ironically unveils the futility and fatuousness of specific bourgeois practices while enlisting at the same time the undeniable sympathy of the reader.

"Un Coeur simple" deliberately refrains from unleashing any direct assault upon the ineffectiveness of organized religion or the narrowness of intellect and attitude that characterizes the typical provincial bourgeois. That any such overt critical confrontation is avoided in the story is attributable to the fact that Flaubert abstains from resorting to his favorite technical device, the *style indirect libre* ["indirect discourse"], in order to fashion the portrait of his main character. The *style indirect libre,* a type of indirect discourse obtained through the momentary association between the consciousness of the character involved and the directing intelligence of the narrator, would have endowed the narrative with a tone radically different than the one achieved in "Un Coeur simple." It is more than likely that Flaubert, intent on portraying Félicité with sympathy and even tenderness, realized that such a technique, in this instance, would impair him in achieving the desired effects. Félicité, unlike Emma Bovary, is incapable of formulating her thoughts or impressions on any appreciably precise or sophisticated level. The collaboration entered upon by Flaubert and Emma Bovary through the *style indirect libre* underscores with particular acuity the consciousness of his protagonist's state of mind, thus mercilessly exposing her to the reader's ridicule as the stupidly ironic victim of her own carefully contrived delusions. . . .

Flaubert's heroine in "Un Coeur simple" escapes the ignominy of such exposure primarily because she never experiences such complicated consciousness of her predicament. Moreover, her aspirations are too indelibly imprinted with simplicity and innocence for them to become so easily the brunt of the author's exploitation. . . .

There is no evidence of any compulsion to make of his simple-minded heroine an object for

> Flaubert endows the heroine of his short story with the kind of homogeneous vision of reality that enables her to retain a remarkably even sense of composure in the face of tragedy and adversity."

derision. To have exploited Félicité's simplicity in the manner that Catherine Leroux's stupidity was singled out in *Madame Bovary* would have reduced "Un Coeur simple" to a cynical commentary on fanaticism and ignorance. Such a single-minded interpretation robs Flaubert's story of its richer dimension.

Flaubert endows the heroine of his short story with the kind of homogeneous vision of reality that enables her to retain a remarkably even sense of composure in the face of tragedy and adversity. Félicité's simple view of life contrasts sharply with Flaubert's complex interpretation of reality. The latter's acute awareness of the complications and contradictions inherent in the world that he sought to comprehend inspired him with the voracious desire for understanding that is discernible in all his fiction. The confusion of change and movement, however, prevented him from pursuing such a goal with the kind of detachment he desired; the much-sought collaboration between his imagination and his practical intelligence never successfully took place, and the final homogeneity or synthesis failed to materialize to the extent that he had wished. Thwarted by the acknowledgment that complete truth remains elusive, Flaubert voiced his frustration as he reaffirmed his stubborn intention to pursue the impossible quest: "Car l'échec de la digestion n'empêche pas sa faim de le pousser vers de nouveaux objects: celle-ci s'exaspère au contraire de l'impossibilité qu'elle éprouve à se satisfaire" ["For a failure in digestion does not keep hunger from turning to new objects: my hunger is aggravated by the very obstacles it encounters"]. To a significant degree, *Madame Bovary* remains perhaps the author's most cogent statement on the

sense of inadequacy resulting from the failure to fashion successfully a homogeneous world from an essentially heterogeneous one. Emma Bovary never succeeds in sustaining her illusory existence for any great length of time because she continually submits her somewhat deficient imaginative powers to the scrutiny of a sordid external reality. She repeatedly becomes aware of her self-deception until she is finally driven to her destruction. Ironically, Félicité, much more ignorant and certainly much less articulate than Emma, achieves a satisfying homogeneity of vision by transforming ordinary reality through her imagination alone.

Félicité's instinctive retreat into the more predictable world of her private imagination is in fact prompted by the overwhelming confusion and bewilderment she experiences when compelled to face the jarring complexities of external reality.... In her insecurity, Félicité accepts Théodore's invitation to dance with him but is rudely shaken when she must resist his crude overtures. Thus, her subsequent withdrawal from the pressing requirements of a complex external reality appears as a defensive reaction to which she has recourse when she intuitively realizes that she is ill-equipped to function effectively under such circumstances. Henceforth, Félicité gazes at reality through her imagination and with her innate common sense. The real irony, of course, is that, despite her ignorance and simple-mindedness, she not only manages to function adequately but she is able, unconsciously, to project her own world outwardly to the point of touching and affecting the lives of others.

Félicité's daily existence, like that of Emma Bovary, is defined by the same kind of boredom, disappointment, and discouragement that mar the security and serenity of an ordered life. Unlike Emma, however, Félicité preserves her equanimity: she proceeds with remarkable resilience to repair whatever havoc may have been wrought by personal tragedy, indifference, and even cruelty. Condemned to perform the simplest chores, she escapes from most of the ravages of boredom by lavishing her attention on others: Mme Aubain, Paul and Virginie, Victor, the *père* Colmiche and Loulou, the parrot. Of all the characters in "Un Coeur simple" it is Félicité who emerges most successfully in the battle against frustration through positive and durable activity.... Ultimately, it is Félicité's constructive attitude that allows her to escape the stultifying effects of an uninteresting existence, for like Emma Bovary and Mme Aubain, she is exposed to the same monotonous routine of provincial life. The protagonist of "Un Coeur simple" is exposed to the cruel indifference and callousness of society that in one instance nearly succeeds in unnerving her to the point of imbalance. Having suffered the ignominy of the mailcoach driver's whiplash, Félicité makes her way painfully to a summit that commands a view of Honfleur, and momentarily yields to Emma's temptation. . . . Fortunately, Félicité's nostalgia is short-lived; the gnawing memory of her misfortune doubtlessly is allowed to surface because of her semi-conscious physical and mental state at the time.

What is frequently conveyed in almost antithetical terms is the fact the Flaubert's heroine in "Un Coeur simple" differs so radically in attitude from his earlier protagonist, Emma Bovary. Flaubert shows Félicité actively resisting the stultification caused by monotony and by the slow, tragic passage of time. While it remains undeniable that the theme is established from the beginning and sustained throughout the narrative, it is interesting to note the coded and even somewhat ambiguous language in which it is cloaked. In *Madame Bovary*, the novelist's intended criticism of the deficient romantic personality and of the mechanized gentry is spelled out in more direct and explicit terms. Flaubert's novels understandably allow more importance to dialogue than do the short stories. In *Madame Bovary*, for example, the spoken language of the characters plays an important role in establishing the kind of private world in which they function. In such stories as "Un Coeur simple," where dialogue is reduced to a strict minimum, Flaubert has recourse rather to symbols in order to evoke or suggest the various attitudes that he intends to portray. It is no small irony that the older, and consequently more mature artist resorts in his later fiction to the utilization of an outwardly more subjective technique of presentation. The highly suggestive passages describing the rooms inhabited by Mme Aubain and the servant convey with effective symbolism the opposing attitudes of immobility and activity, passive resignation and active resistance. . . .

The progressive shrinkage of Félicité's recognizable universe, brought about through the deaths of those she has loved, the eventual loss of part of the Aubain property and the subsequent impairment of her hearing and seeing faculties apparently condemn her to a life of virtually absolute isolation. Yet the opposite effect takes place. The isolation she experiences in a sense enables her to proceed un-

hampered and uninhibited by external forces to fashion the kind of private, homogeneous world that brings about the solace and security that she seeks. As her solitude increases, the powers of her creative imagination also increase. What Victor Brombert calls "the perversion of the Logos" resembles in many ways the nature of the child-poet's vision. Like the child-poet, Félicité creates through her imagination a simplified universe in which the jarring dissonances of a complex external world are conspicuously absent. Félicité's hallucinations or willful distortions of reality are in no way identifiable with the complicated *malaise* endured by Emma Bovary, Frédéric Moreau, and Mâtho. Flaubert's servant in "Un Coeur simple" succeeds in inducing the transformations that allow her to rectify the inequities of reality. This is how, for example, she is permitted to take part with Virginie in the first communion ceremonies. In similar fashion, Flaubert invites the reader to penetrate Félicité's imagination at Virginie's funeral procession. The faithful servant rectifies what she considers to be the arbitrary injustice of reality by her decision to mourn both Mme Aubain's deceased daughter and her own nephew, Victor: "Elle songeait à son neveu, et n'ayant pu lui rendre ces honneurs, avait un surcroît de tristesse, comme si on l'eût enterré avec l'autre" ["She thought of her nephew; and because she had not been able to pay these honours to him her grief was doubled, as though the one were being buried with the other"]. For the most part, Félicité emerges unscathed from her highly imaginative excursions precisely because she does not seek the corroboration of external reality in her experiences. Since she successfully maintains her own sense of equilibrium in the illusory world that she evolves, she never exposes herself to the destructive consciousness of self-deception and ridicule.

When deafness and virtual blindness finally condemn Félicité to the seclusion of the single room she occupies in the Aubain household, attended only by the mère Simon, she escapes progressively from the requirements of the heterogeneous external reality in which all individuals must learn to function. Old age and eventually illness free her from maintaining any kind of relationship with the harsh world of fact. Her mistaking Loulou for the Holy Spirit, indulgently dismissed as the ranting of delirium, conserves intact the illusions nourished by her imagination in more lucid intervals. Thus Félicité's spiritualization of Loulou achieves the status of a poetic metaphor for the Holy Spirit; as such, it emerges as one of the most exalted expressions of

Hugo's romantic synthesis: the sublime residing in the grotesque.

What understandably disturbs the critics who persist in placing "Un Coeur simple" in the same ironic tradition established by Flaubert in his completed novels is that one might suspect a double viewpoint: Félicité grossly misinterprets religious dogma and so, logically, she should be victimized by her own delusions. Yet Félicité's illusory world, as limited as it may appear, provides her with experiences that are as rich and personally satisfying as those of Emma Bovary are flimsy and ultimately corrosive. A comparison of Félicité's and Emma's death scenes verifies the positive value that is unfolded in the short story and the negation that is underscored in the novel. Emma's final agony is counterpointed by the ominous song of the blind man, whose words recall and comment on the dying woman's adulterous life:

> —"L'Aveugle!" s'écria-t-elle. Et Emma se mit à rire, d'un rire atroce, frénétique, désespéré, croyant voir la hideuse face du misérable, qui se dressait dans les ténèbres éternelles comme un épouvantement.

> [—"The blind man!" she cried. And Emma began to laugh, an atrocious, frantic, hopeless laugh, believing she saw the hideous face of that poor soul frightfully standing in the eternal shadows.]

In striking contrast, Félicité's dying moments are depicted as literally enshrined in the brilliant rays of a golden sun and, if anything, are counterpointed by the joyous religious ceremony of the Fête-Dieu, suggesting the triumphal apotheosis of the faithful servant and of her parrot. Among the variegated objects that magnetically attract the attention of the worshippers is the stuffed parrot, Loulou, transformed by his relationship to the expensive vases and colorful flowers that bedeck the altar on which they are placed: "Un sucrier de vermeil avait une couronne de violettes, des pendeloques en pierre d'Alençon brillaient sur la mousse, deux écrans chinois montraient leurs paysages. Loulou, caché sous des roses, ne laissait voir que son front bleu, pareil à une plaque de lapis" ["There was a silver-gilt sugar-basin with a crown of violets; pendants of Alençon stone glittered on the moss, and two Chinese screens displayed their landscapes. Loulou was hidden under roses, and showed nothing but his blue forehead, like a plaque of lapis lazuli"]. The very rhyming of the ceremony—the slow marching, the silence of the crowd, and the kneeling in reverent gesture—acts as a parallel to the slowing beat of Félicité's dying heart. From her bed, she participates in the festivities: "Une vapeur d'azur monta dans la chambre de Félicité. Elle avança les narines, en la humant avec une sensualité mystique; puis ferma les paupières. Ses lèvres souriaient" ["An azure vapour rose up into Félicité's room. Her nostrils met it; she inhaled it sensuously, mystically; and then closed her eyes. Her lips smiled"]. When juxtaposed to the fatuous, pointless dialogue entered into by Homais and Bournisien in the room where Emma lies in state, the death scene of Félicité suggests a striking impression of harmony and respect. . . .

Source: Robert T. Denommé, "Félicité's View of Reality and the Nature of Flaubert's Irony in 'Un Coeur Simple'," in *Studies in Short Fiction,* Vol. 7, No. 4, Fall, 1970, pp. 573-81.

Borge Gedso Madsen

In the following excerpt, Madsen asserts that Flaubert provides a realistic depiction of the setting, incidents, and characters of "A Simple Heart." Madsen concludes by relating Flaubert's pessimistic realism and objective tone to his use of irony.

"Un Coeur Simple," published in 1877 in *Trois Contes,* is a work of Flaubert's maturity. In this realistic *nouvelle* about the disappointments and bereavements of a self-sacrificing, simple-hearted servant girl from Normandy, Flaubert has certainly not given up the pessimism which found such bitter expressions in *Madame Bovary.* But, in spite of the inclusion in "Un Coeur Simple" of at least one very painful episode, and the general depressing effect of the gradual "running down" of Félicité's life, the overall impression which the reader gets from the short story is not exclusively one of bitterness. Perhaps the tone of the work may be tentatively described as one of sad serenity or ironic resignation. Flaubert views his simple-minded main character and her peculiar deity with some irony; but at the same time he is fond enough of her to include in his narrative scenes which are, as we shall see, almost tenderly conceived. This all-inclusiveness (Félicité is viewed with objective realism, with gentle irony, and with unsentimental compassion) lends to the work a richness and mature complexity which are impressive.

That "Un Coeur Simple" is a realistic piece of work there is no mistaking. In the first place, the *nouvelle* is realistically conceived due to the fact that Flaubert, as so often before, took models in actual life for some of his characters. [In his *Flaubert, l'homme et l'oeuvre,* 1932, René Dumesnil observes] that Félicité has traits from a *fille-mère* called Léonie who served in Trouville and also from "mademoiselle Julie," an old faithful servant who worked for the Flaubert family for years. Dumesnil likewise calls attention to the probability that the characters of the two children Paul and Virginie were modelled on Flaubert himself as a child and his sister Caroline. Like Virginie in "Un Coeur Simple," Caroline died young. Even the notorious parrot Loulou had models in real life; Flaubert borrowed specimens, both a live and a stuffed one.

The milieu (*le cadre*) of the short story is realistically depicted throughout, both in the wider sense (the descriptions of the scenery of Normandy) and in the narrower sense (the descriptions of the house of Madame Aubain with the room of Félicité). Flaubert gives more attention, however, to the immediate environment, *i.e.* the house of Madame Aubain, than to rural Norman landscapes. An obvious reason for this would seem to be that Félicité, as the most important character, "stays put" most of the time. She is first of all a *servante*; applying the sociological terminology of [Honore de] Balzac, we might say that in a sense her character is moulded partly by the house of Madame Aubain, and that she perhaps, in her turn, helps to form it—its atmosphere.

The characters in "Un Coeur Simple," including the minor ones, are all described in realistic terms, but, despite the inclusion of some rather unpleasant physical details of illness and disease, not in naturalistic ones. One does not find in "Un Coeur Simple" such starkly naturalistic touches as the description of *L'Aveugle* and the scene of the amputation of Hippolyte's leg in *Madame Bovary*. One should not, however, attempt to make too much of the difference of style between *Madame Bovary* and "Un Coeur Simple" (one is, after all, a full-length novel in several types of style, the other a *nouvelle*) but, perhaps, it is worth noting here that "Un Coeur Simple" does show considerable realistic unity and consistency of style and tone.

As it was indicated above, the characters of the short story are conceived in realistic, even deterministic terms with inclusion, as in the case of illness and death, of reasonably unpleasant physical details. We must learn about Félicité, not only after her arrival at Madame Aubain's house, but also about her childhood: the death of her father and mother, her childhood suffering and loneliness; her disappointing love "affair," which, in a sense, accounts for ("determines") her later desperate clinging to other people and animals. Her emotional

> " . . . The characters of the short story are conceived in realistic, even deterministic terms with inclusion, as in the case of illness and death, of reasonably unpleasant physical details."

(and sexual) life is thwarted in the beginning of the story by the loss of her only love, Théodore, and her parents; but her craving to love is in no way impaired.

When the characters fall ill and die (and many of them do) we get the amount of physical and medical detail which Gustave Flaubert, the son of Doctor Flaubert, believes that good realism calls for. In all justice it must be admitted, however, that Flaubert shows admirable restraint in his enumerations of the symptoms of the several ailments that his characters suffer from. Still we get our details. Suffice it to list just a few of the many examples. At the deathbed of Virginie, Madame Aubain " . . . poussait des hoquets d'agonie" [" . . . was choking with sobs of agony"]. The description of the dead Virginie goes like this: " . . . elle (Félicité) remarqua que la figure avait jauni, les lèvres bleuirent, le nez se pinçait, les yeux s'enfonçaient" [" . . . she noticed that the face had grown yellow, the lips turned blue, the nose was sharper, and the eyes sunk in"]. Even illness of the parrot is observed closely and the appropriate realistic details are given: "Il devint malade, ne pouvait plus parler ni manger. C'était sous sa langue une épaisseur, comme en ont les poules quelquefois. Elle le guérit, en arrachant cette pellicule avec ses ongles" ["He fell ill and could not talk or eat any longer. There was a growth under his tongue, such as fowls have sometimes. She cured him by tearing the pellicle off with her fingernails"]. The characters in "Un Coeur Simple" do not, however, have to fall ill for Flaubert to describe them in realistic terms. At times his descriptions hover between the realistic and the naturalistic (the line of demarcation between the two is, of course, vague). When, at the death of Virginie, Madame

Aubain breaks down and kisses Félicité, for the first and last time forgetting the difference in rank between mistress and servant, the reaction of Félicité is rendered in the following way: "Félicité lui en fut reconnaissante comme d'un bienfait, et désormais la chérit avec un *dévouement bestial* [my italics] et une vénération religieuse" [Félicité was as grateful as though she had received a favour, and cherished her mistress from that moment with the devotion of an animal and a religious worship"].

Worms, an unpleasantly realistic symbol of decay, play an important part in the narrative. Making a nostalgic survey of the dead Virginie's belongings, Madame Aubain and Félicité find a little hat, but ". . . il était tout mangé de vermine" ["it was eaten all over by moth"]. Nor does the sacred bird Loulou, or rather its physical incarnation, escape the ravages of earthly decay: "Bien qu'il ne fût pas un cadavre, les vers le dévoraient . . ." ["Loulou was not a corpse, but the worms devoured him. . ."].

Among the characters of "Un Coeur Simple" Félicité is, of course, of paramount importance; the other characters are merely sketched in by Flaubert. They only interest us in their relations with the servant girl. Madame Aubain is simply Félicité's mistress. Paul and Virginie are merely children that are loved by Félicité. The nephew, Victor, is a young man mothered and later mourned by Félicité. Le père Colmiche is an old sick derelict nursed by Félicité and later prayed for by her. And the parrot Loulou, though it has a birdlike personality of its own, only compels our attention because it is loved by Félicité and becomes her God.

The admirable full-length portrait of the simple soul Félicité offers ample illustration of Flaubert's psychological insight, of his ability to render plausible the naïve workings of a mind entirely different from his own. As the title of the *nouvelle* indicates, Félicité's predominating characteristic is simplicity, combined with a self-effacing devotion to the ones she loves. The following would be a brief summary of the chief components of her character: She is devoutly religious, virtuous, hard-working, economical, efficient, deeply devoted to her mistress and the latter's children, humble to the point of effacing herself. She is ignorant about "bookish" things and the information derived from study (note her ignorance about geography, for instance). She is a muddled thinker, easily confused by irrelevant considerations, all, however, dictated by her great

loyalty to others. Hurrying frantically to Virginie's deathbed, she is suddenly struck by the naïve, domestic fear that the house of Madame Aubain is left unprotected: "La cour n'était pas fermée! si des voleurs s'introduisaient?" ["The courtyard has not been shut up; supposing burglars got in!"] And so she forgets about Virginie for the moment and rushes back to protect the house, like a good servant.

Yet her simplicity is not absolute; it does not extend to the sphere of buying and selling. In bargaining with the tradesmen of Normandy, Félicité gives proof of the considerable practical astuteness of the Norman peasant. No butcher or grocer is going to cheat her! And invariably, when the tradesmen leave her, they are full of respect for her commercial talent and strength of will.

With regard to the realism of incident in "Un Coeur Simple," there is one episode which stands out from all the others in importance; it may almost be said to form the crux of the story. In the terrible scene of the deaf Félicité, on the road in front of the coach, struck down brutally by the whip of the driver, Flaubert focuses all the injustice and brutality that Félicité has suffered. Félicité's deafness and consequent failure to hear the approaching coach and get off the road in time is interpreted by the driver (understandably enough, perhaps, from his point of view, but otherwise, of course, quite erroneously) as spite or defiance; and so furiously he ". . . avec son grand fouet, lui cingla du ventre au chignon un tel coup qu'elle tomba sur le dos" ["gave her such a lash from waist to neck with his big whip that she fell on her back"]. And the coach, moving like "une trombe" ["a hurricane"] passes her by and leaves her bleeding and without understanding on the road. Continuing on her way toward Honfleur with the dead parrot, a little later she realizes the full impact of that terrible experience in a sort of delayed chain reaction in which, in a flash of stupefied insight, all her previous miseries are telescoped into one overwhelming feeling of unbearable pain and defeat: "Alors une faiblesse l'arrêta; et la misère de son enfance, la déception du premier amour, le départ de son neveu, la mort de Virginie, comme les flots d'une marée, revinrent à la fois, et, lui montant à la gorge, l'étouffaient" ["Then a faintness overtook her and she stopped; her wretched childhood, the disillusion of her first love, her nephew's going away, and Virginie's death all came back to her at once like the waves of an oncoming tide, rose to her throat, and choked her"]. This episode is an extremely pessimistic and a very moving one; but it is rendered with the utmost composure by Flaubert, without a trace of sentimentality. In many ways it reminds one of the fate of Hippolyte in *Madame Bovary*. Félicité and Hippolyte are both the helpless victims of the callous, indifferent brutality of the world which crushes them, moving like "une trombe." Félicité is defenseless, in the scene discussed above, because of her deafness which she cannot help, and Hippolyte loses his leg because he is the gullible victim of the "scientific" vanity of Homais and the easily aroused, headless ambition of Charles Bovary.

As it has been indicated above, the tone of the narrative in "Un Coeur Simple" is one of great detachment and objectivity. But some readers would undoubtedly get the impression that a mild irony *vis-à-vis* Félicité and her original metaphysics disengages itself, so to speak, at the end of the story. If irony it is, it is a kind irony, however, not a malicious one like the one Flaubert employs in his satirical account of Emma Bovary's education. . . . But, readers might argue, after all a *parrot* is a somewhat grotesque symbol of the Holy Ghost, and if you make your main character lie on her deathbed blissfully viewing the Holy Ghost in the open heavens in the shape of a gigantic parrot hovering over her head, you might at least *seem* to be implying, ironically and bitterly, that all religion is nothing but delusion. And yet, as we shall see presently, Flaubert's attitude toward this last scene is not mainly ironic.

It is not only the description of Félicité's last moments which is susceptible of an ironic interpretation. The realistic juxtaposition of Félicité's agony and the progression of the quaint religious procession in Madame Aubain's courtyard is presented with a baffling detachment which would unquestionably seem ironic in intent to many readers. The scene is reminiscent of Flaubert's description of "les Comices" in *Madame Bovary*. As in that scene we have a skilful blending of most discordant elements (the love talk between Emma and Rodolphe; the lowing of the cattle; the pompous speech of the official), so in "Un Coeur Simple" Flaubert, in a perfectly realistic way, with impassive composure, arranges somewhat incompatible objects on the *reposoir*: ". . . et des choses rares tiraient les yeux. Un sucrier de vermeil avait une couronne de violettes, des pendeloques en pierres d'Alençon brillaient sur de la mousse, deux écrans chinois montraient leurs paysages. Loulou, caché sous des roses, ne laissait voir que son front bleu, pareil à une plaque de lapis"

[". . . and some rare objects caught the eye. There was a silver-gilt sugar-basin with a crown of violets; pendants of Alençon stone glittered on the moss, and two Chinese screens displayed their landscapes. Loulou was hidden under roses, and showed nothing but his blue forehead, like a plaque of lapis lazuli"].

In conclusion one might ask the question: is "Un Coeur Simple" then, exclusively a bitter, pessimistic, ironic work? In his introduction to *Trois Contes* (Editions Variétés, Avant-Propos, p. 9) René Ristelhueber seems to think so; he observes: "A la fois bref et minutieux, ce récit, sans un rayon de soleil, a quelque chose de poignant et d'amer" ["At once brief and detailed, this tale, without a ray of sun, has a poignant and bitter quality"]. We cannot agree with that. Nor can we, on the other hand, agree with Dumesnil, who remarks in his book on Flaubert: "Dans l'oeuvre de Flaubert, empreinte d'un pessimisme altier, 'Un Coeur Simple' apparaît comme un repos, comme une détente" ["In Flaubert's works, stamped with a proud pessimism, 'A Simple Heart' appears as a rest, as a relaxation"].

It would seem that a more correct critique of "Un Coeur Simple" must try to take account of both of these extreme points of view. We have noted the pessimism of the *nouvelle*, especially in the description of the painful scene of Félicité struck down by the driver, and in the general, cumulatively depressing effect of the "running down" of her life. It has been well said that for many of Flaubert's characters "la vie est une réalité qui se défait" ["life is a reality that self-destructs"]; and certainly the life of Félicité is a case in point. We have likewise noted the possible, but if so, gentle, irony of Félicité's peculiar metaphysics. But we must not forget the title of the work; we must not forget that Félicité is indeed a simple soul. And this is where Flaubert adds tenderness to his pessimistic realism and objectivity. Of all the persons and things which Félicité loved, the only thing which life permits her to keep is the stuffed, worm-eaten parrot. But her humility and great capacity for love find that a more than acceptable object of affection. Since she is devoutly religious, to a simple soul like hers there is nothing strange or irreverent in the fact that the Holy Ghost and the stuffed parrot should merge in her imagination: the thing she loves most in heaven linked to the thing she loves most on earth. If we may be permitted to combine and paraphrase two of the sayings from the Sermon on the Mount, we could say, with Flaubert we believe: Blessed are the poor in spirit and pure in heart, for they shall see (their) God.

Source: Borge Gedso Madsen, "Realism, Irony, and Compassion in Flaubert's 'Un Coeur Simple'," in *The French Review,* Vol. XXVII, No. 4, February, 1954, pp. 253-58.

Sources

Brombert, Victor. "'Un Coeur simple': Tenderness and Irony." In *The Novels of Flaubert: A Study of Themes and Techniques*, Princeton University Press, 1966, pp. 233-45.

Sachs, Murray. "'A Simple Heart'." In *Reference Guide to Short Fiction,* St. James Press, 1994, pp. 899-900.

Starkie, Enid. *Flaubert the Master,* New York: Atheneum, 1971.

Further Reading

Steegmuller, Francis. Introduction to *Madame Bovary,* by Gustave Flaubert, The Modern Library, 1982.
    Steegmuller's comprehensive introduction is very helpful for comparison and contrast and for a general overview of Flaubert's work.

Spunk

Zora Neale Hurston
1925

"Spunk" was only the third short story Zora Neale Hurston published, and it was immediately successful. She had been encouraged to come to New York City by Charles S. Johnson, the editor of the National Urban League's influential magazine, *Opportunity: A Journal of Negro Life,* because Johnson had published her second story, "Drenched in Light," and recognized her talent. At Johnson's urging, Hurston entered "Spunk" in *Opportunity*'s 1925 literary contest and took second prize for fiction. (A play she submitted, *Color Struck,* took second prize for drama.) The story was published in the June 1925 issue of the magazine, and Hurston's career was launched. Later that year, the story was included in *The New Negro: An Interpretation,* an anthology of fiction, poetry, and essays edited by Alain Locke, a former philosophy professor of Hurston's at Howard University. The anthology became one of a handful of important and widely read collections of the Harlem Renaissance, demonstrating the best of the new writing coming out of black America.

The story takes place in a rural, all-black Southern town, much like Eatonville, Florida, where Hurston grew up. It is the story of a confident man who steals a weaker man's wife, and how the husband gets his revenge after death. Like many of Hurston's stories, it deals with the nature of marriage and with a struggle between a strong man and a weak one. Much of the story is told in dialogue, and the characters speak in a Southern African-

American dialect with rich, figurative language. Early critics of Hurston's work were divided on her use of this kind of language: some were delighted that she was celebrating the language she had heard first-hand, and others felt she was advancing her career by presenting demeaning black stereotypes to a white audience.

Author Biography

Zora Neale Hurston's short but dazzling career took her from poverty in rural Florida to the life of the literary elite in New York City and back again. She grew up in Eatonville, Florida, the first officially incorporated all-black township in the United States, and a town much like the one in which "Spunk" takes place. She was born on January 7, in a year that has never been verified but was probably 1901. Her father, John, was a Baptist minister and carpenter; her mother, Lucy Ann, was a former schoolteacher with a small sewing business. Lucy Ann died in 1904, and in 1915 Zora left home to work as a maid for a traveling theatre company.

She found her way to Maryland, where she worked as a waitress and completed high school, and then studied literature and philosophy at Howard University. She published her first short story, "John Redding Goes to Sea," in the university literary magazine. In 1925, at the height of the Harlem Renaissance, she moved to New York City with "$1.50, no job, no friends, and a lot of hope."

Hurston sought out and charmed the Harlem elite with her flamboyant personality, and soon achieved success as a writer. Her short story "Spunk" won second prize in *Opportunity Magazine*'s first literary contest, and was published in the June 1925 issue. The attention led to a scholarship to Barnard College, where she studied anthropology with the famous Franz Boas. She learned to appreciate and collect African-American folklore and, supported by a grant, traveled around the South gathering stories, work she would return to throughout her life.

Hurston was an eccentric, witty, and carefree woman, who lived for many years on gifts from wealthy white friends who found her entertaining and exasperating. With their support she carried on her folklore-collecting and her writing. During the 1930s she produced dozens of short stories, three novels, including the much-admired *Their Eyes Were Watching God* (1937), and two important

collections of folklore, all of which have attracted critical and popular praise. She was a sought-after lecturer at universities, and her short stories were published in the most important magazines of the day. However, as she explains in her autobiography, *Dust Tracks on a Road* (1942), she was never paid enough for her writing to support herself, as was the case for almost all black writers at the time.

Throughout her life, Hurston made a strong impression wherever she went—no one who knew her was neutral about her. She had two brief marriages, won and lost several close friends, and feuded publicly with other prominent African-Americans. Her writing tapered off during the 1940s, and she withdrew from society. By 1950 she had to take on domestic work to make ends meet. She died in a county welfare home in Florida on January 28, 1960, and was buried in an unmarked grave.

Plot Summary

Although there is a third person narrator who tells the story, the actions of the main characters in "Spunk" are interpreted mostly by the men who stand around commenting on what they see as they lounge about their village's one store. The narrator is detached, uninvolved in the action, but the men who speak have opinions about everything. As the story opens, a man and a woman walk arm-in-arm down the street of the village and into the brush. As the men watch the couple walk away, their gossiping makes it clear that the man is Spunk Banks, a "giant of a brown-skinned man" who is known in town and at the saw-mill for his bravery. The identity of the woman is not revealed until a small nervous man enters the store, and Elijah, one of the other men, begins to tease him. He is Joe Kanty, and the woman on Spunk's arm is Joe's wife, Lena. Shamed by Elijah's mockery, Joe takes out a razor and announces that he is going to confront Spunk and get his wife back. He leaves the store in pursuit of the couple, and the men continue to gossip. Elijah tells the story of Joe coming face to face with Spunk and Lena the week before and being too cowardly to act. Although Elijah's friend Walter thinks Spunk is too arrogant, the men all understand why Lena would prefer Spunk to the timid Joe. They are sure that Joe will not have the courage to attack, and that Spunk would never harm him anyway, because Spunk is the greater man.

But the men are wrong. Joe does come up behind Spunk and Lena with his razor, and Spunk shoots him dead. Calmly he tells everyone about the shooting, knowing that no one will challenge him—and no one does, even though he exaggerates the danger he was in, reporting that Joe ''come out there wid a meat axe an' made me kill him.'' Joe was a coward, he says, attacking from behind, and Spunk had no choice. After a swift trial he is set free and takes up again with Lena, who has been waiting for him with love in her eyes.

Soon after, word gets around that Spunk and Lena are about to marry. They have been living together in Lena's house, but Spunk has bought a new house and wants to marry Lena to restore her respectability. One night, as they are getting ready for bed, a black bobcat circles the house howling. Spunk gets his gun—the gun he used to kill Joe—but the animal looks right into his eyes, frightening him so he cannot shoot. Spunk, the man who is known for his fearlessness, is convinced that the bobcat is Joe, come back from Hell to keep him from marrying Lena. Walter, who has always been less admiring of Spunk than the others, believes that the animal probably is Joe, and comments that ''Joe wuz a braver man than Spunk.'' To the surprised Elijah, he explains that for Spunk to fight when he is naturally fearless takes little courage; but for Joe to confront Spunk in spite of his fear is a brave act. Whether the black bobcat (an animal never before seen in the area) really is Joe or not, from that night Spunk lives with fear. Even at the saw-mill, where he has always been able to do the most dangerous work, standing with perfect balance on logs as they move down the conveyor toward the saw, he trembles.

Finally, the inevitable happens. Spunk falls from a log into the saw and is fatally injured. Before he dies, he accuses Joe of having pushed him into the blade—pushed him from the back, like a coward. When Spunk is laid out for burial, the whole village comes to see him and to comfort Lena. As Lena wails loudly for the man she loved, the men drink and make coarse remarks while the women speculate about who will be Lena's next conquest.

Characters

Spunk Banks

The opening words of the story, ''A giant of a brown-skinned man,'' refer to the title character, Spunk Banks, a saw-mill worker with flashy clothes, a

Zora Neale Hurston

guitar, and a way with women. His size is matched by his self-confidence. Not only is he unafraid of the most dangerous jobs at the saw-mill—jobs that have killed other men—he has no hesitation about carrying on with another man's wife right in front of the man and all his friends. The other men treat Spunk with a mixture of respect and fear, and talk admiringly and grudgingly of his courage and quick temper, and of the .45 pistol he carries. Even when he calmly kills Joe, they do not dare challenge him. When Spunk decides to marry Lena, whom he has made a widow, Spunk gets his first taste of fear when confronted with a black bobcat, which he believes is Joe's spirit.

Joe Kanty

Joe Kanty is the opposite of Spunk Banks in every way. He is a small, round-shouldered man with ill-fitting clothes and a nervous disposition. When his wife, Lena, takes up with Spunk, Joe is unable to stand up for himself against Spunk's size and confidence. Even when he meets Spunk and Lena together, he will not or can not fight. Spunk humiliates Joe, and Lena is disgusted with her husband. Finally, Joe gathers his courage and goes after Spunk with a razor. Spunk shoots him dead. Most critics argue that the appearance of a black bobcat near the end of the story represents Joe's

Media Adaptations

- In 1990, playwright George C. Wolfe produced *Spunk,* a musical stage adaptation of three of Hurston's short stories. Although the title ''Spunk'' has come to be associated with the liveliness of Hurston's fiction, the story ''Spunk'' is not included in the program.

return from beyond the grave as he seeks revenge on Spunk.

Lena Kanty

Lena is a small, pretty woman who is married to Joe but in love with Spunk. She has been publicly carrying on with Spunk, seeming not to care about her husband's feelings. When Joe refuses to fight for her, she rejects him totally and walks away with Spunk, but not before asserting her power in a small way by refusing to accept a new house from her lover. She shows some fear when Spunk kills Joe, but she welcomes Spunk when his trial is over. Although she weeps loudly when Spunk is killed, the other women in the village know that she will get over him as quickly as she forgot about Joe.

'Lige

See Elijah Mosley

Elijah Mosley

Among the men lounging in the store when Spunk and Lena walk by is Elijah Mosley, whom his friends call 'Lige. He and the other men function as a kind of narrator, gossiping about what has happened at the mill, or on the street, or in someone's bed. When Joe enters the store, it is 'Lige who goads him with the truth about Lena's infidelity, and after Joe leaves 'Lige tells everyone else about the earlier encounter between Joe and Spunk. He is the first to know that Spunk and Lena plan to marry, and the first to know about the bobcat. Though his role in the action is small, Elijah reports and comments on the action, and he is the most admiring of

all the witnesses. His being first with every detail is a way of vicariously living the exciting life Spunk lives.

Walter Thomas

Elijah Mosley's constant companion in gossip sessions at the store is Walter Thomas, and the dialogue between the two of them makes up most of the story. Walter is always interested in Elijah's news, and is always willing to give opinions about Joe and Spunk and Lena, but he has more reservations about Spunk, and more admiration for Joe, than Elijah has.

Themes

Courage and Cowardice

The most important theme in ''Spunk'' is suggested by its title: since the nineteenth century, the word *spunk* has been slang for feistiness or liveliness. To say of someone, ''She's got spunk,'' is to say that she is spirited, unafraid. Spunk is not only the name of the central character of this story, it is his defining quality, the reason for his name (presumably a nickname). Elijah Mosley praises Spunk's bravery in the opening scene: ''But that's one thing Ah likes about Spunk Banks—he ain't skeered of nothin' on God's green footstool—*nothin*'! He rides that log down at saw-mill jus' like he struts 'round wid another man's wife—jus' don't give a kitty. When Tes Miller got cut to giblets on that circle-saw, Spunk steps right up and starts ridin'. The rest of us was skeered to go near it.'' With every step Spunk takes, every gesture he makes, he shows his confidence and bravery. He saunters, walks leisurely, and speaks in a carefree voice. To the men of the village, he is courage personified.

Immediately after Elijah finishes praising Spunk's actions at the sawmill, Joe Kanty walks into the store where the men are gathered. The contrast is dramatic: ''A round-shouldered figure in overalls much too large came nervously in the door, and the talking ceased.'' Joe has none of Spunk's confidence, even when the subject is his own wife, Lena, whom Spunk has stolen. He stands at the counter ''with his Adam's apple twitching nervously up and down his throat. One could actually *see* the pain he was suffering, his eyes, his face, his hands, and even the dejected slump of his shoulders.'' Where Spunk ''saunters'' and ''strolls,'' Joe ''stumbles'' and ''shambles'' and ''sneaks.'' Behind his back, Elijah tells about an encounter between Spunk and Joe the week before. Even when Spunk claimed Lena as his own, Joe could only mumble in reply, refusing to fight. The men agree that Joe is "timid 'bout fightin'," but disagree about whether that gives Spunk the right to carry on as he does.

Later, when Spunk has killed Joe, the men reassess their notions of bravery. Spunk, the man who "ain't skeered of nothin ," is now the nervous one, "so nervoused up he couldn't shoot" at the bobcat howling outside his window. Walter, who has had his reservations about Spunk all along, claims "he oughter be nervous after what he done," and startles the other men by announcing, "Know what Ah think? Joe wuz a braver man than Spunk." For Spunk to fight, he explains, did not take courage because Spunk has no natural fear, but for Joe to overcome his fear and fight the bigger man was an act of courage.

In the remaining few paragraphs of the story, Hurston presents several more images of fear. One of the men says of Spunk, "I'm skeered of dat man when he gits hot." Elijah hesitates to sit with Spunk's dead body because "Ah'm a li'l bit skittish." One of the men who comes to view the body is Joe's father, "who a few hours before would have been afraid to come within ten feet" of Spunk. None of these men has the courage Joe has finally found. As Walter puts it, "Joe's ready for Spunk an' ain't skeered any more."

Love and Passion

At the center of the conflict between Spunk and Joe is the "small pretty woman" Lena, whom they both love. The exaggerated notion of an "overwhelming passion" is often talked about in movies and stories, but in Joe's and Spunk's case, the description is accurate. Lena's love, and the threat of losing it, makes both men act out of character. Lena is the most important thing in Joe's life, and he sees in Spunk "the man that's got all he ever had. Y'all know Joe ain't never had nothin' nor wanted nothin' besides Lena." The prospect of losing her makes him, a small man with a razor, confront Spunk, a much larger man with a gun. One word for this kind of behavior is *brave,* but another is *crazy,* and Elijah uses this word for Spunk: "Spunk's crazy 'bout Lena." With Joe dead, Spunk is planning to marry Lena, although everyone knows he is the not "the marryin' kind." Thinking that Joe might be coming back as a bobcat to prevent the marriage, Spunk becomes a different, nervous, per-

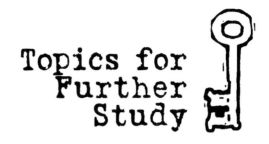

Topics for Further Study

- Find out what you can about how an old-fashioned saw-mill worked. What was the job Spunk was doing when he rode logs near the blade? What amount of steadiness and courage would be required to do this work?

- Investigate the role of the supernatural in African-American folk beliefs, perhaps in Hurston's own collections *Mules and Men* (1935) and *Tell My Horse* (1938). What stories might the townspeople in "Spunk" have heard that would bring them to the conclusion that the bobcat is truly Joe's spirit come back for revenge?

- Do you think "Spunk" is old-fashioned in terms of gender roles? Write a new version of the scene in which Joe confronts Spunk and Lena. Set your scene around the turn of the twenty-first century.

- Hurston has often been praised for having a good ear for the way people speak, and for writing it down accurately and respectfully. For a contrast, read aloud a short passage from "The Goophered Grapevine" (1887) by Charles Chesnutt, which many critics today find to be exaggerated rather than authentic. Do you agree with these critics? Try your hand at writing a short speech in the language you and your friends use. Try to capture the vocabulary, the interesting expressions, and the pronunciation of the way you speak.

son—a person like Joe used to be. Love makes these very different men crazy, and ultimately drives them to kill each other.

Lena also feels love strongly, but it does not overwhelm her. She does love Spunk, and even as her lover is publicly humiliating her husband, Lena looks at Spunk "with her eyes so full of love that they wuz runnin' over." But, like many of Hurston's female characters who seem to be consumed by love, she always holds something back, and when Spunk proposes to build her a new house she asserts her own power and refuses to leave the house that she owns herself. She will give up her love and her body, but she is clear-headed enough to look out for her security. She is not unfeeling: she weeps ''in a frightened manner'' when Joe is killed, and ''deep and loud'' when Spunk dies. But losing love does not destroy her. The viewing of Spunk's body takes place in Lena's house, and already the other women are wondering who will be ''Lena's next.''

Style

Point of View and Narration

''Spunk'' is structured as a series of stories within a story, and it has different levels of narration. At the heart of the story are Spunk, Joe, and Lena—the two men and the woman they both love. Of the three, Lena never speaks on-stage, although well over half of the story is told as direct speech. Joe speaks only once, and the words he says are his last on earth: ''Well, Ah'm goin' after her to-day. Ah'm goin' an' fetch her back. Spunk's done gone too fur.''

Spunk, the central character, speaks three lines, when he takes the other men to see Joe's body and announces calmly, ''Joe come out there wid a meat axe an' made me kill him.''

Most of the action of the story is related by Elijah, gossiping with Walter and the other men at the village store. For Elijah, Spunk's life is admirable, literally the stuff of legends. Elijah tells several stories: the story of Spunk's bravery when Tes Miller is killed at the saw-mill, the story of Joe's earlier confrontation with Spunk and Lena, the story of Spunk and the bobcat. Elijah is also the one who is nearby when Spunk falls into the saw blade and who hears his last words, and he tells that story as well.

Elijah clearly enjoys telling the stories, and tells them well. In fact, once he gets warmed up to a story and is certain of his audience's attention, he is fully capable of embellishing the truth to make the story more interesting. For the story of Joe's confrontation with Spunk, for example, Elijah first poses the idea as a question: ''Didn't he meet Spunk an' Lena face to face one day las' week an' mumble sumthin' to Spunk 'bout lettin' his wife alone?'' Once Walter shows an interest in the story, however, Elijah is able to come up with much more

information, including a detailed dialogue with long quotations from Spunk and Lena—a big step from ''mumbling something.'' Elijah never reveals any affection or consideration for Spunk, Joe, or Lena; they are simply material for his stories.

Tying Elijah's stories together is a third-person narrator who speaks the story's first and last lines but very few in between. The narrator describes actions briefly and gives insightful but unobtrusive analyses based on what can be seen, but does not reveal the inner lives of the characters and does not explain or interpret the story for the reader. Instead, the narrator sets the characters in motion and moves them to places where they can watch each other and talk to each other. The direct speech is memorable and vivid, while the narrator's sections are merely functional, like stage directions in a play.

Colloquialism

When Elijah and the other characters speak, it is in a rich Southern dialect full of folklore and figurative language. A central question in Hurston criticism has been her use of dialectic speech. Many critics have praised her for having a good ear for the way people speak, while others have faulted her for presenting caricatures of real speech that support the negative stereotypes her original white patrons had of African Americans. Whether the way Elijah speaks represents a stereotypical ignorant African American or simply an intelligent and witty rural Southerner may be in the eye of the beholder. In either case, when Hurston quotes Elijah and the others, she attempts to capture not only their characteristic turns of phrase, but their pronunciation as well, as in this line from Elijah: ''He rides that log down at saw-mill jus' like he struts 'round wid another man's wife—jus' don't give a kitty.''

The narrator, however, speaks in an educated, detached voice that could come from anywhere in the country. Instead of colorful phrases like ''don't give a kitty'' or ''passle of wile cats,'' the narrator refers to ''an air of nonchalance'' and ''coarse conjectures.'' The contrast is made startlingly clear in the first two sentences of the story: ''A giant of a brown-skinned man sauntered up the one street of the village and out into the palmetto thickets with a small pretty woman clinging lovingly to his arm. 'Looka theah, folkses!' cried Elijah Mosley, slapping his leg gleefully.'' Hurston's ability to draw as needed on her own two voices, as a rural Southerner and as a college-educated woman in New York City, is put to good use here, to make the different levels of narration clear and distinct.

Compare
&
Contrast

- **1887:** Eatonville was incorporated as an all-black, self-governing community. It provided residents an opportunity to live normal lives without daily struggles with racism. African-American culture thrived without competition.

  1990s: In America's "melting pot," many ethnic groups feel that their distinct cultures are being absorbed and erased because young people are exposed every day to many different cultural influences. Some neighborhoods and communities have established special classes, clubs, and charter schools to preserve and protect their cultural heritage.

- **1925:** Women in the United States had had the right to vote for only five years, and they had few rights in terms of marriage and divorce, employment protection, or property ownership. Most married women, with or without children, were not employed outside the home.

  1990s: Women have few legal impediments to full involvement in the political and economic life of the United States. Most childless women have employment outside their homes.

- **1920s:** Approximately one in nine marriages in the United States ended in divorce.

  1990s: Approximately one in two marriages in the United States ends in divorce.

- **1920s:** The area near Eatonville, Florida, the probable setting for "Spunk," was largely agricultural, with citrus fruit and timber at the center of the economy.

  1990s: Eatonville has been absorbed as a suburb within the Orlando Metropolitan Area, which also includes Walt Disney World. Although there are still farms producing citrus fruit and winter vegetables, the economy is driven by tourism and by the aerospace and electronics industries.

- **1920s:** It was almost impossible for African Americans to earn their living through writing. Publishers did not pay big advances to African-American writers and did not promote their books extensively, and books by African Americans did not tend to sell many copies. Exceptions included *Native Son* (1940) by Richard Wright, and poetry by Langston Hughes.

  1980s and 1990s: Several books by African Americans have become popular and critical successes, making their writers famous and wealthy. Toni Morrison received the Nobel Prize for Literature in 1993; her novel *Beloved* (1988) was awarded the Pulitzer prize. Alice Walker's *The Color Purple* (1983) also received the Pulitzer Prize. Other African-American women writers, including Gloria Naylor, Paule Marshall, Bebe Moore Campbell and Teri McMillan, have written books that were commercially successful and critically acclaimed.

Historical Context

The Harlem Renaissance

When Hurston arrived in New York City in 1925, it was to become a part an intellectual, literary, and artistic movement that came to be known as the Harlem Renaissance. Since the end of World War I, African Americans had been migrating to Harlem, a section of New York City, seeking jobs in the new industrial economy. Soon Harlem was one of the largest black communities in the United States, and it became a center for black intellectuals and artists. The movement was inspired by older, established black intellectuals, including W. E. B. DuBois, who had founded the National Association for the Advancement of Colored People (NAACP) in 1910, and who called for a new racial consciousness and cultural identity. Other mentors included Charles Johnson, editor of *Opportunity: A Journal of Negro Life,* and Alain Locke, who compiled the 1925 anthology of poetry, fiction, and essays called

The New Negro: An Interpretation, which some have called the Bible of the Harlem Renaissance. Throughout the 1920s, these men encouraged the next generation of African-American writers and artists to create new works that presented a realistic view of black life.

Answering the call were many talented and educated young people who were lured to exciting and sophisticated Harlem. During this decade, African-American culture was celebrated everywhere in New York City. Plays about African-American characters, with African-American casts, were produced in Harlem and on Broadway. The famous Cotton Club offered white audiences nightclub entertainment by the best black performers. African-American painters and musicians thrived. Writers, including Claude McKay, Countee Cullen, Langston Hughes, Jean Toomer, James Weldon Johnson, Arna Bontemps, Nella Larsen, and Hurston, produced stories and poems that presented African Americans with respect and pride. The movement faded away with the coming of the Great Depression in the 1930s, but the work it produced greatly influenced later generations of artists, especially during the 1960s and 1970s.

Black Aesthetics, White Patronage

The writers of the Harlem Renaissance were inspired by their own aesthetics and their own wish for self-expression. However, most of their books were published by white publishers for white readers intrigued by stories about African Americans, who seemed foreign and exotic. Some members of this white audience were genuinely interested in the new artists, while others were interested only because the African-American writers were the latest fad. But despite the obvious quality of their work, even the best black writers did not sell many copies of their books and could not command high advances from publishers. Hurston was not unique in being supported for most of her career by wealthy white patrons who gave her money outright or hired her for jobs that required little work; she simply could not earn enough from her writing to support herself. This necessity to appeal to white audiences caused some tension among the Harlem Renaissance writers. They were determined not to echo earlier writers like Charles Chesnutt, who flourished at the end of the nineteenth century and whose work seemed now to be trying too hard to appeal to white stereotypes about African Americans. While some of them hoped that their best writing would demonstrate to white Americans that African Americans

were their intellectual equals, they were determined not to consider white approval or disapproval too much, but to write chiefly for themselves.

Hurston's fiction, as well as her folklore collections, differed from many of the works written during the movement. She did not write about urban or ghetto life, but returned again and again in her writing to the rural life she had known in Eatonville, Florida. With a good ear for speech and dialect, she wrote lines for her characters that sounded the way she heard rural people speaking. Other Harlem Renaissance figures, including Langston Hughes, accused her of using the dialectic speech and the elements of folklore to denigrate her own people and to please whites, who expected unsophisticated language and behavior from African Americans. This controversy, and Hurston's flamboyant disrespect for the more serious and political intellectuals in the movement, contributed to Hurston's gradual withdrawal. By the early 1930s, as the movement itself was waning, she had returned to Florida.

Critical Overview

"Spunk" was received favorably from the very beginning, taking second place in the *Opportunity* literary contest, being published in the magazine, and then being selected for Alain Locke's anthology *The New Negro,* all within a few months. That first success led to others, and Hurston's work was well-regarded for the next fifteen years. Her novels were widely reviewed. Reviewers focused their attention on the local color aspects of the novels and debated whether her characters' dialectical speech was a strength or a weakness. Her autobiography, *Dust Tracks on a Road* (1942), won the Ainsfield Award in Racial Relations. However, she had no great commercial success, and although her works were widely reviewed, there was no serious scholarly criticism of her work during her lifetime. During the civil rights movement of the 1950s and 1960s, writings like "Spunk," depicting rural African Americans speaking in dialect and believing in folk superstitions, fell out of favor with African-American readers. They found the characters too unsophisticated, and associated folklore with the slavery and oppression they hoped to overcome. Hurston's reputation and sales dropped off, and when she died in obscurity in 1960 her works had gone out of print.

A decade later, Hurston and her work were rediscovered, largely through the efforts of poet

A black panther, much like the bobcat Spunk Banks believes is the spirit of Joe Kanty returned from the grave to seek revenge.

and novelist Alice Walker and biographer Robert Hemenway. Walker learned about Hurston through her interest in folklore, and then found in Hurston's fiction the literary foremother she had been seeking. She published an article in 1975 in *Ms.* magazine describing her search for Hurston's unmarked grave. Two years later, Hemenway's biography was published; the book's foreword, written by Walker, ends with this explanation for her efforts to revive Hurston's prominence: "We are a people. A people do not throw their geniuses away. And if they are thrown away, it is our duty as artists and as witnesses for the future to collect them again for the sake of our children, and, if necessary, bone by bone." Hurston's work did become important again, at first primarily to other African-American women and then to a wider readership. Publishers reissued Hurston's books and serious literary criticism began to appear. Hurston is now considered not only an important woman writer or African-American writer, but a major American writer. The Library of America has published two volumes of her work, one of fiction and one of folklore. The Zora Neale Hurston Literary Festival, held annually in Eatonville, Florida, draws large crowds. *Their Eyes Were Watching God* (1937), Hurston's most critically acclaimed book, has become a staple in college literature courses and is often cited as the first black feminist novel.

"Spunk" is widely anthologized in high school and college texts, and in collections of African-American stories, women's stories, and ghost stories. Yet it has attracted little critical attention of its own. Hurston's short stories were never collected and published in book form during her lifetime, so "Spunk" did not appear in print between 1925, when it was included in *The New Negro*, and 1985, when it became the title story in *Spunk: The Selected Short Stories of Zora Neale Hurston.* The story is mentioned in critical surveys written earlier than 1985, including Margaret Perry's *Silence to the Drums: A Survey of the Literature of the Harlem Renaissance* (1976) and Chidi Ikonn's *From Du Bois to Van Vechten: The Early New Negro Literature, 1903-1926* (1981). Both of these critics focus on what Perry calls the "folkloric strains" and Ikonn calls "verifiable folk beliefs." Referring back to the 1925 publications, both assume that their readers have not read the story and give little more than plot summary.

More recent critics have dealt with the story in more telling ways, trying to locate the source of its strength. In their introduction to *The Complete*

Stories, (1995), Henry Louis Gates, Jr., and Sieglinde Lemke point to the complexity of the story's structure, with its "three levels of narration: action (the two protagonists over Lena); judgment (the men watching them and reflecting); and the narrator's comments." Robert Bone's *Down Home: Origins of the Afro-American Short Story* (1988) praises Hurston's "imagination bound to a specific landscape: its people, its folkways, and its pungent idiom." Although Bone finds Hurston's short fiction to be "apprentice work," he finds in "Spunk" "something of the power that is generated by her best fiction."

While critics agree that "Spunk" explores in brief the themes developed more fully in *Their Eyes Were Watching God,* they do not agree about what the themes are. Gates and Lemke find in both stories the themes of "love, jealousy, guilt, superstition, and death," while Lillie P. Howard, author of the Twayne United States Authors volume on Hurston, finds the theme of "hubris punished." Interestingly, for Howard the *hubris* punished is not Spunk's alone. Lena is to blame for her failed marriage, and "she is made to suffer, though her punishment is mild when compared to that of the men. Lena Kanty loses both of the men in her life within a few days." Sam Cornish, reviewing the short stories in the 1985 volume for the *Christian Science Monitor,* is more sympathetic to Lena, seeing in her one of Hurston's young black women "caught between the beginning of the modern world and the oppressive, Victorian atmosphere of the nineteenth-century black and white America."

Criticism

Cynthia Bily

Bily is an instructor of English at Adrian College in Adrian, Michigan. In the following essay, she examines "Spunk" as a story about story-telling.

When Zora Neale Hurston was growing up in Eatonville, Florida, she was surrounded by people who did not value books as much as she did, but who carried within their heads great story collections from the African-American oral tradition. Skillful story-tellers could hold their listeners spellbound for hours, with tales that combined elements of African tradition, the history of slavery, and current events. In Eatonville, as she explains in the introduction to *Mules and Men* (1935), she compiled her first collection of folklore, as everyone knew the same stories. "From the earliest rocking of my cradle, I had known about the capers Brer Rabbit is apt to cut and what the Squinch Owl says from the house top. But it was fitting me like a tight chemise. I couldn't see it for wearing it. It was only when I was off in college, away from my native surroundings, that I could see myself like somebody else and stand off and look at my garment. Then I had to have the spy-glass of Anthropology to look through at that."

Although she had not yet acquired "the spy-glass of Anthropology" when she wrote "Spunk," Hurston already recognized what those stories could provide for a fiction writer. She had always loved hearing the men tell tall tales, and she expected her readers would, too. In *Mules and Men* she remembers a scene of Eatonville that closely resembles scenes of Elijah, Walter and the others in "Spunk": "As early as I could remember it was the habit of the men folks particularly to gather on the store porch of evenings and swap stories." In her autobiography, *Dust Tracks on a Road* (1942), she recalls the scene in greater detail: "Men sat around the store on boxes and benches and passed this world and the next one through their mouths. The right and the wrong, the who, when and why was passed on, and nobody doubted the conclusions. There were no discreet nuances of life on Joe Clarke's porch."

For the men of Eatonville, as for Elijah and Walter, story-telling was an important source of entertainment and a way of processing information about their community. In writing "Spunk," Hurston dealt with issues of courage and love, but on another level she created a story that is itself about the art of story-telling.

"Spunk" is told by a third-person narrator who has no special information about the characters' motivations and feelings, but who is a sharp-eyed and sharp-tongued witness to the events. The narrator, who has the vocabulary and sentence structure of the college-educated Hurston, speaks the first line of the story: "A giant of a brown-skinned man sauntered up the one street of the village and out into the palmetto thickets with a small pretty woman clinging lovingly to his arm." Observations like the fact that Spunk "sauntered" or that Lena clings "lovingly" are typical of this insightful narrator, who also notes that the men in the store try to watch the couple "with an air of nonchalance, but with small success." Nearly everything the narrator says is based on observation of actions and speech, but

What Do I Read Next?

- "The Gilded Six-Bits" (1933), one of Hurston's most popular and well-known stories. Set in Eatonville, it tells of the marriage of Missie May and Joe Banks, and how it is almost destroyed by the lure of wealth.

- *Dust Tracks on a Road* (1942) is Zora Neale Hurston's autobiography. Its early chapters focus on Hurston's early life in Eatonville, Florida, an all-black township that resembles the setting of "Spunk." This telling of her life is as entertaining as it is unreliable—several important facts, including her age and her contributions, are distorted by a writer who was more interested in writing a commercial success than in revealing herself.

- *Their Eyes Were Watching God* (1937), today considered Hurston's masterpiece. The novel begins and ends in Eatonville, Florida, where Janie Crawford struggles to find contentment. After loving and losing three men, she discovers that the key to happiness lies within herself.

- "What White Publishers Won't Print," original-ly published in *Negro Digest* in 1950 and collected in *I Love Myself When I Am Laughing: A Zora Neale Hurston Reader* (1979). Near the end of her career, Hurston laments the difficulties she and other members of ethnic minorities have faced in getting major publishers to publish and promote their stories.

- *A Treasury of Afro-American Folklore: The Oral Literature, Traditions, Recollections, Legends, Tales, Songs, Religious Beliefs, Customs, Sayings, and Humor of Peoples of African Descent in the Americas,* (1976), edited by Harold Courlander, the author and editor of dozens of books of folklore. This volume presents the oral traditions of more than two dozen African-American cultures, and includes maps, photographs and musical scores.

- *Colored People: A Memoir* (1994) by Henry Louis Gates, Jr. Gates remembers growing up in an all-black community in Piedmont, West Virginia, in the 1950s and 1960s, and the "sort of segregated peace" his family enjoyed there.

---

this narrator does not miss the clues in behavior that reveal human character, particularly human frailty.

When Joe Kanty comes into the store, the narrator gives the reader a brief lesson in how much can be learned about people just by watching them. The reader is walked through the interpretation, and the clues that lead up to it: "One could actually *see* the pain he was suffering, his eyes, his face, his hands and even the dejected slump of his shoulders. He set the bottle down upon the counter. He didn't bang it, just eased it out of his hand silently and fiddled with his suspender buckle."

Look carefully at gestures and mannerisms, the narrator seems to say, and you can see into the human heart. A few lines later, the narrator gives another small detail about Joe, and challenges the reader to interpret it correctly. Joe "reached deep down into his trouser pocket and drew out a hollow ground razor, large and shiny, and passed his moistened thumb back and forth over the edge."

This time, it is Elijah who attempts to interpret the action, and he gets it wrong. The narrator's skill at interpreting human behavior contrasts with the lesser skills of the men of the village, particularly Elijah's. He spends his time watching and eavesdropping and gossiping, and more than half of the story is made up of direct speech by the men, who analyze the story of Spunk, Joe and Lena as it unfolds. Very little of the action of the story happens on-stage, in front of the reader. Joe's first confrontation with Spunk is described by Elijah, and his second is described by Spunk and summarized by the narrator. Spunk's bravery at the sawmill, his desire to marry Lena, his fear of the bobcat,

> In 'Spunk' Hurston
> examines the stories men tell
> and finds them unreliable
> and amusing. She uses the
> narrator to point out the
> unreliability of the men's
> version of life in the
> village, and casually
> mentions that the women, who
> 'wondered who would be Lena's
> next,' are better
> interpreters."

and his horrible death are all stories that Elijah brings to Walter and the others.

But unlike the third-person narrator, Elijah-as-narrator is unreliable. Elijah tells a good story, but he is not interested in being a good judge of character or, to put it another way, of his characters. He watches Joe rub his thumb over the razor, but reads the gesture incorrectly. His prediction is that ''He makes that break outa heah to bluff us. He's gonna hide that razor behind the first palmetto root an' sneak back home to bed. Don't tell me nothin' bout that rabbit-foot colored man.''

Of course, he is wrong about what Joe means to do, just as he is wrong about how Spunk will react: ''He might turn him up an' spank him fur gettin' in the way, but Spunk wouldn't shoot no unarmed man.'' Elijah carries on the tradition of the men on the porch in Eatonville and throughout the South. In that tradition, it is not as important to be accurate as it is to be interesting, as Hurston recalls in *Mules and Men*: ''The very next afternoon, as usual, the gregarious part of the town's population gathered on the store porch.... 'Zora,' George Thomas informed me, 'you come to de right place if lies is what you want. Ah'm gointer lie up a nation....' 'Now you gointer hear lies above suspicion,' Gene added.''

Elijah does not try hard to conceal the fact that he makes things up as he goes along. He begins a

typical story with a question, to see whether anyone else has information about the subject: ''Didn't he meet Spunk an' Lena face to face one day las' week an' mumble sumthin' to Spunk about lettin' his wife alone?'' The other men have not heard this one before. Walter asks, ''What did Spunk say?'' and Elijah the story-teller is off again. His story of the encounter is told in rich detail, with long quotations from a conversation that he cannot have actually heard, much less remembered word-for-word. It is easy to see what makes Elijah a good story-teller. He sprinkles his narration with colorful phrases describing ''a passle of wile cats'' and an Adam's apple ''galloping up and down his neck like a race horse.'' His characters speak lines like ''Lena, ain't I yo' husband?'' and ''Lena, youse mine''—lines out of a story. Elijah ends his tale sure that he is right about Joe: ''I'm jus' waiting to see whut he's goin' to say when he gits back.'' Although he is frequently wrong about his interpretations, the men hang on his every word. They would not care to have facts get in the way of a good story.

The narrator steps back to the foreground to open the second of the four parts of ''Spunk,'' to inform the reader that Elijah's stories were inaccurate, that ''Joe Kanty never came back, never.'' This is immediately followed by Spunk's short and inaccurate account of what happened in the thicket: ''Joe come out there wid a meat axe an' made me kill him.'' The men know he is lying, but say nothing. Spunk's account is just another story. At the store later on, ''they all talked of locking him up until the sheriff should come from Orlando, but no one did anything but talk.''

In the third section, Elijah tells tales again, this time about Spunk ''gittin' ready to marry Lena,'' and about the bobcat that has made Spunk fearful. Significantly, Spunk seems to desire marriage, although he is not ''the marryin' kind,'' because he wants to keep Lena from becoming the material for more stories. Elijah explains, ''He don't want folks to keep on talkin' about her—thass the reason he's rushin' so.'' In this section, Walter and the other men do most of the talking, and they seem to be better interpreters than Elijah is. Walter understands the ways in which Joe was brave, and another ''one of the men'' picks up on the important detail of Spunk wobbling on the saw. Unlike Elijah, who thought Joe has nothing to fear from Spunk, this man reports, ''I'm skeered of dat man when he gits hot. He'd beat you full of button holes as quick as he's look atcher.''

When Spunk is killed, the stories stop for a while. The narrator speaks first in section four, reporting, ''The men gathered the next evening in a different mood, no laughter. No badinage this time.'' Using the word *badinage* instead of the simpler *banter* or *repartee,* the narrator draws a clear line separating the narrator's voice from the men's, and a clear distinction between the narrator's reliable reporting and the men's unreliable stories. Elijah tells one last story—the tale of Spunk's last moments of life. He sets this story apart from all the others by telling it simply, with no apparent embellishment, and by telling it away from his usual stage: ''Elijah did not answer until they had left the lighted store and were strolling down the dark street.'' Perhaps he realizes that this story is too important for ''lying,'' or perhaps this is the first story in which he has truly cared about the characters. During the wake, the stories stop. But by the time of the funeral, the men are back to their traditional way of communicating, whispering ''coarse conjectures between guzzles of whiskey.''

In ''Spunk'' Hurston examines the stories men tell and finds them unreliable and amusing. She uses the narrator to point out the unreliability of the men's version of life in the village, and casually mentions that the women, who ''wondered who would be Lena's next,'' are better interpreters. Do the unreliable stories kill Joe and Spunk? Some of the men in the crowd seem to think so, and they glare at Elijah ''accusingly'' when Joe is shot. Years after she wrote ''Spunk,'' when Hurston had equipped herself with ''the spy-glass of Anthropology,'' she learned to value the folk tales and ''lying sessions'' of Eatonville in a new way. It would be interesting to ask her how Elijah, Walter, and the narrator of ''Spunk'' would look under that spy-glass.

Source: Cynthia Bily, Overview of ''Spunk,'' for *Short Stories for Students*, The Gale Group, 1999.

Valerie Traub

In the following excerpt, Traub asserts that ''Spunk'' offers a new perspective on Shakespeare's Hamlet. *Traub argues that, similar to Lena, Gertrude exercises personal prerogative when finding herself defined as ''an object of property.''*

... African-American women writers' return to Shakespearian drama is hardly surprising, for what more obviously status-studded example of Anglo-European patriarchal culture exists to ''signify'' or ''trope'' upon? I will first briefly discuss the way in which Hurston's short story ''Spunk'' rewrites, by means of a few words, Gertrude's marriage to Hamlet's uncle, transforming an action that in Hamlet's mind is equated with adultery and incest into the personal prerogative of any woman who finds herself defined as an object of property. I will then turn in considerably more detail to Gloria Naylor's complex, ambivalent relationship to Shakespeare, and her attempt in *Mama Day* to voice African-American subjectives within the problematic described and enacted by Caliban.

> ''Thass mah house,'' Lena speaks up. ''Papa gimme that.''
>
> ''Well,'' says Spunk, ''doan give up whut's yours, but when youse inside don't forgit youse mine, an' let no other man git outa his place wid you!''

''Spunk'' depicts a struggle among men over ''women-as-property'' that continues even after the men's deaths. ''Cuckolded'' and eventually killed by his wife's lover, Joe returns from the grave for revenge: he pushes his usurper, Spunk, into the blades of a massive saw at the community lumber mill. Yet, inserted within this narrative, working *within* the logic of patriarchal discourse to subvert it, is an unnamed force, conjured up in the final sentences of the story: ''The women ate heartily of the funeral baked meats and wondered who would be Lena's next. The men whispered coarse conjectures between guzzles of whiskey.'' Women heartily consuming funeral baked meats—meats prepared in remembrance of the dismembered Spunk—extends Lena's individual erotic power to a community of women: they too are metaphorically figured as powerfully devouring erotic agents.

In this light, Lena's earlier assertion of property rights, ''thass mah house''—although immediately assimilated by Spunk into his own logic of patriarchal possession (''when youse inside don't forgit youse mine'')—*prefigures* the subversion of the meaning of property and possession by precisely the female erotic power that such symbolic enclosures are meant to contain. Having moved in to Spunk's house after Joe's death, Lena is, at Spunk's death, possessed of house and of herself as sexual object. The trajectory of erotic power within the narrative transforms Lena from male-possessed object to self-possessed subject. By the end of the story, the meaning of the title ''Spunk'' has been transferred and transfigured from male patronymic to Lena's ''spunky'' assertion of erotic power.

The sly reference in ''Spunk'' to funeral baked meats echoes Hamlet's cynical retort to Horatio's admission that the queen's marriage ''followed

> ''Spunk' depicts a struggle among men over 'women-as-property' that continues even after the men's deaths."

hard upon'' the king's funeral: ''Thrift, thrift, Horatio! The funeral bak'd meats / Did coldly furnish forth the marriage tables'' (*Hamlet* 1.2.80-81). Why does ''Spunk'' invoke, through this reference, Shakespeare's play? To call attention, I would argue, to its implicit revision of *Hamlet*'s vilification of female desire. Gertrude's ''adulterous'' marriage becomes newly figured as an exchange fatal to any man who treats woman as his object of property. As in *Hamlet* the men in *Spunk* violently destroy each other, with women's bodies serving as the psychic battleground upon which masculine subjectivity asserts itself or founders; but unlike Gertrude or Ophelia (the woman upon whom Hamlet's anxieties about his mother are projected), Lena is not positioned as the sacrificial victim to male heroism—instead, possessed of self and property, a heroic figure in her own right, she moves on. Even as the men seek to contain Lena's ''predatory'' sexuality between their ''guzzles of whiskey,'' it has, by means of their ''coarse conjectures'' and the women's silent musings, already slipped off the page. Already presumed to be elsewhere, Lena's erotic agency is in excess of what can be said or contained within a patriarchal frame.

Source: Valerie Traub, ''Rainbows of Darkness: Deconstructing Shakespeare in the Work of Gloria Naylor and Zora Neale Hurston,'' in *Cross-Cultural Performances: Differences in Women's Re-Visions of Shakespeare,* edited by Marianne Novy, University of Illinois Press, 1993, pp. 150-64.

Lillie P. Howard

In the following excerpt, Howard discusses the manner in which Hurston explores the issue of marriage in ''Spunk.''

Now that the literary buffs are enthusiastically discovering or rediscovering Zora Neale Hurston (1903-1960), a black woman novelist and folklorist who, like many of her black contemporaries, failed to realize the bright promise of the Harlem Renaissance, a critical look at certain aspects of her fiction may be in order. During her lifetime, much of Hurston's erratic and short-lived fame rested on the publication of her two books of folklore, *Mules and Men* (1935) and *Tell My Horse* (1938), though she also published short stories, plays, essays, four novels—*Jonah's Gourd Vine* (1934), *Their Eyes Were Watching God* (1937), *Moses, Man of the Mountain* (1939), *Seraph on the Suwanee* (1948)—and an autobiography, *Dust Tracks on a Road* (1942). Part of her relative obscurity can be attributed to ill-founded criticism like that of Richard Wright who, in his review of *Their Eyes Were Watching God,* charged Hurston with being unconcerned with the race or class struggle or with the revolutionary traditions of black people in America. Today's readers, having found that Hurston's works deal not only with black problems, but with problems common to all human beings, are puzzled by Wright's charges. Though her fictional landscape differs radically from Wright's her works clearly convey the idea that people, regardless of their color or their peculiar burdens, must inevitably struggle with some of the same life problems. Although several of life's problems interested Hurston, she seemed particularly interested in the problems that beset the state of marriage.

Critics have agreed that a writer's system of values can be determined by a close reading of that writer's works. We can normally determine what qualities an author admires or detests in a character, for instance, by how that writer makes us feel about that character. We can also determine how an author values a character by what he/she allows to happen to that character. Hoyt Trowbridge uses this process to determine that Jane Austen values intelligence, morality, feeling, beauty, and worldly condition (rank and fortune) in her characters. We can use the same procedure to determine what qualities Zora Neale Hurston who, like Austen, confined her studies to small, country villages, considered essential to a good marriage—what qualities she valued in the marriage partners and what qualities she detested.

The marriage relationship and the problems that emanate therefrom are themes in four of Hurston's short stories and in three of her novels. Instead of portraying marriage romantically—all cape jasmine bushes and sweet potatoes—however, Hurston presents it frankly, replete with infidelity, jealousy, violence, and hatred. Of the eleven marriages in the seven works, only three succeed. By looking closely at these three, we can reasonably conclude that Hurston considered courage, honesty, love, trust, respect, understanding, and a willingness to work together essential to a successful marriage. By looking closely at the unsuccessful marriages, we can see that for those who did not subscribe wholeheartedly to Hurston's formula, the consequences could be disastrous.

"Spunk," published in *Opportunity* in June, 1925, is one of the unsuccessful ones. Told in Poe-like fashion, the story examines infidelity, jealousy, violence, and hatred. It is set in an all-black community in Florida where Spunk Banks, Joe and Lena Kanty form a love triangle. Banks, an audacious character who "ain't skeered of nothin' on God's green footstool," woos Lena from her husband and parades around town with her on his arm. Kanty, the weak, cuckolded husband, is shamed and spurred by town gossip to confront Banks and demand his wife back. When he foolishly does so with a mere pocket knife he is killed by Banks. When Banks prepares to marry Lena a few days after Joe's death, he is mysteriously troubled by his conscience. He sees a black bobcat that "walked round and round that house and howled like forty," which he cannot shoot, and he imagines that someone is pushing him into an electric saw at work. Before very long, he is mysteriously caught in the saw—pushed by Joe, he swears—and killed.

Because Joe and Lena Kanty are relatively flat characters and because the narrator is rather closed-lipped, the reader is not privy to information that would explain how the Kanty marriage came to its present state. He does know, however, that Lena is taken with Banks because of his spunk—his determination to conquer and reign over the world—a blatant contrast to Joe's lack of prowess. Too, the reader gets some indication of how he is to feel about the characters by the way each character is portrayed. Spunk Banks, for instance, is described as "A giant of a brown skinned man ..." who "ain't skeered of nothin' on God's green footstool—nothin'! He rides that log down at the sawmill jus' like he struts 'round wid another man's wife—jus' don't give a kitty." He is that kind of man who would "go after *anything* he wanted" and he tells Lena that "Youse mine. From now on Ah works for you an' fights for you an' Ah never wants you to look to nobody for a crumb of bread, a stitch of close or a shingle to go over yo' head, but *me* as long as Ah live." Spunk is clearly a man's man, an absolute necessity in the Hurston world. After he kills Joe, however, he loses some of his spunk, too much to remain one of the chosen. Not only is he so

> "Lena is taken with Banks because of his spunk--his determination to conquer and reign over the world--a blatant contrast to Joe's lack of prowess."

"nervoused up" that he can't shoot the black bob-cat but he believes that the cat is Joe "done sneaked back from Hell!" At work, where he had always reigned supreme, he is now "cussin a blue streak 'cause he 'lowed dat saw wuz wobblin'—almos' got 'im once . . . claimed somebody pushed 'im but 'twant nobody close to 'im." Later, when he is indeed caught in the saw, he claims that "he pushed me—the dirty hound pushed me in the back! . . . It was Joe—the dirty sneak shoved me . . . he didn't dare come to mah face . . . but Ah'll git the son-of-a-wood louse soon's Ah get there an' make hell too hot for him . . . Ah felt him shove me. . . .''

Curiously, as Spunk declines in manliness, Joe Kanty increases in it. While Banks had been a "giant of a brown skinned man," Kanty had simply been a "round shouldered figure in overalls much too large." And while Banks "sauntered up the one street of the Village," Kanty "came nervously in the door" of the local store. After seeing his wife clinging to Banks's arm, Joe "swallowed several times painfully and his lips trembled. . . . He stood there silent with his Adam's apple twitching nervously up and down in his throat. One could actually see the pain he was suffering, his eyes, his face, his hands even the dejected slump in his shoulders." One of the townsmen refers to him as that "rabbit-footed colored man" and another says that he's "timid 'bout fightin'." While Banks loudly proclaims Lena as his, Kanty "sorter whines out 'Lena ain't I yo' husband?''" When Joe does challenge Spunk, he sneaks up and tries to stab him in the back. Clearly there is no comparison between the two.

After Joe is dead, however, one of the townsmen wonders if Joe wasn't a braver man than Spunk:

> Lookit whut he done; took a razor an' went out to fight a man he knowed toted a gun an' wuz a crack shot, too. 'Nother thing Joe wuz skeered of Spunk, scared

plumb stiff! But he went jes' the same. It took him a long time to get his nerve up. 'Tain't nothin' for Spunk to fight when he ain't skeered of nothin'.

And when Banks is killed, the same man says: "If spirits kin fight, there's a powerful tussle goin' on somewhere ovah Jordan 'cause Ah b'leeve Joe's ready for Spunk an' ain't skeered anymore—yas, Ah, b'leeve Joe pushed 'im mahself." Obviously, it is easier to attribute qualities of strength and bravery to Joe Kanty when he is not around, swallowing, slumping, and trembling, to refute the claims. Ironically, both men are quickly forgotten. At Spunk's wake, "The women ate heartily of the funeral baked meats and wondered who would be Lena's next. The men whispered hoarse conjectures between guzzles of whiskey."

By Hurston standards, Joe Kanty is not a MAN; he's one of those puny characters who are more of a nuisance than anything else. Although Banks is a MAN, on the other hand, he is a wrongheaded one, the tragic hero with too much hubris who, by imposing his will upon others (the whole town is frightened of him) without proper regard for their feelings, brings about his own downfall. Too, after Banks kills Kanty, he loses his spunk and thus becomes less than a man. At this point, he would not make an ideal spouse. Lena Kanty does not go unpunished for where she once had two men, she now has none. She at least remains to try again, however. A good marriage for her still remains a distinct possibility.

Source: Lillie P. Howard, "Marriage: Zora Neale Hurston's System of Values," in *CLA Journal,* Vol. XXI, No. 2, December, 1977, pp. 256-68.

Sources

Bone, Robert. "Zora Hurston." In *Down Home: Origins of the Afro-American Short Story,* New York: Columbia University Press, 1988, pp. 144-5.

Cornish, Sam. "Hurston's Tales Illuminate Rural Black Culture." *Christian Science Monitor,* May 31, 1985, p. 23.

Gates, Henry Louis, Jr., and Sieglinde Lemke. Introduction to *The Complete Stories* by Zora Neale Hurston, New York: HarperCollins, 1995, pp. xiv-xv.

Howard, Lillie P. *Zora Neale Hurston,* New York: Twayne, 1980, pp. 64, 71.

Hurston, Zora Neale. *Dust Tracks on a Road,* New York: Arno, 1969, pp. 69-70.

Hurston, Zora Neale. *Mules and Men,* New York: Harper & Row, 1990, pp. 2, 19.

Ikonn‚, Chidi. "Zora Neale Hurston." In *From Du Bois to Van Vechten: The Early New Negro Literature, 1903-1926,* Westport, Conn.: Greenwood Press, 1981, pp. 184-85.

Perry, Margaret. "The Short Story." In *Silence to the Drums: A Survey of the Literature of the Harlem Renaissance,* Westport, Conn.: Greenwood Press, 1976, p. 123.

Walker, Alice. Foreword to *Zora Neale Hurston: A Literary Biography* by Robert Hemenway, University of Illinois Press, 1977, p. xviii.

Further Reading

Davis, Rose Parkman. *Zora Neale Hurston: An Annotated Bibliography and Reference Guide,* Westport, Conn.: Greenwood Press, 1997.
  Compiled by a librarian, this is an exhaustive annotated guide to books, dissertations, articles, chapters, book reviews, children's books and web sites dealing with Hurston's life and work.

Giovanni, Nikki, editor. *Shimmy Shimmy Shimmy Like My Sister Kate: Looking at the Harlem Renaissance Through Poems,* New York: Henry Holt, 1996.
  A highly praised anthology of poetry from Langston Hughes, Richard Wright, Countee Cullen, Gwendolyn Brooks and others, interspersed with Giovanni's perceptive commentary on the poems, history, and biography.

Hemenway, Robert E. *Zora Neale Hurston: A Literary Biography,* University of Illinois Press, 1977.
  The first full-length biography, based on original manuscripts and letters, as well as interviews with Hurston's friends and colleagues. Hemenway is frank about gaps in his research and questions that still need definitive answers.

Howard, Lillie P. *Zora Neale Hurston,* New York: Twayne, 1980.
  A solid overview for the general reader to Hurston's life and work, with chronology, index, and a no-longer-current annotated bibliography.

Walker, Alice. "Looking for Zora." In *In Search of Our Mother's Gardens,* New York: Harcourt Brace Jovanovich, 1984, pp. 93-116. Originally "In Search of Zora Neale Hurston." *Ms. Magazine,* March, 1975, pp. 74-79, 85-89.
  The story of how Alice Walker, searching for her heritage as a writer, located the approximate location of Hurston's unmarked grave and purchased a headstone for it.

Witcover, Paul. *Zora Neale Hurston,* New York: Chelsea House, 1991.
  A richly illustrated biography for young adults, which gives a fascinating look at life during the Harlem Renaissance.

Swimming Lessons

Rohinton Mistry

1987

"Swimming Lessons" is the last story in the collection of short fiction that first brought Rohinton Mistry national attention in Canada and subsequently the United States. The set of eleven stories titled *Tales from Firozsha Baag* [retitled *Swimming Lessons and Other Stories from Firozsha Baag* when it was published in 1989 in the United States] was well received by critics in both countries. As "Swimming Lessons" is positioned as the last story in the collection, it has prompted many reviewers to give it particular attention. An important feature of the story is that its setting moves with the narrator from Bombay to Toronto and allows Mistry to draw deft parallels between the lives of the residents of apartment complexes in both of these crowded, multicultural urban settings. It also gives him an opportunity to explore the writer's uses of memory and events of his past life using the commentary of the narrator's parents, who discuss the manuscript he sends them after living several years in Toronto. While the other stories in the collection focus on the lives, foibles, and crises of the Parsi community in the Bombay housing complex called Firozsha Baag, "Swimming Lessons" shifts the focus to issues of the loneliness, racism, and cultural adjustment of Mistry's Indian immigrant protagonist, a not so thinly veiled autobiographical character. While the two settings are literally worlds apart, the characters of "Swimming Lessons" in the end seem almost comfortably similar to their Indian counterparts in their sad, petty, and often humorous attempts to find

dignity and human connection in the isolating circumstances of modern urban apartment living.

Author Biography

Rohinton Mistry was born in 1952 in Bombay, India's largest city and the most densely populated place in the world. He grew up as a member of Bombay's middle class Parsi community. His father, Behram Mistry, worked in advertising and his mother, Freny Mistry, was a housewife. He obtained a British-style education at the University of Bombay, studying mathematics and economics and receiving a Bachelor of Science degree in 1975. He then married Freny Elavia, a teacher, and immigrated to Canada, settling in Toronto. He worked as a banker to support himself while taking night courses at the University of Toronto and completed a second baccalaureate degree in 1984, majoring in literature and philosophy.

During this period, Mistry became interested in writing. He studied with Mavis Gallant, a writer-in-residence in Toronto's English Department, and won first prize in a short story contest the university inaugurated in 1983. He won this contest again in 1984 and added two Hart House literary prizes and *Canadian Fiction Magazine*'s annual Contributor's Prize to his list of accolades in 1985. He published in numerous literary magazines and was one of the new fiction writers featured in the 1986 volume *Coming Attractions, 4,* published in Ottawa by Oberon Press. The next year, Penguin/Canada published a collection of eleven of Mistry's stories titled *Tales from Firozsha Baag,* which the American publisher Houghton Mifflin picked up in 1989 and retitled *Swimming Lessons and Other Stories from Firozsha Baag.*

This collection, the final episode of which is "Swimming Lessons," centers around an apartment building in Bombay and showcases Mistry's talent for sketching subtle, sympathetic, and often funny character studies of the tenants of the housing complex. It has received positive attention from reviewers, who have praised Mistry's ability to evoke the atmosphere of the Bombay Parsi community and his skill in narrating his stories with wit and compassion.

In 1991 he published his first full-length work, a novel entitled *Such a Long Journey,* which won the Governor General's Award for Canadian fiction

and the Commonwealth Writers Prize. Set in the early 1970s during the creation of Bangladesh from the former East Pakistan, it concerns an upper class Bombay man named Gustad Noble, who is drawn into the politics of this struggle and becomes unhappily involved with Indira Gandhi's government. It was shortlisted (nominated and noted but not chosen) for the prestigious Booker Prize, won the W. H. Smith "Books in Canada First Novel Award," and was quickly translated into several languages.

Mistry's latest work, a novel published in 1995, combines the political themes of *Such a Long Journey* and the character sketches of the Firozsha Baag stories. Titled *A Fine Balance,* it focuses on four people who live in the same apartment in Bombay in the 1970s and describes the effects of the internal political turmoil of the times on their lives. As with his previous work, the critical response was good and Mistry's reputation as one of Canada's premiere young writers has continued to grow.

Plot Summary

"Swimming Lessons" is told from the author's viewpoint except in the italicized portions that use the third person to depict Kersi's parents' responses to the mail he sends from Toronto. These are set in Bombay in his parents' home as they read his communications, first letters and then the manuscript of stories, and discuss their son and his work. Otherwise, the story takes place in an apartment complex in the Don Mills suburb of Toronto, its elevator lobby, its parking lot, and, when the protagonist ventures out to take swimming lessons, the local high school pool.

But it is clear from the opening passages that there is another important setting for this story, namely the memory of the narrator. From the outset, he compares events in his new environment with those back in the Bombay housing complex called Firozsha Baag, where he grew up surrounded by his family and an assortment of quirky, colorful neighbors. In the opening scene, for example, the narrator describes "the old man" (he is never named) who waits for people in the apartment lobby in order to make small talk. As he plays a favorite conversational game, asking people to guess his age, Kersi is reminded of his own grandfather, who had Parkinson's disease and sat on the veranda of their complex waving at anyone who went by.

After introducing the old man, the Portuguese woman in Toronto, and making the first italicized jump-shift to Bombay, the narrator begins to reveal things about himself. He is candid about his erotic urges as he describes spotting two women sunbathing in bikinis beside the parking lot and his attempts to get a closer look. When they turn out to be less than attractive at close quarters, he remembers the swimming lessons he has signed up for, saying he has that "to look forward to."

He recounts a conversation with the attendant at the pool registration desk in which he explains his "non-swimming status" and she in turn explains why she never learned to ride a bicycle. After this there is a long passage of memory based on incidences of swimming, water, and religious festivals relating to water in the narrator's life before immigrating to Canada. He also discusses his newly purchased swimming trunks and recounts a sexual fantasy about them that indicates his high hopes for an erotic encounter at the upcoming swimming lessons. This is followed by another shift to India where the narrator's parents converse about their son in Canada as they write to him. The first section of the story closes with the introduction of Bertha, the building superintendent, who is yelling at her son as he tinkers with his van in the parking lot. The narrator describes her slavic-language tirades and the family's general situation—Bertha's hard work at the apartments, her husband's factory work and occasional binges of "boozing," and the son's seeming lack of any work at all.

The second section opens with the narrator describing his first swimming lesson. There are some bigoted comments from white teenagers as he leaves the locker room. His erotic fantasy does materialize, but only in his mind. He describes his excitement as a woman in the group demonstrates floating face up and he watches her pubic hairs wafting in the water around the edges of her suit. That is the high point. The low point comes when he is asked to paddle to the deep end. He is terrified and almost goes under.

The second lesson is a great disappointment, since the floating woman has shaved her pubic area and no longer reveals anything erotic to Kersi's imagination. He quits. The next italicized portion begins as a Kersi's parents receive a parcel from Canada. It is a copy of the manuscript of stories Kersi has written. His parents are surprised to find that, while he is living in Toronto, the stories are almost all about Bombay. The exception is the last,

which seems to be "Swimming Lessons" itself. Meanwhile time passes in Toronto. Bertha rakes leaves, her son stops working on his van when it gets too cold, the bikini ladies flirt with Kersi in the laundry room, the old man is given a ride in an Oldsmobile by his son, and the Portuguese woman (PW) keeps watch over it all.

As winter deepens the heat falters and then goes off entirely in the apartment complex. Bertha shovels snow, the old man has a stroke and is gone, Bertha's husband and son leave her, the old man returns, and far away in Bombay's Firozsha Baag, Kersi's parents finish their reading of his stories. They like them and are proud, although the father thinks he has focused too much on inconsequential people and his mother thinks he must be homesick since he only writes about Bombay and not Toronto.

Kersi tells in great detail the process of his taking a bath in his apartment. He ruminates on water imagery and finally gets the nerve to go completely under the water, even though it is only in his bathtub. As he is submerging himself he decides he should find out the old man's name. But just as he is looking on the mailbox labels, PW informs him that the old man died in the night. The story ends with an italicized passage, as Kersi's parents are writing to tell him how proud they are of his accomplishment as a writer. They are looking forward to his next book.

Characters

Bertha

Bertha is the apartment building superintendent. She is a hard working middle-aged Yugoslavian woman who spends much of her time trying to get her husband and son to be hard working too. She is demonstrative, loud, and unconcerned about how she is perceived by her neighbors when she yells at her spouse or son. Her husband works in a factory but occasionally yields to alcohol, which Bertha calls "booze," one of her few English slang terms.

Bikini sunbathers

Like most of the characters in "Swimming Lessons," the sunbathers are minor figures who serve primarily to reveal the narrator's thoughts and feelings. First seen from a distance, they are objects of desire as Kersi ogles them. Later he comes to think of them as "horny old cows."

Kersi

See Narrator

Mother and Father

The narrator's parents are the only major characters in the story other than himself. They are presented with complexity both as individuals and as a couple who have lived together for many years. The father at first will not answer Kersi's letters because he dislikes their short and impersonal tone. But when he receives his son's manuscript of stories, he becomes interested and writes to give him suggestions about writing and his subject matter. The mother is less interested in writing theory and criticism. She reads his work with an eye to how her son is feeling personally. The conversation Mistry gives these characters gives him the occasion to discuss literary themes, especially how a writer uses the experiences of his own life to create fiction.

Narrator

The narrator's name is never mentioned in the story, but he is clearly the same Parsi Indian character named Kersi who appears in several of the other stories of the *Swimming Lessons* collection. Although shy, Kersi is becoming progressively "westernized" and enjoys displaying his new cultural knowledge, such as the make and model of the old man's son's car. He is a keen observer of the people in his apartment complex and is beginning to write about them, as is evident from the manuscript he sends to his parents in Bombay. He lives an interior life full of memories of Bombay that he frequently compares to his new life in Canada. He characteristically notices and thinks about the thematic and symbolic meanings of the things he observes.

Old man

Another unnamed character, the old man will soon turn seventy-seven. He sits in his wheelchair by the elevator of the apartment complex and makes small talk with the tenants as they pass in the hall. He seems somewhat senile, but the apartment tenants indulge him and he engages everyone equally. He has a son who visits and takes him for rides.

Portuguese woman

The narrator gives her the designation "PW," making her a blatantly two-dimensional figure. She is nosey and wants the narrator to know the extent of her information about all the goings-on in the apartment building. She is easily insulted when anyone gives her information, since she wants to be the one "in the know."

Themes

Cause and Effect

In looking for the major themes of "Swimming Lessons," it would be a mistake to take the narrator's remarks about cause and effect too literally. It is a noticeable thread in the narrative, but Mistry makes it almost too apparent. The narrator mentions it when he considers his grandfather's osteoporosis and a fall that broke his hip. Did the weakened bone snap and cause his fall or did his fall cause the break? This leads him to wonder if the Bombay Parsi community has the highest divorce rate because it is the most westernized or if it the most westernized because of its divorces. The theme comes up early in the story and continues as he wonders if the waters of Bombay are filthy because of the crowds or if the crowds gather because of the chance to pick through the filth and junk. Which is the cause, which the effect? After raising the question initially, Mistry's narrator drops it. Readers are left with the thought, however, and it haunts other events in the story. Do Bertha's husband and son leave her because she is always yelling at them, or does she yell because she knows they are going to leave? It serves to give an overall sense that life is mysterious and that one cannot figure out why things happen as they do. The theme arises significantly at the end when the narrator's parents wonder if he writes about Bombay because he is lonely in his new home, or if he had to go to the new locale to find his subject matter back in the old one.

Alienation

Any immigrant feels the weight of being "a stranger in a strange land," as the saying goes, but an immigrant of color in modern western society must feel especially alone, lonely, and alienated. This is an important theme in "Swimming Lessons." It is clear that the narrator is isolated and attempting to make connections with other people; but he is not the only character in this condition. The old man dies without anyone in the apartment ever getting to know him. The Portuguese woman (PW) makes her observations and retreats behind her door. The superintendent's family disintegrates. And the narrator makes no acquaintance or friend; the bikini women devolve from distant erotic visions to "horny old cows," and the swimming lessons work out no better. In fact, no character makes any significant human contact with anyone in the story.

Purification

"Water imagery in my life is recurring," says the narrator as he contemplates Chaupatty beach in Bombay in his childhood and the pool where his swimming lessons occur. Usually water and filth are mutually exclusive symbols, but in this story they blend, both in the narrator's present reality and his memory. The sea of his childhood is a grotesque mix of filth, religious symbolic purity, and raw sexual energy. He remembers pre-adolescent street urchins swimming nude with erections and masturbating as his mother tried to teach him to swim. This image is followed by a fantasy of his own erection showing through his trunks and attracting a lover in his swim class. Especially strong images of this mix of purity and impurity occur when the pubic hairs of a woman in the swim class arouse the narrator greatly and later a hair is caught in the drain of the tub as he tests his aquatic courage by submerging himself in his bath. He says he wants to see what is "inside" water. This works well as a symbol of the unconscious mind, an unregulated chaotic mixture of the sacred and the profane.

The Cycle of the Seasons

The artistic patterning of life's experiences is a theme that arises out of the self-consciousness of the narrator in "Swimming Lessons." He wants to know what "the equation" is as he contemplates whether he will experience a "watery rebirth." As it turns out, his focus on water as the source of regeneration has been a false hope. Just as the water in Bombay was a compromised symbol because of the filth in it, so the pool of his swimming lessons fails as a symbol, presumably because he brought "impure" expectations to it. What finally works toward his rebirth in his new country is simply the passing of time. He is new to the phenomenon of the seasons, and pays close attention to it as the story develops. By the end of his narrative, when the old man has died, he has begun to perceive a sense of

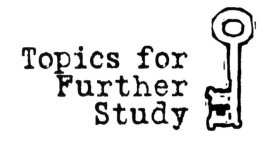

Topics for Further Study

- The Parsis of Bombay that Mistry depicts in his fiction are remnants of the Zoroastrians who came to India from Persia [now called Iran] after the Muslim conquest of that country in the seventh century. Look up the three volume *History of Zoroastrianism* edited by Mary A. Boyce and others (1991) and find out some of the basic tenets of this religion.

- Bombay is the home of one of the most successful steel business families in India, the Tatas. Find out about this famous Parsi industrial family that the narrator's father in "Swimming Lessons" mentions with such obvious pride.

- Sociologist Werner Sollers' 1986 book *Beyond Ethnicity* discusses the tension in the life of immigrants to America (or a big Canadian city like Toronto) regarding "melting," or assimilating the new culture, versus remaining "unmeltable," maintaining native habits and customs. Consider the narrator of "Swimming Lessons" as an immigrant struggling with these tensions.

- The sociology of living in large urban apartment complexes has been studied and discusses extensively. One section of Nicholas Lemann's *The Promised Land* focuses on the problems of African Americans in Chicago's Robert Taylor Homes high-rise apartments in the 1960s. Compare the situation Lemann describes to that of the apartment tenants in "Swimming Lessons."

the ongoing larger natural rhythms created by the cycle of the seasons in Canada.

Style

Point of View

For most of the story, the narrator tells the events. When the typeface becomes italic, the story shifts to Bombay where the narrator's parents discuss their son, his life in Toronto, and, after it arrives in the mail, the manuscript of stories he has written since he immigrated to Canada. One effect of this shift is to give a double vision of the narrator. He is seen as he displays himself and also as his parents see him from halfway around the globe. His self-revelation is sometimes very intimate; he talks about sexual fantasies and very private scenes from his life. But his parents' talk about him also comes close to being embarrassing at points; it has the feel of parents discussing their children when they are not around.

Style

The style of the story is realism; that is, the events in the story are things one would expect to happen in "everyday life." The narrative dwells on encounters between characters in the apartment lobby and mundane conversations in the laundry room. The most dramatic event in the story is the narrator's moment of terror at his swim lesson when the instructor is close by. In other words, there is no great drama, no supernatural agent, not even a direct confrontation between the characters, unless one counts Bertha's bouts of screaming at her husband and son. This kind of low-key realism is often termed "psychological realism" because its focuses on the "inner life," or psychology, of one or two central characters. In "Swimming Lessons" the focus is on the narrator, his human interactions, his sensitivity to social environments, and his perception of images and symbols from "the page of life itself," as he puts it. Things happen, but they are subtle things that must be noticed by careful observation and interpreted by understanding their psychological and symbol significance.

Symbols and Imagery

When the narrator brings up a point about symbols, it reminds readers that he is a writer, the kind of person who thinks about such literary things. He says, "symbols, after all, should be still and gentle as dewdrops, tiny, yet shining with a world of meaning." He has noticed that water imagery has been a constant in his life. His tone is almost that of an excuse—his actual life has handed him the symbol and he apologizes for how obvious it is. All this should also be a hint to look for more subtle symbols throughout the story. Of course, the most striking image pairing in the story is the pubic hairs of the woman in his swim class that arouse him and later the hair he sees caught in the drain plug of his tub. A psychological reading of this image set is that sexuality is under the surface of things. The narrator says, suggestively "The world outside the water I have seen a lot of, it is now time to see what is inside."

The images of two old men, one in Canada and the other the memory of his grandfather in Bombay, are also important in the story. The story opens and closes with the old man and its most significant event is his death. A counterpoint between the ongoing cycle of the seasons and the limited linear time of human life is made clear by that death. And the narrator's mother emphasizes this important symbol when she says grandfather's spirit blessing him is her favorite part of his story.

This leads to a final feature of the story that should be noted. Notice that the mother is discussing the very story the reader is reading as he or she is reading it. The effect is often called "metafiction." The narrator breaks the spell of the narration to draw attention to its "storyness," to discuss it, to speak directly to the reader, to suggest changes, etc. In this case the writer's parents do it, but the effect is the same. "Are you sure, said Father, that you really told him this [about the grandfather's spirit blessing], or you believe you told him because you like the sound of it, you said yourself the other day that he changes and adds and alters things in the stories but he writes it all so beautifully that it seems true, so how can you be sure." Metafiction discloses the artistry of fiction writing and invokes that very question—it seems true, how can you be sure?

Historical Context

Canada

Since the 1960s, and particularly since 1980, Canada has been embroiled in a series of disputes arising out of efforts to "patriate" and modernize Canada's constitution. Quebec nationalists, provincial premiers, and, more recently, feminists and aboriginal leaders have sought and sometimes won major victories as Canadians have attempted to transform their constitution and move from a commonwealth based in British law to an independent republic.

India

An ongoing conflict between India and Pakistan after independence from Great Britain came over Kashmir in 1947-49. With independence and partition, the numerous states had to choose to join either Hindu India or Muslim Pakistan. Contiguous to both India and West Pakistan, Kashmir was ruled by a Hindu prince, but the majority of its population was Muslim. In 1947, Pakistan invaded Kashmir in support of an uprising by Muslim peasants. The maharajah fled to Delhi, where he signed papers giving Kashmir to India. Indian troops defended the former princely state, which drew the Pakistani army into the conflict. Fighting continued in Kashmir until a United Nations commission arranged a truce in January 1949. Kashmir was then divided along the cease-fire line, with India holding about two-thirds and Pakistan the remainder. Periodic fighting has broken the uneasy peace often since then and India and Pakistan remain bitter enemies.

Bombay

Greater Bombay, of which the southernmost part is the island of Bombay, was formed into a metropolitan municipal organization in 1957, when it was officially renamed Mumbai. About two-thirds of the population is concentrated on Bombay Island, which has an area of 26 square miles. Bombay has one of the highest population densities in the world, in some areas reaching 1,500 persons per square mile. The city attracts a large number of migrants, particularly from the states of Maharashtra, Gujarat, and Madhya Pradesh. The principal languages spoken are Marathi, Gujarati, and Hindi. Of all of India's huge cities, Bombay offers the greatest religious diversity. More than half its population is Hindu; the rest is divided among Parsis, Christians, Jains, Muslims, and others.

Critical Overview

Mistry's "Swimming Lessons" is the concluding story of *Tales from Firozsha Baag,* the collection that first brought him critical attention, but most commentators initially ignored this particular story. Writing in *Canadian Literature,* Amin Malak, for example, chose to discuss "Squatter" and "Lend Me Your Light," presumably to showcase both the Parsi Indian and Canadian immigrant elements of Mistry's work. But he never mentions the last story. He does make flattering literary comparisons to Mistry's work that later reviewers echo. He writes that "following the models of psychological realism set by Chekhov and Joyce, Mistry reveals a knack for generating humour in the midst of trage-

dy," and concludes that he "adroitly blends tragedy with irony, cynicism with humour, skepticism with belief."

When the collection was reprinted in the United States in 1989, two years after its Canadian debut, it was reviewed twice in the *New York Times,* first by Michiko Kakutani in February and then more extensively by Hope Cooke in the March 5th *New York Times Book Review.* Both reviewers discuss the final story, probably since the American edition retitled the collection, *Swimming Lessons and Other Stories from Firozsha Baag.* Kakutani notes that it was in the book's last tale that the narrator is revealed as a fictionalized surrogate for the author, and Cooke points out that Mistry "steps out of the frame" in the final story to discuss issues of symbolism and metaphor in fiction and his artistic intentions as a writer.

Both reviewers are very positive. Kakutani stresses Mistry's masterly evocation of his characters' "epiphany" moments, those sudden flashes of understanding about the world and one's place in it that were named and perfected in the stories of James Joyce. She concludes that Mistry's best stories "pivot around incidents that reveal to the characters some unforeseen truth about their lives." Hope Cooke, on the other hand, focuses on Mistry's humor and compassion for his characters, attributes placing him more in the company of Chekhov than Joyce. She suggests that the light, life-affirming quality of his stories is "astonishing, given the horrifying, stunted lives he depicts."

Janette Turner Hospital, writing in the *Los Angeles Times Book Review*, is less approving in her assessment of the collection. It is her opinion that:

> There are weaknesses in the stories, moments when the reader is conscious that this is a first collection from a young writer. Mistry is imitative of Indian novelist Anita Desai in his depiction of sudden and grotesque incursions of violence into the community, but he has the habit of predictably and rather portentously foreshadowing these events (a splat of betel juice on a white cloth prefigures a murder; a rat bludgeoned with a cricket bat precedes the bludgeoning of a starving servant) and in general there is a tendency toward heavy-handed symbolism.

Her discussion of the story "Swimming Lessons" points out that, while the narrator alludes to racist remarks others make about him, he is unaware of his own sexist remarks about several of the women he encounters (or more accurately, stares at) in the course of the story. In general, she likes the stories set in Firozsha Baag more than the Toronto

A view of Marine Drive from Malibu Hill in Bombay, India.

ones, but she predicts that "significant" work about Mistry's Canadian experiences might be yet to come.

In an interview with Mistry in *The Canadian Fiction Magazine*, Geoff Hancock brings out interesting comments from him regarding his "double consciousness" as a resident alien Canadian, his sense of the difference between Canada and the United States (which he obviously sees as a very violent society), and his major literary influences. In this interview he confirms those who saw Joyce and Chekhov as important models for his work and adds V. S. Naipaul, R. K. Narayan, Bernard Malamud, and John Cheever to the list. He makes it very clear

that the Kersi/narrator figure of "Swimming Lessons" is not himself but a fictional character. He notes that the parents in the story say they would like to learn more about how he lives in Canada; his next book did not fulfill that wish but returned to the Bombay Parsi community of the earlier stories. The interview is noteworthy as well for his insistence that both politics and religion are of minor importance in his work.

Finally, a long article by Keith Garebian in *The Canadian Forum* is worth mentioning because of its early, strong evaluation of Mistry as an important new writer based on his performance in *Swimming*

Lessons and Other Stories from Firozsha Baag. In "In the Aftermath of Empire: Identities in the Commonwealth of Literature," he says, "in short, Mistry's is a tour de force first collection, on a higher order than V. S. Naipaul's first collection, *Miguel Street.*" This is a robust endorsement and has certainly helped bring attention to Mistry's work.

Criticism

Thomas E. Barden

Barden is a professor of American Studies and the Director of Graduate Studies at the University of Toledo. In the following essay, he examines Mistry's use of humor and symbolism.

Rohinton Mistry's "Swimming Lessons" is not very dramatic. Very little actually happens in the story and the narrator seems to miss a lot of what does happen until other characters point it out to him. There are some minor social interactions, numerous finely-turned descriptions of scenes from the narrator's daily life, and several cutaways to his memories and scenes of his mother and father in Bombay. But altogether, it is certainly not the short story as envisioned by Edgar Allen Poe, who invented the genre and thought it should focus on a single compelling dramatic event. Nor is it like the short fiction of James Joyce, whose addition to the genre was the concept of the "epiphany," or sudden psychological realization on the part of a central character, as an alternative to Poe's single effect.

Mistry's closest historical model is the turn-of-the-century Russian writer and dramatist Anton Chekhov, whose "psychological realism" chronicled the ordinary lives of pre-revolutionary Russia's middle class. While avoiding dramatic scenes, Chekhov gave readers insights into the hearts and minds of his believable and sympathetic, if shabby, characters. Likewise, Mistry explores the loneliness and anxieties of his modern ensemble of unremarkable people. His characters fill today's sterile apartment complexes rather than estates on the outskirts of Moscow, but the feeling is the same. Nothing happens, sentences never quite get completed, even the title event of the story, the swimming lessons, don't work out and are quietly dropped. Just be-

neath the surface, however, the characters lead lives of quiet desperation and make bumbling attempts to reach out to each other. They engage our sympathy because Mistry makes them real and likeable despite their pettiness and quirks.

One of the principal ways he does this is through his subtle use of humor. Like Chekhov, Mistry is essentially a comic writer. His characters' unfulfilled longings and failures to communicate would be merely depressing if he didn't convey their optimism, energy, and ability to endure life's blows with dignity. One need only think of the large-bosomed, muscular Bertha's overture to the reticent narrator figure to see how integral comedy is to "Swimming Lessons." Kersi, who has already revealed to us his tendency to conjure up erotic daydreams, speaks to her about the heat going out in his flat. In a great flurry of thickly accented English she scares him with her broad sexual humor. "Nothing, not to worry about anything. . . . Radiator no work, you tell me. You feel cold, you come see me, I keep you warm." His response is understated and yet precisely phrased in Mistry's language. "I step back, and she advances, her breasts preceding her like the gallant prows of two ice-breakers."

The image works because it is weird, funny, and symbolic at the same time. She will "break the ice," as the cliche goes, and combine her business as apartment manager with pleasure. Mistry's narrator then adds another detail. "She looks at the old man to see if he is appreciating the act." We are left with two possibilities—that she is as repressed and frustrated as the narrator, or she is only joking. Or, and here we begin to rise to Mistry's bait and psychoanalyze her, maybe she only thinks she is joking. The next thing we learn about her is that she was screaming loudly at her husband. Not long after this her husband and son leave her. Her complexity as a character deepens and she becomes both a stereotypical Eastern European comic figure and a realistic, suffering human being facing her coming old age alone.

Another example of Mistry's comic touch in "Swimming Lessons" is the Portuguese Woman, whom he reduces to a two-dimensional cliche soon after introducing her into the narrative. She becomes "PW," a hovering, snooping presence whose only joy in life is waiting by the elevator and keeping absolutely current about events in the apartment complex. In one of the few threads of the story

What Do I Read Next?

- *Such a Long Journey* (1991) is Mistry's first full-length novel. It is about an ordinary middle class man from Bombay's Parsi community named Gustad Noble who becomes unwillingly entangled in the corruption of Indian national politics.

- *Dubliners* (1914), James Joyce's famous short story collection about the people of Ireland's capital city, is a work Mistry has said was very influential on him. Like Mistry, Joyce was living away from the city he depicted when he wrote and relied heavily on his personal memories of his hometown.

- *Midnight's Children* (1981), which first brought Salman Rushdie a wide audience and won Britain's Booker Prize, is an allegory about the birth of independent India. It is a good introduction to this important Indian writer.

- *The Things They Carried* (1990), by Tim O'Brien, is a collection of interrelated short stories about a platoon of soldiers in the Vietnam war. This powerful set of narratives, like Mistry's work, focuses on memory and the relationship between individuals and the groups to which they belong.

- Alice Munro's 1990 *Friend of My Youth* is a good introduction to a Canadian writer many critics have compared to Rohinton Mistry. Her short story collections depict the rich human connections of small town life in Ontario, Canada.

- Starting in the 1930s, R. K. Narayan wrote tales of everyday life in the fictional South Indian village of Malgudi, often said to be his hometown of Mysore. *Swami and Friends* (1935), his first collection of Malgudi stories, is a good place to start reading Narayan, India's best known English language writer.

- The stories of Russian writer and playwright Anton Chekhov are similar to Mistry's stories in their sympathy with the lives and struggles of unspectacular middle-class people. Some outstanding stories are "A Dreary Story," "The Butterfly," "Terror," "Lady with a Pet Dog," and "In the Hollow."

---

that builds to a climax, the narrator increasingly mocks her until she realizes she is being mocked. She is incensed because he is a member of a more recent and "less acceptable" immigrant group than her own yet seems to understand the chaotic scenes going on around him. When she tells Kersi two women were sunbathing in bikinis by the parking lot, he responds by saying "That's nice." When she tells him Bertha filled six big black garbage bags with autumn leaves in her frenzy of work that day, he responds with, "Six bags! Wow!" The finale of these exchanges comes when she informs him that the old man's son came to take him on a drive in his big beautiful American car. "I see my chance," he says, and shoots back at PW, "Olds Ninety-Eight." His comment on this exchange reveals the power struggle that he knows has been occurring. "She does not like this at all, my giving her information. She is visibly nettled, and retreats with a sour face."

As with Bertha, the comic atmosphere takes a turn and we see a psychological reality behind the two-dimensional figure of PW. She yearns for some measure of respect, some position in the apartment complex. She wants to have something of importance, even if it is only the latest news.

One critic of the story took Mistry to task because he "frequently makes extremely sexist observations about women." But the over-wrought political correctness of this criticism misses an important point. These observations are essential to the humor that permeates "Swimming Lessons." Furthermore, they are indispensable to its psychological realism. It is true that the narrator is constantly ogling women, but it is always only from a distance and in his imagination. And things never work out for him in this area. The bikini sunbathers turn out to be middle-aged women with varicose veins and sagging bottoms. They become like the comic Bertha when they take on the role of sexual aggressors in the laundromat. Kersi has hesitated to remove their clothes, which have finished drying in the unit's only two dryers, because he thinks it will offend them. When the women come in, they tell him he needn't have waited, that he should have taken them out. When one of them suggestively adds, "You can touch my things any time you like," the narrator is not pleased. This is not his idea of a good erotic offer. His disgusted response is to call her a "horny old cow," not to her face, of course.

As this case illustrates, the humor in Mistry's narrative is characteristic of the sort that Sigmund Freud noted in his 1905 treatise "Jokes and Their Relation to the Unconscious." Freud suggested that the psychological sources of comedy are those things we have deep anxieties about, sex, nudity, violence, death, etc. This idea helps explain Kersi's bumbling encounters and lonely fantasies, which are funny but also embarrassing and usually of a sexual nature. Akin to the bikini sunbathers' daydream is his fantasy of meeting a sexual partner at his swimming lessons. When he buys new swimming trunks he worries that they will be too skimpy to cover him sufficiently if he becomes aroused at the lessons. With this thought he launches into a confession to the reader that he hopes he will encounter a gorgeous woman, become aroused, and thus attract a fantasy partner, who will be unable to resist his "delectable Asian brown body."

This confession prepares the reader for his account of the swimming lessons. Knowing his high romantic expectations gives us a simultaneous interior and exterior view of the subsequent events. On arrival, Kersi is immediately disappointed that his dream lover is not among the students, but he quickly settles for a less than ideal substitute. His lovingly detailed description of her partially exposed pubis around the edges of her bathing suit (probably what the critic of his sexist observations was referring to) reveals his dreamy disconnectedness to the actual scene he is in. No wonder he doesn't learn to swim! Later, the instructor has him go to the deep end helped along by a pole and net, but he is terrified, almost sinks to the bottom, and accuses the teacher of being "an irresponsible person," again, not to his face.

When the object of his desire shows up at the next lesson having shaved her pubic area, he loses

> " Just beneath the surface, however, the characters lead lives of quiet desperation and make bumbling attempts to reach out to each other. They engage our sympathy because Mistry makes them real and likeable despite their pettiness and quirks."

heart for the entire thing and drops out. Reality and fantasy do not seem to come together very well for the narrator. But from our reader's perspective, we grasp the Chekhovian comic-sadness of this lonely but persevering immigrant. He is trying to have a life. These sad-comic scenarios suggest that there is both a surface and a deeper symbolic level to every character and every element of the story. The old man in the lobby playing his guessing game about his age is just a "slice of life" in the apartment complex; but he also becomes emblematic of a general human longing for company and communication. The narrator begins to realize this after he associates him with his own grandfather back in India and remembers his mother's advice that one should be nice to old people because they can bestow blessings on people, even after death. But when he resolves to find out the old man's name, it is too late. He has died.

Mistry discloses his view of symbolism in fiction early on in the story when his narrator muses aloud that "symbols, after all, should be still and gentle as dewdrops, tiny, yet shining with a world of meaning." This is perhaps the best possible literary gloss on "Swimming Lessons," since it comes from the author's surrogate himself. The writer declares that he crafts his work to contain "worlds of meaning." But his narrator immediately goes on to pose a problem by asking—"But what happens when, on the page of life itself, one encounters the ever-moving, all-engirdling sprawl of the filthy sea?" Beneath this beautiful sentence lies a defining issue of psychological realism. How does a writer depict "real life" as he or she sees it, but also provide the symbolic meaning essential for successful fiction?

The answer is to find those things in reality that innately function at a symbolic level. And then, of course, he/she must write so precisely that readers will not say, as Kersi puts it, "how obvious, how skilless." Water as a symbol, for example, is important enough for the narrator to single it out for comment. Kersi says "water imagery in my life is recurring." With a title like "Swimming Lessons" this should not be unexpected, but in choosing water, Mistry consciously plays with our symbolic expectations. Ordinarily, water equals purity. Going under the water, as in a baptism, symbolizes death to an old life and rebirth to a new one. These are standard western symbolic meanings, but Mistry blurs them and disrupts our expectations in subtle ways. In his symbolic lexicon, water is not only Judeo-Christian but also Zoroastrian, and he provides us with fitting analogs in the story. The squeaky clean high school pool in Toronto is juxtaposed to the filthy sea of Bombay. To the western mind water is pure. To the Parsi tradition only fire is wholly pure; water may be good and bad simultaneously, reflecting the ever-present struggle between good and bad that is the bedrock of the Parsi faith. Just as Ahriman and Ahura Mazda struggle at the cosmic level over good and evil, so water can be religiously clean but grossly polluted in actuality.

In fact, this water-borne struggle between purity and filth is woven through the story. Freud would appreciate how blatantly erotic images keep popping up and "dirtying" the situation whenever water is invoked in the narration. A telling example, and surely the most startling water image in "Swimming Lessons," is that of the guttersnipes—the naked Bombay urchins who used to expose their "buoyant little penises" in the garbage-strewn waters of Chaupatty Bay when he was a boy. They would splash around pretending to masturbate as Kersi's "Mummy" tried to teach him to swim. After such an image, the chlorine-clean pool and the female student's out-of-place pubic hairs seem tame. Later in the story, when Kersi overcomes his fear of going under water and totally submerges himself in his bath tub, he finds a strikingly similar image to the one that excited him so much in the pool. As he opens his eyes to look around in his newly conquered underwater realm, he discovers a hair caught in the tub drain. He describes it in very similar wording to the student's pubic hairs.

The numerous scenes that pit purity against dirt, the body, and sex lend an unmistakable Freudian tone to the story. The narrator drops hints about all of this, the most obvious being his concluding comment on the bath tub episode. Kersi says, "The world outside the water I have seen a lot of, it is now time to see what is inside." This thinly veiled reference to the unconscious points the reader to the psycho-symbolism of the story and heightens reader interest in Kersi by presenting him in all his complexity, "inside and out."

Of course, sex is not the only sub-text of "Swimming Lessons." Although his frustrated libido is the most obvious facet of the narrator's interior life, there are other things going on in there. As Freud's student Carl Jung pointed out, there are human motivators besides sex. An important one in "Swimming Lessons" turns out to be the yearly change of the seasons. For writers from temperate climates, this has been a time-honored trope. James Joyce, for example, used winter to stand for deadness of the soul in "The Dead," the final story of his *Dubliners* sequence. But to the immigrant Kersi (and in the hands of his immigrant creator Mistry), the symbol seems fresh and new. That the seasons anchor the story can be readily seen by noting how the first sentences of so many paragraphs remark on them. Kersi recalls that he read about snow and winter in British adventure books when he was a boy in Bombay (a tropical city on a parallel latitude to Jamaica). But in Toronto he experiences the real thing.

After taking us around a full year, through a rough winter, and to the symbolic end point of the old man's death, Kersi blithely states, "The dwindled days of winter are all but forgotten. . . . I resume my evening walks, it's spring and a vigorous thaw is on." The elevator door has been oiled and no longer squeaks. He remembers that the spring class for adult non-swimmers will begin in a few days at the high school and, as hope springs eternal in the new blossoming year, he decides to sign up and try again. Here is a symbol readily available from, as Kersi put it, "the page of life itself."

Source: Thomas E. Barden, Overview of "Swimming Lessons," for *Short Stories for Students*, The Gale Group, 1999.

Elisabeth Piedmont-Marton

In the following essay, Piedmont-Marton compares and contrasts the two-halves of the "split screen" of "Swimming Lessons," Toronto and Bombay, and the narrator's perception of events in his life with reality.

In "Swimming Lessons" a young Indian immigrant, Kersi, describes his daily life in an apartment building in Toronto. Woven into his narrative, however, are imagined scenes from his parent's apartment in Bombay. The story is constructed like a split screen, with the narrator's life and story telling on one side, and his parents ten thousand miles away reading his letters and stories and commenting on them. The swimming lessons that the narrator signs up for are also a metaphor for his attempts to negotiate the foreign waters of his adopted country.

The story opens in *media res,* or in the middle of things. The narrator, whose name is not revealed but is recognizable from the preceding stories in the volume, is describing the cast of characters who live in his building, but he does not reveal his writerly ambitions. He mentions his family back in Firozsha Baag, in Bombay, but his attention is focused on his late grandfather. He does not reveal anything about his parents' lives at the present or about his relationship with them. It's the old man who sits in the lobby of the apartment building that brings the narrator's thoughts back to his childhood in India: "He reminds me of Grandpa as he sits on the sofa in the lobby staring vacantly at the parking lot." When he recalls his grandfather's decline from Parkinson's disease, osteoporosis, and finally lung cancer, the narrator expresses regret that he should have done more to ease his last days. Twice he says, "I should have gone to see him more often." Visiting his grandfather would have been all the more important because, as his mother said, "the blessings of an old person were the most valuable and potent of all, they would last my whole life long."

When the scene suddenly shifts to India, it is unclear whether Kersi is present in this memory, if he is imagining it, or if it is happening during the same time period when he introduces readers to his neighbors, like the old man and the Portuguese Woman. Soon though, it becomes apparent that the scene is Kersi's parents' apartment on the day they receive a letter from him in Toronto. The letter fails to live up to its promise however, and both of his

> For Kersi, swimming and water imagery are important themes in his life, and anticipating his first adult swimming lesson prompts him to revisit his attempts at swimming as a child in India."

parents are disappointed that their son chose only to write about the weather and what his apartment looks like. Since readers have had a glimpse of Kersi's close observations of the rich details of his life in Canada, they, too, may wonder why, as his father says, "everything about his life is locked in silence and secrecy."

The dramatic contrast between Bombay and Toronto is underscored by another striking disparity. Kersi's inner life is rich with detail and humor, while his outer life, to all observers, must appear lonely and isolated. His father isn't the only one who thinks he lives a life "locked in silence and secrecy." For Kersi, for example, an encounter with some women in the elevator is filled with heroic details and romantic possibilities. After watching the two women sunbathing from his window, Kersi races downstairs to arrange an accidental meeting. But the women are not what they had seemed to be from the window, and standing in the elevator with them, he is disappointed to see that they do not resemble the characters he has created in the ongoing story in his head. "The elevator arrives and I hold it open, inviting them in with what I think is a gallant flourish. Under the fluorescent glare in the elevator I see their wrinkled skin, aging hands, sagging bottoms, varicose veins. The lustrous trick of sun and lotion and distance has ended." The women have no way of knowing what role they have played in, and have failed the audition for, Kersi's inner life.

Another small episode also assumes unusual significance for the narrator. Kersi has signed up for evening swimming lessons at the local high school.

When he registers he is struck with the friendliness of the woman at the desk, who, unbeknownst to her, gives him an opportunity to tell part of his story out loud: "The woman at the registration desk is quite friendly. She even gives me the opening to satisfy the compulsion I have about explaining my non-swimming status." For Kersi, swimming and water imagery are important themes in his life, and anticipating his first adult swimming lesson prompts him to revisit his attempts at swimming as a child in India. When he explains that "The art of swimming had been trapped between the devil and the deep blue sea," and that "water imagery in my life is recurring," the narrator reveals his ambitions as a writer. It's not just his failure to learn how to swim that bothers Kersi, what's worse is his inability to interpret and arrange the images and connotations associated with water and swimming: "The universal symbol of life and regeneration did nothing but frustrate me. Perhaps the swimming pool will overturn that failure." The narrator's memories of swimming in the Bay of Chaupatty are inseparable from his fears and feelings of inadequacy, and these insecurities apply to swimming as well as writing and interpreting: "When images and symbols abound in this manner, sprawling or rolling across the page without guile or artifice, one is prone to say, how obvious, how skilless; symbols, after all, should be still and gentle as dewdrops, tiny, yet shining with a world of meaning."

Kersi's swimming lessons will require him to move from the familiar world of the apartment building and his own imagination to the frightening public world where he risks and encounters, failure, embarrassment, and racism. He arrives at the pool for his first swimming lesson weighed down with fears and unreasonable expectations, burdened with old stories from his past as well as the hopeful beginnings of new stories. Kersi's memories of his childhood swimming excursions evoke the crowded, filthy, and vaguely menacing atmosphere of the public beach near his home in Bombay. Obstacles to swimming there included the filth generated by crowds of "street urchins and beggars and beachcombers," and by all the "religious festivals [that] used the sea as a repository for their finales." But for Kersi, the worst thing about trying to swim in the Bay of Chaupatty "was the guttersnipes, like naked fish with their little buoyant penises, taunting me with their skills, swimming underwater and emerging unexpectedly all around me." Years later, in Toronto, he converts the sexual element of his

memories into an erotic fantasy of his own about meeting a gorgeous young woman in the class.

The narrator's adult swimming lessons are no more successful than his childhood attempts, but on the metaphorical level he makes more progress. Terrified after the first class, he returns only because he hopes to get another glimpse of "the straying curls of brown pubic hair" of one of the women in the class. When even this doesn't happen, Kersi feels like "the weight of this disappointment makes the water less manageable, more lung-penetrating," and he never returns to class. Though he has failed to learn to swim once again, the narrator may have made some progress in negotiating the deep waters of fashioning his solitary immigrant's life, "locked in silence and secrecy," into the writer's life to which aspires. Back in the apartment in Bombay, his parents receive a surprise from the postman: not the usual bland and uncommunicative letter from their son, but a parcel, a book of stories. In this scene, the narrator imagines his parents' joy and his father's pride at discovering that their son is a writer. Imagining his parents as readers of his work keeps Kersi connected to his childhood in India while he struggles to find his way alone in a strange country.

Source: Elisabeth Piedmont-Marton, Overview of "Swimming Lessons," for *Short Stories for Students,* The Gale Group, 1999.

Peter J. Bailey

In the following excerpt, Bailey notes that Mistry has managed to "epitomize the important difference necessary to render fiction individual" and "distinctive."

. . . The other stories dealing with the ambiguities of emigration follow Kersi from his childhood disillusionments with the Firozsha Baag residents through his move to Toronto, the dynamic of the collection moving the action progressively away from Bombay to Canada. By the closing story, "Swimming Lessons," Firozsha Baag has been replaced by the grim "Don Mills, Ontario, Canada" apartment building where Kersi lives among strangers, watching alien snowflakes fall and indulging himself in sexual fantasies about the women taking swimming lessons with him at an indoor high school pool. The exotic, densely-consonated Indian words which lent such strangeness to the early stories have given way to the ''gutang-khutang'' sound the building's elevator makes, and Bombay exists only as a truncated echo in Kersi's parents' letters, which admonish him to ''say prayers and do *kusti* at least twice a day,'' and which comment on the very stories the reader has come to the end of. Kersi must be ''so unhappy there,'' his mother concludes, because ''all his stories are about Bombay, he remembers every little thing about his childhood, he is thinking about it all the time even though he is ten thousand miles away, my poor son, I think he misses his home and us and everything he left behind, because if he likes it over there why would he not write stories about that, there must be so many new ideas that his new life could give him.''

''Swimming Lessons'' movingly dramatizes both the truth and error of Kersi's mother's opinion; *Swimming Lessons and Other Stories from Firozsha Baag* anatomizes the process which has left Kersi dreaming of one culture, living in another, and feeling himself a citizen of neither. In this stunning first work of fiction, Mistry manages to epitomize the ''important difference'' necessary to render fiction individual, distinctive, even as it affectingly enacts the protagonist/author surrendering up that ''different viewpoint.'' His book renders simultaneously what is saved and what is lost.

Source: Peter J. Bailey, ''Fiction and Difference,'' in *The North American Review,* Vol. 274, No. 4, December, 1989, pp. 61–64.

Sources

Cooke, Hope. ''Beehive in Bombay.'' *The New York Times Book Review,* March 5, 1989, p. 26.

Garebian, Keith. ''In the Aftermath of Empire: Identities in the Commonwealth of Literature.'' *Canadian Forum,* Vol. LXVIII, No. 780, April, 1989, pp. 25-33.

Hancock, Geoff. ''An Interview with Rohinton Mistry.'' *Canadian Fiction Magazine,* No. 65, 1989, pp. 143-50.

Hospital, Janette Turner. ''Living in Toronto, Dreaming of Bombay.'' *Los Angeles Times Book Review,* March 5, 1989, pp. 2, 11.

Kakutani, Michiko. ''Tales from a Bombay Apartment Complex.'' *The New York Times,* February 3, 1989, p. C32.

Malak, Amin. ''Images of India.'' *Canadian Literature,* No. 119, Winter, 1988, pp. 101-03.

A Very Old Man with Enormous Wings

Gabriel Garcia Marquez

1968

Written in 1968, "Un señor muy viejo con alas enormes" ("A Very Old Man with Enormous Wings") is typical of a style known as "magic realism," which is closely associated with its author, the Colombian novelist Gabriel Garcia Marquez. This imaginative style combines realistic, everyday details with elements of fantasy, blurring the reader's usual distinctions between reality and magic. But unlike other works of the imagination such as fairy tales or folk legends, stories of magic realism lead to no clear morals or simple truths; they present a rich and vivid world of magical possibilities, while frustrating and complicating the reader's efforts to fix a definite meaning to events.

Very simply stated, this is the story of what happens when an angel comes to town. But while it is subtitled "A Tale for Children," it is by no means a simple story. The setting is no ordinary town, and its visitor is no ordinary angel—indeed, he may very well not be an angel at all. In most respects, he seems disappointingly ordinary and human, despite his extraordinary appearance. Because he contradicts their expectations, the characters we meet seem thoroughly incapable of understanding him; their conventional wisdom and superstitious beliefs lead them into absurd explanations for his sudden visit, and they treat him in a manner that seems cruel, unjust, and ignorant.

Magic realism has been a popular and influential form, attracting a wide readership and a great

deal of interest from literary scholars. Drawing on the stories and legends of his rural South American childhood, as well as his study of the sophisticated techniques of modernist writers, Garcia Marquez creates a rich and suggestive fictional landscape that challenges traditional modes of thought and focuses the reader's attention on the difficult, elusive work of making sense of the world.

Author Biography

Gabriel Jose Garcia Marquez was born on March 6, 1928, in Aracataca, Colombia, a small town in a farming region near the Caribbean coast. His birth came just as this region entered a sudden economic decline after twenty years of relative prosperity. His father, an out-of-work telegraph operator, relocated, leaving young Gabriel to be raised by his grandparents for the first eight years of his life.

These early circumstances are significant, for they seem to have had a profound influence on the mature writer's work. Garcia Marquez has said that he had learned everything important in his life by the time he was eight years old, and that nothing in his writing is purely a product of "fantasy." As a boy, he delighted in his grandfather's storytelling, from which he heard local legends and history; from his grandmother and the other villagers, he absorbed a wealth of traditions, superstitions, and folk beliefs. Drawing heavily on such sources, Garcia Marquez has developed an imaginative style literary critics call "magic realism." Many of his stories, including the celebrated epic novel *Cien años de soledad* (*One Hundred Years of Solitude* 1967), are set in a fictional village named "Macondo"— which seems to be based on Aracataca, and in some ways reflects the rich, confusing world of childhood as well. Like the unnamed villages in "A Very Old Man with Enormous Wings" and "The Handsomest Drowned Man in the World," Macondo seems to be half-real and half-mythical, a place where dreams and the supernatural are blended with the details of everyday life, and where the most extraordinary events are somehow accepted as "normal," even if they can't be adequately explained. Old men, like the winged gentleman in "A Very Old Man with Enormous Wings," are frequent characters in Garcia Marquez's writing, leading critics to speculate that they may all be derived, in part, from the author's own grandfather.

Garcia Marquez rejoined his family in Bogota, moving from a tropical village to a cold city high in the Andes mountains; he graduated from high school in 1946, and entered the National University in Bogota as a law student in 1947. However, the following year marked the beginning of *la violencia,* a decade-long period of civil warfare in Colombia, which would disrupt his life in many ways. When violence in Bogota caused the university to close, Garcia Marquez transferred to the University of Cartagena (near Aracataca on the northern coast) to continue his law studies. While there he also took a job as a journalist and began to write fiction seriously. In 1950 he dropped out of law school and moved to nearby Barranquilla. He found newspaper work and joined a circle of local writers who admired the work of European and American modernist authors (including James Joyce, Franz Kafka, Virginia Woolf, William Faulkner, and Ernest Hemingway), and who sought to apply their styles and techniques to Latin American settings and themes in their own writings. García Márquez has acknowledged the particular influence of Faulkner and Hemingway on his own early work, and critics often compare his fictional creation of "Macondo" to that of Yoknapatawpha County, the recurring setting for many of Faulkner's novels and short stories.

For fifteen years, Garcia Marquez made a modest living as a journalist and published several short stories. His first novella, *La hojarasca,* was published in 1955; it was translated into English in 1972 as the title piece in *Leaf Storm and Other Stories,* which included a translation of the story "The Handsomest Drowned Man in the World." That same year a Bogota newspaper, *El Espectador,* sent him to Switzerland as a correspondent, but the paper was soon shut down by the military government, stranding Garcia Marquez in Europe for several years in relative poverty. A second novel, *El colonel no tiene quien le escriba* (*No One Writes to the Colonel*), was published in 1961, followed by a collection of short stories, *Los funerales de la Mamá Grande* (*Big Mama's Funeral*), in 1962. By this time, his writing had received some critical approval but had made very little impact outside of Colombia, and García Márquez apparently resolved not to write any more fiction. However, three years later he began working on *One Hundred Years of Solitude.* When it was published in April, 1967, it became an international sensation: after years of frustration, Garcia Marquez was an "overnight success." In the process, he not only found a vast audience for his own writing, but helped spark a boom-period for Latin American literature in general. Western critics took a new interest in the region and began to recognize the achievements of such writers as Julio Cortazar, Ernesto Sabato, Jorge Luis Borges, Pablo Neruda, Carlos Fuentes, and Mario Vargas Llosa—all of whom came to enjoy much wider readership than they had found before García Márquez's breakthrough. A second story collection, *La increíble y triste historia de la candida Eréndira y de su abuela desalmada* (*The Incredible and Sad Story of Innocent Eréndira and Her Heartless Grandmother*), which includes ''A Very Old Man with Enormous Wings,'' was published in 1972. García Márquez's later novels include *El otoño del patriarca* (*The Autumn of the Patriarch*, 1975), *Crónica de una muerte anunciada* (*Chronicle of a Death Foretold*, 1981), *El amor en los timepos del cólera* (*Love in the Time of Cholera*, 1985), and *El general en su laberinto* (*The General in His Labyrinth*, 1989). Among his many honors is the Nobel Prize for Literature, which he received in 1982.

Plot Summary

While Garcia Marquez makes no divisions in the text, this discussion will consider the plot in four separate stages. The story begins with the ''old man's'' arrival and ends with his departure. The intervening period, which covers several years, may be divided into two stages: the brief sensation caused by his appearance and a long period of declining interest in which the strange visitor is all but forgotten.

Arrival

The setting is an unnamed coastal village, at an unspecified time in the past. A long rainstorm has washed crabs up from the beach into Pelayo's house, creating an odor he thinks may be affecting his sick newborn child. Disposing of their carcasses, he sees a figure groaning on the ground in his courtyard; as he moves closer, he discovers it to be ''an old man, a very old man, lying face down in the mud, who, in spite of his tremendous efforts, couldn't get up, impeded by his enormous wings.'' Staring at this pitiful ''bird-man,'' Pelayo and his wife Elisenda begin to overcome their amazement, and even find him familiar, despite those mysterious wings. While they can't understand his language, he seems to

have ''a strong sailor's voice,'' and at first they decide he is a shipwrecked foreign sailor, somehow managing to overlook the need to explain his wings. But a neighbor soon ''corrects'' them, stating confidently that he is an angel. Assuming he is nothing but trouble, she advises them to kill him. Not having the heart for it, Pelayo instead locks the old man in his chicken coop, still planning to dispose of him, only now by setting him to sea on a raft. He and Elisenda wake the next morning to find a crowd of neighbors in the courtyard and a far more complicated situation on their hands; suddenly, ''everyone knew that a flesh-and-blood angel was held captive in Pelayo's house.''

Sensation

The villagers treat the old man like a ''circus animal''; they toss him food and speculate about what should be done with him. Some think he should be made ''mayor of the world,'' others want him to be a ''five-star general in order to win all wars,'' and still others hope he will father a super-race of ''winged wise men who could take charge of the universe.'' The village priest arrives to inspect the captive, and presumably to make a more reasoned judgment on his nature. Father Gonzaga suspects ''an impostor'' at once and finds the old man's pathetic appearance to be strongly at odds with the church's traditional image of heavenly messengers. Finding the old man smelly and decrepit, his battered wings infested with insects, and showing no knowledge of church etiquette, the priest concludes that ''nothing about him measured up to the proud dignity of angels.'' Despite his skepticism, he refuses to give a definitive ruling on the old man, choosing instead to write letters to his church superiors and wait for a written verdict from scholars in the Vatican. In the meantime, he warns the villagers against reaching any rash conclusions.

But word of the ''angel'' has already traveled too far, drawing fantastic crowds and creating a carnival atmosphere; events unfold quickly, described in language that suggests the exaggerated, dreamlike world of fairy-tales.

Surrounded by all this hectic activity, the old man takes ''no part in his own act,'' keeping to himself and tolerating the abuses and indignities of his treatment with a patience that seems to be ''[h]is only supernatural virtue.'' Drawn by the crowds, traveling circuses and carnivals arrive in town—

including one that provides formidable competition for the puzzling attraction of "a haughty angel who scarcely deigned to look at mortals."

Decline

The new sensation is "the spider-woman," whose fantastic nature includes none of the majesty we associate with angels; she represents a kind of "magic" familiar from fairy-tales and folk legends. When still a girl, she once disobeyed her parents by going dancing; later, on the way home, she was struck by lightning and changed into a giant tarantula, retaining her human head. As a spectacle, she appeals to the crowd in ways the old man cannot, and even charges a lower admission price. Significantly, she speaks to her visitors, explaining the meaning of her monstrous appearance; her sad story is easy to understand, and points to a clear moral (children should obey their parents), one her audience already believes to be true. In contrast, the old man does nothing to explain himself, teaches nothing, and doesn't even entertain people; rather than confirming their beliefs, his mysterious nature challenges all the expectations it creates. He does perform some miracles, but they are equally puzzling, seeming to be either practical jokes or the result of some "mental disorder." These disappointing miracles "had already ruined the angel's reputation, when the woman who had been changed into a spider finally crushed him completely." The crowds disappear from Pelayo and Elisenda's courtyard as suddenly as they had come, and the unexplained mystery of the "bird-man" is quickly forgotten.

Still, thanks to the now-departed paying customers, Pelayo and Elisenda are now wealthy. They rebuild their home as "a two-story mansion with balconies and gardens and high netting so that crabs wouldn't get in during the winter, and with iron bars on the windows so that angels wouldn't get in," and settle into a life of luxury. But the ruined chicken coop and its ancient captive remain; as the years pass, the couple's growing child plays in the courtyard with the old man, who stubbornly survives despite his infirmities and neglect. When a doctor comes to examine him, he is amazed that the old man is still alive, and also by "the logic of his wings," which seem so natural that the doctor wonders why everyone doesn't have them. Even the bird-man's mystery and wonder grow so familiar that he eventually becomes a simple nuisance: a

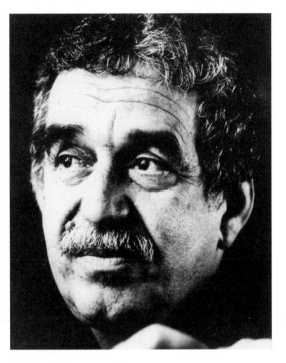

Gabriel Garcia Marquez

disagreeable old man, "dragging himself about here and there," always underfoot. Elisenda seems to find him everywhere in the house, as if he were duplicating himself just to annoy her; at one point she grows so "exasperated and unhinged" she screams that she is living in a "hell full of angels." Finally the old man's health deteriorates even further, and he seems to be near death.

Departure

As winter gives way to the sunny days of spring, the old man's condition begins to improve. He seems to sense a change taking place in himself, and to know what it means. He tries to stay out of the family's sight, sitting motionless for days in the corner of the courtyard; at night, he quietly sings sailor's songs to himself. Stiff new feathers begin to grow from his wings, and one morning Elisenda sees him trying them out in the courtyard. His first efforts to fly are clumsy, consisting of "ungainly flapping that slipped on the light and couldn't get a grip on the air," but he finally manages to take off. Elisenda sighs with relief, "for herself and for him," as she watches him disappear, "no longer an annoyance in her life but an imaginary dot on the horizon of the sea."

Characters

Bird-man

See Very old man with enormous wings

Elisenda

In her marriage to Pelayo, Elisenda takes an active part in decision-making. Her husband runs to get her as soon as he discovers the old man, and they try to make sense of him together, apparently sharing the same reactions. It is she who first conceives of charging the villagers admission to see the "angel," an idea which makes the couple wealthy. At the end of the story, she is the mistress of an impressive mansion, dressed in the finest fashions. Yet the old man seems to be a constant annoyance to her, a feeling that only intensifies over time. He is useless and infuriating to her, "dragging himself about here and there like a stray dying man"; she seems to be constantly shooing him out of her way. She eventually grows so "exasperated and unhinged" that she screams that she is living in a "hell full of angels." Elisenda is also the only witness to the old man's departure, watching silently from the kitchen window as he tries out his newly regrown wings. Her reaction as he disappears over the horizon shows a measure of sympathy for the "senile vulture," as well as her hope that her own life will return to normal: she lets out a sigh of relief "for herself, and for him."

Father Gonzaga

A former woodcutter, Father Gonzaga is the village priest whose religious training and standing in the community make him a moral and intellectual authority. Of all the characters, he seems uniquely qualified to pass judgment on the strange visitor and to determine whether he is really one of God's angels or "just a Norwegian with wings." However, his understanding of church doctrine leads him to no solid conclusions. He counsels the villagers to withhold their own judgment until he can receive a definitive answer from scholars in the Vatican. Father Gonzaga is never able to provide an explanation, and he loses sleep over the mystery until his parishioners eventually lose interest in the old man entirely.

Examining the angel-like creature, Father Gonzaga immediately suspects that he is "an impostor." The old man's unbearable odor, his derelict condition, and his undignified appearance all make him seem "much too human" to accept as a perfect immortal or member of a divine race. But rather than make a judgment from the evidence of his senses (and knowing that the devil likes to trick people with appearances), he applies a series of tests to the old man, presumably based on church teachings about the nature of angels. First, he greets the old man in Latin; the lack of a response is yet another suspicious sign, for it shows that the "angel" doesn't "understand the language of God or know how to greet His ministers." A series of letters from higher church authorities results in further "tests" of divinity (Does the old man have a belly-button? Does his language seem related to the biblical dialect of Aramaic?) but fail to lead him to any final judgment. Unable to provide the answer that they seek from him, the Father can only warn his flock not to jump to any conclusions—a warning which they ignore with enthusiasm.

As a comic authority figure Father Gonzaga is open to a variety of interpretations. He is clearly ineffective in his role as a spiritual authority and as a source of wisdom and enlightenment. His superiors in the church hierarchy prove no more helpful and seem to be obsessed with obscure theological abstractions, such as how many angels can fit on the head of a pin. Such factors suggest at least a mildly satirical view of the Catholic Church and perhaps of organized religion in general. To some critics, Father Gonzaga's means of inquiry are also a parody of the scientific method, while his fruitless correspondence with church scholars reflects the uselessness of bureaucracies everywhere. And other critics even see a reflection of themselves—the figure of the cultural authority, whose profession makes him unwilling to admit the obvious limits of his understanding.

Old man

See Very old man with enormous wings

Pelayo

It is Pelayo, the town bailiff, who discovers the old man with wings struggling face down in the courtyard of his home after a storm. As the strange visitor begins to attract crowds, Pelayo and his wife, Elisenda, exhibit him as a carnival attraction. Though the old man proves to be only a temporary sensation, he creates a highly profitable windfall for the young couple. In "less than a week they had crammed their rooms with money" from paid admissions; they quickly earn enough to rebuild their house as a mansion and to live in luxury by village standards. Pelayo quits his job and sets up a rabbit warren on the edge of town, trading a minor administrative position for the leisurely life of a gamekeeping squire. While Pelayo's discovery of the winged being brings him great fortune, it also brings confusion and complication into his life. It is not the sort of luck he hopes to see repeated. When he and Elisenda design their new home, they are careful to include "iron bars on the windows so that angels wouldn't get in."

Spider-woman

The centerpiece of a traveling carnival, the "woman who had been changed into a spider for disobeying her parents" proves to be a more popular attraction than the old man, causing the villagers to lose interest in him and putting an end to Pelayo and Elisenda's profitable courtyard business. As a young girl, she had once gone dancing all night against her parents' wishes; later, while walking home, she was allegedly struck by lightning and transformed into "a frightful tarantula the size of a ram . . . with the head of a sad maiden." Compared to the baffling old man, the spider-woman provides a far more satisfying spectacle. While she is at least as grotesque and fantastic as the "bird-man," she charges a lower admission price; more importantly, she is willing to communicate freely with her visitors, recounting her sad experience and inspiring sympathy for her fate. The "meaning" of her story is easy to grasp and teaches a clear moral lesson— one that confirms the villagers' conventional beliefs. In contrast, the old man makes no attempt to explain himself and seems to contradict all religious and folk beliefs about the nature of angels. His very existence raises disturbing questions, but he offers no reassuring answers.

Very old man with enormous wings

The old man is the story's central character and its central mystery. He is given no name but is precisely described in the title, which includes everything that can be said about him with any assurance: he is an extremely old man, in failing health, with all the frailties and limitations of human old age, and he has a huge pair of bird's wings growing from his back. We follow the other characters in their comic efforts to explain him, to assign some "meaning" to his sudden appearance, and finally to just put up with his annoying presence, but when he flies away at the story's end, the mystery remains.

The very idea of a "winged humanoid" evokes the image of angels, and most of the "wise" villagers quickly assume that he *is* an angel. But every-

Media Adaptations

- "A Very Old Man with Enormous Wings" was adapted, with some modifications, as a film with the same title in 1988, in a Spanish production directed by Fernando Birri. Starring Daisy Granados, Asdrubal Melendez, and Luis Alberto Ramiriz, the film is available with English subtitles on Fox/Lorber Home Video, Facets Multimedia, Inc., or from Ingram International Films.

thing about him seems to contradict traditional stereotypes of heavenly power and immortal perfection. When Pelayo first finds him in the courtyard, apparently blown out of the sky by a strong rainstorm, his condition is pathetic: he lies "face down in the mud," "dressed like a ragpicker," and tangled in his half-plucked, bug-infested wings. The narrator tells us directly that this "pitiful condition of a drenched great-grandfather had taken away any sense of grandeur he might have had," and Father Gonzaga underscores the point later, when he observes that "nothing about him measured up to the proud dignity of angels." Nor do the villagers allow him any dignity or respect; throughout the story, they treat him "without the slightest reverence." He is displayed like a circus animal or sideshow freak; poked, plucked, and prodded; branded with a hot iron; pelted with stones and garbage; and held prisoner for years in a filthy, battered chicken coop, exposed to the elements. Though he is the source of the family's great fortune, Elisenda comes to find him an intolerable annoyance, becoming "exasperated and unhinged" by his presence. He is understandably "standoffish" toward people, tolerating only the company of the couple's young child, and the villagers come to think of him as "a haughty angel who scarcely deigned to look at mortals." Given his cruel captivity, the reader can only agree when the narrator observes that his "only supernatural virtue seemed to be patience." Even this virtue is later deprived of any otherworldly greatness; it becomes merely "the patience of a dog who had no illusions."

The old man is described in imagery of earthly poverty and human weakness, contradicting traditional heavenly stereotypes. Even the birds with which he is compared to are ignoble ones (''buzzard wings,'' ''a huge decrepit hen,'' ''a senile vulture''). Yet there is clearly something of the magical about him beyond his unexplained wings and mysterious origin. He does, after all, perform miracles—but they, too, fail to satisfy expectations. The blind man's sight isn't restored, but he suddenly grows three new teeth; the leper's sores aren't cured, but sunflowers begin growing from them. These are ''consolation miracles,'' which show ''a certain mental disorder,'' as if senility had caused his magic powers to misfire. Alternately, they could be practical jokes, a form of ''mocking fun'' to avenge his abuse by the crowd. Their sick child recovers when Pelayo and Elisenda take in the old man, but this could be coincidence, or perhaps another case of failed magic (if, as the neighbor woman believes, he is an angel of death sent to take the baby). And, despite his obvious infirmities, he is possessed of a surprising inner strength. His health seems to be in irreversible decline throughout; a doctor's examination finds it ''impossible for him to be alive,'' and very late in the story his death appears imminent. Yet with the coming of spring, after years of uselessness, his wings grow new feathers and regain their strength, allowing him to escape the village forever.

Although his wings make him a creature of the sky and he is clearly not at home on land, the old man also has some association with the sea. He comes from the sea (or at least from over it), washed up with a tide of crabs by a three-day storm; his first attempts to fly away are accompanied by ''a wind that seemed to come from the high seas.'' Pelayo and Elisenda first take him for a foreign sailor (perhaps because they detect ''a strong sailor's voice'' in his incomprehensible speech), and an early plan called for him to be set out to sea on a raft with provisions. As his wings begin to regenerate, he sings ''sea chanteys'' under the stars. Critics disagree in their interpretations of this connection and in their judgments on its significance. But in García Márquez's other works, they often find the sea to be an important theme or symbol, both as a natural force of great power (equally capable of bringing rich gifts or terrible destruction), and as a force associated with the supernatural. Several of his stories include episodes where unusual strangers from the ''outside world'' appear in a small town and have a strong effect on its people. Very often, these remarkable visitors arrive by sea.

The old man is also connected in some way with Pelayo and Elisenda's child. The newborn is ill when he first appears, but quickly recovers when the ''angel'' takes up residence. The ''wise neighbor woman'' believes that he was sent to takes the child's life. Both the child and the old man come down with chicken pox at the same time, and the old man uncharacteristically allows the child to play with and around him, tolerating ''ingenious infamies'' with patience. But beyond these details, the connection or bond between the two is not developed.

Because the old man is a misunderstood outsider subjected to cruel mistreatment, he becomes primarily a figure of pity—a strange emotion for an ''angel'' to inspire. He has enough magical qualities to let the reader see him, at least potentially, as a figure of wonder, but his very human vulnerability keeps this from being much more than a suggestion. Finally, there is at least an equal suggestion of a potential ''dark side.'' Pelayo's first impression is that of having seen a ''nightmare,'' and the ''mental disorder'' of the old man's miracles suggests that his ''magic powers'' are uncontrollable, making him dangerous. When burned with a branding iron, his startled wing-flapping creates ''a whirlwind of chicken dung and lunar dust,'' ''a gale of panic that did not seem to be of this world.'' It is almost a moment of terror; when he calms down, the villagers regard him with renewed caution and fear: ''his passivity was not that of a hero taking his ease, but that of a cataclysm in repose.'' And though his visit brings truly miraculous results for Pelayo and Elisenda by making them fabulously wealthy, it also seems to be a frightful and unnerving experience for them. Elisenda comes to feel that she lives in ''a hell full of angels,'' and when they design their dream home, the couple make sure to ''angel-proof'' it with iron bars.

Themes

Doubt and Ambiguity
One of this story's difficult aspects is the sense of uncertainty it creates by leaving important facts

unresolved and seeming to offer several possible interpretations for its events. The reader is never allowed to doubt that the old man and his strange wings are as "real" as anything else in the story; yet the reader can never be sure just *what* he is—a heavenly angel, a sad human who happens to have wings, or perhaps some other, unexplained possibility. This deliberate uncertainty can leave readers feeling a bit cheated—particularly in what seems to be a fairy tale. Stories are expected to have clear-cut meanings, and the author is expected to reveal them to the reader; if not, there is a tendency to feel he has failed in his storytelling, or that his audience has failed as readers. But in works of realism (and many other forms), ambiguity is often used as an intentional effect, to make a story seem less "story-like," and more like life itself. It reflects the understanding that real life is far more uncertain than the stories in books, and often forces readers to choose among several, equally possible explanations of events. As characters in daily life, readers seldom know "the whole story"—but it is traditional to expect writers to tie all tales neatly together for our understanding. While it complicates the task of the reader, the skillful, suggestive use of ambiguity is often admired by critics, and is usually considered to be one of the most appealing features of "magic realism."

Even in stories dealing with magic or the supernatural, there are rules a writer is expected to follow—for example, that there must always be a clear distinction between magical events and "normal" ones, and that the nature and significance of all characters is eventually made known to the reader. But as a magic realist, Garcia Marquez insists on breaking these rules as well. Without its fantastic elements, there is no story; yet the reader is never sure just how to take them, and how far to trust the narrator. Sometimes, he makes it obvious that the villagers' magical beliefs are in fact ridiculous delusions; but at other times, the reader seems expected to take logically impossible events at face value. The changing of a human into a giant spider, a man who can't sleep because "the noise of the stars" disturbs him—are these things that "really happened?" Can they be dismissed as mere hallucinations? Are they poetic images, meant to be interpreted on some level beyond their literal meaning? Like the old man with his miracles, Garcia Marquez may be suspected of having a kind of "mocking fun" with the reader, suggesting all sorts of miraculous possibilities, then stubbornly contradicting all

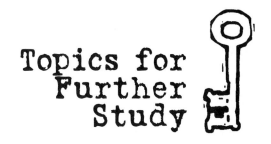

Topics for Further Study

- Look into other forms of "fantastic" literature, such as fairy tales, science fiction, mythology, superhero comics, or folk legends. Choose specific works of at least two different types and compare their styles and techniques to those of "magic realism" as represented by this story.

- Compare the manner in which García Márquez treats the traditional idea of angels in "A Very Old Man with Enormous Wings" with the way angels are represented or interpreted elsewhere, in some other work or media. Potential sources include feature films, television shows, religious or inspirational literature, and advertising.

- Be an amateur "magic realist," loosely following the formula García Márquez employed for "A Very Old Man with Enormous Wings." For this assignment, your "village" is any other story you have already studied; the "angel" will be another character you introduce from "outside" the story, chosen because he or she seems totally alien to the sense of the story as you have come to know it. It could be a character from outside literature: a pop culture celebrity, a representative from another time or culture–anyone who seems not to belong at all in the world constructed by the author of your story. Re-write or outline the story, incorporating the viewpoint of your new character and making the other characters respond to their ill-fitting new companion.

the expectations he creates. In appreciating such a story, it may be necessary to limit one's reliance on clear meanings and moral lessons, and to be prepared to enjoy the sheer wealth of possibility and comic misunderstanding that is presented.

The Problem of Interpretation

One effect of ambiguity is to focus attention on the uncertain nature of all efforts to assign meaning to events. The troublesome nature of *interpretation* has been a matter of intense interest for literary critics in the years since this story was written—which may be one reason Garcia Marquez remains a popular subject of scholarly attention. Many theorists stress that all ''readings'' (whether of texts, or of life itself) are strongly influenced by their context, and by the specific interests and point of view of the person making the judgment. While one may detect such influence in the opinions of others, it usually operates unconsciously in the self; the assumptions behind one's own thinking are so familiar that one tends not to even recognize them *as* assumptions. Some critics go so far as to suggest that all explanations are actually *inventions,* and that ''true meanings'' can never be reliably determined. While one may not choose to embrace so extreme a position, the speculation serves as a reminder that confident pronouncements about the world are seldom, if ever, as rational or disinterested as one believes them to be. The villagers' quirky thought-patterns may be seen as a parody of this universal human tendency. They ''talk themselves into'' all kinds of wild speculations, clinging to irrational notions (such as the ''fact'' that mothballs are the proper food for angels) and leaping to impossible conclusions (for example, that the old man should be named ''mayor of the world.'') It seems that, once they get an idea into their heads, they willfully convince themselves of its truth and ignore any evidence to the contrary—unless a more appealing version of the truth comes along. Their folly is a kind of exaggerated ignorance, which Garcia Marquez uses consistently for comic effect; but in their unquestioning application of ''conventional wisdom,'' and their stubborn faith in their own ideas, they reflect habits of mind that can be recognized in all cultures.

On another level, the author may be seen as placing the reader in much the same position—forcing the reader to accept interpretations that seem absurd, or to give up any hope of understanding events. In this sense, it might be said that the story's meaning lies in the manner it denies any clear meanings, complicating the reader's efforts to understand, and showing usual means of determining the truth in a strange, uncertain light. The context of literature may tempt one to ''read into'' these odd characters, looking for symbolic meanings and creatively-coded messages from the author. Nothing prevents the reader from doing so, but there are few clues or hints to help and no obvious way to confirm or deny any interpretation one may construct. The reader can't be sure if he is *finding*

the story's meaning or making one up; he may even wonder if the story has a meaning at all. Garcia Marquez presents a rich mystery, which engages the reader's thinking and seems to ''make sense'' in the manner of fairy tales; then he leaves the reader to decide its meaning for himself. However one goes about the job, he is never allowed to escape the suspicion that he may, in his own way, wind up being as foolish and gullible as the villagers.

Style

Imagery

In establishing the character of the old man, Garcia Marquez plays against traditional stereotypes of angels. Angels are supernatural creatures and are expected them to be presented in images that convey grandeur, perfection, wisdom, and grace. By definition, angels are contrasted with humans; though they resemble humans physically, they are *super-human* in every conceivable way. But like Father Gonzaga, the reader's first response to the old man is likely to be that he is ''much too human.'' Instead of presenting a majestic, awe-inspiring figure, Garcia Marquez describes a creature with mortal weaknesses and senility (''a drenched great-grandfather''), in circumstances without any trace of reverence or dignity. While his feathered wings invite comparisons with birds, even this imagery is common and debased; he is ''a senile vulture'' or a ''decrepit hen,'' not a soaring eagle or an elegant swan. While the villagers face the problem of understanding an apparent ''angel'' who fits none of their expectations for the type, the reader finds himself placed by the author in the same position.

Also unusual is the way Garcia Marquez combines different types of imagery. The opening line reveals that it is ''the third day of rain,'' and a few lines later this information is repeated in another form: ''The world had been sad since Tuesday.'' One is a direct statement of fact, which might appear in a weather report; the other is a poetic image, projecting human emotions onto the weather and individual feelings onto the entire world. Expressed in other terms, the reader accepts the first version as ''real,'' while the second version (if taken at face value) is ''magical,'' involving a logically-impossible connection between human feelings and the weather. Both attitudes are familiar to readers, who know to read a factual account in a rational, literal frame of mind, and to suspend disbelief in a more imaginative story, where descriptions are expected to be used for their creative, suggestive effects. But Garcia Marquez never allows the reader to settle comfortably into one attitude or the other; throughout the story, realistic and magical details are combined, seeming to suggest that both attitudes are valid, and that neither one is sufficient by itself.

Narration

The ambiguity within the story is reinforced by inconsistencies in the narrative voice. The narrator is, after all, the "person" presenting all this odd imagery to the reader, and readers habitually look to the narrator for clues to help find a proper interpretation. For example, when the narrator states that Father Gonzaga's letters to his church superiors "might have come and gone until the end of time" without reaching a conclusion, he confirms the reader's suspicion that the priest's approach is futile, despite his confident assurances to the crowd. Narrators don't just present facts; they also give direction as to "how to take" the information we receive

This narrator, however, seems to direct the reader all over the map and to be inconsistent in his own attitude to events. The villagers' wild ideas about the old man are often presented as obvious delusions, characterized as "frivolous" or "simple" by the narrator. But at other times, he seems no more skeptical than the villagers. For example, the story of the spider-woman seems far more fantastic than that of an old man with wings, but the narrator gives no suggestion that her transformation is particularly unusual and seems to expect the reader to accept this frankly "magical" event as if it presented no mystery at all. Though they are wise in ways the villagers are not, and see through the various fanciful interpretations of the visitor, readers come to feel that the narrator may not fully understand the old man himself. Such an unreliable storyteller makes a mystery even more mysterious, complicating efforts to fix a definite meaning to the tale.

Historical Context

The Lack of a Context

The time and place of this story are undetermined. The characters' names suggest a Spanish-speaking country, and a reference to airplanes indicates that we are somewhere in the twentieth century; but beyond these minor details, we seem to be in the "once-upon-a-time" world of fairy tales. The narrator tells of events in the past, using the phrase "in those times" in a manner common to myths and legends. These associations help prepare the reader for the story's "magical" elements by suggesting that this is not a factual history to be taken literally, but a tale of the imagination where the usual rules may be suspended.

Such an "undetermined" setting is common in Garcia Marquez's fiction. While he is often outspoken in his journalism and takes a public stand on many political issues, references to contemporary history in his fiction tend to be indirect and uncertain. Critics have tried to trace such connections (for example, by suggesting that a character in one of his novels is modeled on a certain South American dictator), but the author's decision to write in this manner indicates that such "messages" are not his primary concern. By its nature, the story is not tied to any particular time or place; like legends from a mythical golden age in the past, it calls our attention to timeless, universal themes, applying in a general way to all times and places.

The Context of Reception

While the story shows no direct evidence of historical context, it was, of course, written in a particular time and place. And like all artistic productions, its "success" has depended not only on its artistic merits, but on its ability to attract an audience and to gain acceptance from critics and scholars. Unlike the writing itself, the *reception* of a work involves factors largely outside the author's control, factors usually having much to do with historical and cultural context.

The extremes of popular and critical reception can be seen in the stereotype of the "starving artist," who works without reward for years then suddenly (perhaps only in death) receives widespread, long-overdue recognition. This is the "tragic genius," ahead of his time—"the world was not ready" for the work he produced. The type does not fit Garcia Marquez exactly, but he did labor in relative obscurity for many years, then suddenly became an international phenomenon: a best-selling author who was also praised by prominent intellectuals, even being heralded as the vanguard of a revolution in Latin American literature. Such sudden enthusiasm, for however deserving an artist, indicates that the world somehow *was* ready for Garcia Marquez in 1967, when the publication of

One Hundred Years of Solitude brought him instant fame, as well as intense scrutiny.

The Garcia Marquez ''boom'' was fueled by a number of developments, both in popular culture and in critical scholarship, which made it easier for many readers to embrace a work of ''magic realism,'' and an author from a non-Western culture. The late 1960s are usually characterized as a period of intense cultural change, in which traditional values of all kinds were challenged, and alternative ways of living were widely explored. College campuses were a particular focus for this controversy, most famously in occasional violent confrontations between law enforcement and student political protesters. But it also found expression through passionate debates within the scholarly disciplines, debates in which the most basic assumptions were questioned, and apparently radical changes were given serious consideration. In literature departments, one result was an effort to expand the ''canon''—the list of ''classic'' works (sometimes listed in an official document, sometimes found in the unspoken, shared assumptions of faculty members) whose study is traditionally considered to form the necessary basis of a liberal arts education. Critics charged that, with few if any exceptions, the canon had excluded women and people of color from the roll of ''great authors,'' as well as writers from poor or working-class backgrounds and those from non-European cultures. Efforts to expand the canon, to include a more diverse blend of cultural voices among the works considered worthy of serious scholarship, have continued for over thirty years. Garcia Marquez can be seen as an early beneficiary of this trend; Latin American writers had long been neglected, and his work could be shown to include many of the elements critics had praised in European and North American works. He thus made an early ''test case'' for expanding the canon, an example of a non-Western writer who deserved to be honored on a level equal to his Western contemporaries. His recognition encouraged the ''discovery'' of many more Latin American authors and contributed to an explosion of scholarship on the region's literary heritage.

Finally, this story has a context within Garcia Marquez's own career. It was written in 1968, a year after his sudden fame. One interpretation of ''A Very Old Man with Enormous Wings'' sees it as an exaggerated, satirical account of his own experience with instant celebrity; or, in a more general way, as a commentary on the position of the creative artist in modern culture. In this reading, the ''old man'' is the artist, while his ''wings'' stand for transcendence, greatness, truth, beauty—whatever elusive qualities we think of as being valuable in art. The villagers, in turn, are ''the public,'' who are greedy for whatever ''magic'' he might bring them—but who insist on having it on their own terms. Rather than accepting him as he is, with all his quirks and contradictions, they treat him as a carnival attraction and look for ways to profit from his odd celebrity. They misunderstand him completely, yet confidently ''explain'' him with wild, illogical speculations. And given a choice, they prefer the kind of magic offered by sensations like the spider-woman—flashy and easy to understand, fitting in comfortably with their beliefs, presenting no awkward difficulties or mysteries. However ''magical'' they may be, such creatures as artists and angels just aren't made for everyday life; ultimately, they are an annoyance and an embarrassment to the rest of us. This is, of course, only one of many possible interpretations, for a story that seems designed to resist any single, clear explanation. But it does show another way in which context (cultural, historical, and personal) can find its way into a story which seems, on the surface, to have been written from no particular time or place.

Critical Overview

''A Very Old Man with Enormous Wings'' was written in 1968, in the wake of its author's sudden fame. The story's timing has led some critics to suggest that it may, at least in part, be a comic treatment of Garcia Marquez's own experience as a writer, or an allegory for the condition of creative artists in general. In this reading, the old man represents the artist, and his experience in the village is a satirical account of the way a work is received by the public. While his wings mark him as extraordinary, in other ways he fails to meet the villagers' impossible expectations; and while they feel a need to account for him, this proves to be a difficult, complex, and uncertain task. Instead, they misinterpret him wildly, and abuse and exploit him as a carnival freak. By insisting on simple, dramatic ''miracles'' that fit comfortably with their beliefs, they give up all chance of understanding whatever ''magic'' he *does* possess and soon lose interest in him. However, it must be stressed that this is only one possible interpretation for this complex story. Other critics have argued that, however appealing, it is far too simple, ''neat,'' and logical to fully account for a tale so rich in invention and suggestion; and even those who advance such a reading point out that is just one of several levels on which meaning can be found.

While Garcia Marquez's early short stories, written in the late 1940s and early 1950s, were generally considered unsuccessful for their overly self-conscious use of unconventional narrative techniques, his later stories employ many of the same narrative strategies that have made Garcia Marquez one of the twentieth century's most influential authors, prompting critics to compare him to the likes of William Faulkner and Franz Kafka.

Criticism

Tom Faulkner

A freelance writer and copyeditor, Faulkner is pursuing an M.A. in English at Wayne State University. In the following essay, he explores the peculiar effects of magic realism as a literary style employed in "A Very Old Man with Enormous Wings."

The style of writing referred to as "magic realism" is marked by its imaginative content, vivid effects, and lingering mystery. In combining fantastic elements with realistic details, a writer like Garcia Marquez can create a fictional "world" where the miraculous and the everyday live side-by-side—where fact and illusion, science and folklore, history and dream, seem equally "real," and are often hard to distinguish. The form clearly allows writers to stretch the limits of possibility and to be richly inventive; however, it involves more than the creation of attractive fantasies. The village in "A Very Old Man with Enormous Wings" may be appealing in some ways, but it is also a complex, difficult, even disturbing fantasy. Beyond imagination, the successful creation of such a world in the reader's mind requires skillful use of the same tools and techniques familiar in more conventional, less "magical" types of fiction. Garcia Marquez not only combines realistic details with fantastic ones, but seems to give them both equal weight, an equal claim to reality or truth in the reader's mind.

In the character of the "bird-man," we can see this style at work and experience the charming (but unsettling) effect it often has on readers. His mysterious nature is the story's central "problem," the source of its energy and tension. We know, of course, that human beings don't have wings; logi-

cally, such a character must be either a monster or a miracle—if he exists at all. Yet when the doctor examines the old man, what most impresses him is "the logic of his wings," which "seemed so natural on that completely human organism that he couldn't understand why other men didn't have them too." Logic and science insist that such a creature must be *supernatural,* but Garcia Marquez presents him as entirely "natural"; much like the doctor, once we've "seen" him, it's as if winged old men were common, even unremarkable, visitors. We see how, despite "the inconvenience of the wings," Pelayo and Elisenda "very soon overcame their surprise and in the end found him familiar." As readers, we are guided to the same kind of acceptance. No one questions the old man's existence, or the reality of his wings, not even the narrator (except, perhaps, in the final line, when the old man becomes "an imaginary dot on the horizon of the sea"). He may or may not be an angel, but he is unquestionably an old man with wings, as "real" as anyone else in the story.

Several techniques contribute to the old man's vivid "existence." Detailed sensory imagery is a standard means for writers to reinforce a character's "reality" to the reader, and Garcia Marquez not only makes us "see" the old man (right down to the "few faded hairs left on his bald skull" and the parasites picking through his ruined feathers), but also "smell" him, "feel" the texture of his wings, and "hear" his whistling heartbeat. The rich imagery also works to undermine supernatural stereotypes, contradicting our usual ideas about angels and denying the old man any of the heroic or exalted qualities we expect. He is described not only in human, earthly terms, but in terms of extreme weakness and poverty ("dressed like a ragpicker," "his pitiful condition of a drenched great-grandfather"). When he is compared to birds, they are not exotic eagles or dazzling peacocks, but common species with less-than-noble reputations (his "buzzard wings," "a decrepit hen," "a senile vulture"). As Father Gonzaga observes (and by the author's design), "nothing about him measured up to the proud dignity of angels." He thus becomes real the more we see him as *human,* a creature closer to our own experience and understanding—not a shining, mythical being but a frail, suffering, even pathetic fellow, who happens to have a few physical quirks.

The problem Garcia Marquez presents us is not just "What if angels were real?" but "What if they were real, and nothing like we expect them to be?"

What Do I Read Next?

- Readers who enjoy this story may wish to explore Garcia Marquez's other works. *Big Mama's Funeral* (1962) and *The Incredible and Sad Story of Innocent Erendira and Her Heartless Grandmother* (1972) are collections of short stories, many of which also embody principles of magic realism. The novel *One Hundred Years of Solitude* (1967) depicts the marvelous village of Macondo through a complex history that spans three generations of the town's leading family. Here, as in *Love in the Time of Cholera* (written in 1985, and set in an unnamed town), Garcia Marquez creates a dreamlike, many-layered landscape, realized in far more detail than is possible for the village in this brief tale. To many critics, *One Hundred Years of Solitude* still represents the highest achievement of magic realism.

- *Labyrinths* (1962) by Jorge Luis Borges is a collection of short fictions, essays, and "parables" that presents interesting parallels and contrasts to the style of Garcia Marquez. Borges is not strictly considered a "magic realist," having already achieved considerable recognition before Garcia Marquez's success; however, he does show many of the same influences and concerns, and indeed may have influenced the younger writer. Borges seems fascinated by paradox and the human thirst for meaning; through short, tightly structured narratives, he develops a variety of inventive contradictions, full of hidden insights and unexpected turns.

- Since the appearance of Garcia Marquez's works, writers from many traditions have continued to test the boundaries of fantasy and reality, in innovative works that suggest the influence of magic realism, or at least seem to arise from similar sources and concerns. Among the many such works that employ an American setting are Max Apple's *The Oranging of America* (1976), a collection of modern fables that explores various aspects of "the American Dream" and its modern myths of success, and *Mumbo Jumbo* (1970) by Ishmael Reed, a satiric "HooDoo detective novel" that is also an ambitious, mythical reimagination of the history of Africans in America.

- Readers might be interested in a novel which is quite similar in theme to "A Very Old Man with Enormous Wings": that work of fiction is *The Wonderful Visit* (1895), by H. G. Wells, author of *The Time Machine, The Island of Dr. Moreau, The Invisible Man,* and other distinguished works of the imagination. *The Wonderful Visit,* which concerns the wounding and capture of an angel by rural English villagers, has been described by critic Kenneth Young as "an ironical study of life in the English countryside. . . . The satire—on ownership, on the ugliness of people's lives—is gentle, though there is a dark passage on 'the readiness of you Human Beings to inflict pain'."

He creates a tension between the old man's magical and human qualities, leaving us unable to fit the character into a comfortable mental category. The old man is far too human and decrepit to match our cultural image of angels: perfect, powerful, majestic, immortal. Nor does he appear to be a heavenly messenger, sent by God as a sign of momentous changes; his presence seems to be purely an accident of the weather, without purpose or meaning. Nonetheless, he certainly has his magical qualities, and is even credited with miracles (though, like everything else about him, they are disturbing, and fail to satisfy expectations). However miraculous his nature, origins, or abilities may be, he is stranded here, and relatively powerless—an exile from his former life, at the mercy of strangers. The villagers must somehow account for him, and because no one understands his language, he is unable (and apparently unwilling) to explain himself. Several possible interpretations arise, but most of them are clearly absurd, telling us more about the villagers' superstitions and beliefs than about the old man's "true nature." They are rendered with playful humor, ensuring that the reader will appreciate the irrational and illusory basis of such "folk wisdom." Yet our "superior," conventional methods of logic and reason don't seem any more useful in reaching a secure explanation. The old man remains a stubborn, intriguing mystery, both magical *and* ordinary, impossible to decipher but undeniably *there.*

This uncertainty (or *ambiguity*) applies not just to the old man, but evidently to life itself, as it is lived in this timeless, nameless village. It seems to be a place where just about anything can happen (for example, a young woman can be changed into a spider for disobeying her parents)—or at least, it is a place where everyone is quite willing to *believe* such things happen and to act as though they *do* happen. This impression is partly a result of Garcia Marquez's use of narrative voice. For the most part, the story seems to be told by the standard "omniscient observer" of third person fiction—a narrator who knows all the necessary facts, and can be trusted to present them reliably. When such narration expresses an opinion, the reader tends to accept it as a correct interpretation. This narrator may seem to fit the type at first, but later appears to change his point of view, and even his opinions of events. The narrator seems to endorse the villagers' thinking at times (for example, reporting without comment that the old man has a "strong sailor's voice," even though we have no evidence for this assumption of Pelayo and Elisenda's), but at other times, he seems almost contemptuous of their irrational ideas. (A few lines later, when he describes how the couple "skipped over the inconvenience of the wings" and "quite intelligently" decided that he was nothing but a sailor, the intent seems to be strongly sarcastic.) We might entertain hope that Father Gonzaga's correspondence with church leaders will eventually produce an explanation—until the narrator comments that those "meager letters might have come and gone until the end of time" without result. In such ways, readers come to rely on the narrator for clues about "how to take" elements in the story that may be unclear. But this narrator seems determined to be untrustworthy, and leaves us uncertain about important events. Without telling us *how,* he treats everything that happens as though it "makes sense." Though he is habitually ironic in his view of the "wise" villagers' beliefs, he describes the supernatural experience of the "spider-woman" in simple factual terms, seeming to accept it as readily as

his characters do. Are we to conclude that this fantastic transformation from human to spider actually happened? Or that the narrator is now as deluded as the villagers? Or even that he is purposely lying to us? At such moments, the narration seems to parody the style of traditional fairy tales; as the label "magic realism" suggests, some elements of the story seem meant to be approached with the simplistic "logic" of fantasy, while others are depicted with all the complexity and imperfection that mark "real life."

Garcia Marquez not only combines realistic details with fantastic ones, but seems to give them both equal weight, an equal claim to "reality" or "truth" in the reader's mind. Dreamlike, poetic descriptions are presented matter-of-factly; like winged old men who fall from the sky, they are treated more as everyday realities than as bizarre impossibilities. When we learn that a character is deprived of sleep "because the noise of the stars disturbed him," it seems to be merely a symptom quoted from his medical chart, perhaps even a common cause of insomnia, not an obvious delusion or a feat of supernatural hearing. As in the similar case of the "poor woman who since childhood had been counting her heartbeats and had run out of numbers," the narrator gives no indication that any particular explanation is required, almost assuming that the reader will accept these odd riddles without question. Traditionally, we aren't meant to take such language literally (as a description of factual events), but poetically (or *figuratively*), as a creative key to some idea or state of mind, which we must interpret for ourselves. (The insomniac, for example, might be said to "really" be experiencing hallucinations due to mental illness, or perhaps a feeling of isolation and insignificance in the cosmos—but not actually listening to stars.) But here, such "magical" descriptions seem to be offered as straightforward accounts of "normal" (if rare and unusual) occurrences (his ears are sensitive, and those stars are just too loud!)—events whose "real meaning" need not, or cannot, be determined, but which must nonetheless be accepted as "real."

The mixture of different kinds of imagery, and different narrative attitudes, serves to heighten the reader's uncertainty. Realistic and magical descriptions are often combined, as if they are inseparable aspects of the same events. Thus, we are not only told that it is "the third day of rain," but also, a few lines later, that "[t]he world had been sad since Tuesday." By combining factual and imaginative descriptions, and seeming to treat them with equal credibility, the author suggests that both ''ways of knowing'' are valid, perhaps even necessary to achieving a balanced understanding. Magic seems to lie just beneath the surface of the story, waiting to break through, almost beyond the narrator's control. For example, a description of the old man's undignified captivity lingers over factual, everyday details (his diet of eggplant mush, the crowd tossing stones to get him to react, the hens pecking through his feathers); but the insects infesting his wings are suddenly described as ''stellar parasites''—a poetic image, not a ''factual'' one (at least until there is any evidence of insects living on stars). If we approach the story expecting to be charmed by a fairy tale, the factual descriptions seem ''too real;'' they spoil the ''magical'' effect we hope for, by allowing the unpleasant and inconvenient details of everyday life to intrude on our imaginative landscape. But if we read with a ''realistic'' frame of mind, looking for solid facts and logical explanations, the strange poetic images only frustrate us, and may cause us to question other apparent ''facts.'' The magical touches may dazzle us, but they can also make us feel like the old man in his early efforts to fly: that we are ''slip[ping] on the light,'' unable to ''get a grip on the air.'' We must somehow accept the events our narrator presents (at least temporarily), in order to continue reading at all, and have any hope of making sense of the tale. But we are never sure whether to ''accept'' them as real events, mass hallucinations, symbolic stand-ins for some ''other'' story the author has in mind, or the unreal ''magic'' of legends and fairy tales. We cannot choose between reality and magic; Garcia Marquez insists on giving us both, even in the most minor details. When the startled bird-man suddenly flaps his wings, he creates a ''whirlwind'' in the courtyard, with a dustcloud composed of both (earthly) chicken dung and (heavenly) ''lunar dust'': even the dirt on the ground is shown to be both humble and marvelous at once.

Typical of the style, this story's tone seems both playful and serious. The striking images and sudden surprises stimulate the reader's senses and imagination, but also frustrate and complicate our efforts to fix a definite meaning to events. Works of magic realism are both praised and criticized for their ''childlike wonder,'' their depiction of a world of almost-infinite possibilities, where the supernatural and the everyday take on the same vivid intensity. But they are not fairy tales or two-dimensional fantasies; they offer no clear lessons, simple

events, or sharp distinctions between reality and magic. ''Wondering'' includes both delight and *confusion,* the struggle to comprehend experiences that challenge our understanding, and don't fit our accustomed map of reality. Far more things are possible in the world of magic realism, including miracles, contradictions, and logical impossibilities—but this also means that more *meanings* are possible, and that all meanings will be elusive and uncertain.

Source: Tom Faulkner, Overview of ''A Very Old Man with Enormous Wings,'' for *Short Stories for Students,* The Gale Group, 1999.

Mark Millington

Millington is Lecturer in Latin American Studies at the University of Nottingham, England. In the following excerpt, he provides an overview of the symmetrical structure of the stories in The Incredible and Sad Story of the Innocent Erendira and her Heartless Grandmother, *including ''A Very Old Man with Enormous Wings,'' detailing the opening of each story with the arrival of an invading presence which causes widespread change in the life patterns of the characters, and the conclusion with a departure which completes the natural cycle. Millington also focuses on the narrative structure of the stories, which incorporates cultural knowledge frames and partial narrator authority to emphasize the relation between the narrative world and the actual world.*

I am going to begin with beginnings. Each story in [*The Incredible and Sad Story of the Innocent Evendira and her Heartless Grandmother* (*ISS*)] begins with an arrival—a space or a consciousness is invaded by an unknown presence. But the nature of the invading presence differs: in ''Constant Death'' and ''Blacamán'' it is human (Onésimo Sánchez and Blacamán respectively); in ''Very Old Man'' it is part-human (the bird-man); in ''Drowned Man'' it was formerly human (Esteban's corpse); in ''Sea'' and ''Incredible Story'' it is a natural phenomenon (the smell of roses and a wind respectively); and in ''Last Journey'' it is an object (the ghost ship). But in four of the stories the source of the invading presence is the same: in one way or another, the sea is associated with the arrival in ''Very Old Man,'' ''Sea,'' ''Drowned Man'' and ''Last Journey,'' and in the first two of these the invading presence returns to the sea at the end. And in all of the stories the arrival has the same extraordinary effect—it becomes the focus of widespread, sometimes all-absorbing, attention—and in each case the arrival represents the inception of a series of events that will occupy the remainder of the story. The effect of the arrival is to disrupt—it introduces instability into a preexistent situation, and that instability produces interest and also movement. The interest stimulated by the new arrival centres on a common reaction in several stories: the need to discover the meaning of the disruption. But the invading presence also seems to produce a release of energy in the characters and so to create a new pattern of life. In both respects the arrival is a beginning—a point of inception.

The fact that in certain stories the characters need to interpret the arrival, to establish the meaning of the invading presence, is a sign of the destabilizing character of the event. The diversity of the interpretations and the confusion felt is most graphically apparent in "Very Old Man." Here the desire to understand is powerful but the capacity to comprehend minimal: the bird-man is variously seen by the villagers as a nightmare, a shipwrecked sailor, an angel and a circus animal; and their confusion is shared by the chain of ecclesiastical interpreters extending up to the Vatican, which is notable for its failure to produce even a conjectural interpretation. The same overloading of interpretative skills is evident in "Drowned Man," where the desire to establish whether Esteban is human is simply swept aside by unquestioning awe in the face of his extraordinary beauty. In both of these cases (and in the other stories with inanimate invasions) the new arrival sets up no dialogue with the community that is invaded—the bird-man and Esteban simply arrive and are observed. They provide no self-explanation, and that accounts, in part, for the disputes that arise as to their nature and even existence (examples of the latter are in "Sea" and "Last Journey"). In each case, the interpretations are attempts to accommodate the unknown within everyday frames of knowledge. Given the nature of the new arrivals, the interpretations are not surprising, though they are certainly not definitive either. They also provide a valuable means of assessing the workings of characters' minds, that is, their capacity for rational thought, and this factor is crucial for the reader's response, in potentially stimulating an ironic view of characters.

More important than the question of characters' interpretations is the new direction that their lives take. The change results from the instability that the new arrivals produce, since characters are stimulat-

> " . . . The bird-man's arrival involves Pelayo and Elisenda willy nilly in trying to cope with the sheer physical problem of crowds of onlookers, and that problem leads to their financial triumph, the building of a luxurious house and a new job for Pelayo: life is transformed. . . ."

ed to undertake action, and action means change. It is not that any specific response is demanded, any inescapable action forced upon them, but that a field of possibility is opened up. . . . In "Very Old Man" the bird-man's arrival involves Pelayo and Elisenda willy nilly in trying to cope with the sheer physical problem of crowds of onlookers, and that problem leads to their financial triumph, the building of a luxurious house and a new job for Pelayo: life is transformed. . . .

The structure so far isolated, therefore, involves various kinds of invasion or arrival, which sometimes stimulate interpretation but which, above all, destabilize a preexistent situation and lead to the inception of new movement, new courses of action. And the remarkable feature of the new movement in *ISS* is that the individuals involved, who first perceive the intruding presence, are frequently joined by the whole community—a broad expansion takes place, which makes the disequilibrium a shared and festive event. There is a multiplication of interest which often extends beyond the bounds of the local population. The fair motif is central to this expansion. In "Very Old Man" the bird-man's arrival initially affects only Pelayo and Elisenda, but overnight there is a large influx of people from the neighbourhood and subsequently of huge crowds of people from far and wide who stretch in a line over the horizon waiting to see the prodigy. This influx brings with it a variety of fairground performers from around the Caribbean who temporarily transform the community—life undergoes a process of carnivalization. . . .

This move into expansion and carnivalization amplifies the localized effects of new arrivals; it is a consistent structural motif throughout *ISS*, but there is no precise repetition of detail in each story; it is a general rhythm and developmental strategy. . . .

Given that some of the stories do not rely heavily on strong causal links to sustain forward movement, it is interesting to consider how endings are achieved. If there is little causal emphasis, what relation can an ending have with what precedes it? Is there any evidence to suggest that the endings in *ISS* act as points of culmination or resolution? And, if not, how does each story create a "sense of an ending"? The key factor here is departure. Most of the stories rely on departures to provide a "sense of an ending," that is to create an impression that a "natural" cycle has been completed: the departure terminates what the arrival inaugurated, which is something that readers can accept by drawing on cultural knowledge and without needing an explanation of how or why it came about. "Very Old Man" ends with the growth of the bird-man's feathers which creates the possibility of flight and departure. . . .

[The] ending of "Very Old Man" (not untypically) seems to be underdetermined; it is pointless to ask why the bird-man's feathers grow and why he flies away, since there is no cause other than the need to provide a narrative ending.

This type of ending leaves us with a global structure as a basis for most of the stories: arrival—reaction and expansion—departure. But the symmetry of this structure is deceptively attractive. It is deceptive because it provides a neat representation which fails to take into account an important aspect of the stories: their elusiveness. It is not that this structure is wrong, simply that it does not tell us enough. Above all, this pattern seems "closed," where the stories are teasingly "open" —that is, they are thematically reticent while foregrounding elements of a highly imaginative and problematic sort. There is a need, therefore, to question any simple, closed representation. One way to modify the neatness of the first representation is by looking at the reversals which contribute to the instability of the stories; and one way to begin trying to make sense of their openness—without reducing the stories to statements of what they are "about," which would impose closure from "outside"—is to examine the fair motif. . . .

The fair motif is, or accompanies, an intrusion into the narrative space in *ISS*—it constitutes or reinforces a radical disequilibrium in life patterns; in this way it represents a potential opening or transformation. And in that connection the fair motif can be examined in the light of what [Mikhail] Bakhtin [in *Problems of Dostoevsky's Poetics,* translated by R. W. Rotsel, 1973] calls popular-festive forms or carnivals. Bakhtin's theorization is useful:

> Carnival is a pageant without a stage and without a division into performers and spectators. In the carnival everyone is an active participant, everyone communes in the carnival act. Carnival is not contemplated, it is, strictly speaking, not even played out; its participants *live* in it, they live according to its laws, as long as those laws are in force, i.e. they live a *carnivalistic life.* The carnivalistic life is life drawn out of its *usual rut,* it is to a degree "life turned inside out," "life the wrong way round" ("monde á l'envers").

The laws, prohibitions and restrictions which determine the system and order of normal, i.e. non-carnival, life are for the period of carnival suspended; above all, the hierarchical system and all the connected forms of fear, awe, piety, etiquette, etc. are suspended, i.e. everything that is determined by social-hierarchical inequality among people, or any other form of inequality, including age. . . . Carnival celebrates change itself, the very process of replaceability. . . .

The stress here is on newness, on the potential for change, on living in a radically different way from before, if only for the duration of the festivity. In that perspective the fairs or carnivals of *ISS* are recognizable as stimuli for change ("Sea" and "Very Old Man") or as ways of life ("Blacamán" and "Incredible Story").

But the key question is: "How much really changes or is transformed in *ISS*?" . . . In "Very Old Man" there is real transformation; the fair builds on and exceeds the arbitrary arrival of the bird-man and it helps Pelayo and Elisenda to gain new social status by allowing them to earn money from the curiosity the bird-man is. Here the change outlasts the festivity. . . .

I will end by attempting to analyse the structure of the narrative space created in *ISS*. I want to suggest a way of understanding the kind of narrative world that exists in *ISS*; that is, by trying to establish the nature and consistency of the relations that hold between the actual world and the narrative world, I want to propose an analytical approach to the comprehension of the stories' narrative space.

In discussing the way all discourse is comprehended [in "Semantic macro-Structures and Knowledged Frames in Discourse Comprehension," in *Cognitive Processes in Comprehension,* ed. M. A. Just and P. A. Carpenter, 1977], Teun van Dijk has stressed the importance of knowledge frames. He defines these as follows:

> Frames are knowledge representations about the "world" which enable us to perform such basic cognitive acts as perception, action, and language comprehension.

We propose that frames define units or chunks of concepts which are not essentially, but *typically,* related. Some intuitive examples may clarify this point. Conceptually, there is no immediate or essential relation between the concept of "table" and the concept of "cereal," nor between "soap" and "water," nor between "waitress" and "menu." They are distinct and do not presuppose each other. Yet, they are organized by the frames of "breakfast," "washing" and "restaurant," respectively. They usually denote certain normal courses of events or courses of actions involving several objects, persons, properties, relations, and facts. . . . It is in this sense that frames are higher-level organizing principles. They unify concepts of various types and at various levels of representation under the constraint of typicality and normality. . . . Frames . . . are conventional and general. Most members of a society or culture have approximately the same set of frames.

Van Dijk points out that these frames act as a crucial part of our horizon of expectation and comprehension in processing all discourse (including literature), and it is clear that they complement whatever conventions may hold within any specific discourse. The reliance of discourse on knowledge frames is evident in its capacity to be comprehended without recourse to totalizing explanation. Discourse is efficient and concise; it can elide information precisely because it can rely on triggering knowledge frames in its audience—it can rely on shared experience. This is a basic assumption which is operative in discourse processing by default; that is, unless there is any indication to the contrary, it seems that normal knowledge frames are operative.

This basic assumption is apparent in innumerable details of *ISS*: the reader can be relied upon to attach the appropriate frame to single actions that in global terms form part of, for instance, having breakfast, making love, or attempting murder. Similarly, global action need only be alluded to for a knowledge frame to fill it out: playing draughts,

selling a patent medicine, attempting to corrupt a politician. These bits of knowledge are trivial because they correspond to a possible or actual world of experience, and the input of information by the reader is, therefore, effortless, even unconscious, whatever the specific detail of the narrative.

But the key point is that much of the force of *ISS* derives from the deviation from knowledge frames. If one defines a "possible world" as one that is constructed and comprehended in terms of knowledge frames of the actual world (in specific combination or permutation), then it is evident that *ISS* constructs only partially possible worlds; it blurs or subverts the normal structures of the actual world. Some examples of blurring or subversive phenomena or actions which are "facts" within the stories will make the point more clearly. In "Very Old Man" the spider-woman has an explanation for her condition: she is not a fairground curiosity; her condition is real just as that of the bird-man himself is real, and this blurs the normal distinction between the fair ground and the real world. . . . In "Very Old Man," a cultural knowledge frame is subverted when it becomes obvious that the supposed angel displays only one feature characteristic of an angel: he has wings. Otherwise he is physically unimpressive, withdrawn, passive, fails to understand Latin and is ultimately a domestic nuisance. . . .

[Often] the knowledge frames of the actual world are indispensable in reading, but there are also significant deviations from or transgressions of this ensemble of structured knowledge. So, in part, *ISS* aligned with and, in part, sits athwart actual knowledge frames. And the area of discrepancy does sometimes extend to the conscious actions and the minds of characters. Not only is there no rational critique of events by characters from within the stories—that is a viewpoint potentially equivalent to that of the reader—but the characters frequently add to the number of deviations. . . .

In this way the narrative space seems rather idiosyncratic. And so a final question must be posed concerning the position of narrators. The narrators' position could theoretically provide a gauge of events or behaviour; it could align the global point of view with that of the reader and his/her knowledge frames; it could constitute an internal reference point of critical distance. In fact, the question of the narrators' position is quite complex. In the first place the authority and mediation of the narrators in *ISS* is more or less uniform. This is the case regardless of whether the narrator speaks with a first or a third person voice, though the latter is more common. . . . This authority and mediating power—plus the capacity to name and classify, and the control of chronological progress—doubtless create a certain consistency and clarity. But the question is to see how that authority and mediation are used. Do they carry out the task of distancing critique? The answer is that they do not. The narrators' authority is partial; it is used to register scenes and to fill in certain contextual gaps, but it is not used to justify, explain or question what the characters do or what phenomena are. . . . [The] narrators' silence, the lack of authoritative, rational discourse, is an important feature. The narrators do not rationalize; they do not analyse; they rather present events as if they were "simple facts," even if these "facts" deviate substantially from our knowledge frames. This is curious in so far as their authority seems to imply a capacity for rationalizing distance; but, in fact, the narrators' viewpoint is closer to the characters than to the reader. Very often the "seeing eye" of narration is that of one aligned with a character's viewpoint or with an amalgamation of characters' viewpoints. And this is hardly surprising since the narrative structure, the relations between narrative world and actual world, would be inconsistent and simplified if the narrators cut through the complexities of the other features I have described. The gaps and uncertainties are crucial and exist in terms of the relation actual/narrative worlds. To have recourse to such labels as fairy stories or children's stories to describe *ISS* would be to seek security and closure by removing the stories into an unworldly, "purely literary" frame of reference (if such a concept is anything more than wishful thinking). The fissures in our knowledge frames that are created, and the consequent uncertainty potentially stimulated in our reading, are surely consistent with the basic thrust of the fair or carnival motif: namely, to open up and transform.

Source: Mark Millington, "Aspects of Narrative Structure in *The Incredible and Sad Story of the Innocent Erendira and her Heartless Grandmother*" in *Gabriel Garcia Marquez: New Readings,* edited by Bernard McGuirk and Richard Cardwell, Cambridge University Press, 1987, pp. 117–33.

John Gerlach

In the following excerpt, Gerlach examines "A Very Old Man with Enormous Wings" as a fantasy in which Garcia Marquez employs language, similes, and satire to both destroy and evoke an appropriate reaction to a mythic subject. Gerlach also offers his interpretation of the role of the narrator, asserting that the narrator uses two levels of distortion to
contrast the human folly of the villagers with the more desirable traits (such as patience) of the old man.

Is fantasy dependent on certain themes, and, if so, might these themes be exhausted? My own response to one story, Gabriel Garcia Marquez's "A Very Old Man with Enormous Wings," a story in which theme and the atmosphere of a fantasy that emerges from the theme are, if anything, negatively correlated, leads me to suspect that fantasy is not closely tied to theme, so that fantasies may be created in any age, without reference to theme.

The story might best be described by starting at the end. At the conclusion, an old man flaps like a senile vulture away from the village where for years he has been held captive. The woman who has grudgingly taken care of him watches him open a furrow in the vegetable patch with his fingernails in his first attempt to rise. She sees him nearly knock down a shed with his "ungainly flapping." As he gains altitude and begins to disappear, she watches "until it was no longer possible for her to see him, because then he was no longer an annoyance in her life but an imaginary dot." George McMurray, in his recent study of Gabriel Garcia Marquez [*Gabriel Garcia Marquez,* 1977], focuses on this final image and concludes that for the reader (and the villagers) the story is a "cathartic destruction of antiquated myths." My own reaction was quite different: I had the prescribed catharsis, but I came away with my taste for myth and the supernatural intact. I could see how McMurray arrived at his conclusion, because this particular Icarus, with his "few faded hairs left on his bald skull" and the air of a "drenched great-grandfather," would hardly seem to inspire wonder. But I felt as if I had witnessed the beginning of a myth, not its end, and the story had evoked for me the sense of wonder and marvel that one associates with myth at its inception.

Whether the story is best designated as a myth or as a fantasy is another matter. Myths present "supernatural episodes as a means of interpreting natural events in an effort to make concrete and particular a special perception of man or a cosmic view," as [C. Hugh Holman, in his 1972] *A Handbook to Literature* would have it. The old man of Garcia Marquez's story does not stimulate the villagers to interpret anything. He is dropped into their existence unexplained, and leaves unexplained, clarifying nothing. It would be more accurate to consider the work a fantasy on the grounds that the story deals, to use the handbook's terms again, with an "incredible and unreal character." I will eventually apply a more contemporary definition of fantasy to the story, [Tzvetan] Todorov's definition [in *The Fantastic: A Structural Approach to a Literary Genre,* trans. Richard Howard, 1973], but for the moment I prefer to pursue further the consequences of McMurray's approach. His view implies that the subject of myth, or, as I will have it, fantasy, determines our reactions. If the text parodies a mythic subject, then the reader would appropriately respond, not with an elevated sense of wonder, but with amusement at the exposure of nonsense. Since the subject matter in Garcia Marquez's story does not diminish my own appreciation of the marvelous, I am left to conclude either that McMurray has misread the text or that the effect of a fantasy is not dependent on the subject. I have concluded that both propositions are true. McMurray has misrepresented the text, and, even so, something other than theme or subject matter creates what the reader responds to in a fantasy. "A Very Old Man with Enormous Wings" can be used to show that, as Todorov has predicted, the manner of telling, not the matter, creates the fantasy.

McMurray's points should first be dealt with in more detail. His interpretation is brief, but his argument is easily extended. Part of Garcia Marquez's strategy, as McMurray suggests, was undeniably to diminish the grandeur of this unearthly winged creature. Similes used to describe him do not even grant him human attributes: matched with the villagers who stood around his cage he looked "like a huge decrepit hen among fascinated chickens." Later it is said that he tolerates a child's "ingenious infamies with the patience of a dog who had no illusions." A complex simile, to be sure, for the narrator is saying not only that the old man is like a dog, but also that the dog with his patience and lack of illusions is like a human being. Nevertheless, the effect of the simile is to emphasize the analogy to an animal. The syntax of the sentence which reveals the old man's wings also diminishes rather than ennobles him. Pelayo, the man who found him, heard something moving and groaning in the courtyard that he had recently cleaned of crabs and the stench they left behind. Pelayo "had to go very close to see that it was an old man, a very old man, lying face down in the mud, who, in spite of his tremendous efforts, couldn't get up, impeded by his enormous wings." The long sentence, with its hesitations that duplicate in the reader the efforts of the old man, relegates the marvel of his wings to the terminal subordinate clause. Rhetorical decisions

> The narrator's motive in telling the story would seem to be satiric rather than inspirational. The credulity of mankind and greed--Pelayo's wife begins to charge admission to see the old man-- are apparently the narrator's targets."

such as these have just as much effect on us as the content. It would seem that both the language and the content are pushing the reader in the direction that McMurray has outlined. The supernatural is described as something ordinary or, even more precisely, foul and repellent.

McMurray's analysis can be extended further. The narrator's motive in telling the story would seem to be satiric rather than inspirational. The credulity of mankind and greed—Pelayo's wife begins to charge admission to see the old man—are apparently the narrator's targets. The church is too, for the attempts of ecclesiastical bureaucrats to discover through correspondence with the resident priest whether or not the winged creature is an angel are bogged down by their desire to find out "if the prisoner had a navel, if his dialect had any connection with Aramaic, how many times he could fit on the head of a pin, or whether he wasn't just a Norwegian with wings." Furthermore, the narrator's exaggerated manner of description seems to undercut even further our response to the old man. When Pelayo and his wife Elisenda first speak to the old man, "he answered in an incomprehensible dialect with a strong sailor's voice." What it is that makes the voice sound like that of a sailor is not questioned by the narrator, who simply mirrors what is presumably the illogic of Pelayo and Elisenda. The narrator's complicity in this fabrication extends beyond mirroring. He notes that Pelayo and Elisenda "skipped over the inconvenience of the wings and quite intelligently concluded that he was a lonely castaway." Since wings are certainly more than an "inconvenience," and the logical processes of Pelayo

> The winged man's humanity is underlined by a foil the narrator creates--a woman who has been changed into a spider."

and Elisenda are therefore something less than intelligent, we have a narrator who, instead of striving to establish the credibility of this supernatural creature, is emphasizing the credulity of the villagers.

Similes that demean, satire, playful logic—it would seem that Garcia Marquez is not about to honor a myth. Yet none of these devices totally cancels out the mystery. The diminishing suggested by these devices does not represent all of the truth about the old man and his wings. However decrepit the old man is, he does renew himself. When he arrived he seemed close to death, and several years later a doctor listening to the old man's heart concludes that it is impossible for him to be alive; yet after his release from his cage and with the onset of sunny days, stiff feathers begin to grow on his wings. Although the narrator continues to denigrate, calling the new growth "scarecrow feathers" that look like "another misfortune of decrepitude," the feathers do allow the old man to fly away. Something about the old man is greater than the narrator's estimation of him.

Other devices that the narrator used to increase rather than decrease our respect for the old man also need to be considered. When compared to those around him the old man becomes the model of patience, trying the best he can to "get comfortable in his borrowed nest, befuddled by the hellish heat of the oil lamps and sacramental candles that had been placed along the wire." He refuses to eat the mothballs that one of the villagers thinks is the "food prescribed for angels," and subsists on eggplant mush. If he is "befuddled," that term has ironic value, for it is those that regard him who are confused.

Contrast with what seems to be even the sanest of mortals is illustrative. Father Gonzaga is the figure presented by the narrator as the most sane. He is not, as his parishioners are, ready to make the old man the mayor of the world or a "five-star general in order to win all wars," nor does he want to put him out to stud to create "a race of winged wise men who could take charge of the universe." Father Gonzaga "had been a robust woodcutter" and so by implication is more realistic. He soberly approaches the old man and says good morning in Latin. Father Gonzaga has "his first suspicion of an imposter" when he saw that the old man "did not understand the language of God or know how to greet His ministers," and it is at this point we realize that Father Gonzaga is the one who fails the test, not the old man. Father Gonzaga notices that "seen close up" the old man "was much too human," and so the priest warns his parishioners not to be taken in. In the light of Father Gonzaga's response, the comment that the old man is "too human" is particularly telling. Gonzaga's rationalism obscures his realization that although the winged gentleman may not meet doctrinal specifications, he still is miraculous. What begins to emerge is an image of the old man as someone possibly more human and reasonable than members of the wingless species.

The winged man's humanity is underlined by a foil the narrator creates—a woman who has been changed into a spider. Her presence distracts the villagers, and they cease to pay attention to the old man. Her exhibit costs less, and unlike the old man, she talks about her affliction. Where the old man refused, she encourages responses, readily accepting meatballs tossed into her mouth. There is nothing ambiguous or submerged about our perception of her. The old man's wings were slowly revealed; we are told bluntly that this woman is "a frightful tarantula the size of a ram . . . with the head of a sad maiden." Though the narrator does not exaggerate the catalogue of her strangeness, she is in fact more grotesque than the old man.

The narrator's description of the villagers' response to her is familiar: once again the logic of the villagers is suspect; the crowd regards her a spectacle full of "human truth," a "fearful lesson." The facts of the lesson, however, are these: a lightning bolt of brimstone changed her form because she had been dancing all night without her parents' permission. The narrator's indirect exposure of the triviality of what the crowd considers a basic truth alters our response to the old man. We begin to admire more his silence and even his diet.

The way the villagers treat him is ultimately the best clue to how we should regard him. They poke, they prod, and at one point they burn him with a branding iron. Up until this point pain itself has seemed unreal. Those with ailments who come to be cured have only the most fanciful of afflictions, such as that of an old man "who couldn't sleep because the noise of the stars disturbed him" and that of "a poor woman who since childhood had been counting her heartbeats and had run out of numbers." But the old man with wings responds with true pain, ranting in his "hermetic language," tears in his eyes, flapping his wings to create "a whirlwind of chicken dung and lunar dust." The villagers take the old man as no more than a creature of fiction, hence not subject to pain. They may not see the old man's humanity, but the reader should.

What I hope is emerging is a more complete sense of the role of the narrator. His denigrations of the protagonist have been systematic but not exclusive. He distorts by alternately exaggerating and understating. What could be called the outer or secondary level of distortion is the product of the narrator's supposed sympathy with the viewpoint of the villagers. This level, whose function is basically satiric, leads the narrator to call wings "inconvenient" or to exaggerate the church's concern in terms of the medieval problem of calculating the number of angels on the head of a pin. The narrator takes the viewpoint of the villagers themselves, pretending to be alternately detached or supportive, but everywhere he exposes irrationality and superstition. Underneath this level, however, is another, an inner or primary level of distortion, which grows from one central fact—there is an old man with enormous wings. That conception embodies even in its grammatical form a paradox in the contrast between "old" and "enormous," for we would not expect anything so powerfully endowed to be so decrepit. Beyond this paradox is a kind of simplicity and unarguable solidity. The nature of the wings themselves does not change; what changes is our perception of their naturalness. By the end of the story, a doctor examines the old man and is surprised by "the logic of his wings," and the reader is prepared for a similar realization. These wings, as the doctor puts it, seem "so natural on that completely human organism that he couldn't understand why other men didn't have them too." This old man, with his muteness, his patience, is in some ways more human, more natural, and even more believable, than anyone else in the story. The secondary level of distortion playfully exposes human folly; the primary level by contrast defines more desirable human traits.

At this point it is appropriate to define the genre of the work more precisely. The definition will allow us to see how the two levels of distortion work together to create the effects we associate with fantasy. Within the last few years, several critics, in particular W. R. Irwin [*The Game of the Impossible: A Rhetoric of Fantasy*, 1976], Eric S. Rabkin [*The Fantastic in Literature*, 1976], and Tzvetan Todorov, have attempted to describe fantasy as a genre. Of the three, Todorov's analysis provides the most instructive standards to apply to Garcia Marquez's story. The fit is not perfect; Todorov, I believe, concludes that "fantasy" narrowly defined is hardly being written anymore. But even the divergence between "A Very Old Man with Enormous Wings" and Todorov's principles is in itself enlightening.

Todorov assumes that, first, fantasies produce the effect of hesitation. The reader is never wholly sure whether he is confronting a supernatural event or something that can be rationally explained. If the reader is able to conclude the event is explicable solely on the supernatural level, the story belongs to another genre, the marvelous, and, if the reader chooses the rational explanation, the story falls into the genre of the "uncanny." Second, the reader usually participates in the story through the medium of a character who believes in reason and order, so that the reader experiences the hesitation through the character's eyes. Third, the reader must not be able to explain away the supernatural events by considering them allegorical or poetic. In this case the reader would conclude that the supernatural is merely a shorthand for an idea, hence not to be taken literally. One of the clues to allegory is that no one in the story takes an aberration to be unusual, and so there is no sense of hesitation.

In the case of the Garcia Marquez story, it is simpler to deal with the second point first. There is no character recounting for us his experiences. There is an implied narrator, and this narrator is a direct inversion of the sort of character that Todorov has posited. This is no rational human, but a creator of exaggerations. The hesitation that Todorov speaks of as his first point, then, derives in this story not from the doubts of a character, but from our doubts about what the narrator is saying. Todorov's analysis allows us to see the ingenuity of what Garcia Marquez has done. Garcia Marquez has taken what would normally be the index of normality, the village folk, and made them the greatest of exaggerators. The unreal character, in contrast, begins to appear normal and harmless. Garcia Marquez has managed to make his central contrary-to-fact situation, the old man with wings (what I have been calling the primary level of distortion), seems altogether more rational and ordinary than the villagers. Those who follow Rabkin's definition of fantasy should be pleased, for the effect that I have described is replete with what Rabkin calls 180-degree turns in perspective, the undermining of established expectations. As for the matter of allegory, it is possible that the wings themselves might be taken as allegorical evidence of the true dignity of man. What prevents us from taking the wings as allegory is the very insistence on the decrepitude of the old man, and elaboration of the reality of the wings, the "stellar parasites" in them. In the same way, the characters both are and are not taking the old man as unusual, so that the wings both are and are not allegorical. It is not that Garcia Marquez is making hash of Todorov's categories. What he is doing by his exaggerations is creating the maximum doubt and hesitation about not only the supernatural but the natural as well.

We should now be able to reconsider some of the questions originally raised by McMurray's interpretation. Although it might be possible to contend that McMurray's reading of the text failed to take into account the double role of the narrator and the two levels of distortion, and hence he did not see the extent to which Garcia Marquez has shifted our sympathies toward the old man and located the antiquated, exhausted view in the perception of the villagers, such a view does not fully account for the energy of the story. Arriving at the truth of the story and feeling its impact do not automatically result from peeling off the secondary layer of distortion and getting at the primary. It is not possible to take either level as the ultimate truth. The positive values may seem to be vested in the primary level, for Garcia Marquez has made muteness and patience seem truly supernatural virtues, and by implication exaggeration the expression of human fallibility. But the center of the story is still an exaggeration. Men do not have wings. The process of distortion itself is the vehicle of our approach to the story. The very act of reading and interpreting the story rests not on muteness and patience, but on the appreciation of exaggeration. In reading the story the reader does not respond only to the truth of a particular idea, in the case of this story, for instance, the idea that there is an indestructible, winged aspect of man that can fly despite its own aging or the lack of appreciation from ordinary men. The story is a whole, not a set of levels, and what causes the reader

to respond, in the terms that Todorov has established, is the reader's hesitation over what is real.

This hesitation is built up from the minutest details, as can be shown in one isolated segment, the ending. Even slight distortions in language are significant. The concluding phrase states that the old man "was no longer an annoyance in [Elisenda's] life but an imaginary dot on the horizon of the sea." The antithesis of "annoyance" and "dot," contrasting an abstraction with something at least barely visible, might make us grammatically uncomfortable, but the mismatch reproduces the quality of the story itself. It is as if there were a rather easy flow between our feelings and the things we find about us, so that a thought might suddenly take a substance as real as our own, or just as suddenly disappear. The energy created by unusual phrases works in the same way. The idea of modifying "dot" by the adjective "imaginary" is plausible in that the dot may be so small that it is nearly imaginary, but the conjunction of the two terms is also implausible; it has something of the force of an oxymoron, for Elisenda is simultaneously seeing and merely imagining. "Imaginary" is also apt in that the old man is by our standards rightly considered imaginary. Structurally the close is effective because it complements the opening—the character was visually constructed piece by piece for us, and now visually recedes into nothingness. Viewed from one perspective, humankind is relieved of a burden. Viewed from another, a creature more perfect, more logical than man has achieved his freedom. The fact that the old man has escaped from the perspective of the characters means to the characters that he does not exist, he may be ignored. But we have seen him endure over a period of time and can imagine him perhaps going back to whatever imaginary place it is that he lives in, one that has as much validity to it as this imaginary town into which he has fallen.

The cluster of possibilities here matches the possibilities advanced in the rest of the story. Clusters such as this give the story its power and create the effects we identify with fantasy; the clusters work much the same way as the hesitation over the natural and the supernatural. Because the effect of the story, the sense in which it is a fantasy, is created by the treatment, not by the subject or theme, the number of fantasies that can still be written should be endless. At one time myths may have been man's way of imagining the unimaginable, but now, even though literal mythmaking is no longer used to explain the world around us, the sense of wonder that myth brings with it need not in consequence be abandoned. It does not matter that we cannot take the fanciful as literally as man might once have, nor does it matter that the subject of a myth is decrepit, toothless, and featherless. The sense of wonder that a myth or a fantasy evokes inheres not in the subject, but in the telling. Fantasy is more the *how* than the *what*.

Put in terms of Todorov's discussion, fantasy is created initially by something significantly contrary to the ordinary. The task of the reader is to naturalize, to recuperate, that is, to make intelligible, this break from the norms of the reader's experience. The most significant thing about the genre is that the break should not readily be bridged; the circuits must be kept open as long as possible. In Todorov's words, the hesitation must continue. What the reader ends up recuperating is ultimately the process, the broken circuit itself. It is not what the break is about, it is that there *is* a continuous break that makes a fantasy. Since fantasy is a process, not a result, its resources are endless, and it is in no way dependent on the fashion of the conventions it adapts.

The final matter to consider is the effect of parody in the genre. Does the parody of a myth or fantasy make the story a last gasp, as the Russian formalists have asserted in other cases, of a genre that is about to expire or assume a new form? I think not. Parody is not central to this story. The mention of stellar bugs and scratchings is only a way for the narrator to make the mystery of the old man more, not less, incredible. There are parodic elements, but this is not a parody as such. What one ultimately grasps in a fantasy is the potential of language to construct a world partly, but not wholly, like our own. Fantasy is the logical extension, the wings, of language itself. Literature in general and fantasy in particular are the magic which our customary language so dimly represents.

Source: John Gerlach, ''The Logic of Wings: Garcia Marquez, Todorov, and the Endless Resources of Fantasy,'' in *Bridges to Fantasy,* George E. Slusser, Eric S. Rabkin, and Robert Scholes, eds., Southern Illinois University Press, 1982, pp. 121–29.

Further Reading

Bell-Villada, Gene H. *Garcia Marquez: The Man and His Work,* University of North Carolina Press, 1984.
    Bell-Villada explores various aspects of Garcia Marquez's work, with chapters focusing on his short fiction, his early development as a writer, and his novels.

Williams, Raymond. *Gabriel Garcia Marquez,* Twayne Publishers, 1984.
    A volume of criticism covering Garcia Marquez's career up to the time of its publication, including chapters analyzing each of his novels and most of the short stories. Williams also includes a biographical introduction, and a survey of the author's work as a journalist.

Glossary of Literary Terms

A

Aestheticism: A literary and artistic movement of the nineteenth century. Followers of the movement believed that art should not be mixed with social, political, or moral teaching. The statement ''art for art's sake'' is a good summary of aestheticism. The movement had its roots in France, but it gained widespread importance in England in the last half of the nineteenth century, where it helped change the Victorian practice of including moral lessons in literature. Edgar Allan Poe is one of the best-known American ''aesthetes.''

Allegory: A narrative technique in which characters representing things or abstract ideas are used to convey a message or teach a lesson. Allegory is typically used to teach moral, ethical, or religious lessons but is sometimes used for satiric or political purposes. Many fairy tales are allegories.

Allusion: A reference to a familiar literary or historical person or event, used to make an idea more easily understood. Joyce Carol Oates's story ''Where Are You Going, Where Have You Been?'' exhibits several allusions to popular music.

Analogy: A comparison of two things made to explain something unfamiliar through its similarities to something familiar, or to prove one point based on the acceptance of another. Similes and metaphors are types of analogies.

Antagonist: The major character in a narrative or drama who works against the hero or protagonist. The Misfit in Flannery O'Connor's story ''A Good Man Is Hard to Find'' serves as the antagonist for the Grandmother.

Anthology: A collection of similar works of literature, art, or music. Zora Neale Hurston's ''The Eatonville Anthology'' is a collection of stories that take place in the same town.

Anthropomorphism: The presentation of animals or objects in human shape or with human characteristics. The term is derived from the Greek word for ''human form.'' The fur necklet in Katherine Mansfield's story ''Miss Brill'' has anthropomorphic characteristics.

Anti-hero: A central character in a work of literature who lacks traditional heroic qualities such as courage, physical prowess, and fortitude. Anti-heroes typically distrust conventional values and are unable to commit themselves to any ideals. They generally feel helpless in a world over which they have no control. Anti-heroes usually accept, and often celebrate, their positions as social outcasts. A well-known anti-hero is Walter Mitty in James Thurber's story ''The Secret Life of Walter Mitty.''

Archetype: The word archetype is commonly used to describe an original pattern or model from which all other things of the same kind are made. Archetypes are the literary images that grow out of the ''collective unconscious,'' a theory proposed by psychologist Carl Jung. They appear in literature as incidents and plots that repeat basic patterns of life. They may also appear as stereotyped characters. The ''schlemiel'' of Yiddish literature is an archetype.

Autobiography: A narrative in which an individual tells his or her life story. Examples include Benjamin Franklin's *Autobiography* and Amy Hempel's story ''In the Cemetery Where Al Jolson Is Buried,'' which has autobiographical characteristics even though it is a work of fiction.

Avant-garde: A literary term that describes new writing that rejects traditional approaches to literature in favor of innovations in style or content. Twentieth-century examples of the literary *avant-garde* include the modernists and the minimalists.

B

Belles-lettres: A French term meaning ''fine letters'' or ''beautiful writing.'' It is often used as a synonym for literature, typically referring to imaginative and artistic rather than scientific or expository writing. Current usage sometimes restricts the meaning to light or humorous writing and appreciative essays about literature. Lewis Carroll's *Alice in Wonderland* epitomizes the realm of belles-lettres.

Bildungsroman: A German word meaning ''novel of development.'' The *bildungsroman* is a study of the maturation of a youthful character, typically brought about through a series of social or sexual encounters that lead to self-awareness. J. D. Salinger's *Catcher in the Rye* is a *bildungsroman*, and Doris Lessing's story ''Through the Tunnel'' exhibits characteristics of a *bildungsroman* as well.

Black Aesthetic Movement: A period of artistic and literary development among African Americans in the 1960s and early 1970s. This was the first major African-American artistic movement since the Harlem Renaissance and was closely paralleled by the civil rights and black power movements. The black aesthetic writers attempted to produce works of art that would be meaningful to the black masses. Key figures in black aesthetics included one of its founders, poet and playwright Amiri Baraka, formerly known as LeRoi Jones; poet and essayist Haki R. Madhubuti, formerly Don L. Lee; poet and playwright Sonia Sanchez; and dramatist Ed Bullins. Works representative of the Black Aesthetic Movement include Amiri Baraka's play *Dutchman,* a 1964 Obie award-winner.

Black Humor: Writing that places grotesque elements side by side with humorous ones in an attempt to shock the reader, forcing him or her to laugh at the horrifying reality of a disordered world. ''Lamb to the Slaughter,'' by Roald Dahl, in which a placid housewife murders her husband and serves the murder weapon to the investigating policemen, is an example of black humor.

C

Catharsis: The release or purging of unwanted emotions—specifically fear and pity—brought about by exposure to art. The term was first used by the Greek philosopher Aristotle in his *Poetics* to refer to the desired effect of tragedy on spectators.

Character: Broadly speaking, a person in a literary work. The actions of characters are what constitute the plot of a story, novel, or poem. There are numerous types of characters, ranging from simple, stereotypical figures to intricate, multifaceted ones. ''Characterization'' is the process by which an author creates vivid, believable characters in a work of art. This may be done in a variety of ways, including (1) direct description of the character by the narrator; (2) the direct presentation of the speech, thoughts, or actions of the character; and (3) the responses of other characters to the character. The term ''character'' also refers to a form originated by the ancient Greek writer Theophrastus that later became popular in the seventeenth and eighteenth centuries. It is a short essay or sketch of a person who prominently displays a specific attribute or quality, such as miserliness or ambition. ''Miss Brill,'' a story by Katherine Mansfield, is an example of a character sketch.

Classical: In its strictest definition in literary criticism, classicism refers to works of ancient Greek or Roman literature. The term may also be used to describe a literary work of recognized importance (a ''classic'') from any time period or literature that exhibits the traits of classicism. Examples of later works and authors now described as classical include French literature of the seventeenth century, Western novels of the nineteenth century, and American fiction of the mid-nineteenth century such as that written by James Fenimore Cooper and Mark Twain.

Climax: The turning point in a narrative, the moment when the conflict is at its most intense. Typically, the structure of stories, novels, and plays is one of rising action, in which tension builds to the climax, followed by falling action, in which tension lessens as the story moves to its conclusion.

Comedy: One of two major types of drama, the other being tragedy. Its aim is to amuse, and it typically ends happily. Comedy assumes many forms, such as farce and burlesque, and uses a variety of techniques, from parody to satire. In a restricted sense the term comedy refers only to dramatic presentations, but in general usage it is commonly applied to nondramatic works as well.

Comic Relief: The use of humor to lighten the mood of a serious or tragic story, especially in plays. The technique is very common in Elizabethan works, and can be an integral part of the plot or simply a brief event designed to break the tension of the scene.

Conflict: The conflict in a work of fiction is the issue to be resolved in the story. It usually occurs between two characters, the protagonist and the antagonist, or between the protagonist and society or the protagonist and himself or herself. The conflict in Washington Irving's story "The Devil and Tom Walker" is that the Devil wants Tom Walker's soul but Tom does not want to go to hell.

Criticism: The systematic study and evaluation of literary works, usually based on a specific method or set of principles. An important part of literary studies since ancient times, the practice of criticism has given rise to numerous theories, methods, and "schools," sometimes producing conflicting, even contradictory, interpretations of literature in general as well as of individual works. Even such basic issues as what constitutes a poem or a novel have been the subject of much criticism over the centuries. Seminal texts of literary criticism include Plato's *Republic,* Aristotle's *Poetics,* Sir Philip Sidney's *The Defence of Poesie,* and John Dryden's *Of Dramatic Poesie.* Contemporary schools of criticism include deconstruction, feminist, psychoanalytic, poststructuralist, new historicist, postcolonialist, and reader-response.

D

Deconstruction: A method of literary criticism characterized by multiple conflicting interpretations of a given work. Deconstructionists consider the impact of the language of a work and suggest that the true meaning of the work is not necessarily the meaning that the author intended.

Deduction: The process of reaching a conclusion through reasoning from general premises to a specific premise. Arthur Conan Doyle's character Sherlock Holmes often used deductive reasoning to solve mysteries.

Denotation: The definition of a word, apart from the impressions or feelings it creates in the reader. The word "apartheid" denotes a political and economic policy of segregation by race, but its connotations—oppression, slavery, inequality—are numerous.

Denouement: A French word meaning "the unknotting." In literature, it denotes the resolution of conflict in fiction or drama. The *denouement* follows the climax and provides an outcome to the primary plot situation as well as an explanation of secondary plot complications. A well-known example of *denouement* is the last scene of the play *As You Like It* by William Shakespeare, in which couples are married, an evildoer repents, the identities of two disguised characters are revealed, and a ruler is restored to power. Also known as "falling action."

Detective Story: A narrative about the solution of a mystery or the identification of a criminal. The conventions of the detective story include the detective's scrupulous use of logic in solving the mystery; incompetent or ineffectual police; a suspect who appears guilty at first but is later proved innocent; and the detective's friend or confidant—often the narrator—whose slowness in interpreting clues emphasizes by contrast the detective's brilliance. Edgar Allan Poe's "Murders in the Rue Morgue" is commonly regarded as the earliest example of this type of story. Other practitioners are Arthur Conan Doyle, Dashiell Hammett, and Agatha Christie.

Dialogue: Dialogue is conversation between people in a literary work. In its most restricted sense, it refers specifically to the speech of characters in a drama. As a specific literary genre, a "dialogue" is a composition in which characters debate an issue or idea.

Didactic: A term used to describe works of literature that aim to teach a moral, religious, political, or practical lesson. Although didactic elements are often found in artistically pleasing works, the term "didactic" usually refers to literature in which the message is more important than the form. The term may also be used to criticize a work that the critic finds "overly didactic," that is, heavy-handed in its delivery of a lesson. An example of didactic literature is John Bunyan's *Pilgrim's Progress.*

Dramatic Irony: Occurs when the reader of a work of literature knows something that a character in the work itself does not know. The irony is in the contrast between the intended meaning of the statements or actions of a character and the additional information understood by the audience.

Dystopia: An imaginary place in a work of fiction where the characters lead dehumanized, fearful lives. **George Orwell's** *Nineteen Eighty-four,* and Margaret Atwood's *Handmaid's Tale* portray versions of dystopia.

E

Edwardian: Describes cultural conventions identified with the period of the reign of Edward VII of England (1901-1910). Writers of the Edwardian Age typically displayed a strong reaction against the propriety and conservatism of the Victorian Age. Their work often exhibits distrust of authority in religion, politics, and art and expresses strong doubts about the soundness of conventional values. Writers of this era include E. M. Forster, H. G. Wells, and Joseph Conrad.

Empathy: A sense of shared experience, including emotional and physical feelings, with someone or something other than oneself. Empathy is often used to describe the response of a reader to a literary character.

Epilogue: A concluding statement or section of a literary work. In dramas, particularly those of the seventeenth and eighteenth centuries, the epilogue is a closing speech, often in verse, delivered by an actor at the end of a play and spoken directly to the audience.

Epiphany: A sudden revelation of truth inspired by a seemingly trivial incident. The term was widely used by James Joyce in his critical writings, and the stories in Joyce's *Dubliners* are commonly called ''epiphanies.''

Epistolary Novel: A novel in the form of letters. The form was particularly popular in the eighteenth century. The form can also be applied to short stories, as in Edwidge Danticat's ''Children of the Sea.''

Epithet: A word or phrase, often disparaging or abusive, that expresses a character trait of someone or something. ''The Napoleon of crime'' is an epithet applied to Professor Moriarty, arch-rival of Sherlock Holmes in Arthur Conan Doyle's series of detective stories.

Existentialism: A predominantly twentieth-century philosophy concerned with the nature and perception of human existence. There are two major strains of existentialist thought: atheistic and Christian. Followers of atheistic existentialism believe that the individual is alone in a godless universe and that the basic human condition is one of suffering and loneliness. Nevertheless, because there are no fixed values, individuals can create their own characters—indeed, they can shape themselves—through the exercise of free will. The atheistic strain culminates in and is popularly associated with the works of Jean-Paul Sartre. The Christian existentialists, on the other hand, believe that only in God may people find freedom from life's anguish. The two strains hold certain beliefs in common: that existence cannot be fully understood or described through empirical effort; that anguish is a universal element of life; that individuals must bear responsibility for their actions; and that there is no common standard of behavior or perception for religious and ethical matters. Existentialist thought figures prominently in the works of such authors as Franz Kafka, Fyodor Dostoyevsky, and Albert Camus.

Expatriatism: The practice of leaving one's country to live for an extended period in another country. Literary expatriates include Irish author James Joyce who moved to Italy and France, American writers James Baldwin, Ernest Hemingway, Gertrude Stein, and F. Scott Fitzgerald who lived and wrote in Paris, and Polish novelist Joseph Conrad in England.

Exposition: Writing intended to explain the nature of an idea, thing, or theme. Expository writing is often combined with description, narration, or argument.

Expressionism: An indistinct literary term, originally used to describe an early twentieth-century school of German painting. The term applies to almost any mode of unconventional, highly subjective writing that distorts reality in some way. Advocates of Expressionism include Federico Garcia Lorca, Eugene O'Neill, Franz Kafka, and James Joyce.

F

Fable: A prose or verse narrative intended to convey a moral. Animals or inanimate objects with human characteristics often serve as characters in fables. A famous fable is Aesop's "The Tortoise and the Hare."

Fantasy: A literary form related to mythology and folklore. Fantasy literature is typically set in non-existent realms and features supernatural beings. Notable examples of literature with elements of fantasy are Gabriel Garcia Marquez's story "The Handsomest Drowned Man in the World" and Ursula K. LeGuin's "The Ones Who Walk Away from Omelas."

Farce: A type of comedy characterized by broad humor, outlandish incidents, and often vulgar subject matter. Much of the comedy in film and television could more accurately be described as farce.

Fiction: Any story that is the product of imagination rather than a documentation of fact. Characters and events in such narratives may be based in real life but their ultimate form and configuration is a creation of the author.

Figurative Language: A technique in which an author uses figures of speech such as hyperbole, irony, metaphor, or simile for a particular effect. Figurative language is the opposite of literal language, in which every word is truthful, accurate, and free of exaggeration or embellishment.

Flashback: A device used in literature to present action that occurred before the beginning of the story. Flashbacks are often introduced as the dreams or recollections of one or more characters.

Foil: A character in a work of literature whose physical or psychological qualities contrast strongly with, and therefore highlight, the corresponding qualities of another character. In his Sherlock Holmes stories, Arthur Conan Doyle portrayed Dr. Watson as a man of normal habits and intelligence, making him a foil for the eccentric and unusually perceptive Sherlock Holmes.

Folklore: Traditions and myths preserved in a culture or group of people. Typically, these are passed on by word of mouth in various forms—such as legends, songs, and proverbs—or preserved in customs and ceremonies. Washington Irving, in "The Devil and Tom Walker" and many of his other stories, incorporates many elements of the folklore of New England and Germany.

Folktale: A story originating in oral tradition. Folktales fall into a variety of categories, including legends, ghost stories, fairy tales, fables, and anecdotes based on historical figures and events.

Foreshadowing: A device used in literature to create expectation or to set up an explanation of later developments. Edgar Allan Poe uses foreshadowing to create suspense in "The Fall of the House of Usher" when the narrator comments on the crumbling state of disrepair in which he finds the house.

G

Genre: A category of literary work. Genre may refer to both the content of a given work—tragedy, comedy, horror, science fiction—and to its form, such as poetry, novel, or drama.

Gilded Age: A period in American history during the 1870s and after characterized by political corruption and materialism. A number of important novels of social and political criticism were written during this time. Henry James and Kate Chopin are two writers who were prominent during the Gilded Age.

Gothicism: In literature, works characterized by a taste for medieval or morbid characters and situations. A gothic novel prominently features elements of horror, the supernatural, gloom, and violence: clanking chains, terror, ghosts, medieval castles, and unexplained phenomena. The term "gothic novel" is also applied to novels that lack elements of the traditional Gothic setting but that create a similar atmosphere of terror or dread. The term can also be applied to stories, plays, and poems. Mary Shelley's *Frankenstein* and Joyce Carol Oates's *Bellefleur* are both gothic novels.

Grotesque: In literature, a work that is characterized by exaggeration, deformity, freakishness, and disorder. The grotesque often includes an element of comic absurdity. Examples of the grotesque can be found in the works of Edgar Allan Poe, Flannery O'Connor, Joseph Heller, and Shirley Jackson.

H

Harlem Renaissance: The Harlem Renaissance of the 1920s is generally considered the first significant movement of black writers and artists in the United States. During this period, new and established black writers, many of whom lived in the region of New York City known as Harlem, published more fiction and poetry than ever before, the first influential black literary journals were established, and black authors and artists received their first widespread recognition and serious critical appraisal. Among the major writers associated with this period are Countee Cullen, Langston Hughes, Arna Bontemps, and Zora Neale Hurston.

Hero/Heroine: The principal sympathetic character in a literary work. Heroes and heroines typically exhibit admirable traits: idealism, courage, and integrity, for example. Famous heroes and heroines of literature include Charles Dickens's Oliver Twist, Margaret Mitchell's Scarlett O'Hara, and the anonymous narrator in Ralph Ellison's *Invisible Man.*

Hyperbole: Deliberate exaggeration used to achieve an effect. In William Shakespeare's *Macbeth,* Lady Macbeth hyperbolizes when she says, "All the perfumes of Arabia could not sweeten this little hand."

I

Image: A concrete representation of an object or sensory experience. Typically, such a representation helps evoke the feelings associated with the object or experience itself. Images are either "literal" or "figurative." Literal images are especially concrete and involve little or no extension of the obvious meaning of the words used to express them. Figurative images do not follow the literal meaning of the words exactly. Images in literature are usually visual, but the term "image" can also refer to the representation of any sensory experience.

Imagery: The array of images in a literary work. Also used to convey the author's overall use of figurative language in a work.

In medias res: A Latin term meaning "in the middle of things." It refers to the technique of beginning a story at its midpoint and then using various flashback devices to reveal previous action. This technique originated in such epics as Virgil's *Aeneid.*

Interior Monologue: A narrative technique in which characters' thoughts are revealed in a way that appears to be uncontrolled by the author. The interior monologue typically aims to reveal the inner self of a character. It portrays emotional experiences as they occur at both a conscious and unconscious level. One of the best-known interior monologues in English is the Molly Bloom section at the close of James Joyce's *Ulysses.* Katherine Anne Porter's "The Jilting of Granny Weatherall" is also told in the form of an interior monologue.

Irony: In literary criticism, the effect of language in which the intended meaning is the opposite of what is stated. The title of Jonathan Swift's "A Modest Proposal" is ironic because what Swift proposes in this essay is cannibalism—hardly "modest."

J

Jargon: Language that is used or understood only by a select group of people. Jargon may refer to terminology used in a certain profession, such as computer jargon, or it may refer to any nonsensical language that is not understood by most people. Anthony Burgess's *A Clockwork Orange* and James Thurber's "The Secret Life of Walter Mitty" both use jargon.

K

Knickerbocker Group: An indistinct group of New York writers of the first half of the nineteenth century. Members of the group were linked only by location and a common theme: New York life. Two famous members of the Knickerbocker Group were Washington Irving and William Cullen Bryant. The group's name derives from Irving's *Knickerbocker's History of New York.*

L

Literal Language: An author uses literal language when he or she writes without exaggerating or embellishing the subject matter and without any tools of figurative language. To say "He ran very quickly down the street" is to use literal language, whereas to say "He ran like a hare down the street" would be using figurative language.

Literature: Literature is broadly defined as any written or spoken material, but the term most often refers to creative works. Literature includes poetry, drama, fiction, and many kinds of nonfiction writing, as well as oral, dramatic, and broadcast compositions not necessarily preserved in a written format, such as films and television programs.

Lost Generation: A term first used by Gertrude Stein to describe the post-World War I generation of American writers: men and women haunted by a sense of betrayal and emptiness brought about by the destructiveness of the war. The term is commonly applied to Hart Crane, Ernest Hemingway, F. Scott Fitzgerald, and others.

M

Magic Realism: A form of literature that incorporates fantasy elements or supernatural occurrences into the narrative and accepts them as truth. Gabriel Garcia Marquez and Laura Esquivel are two writers known for their works of magic realism.

Metaphor: A figure of speech that expresses an idea through the image of another object. Metaphors suggest the essence of the first object by identifying it with certain qualities of the second object. An example is "But soft, what light through yonder window breaks?/ It is the east, and Juliet is the sun" in William Shakespeare's *Romeo and Juliet.* Here, Juliet, the first object, is identified with qualities of the second object, the sun.

Minimalism: A literary style characterized by spare, simple prose with few elaborations. In minimalism, the main theme of the work is often never discussed directly. Amy Hempel and Ernest Hemingway are two writers known for their works of minimalism.

Modernism: Modern literary practices. Also, the principles of a literary school that lasted from roughly the beginning of the twentieth century until the end of World War II. Modernism is defined by its rejection of the literary conventions of the nineteenth century and by its opposition to conventional morality, taste, traditions, and economic values. Many writers are associated with the concepts of modernism, including Albert Camus, D. H. Lawrence, Ernest Hemingway, William Faulkner, Eugene O'Neill, and James Joyce.

Monologue: A composition, written or oral, by a single individual. More specifically, a speech given by a single individual in a drama or other public entertainment. It has no set length, although it is usually several or more lines long. "I Stand Here Ironing" by Tillie Olsen is an example of a story written in the form of a monologue.

Mood: The prevailing emotions of a work or of the author in his or her creation of the work. The mood of a work is not always what might be expected based on its subject matter.

Motif: A theme, character type, image, metaphor, or other verbal element that recurs throughout a single work of literature or occurs in a number of different works over a period of time. For example, the color white in Herman Melville's *Moby Dick* is a "specific" *motif,* while the trials of star-crossed lovers is a "conventional" *motif* from the literature of all periods.

N

Narration: The telling of a series of events, real or invented. A narration may be either a simple narrative, in which the events are recounted chronologically, or a narrative with a plot, in which the account is given in a style reflecting the author's artistic concept of the story. Narration is sometimes used as a synonym for "storyline."

Narrative: A verse or prose accounting of an event or sequence of events, real or invented. The term is also used as an adjective in the sense "method of narration." For example, in literary criticism, the expression "narrative technique" usually refers to the way the author structures and presents his or her story. Different narrative forms include diaries, travelogues, novels, ballads, epics, short stories, and other fictional forms.

Narrator: The teller of a story. The narrator may be the author or a character in the story through whom the author speaks. Huckleberry Finn is the narrator of Mark Twain's *The Adventures of Huckleberry Finn.*

Novella: An Italian term meaning "story." This term has been especially used to describe fourteenth-century Italian tales, but it also refers to modern short novels. Modern novellas include Leo Tolstoy's *The Death of Ivan Ilich,* Fyodor Dostoyevsky's *Notes from the Underground,* and Joseph Conrad's *Heart of Darkness.*

O

Oedipus Complex: A son's romantic obsession with his mother. The phrase is derived from the story of the ancient Theban hero Oedipus, who unknowingly killed his father and married his mother, and was popularized by Sigmund Freud's theory of psychoanalysis. Literary occurrences of the Oedipus complex include Sophocles' *Oedipus Rex* and D. H. Lawrence's "The Rocking-Horse Winner."

Onomatopoeia: The use of words whose sounds express or suggest their meaning. In its simplest sense, onomatopoeia may be represented by words that mimic the sounds they denote such as "hiss" or "meow." At a more subtle level, the pattern and rhythm of sounds and rhymes of a line or poem may be onomatopoeic.

Oral Tradition: A process by which songs, ballads, folklore, and other material are transmitted by word of mouth. The tradition of oral transmission predates the written record systems of literate society.

Oral transmission preserves material sometimes over generations, although often with variations. Memory plays a large part in the recitation and preservation of orally transmitted material. Native American myths and legends, and African folktales told by plantation slaves are examples of orally transmitted literature.

P

Parable: A story intended to teach a moral lesson or answer an ethical question. Examples of parables are the stories told by Jesus Christ in the New Testament, notably ''The Prodigal Son,'' but parables also are used in Sufism, rabbinic literature, Hasidism, and Zen Buddhism. Isaac Bashevis Singer's story ''Gimpel the Fool'' exhibits characteristics of a parable.

Paradox: A statement that appears illogical or contradictory at first, but may actually point to an underlying truth. A literary example of a paradox is George Orwell's statement ''All animals are equal, but some animals are more equal than others'' in *Animal Farm.*

Parody: In literature, this term refers to an imitation of a serious literary work or the signature style of a particular author in a ridiculous manner. A typical parody adopts the style of the original and applies it to an inappropriate subject for humorous effect. Parody is a form of satire and could be considered the literary equivalent of a caricature or cartoon. Henry Fielding's *Shamela* is a parody of Samuel Richardson's *Pamela.*

Persona: A Latin term meaning ''mask.'' Personae are the characters in a fictional work of literature. The persona generally functions as a mask through which the author tells a story in a voice other than his or her own. A persona is usually either a character in a story who acts as a narrator or an ''implied author,'' a voice created by the author to act as the narrator for himself or herself. The persona in Charlotte Perkins Gilman's story ''The Yellow Wallpaper'' is the unnamed young mother experiencing a mental breakdown.

Personification: A figure of speech that gives human qualities to abstract ideas, animals, and inanimate objects. To say that ''the sun is smiling'' is to personify the sun.

Plot: The pattern of events in a narrative or drama. In its simplest sense, the plot guides the author in composing the work and helps the reader follow the work. Typically, plots exhibit causality and unity and have a beginning, a middle, and an end. Sometimes, however, a plot may consist of a series of disconnected events, in which case it is known as an ''episodic plot.''

Poetic Justice: An outcome in a literary work, not necessarily a poem, in which the good are rewarded and the evil are punished, especially in ways that particularly fit their virtues or crimes. For example, a murderer may himself be murdered, or a thief will find himself penniless.

Poetic License: Distortions of fact and literary convention made by a writer—not always a poet—for the sake of the effect gained. Poetic license is closely related to the concept of ''artistic freedom.'' An author exercises poetic license by saying that a pile of money ''reaches as high as a mountain'' when the pile is actually only a foot or two high.

Point of View: The narrative perspective from which a literary work is presented to the reader. There are four traditional points of view. The ''third person omniscient'' gives the reader a ''godlike'' perspective, unrestricted by time or place, from which to see actions and look into the minds of characters. This allows the author to comment openly on characters and events in the work. The ''third person'' point of view presents the events of the story from outside of any single character's perception, much like the omniscient point of view, but the reader must understand the action as it takes place and without any special insight into characters' minds or motivations. The ''first person'' or ''personal'' point of view relates events as they are perceived by a single character. The main character ''tells'' the story and may offer opinions about the action and characters which differ from those of the author. Much less common than omniscient, third person, and first person is the ''second person'' point of view, wherein the author tells the story as if it is happening to the reader. James Thurber employs the omniscient point of view in his short story ''The Secret Life of Walter Mitty.'' Ernest Hemingway's ''A Clean, Well-Lighted Place'' is a short story told from the third person point of view. Mark Twain's novel *Huckleberry Finn* is presented from the first person viewpoint. Jay McInerney's *Bright Lights, Big City* is an example of a novel which uses the second person point of view.

Pornography: Writing intended to provoke feelings of lust in the reader. Such works are often condemned by critics and teachers, but those which can be shown to have literary value are viewed less harshly. Literary works that have been described as pornographic include D. H. Lawrence's *Lady Chatterley's Lover* and James Joyce's *Ulysses.*

Post-Aesthetic Movement: An artistic response made by African Americans to the black aesthetic movement of the 1960s and early 1970s. Writers since that time have adopted a somewhat different tone in their work, with less emphasis placed on the disparity between black and white in the United States. In the words of post-aesthetic authors such as Toni Morrison, John Edgar Wideman, and Kristin Hunter, African Americans are portrayed as looking inward for answers to their own questions, rather than always looking to the outside world. Two well-known examples of works produced as part of the post-aesthetic movement are the Pulitzer Prize-winning novels *The Color Purple* by Alice Walker and *Beloved* by Toni Morrison.

Postmodernism: Writing from the 1960s forward characterized by experimentation and application of modernist elements, which include existentialism and alienation. Postmodernists have gone a step further in the rejection of tradition begun with the modernists by also rejecting traditional forms, preferring the anti-novel over the novel and the anti-hero over the hero. Postmodern writers include Thomas Pynchon, Margaret Drabble, and Gabriel Garcia Marquez.

Prologue: An introductory section of a literary work. It often contains information establishing the situation of the characters or presents information about the setting, time period, or action. In drama, the prologue is spoken by a chorus or by one of the principal characters.

Prose: A literary medium that attempts to mirror the language of everyday speech. It is distinguished from poetry by its use of unmetered, unrhymed language consisting of logically related sentences. Prose is usually grouped into paragraphs that form a cohesive whole such as an essay or a novel. The term is sometimes used to mean an author's general writing.

Protagonist: The central character of a story who serves as a focus for its themes and incidents and as the principal rationale for its development. The protagonist is sometimes referred to in discussions of modern literature as the hero or anti-hero. Well-known protagonists are Hamlet in William Shakespeare's *Hamlet* and Jay Gatsby in F. Scott Fitzgerald's *The Great Gatsby.*

R

Realism: A nineteenth-century European literary movement that sought to portray familiar characters, situations, and settings in a realistic manner. This was done primarily by using an objective narrative point of view and through the buildup of accurate detail. The standard for success of any realistic work depends on how faithfully it transfers common experience into fictional forms. The realistic method may be altered or extended, as in stream of consciousness writing, to record highly subjective experience. Contemporary authors who often write in a realistic way include Nadine Gordimer and Grace Paley.

Resolution: The portion of a story following the climax, in which the conflict is resolved. The resolution of Jane Austen's *Northanger Abbey* is neatly summed up in the following sentence: "Henry and Catherine were married, the bells rang and everybody smiled."

Rising Action: The part of a drama where the plot becomes increasingly complicated. Rising action leads up to the climax, or turning point, of a drama. The final "chase scene" of an action film is generally the rising action which culminates in the film's climax.

Roman a clef: A French phrase meaning "novel with a key." It refers to a narrative in which real persons are portrayed under fictitious names. Jack Kerouac, for example, portrayed various his friends under fictitious names in the novel *On the Road.* D. H. Lawrence based "The Rocking-Horse Winner" on a family he knew.

Romanticism: This term has two widely accepted meanings. In historical criticism, it refers to a European intellectual and artistic movement of the late eighteenth and early nineteenth centuries that sought greater freedom of personal expression than that allowed by the strict rules of literary form and logic of the eighteenth-century neoclassicists. The Romantics preferred emotional and imaginative expression to rational analysis. They considered the individual to be at the center of all experience and so placed him or her at the center of their art. The Romantics believed that the creative imagination reveals nobler truths—unique feelings and attitudes—than those that could be discovered by logic or by scientific examination. "Romanticism" is also used as a general term to refer to a type of sensibility found in all periods of literary history and usually considered to be in opposition to the principles of classicism. In this sense, Romanticism signifies any work or philosophy in which the exotic or dreamlike figure strongly, or that is devoted to individualistic expression, self-analysis, or a pursuit of a higher realm of knowledge than can be discovered by human reason. Prominent Romantics include Jean-Jacques Rousseau, William Wordsworth, John Keats, Lord Byron, and Johann Wolfgang von Goethe.

S

Satire: A work that uses ridicule, humor, and wit to criticize and provoke change in human nature and institutions. Voltaire's novella *Candide* and Jonathan Swift's essay ''A Modest Proposal'' are both satires. Flannery O'Connor's portrayal of the family in ''A Good Man Is Hard to Find'' is a satire of a modern, Southern, American family.

Science Fiction: A type of narrative based upon real or imagined scientific theories and technology. Science fiction is often peopled with alien creatures and set on other planets or in different dimensions. Popular writers of science fiction are Isaac Asimov, Karel Capek, Ray Bradbury, and Ursula K. Le Guin.

Setting: The time, place, and culture in which the action of a narrative takes place. The elements of setting may include geographic location, characters's physical and mental environments, prevailing cultural attitudes, or the historical time in which the action takes place.

Short Story: A fictional prose narrative shorter and more focused than a novella. The short story usually deals with a single episode and often a single character. The ''tone,'' the author's attitude toward his or her subject and audience, is uniform throughout. The short story frequently also lacks *denouement*, ending instead at its climax.

Signifying Monkey: A popular trickster figure in black folklore, with hundreds of tales about this character documented since the 19th century. Henry Louis Gates Jr. examines the history of the signifying monkey in *The Signifying Monkey: Towards a Theory of Afro-American Literary Criticism,* published in 1988.

Simile: A comparison, usually using ''like'' or ''as,'' of two essentially dissimilar things, as in ''coffee as cold as ice'' or ''He sounded like a broken record.'' The title of Ernest Hemingway's ''Hills Like White Elephants'' contains a simile.

Social Realism: The Socialist Realism school of literary theory was proposed by Maxim Gorky and established as a dogma by the first Soviet Congress of Writers. It demanded adherence to a communist worldview in works of literature. Its doctrines required an objective viewpoint comprehensible to the working classes and themes of social struggle featuring strong proletarian heroes. Gabriel Garcia Marquez's stories exhibit some characteristics of Socialist Realism.

Stereotype: A stereotype was originally the name for a duplication made during the printing process; this led to its modern definition as a person or thing that is (or is assumed to be) the same as all others of its type. Common stereotypical characters include the absent-minded professor, the nagging wife, the troublemaking teenager, and the kindhearted grandmother.

Stream of Consciousness: A narrative technique for rendering the inward experience of a character. This technique is designed to give the impression of an ever-changing series of thoughts, emotions, images, and memories in the spontaneous and seemingly illogical order that they occur in life. The textbook example of stream of consciousness is the last section of James Joyce's *Ulysses*.

Structure: The form taken by a piece of literature. The structure may be made obvious for ease of understanding, as in nonfiction works, or may obscured for artistic purposes, as in some poetry or seemingly ''unstructured'' prose.

Style: A writer's distinctive manner of arranging words to suit his or her ideas and purpose in writing. The unique imprint of the author's personality upon his or her writing, style is the product of an author's way of arranging ideas and his or her use of diction, different sentence structures, rhythm, figures of speech, rhetorical principles, and other elements of composition.

Suspense: A literary device in which the author maintains the audience's attention through the build-up of events, the outcome of which will soon be revealed. Suspense in William Shakespeare's *Hamlet* is sustained throughout by the question of whether or not the Prince will achieve what he has been instructed to do and of what he intends to do.

Symbol: Something that suggests or stands for something else without losing its original identity. In literature, symbols combine their literal meaning with the suggestion of an abstract concept. Literary symbols are of two types: those that carry complex associations of meaning no matter what their contexts, and those that derive their suggestive meaning from their functions in specific literary works. Examples of symbols are sunshine suggesting happiness, rain suggesting sorrow, and storm clouds suggesting despair.

T

Tale: A story told by a narrator with a simple plot and little character development. Tales are usually relatively short and often carry a simple message. Examples of tales can be found in the works of Saki, Anton Chekhov, Guy de Maupassant, and O. Henry.

Tall Tale: A humorous tale told in a straightforward, credible tone but relating absolutely impossible events or feats of the characters. Such tales were commonly told of frontier adventures during the settlement of the west in the United States. Literary use of tall tales can be found in Washington Irving's *History of New York,* Mark Twain's *Life on the Mississippi,* and in the German R. F. Raspe's *Baron Munchausen's Narratives of His Marvellous Travels and Campaigns in Russia.*

Theme: The main point of a work of literature. The term is used interchangeably with thesis. Many works have multiple themes. One of the themes of Nathaniel Hawthorne's ''Young Goodman Brown'' is loss of faith.

Tone: The author's attitude toward his or her audience may be deduced from the tone of the work. A formal tone may create distance or convey politeness, while an informal tone may encourage a friendly, intimate, or intrusive feeling in the reader. The author's attitude toward his or her subject matter may also be deduced from the tone of the words he or she uses in discussing it. The tone of John F. Kennedy's speech which included the appeal to ''ask not what your country can do for you'' was intended to instill feelings of camaraderie and national pride in listeners.

Tragedy: A drama in prose or poetry about a noble, courageous hero of excellent character who, be-cause of some tragic character flaw, brings ruin upon him- or herself. Tragedy treats its subjects in a dignified and serious manner, using poetic language to help evoke pity and fear and bring about catharsis, a purging of these emotions. The tragic form was practiced extensively by the ancient Greeks. The classical form of tragedy was revived in the sixteenth century; it flourished especially on the Elizabethan stage. In modern times, dramatists have attempted to adapt the form to the needs of modern society by drawing their heroes from the ranks of ordinary men and women and defining the nobility of these heroes in terms of spirit rather than exalted social standing. Some contemporary works that are thought of as tragedies include *The Great Gatsby* by F. Scott Fitzgerald, and *The Sound and the Fury* by William Faulkner.

Tragic Flaw: In a tragedy, the quality within the hero or heroine which leads to his or her downfall. Examples of the tragic flaw include Othello's jealousy and Hamlet's indecisiveness, although most great tragedies defy such simple interpretation.

U

Utopia: A fictional perfect place, such as ''paradise'' or ''heaven.'' An early literary utopia was described in Plato's *Republic,* and in modern literature, Ursula K. Le Guin depicts a utopia in ''The Ones Who Walk Away from Omelas.''

V

Victorian: Refers broadly to the reign of Queen Victoria of England (1837-1901) and to anything with qualities typical of that era. For example, the qualities of smug narrow-mindedness, bourgeois materialism, faith in social progress, and priggish morality are often considered Victorian. In literature, the Victorian Period was the great age of the English novel, and the latter part of the era saw the rise of movements such as decadence and symbolism.

Cumulative Author/Title Index

Nationality/Ethnicity Index

Subject/Theme Index